MEASURING THE MOSAIC:
AN INTELLECTUAL BIOGRAPHY OF JOHN PORTER

Measuring the Mosaic is a comprehensive intellectual biography of John Porter (1921–1979), author of *The Vertical Mosaic* (1965), pre-eminent Canadian sociologist of his time, and one of Canada's most celebrated scholars. In the first biography of this important figure, Rick Helmes-Hayes provides a detailed account of Porter's life and an in-depth analysis of his extensive writings on class, power, educational opportunity, social mobility, and democracy.

While assessing Porter's place in the historical development of social science in Canada, Helmes-Hayes also examines the economic, social, political and scholarly circumstances – including the Depression, World War II, postwar reconstruction, the baby boom, and the growth of universities – that shaped Porter's political and academic views. Using extensive archival research, correspondence, and over fifty original interviews with family, colleagues, and friends, *Measuring the Mosaic* stresses Porter's remarkable contributions as a scholar, academic statesman, senior administrator at Carleton University, and as an engaged and practical public intellectual.

RICK HELMES-HAYES is an associate professor in the Department of Sociology at the University of Waterloo.

RICK HELMES-HAYES

Measuring the Mosaic

An Intellectual Biography of John Porter

UNIVERSITY OF TORONTO PRESS
Toronto Buffalo London

© University of Toronto Press Incorporated 2010
Toronto Buffalo London
www.utppublishing.com
Printed in Canada

ISBN 978-0-8020-9703-3 (cloth)
ISBN 978-0-8020-9648-7 (paper)

Printed on acid-free paper with vegetable-based inks

Library and Archives Canada Cataloguing in Publication

Helmes-Hayes, Richard C. (Richard Charles), 1951–
Measuring the mosaic : an intellectual biography of John Porter /
Rick Helmes-Hayes.

Includes bibliographical references and index.
ISBN 978-0-8020-9703-3 (bound).   ISBN 978-0-8020-9648-7 (pbk.)

1. Porter, John, 1921–1979.   2. Sociology – Canada.   3. Porter, John,
1921–1979. Vertical mosaic.   4. Sociologist – Canada – Biography.   I. Title.

HM479.P668H44 2009   301.092   C2009-905702-6

This book has been published with the help of a grant from the Canadian
Federation for the Humanities and Social Sciences, through the Aid to
Scholarly Publications Program, using funds provided by the Social
Sciences and Humanities Research Council of Canada.

University of Toronto Press acknowledges the financial assistance to its
publishing program of the Canada Council for the Arts and the Ontario
Arts Council.

 Canada Council   Conseil des Arts    ONTARIO ARTS COUNCIL
for the Arts   du Canada   CONSEIL DES ARTS DE L'ONTARIO

University of Toronto Press acknowledges the financial support for its
publishing activities of the Government of Canada through the Book
Publishing Industry Development Program (BPIDP).

For Pamela

If we neither neglect great names nor defer to them, but seek, to the best of our ability, to take their measure, we are then better placed to take our own.

– John Plamenatz

Foreword

WALLACE CLEMENT

John Porter wrote the foreword to my first book, *The Canadian Corporate Elite* (1975), a study based on my master's thesis, which he had supervised. In his foreword, John deemed me to be 'not wholly in the company of the carpers,' a term he used to characterize much of the 'radical criticism' of the late 1960s and early 1970s. Rick Helmes-Hayes has asked me to write a foreword to his biography of Porter, which began as a post-doctoral project in 1986, nominally under my supervision. More than two decades later, that project has come to fruition. It proved to be a more demanding scholarly task than Rick originally anticipated. Helmes-Hayes is far from a 'carper.' As you will see, his analytical biography is respectful, empirically rich, and in-depth.

After completing a PhD on the foundations of Canadian sociology at the University of Toronto, Rick Helmes-Hayes came to Carleton University to do his post-doctoral research. We worked together on the reissuing of Porter's *The Measure of Canadian Society* (1987). I am now older than John was when he passed away. It makes me conscious of just how young he was at his passing and how little time he had in academia given his late start, serious illness along the way, and premature departure. The detailed documenting of this unique journey makes Rick Helmes-Hayes's narration a compelling read. He has taken great scholarly care with his craft. The biography reveals the life of a fascinating person who touched many lives and lived in disruptive times. Porter's accomplishments were impressive; he pioneered macro-level social science research in Canada, setting a new standard for scholarship in the fledgling discipline of Canadian sociology, and instantly gained international recognition.

Rick Helmes-Hayes describes the 'village' that raised this book – an amazing array of supporters, informants, and assistants. It is a vast undertaking, digging into Porter's roots and historical contexts – the Great Depression, the Second World War, and the 'Golden Years' that followed. These peculiar conjunctures made it possible for this working-class, migrant youth with little formal education to complete a London School of Economics degree. John Porter finessed multiple cracks in the class structure into a university professorship and, eventually, reached the pinnacle of Canadian social science scholarship.

Where John and I differed analytically was in our views about separate, competing elites. There was no difference in our opinions on reconstructing the economic elite (the subject of my master's thesis). It was when I extended my study to include the three chapters on the media elite (while John was at Harvard and I was doing my doctoral course work) that we had a difference, as reflected in his preface to my book. I argued that the two elites overlapped sufficiently to be called a 'corporate elite,' thus challenging the separate elite model John promoted so strongly, especially in the conclusion to *The Vertical Mosaic*, where he invoked the classical elite theorists Mosca, Pareto, and Michels. I was more inclined to the 'power elite' model of C. Wright Mills, who argued, for the postwar conjuncture, that a power elite had formed in the United States, characterized by the 'military-industrial complex.' In part this was a result of different 'framings.' John followed Raymond Aron's distinction between Soviet or totalitarian systems and the so-called Western one based on competing, balanced elites, underwritten by a Weberian rational-legal world view. I was beginning to frame my analysis in terms of a ruling class, trying to escape the separation inherent in an elite/mass model by using a more relational understanding of class and power. This difference is fundamental to the major criticism of *The Vertical Mosaic* as a whole, namely the relationship between its two parts: The Structure of Class and The Structure of Power. Related to this was Porter's conception of class in distributional rather than relational terms (sometimes referred to as the difference between opportunity and structure or condition).

This framing difference is basic to Rick Helmes-Hayes's decision to characterize Porter as a New Liberal. This novel claim by Helmes-Hayes runs throughout the book, traced carefully back to Porter's undergraduate days at the London School of Economics and its influences on his development. In contrast, I have been more convinced by the views of C.B. Macpherson and his focus on the contradictions between liberalism and democracy. Within New Liberalism inequality is a distributional social problem, remedied by greater equality of opportunity and merit principles rather than inequality structured by relations of power and production fundamental to the transformation of capitalism. In addition, Porter came to accept the post-capitalist claims of the new managerialism (Berle and Means)[1] and knowledge-based post-industrial society (Daniel Bell)[2] current in the 1960s in the United States. For me, Helmes-Hayes's insight into the foundations of Porter's assumptions and values is his single most notable contribution, beyond the detailed documentation of Porter's life and work. I also think it was Porter's crisis with New Liberalism, reflected in the McInnis Lectures at York University and published in *The Measure of Canadian Society* that motivated the changes to his thinking about social justice toward the end of his life. It can also be interpreted as a return to his moment of social democratic enthusiasm best illustrated in his 1961 essay 'Power and Freedom in Canadian Democracy.' The McInnis Lectures reflect the failure of public education and the disappointments of post-industrialism, two of the pillars in John's earlier vision. Still, he adopted John Rawls's version of justice, one that emphasizes equality of opportunity rather than equality of condition.

Helmes-Hayes's insight into Porter's New Liberalism effectively accounts for his post–*Vertical Mosaic* focus on occupational prestige rankings, social status, social mobility, and especially educational aspirations and achievement. Ethnicity (the mosaic) was a barrier to the equal distribution of benefits and anything that reinforced such ascriptive barriers (including multiculturalism) was to be opposed. When ascription gets in the way of achievement, there is a basic problem for New Liberalism, not only for the individual but for the release of talent and its maximized utility for the society. In his later work with Marion Porter and Bernard Blishen, *Does Money Matter?*, gender-based inequalities were revealed as key barriers to educational merit when smart young women did not realize their full talents.

What does Helmes-Hayes mean when he identifies John Porter as a 'New Liberal practical intellectual'? For Porter, scholarship was about 'both explanation and evaluation.' Engagement meant taking on the

---

1 A. Berle and G. Means, *The Modern Corporation and Private Property* (New York: Macmillan, 1948)
2 D. Bell, *The End of Ideology* (New York: Free Press, 1962), and *The Coming of Post-Industrial Society* (New York: Basic, 1973).

prevailing ideas of the day. That was a scholarly obligation or a 'vocation.' The New Liberalism is presented as a project to 'rescue liberalism' in its classic form from itself.

Helmes-Hayes builds a compelling case about the New Liberalism and Porter's fit with it. It is built on a duality of 'both a political perspective and a scholarly orientation' that is politically characterized as 'liberal socialism' and in scholarly terms as engaged; that is, it is 'value-laden.' This account resonates especially with Porter's uneasy connection with scientific (American) sociology; he rejected its professed value neutrality yet admired its methodologies. Put in positive terms, if New Liberalism valued 'inclusive, rational, and egalitarian' practices owing to 'equality, freedom, rights, and universality' accomplished through a 'positive' state leading to progress, then that was the essence of Porter's position. The term captures the force that drove his research and teachings. Helmes-Hayes documents the roots of this tradition, its conflict with classic liberalism, and its resonance with other influences in Porter's life.

This book is a major contribution to Canadian scholarship and Canadian sociology. It is critical in the best sense of the word, meaning to delve to the roots and examine the assumptions of thoughts, arguments, and evidence. Sociologists, students of sociology, and informed readers will learn a great deal about the intersection of biography and history. They will also learn about the motives and complexity of social research through an in-depth examination of the career of Canada's greatest sociologist. John Porter's thoughts continue to be foils against which we can sharpen our analytical and intellectual capacities.

John and Marion's children, Tony and Ann (both of whom became established as successful political science professors well after John's death), will be ambivalent about this intimate portrayal of their parents. It is revealing and they are private people. In the end, this intellectual biography stands as a lasting legacy to the remarkable life of a public intellectual. We are all rewarded by the monk's work Rick has undertaken, as I have been enriched by my fortunate association with John Porter and his family.

Wallace Clement
Ottawa, 2009

Contents

Preface

The date 12 May 1965 must surely rank as one of the most significant in the history of Canadian sociology. On that day, John Porter's magnum opus, *The Vertical Mosaic*, first appeared on bookstore shelves. The volume, subtitled *An Analysis of Social Class and Power in Canada*, sold out its initial run of 1,500 copies within three weeks of publication.[1] Indeed, it became an instant classic and went on to sell more than 110,000 copies, far more than any other volume produced in the long and distinguished history of the University of Toronto Press. It remained in print until after the turn of the twenty-first century – again, a span as long or longer than any other book produced by the Press – and was recently chosen as one of the ten 'most important' book-length, English-language sociological works published in Canada in the twentieth century.[2] The scholarly impact of *The Vertical Mosaic* was immediate, profound, and long lasting. It legitimated sociology in the Canadian scholarly community, changed the basic nature of the discipline – so that it became more macrosociological in orientation and more focused on issues of class and power – and set much of Canadian sociology's agenda for the next ten to fifteen years.[3]

The influence of the book stemmed from two sources. First, it provided an authoritative empirical description of the national structure of class and power in Canada that demonstrated that the country – counter to popular belief – was neither egalitarian nor democratic. Second, Porter presented these data using the insightful image of Canada as a 'vertical mosaic.' This suggestive phrase crystallized in two words the complex reality of Canada as a hierarchical patchwork of classes and ethnic groups, and immediately gained wide popular and academic usage. Today, more than four decades later, the imagery of the vertical mosaic retains a prominent place in the language of social commentary in this country because, while some of the patterns of social inequality that Porter identified in *The Vertical Mosaic* have changed, many of Canada's basic structural features, including class and ethnic inequality, remain firmly in place.[4]

John Porter built on the reputation that *The Vertical Mosaic* garnered him and went on to become the most well-known and influential English-language sociologist of his generation in Canada, perhaps of all time.[5] Certainly, his work is as foundational as any in Canadian social science and his legacy remarkable by any standard. He penned one of the most important and influential books in the history of Canadian social science, contributed to the maturation of the discipline in the 1960s and 1970s, and (with a series of collaborators) subsequently completed a triumvirate of influential studies of key aspects of Canadian social life – occupational prestige, educational and occupational opportunity, and social mobility – that played a leading role in the establishment of the survey research tradition in Canada.[6] So important were these works that in a recent compilation of the seventeen 'most important' books and articles in English-language Canadian sociology from the twentieth century, Porter's name is the only one to appear three times: for *The Vertical Mosaic*; for an article on occupational prestige co-authored with Peter Pineo; and for *Ascription and Achievement*, co-authored with Monica Boyd, John Goyder, Frank Jones, Hugh McRoberts, and Peter Pineo.[7]

The book in your hands is my attempt to tell John Porter's life story and to understand his scholarly contributions, especially *The Vertical Mosaic*, in the context of Canadian society and the Canadian sociology of his time. Given that I am writing such a book, I should confess at the outset that I never met John Porter. I was once offered the chance to do so and it is without question the greatest irony of my academic career that I declined. The opportunity arose in the fall of 1977 when for a year I was a PhD student in kinesiology at the University of Waterloo, specializing in the area of the sociology of sport. The kinesiology department was not much to my liking, but I was able to find lots of intellectual stimulation and encouragement in the sociology department, where I took courses with Jim Curtis and Ben Agger. I had done my MA at Queen's University, where my mentor, Richard Gruneau, had introduced me to classical Marxism and its then-contemporary interpreters, as well as to proponents of the new Canadian social history and political economy. I had minored in history during my undergraduate days at Queen's, so I was especially interested when, in Gruneau's seminar on Canadian intellectual history, we read the work of some of the country's most famous and influential mainstream historians and economists: Donald Creighton, Harold Innis, and Arthur Lower among others. Even more appealing was the work of two other groups of scholars: social critics from an earlier era such as George Grant, C.B. Macpherson, H. Clare Pentland, and Stanley Ryerson who had recently been 'rediscovered'; and a new generation of radical historians, political economists, and social theorists such as Wallace Clement, Greg Kealey, Leo Panitch, and Gary Teeple. Thanks in part to these classes and my subsequent interactions with Agger and Curtis at Waterloo, I developed a deep appreciation of the salience of class as a central and contested variable in the literature of Canadian history and social science.

The result of this experience was that I came to be preoccupied with issues of class inequality and social justice and, like many who are exposed to Karl Marx's powerful and compelling writings in their formative intellectual years, I bought into Marxism root and branch. Indeed, with many of my left-wing graduate student friends, I came to be absolutely certain of the moral and scholarly superiority of Marxism relative to the weak-kneed inferiority of what we disparagingly referred to as mainstream, 'liberal' scholarship. So, when one October day Jim Curtis stopped me in the hall of the sociology department to invite me to meet John Porter at a wine and cheese party that afternoon – Porter was to receive an honorary degree from the University of Waterloo the following day – I haughtily declined. I still remember my condescending reply to the bemused Curtis: 'No,' I said dismissively, 'I am not interested in attending a function in honour of a liberal apologist for the system.' And, with that pronouncement, I turned and sauntered off, my ego, scruffy beard, long hair, and second-hand army fatigues having struck what I imagined was a little blow in the class struggle. I did not realize, of course, how profoundly foolish this act would later seem.

In fact, beginning with my PhD dissertation, I have spent a good portion of my academic career writing about John Porter and his work. The result of these efforts is *Measuring the Mosaic*: an intellectual biography that documents and assesses John Arthur Porter's remarkable contribution to Canada's intellectual and political life.

At the outset, the prospect of writing this book was daunting. Not only was it an enormous undertaking but also I was aware that for many people – not just family and friends – I was dealing with a sacred trust of sorts. Many of his colleagues and students regarded him as an icon, a myth even. As Dennis Forcese put it, 'I admired his work for its substance, but also for its symbolism ... To me the myth of John Porter is as important, more important, than the reality, whatever that reality may have been.'[8]

This mythic or iconic status was a double-edged sword. Lots of people knew him and his work, so knowledgeable sources were ready to hand, and I experienced no difficulty getting people to talk about Porter, his work, his contribution, his times, and so forth. However, his iconic status was sufficiently sobering and intimidating that in the early stages I often thought that I should have left the project to someone more senior and experienced, or at least someone who had first-hand knowledge of Porter and his generation. However, I soon realized that whatever the abstract merits of such a situation, the reality was that the book would not be written unless I wrote it myself. Canadian sociologists of Porter's generation were too busy doing sociology to be very self-reflective in the sense of being interested in documenting and assessing their own generation's contribution to the development of the discipline. For their part, more recent cohorts of Canadian sociologists do not regard the history of the discipline as a priority. I suspect that had I left the task to other people, it would have been a long time before it got done – if it got done at all.

One final point: John Porter is a key figure in the history of Canadian social science and this book documents and assesses the impact of his scholarly efforts. Had he reached the normal three score and ten years or more, he would have lived into the 1990s. I would have been able to interview him and, doubtless, write a richer, more nuanced and accurate account of his life and work. There is a lesson for the discipline here. The cohorts of Canadian sociologists who built and then stewarded the discipline during the key period of the 1960s and 1970s have reached retirement age. Some key figures have died and many more will do so over the next few years. We have a responsibility to seek out these scholars, interview them, and archive the most significant of their papers (files, course notes, correspondence) so that we have as many first-person accounts of the development of the discipline as possible. If this task not completed soon, it never will be. Aside from whatever benefits might accrue to the discipline from John Porter's biography, I hope that it spurs other scholars to write the history of the discipline. It is interesting and important work.

Acknowledgments

In 1992, I submitted to the Social Sciences and Humanities Research Council of Canada an application for a research grant to complete this book. I had started the project in 1986 while a postdoctoral fellow at Carleton University but needed money to complete my work. Later that year, I received the welcome news that my application was successful. I tell this story because it allows me to highlight a comment made by one of the scholars who reviewed my proposal. It has come to mind many times while I chipped away at this project. In my original optimism and naïveté, I wrote that I expected to complete a draft of the book in three to five years. The reviewer argued that this was highly unlikely. The type of work in which I was engaged – archival research, interviews, textual analysis – was, he or she said, 'monk's work' and would take much longer than I anticipated.

The reviewer was right. 'Monk's work' it has been: slow, incredibly labour intensive, and mostly solitary. But it has been endlessly interesting and rewarding as well. The detective work involved in writing a biography is a stimulating challenge, and the lure of archival research – What piece of the puzzle might I find in the next dusty box? – is for me irresistible. Moreover, since remarkable people like John Porter have interesting and accomplished friends, the project afforded me the opportunity to interview senior scholars and influential public figures I would otherwise never have had the privilege to meet. It was a welcome bonus to discover that to a person they saw my project as worthwhile and were pleased to offer moral and other kinds of support to help me undertake it. Sadly, since the book took much longer to finish than I had hoped and planned – over twenty years of sporadic, mostly part-time effort – several people who gave generously of their time and expertise have since died. I would like to mention six of them in particular.

Without question, the most important is Marion Porter. It is unfortunate that Marion will not see the book in print. She remained devoted to her husband and his work long after he died – a vigilant guardian of his image and reputation – and was pleased when she learned I was to write a book on his life's work. She was a bit reticent at first, especially when she thought I was too concerned about her husband's personal life rather than his work, but with some reassurance from Wallace Clement she soon came to be a source of much information and insight. Indeed, for about ten years as I worked in fits and starts, she was her husband's proxy, correcting errors and filling in gaps in my account. She was helpful and knowledgeable, if blunt, in her criticism, but never tried to overrule my interpretations. She was open and honest in helping me to construct and tell her husband's story and, near the end of her life, brave enough to let me tell her own difficult story as well. I owe her a great deal. Two other family members who died before I finished the project were Eileen Jones, John's elder sister, and Alan Porter, his younger brother. Eileen was a gracious host and proud sibling when I interviewed her at her home in North Wales in the summer of 1989, opening her heart about the family's difficult experiences during the Depression and World War II in a way that I had no right to expect. Alan Porter was helpful and informative, though less knowledgeable about the family's history than Eileen. Two other generous confidantes who have since died were Beattie MacLean, Porter's former high school teacher, mentor, and friend, and R.A.J. 'Bob' Phillips, Porter's best friend. Professor MacLean, who shared John's love of poetry, not only provided me with copies of some of their wartime correspondence and wrote long letters in response to my questions about the young 'Jack' Porter, but also read critically through chapters 1 and 2. For his part, Bob Phillips consented to an in-depth interview, wrote extensive comments on all but the last chapter of the manuscript, and invited me to his home for a long discussion of his critical remarks. His insights afforded me an understanding of John Porter's life and personality that can come only from the perspective of a close friend of thirty years. A final special mention must go to my colleague, the late Jim Curtis. Jim, surely one of the wisest of Canadian sociologists, was not just my colleague but also my mentor and friend for nearly thirty years. He encouraged me throughout the writing and then, in typically careful and insightful fashion, read the completed first draft in 2004. I could not have asked for a better critic. I benefited greatly from his knowledge, wisdom, and good humour.

In addition to these people, five others deserve special mention: Wallace Clement, Ron Lambert, Roberta Hamilton, Ann Porter, and Tony Porter. From the beginning, Wallace Clement has been interested, encouraging, and helpful. I interviewed him three times, and once the draft was (finally) complete, he read it and offered many useful comments. Graciously, he also agreed to write the foreword. My former colleague Ron Lambert, who is now retired, demonstrated both his friendship and his commitment to scholarship by reading the first draft. His comments helped me to rethink and rewrite it in ways, great and small, that made it much better. Queen's University sociologist Roberta Hamilton, in an act of tremendous and unsolicited scholarly generosity and personal kindness, acted as a 'ghost editor' of the penultimate draft, demonstrating consummate skill as both a coach and supporter at a time when I was in desperate need of both. John and Marion Porter's children, Ann and Tony, now university professors themselves, also deserve special thanks. They were helpful when, toward the end of the project, I asked them to fill in missing pieces about their parents' careers and personal lives. Not only did they allow me to interview them but they also granted me access to some of their father's private correspondence that had not been donated to Library and Archives Canada. In addition, each read the manuscript and offered insightful commentary. I should mention that Ann Porter had serious reservations about my analysis of her father and his work. Her generous cooperation – providing me with materials, granting me an interview, reading the draft – should not be interpreted as an endorsement of my claims about her parents or their work.

Many people read drafts of one or more chapters, filling in blank spots, correcting errors, and challenging my interpretations of people and events: Carl Amberg, Douglas Anglin, Maria Barrados, William Beckel, Bernard Blishen, Monica Boyd, Raymond Breton, David Brown, Ian Campbell, James Downey, Margrit Eichler, David Farr, Barry Ferguson, Paul Fox, James Gibson, Scott Gordon, John Goyder, Naomi Griffiths, Ann Hall, Roberta Hamilton, Geoffrey Hayes, Frank Jones, Bruce McFarlane, Kenneth McRae, Hugh McRoberts, John Myles, Michael Oliver, Peter Pineo, Tom Ryan, Jean-Philippe Warren, and Don Whyte. St. Jude Thaddeus helped out when it was most needed near the end.

I would like as well to acknowledge the assistance of the librarians and archivists at the London School of Economics, Harvard University, the University of Chicago, Queen's University, McGill University, Memorial University of Newfoundland, the University of British Columbia, the University of Toronto and, above all, the University of Waterloo, Library and Archives Canada, and Carleton University.

Financial assistance for the project was furnished by the Social Sciences and Humanities Research Council of Canada, which provided me with a two-year postdoctoral fellowship (1986–7) and a research grant (no. 410–93-0642) that covered many of my research expenses 1993–9. Memorial University of Newfoundland paid for a research trip to England and Wales (1989). The University of Waterloo provided me with some research funds and a travel grant. The Dean of Arts helped to pay a professional to create the index.

Several graduate and undergraduate students at the University of Waterloo either transcribed interviews or did library research. My thanks to Nerida Bullock, Fatima Camara, Shane Dixon, Marcela Granick, Kate Hano, Gina Heins, Kathleen McSpurren, Susan Phillips, Mike Tansca, and Tomasz Tomza. A special thank you in this regard to my good friend, the late Shawn Mann.

The people at the University of Toronto Press, Virgil Duff and Anne Laughlin in particular, were very helpful and exhibited great professionalism throughout the production process. Special mention should go to Camilla Blakeley, my copy editor, who not only taught me a good deal about writing but made the process of revising the manuscript a truly positive experience. I would also like to thank the scholars who reviewed the manuscript for the Press. Their comments and suggestions were extremely thoughtful and useful.

My mother, Helen Duncan, was supportive the entire time. Indeed, she was always curious about the project and, better yet, listened carefully when I gave over-long answers to her questions about how the book was coming along. My father and stepmother, Charlie and Doris Helmes, welcomed me into their Ottawa home on many occasions when I needed a place to stay while doing research at Library and Archives Canada and invariably prepared a daily gourmet meal to bolster this 'monk's' sometimes flagging faith that the book would ever be completed. My best friend, Jim McLachlan, kept my spirits up by letting me beat him at golf on the days we decided, wisely, that work could wait.

Finally, and most of all, of course, I want to thank my sons, Graham and Kevin, and my wife, Pamela. In their own individual and very different ways, Graham and Kevin kept me grounded and family oriented as only kids can, and made me a much better dad and person. Without question, however, the person who deserves the biggest thank you of all is my wife, Pam. Though she never had the opportunity to go to university, she has spent most of her career working at the University of Toronto and the University of Waterloo. Pam values and understands the mission and importance of the university and has always done what she could to further its work. I have benefited direcly from her devotion to its cause. She never complained when she had to cover my share of our mutual domestic responsibilities when I went off to Ottawa or England or Boston to do research or when I had to spend evenings and weekends at my desk. Most important, despite the evidence, she never lost her faith in me during all the years that the book was more chimerical than real. Perhaps most amazing of all, for several years near the end, she refrained from laughing out loud when I kept saying that it was 'almost done.' Well, it's done now and would like to dedicate the book to her as a way of saying 'Thanks for everything.'

One last remark: My chief goal as I undertook this project was to get the story 'right,' to maximize the likelihood that when scholars and others – most important John Porter's family, friends, and colleagues – read the finished product they would judge my account and assessment to be accurate and fair. Each of the people mentioned above helped me to construct this account of John Porter's life and work. However, given that the contents of the book do not have either the official or the unofficial blessing of any of them, I should stress that any shortcomings or errors that remain, despite their best efforts and mine, are my responsibility.

MEASURING THE MOSAIC:
AN INTELLECTUAL BIOGRAPHY OF JOHN PORTER

Introduction

When John Porter died prematurely in the summer of 1979, he was just fifty-seven years old. Despite his relative youth, he had already spent nearly three decades as a faculty member at Carleton University, studying Canadian society and writing influential pieces about key aspects of the country's social structure. The era during which he wrote, the 1950s, '60s, and '70s, was a period of continuous and fundamental social change in Canada: rapid population growth; remarkable, if sporadic, economic development; substantial industrialization; ever greater integration of Canada into the orbit of the American economy and its culture; the youth movement; the women's movement; the Quiet Revolution and the growth of separatism in Quebec; the massive growth of education and the welfare state – to list just a few of many developments. Porter was very interested in the nature and impact of these changes and often front and centre in scholarly and social policy debates that examined their implications for Canada. Indeed, over his career, he undertook a series of major (often collaborative) research projects – *The Vertical Mosaic*, 'Occupational Prestige in Canada,' *Towards 2000*, *Stations and Callings*, and *Ascription and Achievement* – that examined these developments in depth.[1]

For its part, Canadian sociology underwent an equally remarkable transformation during this period. Between 1949 and 1979 it grew from a relatively small and marginalized community of about fifty scholars scattered across the country to a full partner in the Canadian social science enterprise: 1,000 university-based scholars, departments in every university in the country, two scholarly-professional organizations, a sophisticated research enterprise with its own journals, and so forth. Porter figured prominently in a number of these developments.

In the nearly three decades since Porter died, Canadian society and Canadian sociology have, of course, changed again. Porter's work is now part of the discipline's past, but this is not because Canadians have solved the problems with which he struggled. Indeed, social inequalities abound and Canadian society seems just as unequal, irrational and unjust as it was forty years ago, and many of Porter's more abstract and moralistic ruminations on these themes, which I discuss in the concluding chapters of the book, remain relevant and timely. However, because those ruminations were often deeply embedded in empirical evidence that is now outdated, his contributions no longer seem as directly useful as they once did. That said, we should not allow them to fade from collective memory, either in Canadian sociology or in Canadian society more generally. The danger of Porter and *The Vertical Mosaic* becoming just a footnote is very real. Thirty, perhaps even twenty, years ago, it was impossible for any well-rounded undergraduate sociology or political science student to finish a degree at a Canadian university without becoming familiar with *The Vertical Mosaic*. Today few undergraduates have heard of it. Worse yet, many sociology graduate students seem little better informed. Some have *heard* of the book, but few have actually *read* it. In such circumstances, a full-scale intellectual biography of John Porter, especially one that includes a detailed description and assessment of *The Vertical Mosaic*, seems appropriate and timely: a necessary part of the history of the discipline and a well-deserved tribute to one of the great figures of Canadian social science.[2] Over twenty-five years of social change and social science scholarship since his death provide an historical perspective on his legacy that allows us to appreciate the enormity of his accomplishments while acknowledging that the country has changed and the discipline has moved on.

I would like to make two further points before I describe more specifically the purposes of this volume. First, I have just suggested that I regard *Measuring the Mosaic* as a tribute to John Porter. And it is. But it is not a celebration. I began this project with enormous respect for John Porter's contribution to Canadian sociology, and my admiration grew as I worked to put together an account of his life story and intellectual contribution. He was a gifted and hardworking scholar, a thoughtful, principled citizen of his university, his discipline, and his country, and a landmark on Canada's intellectual landscape for well over two decades. He contributed more than any other sociologist of his generation to the strength and legitimacy of the discipline and added much to the quality of intellectual discourse in Canadian social science. But like the rest of us, John Porter had academic feet of clay, and parts of this study are given over to a respectful but critical analysis of his work.

Second, I think it worth noting that at one point in his career Porter denied that he was an appropriate subject for an intellectual biography. Over the summer and fall of 1976, Wallace Clement, then Porter's PhD student, discussed with him the prospect of writing such a book. Porter's immediate response, while not entirely dismissive, is probably best characterized as ambivalent. He stated that such a book was neither warranted nor of any interest to the public; indeed, he claimed that there were others 'more deserving of such attention.' Clement was not easily deterred, however, and pressed him further. It is in my view revealing that Porter did not encourage Clement but did not rule out the possibility either. I think that by this time in his career he had a sense of his rightful place in the discipline that made the prospect of an intellectual biography a reasonable one.[3] In any case, when Clement first broached the subject, nothing was done. They decided the project was premature but instead determined to carry out a series of tape-recorded interviews that would allow Porter to provide a first-person account of his life and work should Clement ever decide to revisit the project.[4] Unfortunately, the interviews never took place. Clement completed his PhD thesis, took a position as a faculty member at McMaster University, and became busy with other research. Three years later, Porter died of a heart attack and his life story was never recorded.

Intellectual Biography

Above I referred to this volume as an 'intellectual biography.' I should specify what I mean by that term, for such books can take a variety of forms.

First, and most obviously, I tell the story of John Porter's life, focusing in particular on events and experiences that relate directly to his development as an intellectual and help us to understand and appreciate his activities as a scholar.

In assessing his intellectual contribution, I concentrate on his written work, especially the published pieces, focusing in particular on his major published writings: 'Power and Freedom in Canadian Democracy,' 'Occupational Prestige in Canada,' *Towards 2000, Stations and Callings, Ascription and Achievement*, the McInnis Lectures, and, above all, *The*

Vertical Mosaic.[5] But I also rely, of course, on other sources of information – unpublished writings, interviews, correspondence with his colleagues and friends, the secondary literature, and so on.

The biography is somewhat unusual because so much of the narrative focuses on one book: *The Vertical Mosaic*. I describe in detail both its contents and how it was written, and carefully assess the response it generated. In addition, I examine the impact the work had on Porter's life and subsequent writing. My account is skewed in this way because *The Vertical Mosaic* was without question the most important thing John Porter wrote. It was his entrée into the pantheon of Canadian sociology and the Canadian social science hall of fame. In my estimation, this means that a good deal of Porter's life as a scholar *has* to be written with *The Vertical Mosaic* front and centre. Its publication constituted the defining moment in John Porter's academic life, so we must understand him in relation to it in the same way that we understand it in relation to him. In a sense, he was as much a product of the book as, in the beginning, the book was his product.

While this work is an intellectual biography of John Porter, it necessarily deals with several aspects of the history of English-language Canadian sociology during the 1950s, '60s, and '70s. The release of *The Vertical Mosaic* in 1965 constituted a defining moment in the life of John Porter, but it was no less a defining moment in the history of Canadian sociology. For decades, sociology in English Canada had languished in a largely underdeveloped state, neglected, maligned even, by scholars from the more traditional and established disciplines. Most historians, political scientists, economists, and philosophers, it seems, regarded sociology with disinterest or disdain. In their view, nothing significant could be learned or researched via sociology that could not be learned or researched in a more rigorous and sophisticated way through one of the classical disciplines of study. The appearance of *The Vertical Mosaic* changed everything. Suddenly, English-language Canadian sociology had both a showpiece and a validation. In a sense, the publication of *The Vertical Mosaic* marked the coming of age of the discipline in English Canada.[6] It demonstrated that sociologists had something worthwhile to say and the book stepped into the very front rank of must-read books in Canadian social science. Given the significance of Porter and his work for Canadian sociology, I saw it as important to put Porter's scholarly contributions into their socio-historical context. Every scholar writes from a particular perspective, from a standpoint framed by personal experiences and scholarly training, and under the influence of particular historical events, cultural practices, intellectual icons, and the like. Indeed, the standpoints of intellectuals are especially complex because scholars are subject to the influence of specifically academic schools of thought – ways of describing, constructing, and discussing the world – that are different from the so-called common-sense ways of doing and seeing things that most people share.

As I pieced together my account of the relevant details of Porter's private life I ferreted out as much useful information as possible about the nature and sources of his scholarly world view. I therefore had to describe the development of Canadian sociology, outline the more general Canadian university culture of the period, and describe selected social, economic, and political events and trends of the era, especially those that had a direct impact on Porter's agenda and approach. It is for this reason that I deal in some detail with the Depression, World War II, the postwar boom, the rapid-growth phase of universities in the 1960s, and so on. These were the key social events that framed and contoured Porter's personal and scholarly life, just as they framed and contoured the experiences of his entire generation. I try to link these events to his biography and scholarly works. As I describe Porter's work and contributions, I document in detail how he came to write each of his works, trying to determine not just what led him to take on certain projects at particular times but also what caused him to approach them as he did.

The Structure of the Book

I decided early on that I would write a chronological narrative. That is, rather than divide the work into sections focused exclusively on Porter's life, times, or work, I would weave the three together.

Chapter 1 describes his childhood and teenage years in Vancouver, Canada, and London, England (1921–41), and chapter 2 describes the time he spent in the Canadian Army during and after World War II (1941–6). In these chapters I try to understand how these experiences influenced his personal development and contributed to the formation of the intellectual and political views he later held as a scholar.

Chapter 3 documents the details of his formal education at the London School of Economics and Political Science (1946–9) and examines the impact of this relatively brief but influential period of formal schooling. The ideas of Leonard Hobhouse, a New Liberal sociologist and political philosopher, figure prominently in the account.

Chapters 4 through 8 focus on Porter's masterwork, *The Vertical Mosaic*. After graduating from the LSE in 1949, Porter returned to Canada for a visit. While in Ottawa, he accepted a teaching position at Carleton College (later Carleton University). At the time, Carleton was a new and precarious enterprise and Canadian sociology a small and marginal part of the nation's scholarly community. Since these circumstances help to explain some of Porter's early interests and efforts as a scholar, I use chapter 4 to provide the social and political context of Canada in 1939–63 as the background for understanding Porter's early academic career. Chapter 5 outlines the growth and development of Carleton and describes the genesis of *The Vertical Mosaic*. Porter was prompted to write the book in part because of pressure from the president of Carleton, who demanded that Porter either get a PhD or publish a major work. Under the impetus of this not-so-veiled threat, Porter made the fateful decision to begin work on the structure of class and power in Canada, research that eventually culminated in *The Vertical Mosaic*. The next three chapters deal directly with one or another aspect of this event. Chapter 6 describes Porter's long struggle to write the book – a massive undertaking, given the limited resources available to him at the time – and examines Porter's growing reputation in the Canadian social science community. Chapter 7 describes in detail the contents of *The Vertical Mosaic*. Chapter 8 provides a detailed conceptual, substantive, methodological, and theoretical critique and outlines the public and scholarly response it generated over the next decade.

Chapters 9 through 15 focus on Porter's post-*Mosaic* scholarly career. Chapter 9 describes selected social, economic, ideological, and political changes that altered the landscape of the nation during the period and, in turn, influenced the growth and development of the Canadian university system and transformed Canadian sociology. Chapter 10 picks up the biographical thread by describing Porter's time as a fellow at the Institute for Labour Studies at the International Labour Organization in Geneva and, for one unhappy year, as a faculty member at the University of Toronto. As well, it details the process of writing, with Peter Pineo, their influential study, 'Occupational prestige in Canada.' Chapter 11 describes the writing, with Marion Porter and Bernard Blishen, of *Stations and Callings*, a massive empirical study of the educational aspirations and attainment of Ontario primary and secondary school students. Chapter 12 does the same thing for *Ascription and Achievement*, the landmark study of social mobility that Porter co-authored with Monica Boyd, John Goyder, Frank Jones, Hugh McRoberts, and

Peter Pineo. In these chapters I make three basic claims. First, while none of these studies earned the kind of plaudits garnered by *The Vertical Mosaic*, each constituted a major contribution to the growth and maturation of Canadian sociology. Second, each allowed Porter to follow up on one or the other of the key themes in *The Vertical Mosaic*. Third, along with other work and activities, they constitute evidence of Porter's desire to be a 'practical, engaged intellectual,' one who examined Canadian society not from the point of view of the detached, objective scholar but from that of an engaged scholar-citizen committed to making the nation more just, rational, and humane. Chapter 13 continues the narrative of Porter's post-*Mosaic* career by describing the bittersweet period he spent as a senior university administrator at Carleton, including an account of his failed bid to become president of the university in 1978. Chapter 14 examines the substantial scholarly and personal role that Marion Porter played as John's intellectual partner. Chapter 15 describes his scholarly and other activities during the last months of his life, after leaving the vice-presidency of Carleton.

The book concludes with an afterword that examines Porter's legacy and significance as a practical intellectual, specifically as a practitioner of the British tradition of New Liberal political thought and policy-relevant, morally driven scholarship. The New Liberalism, which had its roots in the work of John Stuart Mill, T.H. Green, and others, reached prominence in England during the last years of the nineteenth century and the first of the twentieth through the efforts of scholars like J.A. Hobson and – most important for my purposes – L.T. Hobhouse and Morris Ginsberg. Porter studied with Ginsberg, T.H. Marshall, and other New Liberal thinkers at LSE. The tradition had an early start in Canada at Queen's University and the University of Toronto, but had more influence in the Canadian civil service than in academia until after World War II. I argue in this final chapter that Porter's work can be fruitfully understood by placing it in this tradition, a tradition of service that combined scholarly and political work in an effort – regarded at one and the same time as both a duty and a mission – to make Canada a more rational, humane, and democratic country.

1 Growing Up in Vancouver and London, 1921–1941

The Vancouver Years, 1921–1937

John Arthur Walker Porter was born in Vancouver, British Columbia, on 12 November 1921, the second of three children born to Arthur Porter and Ethel Cuffin. His childhood and teenage years were difficult – marred by poverty and family dissolution – leaving a permanent mark on the quiet, sensitive young man who would become Canada's premier sociologist. According to family lore, the source of the problems was Arthur.

Arthur and Ethel had immigrated to Canada as children – Arthur from England, Ethel from Wales.[1] Arthur was born in Brentford, England, in 1898. He was given up for adoption at birth by his mother and grew up as the unofficially adopted son of Cornelius Edward Porter, an accountant, and Annie Mayo.[2] Cornelius and Annie moved to Canada soon after the turn of the century and settled in Toronto. Both were devout Christians, enthusiastic members of the Salvation Army who, on Sundays, often left their very young son to fend for himself all day while they went out to preach. Arthur seems to have become alienated from his parents at a very early age for in 1912, when he was just fourteen, he left and headed west to Vancouver. There he worked for a year as a clerk at Spencer's, a large department store, before getting a job as a messenger and subsequently clerk at McDougall and Cowans, a stock-broking firm.[3] Sometime in 1915 or 1916 he joined the Canadian Army and, according to his daughter, Eileen Jones, served for the balance of the war, including some time overseas.[4] Upon returning to Canada at war's end, he obtained a position as a clerk at Pemberton and Son, a large insurance, investment, and property management firm in central

Vancouver.[5] It was while working at Pemberton's that he met Ethel Cuffin.

Ethel Cuffin, three years Arthur's senior, was born in Newport, Wales, the daughter of John Cuffin and Eva Tink, also active members of the Salvation Army.[6] When she was still quite young, the family moved from Newport to Wrexham in North Wales, where her father had secured a job as manager of a brick manufacturing plant. A bright child, she earned a scholarship to attend a local high school but was unable to finish her course of studies because when she was fifteen, the family emigrated to the United States. They lived briefly in Jacksonville, Florida and Missoula, Montana – where she finally completed secondary school.[7] In 1914, just as World War I broke out, the family moved again – to Vancouver. Within a couple of years, her father, John, was able to re-establish himself, obtaining a position as the supervisor of a brickworks owned by Coughlan's, one of the city's largest construction and ship-building firms.[8] Ethel attended normal school and worked briefly as a cashier at Spencer's before taking a job as an elementary school teacher.[9] Sometime during this period, she met Arthur Porter at a Salvation Army social function.[10] They married on 11 September 1919.[11]

Arthur and Ethel decided to stay in Vancouver, a beautiful and promising city then at the height of a long economic boom. Two decades earlier, Vancouver had been a comparatively small and undeveloped economic centre and Victoria had claimed pride of place as British Columbia's political, economic, and cultural capital and largest city. By the early 1920s, however, Vancouver's population had grown rapidly to 120,000 and it had become a manufacturing and transportation hub.[12] It soon supplanted Victoria as the province's most important city. Much of Vancouver's population growth had occurred via immigration from the British Isles and the city had a decidedly English cultural orientation.[13] As late as 1922, for example, people still drove on the left side of the road.[14]

Soon after marrying, Arthur and Ethel decided to start a family. Eileen, their first child, was born in 1920, and John a year later. Ethel left her teaching job to look after the children. For the first few years, the family managed on Arthur's salary as a clerk,[15] and they lived in a series of small rented houses in the Grandview area, a working-class neighbourhood a couple of blocks east of the massive Canadian Northern Railway yards at the end of False Creek.[16] By the middle of the decade, things had taken a turn for the better. They moved briefly to Kitsilano for 1924 and 1925 and then to a new house on Larch Street in Kerrisdale, a burgeoning, middle-class neighbourhood in southwest Vancouver. They remained in Kerrisdale for five years, until 1930, just after the sudden onset of the Depression.[17] For the Porters, like many families, the Depression changed everything.

During the Depression, Canada's economy collapsed almost completely. Between 1929 and 1933, the gross national product dropped by nearly a third, national income dropped by half, and more than one in four adults was unemployed.[18] R.B. Bennett's Conservative government, which had replaced Mackenzie King's Liberals as Canada's governing party in 1930, tried a variety of corrective and palliative measures, but to no avail.[19] Through the thirties, little changed; unemployment rates remained high, farmers struggled with dust and foreclosures, and hundreds of thousands of Canadians lived on meagre relief payments provided by municipalities.[20]

Circumstances were particularly dire in Vancouver. The city's construction industry ground to a halt, sawmills closed, and wheat sales shrank. Thousands of workers lost their jobs and the situation worsened considerably as hundreds of labourers from outlying lumber and mining communities flocked to the city looking for work and assistance. By the winter of 1932–3, approximately 40,000 of the city's residents depended entirely on municipal relief.[21] The Porters were among them. Sometime in late 1930 or early 1931, Arthur lost his job and the family ended up on the dole. Though only eight or nine years old at the time, John never forgot the experience. For the balance of his life, he retained vivid and bitter memories of the humiliation of standing in line with his father to collect their weekly allotment of staples.[22] The system was intentionally shaming: 'Unemployed families in need of relief did not receive a cash payment. The head of the family had to line up on relief day and receive groceries which were carried home in a gunny sack. It was intended to be humiliating since all the neighbours would know who was on relief and it was assumed that unemployed people could not be trusted to handle money properly.'[23] Eric Kelly, one of Porter's elementary school teachers, recalls that the Depression hit the working-class neighbourhood where the Porters lived 'with great severity': 'Teachers ... paid money into a "shoe fund" [for] ... students who had not proper footwear to be able to go to school.'[24]

Those on relief in Vancouver found it even more difficult to make ends meet than did those in most other Canadian urban centres. The city had the third highest cost of living in Canada,[25] but ranked only twenty-fifth in terms of the monthly welfare allowances it provided to needy families.[26] As a family of five, the Porters would have received a monthly maximum of about $38 for food, fuel, and rent, compared to $50 in Edmonton and nearly $60 in Toronto and Calgary.[27] At the time, a loaf of bread cost 6 cents, milk was 10 cents a quart, and rent for a two-bedroom apartment was approximately $22–25 per month, so the allowance would have covered only about half their expenses.[28] Even with such careful expenditure of public money, however, by 1935 the City of Vancouver was nearly bankrupt.[29]

Desperate conditions in Vancouver and across the country spawned a good deal of political activity, ranging from occasional outbursts of brute violence on the part of the unemployed to the formation of new political organizations and parties to advocate on behalf of the disadvantaged. Perhaps the most important of such groups was the Co-operative Commonwealth Federation (CCF), founded in 1933. This left-wing party brought together embattled farmers, unemployed workers, and progressive intellectuals; many of these last were members of the Fabian Society, an English socialist organization that had been crucial in helping to establish the British Labour Party. Not surprisingly, the CCF's pro-labour, pro-farmer policies spurred some immediate, if modest, electoral success – seven seats in the federal election of 1935.[30] More important, however, in the following decades the party helped to spearhead the movement that eventually succeeded in creating a national welfare state. Porter, who was just twelve years old in 1933 when the CCF proclaimed its radical 'Regina Manifesto,' later came to play a prominent role in the writing of *Social Purpose for Canada*, the paper foundation of the New Democratic Party (NDP), successor to the CCF.[31]

If the widespread poverty and unemployment that plagued the country during the 1930s suggest that Arthur Porter might be excused for failing to provide for his family, his children did not see it that way. He is a shadowy and unwelcome figure in the family's collective memory, remembered as an irresponsible parent who was unwilling to work enough to build a solid career and support his family.[32] As John put it thirty years later when speaking with a journalist, Arthur 'did some clerical work but had no inclination to do anything very much.'[33] Alan, John's brother, said much the same thing: 'We were poor, there is no question about that, and I suspect that it was mainly due to my father's irresponsibility … He had [a] "reluctance" to develop a real career [and] was unstable, I suppose, in that respect.'[34]

When Arthur lost his job, the Porters moved to Chilliwack, a small community just a few miles southeast of Vancouver.[35] Ethel was pregnant with their third child, Alan, but shortly after they moved to Chilliwack, she discovered that Arthur had become involved in an affair, one of many over the course of their marriage. She forced him to leave, but he returned after a few weeks, the rift between them apparently repaired. Though the situation stabilized and the family remained together for some years thereafter, the move to Chilliwack proved fruitless – Arthur could not find a full-time job – and about a year later they pulled up stakes, returning once again to Vancouver. Finally, in 1932, in a stroke of luck and with no little irony, Arthur found a job with the Municipal Assistance Board of Vancouver, helping people on the dole. Despite this good fortune and the financial stability it brought, the Porters moved each year for the next five, always within the bounds of the familiar working-class residential area of Knight Road, not far from where they had begun their sojourn as a family a decade and a half earlier.[36] John and Eileen settled in at Lord Selkirk Elementary School.[37]

John remembered these early years at school as the only truly happy part of his childhood.[38] With great encouragement from his mother, he proved to be an exceptionally able pupil and, in his final year at Lord Selkirk, won an award as the outstanding student in his grade.[39] He then followed Eileen to nearby John Oliver High School, at the corner of 41st and Fraser Streets. In the 1930s, John Oliver was Vancouver's largest secondary school, with an enrolment of 1,800–2,000 mostly working-class students.[40] In his first year there, 1935, he obtained an average of 84 per cent, including 98 per cent in algebra and 87 per cent in social studies.[41] His intelligence and sensitivity, coupled with his love of reading and his facility with the written word, were already in evidence.[42] His English teacher, Beattie MacLean, recalled that he very soon recognized John as 'an outstanding ... student, obviously possessed of a very high IQ. His participation in class discussions and his writing showed a maturity far beyond that of the average 14- or 15-year-old boy or girl. He stood out as an independent thinker, somewhat "left" leaning, and already possessed of considerable talent in verse-writing.'[43] In fact, English was Porter's favourite subject and his creative writing skills were so remarkable that many years later, MacLean lamented his young protégé's choice of sociology over English literature, believing that he had forfeited an opportunity to become Canada's greatest poet.[44] Eileen remembers her brother recounting a story about a composition he had written for MacLean's English class. Apparently, MacLean raved about it to John's classmates: 'I must read this out. I must read this out.

This is wonderful – to think that one of my students has written a thing like this.'[45] From this beginning, MacLean and Porter, originally teacher and student, eventually became good friends, maintaining a correspondence long after Porter moved to England. MacLean acted as John's literary mentor for years, and during World War II, when MacLean was posted to England, he became a frequent and welcome visitor to the Porter family home on Pilgrim's Way in Paentre Maelor, a housing estate near Wrexham in North Wales.

The half-decade or so of relative family stability in the Porter home came to an abrupt end in the fall of 1937. Arthur began yet another affair and left for England, abandoning Ethel and the three children.[46] His departure left them virtually penniless, for he had taken out a chattel mortgage on the furniture before leaving. Since Ethel was unable to make the payments – John's paper route was the family's only cash income – bailiffs seized most of their belongings.[47] Not long after, Arthur telegraphed Ethel, inviting her to follow him to England.[48] Curiously, she decided to go, but having collapsed emotionally in the wake of her husband's departure, she was incapable of arranging the trip.[49] It fell to John and Eileen – then fifteen and sixteen, respectively – to organize the family's exodus via train to Halifax and from there by ship to England.[50]

The London Years, 1937–1941

Once they arrived in London, Arthur helped them to find a flat in Catford, in the southeastern part of the city.[51] Ethel remained deeply depressed and could not work, so for the next two years, it fell to Eileen and John to support the family, apparently with some help from Arthur, who had found a job with a welfare agency in London.[52] Eileen took a job as a librarian for Boots Chemists – it was common practice for pharmacies to have small lending libraries in those days – while John worked at a variety of odd jobs: as a packer in a factory, as an amateur social worker, and as a management trainee for Littlewood's department store.[53] During these years, John matured tremendously. He assumed a quasi-paternal role with his brother and helped handle many of the family's problems as they settled into life in Depression-era London.[54] In a letter to MacLean written three years after arriving in England, he mused that the intervening period had been the 'fullest' of his life and remarked that he found it hard to believe 'that anyone [he had gone] to school with could still be studying.'[55]

Not until 1939, two full years after they arrived in London and just a few months after the outbreak of World War II, did Ethel recover sufficiently to begin working again, in a full-time position procured with Arthur's help as a clerk-administrator for the Women's Voluntary Service in Lambeth.[56] Her job, once the Blitzkrieg began, was to help resettle people who had been forced out of their homes by the bombing.[57] Ironically, the Porters themselves soon joined the ranks of the 'bombed-outs,' and John and Eileen grew increasingly restive about the dangers of staying in London. Soon, Alan and Ethel were sent to live with relatives in Wrexham.[58] Once safe in Wales, Ethel found a job at a Royal Ordinance Factory making munitions for the duration of the war.[59]

Arthur kept in touch with the family during these early years, and John lived with him briefly during the Blitz,[60] but there is no evidence Arthur intended to return to his wife and children or that John or Eileen changed their very negative opinion of their father. Arthur's actions scarred all of them permanently, Ethel in particular. For the rest of her life she would 'collapse' whenever in the presence of her eldest son or daughter, demanding to be cared for by them.[61] Later in his life Porter came to resent this, but early on it helped to establish a very strong bond between them.[62] Ethel had a tremendously positive, long-term influence on her son's intellectual and emotional development, but it could not make up entirely for the damage Arthur had done to his eldest son. The impressionable young 'Jack' Porter could neither fathom nor forgive his father's decision to desert the family.[63] Years later, in wartime letters home to his mother, he would bristle about Arthur's behaviour: 'Dad must help and if I return and find things different to what I expect, and through his despicable neglect Alan in any way suffers, he will have to face a very irate person. I am losing most of my scruples, and often I think I am killing better [men] than he.'[64] This bitterness never dissipated. A decade later, when Marion gave birth to their first child, Tony, John refused Arthur's request for a picture of his grandson. The letter bearing the request was immediately torn up and thrown away.[65]

According to Marion Porter, the 'painful experiences' her husband endured as a child 'haunted him most of his adult life.'[66] Others, too, noted the deep impact of the poverty and family instability he endured as a child. As Pauline Jewett put it, 'It would be impossible to overestimate the negative impact that his boyhood had on him.' According to her, John's early experiences manifested themselves in a pessimistic outlook on life. 'Where Marion and I would see the doughnut,' she said, 'John would see the hole.'[67] His friend, political scientist Paul Fox, concurred, but noted that one of the reasons John succeeded as an academic was that he possessed a passion unknown to middle-class intellectuals of the time, a passion born of his poverty-stricken background. 'It took somebody who suffered under the class system,' Fox said, 'to change it.'[68]

While the London years were difficult, there were happy times as well. After working at odd jobs for two years, Porter finally found something he really liked – a job at a London newspaper, the *Daily Sketch*.[69] This position not only afforded him the opportunity to do some writing but also satisfied his craving for intellectual stimulation – something that had been denied him at other jobs. As he wrote to Beattie MacLean, 'The longing to learn burns constantly in me, and I try, though it is very hard at this time, to read and write, trying always to improve my style.'[70] But his budding career as a newspaper man lasted less than two years, cut short by World War II.

World War II Begins

On 3 September 1939, following a series of escalating diplomatic confrontations with Germany over the invasion of Austria and Poland, Britain's prime minister, Neville Chamberlain, declared war on Germany.[71] That winter Hitler made no further moves, but in the spring of 1940 he quickly overran Denmark, Norway, Finland, Holland, Luxembourg, and France. To press his advantage, and in preparation for a prospective all-out invasion of England in the autumn of 1940, Hitler initiated a massive air assault on the island. Initial raids carried out in mid-August 1940 were intended to destroy the RAF Fighter Command and decimate England's network of fighter factories.[72] Only an RAF victory in the Battle of Britain, a spectacular and pivotal aerial combat over London and south England in mid-September, forestalled his plan for an imminent invasion of the island. But the bombing did not stop. Indeed, the frequency and scale of air raids intensified. Now, however, they took place only at night and focused for the most part on London. For the next eight months, until Hitler finally shifted his attentions east to Russia, the Blitzkrieg raged nightly.

Hitler's bombers did massive physical damage to the city. Large sections of central London were demolished and 1.5 million of the city's population of 8 million were made homeless. For some people, the ordeal of homelessness – being counted among the bombed-outs

– lasted just a few days or weeks, but for tens of thousands it lasted months, even years.[73] Many middle-class Londoners were able to retreat to private underground shelters – so-called Andersons – built in their back gardens, but working-class residents of central London were not so fortunate. They had to spend their nights in subway stations and other shelters, grim places with few or no toilets or other amenities. At the massive Tilbury shelter in the working-class neighbourhood of Stepney, for example, 16,000 people crowded together in filth and dampness each night for months on end.[74] The psychological strain in the city was tremendous; the rain of bombs destroyed people's homes and businesses and took a devastating toll in human lives. More than 30,000 Londoners died and many times that number were injured.[75]

Porter and his family were not spared the suffering; indeed, they were bombed out three times. John described one such occasion in a letter to Beattie MacLean.

> It was a particularly heavy night ... Every time they dropped one we threw ourselves on the floor. Mothers would instinctively cover their small children with their own bodies. What a pathetic sight. About 2 AM activity increased ... Amid the din of guns we heard a bomb coming – louder and closer than anything we had ever heard.... It finally came to earth across the street – an aerial torpedo which demolished 2 1/2 houses, burying a number of people. Our house rocked. We piled on top of each other to avoid being cut by glass which flew in all directions ... By now ARP men were on the scene, doors were broken open and out we walked, but not to safety ... Without anything but our clothes, my mother, little brother ... my sister and I ran through the hail of shrapnel to the [first aid] post.[76]

Porter often marvelled that he had escaped with his life. 'It seems so ridiculous to look forward beyond the very minute in which you live,' he wrote to MacLean. 'I never was a fatalist, but I should like to know what dread hand keeps me clear of falling bombs.'[77]

During the first six months of the Blitz, Porter continued to work at the *Sketch*. Indeed, as the war intensified, and senior reporters left to join the armed forces, he was given the chance to work as a junior reporter, covering the Blitz.[78] He took full advantage of the opportunity, supplementing his practical training at the paper during the day with journalism courses at Regent Street Polytechnic in the evening.[79] In his spare time he and a colleague, R. Alwyn Raymond, drew on their experiences to write 'London's Story', a first-hand, ethnographic account of the Blitz. The scope and quality of this project are impressive, especially considering that Porter was an eighteen-year-old high school dropout.[80]

A fascinating, 200-page eyewitness account, 'London's Story' provides a glimpse of the bravery and ingenuity exhibited by ordinary Londoners as they struggled to deal with the bombing and its horrific after-effects.[81] As well, it provides a peephole through which we can get a sense of Porter's ideas and attitudes at the time. One of the most obvious features of the manuscript is its political tone. Raymond and Porter are clearly alive to political and social issues and make many comments critical of individual politicians, the Conservative Party, the Labour Party and, above all, England's class system. In their telling of the tale, they are highly complimentary of the efforts of the 'average' Londoner – the lorry driver, the factory worker, and the shop clerk – but the wealthy receive no such plaudits. They are often portrayed as selfish and uncaring, little concerned to share the burdens of war. As an example, Porter and Raymond remark that during the Blitz it became customary for motorists to offer rides to pedestrians stranded at crowded bus and tram shelters. The very wealthy, especially those in chauffeur-driven limousines, were less likely than others to be good Samaritans: 'Stately old ladies with room enough for at least six people would sail majestically and indifferently past miserable, tired, rain-soaked crowds. When signalled to stop, they seemed shocked to think that their serene presence should be disturbed by lowly strangers.'[82] Porter and Raymond were equally critical of the measures the wealthy took to avoid the nightly bombing:

> For the more elite section of the population a luxury train with sleeping and restaurant cars was used. It was hired by a group of businessmen, and, with its staff of attendants, left a main London terminus every night, and parked in a siding of a branch line in the country. After a night in the sleeper the various components of the back-bone of Britain would saunter along to the dining car for breakfast, and when the 'all clear' had been signalled from London, the train with its precious cargo, their indomitable spirit unbroken, would return to the capital.
>
> For the brave plutocrats who gallantly decided to stay in London at night, underground, bomb-proof, sound-proof, guinea-a-night bedrooms were at their disposal … They were called in the morning with a cup of tea, and the information that 'the raiders-passed signal has now been sounded.'[83]

While Porter enjoyed this kind of work, he realized that as the war grew in scale his days as a reporter were numbered. He was British citizen subject to conscription and on 24 February 1941, about six months after the Blitz began and just three months into his twentieth year, he enlisted. Rather than joining a British unit, however, he signed on with the Vancouver-based Seaforth Highlanders Regiment of the Canadian Army.[84] Though he later insisted that World War II had been worth fighting because it saved the world from fascism, patriotism was not the proximate cause of his decision to join the Seaforths.[85] Just a few months earlier, he had written to Beattie MacLean saying that he did *not* intend to join the Army. If it became necessary, he wrote, he would join the Merchant Navy.[86] When he realized he was going to be called up anyway, however, he took a quick and pragmatic glance at his wallet and decided to sign on with the Canadian Army. The pay was better.[87]

2 The Army Years, 1941–1946

From 1939 to 1945, Canada was a nation at war. Some 1.1 million men and women out of a population of 11 million served in the country's Armed Forces and, of those, 42,042 lost their lives.[1] John Porter was lucky; even though he spent over a year in and around the fighting in Sicily and Italy, his only injury was a concussion sustained in a motorcycle accident while doing basic training in Surrey.[2] However, while he made it through the war physically unscathed, it influenced him deeply. A sensitive and artistic young man, he enlisted reluctantly. He was certain of the justice of the Allied cause and committed to the fight against fascism, but loath to leave his promising job at the *Sketch* for the risky life of an infantryman. Especially during his early years of service, he found military training and duties boring and chafed under the discipline and regimentation of army life. Letters home to his family complain of despondency, even depression. To cope, he treated his day-to-day duties with a cynical 'detached amusement' while simultaneously finding as much time as possible to pursue the literary pastimes he had enjoyed in civilian life.[3] Later, when he moved into the Intelligence Corps, his spirits improved markedly, not only because the work suited him better but because military discipline was less formal.[4] Though he continued to manifest a tendency to become depressed, he nonetheless served effectively and resourcefully during his career in the Intelligence Corps and ultimately earned the rank of captain.

Learning to Be a Soldier: Training in England, 1941–1943

When Canada entered the war in September 1939, its armed forces were poorly prepared.[5] The Permanent Force of Army, Navy, and Air Force personnel numbered less than 10,000 and reserves were in each case poorly trained and ill equipped.[6] The declaration of war changed the manpower situation dramatically. Regiments mobilized quickly, Canadians volunteered by the thousands, and within a month the Army alone had swelled to 60,000.[7] All across the country, armouries and parade squares came to life as recruits learned the rudiments of drill. Equipment from World War I, much of it obsolete, was cleaned up and pressed into service – and still there were great shortages. Canadian author Farley Mowat was at the time an intelligence officer with the Hastings and Prince Edward Regiment, or the 'Hasty P's' as they were better known. In *The Regiment*, he recalled the scene at his regiment's training facility in Trenton, Ontario:

> A man who had been a railroad hand four days previously now stood on the open land behind the Cold Storage Building ... shouting drill orders to his platoon. The men wore ... bright sweaters, worn jackets, flannel trousers, and grease-stained mechanic's overalls. On their shoulders, they carried lengths of wood, broomsticks or pieces of planking shaped roughly to resemble the Lee-Enfield, for there were not even enough antiquated rifles to go around.[8]

Porter's regiment, the Vancouver-based Seaforth Highlanders of Canada, was among the first to mobilize and on 10 December 1939 a contingent of them sailed from Halifax, part of a force of 23,000 Canadian troops that arrived in England over the Christmas holiday and into the new year of 1940.[9] Though eager, most were just civilians in uniform, having received only rudimentary training before leaving Canada. They were therefore immediately shipped to Aldershot, the main Canadian Forces training base in England, to begin supplementary training.[10]

Aldershot, set in the gently rolling countryside of Hampshire about forty miles southwest of London, was England's largest peacetime military base and had long been a military training centre. In fact, many Canadians had trained there during World War I.[11] The area offered varied terrain – ploughed and unploughed fields, forested areas, marshes and ponds – and small towns and quaint villages dotted the landscape roundabout. The base itself, however, was quite dismal. Mowat once described it as a set of 'frigid barrack blocks ... almost as bleak as the hutments of Depression labour camps,' perhaps an overstatement but no doubt the amenities were poor, especially compared to what most

Canadians had enjoyed back home.[12] Originally constructed during the Crimean War, the barracks were rebuilt in the 1890s. Though now made of brick rather than wood, they remained quite primitive; many had no provisions for hot water or showers, some even lacked indoor plumbing. Worse, the barracks were not insulated and lacked central heating. This proved to be a huge problem because, as it happened, the winter of 1939–40 was the coldest since 1894.[13] The only source of heat in each dormitory was a small coal-burning stove or open fireplace, and since fuel was strictly rationed and of low quality, trainees were never warm. Recruits scavenged everywhere for fuel and, to great local consternation, 'liberated' many wooden park benches and bus stop seats to feed dormitory fires.[14] Yet even these measures could not prevent many of the first arrivals from developing cold-related maladies.[15] Conditions had improved by the time Porter arrived in February of 1941, but Aldershot remained an unpleasant place to live for any extended period.

Basic Training

Basic infantry training was an imposing round of exercise, instruction, and drills designed to turn civilians into soldiers as quickly as possible. The most important aspects of this training, and the ones taught first, were individual skills. These were typically taught in two phases, basic and advanced, each taking six weeks. Advanced skills involved some platoon-level tactics and battle drill.[16]

The day began with reveille at six in the morning. Physical fitness training was first: sit-ups, push-ups, running, and callisthenics for a half-hour or so before returning to barracks. Breakfast was next, followed by parade at eight o'clock. There troops were put into groups, some to engage in further training exercises, others to carry out 'fatigue' duties such as cleaning or kitchen work. Morning sessions involved basic drill – marching in formation on the parade square – combined with skills training. Some skills training activities were combat related, and others were technical or job related. Early in the war, combat-related training was very simple: range practice, field craft, first aid, and map-reading exercises.[17] As the war progressed, it became more specialized and demanding. Recruits were put through realistic battle drill, learned military tactics and unarmed combat and, as a last measure, were exposed to live-firing exercises designed to simulate battle conditions.[18] Afternoons were given over to technical training: everything from repairing a rifle to running a field radio. In Porter's case, long hours were spent on a motorcycle, navigating the lanes and hedgerows of the English countryside with map and compass. As a security precaution, and to force trainees to find their way 'blind,' all road signs had been removed.[19] All of this training was supplemented by extended route marches – often ten miles or more – intended to build stamina. After dinner trainees usually had some free time, but sometimes they had to undergo night-time skills training.[20] For example, Porter had to learn to get from place to place on his motorcycle in the pitch dark without benefit of a headlight, again to simulate battle conditions.

Subsequent phases of basic training involved ever more complex unit-based activities, culminating in battalion-level field exercises, but the first contingent of Canadians did not get to this group level of training right away. Originally, the 1st Canadian Division was to have joined the British Expeditionary Force in France in late summer of 1940. The speed of Hitler's advance through continental Europe, combined with the Allied defeat at Dunkirk in early June 1940, changed everything, however, and the primary objective of the Allied command became the defence of England against imminent German invasion.[21] To this end, British and Canadian troops were stationed in strategic defensive locations, concentrated most heavily on the southern coast.[22] The threat of a German invasion diminished when the RAF won the Battle of Britain in September and lessened further with the onset of winter, but it did not dissipate entirely until the Germans opened the Eastern Front in June 1941.[23] Until then, the key responsibility given to the Canadian Army Overseas was the defence of England.

It was in the context of waning fears of an immediate German invasion that Porter enlisted in late February 1941 and completed basic training.[24] The steady diet of calisthenics, drill, sports, and forced marches in the English countryside must have been trying for him. He was a bookish sort, completely uninterested in physical exercise and sports. When he enlisted, he was reed thin – a mere 131 pounds spread over a 5-foot, 10-inch frame.[25] Nonetheless, at nineteen years old, he was sufficiently resilient that he completed basic training without incident.

His next stop was Princeton Street School in Witley, where he received language instruction and clerical training.[26] He completed the course in August and, after spending three weeks in hospital with diphtheria and dental problems, returned to Aldershot.[27] There he worked as a clerk until early December.[28] At that point he was once again transferred, this time to the 1st Canadian Division Infantry Reinforcement Unit.[29] This began his shift into intelligence work.

The first step was a brief Intelligence Corps interrogation course, where he did well. His instructor noted that his German was good, that he had 'a good grasp of enemy organization,' and that he had 'worked hard and intelligently and learnt a great deal during the week.'[30] Presumably on the basis of this positive first experience, in mid-March 1942, he was transferred to the Intelligence and Field Security Pool and in late April was sent to a two-week course for potential field security personnel at CMHQ in London.[31] Again, his instructor judged him to be an excellent candidate: 'An intelligent and resourceful man with likeable personality. Will make good FSP [Field Service Personnel].'[32] Shortly thereafter, on 9 May 1942, Porter received his first permanent intelligence posting: Field Security Section No. 1, commanded by Lieutenant W.A.C. 'Bill' Cooper.[33]

Canada's Intelligence Corps, not officially established until October 1942,[34] had four parts: air reconnaissance, wireless intelligence, battle intelligence, and counter-intelligence. Porter worked as a field security operative in counter-intelligence, the main purpose of which was to maintain the security and safety of Canadian troops by preventing acts of espionage or sabotage. In the lead-up to a battle, this meant making sure that troops kept their orders and objectives secret. Once engaged in battle, of course, counter-intelligence duties changed: monitoring access to military areas, monitoring civilians in and around military establishments, keeping an eye on the press, and controlling the assembly and movement of troops.[35] For its part, once in the field, Porter's unit was responsible for the interrogation of captured Axis soldiers and Fascist collaborators.

The decision taken by the Allied command to assign the 1st Canadian Division the task of defending Britain against the threat of an immediate invasion meant that the Canadian Army Overseas did not see action until the war was well along.[36] Only when the threat of invasion faded over late 1940 and into 1941 did the Allied command rethink its role. Their decision – to train the Canadians as an assault force – did not go over well with the troops. They had been in England for nearly two years and, while they believed they had been engaged in an important mission – 'securing the citadel of freedom against imminent peril' – the change in orders greatly lessened their sense of purpose. As the winter of 1941 gave way to the spring of 1942, morale declined accordingly.[37]

Porter, still stuck at Aldershot, groused to family and friends about his lot. Not only did he feel 'as out of place as a palm tree on an iceberg,' but, like other Canadian soldiers, he was upset and impatient about marking time in England.[38] The war he knew was no more than 'a doubt at a distance.'[39] As well, he resented the ubiquitous discipline of army life and found it impossible to stay 'parade square presentable' – buttons polished, uniform ironed, shoes shined.[40] So stultifying was the day-to-day routine of military training that he became bored and increasingly depressed, a recurring problem during his Army and student days. As early as July 1941 he wrote to Beattie MacLean that he had 'lapsed into an indifferent, listless frame of mind ... I long for [my] days ... on the *Sketch*, when my mind was active and when I thought of little more than making a career for myself. Now I don't care.' Like many people, he despaired that the war would go on for a very long time and that the Army would turn him into 'a perfect automaton.'[41] He also had trouble coming to terms with the Army's formal structure of privilege and command. Years later, he confided to Pauline Jewett that his egalitarian sensibilities were offended by the preferential treatment he received as an officer. He was proud of having earned his captain's bars, he said, but felt just as uncomfortable giving orders as taking them.[42]

It is understandable how Porter became increasingly restless and unhappy during this period of extended inaction and insecurity, suspended between the war on one hand and his 'real' life on the other. But it could have been much worse. While other Canadian soldiers were thousands of miles from their loved ones, he was close to home and family, able to go to London or Wales on leave, and, from time to time, the family would come to Aldershot for a visit.[43] Moreover, unlike Allied front-line troops living in the mud and snow of Russia or the heat and dust of North Africa, he was living in the relative comfort of the barracks at Aldershot. In fact, during part of his training, he was lucky enough to be billeted with a British family, the Bartholomews of Hailsham, from whom he picked up a lifelong interest in classical music.[44] And while his days were filled with mundane clerical tasks, he had the leisure to pursue his literary interests, particularly his poetry, which he sent to Beattie McLean, in hopes of having it published in Canada.[45]

Indeed, at this point in his life, Porter's literary endeavours were central to his identity. He saw himself as a writer: trapped in a khaki prison, to be sure, but a writer nonetheless. Letters to his family and friends often mention what he is reading and discuss his writing in progress. They reveal, as well, his views on culture and the arts in general. In one letter to Ethel, for example, he mentions a female friend with whom he regularly discussed poetry: 'Thank God my last six months in the Army have not altogether been barren of intellectual companionship. Probably I have been saved from going crazy by it.'[46] John Grist, Porter's friend from LSE days and himself a veteran, noted that John was a quiet, reserved, bookish sort, an atypical soldier who, after reading the work of the German poet Rainer Maria Rilke in Italian, set out to translate it into English.[47] This explains why John got along so well with his friend and sometime commanding officer, Porter (Peter) Cole, who later became a professor of English literature: 'I think he liked me as much as I liked him because we were both oddballs and ... intelligent men ... We could talk about most anything under the sun.'[48] Dodie Cole, Peter's wife, recalled that both of them 'could quote whole poems by John Donne and other great poets.' It was 'very rare,' she said, in the Armed Forces in the middle of the war that they had the opportunity to talk about such things and, in so doing, 'refresh' and 'elevate' themselves.[49]

Porter's deep interest in literature suggests that we should examine his literary efforts of the period, not to determine where they fall within the traditions of Western literature or to assess their merit as art but to see what they reveal of his personality, hopes, ideals, and intellectual orientation as a young man.[50]

Parenthetically, it is worth noting that years later, Porter's interest in poetry had a happy and unintended consequence. In 1957–8, John spent a year at the University of Toronto as a visiting scholar. At the time, the Porter children, Tony and Ann, were still small, and one of their babysitters was a sixteen-year-old budding poet, a high school student who was Marion's 'half-cousin.' Marion recalls that John was 'very impressed with her poetry' and 'encouraged her to send her poems to the *Canadian Forum*.'[51] Decades later, I met the 'young poet.' With great fondness, she recounted the same story: 'I recall John urging me to send my early poetry to the *Canadian Forum* (where, miraculously, it was published).' Thus did Gwendolyn MacEwen get her start.[52]

Poet in a Khaki Prison

John Porter's wartime writing, mostly poetry, reveals him to be a sensitive and empathetic observer who could create strong, provocative images and compelling turns of phrase, a skill he later turned to advantage in his sociological writing. The best illustration of this, of course, is 'the vertical mosaic,' but there are others. He once captured the essence of patterns of immigration and emigration in Canada – people often used the country as a stopover before moving on to the United States – by referring to it as a 'demographic railway station.' Even routine academic meetings could be enlivened by his creative wit and literary skills, as a brief introductory speech to a university computing conference clearly demonstrates:

> You meet at the summer solstice, a point in the ritual calendar for dreams, flights of fancy and even downright madness. What more auspicious time for a computing conference? Do not computers perform great feats of magic? Are there not little sprites at the other end of the terminal that answer back and ask how you can make such a silly mistake, and deny you access to their great Fairy Queen ...? There is a line from *A Midsummer Night's Dream* which goes 'Bless the Bottom! Bless thee! Thou art translated.' Now wouldn't that make a refreshing message for the harassed logger-on?[53]

Porter's concern for clarity and creative wordsmithing originated with his literary interests as a young man and never left him.

A basic set of ideas lies at the core of Porter's wartime writing, his poetry in particular. These ideas provide continuity from one phase and type of writing to another, while shifts of mood and theme act as barometers of his response to particular wartime experiences. It is important that we take this early creative writing seriously and treat it as a part of his oeuvre for two reasons. To begin, although it is likely that his poetry took on an exaggerated importance for him during the war, a significance it did not retain later in his life.[54] I concur with Marion Porter that at the time his poetry was important to him and, with her, I argue that it provides good insights into his character and beliefs. 'The sentiments [he expressed] about death and the despair of the world might be seen as the posturing of a young man,' she wrote, 'but I am sure the feelings were genuine.'[55] There is another reason for taking them seriously. In another form it is precisely the ideals held by the young poet Jack Porter that many years later the scholar John Porter put to the test repeatedly when he became a social scientist.

Just twenty poems and a few scraps of prose fiction remain of what must have been a much larger body of work Porter wrote during the war.[56] The first of his war poems, 'Death's House,' was written in June 1942, the last, 'From Old Cities,' in mid-1945, around the time the Allies occupied Germany. These three years were an emotionally charged and difficult time of personal development for him, and his poetry, prose, and letters to his mother and Beattie MacLean reveal this clearly. Most of his poetry is romantic and serious, often melodramatic, sometimes morose. We learn from it that he was a sensitive, observant individual, depressed and embittered by his life in the Army. Those feelings are clearly portrayed in a letter to MacLean, written November 1941, just nine months after he enlisted:

> Your letters to me are a light in the perpetual blackout in which I seem to grope, getting nowhere, attaining nothing. How despondent all my letters to you must seem, and yet I can't help it. Everything around me is foreign to my nature; the people I am with (they are better than I) always upset me. I wish I could acquire their indifferent attitude to life. Although they don't like the regimentation any more than I do, their reaction is not quite so bitter.[57]

A letter to his mother written two years later reveals the same feelings: 'Most of my thoughts nowadays are purely morbid and sensual. I seem to have sunken terribly, and to have become indifferent and disinterested … I am depressed. But that is nothing new. You know how often in the past I have been subject to these fits of depression.'[58]

His poetry likewise shows that he was troubled by his difficult situation and confused about how he 'should' respond. For example, in 'Death's House,' written in June, 1942, Porter evokes a grisly tour of a makeshift morgue where 'death reigns.' Life is portrayed as a 'tragedy' and a 'paradox' born of 'inhumanity.'[59] People of all ages, their faces once full of 'vigorous life,' are now condemned to 'death's solitude.' Saddest of all, he writes, people seem incapable of learning from their mistakes. Turning to the inert bodies of aged victims in death's house, he asks what we might learn from the dead:

> What of this thing called Life?
> If your cold lips could but relate to Youth
> What lies beyond
>
> But No, Man's lot was not
> To dwell in commune
> Age to guide or Youth to aid.[60]

Still, while pessimistic, he does not despair. There is a solution to the problems of inhumanity, irrationality, and wasted potential that trouble humanity. Even at this relatively early stage in his life, Porter champions a thoughtful 'middle path':

> Youth beset with Life's perplexities
> Not yet corrupt with miscarried wisdom
> But striving for the middle path
> That makes life easy ...[61]

But what does it mean to follow a middle path? To begin, he writes, it means thinking carefully in a general, abstract sense: be rational, arrive at morally acceptable views, and then act on them. But Porter's vision of humane rationality is more specific, as can be seen in 'Hospital Ship,' which he wrote after watching wounded soldiers disembark from a troop ship at Bristol in December 1942:

> We are tied in one vast continent of life,
> Each to the other indispensable ...
> Each man is a part of everyman
> Here and beyond.
> There are no colours, classes,
> Creeds, sexes, nationalities,
> Schools of thought;
> No possessions, no destitution,
> No power, no weakness –
> All men shall be one –
> A one-man-ness.
>
> Each man shall see in every man
> Himself.
> Each know himself and in
> Himself know everyman ...
>
> There is no better or worse,
> Just a being.
> This shall be no man and every man –
> The realization of some master's Mind.

Porter here offers injunctions against racism, sexism, and nationalism and makes the point that materialism, avarice, and power seeking must be eliminated if we are collectively to realize Utopia – his 'one-man-ness.'[62]

The conclusion of this poem suggests that Porter was in some way religious. So, too, does the last stanza of 'Majella Moon,' written in February 1944:

> Here in the night's neutrality
> Beyond all man's violation
> I am the austere assurance
> Of a God and His creation.[63]

And in a letter to Beattie MacLean, he writes that the glorification of the sordidness and immorality of war 'seems so out of line with what God really meant Man to be.'[64] Though these passages hint that the solution to human problems might rest with faith in some sort of a higher being, Porter was never religious. When he enlisted in 1941, he described himself as a member of the Church of England, but his declaration on demobilization indicates that he had no religious affiliation. No genuine shift is evident, however, and war made no difference to his views for he was never a religious person despite growing up in a Salvation Army family. Indeed, according to Ann Porter, her father, while morally principled, was 'militantly anti-religious' and a 'very strong atheist.'[65]

The unifying themes that run throughout Porter's wartime writing, perhaps best captured by the phrase 'humane rationality,' contrast with some shifts of tone and subject matter. The poems he wrote before June 1943, when he finally embarked for Sicily, are more positive than those he wrote later. Early on, he was bored and frustrated by army life but safe. As he came closer to shipping out, his poetry dealt increasingly with destiny and physical and spiritual death. It was during this period that Porter wrote 'If I Should Die,' his own favourite work:

> If I should die
> And witness not the brass cheering
> Of long awaited heroes,
> The thousand handshakes
> And sudden eager kisses,
> Remember that I loved.
>
> Remember,
> I did not enter this war with hate,
> Desiring the flesh of my brother,
> Or by the shell dissection of his body
> Hope to clear the common conscience of the world,

But rather I had hoped for a rebirth.
And this was the agony that precedes
Birth of all life.
And since I cannot see this offspring
Conceived through death,
I must die with those memories of love.
Such memories cannot be extinguished
By the gun's flash,
Or the eye's picture
Of a fallen comrade's hand raised
In final supplication.
They outlive all this, but I die with the leaden burn.

Remember also that I die,
Knowing
That what I loved still lives unchangeable
By lead or metal.[66]

The poet's mental image of war would soon become very real. The Allies had suffered repeated and devastating defeats in Europe and Africa throughout 1940 and 1941, but beginning in the fall of 1942, they began to turn the tide. Montgomery's 8th British Army defeated Rommel's Afrika Korps at El Alamein in North Africa and the Russians forced the German 6th Army to surrender at Stalingrad.[67] In the aftermath of these successes, Roosevelt and Churchill agreed to open a second European front; Italy would be invaded from the south.[68] This action would be a combined and decisive Allied effort, intended to knock Italy out of the war. As well, it would force Germany to divert troops from France, support Russia's effort on the Eastern Front, give the Allies control of the Mediterranean, and – most important – allow time for the preparation of the D-Day offensive, slated for early 1944.[69] Immediately after this decision was taken, the Canadian government pressured Churchill to include Canadian troops in the invasion force.[70] He eventually relented, and the 1st Canadian Division and the 1st Canadian Tank Brigade were inserted into the order of battle.[71] By this time, the 1st Canadian Army was an impressive force: nearly 220,000 soldiers, including 98,000 in fighting formations of infantry, armour, and artillery that had gone through extensive combined operations training.[72] For his part, during the last half of 1942 Porter took more field security courses and in December, nearly two years into his career, received his first promotion, to corporal.[73] He then spent the early months of 1943 on course in London and at 1st Division Headquarters.[74]

'Well and Truly Bloodied': In Action in Sicily and Italy, 1943–1944

John Arthur Porter's war lost its chimerical quality on 28 June 1943, when he boarded the HMS *Circassia*, an armed merchant cruiser converted to wartime service by the British Admiralty, and set sail for the Mediterranean. Twelve days later, at dawn on 10 July, the fleet, 2,600 ships strong, arrived in Italy and the Allied troops stormed the coast.[75]

The assault was a massive undertaking; 160,000 men, 14,000 vehicles, 600 tanks, and 1,800 guns had to be put ashore over a four-day period.[76] To everyone's surprise, the landing went largely uncontested. The coast was poorly defended and all initial objectives were taken easily. At Pachino, where the Canadians landed, 'most soldiers had no need to fire their weapons at all while taking 700 Italian and 20 German prisoners.'[77] In less than a day, supplies were being brought on to the beaches and supply lines had been established well inland with perfect security.[78]

Their initial objectives gained, the assault force moved north. The 1st Canadian Division was assigned the job of clearing the rugged north–south central strip of the island, the 'crocodile's back.' The first seventy miles – Pachino to Piazza Armerina – went well; Italian troops offered only perfunctory resistance. Heat, dust, topography, and the need for speed of movement soon became formidable foes,[79] but in a letter to his mother, Porter expressed deep satisfaction regarding the success of this first phase of the Allied mission. 'It is ... interesting,' he wrote, 'to witness ... the breaking up of Fascism and it is grand to feel that you are taking part in it. There is no doubt it is rotten.'[80]

Early successes in southern Sicily proved misleading, however. Though Mussolini was deposed on 25 July, and his replacement, Marshal Petro Badoglio, soon surrendered to the Allies, Germany continued to resist. Canadian troops had to fight hard to push the Germans northward toward Italy, and it took three full weeks before they could rendezvous with the main body of Montgomery's British forces at Adrano, near the base of Mount Etna in the northeastern part of the island, their task accomplished.[81] In *The Regiment*, Mowat argues that it was during this march north that the 'phoney war' – Porter's 'doubt at a distance' – became all too real and Canadian troops such as the Seaforths lost their innocence. Of the thirty-eight days it took them to make their 125-mile trek, they had to fight on twenty-nine. They did their job with great distinction but were 'well and truly bloodied' in the process, suffering 2,434 casualties, including 485 dead.[82] British and American troops handled the final push into Messina at the northern tip of the island.[83]

As the Allies pushed north, Porter was sent, now as Sergeant Porter, to divisional headquarters at nearby Francoforte.[84] There, Field Security Section No. 1 made final preparations for its role in the 1st Canadian Division's next major task, a part in Operation Baytown: the invasion of Italy.[85]

It is difficult to get a clear picture of Porter's personal role in the month-long Sicilian campaign, but we know from S.R. Elliot's description of the activities of the Canadian Intelligence Corps that field security personnel like Porter were seldom in forward positions. Instead, they worked out of divisional headquarters in the rear, finding, capturing, and interrogating enemy soldiers and Fascist sympathizers once an area had been cleared and secured by advancing troops. Field security personnel would head first for the town hall, the police station, and then Fascist headquarters hoping to find sensitive information.[86] If they were lucky and officials had not destroyed or spirited away their records, they would discover lists of local collaborators and operatives, which they could then use to corroborate and supplement their own blacklists.[87] Other regular duties included keeping refugees clear of transportation routes so that troops and supplies could move quickly, curtailing black market operations, and supervising curfews. On occasion, field security personnel would arrive in advance of Allied Military Government and be called on to feed and house refugees, restore water and power supplies, and the like.[88]

Just as the 1st Canadian Division prepared to embark on Operation Baytown in early September 1943, Porter became ill with hepatitis and was sent to hospital in North Africa.[89] While it was peaceful, he found the experience very upsetting. The poverty, devastation, and death he had witnessed in Sicily, combined with the suffering of the sick and injured soldiers he saw in the hospital, led him into a period of lethargy and depression. He wrote to his mother that he had hoped to find some 'new inspiration for writing' away from the fighting, but his illness and the stress of his experiences in Sicily made it difficult. All he had been able to do, he wrote, was compose a 'very cynical poem.' Frustrated, he passed the bulk of his time in the hospital reading 'cheap novels.' 'Mozart and Bach, Shaw and Stephen Spender are only weak reflections of a dim past … None of them seem right, and to have come out here armed with all their spectacular philosophies makes the lesson a difficult one to learn and everything of the past is a delusion … If I get back I must start afresh. Goodness knows where, but certainly not where I left off.'[90]

It took him over a month to recuperate and he did not rejoin his field security unit at Campobasso until early in November.[91] Canadian troops were not sent into action until late in the month, but when they were, it was a grim and challenging assignment they faced.[92] The battle they entered, a fight for control of the Moro River valley, was the most difficult and costly action of the Italian campaign, culminating in a deadly, week-long struggle over the port city of Ortona on the Adriatic coast in December 1943.[93] During the initial phase of this month-long struggle, Porter's field security unit worked out of Campobasso, but in December his unit moved to San Vito Chietino, right on the edge of the heavy fighting in Ortona.[94] Most of his work during the period was routine, but at one point, in what was probably the most dangerous episode of his military career, Porter and his friend Peter Johnson liberated a nearby village, even though 'they had gone ahead of the unit and were cut off because a bridge over which they had crossed was destroyed behind them.'[95]

Porter recorded his feelings about Ortona in two poems, both written after he visited a nearby Allied military cemetery:

Our comrades who lie
Mute in the Adriatic orange groves
Marked by rude engraved crosses
Shall not be forgotten when we have left you
To the warm sun, and the peasants' foolish chatter.
…
Each with our own awareness of the danger
And private undefinable explanations of duty
Can understand the fineness of your sacrifice.

You of our comrades, passing in the haste of the moment,
Will have life always
In memory's fire – and not forgotten
When we have left.[96]

Whatever other feelings he now had about the war, cynicism was not among them.[97] Porter meant it when he said he wouldn't forget. Years later, after he had moved to Ottawa, married, and had children, the family would attend the Remembrance Day services at the Cenotaph and two decades later, when the Porters twice went to Europe to live and travel, the family visited not only cemeteries where Canadian soldiers were buried but also Ortona, Normandy, and other battle sites.[98] Ann recalls that her father wanted to impress upon them 'the lives lost … [and] the historical significance' of the war.[99]

Victory and Denouement, 1944–1946

The battle for Italy did not end with Ortona, of course. The Germans withdrew to a newly prepared line of defence – the Gustav Line at the mouth of the Liri River valley northwest of Ortona – and dug in. The Americans made an attempt to end the stalemate in northwestern Italy by landing at Anzio on the western coast in January 1944 but were unable to break through toward Rome. The Allies had to hunker down and wait until spring. The 1st Canadian Division spent a miserable winter in the wind and cold of east-central Italy near Ortona.[100] Porter's unit spent the entire period attached to 1st Canadian Corps headquarters.[101] Finally, in late April, the weather improved and the 1st Canadian Division, including Porter's field security section, moved to Campobasso to undertake training prior to a new offensive planned for May. At this point, Porter was promoted to acting company sergeant major and transferred to Field Security Section No. 11, where he served for the next three months.[102]

The major objective of the May offensive was to gain control of Rome. The Germans had used the winter to shore up their defences, but the Allies eventually breached them.[103] On 4 June 1944, American troops occupied the Eternal City.[104] Just two days later, the Allies landed at Normandy, and at that point the 1st Canadian Division stood down, spending June and July on reserve in the Volturno River valley.[105] Porter, now with his new section, was busy elsewhere. So many Italian refugees were clogging the roads that they were interfering with Allied military operations. Several field security detachments, including No. 11, were reassigned to deal with these and related problems.[106]

As the fall and winter months of 1944–45 ebbed away, the 1st Canadian Corps did its part in an effort to consolidate the Allied hold on northern Italy and encircle the Germans before they could escape.[107]

The effort was unsuccessful, however, and the force had to winter near the Senio River in northern Italy.[108]

Porter did not take part in these events. Just as the 1st Canadian Corps headed into action to help consolidate the Allied hold on northern Italy, he received a promotion to company sergeant-major and was ordered to return to Aldershot to begin officer training.[109] Instruction commenced on 1 October 1944, and he spent the next three and a half months as an officer cadet.[110] Canadian military historian Geoffrey Hayes notes that it was a major accomplishment to be selected: '[Porter's] obvious intelligence and considerable military experience made him an ideal candidate for officer training at that time. Even with the considerable innovations in officer selection that went on through the war, it was still a substantial achievement to be commissioned after service in the enlisted ranks, particularly [since] he didn't have high school senior matriculation.'[111] The course went well – on 23 February 1945 he was promoted to lieutenant – but his evaluation, written by his chief instructor, Major P.G.S. Sanderson, was curious indeed.[112] Sanderson described Porter as a 'conscientious, hard worker' who had 'done well,' yet he estimated that the young officer demonstrated only 'average' powers of leadership and a 'fair' capacity to express himself verbally. Most unexpectedly in light of Porter's future academic accomplishments, Sanderson wrote that his young charge appeared 'rather slow-witted.'[113]

Not surprisingly, while he was at Aldershot Porter's spirits improved. He was out of danger and near home, with time off on the weekends to visit London and Wales, and was engaged in intellectual work among well-educated people with whom he could share his literary interests. During this period he met R.A.J. (Bob) Phillips, a staff member at the Intelligence School with whom he became lifelong friends.[114] As well, Beattie MacLean arrived from Canada at Christmas 1944, and they were able to spend considerable time together while on leave in London. Forty-five years later, MacLean recalled these good times: 'We spent several weekends in London together, often attending theatre and concert productions ... [Often we walked] along The Embankment, indulging in most stimulating conversation for hours into the night ... I did not note depression or melancholy in Jack; indeed, he had a most captivating sense of humour, although tinged with black humour.'[115]

There is some evidence that Porter's sociology career began during this interlude at Aldershot – even before. In the Porter papers at Library and Archives Canada is a notebook written in his hand and dated 1944 that contains notes from the works of Durkheim, Freud, Westermarck and others.[116] And, Wallace Clement remembers Porter telling him that at the suggestion of a wartime Italian girlfriend he had read Antonio Gramsci's *Prison Notebooks*.[117] We know that as early as 1943 his intellectual interests had expanded beyond English literature to philosophy and related subjects for, in a letter to his mother written in June of that year, he mentions that while travelling by train from Wales to London he discussed the ideas of Buddha and Confucius with his friend Peter Johnson.[118] As well, in late 1944 or early 1945, he began to read and discuss seriously the kinds of political issues reported in the *New Statesman* and the *Nation*.[119] This suggests he was not only becoming more politically aware but also more concerned to intellectualize his developing political interests – perhaps with some assistance from sociology, philosophy, and political science.

After earning his commission, Porter received a posting to the Netherlands and spent time in Deventer and the Hague.[120] He did not join either of his two former units but was assigned to a pool of field security officers. In that capacity he accompanied the 1st Canadian Army when it embarked on its first and only campaign as an all-Canadian force under Canadian command: clearing the northern and western parts of the Netherlands.[121] Since August 1944, the Allies had been closing the ring around Germany. As 1944 drew to a close and 1945 dawned, the Russians pushed toward Berlin from the east while the Allies advanced both in Italy and on the Western Front. Finally, in early May 1945, Hitler's last defences crumbled and the war ended.[122]

There was much to do to establish proper peacetime government in occupied Europe. Most Canadian forces spent the months until repatriation and demobilization in the Netherlands.[123] By contrast, Porter spent the period in Germany. He was first stationed in Oldenburg, near Hamburg. About a month before he left for England, he was moved to Nienburg, near Hanover.[124] There he was assigned to the 1st Canadian Army Refugee Interrogation Team, attached to the 2nd Canadian Infantry Division.[125] Throughout the period his chief tasks related to the 'massive flow of refugees' then creating transportation and security problems all across Europe. Geoffrey Hayes notes that in Holland, 'many Dutch civilians were trying to return home from forced labour assignments in Germany,' while at the same time 'thousands of German soldiers [who had] surrendered … had to be marched back to the German frontier' before being interrogated and processed by the occupying Allied Army. All of this had to be documented, studied, managed, and reported on, entailing long hours of interviewing and report writing for Porter and his colleagues in field security.[126] Writing from Oldenburg in mid-June, he complained to his mother that he was 'up to [his] neck in work' with 'no respite' in sight.[127]

Initially, Porter had an 'intense' dislike for his job in Oldenburg because he was stuck behind a desk all day.[128] Eventually, though, he came to enjoy the work despite complaining that he had 'never worked so hard in [his] life.'[129] One of the attractions of the location was that he was able to do considerable 'swanning' – travelling and sightseeing – over the summer.[130] A more serious concern than his immediate job situation was the stress of planning his post-Army life. So uncertain was he about what to do – or what the Army might order him to do – that he grew anxious and despondent. One of his friends, in receipt of a letter from Porter written from Oldenburg during this period, replied: 'Your letter was vile. They usually are depressing but this is the worst. You have been working too hard and you are a damn fool. I am glad to see you have your third pip; it will ... enable you to make a much more spectacular leap from Waterloo Bridge.'[131]

It is understandable that Porter would fret about his future. Ironically, after all his complaints about life in the Army, his biggest worry once the war was over was leaving the service. He had become so accustomed to the Army organizing his affairs that he confessed to feeling 'honestly ... afraid of the insecurity of civilian life.' He even toyed briefly with staying on, though he soon discounted the prospect when he discovered it might mean being sent to Japan as part of the Allied occupying forces.[132] Indeed, the appeal of civilian life soon grew strong and he began to consider other options. Keen to return to journalism and very taken with Italy, he checked into the possibility of working for one of the European wire services in Rome and made a similar enquiry about returning to London and a job at the *Daily Sketch*.[133] Neither prospect came to anything. When in late June he received notification that if he took the repatriation draft and returned to Canada he would not have to go to Japan, he consequently took the opportunity.[134] 'I have had enough of the Army,' he wrote, 'and if I stayed in the occupation forces it would merely be an acknowledgement of my own lack of confidence. So I am going to take the repat draft when it comes along.' Another possibility that he had kept in mind throughout the summer was a return to school. He discovered that he could get an allowance for himself and his family if he returned to Canada to attend university and since he surmised that a return to school would be his best option, the one that would cause the fewest regrets, he looked into the possibility of moving to Vancouver to attend the University of British Columbia.[135] But there were problems with this choice. His mother would have had to obtain a legal separation from Arthur and get some sort of assurance that Arthur would provide her with a stable monthly income. Arthur had joined the Navy during the war and thus had a regular salary, but John was not optimistic his father could be counted on to keep any promises he made.[136] However, shortly after being sent back to England in late July, another opportunity arose.[137] One day in early August, while walking along a London sidewalk, he bumped into his former commanding officer, Bill Cooper. They chatted about Porter's prospects for a few minutes, at which point Cooper offered to introduce John to a colleague then working in the Historical Section of the Canadian Army. Porter leapt at the opportunity and after the three of them met a few days later, Cooper's colleague offered Porter a job. He accepted immediately, and they submitted the paperwork requesting the transfer. Porter waited anxiously for the Army's decision.[138]

When he wrote to his mother to tell her of this new development, he gave three reasons for applying to the Historical Section. First, he said, if the application were successful, he would not have to be repatriated to Canada and the family could stay in England. Second, he had discovered that it was highly unlikely that he would be able to get into university without high school matriculation papers. Were he to take the job with the Historical Section, he would be able to remedy that deficiency by attending night school in London. Moreover, the job would provide some welcome professional experience and allow him to interact with the many university professors working on the project. This, he thought, might help him to 'get some irons in the fire' about getting into university. Third, and finally, in London he could continue to explore job prospects in the newspaper world.[139] Word soon came that his transfer had been approved and, on 30 August 1945, he was posted to the Historical Section.[140]

For the next ten months Porter lived in a rented room in Chelsea in London's West End and worked as part of a team headed by the Canadian historian Colonel C.P. Stacey, then compiling the official history of the Canadian army's involvement in the war.[141] Porter helped draft two chapters of the second volume, *The Canadians in Italy, 1943–1945*, and one chapter of the third, *The Victory Campaign: The Operations in Northwest Europe, 1944–1945*. At the same time, he studied for the London Matriculation Examination, attending Regent Street Polytechnic in the evenings in hopes of ultimately getting a place at the University of London.[142]

Porter achieved his goal, though only after great effort and many moments of self-doubt. Such was the struggle required to keep up with this double workload over the fall and winter that his mother, who saw him from time to time, noted that he seemed very tired and anxious: 'He is working very hard, and seems rather tired. His work demands a great deal of concentration, and his night study in addition is taking a lot out of him.' But it would all be worth it, she thought, if he qualified to enter the University of London in the fall.[143] One great help to him at this time was his former commanding officer, Peter Cole, with whom he had become fast friends. Peter and Dodie Cole lived in a cottage near Oxford, where Peter was studying for his doctorate in English literature. Porter visited them nearly every weekend, and Cole worked hard to buoy what he perceived as John's flagging spirits by writing to him almost daily – sometimes in Italian, sometimes with a bit of doggerel he had composed – during the spring and early summer.[144] This support from friends and family, combined with lots of hard work, eventually paid off. In mid-summer he successfully sat the matriculation exams and shortly thereafter the entrance examination for the University of London.[145] On 18 September 1946, he received notice that he could register as a full-time student at the LSE, a college of the University of London, proceeding to a degree in economics.[146] In October, a full ten years after leaving John Oliver High School, he once again became a student – this time at the prestigious London School of Economics and Political Science. He did not formally retire from active service until 8 November 1946, but by that time Captain John Porter's challenging and formative new life as a student was already well underway.[147]

Porter left the service a changed man. Life as a soldier had not altered his basic personality or temperament, but it had influenced him in other ways. He had found his years in the service difficult because essential elements of army life – hierarchy, regimentation, routine – and unavoidable aspects of war – violence, irrationality, and suffering – were completely foreign to his basic temperament, outlook, and values. As his daughter, Ann, put it, 'He was a very gentle man and [being a soldier] was very counter to his nature.'[148] He had no doubts that the war was necessary and just, but struggled throughout his military career with feelings of despondency brought on by the grim reality of wartime life as a soldier. In later years he seldom mentioned the war or his time as a soldier to his family, but there is no doubt the experience stayed with him.[149] It was Ann's view that 'a lot of things happened [during the war] that obviously had a huge impact on him that he didn't want to talk about very much.'[150] Perhaps, like many veterans, he pushed it to the back of his mind, always aware of it but having no desire to bring back powerful, painful memories or to glorify war by discussing it with his children. My uncle, the late Russell Wolsey, also served in the Canadian Infantry during World War II and he, too, was reluctant to talk about his experiences. A few years before he died, my father took him to the Museum of Civilization in Hull, Quebec, just across the Ottawa River from the parliament buildings. Russ was in his early eighties then and used a wheelchair. As they moved through the exhibition to the gallery where paintings from World War II were displayed, he became increasingly sombre. They stopped in front of one particularly graphic portrayal of a battle in Holland and my father asked if he recognized it. His voice cracking, his eyes filling with tears, he replied, 'I was there. I saw that. I don't want to see any more.' [151] Certainly, the war remained for Porter a point of moral and social reference. Two decades after leaving the service, he counselled his young son, Tony, against joining the scouting movement because of its military overtones.[152] Likewise, a full thirty years after the war, he dredged up his very negative feelings about the Army in a memorandum against the prospect of faculty unionization at Carleton. 'Since my unhappy years as a soldier,' he said, 'I have hated discipline and regimentation, so perhaps I have an irrational fear of the effect of unionization on the intellectual life which the university has traditionally harboured.'[153]

Despite his distaste for Army life, he put together a highly successful career as a soldier. By virtue of intelligence and hard work, he became an officer in spite of his class background, bolstering his confidence and perhaps convincing him of the benefits of meritocratic liberalism. As Geoffrey Hayes has pointed out, 'From its very beginnings, the Canadian Army's officer corps was to have been a meritocracy, its members judged not by basis of social status or wealth, but by merit. There [was] a series of debates on that issue throughout the war: how to measure merit? In the end, however, the system judged Porter worthy of commissioned rank. Surely this is worth considering when one looks for the basis of his ideas later on.'[154] His work with the Intelligence Corps and the Historical Section allowed him to develop research and writing skills that prepared him for an academic career. Years later, he remarked to Marion and others that his time with Colonel Stacey was especially valuable in this regard.[155]

Perhaps most important from a personal point of view, the time he spent in the service helped him to mature as a young man and to come to a more balanced and healthy relationship with his mother. When his father abandoned the family during the Depression, John assumed many family responsibilities. Forced to quit school, he worked for a number of years to support the family and took on a quasi-parental role with his brother. After war broke out and he joined the Army, he continued to support the family, sending a portion of his pay to his mother.[156] In his letters home he constantly enquired about the welfare of his brother, Alan, and sister, Eileen. Partly as a consequence of taking on these responsibilities, he developed an unusually close relationship with his mother. During the war, they wrote to each other frequently, and his letters spoke to her in a very open way about his deepest feelings. Ethel responded in kind. She saw in her son a special intelligence and sensitivity and nurtured it as best she could. As well, she fostered in him a deep sense of self-confidence. Decades later, Marion Porter noted in this regard that though John's early life had been difficult, and that he was 'somewhat shy' by nature, his mother instilled in him the notion that he could accomplish anything.[157] 'He had the greatest inner self-confidence of any person I have ever known,' she wrote. 'From an early age, his mother told him that he was special and that if he wanted to, he could become Prime Minister or anything else that interested him. He truly believed that if he turned his attention to any task, he could master it.'[158] This was a great gift. Porter's sensitivity and tendency toward self-doubt and depression as a young man might easily have become impediments had it not been for the strength of her support. At the same time, he walked a fine line with his mother. According to his sister, Eileen, Ethel almost stifled him and, ironically enough, it was the Army that 'saved' him: 'He didn't like the Army but … the Army got him away from home, which was a great thing … I don't think he realized how much Mother was leaning on him, depending on him.… [S]he encouraged him all the way. But … he would have been too tied to her and would never have made the success of his life that he did when he had to leave home and go in the Army. In a way, it was a blessing for him.'[159]

The years Porter spent in the Army gave him the right as a veteran to claim the tuition credits he used to attend the LSE after the war. Without these credits, his class background was such that he could never have afforded to go to university and his life would have taken an entirely different path.

3 The LSE Years, 1946–1949

The London School of Economics and Political Science sits stoically amid the frenetic bustle of commercial London, close by the west end of Waterloo Bridge.[1] Its location in the jumble of lanes and avenues around Houghton Street makes it a short walk to many of the city's landmarks: Parliament, Whitehall, the Royal Courts of Justice and, of special importance to students and faculty of the LSE, the British Museum and the rest of the University of London. In the late 1940s, when John Porter studied there, a fortunate conjunction of unique and remarkable circumstances – a cadre of world-famous scholars, a mature and committed student body, and a general sense of postwar optimism – made it among the best and most exciting places in the world to study the social sciences.[2] Years later, Porter recalled that the intellectual excellence and political vibrancy of the LSE had a powerful formative impact on his development as a scholar, equivalent to a graduate school experience.[3] Writing in 1987, his student, Wallace Clement, agreed. During the LSE years, Clement wrote, Porter 'consolidated the principles, values, and ideas which were to guide his [entire] career.'[4]

The School was founded in 1895 largely through the efforts of the British Fabian Society, Sidney Webb in particular, and W.A.S. Hewins, the LSE's first director.[5] England at the time had few social science appointments and almost no opportunities to do social science research.[6] Webb and his like-minded fellow travellers hoped the LSE would fill this void and become 'the first British university devoted to the study of the social sciences.'[7] From the outset, in keeping with the Fabians' practical political orientation, Webb championed the LSE as a place where intellectuals could be trained to generate scientific data that could be used in the service of society. As well, and in spite of his own socialist preferences, Webb intended the LSE to be a place of free enquiry.[8] And he prevailed – though only after overcoming substantial resistance from members of the Fabian Society who wanted the School to be a setting for the propagation of Fabian political doctrine. Thus, when the school first opened it boasted a highly respected and politically eclectic faculty, with Fabians 'a distinct minority' among them.[9]

The author of the definitive history of the LSE, Ralf Dahrendorf, has noted that at the beginning the LSE was a modest, highly tenuous enterprise – a dozen faculty teaching a slate of evening courses to between 200 and 300 part-time students in rented quarters at Adelphi Terrace.[10] And for the first few years, it remained that way, 'a flimsy institution … more an arrangement and a promise than a university.'[11] By the time Porter enrolled in 1946, however, the School had a stellar international reputation and had grown to many times its original size. The campus, comprising about a dozen buildings, was quintessentially urban – cramped and patchwork – having expanded in fits and starts by taking over buildings in the Clare Market area as they became available.[12] 'I hated the place,' said one graduate. 'The building itself [was] a charmless pile, like the head office of a minor insurance company, hidden away in a back street.'[13] But whatever the School lacked by way of physical amenities, it more than made up for in other ways, most importantly in terms of its teaching staff. In fact, the immediate postwar period proved to be the LSE's golden years and few places in the world could match its roster of academic stars: anthropologist Raymond Firth, economists Lionel Robbins and Friedrich von Hayek, philosopher Karl Popper, historians Arnold Toynbee and R.H. Tawney, political scientists Harold Laski and T.H. Marshall, and sociologist Morris Ginsberg.[14]

Sociology at the LSE, 1907–1946

The first permanent chair in sociology at the LSE was established in 1907 when Martin White, a wealthy Scottish landowner and friend of two pioneers of British sociology, Patrick Geddes and Victor Branford, provided an endowment to fund it.[15] Leonard Trelawney Hobhouse, the former political editor of the London *Tribune* and a man with strong academic and political credentials, became the first incumbent. Hobhouse had attended Marlborough and Oxford on scholarships and then taught at Corpus Christi and Merton colleges before leaving academia for the *Manchester Guardian* and reform work. Nonetheless, he retained his academic interests and connections and, by 1907, when he assumed the chair, was a prominent member of the British Sociological Society, had served as editor of its *Sociological Review,* and written a half-dozen books, including *The Labour Movement, The Theory of Knowledge, Mind in Evolution,* and *Morals in Evolution.*[16]

Hobhouse's job as occupant of the Martin White Chair was not an easy one, for it required a scholar of great industry, wide learning, and political savvy. The last was important because at the time British sociology was intellectually and organizationally balkanized without a clear, shared definition of its nature and purposes. Indeed, it was less a discipline than a movement and its practitioners had not sorted out whether it was an historical, theoretical, philosophical enterprise or a science, whether it was separate from social work, or if and how it was related to economics, political economy, and biology (especially evolution and eugenics).[17] As a scholar, Hobhouse showed well. He published at an impressive rate throughout his career and, as Sir Sidney Caine has pointed out, 'contributed to the development of thought in areas of study which by [the mid-1960s] were covered in the LSE by five professors of sociology, three of social anthropology, two of social administration, one of social psychology and one of logic and scientific method.'[18] However, Hobhouse's attempts during the early years to make his own style of sociology dominant both at the LSE and in England more generally led to considerable tension with the Fabians and others who had a stake in the development of the discipline and contributed, in turn, to its slow institutional growth all across the country.[19]

After Hobhouse's appointment, there was no growth in university sociology for a long time. Morris Ginsberg, Hobhouse's student and follower, eventually took over the Martin White Chair when Hobhouse died in 1927 and, like his mentor, earned numerous academic honours.[20] But for years he remained the only scholar to hold a sociology chair in Britain.[21] Not until after World War II, approximately coincident with Porter's arrival, did the situation change markedly. At that point, the School hired three outstanding young sociologists – Donald MacRae, David Glass, and Jean Floud – who, in combination with short-term appointments such as Edward Shils and resident luminaries Marshall, Laski, and Tawney, put the School in a position where, according to Ralf Dahrendorf, its sociology program could 'move into the same small premier league' as Harvard, Columbia and Chicago.[22]

The vitality and excellence of the LSE in the postwar years was especially remarkable given the economic conditions under which it operated. London had been hard hit during the war. Everywhere were smashed and blackened architectural monuments to the Blitz: mangled public buildings, disembowelled factories, shattered private homes. And everywhere the job of rebuilding was slow and painful. Clement Atlee's newly elected Labour government had few resources on which to draw because the British economy lay in ruins, much of its industrial plant woefully out of date. Even basic items such as foodstuffs, housing, and coal remained scarce for some years after the signing of the armistice.[23]

Fortunately, despite the intensive bombing of central London and some direct hits in the immediate area, the School's buildings survived intact so, after a quick cleaning and a facelift, it was able to reopen in October 1945.[24] But conditions were difficult. The government poured as much money as possible into education in order to accommodate qualified service personnel, and they made money available to refurbish existing facilities and build new ones, but in Clare Market space was at a premium and the School had to wait until buildings became available.[25] As a result, when the doors reopened and veterans poured in by the hundreds, classrooms and other facilities were stretched to their limits and beyond.[26] Class sizes increased tremendously, of course, and due to the influx of ex-servicemen the gender balance was highly skewed; four of every five students were male. On the plus side, the provision of education benefits to veterans like Porter meant that the student body contained more working- and lower middle-class people than ever before.[27]

Graduates from the time have conflicting recollections of the student culture they created.[28] In his centenary history of the LSE, Dahrendorf claims that for about fifteen years after the war the School was a 'magnetically attractive setting' for students in the social sciences, where they not only learned a good deal but also had fun.[29] But others have different stories. Some claim that students arrived at Houghton Street intent on getting an education as quickly as possible so they could get on with their interrupted lives. That was Canadian sociologist Anthony Richmond's memory: 'The academic standards were exceedingly high and the competition tough. There was little time for any kind of activity except studying.'[30] Others remember being serious and practical but less careerist than Richmond. They went to the LSE not just to kick-start their careers but with altruistic social purposes in mind. For them it was a time to look unashamedly toward the possibility of building a better world. 'Overwhelmingly,' recalls Ken Braidwood, 'we were eager for change ... We looked for a new order which would see an end of the wars and debauching poverty which had seared the 20s and 30s, a new order which would capture economic prosperity with social fairness. These were our goals and we went to LSE to learn how to score them.'[31] For his part, Porter shared Braidwood's sense of the student and wider culture at the LSE after the war. As he recalled them, 'The war years were a watershed between the age when social forces were pretty much left to themselves to confer benefit or distress as they might ... [It was a] period of optimism when it was felt that the social environment could be controlled, that depressions could be made a thing of the past, and distributive justice was a matter of social engineering.'[32]

A collective eagerness to debate the details of social reconstruction created a vibrant political environment on campus. Students and faculty debated issues in the classrooms, of course, but student-run political societies and even student residences acted as forums for the daily exchange of ideas.[33] During his first year, Porter lived at Passfield Hall, the first student residence built at the LSE, and he recalled great benefit from the experience:

> [Passfield Hall] accommodated around sixty people who must have been chosen on the basis of national quotas because we were like a miniature United Nations. The discussions were intense and, as with all university groups, ranged over the major issues of the day. We did not much care how our universities were governed ... Our enthusiasms were about social inequality at home, ... the end of colonialism abroad and ... the removal of the final remnants of Fascism in Europe.[34]

This, then, was the student life into which Porter plunged when he arrived at Clare Market. A dynamic student culture and excellent teaching, all in the welter of Britain's postwar political turmoil and economic restructuring, created an exciting environment in which to learn. Porter's classmate, Reginald Robson, who later taught at UBC, recalls its profound impact: 'Intellectually, to me, it was an extremely exciting and challenging place to be at that time; over the three years I spent there, it had the effect of challenging some of the most basic elements of my value system and resulted in my having to re-think where I stood and why.'[35] It certainly had a long-lasting impact on Porter. It was there that Leonard Hobhouse's New Liberal politics and sociology were etched deeply into his developing intellectual consciousness.

Porter's Course Work, 1946–1949

On the model of scholarship operative at the LSE after World War II, students 'read' for a degree; that is, they spent their time in the library reading on their own in their particular areas of study. Faculty offered lectures on an ongoing, if sometimes irregular, basis and students attended those lecture series listed in the calendar as appropriate for their chosen subject areas, but there was no compulsion to do so. Professors did not take attendance and term work did not count.[36] One of Porter's student colleagues at the time, eminent Canadian political scientist Paul Fox, recalls the entire system as 'chaotic.' He remembered it as difficult even to find out 'what the lectures were and where.' Without any other announcement, he said, 'some school porter would go out with a thumbtack and a list and put it ... on a notice board and you would go along and find out that the great Professor Laski was going to lecture on Mondays at 11 on the history of socialism.'[37] The assessment of student progress was handled very differently as well. When students felt ready, they sat for the examinations appropriate to the degree for which they were studying. This usually occurred at the end of the first year of study and then again, two years later, at the end of the third and final year.[38]

Porter registered as an economics student and in his first year took courses in five subjects: logic, geography, political science, English economic history, and economics. The economics courses were required for his degree program, of course, but he was not much interested in them. Like other students in sociology, he took them only because he had to.[39] There was no degree program in sociology, so those wanting to major in the subject had to take a BA in economics and specialize in sociology during their second and third years.[40] Although he did not particularly enjoy his economics courses, Porter's exposure to the field had two long-term benefits. It later allowed him to hold his own in arguments with economists and, perhaps more important, to gain a solid knowledge of liberal economic theory, including its neoclassical and Keynesian variants, ideas central to the New Liberalism.[41]

The only first-year course that seems to have had much long-term impact on him was a twenty-four-lecture analysis of the British constitution, taught jointly by K.B. Smellie and Harold Laski.[42] Laski was, for Porter, by far the more important of the two. Widely regarded as the dominant presence in the School, Laski was by all accounts a remarkable teacher.[43] Certainly Porter was impressed by his progressive

political ideas, especially those concerning the role of the interventionist state, and often drew on them in later years. In a 1950 interview,
Porter mentioned Laski as one of three scholars who had especially
impressed him during his time at the LSE and, according to Virginia MacDonald, one of Porter's early students at Carleton College, he
made frequent mention of Laski in his lectures.[44] So great was Porter's
respect, said MacDonald, that the day they announced Laski's death
– 24 March 1950 – she expected that 'John would come in [wearing] a
black armband.'[45]

In June 1947, Porter concluded his first year of study by successfully
sitting the LSE's annual Special Intermediate B.Sc. (Econ.) Examination.
This entitled him to begin the second phase of his undergraduate education that autumn.

Completing first year must have been a tremendous relief. Before entering the LSE, he had persevered through a year of evening classes at
Regent Street Polytechnic while working full time during the day at
the Historical Section. He had then passed the entrance examination
and survived the intimidating academic challenge of his first year at
university – all after ten years away from formal schooling and while
in competition with some of the finest students in postwar England.
Moreover, he had become active in the School's social and political life
and joined the staff of LSE's student-run literary and political magazine, the *Clare Market Review*.[46] But problems in his personal life made
his last two years at LSE less enjoyable than they might have been.

Around the time Porter returned to London from Germany, perhaps
while working for Stacey in the Historical Section, he met Elizabeth
Edith Stalker, a young naval officer from a relatively well-to-do military
family from Prestatyn, a small coastal town about twenty-five miles
northwest of Porter's family home in Wrexham.[47] Elizabeth's parents
were Lieutenant Douglas Stalker, a career officer in the Highland Light
Infantry who had died shortly after World War I, and Edith Mary
Hume. Douglas Stalker had received a number of postings, including
India. During World War I, he had been captured by the Germans and
spent some time in a POW camp in France. By the time the war was
over, he was quite ill and died shortly after returning to Great Britain.
After her husband's death, Edith took Elizabeth to Prestatyn, North
Wales, where they lived with Edith's mother. Elizabeth was an expres-
sive child, very interested in fashion and the arts, and when World War
II broke out she was enrolled in art school in Liverpool. As soon as war
was declared she volunteered for the Navy, attending the Royal Naval

College at Greenwich. She was stationed at Brighton during the Battle of Britain and subsequently at Troon, Scotland, where she served as a 'torpedoman' and earned the rank of lieutenant.

John and Elizabeth met because of a bicycle. One of Elizabeth's friends had lent out Elizabeth's bicycle without her permission. Elizabeth was angry about it and the friend, to mollify her, invited her to a military ball. It was there she met John Porter.[48] John was quite taken with the attractive, outgoing Elizabeth and, after what Dodie Cole referred to as a 'short and passionate' courtship, they were married.[49] The wedding was a formal military affair held in the parish church in Prestatyn on 18 December 1946 at the end of Porter's first term at LSE.[50] The marriage did not get off to a good start – a number of the guests had possessions stolen from their hotel rooms while the ceremony and the reception took place – and lasted only a year.[51]

In retrospect, it is not surprising. The vivacious, strong-willed Elizabeth came from a privileged upper-middle-class family. She loved parties and fancy clothes, had done a good deal of travelling, and, saving her time in the Navy, had never worked. She had been a student at a school for fine arts before the war. John was an altogether different sort of person – intense, reserved, and cerebral – and his life offered a stark contrast to Elizabeth's. The eldest son in a working-class family that had once been on the dole, he had been forced to drop out of high school in order to help support his struggling family. The class difference between them was revealed quite vividly in their search for a wedding ring. When John asked Elizabeth what kind of wedding ring she wanted, she replied, in honour of his Canadian roots, 'One with maple leaves on it.' When, after a fruitless search in the jewellery shops of London, John returned to tell her that nothing of the sort was available, she replied, nonplussed, 'Well, then, have one made.'[52] To Elizabeth, who came from a well-off family, if one could not find what one wanted, one simply had it made. This would never have occurred as a reasonable prospect to someone like John, who did not have the resources to order custom jewellery.

It did not take long for troubles to surface once they were married. John apparently did not tell Elizabeth about his bouts of depression until after they were married, which angered her,[53] and though the first few months seem to have been relatively peaceful, differences of class and temperament – combined, I suspect, with conflicting expectations about gender roles – created sufficient animosity between them that by Christmas Day 1947 Elizabeth refused to have anything further to do with John.[54] Sad as this was, it was not unlike many other war-inspired marriages that did not last the peace. Both of them would probably have moved on with relative ease were it not for a complication: Elizabeth was pregnant. Attempts at negotiation and reconciliation failed. Elizabeth gave birth to their daughter, Fiona, the following spring.[55] John saw Fiona only once, very briefly, a few days after she was born.[56] He would not see her again for many years. It was in the context of this turmoil, and carrying the emotional freight it generated, that he completed his last two years of study.

Porter's contemporaries at the LSE, students and instructors alike, remember him well. Donald Chesworth recalled his physical appearance:

> Tall [and] thinnish ... He used to have a kind of trousers made out of cavalry twill [in an] officer's style ... He was what could be called neat, trim, and orderly ... in appearance and in his way of doing things. He had a slightly hatchet face and much of the time looked rather dour, but fairly easily a rather nice smile came over the dour face.[57]

Teachers and fellow students shared a recollection of him as serious, hard working, and astute. Paul Fox, then a PhD candidate, recalled John as 'a great reader.' 'He really read the stuff and then he thought about it.'[58] Similarly, Donald MacRae, then a lecturer and later director of the School, recalled him as an excellent pupil, 'competent ... all the time.' He never just *did* his homework, said MacRae; he took the time to 'master' it.[59] However, friends remember him as 'reserved,' 'taciturn,' and 'self-contained.'[60] 'In a generation of brilliant students,' said MacRae, '[Porter] did not mingle very much.'[61] Edward Shils, another of his instructors, said something similar. He recalled being favourably impressed with Porter's 'intellectual ambition and intelligence,' but also noted that he was 'shy and retiring' to the point of 'reticence.'[62] As a consequence, '[Porter] did not leave a very pronounced impression on me of his intellectual force or vitality. I could see that he had an acute intelligence but he was not expansive in his conversations with me. Hence when his book [*The Vertical Mosaic*] appeared I was not surprised but I can also say that I did not anticipate it in the way in which one sometimes anticipates a work of first importance from one of one's research students.'[63]

Long-time friends John and Gill Grist remember Porter as not just reserved but moody, sometimes to the point of being morose. In his down periods, John Grist said, he was 'a depressive influence, not to be encouraged.' 'I moved out [of our shared flat] going up to take my final examinations,' he said, because 'I just couldn't stand it.'[64] Indeed, according to Fox, Porter was often critical and pessimistic – 'an angry young man with a chip on his shoulder.'[65] Porter's moodiness sometimes manifested itself in his work habits. Spasms of frenzied effort, fuelled by feelings of confidence, would be punctuated by periods of lethargy, pessimism, even depression. It was a pattern he had demonstrated during his days in the Army. An intense, introspective person, the rapid breakdown of his marriage probably meant that at times school just did not seem very important, but as a young *intellectual*, the politically and intellectually charged environment at the LSE seemed to challenge and stimulate him sufficiently to break out of his melancholy and press on.

Whatever his personal difficulties, Porter benefited greatly from the opportunity to attend lectures given by some of the most accomplished scholars of his time, and he received an excellent, broad-based orientation to the social sciences. There is no evidence at this point of an elective affinity between Porter and his later calling. In fact, he still wanted to be a writer and took sociology only because 'he thought that it would help him understand society.'[66] Of the many courses he took in economics, political science, ethics, social and political theory, social psychology, and history over the next two years, those taught by Shils, MacRae, Marshall, Laski and, in particular, Ginsberg had the greatest and most enduring impact. Through Ginsberg in particular he came to be deeply influenced by Hobhousian ideas. (In the afterword I pick up on this theme, looking at the links between Porter's written work and the writings of the New Liberals, Hobhouse and Ginsberg in particular. I conclude that Porter is best understood as a New Liberal 'practical intellectual.')

Porter appears to have taken two of Shils' courses: 'Urban Society' (co-taught with David Glass) and 'Sociological Research.'[67] While the only place Porter drew directly on Shils' work is in the chapter of *The Vertical Mosaic* dealing with ideological elites, he apparently admired the scholar's empirical style of sociology.[68] In the ten-lecture urban studies course taught by Shils and Glass they reviewed the early history of the tradition, beginning with studies by German ethnographers in the early nineteenth century and finishing with the contemporary work of the Chicago School, including W. Lloyd Warner's *Yankee City* studies.[69] Among the subjects broached in the course was class inequality, and its treatment doubtless informed Porter's views on the subject and how to study it.[70] The study of class was central to the entire intellectual ambience of the LSE, and several faculty members were doing research in the area at the time. Marshall and Ginsberg had just edited a set of British Institute of Sociology conference papers entitled *Class Conflict and Social Stratification*, Marshall was writing *Citizenship and Social Class and Other Essays,* and David Glass and Jean Floud were in the midst of notable work on social mobility.[71] Though there is no evidence Porter attended it, Floud taught a course entitled 'Property and Social Class in Modern Society' that dealt with the nature and significance of private property, forms of ownership, the implications of public and private corporate ownership, the relationship of property to class, and the like – themes at the core of Porter's scholarly interests. The reading list included a number of sources Porter later employed in *The Vertical Mosaic*: H. Campion's *Public and Private Property in Great Britain*, A.A. Berle and G.C. Means' *The Modern Corporation and Private Property*, Tawney's *The Acquisitive Society*, Marshall's *Social Stratification and Class Conflict*, and works by Marx and Weber.[72] Anthony Richmond has noted that the work of Glass and Floud would have been 'directly relevant to Porter's later interests' and might have constituted 'a model for Porter's later work on ascription and achievement in Canada.'[73]

More important than the urban studies course was Shils' seminar in research methods. During this twenty-lecture course Shils reviewed recent (mostly American) developments in the various empirical research traditions. There are no notes from Shils' course among Porter's student notes, but years later Porter hinted that he had attended the class. In reminiscing about his time at the LSE, he wrote, 'Edward Shils had recently come from Chicago, and through a seminar in sociological research put sociology students into contact with the developing empirical work in the United States.'[74] Methodology was central to the course; among other sources, Shils used George Lundberg's *Social Research,* Hadley Cantril's *Gauging Public Opinion,* P.V. Young's *Scientific Social Surveys and Research,* and Gordon Allport's *The Use of Personal Documents in Psychological Science.*[75] The seminar was crucial because it exposed British students to mainstream American sociology at a time when many faculty members at the LSE – and in Great Britain more generally – regarded American-style sociology with great suspicion, if not disdain. They saw Chicago sociology as too narrowly empirical in orientation and were unconvinced by Parsons' 'weirdly unwieldy and polysyllabic' functionalism.[76] So Shils' course was a boon to students interested in modern American methods. Ginsberg taught the core theory and methods course, but many students regarded it as boring and out of date. Indeed, according to Richmond, most of them regarded Shils as the only real sociologist on the staff.[77] In such an environment, Porter's contact with Shils was doubly significant. It marked his initial encounter with a sophisticated advocate of American sociology and its scientific methodology, and constituted his first exposure to an expert analysis of the theoretical and methodological works of Max Weber, on whose work he drew heavily later in his career.[78]

Another notable figure at the School was the Christian socialist historian R.H. Tawney. According to Norman Dennis and A.H. Halsey, Tawney is 'the crowning figure of ethical socialism in the twentieth century' whose works, *The Acquisitive Society*, published in 1921, and *Equality*, published in 1931, constitute 'the best and probably the most widely influential modern statement[s] of democratic socialism.'[79] It is difficult to gauge directly Tawney's influence on Porter, for there is no evidence he sat in on any of Tawney's courses. However, we know that he occasionally attended an informal seminar that Tawney hosted at his very untidy London apartment. At these affairs, said Donald Chesworth, 'Tawney, apart from talking, served tea and fruitcake, not just to favoured students and gate-crashers, but also to the mice which inhabited [his] Mews flat.'[80] Tawney's writings regularly appeared on the reading lists of courses at LSE and, like T.H. Marshall, Tawney wrote about the history of rights, especially property rights, and their relation to the development and maintenance of the class system. He criticized the irrationality and injustice of 'non-functional' private property (rights without service) and advocated Keynesian economics, the development of a generous welfare state, and a limited form of public ownership of the means of production in British society. In this regard, though Dennis and Halsey refer to him as an 'ethical socialist,' many of his ideas are similar to those of New Liberals such as Hobhouse, Ginsberg, and John Hobson.[81] Indeed, Tawney worked with Hobhouse at the *Manchester Guardian* and, according to Dennis and Halsey, drew much of his inspiration from Hobhouse's New Liberalism.[82]

MacRae's twelve-lecture course entitled 'Political Sociology' seems to have had an even greater immediate and tangible impact on the young John Porter.[83] Though the lectures dealt with a lengthy list of theorists, among them Plato, Machiavelli, Aquinas, Marx, Weber, Mannheim, and MacIver, Porter's notes indicate that MacRae paid most attention to Michels and the elite theorists. Porter may have used MacRae's lectures to prepare a half-course in political science he taught at Carleton

College in 1949–50, and the elite theorists occupied an important place in his discussion of power in *The Vertical Mosaic*.

Laski offered a second-year course entitled 'Political and Social Theory' that dealt with classical themes in the discipline: property, power, equality, education, individual rights, and the nature and role of the state. These concepts were much in the public consciousness and central to public debates in England during the postwar period, and Laski's reading list, which included Hobhouse's *The Elements of Social Justice*, MacIver's *The Modern State* (a New Liberal treatment of the issue), Hayek's *The Road to Serfdom*, E.F. Carritt's *Morals and Politics*, and Laski's own *A Grammar of Politics*, gave his students, John Porter among them, much to think about.[84] According to Porter's notes, it was Laski's view that in modern society the state had replaced the Church as society's 'supreme coercive power' – as Laski's little aphorism suggests: 'If the Church damns you, you might be damned. If the state hangs you, you will be hanged.' According to Laski, social order was maintained by 'making men keep laws,' but power was unevenly distributed and tended to be exercised in favour of the 'inner circle' and 'the protection of property.' True freedom, Laski said, was the result of 'economic well-being' and could expand only 'where members of society have an equal interest in its outcome.' Echoing the New Liberal ideas of the time, he claimed that each citizen had a number of 'natural rights': the right to work, a reasonable wage, education that would make leisure self-fulfilling, and so forth. Though Porter's student files contain notes from only a few of Laski's nineteen lectures, and these are very brief, it is difficult to believe that he abandoned the course part way through.[85] Its themes became central to Porter's scholarly and political interests – in *Social Purpose for Canada*, *The Vertical Mosaic*, and the McInnis Lectures, for instance[86] – and it is likely that, as in the case of Laski's course on the British constitution, his notes found their way into Porter's Carleton College political science lectures in the early 1950s.

The only teachers more important to Porter than Laski were T.H. Marshall and Morris Ginsberg. Marshall, who held a chair as professor of social institutions, was Porter's tutor during his last two years.[87] A great admirer of Hobhouse, he was second only to Ginsberg in seniority.[88] According to Richmond, Marshall was generally 'held in higher esteem by the students than Ginsberg' even though some of them regarded his comparative institutions course as uneven: 'second-hand history and anthropology [that was] rather uninspiring.'[89] But Marshall's forty-lecture course, 'Comparative Social Institutions,' clearly piqued Porter's interest. The course was divided into two parts. The first dealt with the institutional aspects of social structure, including justice, property, and social stratification; the second dealt with the contemporary social structure of England. The reading list included, among other works, Hobhouse's *Morals in Evolution*, Ginsberg's *Sociology*, MacIver's *Society*, and A.M. Carr-Saunders and D. Caradog Jones' *A Survey of the Social Structure of England and Wales*.[90] Porter took extensive notes at the lectures and many of them bear signs of close reading.[91] Particularly influential was Marshall's concept of citizenship, which, according to Dennis and Halsey, he took from Hobhouse: '[Marshall] offered a theory of ethical socialism, conceptualized as citizenship, which is sociologically more defensible than the Hobhousian theory of progress, for while it gives due weight to the autonomously moral, corrects Hobhouse's overemphasis on it.'[92] Marshall's writing on citizenship became central to Porter's thinking about how to construct a workable liberal democracy.[93]

Marshall argued that citizenship was an ascribed status. All citizens, he argued, are automatically granted at birth a basic minimum of rights (and duties) by virtue of their citizenship. Historically, this minimum had been extended in two ways: first, to more people, so that no one would be excluded by virtue of an ascribed characteristic and, second, to a wider range of rights. One of the most important developments in this dual process was the replacement of 'status' by 'contract.' People realized that the rules that had created social order over time were not the result of some sort of immanent, unalterable set of natural laws but rather a consequence of purposive action by individuals.[94] According to Marshall, the transformation from status to contract constituted a rough index of social progress and occurred in stages. The British case, on which Marshall focused in detail, had three stages. Economic rights (property and contract) emerged first. Political rights emerged next. Here the extension of the franchise was especially important, for it prevented the arbitrary wielding of power. Civil and social rights emerged last. They were necessary, Marshall argued, here sounding much like Hobhouse and the New Liberals, because universal and abstract rights such as property rights and the freedom of contract meant little when many people had no property and, as labourers, had no choice but to enter into disadvantageous contracts with powerful property owners.[95] Economic and political rights were important and necessary indicators of progress, but to Marshall clearly insufficient unless they were supplemented by social rights that guaranteed a minimally equal standard of living for all.[96] These ideas, particularly the notion that it was possible to measure social progress through the development and spread of rights and improved standards of living, came to constitute a central aspect of Porter's beliefs.

However, as important as these ideas and scholars were, none seems to have had the impact on Porter of the New Liberal sociology and politics of Morris Ginsberg. Ginsberg's omnivorous conception of sociology addressed the same ideas examined by Shils, MacRae, Laski, and Marshall, but unlike the others, Ginsberg was a true disciple of Hobhouse. It was Ginsberg, I think, who acted as Porter's link to the New Liberal political theory and sociological practice that Hobhouse propounded in the first part of the twentieth century. Ginsberg was the senior sociologist on staff at the LSE and, according to Richmond, made certain that Hobhousian concerns and views were well represented in the curriculum.[97] In this regard, said A.H. Halsey, another of Ginsberg's postwar students, the sociology curriculum at the LSE in the late 1940s and early 1950s grew out of a different intellectual dynamic from that at other schools: 'Sociology in the now received view is continental in origin. It has been the European reply to Marxism. Is that the subject which was taught ... at LSE in the late 1940s? Certainly not directly. On the contrary, the LSE syllabus still rehearsed the 19th century battles between the statistical empiricism of the London Statistical Society and the synthetic or orthogenic evolutionism espoused by L.T. Hobhouse.'[98]

Dahrendorf describes the peculiarity or particularity of postwar sociology at the LSE by drawing on Colin Crouch's words. According to Crouch, the curriculum gave considerable weight to the traditional approach of Ginsberg but tempered it with the transitional, modernizing influence of Marshall and Glass: 'What, then, was peculiar about LSE sociology in the narrower sense? The combination of ... "evolutionary sociology, citizenship sociology ... and political arithmetic" of Ginsberg, Marshall and Glass.'[99] Most students regarded Ginsberg's sociology as boring and out of date, indeed, irrelevant, but John Porter did not share this view.

The Hobhouse Connection: Ginsberg, Porter, and the New Liberalism

The New Liberalism

According to the New Liberalism, the minimalist conception of the state and the negative conception of rights that constituted the basis of classical, laissez-faire liberalism during the eighteenth and nineteenth centuries were outmoded.[100] The 'free' market had not produced and would never produce a society that was sufficiently equal, free, just, and rational that people could realize their individual and collective potential. Instead, it created ubiquitous and hidebound class inequalities in living standards and mobility opportunities. In place of the market, the minimalist state, and the negative conception of rights, the New Liberals, beginning with John Stuart Mill in the 1860s and culminating with Graham Wallas, John Hobson, Leonard Hobhouse, and others in the 1920s and '30s, proposed a new kind of liberal market society. Central to the new society was the positive state: a powerful central government aided by a technically competent, merit-based civil service staffed by knowledgeable experts who would oversee the market and manage an economy comprising elements of public and private enterprise. Increasingly comprehensive welfare state measures would improve the living standards of the poor and provide them with real opportunities for social mobility. The New Liberals regarded society as an organic, collective whole and argued that it was possible to talk meaningfully about a collective *societal* interest and the *common* good. That is, like individuals, society had rights and could use those rights to appropriate societally produced surpluses from those who, as individuals, benefited unduly from collectively generated surpluses, profits, and benefits. These appropriated resources could then be used for the common good.

A second part of the New Liberalism was a novel conception of the scholar as an engaged, practical intellectual. His or her purpose was to identify the societal or collective good, work toward that good, and measure the progress so achieved. Hobhouse, an especially influential figure in this tradition, claimed that one part of the New Liberalism, intimately tied to the conception of the engaged, practical intellectual, was a value-infused, empirically informed, activist sociology. As Hobhouse described it, New Liberal sociology had three essential purposes. First, it would provide a comprehensive description and explanation of 'orthogenic evolution,' that is, the unfolding of social and moral progress as manifested in the increasing 'unity of mankind' and the establishment of a 'rational harmony' in society. Second, it would be a social mechanism for the creation of a collective moral (philosophical) and scientific (empirical) self-understanding that could be used by intellectuals, the public, and the state to guide orthogenic evolution. Third, it would develop ways of empirically measuring the societal progress created by orthogenic evolution. Through Hobhouse and Ginsberg, the

New Liberalism had a major impact on British sociology during the early decades of the twentieth century, especially at the LSE.[101] By the end of World War II, however, this influence had waned. Indeed, according to John Westergaard and Basil Bernstein, both students at the LSE at the time, 'the spirit of Hobhouse (both liberal and evolutionist) was moribund.'[102]

Porter's Course Work with Ginsberg

Porter attended part or all of five sets of lectures given by Ginsberg during his last two years at LSE. The majority were two-term courses. This means that he took as many courses from Ginsberg as from Shils, Laski, MacRae, and Marshall combined. The five courses Porter took from Ginsberg between October 1947 and May 1949 were 'The Relationship between Psycho-Analysis and Sociology,'[103] 'Ethics,' 'Comparative Morals and Religion,' and, most important, 'Theories and Methods of Sociology,' and 'Social Philosophy.'

The twenty-lecture theory and methods course was not a conventional review of the standard methodological and theoretical approaches in the field. Though the recommended readings in the LSE calendar contained some standard methods-related books – among them A.L. Bowley's *The Measurement of Social Phenomena* and the Webbs' *Methods of Social Study* – Ginsberg dealt with methods only sparingly. As well, he handled the theoretical materials in an idiosyncratic way. The calendar lists Hobhouse's *Social Development,* MacIver's *Society,* and Pitirim Sorokin's *Contemporary Sociological Theories* as books recommended for the course, but Porter's notes indicate that he dealt with the corpus of theory very selectively.[104] He touched on Weber only briefly and apparently ignored not only Parsons and the American functionalists but also the British functionalist anthropologists Radcliffe-Brown and Malinowski, despite their high profile at the LSE and elsewhere. Those he focused on were Hobhouse, Durkheim, Kant, Hegel, Comte, and Marx. According to Porter's files, the course reading list contained sixteen books, including three by or about Hobhouse, two by or about Durkheim, and two by or about Marx.[105]

The first part of the course was taken up with the philosophy of knowledge or, perhaps more accurately, the philosophy of history. Ginsberg drew on a variety of thinkers in order to discuss the relationships between sociology and other social science disciplines, a definition of positivism (Comte, Durkheim), the utility of evolutionary theory (Hobhouse, Westermarck, Spencer), the relative merits of the work of Comte and Marx, and so forth. Ginsberg thought Marx's work important in theoretical and political terms but ultimately unconvincing. Porter's later disavowal of Marx in *The Vertical Mosaic* and elsewhere may have been fuelled by Ginsberg's remarks as well as by the political activities of the student Communists at the LSE and the anti-Marxist writings of Karl Popper and Fritz Hayek, but there is no definitive evidence.[106]

Ginsberg's social philosophy course showcased his particular interpretation of sociology and in many respects repeated basic messages from the ethics and theories and methods courses. His major concern was the role sociology could play in resolving problems of morality, in answering the question 'How shall we live?' Once again, he drew on many New Liberal sources to develop his argument. Books listed in the course description in the calendar included T.H. Green's *Lectures in the Principles of Political Obligation,* J.A. Hobson's *Wealth and Life,* and Hobhouse's *Elements of Social Justice,* as well as Laski's *A Grammar of Politics.*[107] Porter's notes indicate that Ginsberg established the problematic for the course right at the outset. According to Ginsberg, the malaise of the post–World War II period – a 'feeling of impatience with the Liberal Spirit' – was similar to that which characterized the period after World War I. During such times, Ginsberg said, people felt a compulsion to organize social life in a way that was morally appropriate but differed over both what the good life was and how best to realize it. The root of the problem, as defined by Ginsberg according to Porter's notes, is that people feel there is no set of absolute moral principles to guide their lives: '[This malaise] arises from [the] difficulty of applying ultimate moral principles to the solution of modern problems. [There is a] feeling that [the] teachings of the great religions have failed to deal with problems today ... [This] also applies to philosophical writers who fail to show how to move from principle to action in life.'[108] Ginsberg argued that this was one place where sociology could make a major contribution.

He noted that the question 'What is to be done?' involved factual and ethical considerations regarding both means and ends and argued that social philosophy, which he saw as a constituent part of the more inclusive discipline of sociology, could and must play a pivotal role in helping to separate those considerations when they inevitably became entangled. On the question of ends, he eschewed moral relativism and argued, following Hobhouse, that there existed a set of absolute moral standards. It was therefore possible to judge the degree to which society had moved in the direction of progress. As I note in detail in the afterword, Porter found this view compelling and adopted it as a part of his sociological world view. He pursued ideas about the possibility of measuring progress throughout his career, but at most length in some reflective essays he wrote near the end of his life (see afterword).

If Porter was taken with the sociological and political ideas of New Liberalism while at the LSE, he was influenced by other currents of thought as well. The most widely noted is Fabanism, and scholars such as Dennis Wilcox-Magill and Frank Vallee have argued that Porter is best understood as a Fabian.[109] This interpretation makes some sense. Porter left the LSE with what could be seen as a Fabianesque scholarly political orientation: rationalist, empirical, humanist, socialist. As well, he had a 'practical' political orientation that favoured the prosecution of empirical social science relevant to the development of a strong, progressive welfare state. But all of these elements of Porter's perspective have non-Fabian roots, in particular in the New Liberalism, and Porter rejected too many aspects of Fabianism for it to make sense for us to label him in this way.

In fact, it is difficult to judge how potent Fabianism might have been at the LSE after the war. Some, such as MacRae, thought it a spent force.[110] This was Shils' view as well. 'Fabianism, *au pied de la lettre*,' he said, 'probably had few followers.'[111] But others disagreed. Reginald Robson, who was a friend of Porter at LSE, challenged the claim that Fabianism was 'pretty much dead.'[112] John Westergaard, also a student at the time, concurred. 'Classical Fabianism,' Westergaard wrote, remained important at the School because it prioritized 'empirical, policy-relevant investigation,' a task it had taken over from 'the Blue Book and "political arithmetic" tradition.'[113] Porter shared the latter view. In his recollection, 'the traditions of LSE established by Sidney and Beatrice Webb were most salient at that time.'[114]

My own view is that while the intellectual-political ambience at the School remained rooted in Fabianism and while its *symbolic* presence remained strong – witness the Shaw Library, for example – classical Fabianism had long since been critiqued and modified. So, for example, Porter's student colleague Anthony Richmond could reasonably say that at that the time people often claimed that, minus the impediments of the details of classical Fabianism, 'we are all Fabians now.'[115] In a similar fashion, Frank Vallee noted, 'I don't think I ever heard him use the term "Fabian," [but] there is no doubt that he was very much influenced by the Fabian view of reality and rationalism. But rationalism informed with a kind of passion.'[116]

But classical Fabianism by no means dominated the scene. Instead, there was an intellectual stew, good portions of which shared many of the progressive, meliorist, left-liberal/socialist assumptions, features, and goals of the classical Fabians without being Fabian per se. In the words of John Westergaard, there was 'a common climate of opinion around much ... academic work in social science' that blended 'Marxism, ... labour-radicalism, and ... Blue Book reformist social enquiry.'[117] Dahrendorf came to a similar conclusion:

> From the 1920s to the 1950s at least, the London School of Economics has had a powerful influence at home and, even more so, abroad. This influence is variously described as socialism, Fabianism, the Welfare State; perhaps social democracy would be a more appropriate notion if it were not so alien to British political discourse. What is meant is the combination of Westminster-style democratic institutions with a benevolent interventionist government guided by a view of the good or just society. A little Laski, so to speak, a little Beveridge, some Tawney, and a lot of Pierre Trudeau, the long-serving Canadian Prime Minister with an LSE past.[118]

Porter's teachers offer a collective case in point. They shared a common intellectual currency. 'There was,' said John Owen, author of *L.T. Hobhouse: Sociologist*, 'an intellectual affinity between Hobhouse, Tawney, Ginsberg, MacRae and Marshall.'[119] In my estimation, their ideas encouraged Porter to develop an orientation to sociology that was based on what MacRae referred to as a set of 'common humane assumptions and, in the centre, ... liberal socialism.'[120] Progressive social change could take a variety of specific institutional forms but, as MacRae put it, people generally agreed to disagree 'within certain parameters.'[121] The elements of this common currency, at least among those who were important to Porter, included the following. All had an interest in and worked at the macrosociological level of analysis and each favoured a multidisciplinary approach to the study of social phenomena, even if they did not agree on what disciplines should be stressed.[122] Not all focused on philosophical issues as much as Ginsberg, but each had an interest in such problems. They also shared a basically progressive, Whig view of history. Finally, all were rationalists, humanists, and pragmatists who shared the conviction that sociology could be used as a tool not just for understanding the world but also for changing it. An analysis of Porter's LSE student notes bears out this sense of the place of Fabianism per se. Fabian publications were found only in scattered places on course reading lists and Fabians were not often cited in lectures. So Fabianism was only one of the threads, and a background colour at that, in the complicated tapestry of intellectual influences that shaped Porter's scholarly world view.[123]

In fact, Porter *rejected* some basic aspects of Fabian political and sociological thought.[124] First, he harboured grave doubts about the Fabians' widespread faith in the efficacy of social engineering by social scientists. In a critique of the mental health movement written just a few years after he left the LSE, he rejected its premise that 'an electorate sufficiently aware of mental health criteria ... would elect well-adjusted individuals to office' and that 'in the main these would be social scientists' who would be able to 'get on with the job of helping the people ... to live peacefully together.' Indeed, Porter said, 'It might be that there is an even greater danger in having the world run by social scientists now than there was forty years ago.'[125] Second, Porter was respectful of the Webbs' contribution to English politics and sociology, including their sponsorship of people like William Beveridge.[126] However, he regarded the Fabians as too bureaucratic and *dirigiste*, and at one point referred to Sidney Webb as an 'apparatchik.'[127] Another, related disagreement concerned the Fabians' faith in the possibility of progress. Unlike them, Porter did not believe it would come naturally or easily but would occur only with great effort and at 'glacial' speed.[128] And it should not come via top-down social engineering and the false democracy of manipulated consent. Instead, following Hobhouse, Tawney, and Marshall, Porter preferred the model of the engaged intellectual, working to educate policy makers, politicians, and the public by undertaking policy-relevant research, stimulating academic and social debate, working with government, and so forth. And unlike the Fabians, Porter was deeply influenced by the anti-rationalist writings of the elite theorists and Freud. An element of anti-rationalism remained a pervasive, if subsidiary, aspect of his world view for much of his career.[129] Finally, the Fabians were socialists, devout and unequivocal; Porter was not. He was throughout his career a liberal, though he vacillated from one version of the doctrine to another during his adult life. Hobhouse's influence is crucial here. His radical version of liberalism was a broad one that allowed Porter at some points in his career to stress the radical and socialistic parts of the doctrine and at others to emphasize its more traditional and individualistic aspects. For his part, Laski the Marxist saw the liberal socialism of Hobhouse as very far left indeed. 'To any of you who want a good introduction to socialist ideas,' Laski once said, 'get a little book in the Home University

Library, by Professor Hobhouse, entitled *Liberalism*.'[130] For their part, Dennis and Halsey argue that Hobhouse belongs with William Cobbett, Robert Owen, G.D.H. Cole, R.H. Tawney, and others in what they refer to as the tradition of 'English ethical socialism,' a pigeonhole that suggests the boundaries between left liberalism and social democracy are blurred and permeable indeed.

It seems, then, that the most foundational of Porter's beliefs, the ones most central to his sociology and politics and those he retained the longest, came not from Fabianism but from the New Liberalism as presented by Marshall and Ginsberg. Even during Porter's later years, when he was increasingly influenced by American mainstream sociology – scientific research and data analysis techniques, modernization theory, postindustrialism, the end-of-ideology thesis, and so forth – the New Liberalism remained at the core of his sense of the nature and purpose of sociology. Most important, he remained more politically radical than his American contemporaries and rejected the notion of value freedom, a key element of American scientific sociology.

It is peculiar that other scholars have not noticed the connection from Hobhouse through Ginsberg to Porter because Porter specifically pointed it out in his 'research biography' of *The Vertical Mosaic*.[131] The most likely reason for this oversight is that there exists a plausible alternative interpretation: the Fabian one sketched above. Perhaps, too, since Porter generally limited his use of secondary sources to the data reported in empirical research monographs and often wrote without making reference to theoretical treatises, particularly the classical literature, his debts to Hobhouse and other early theoreticians were obscured.

In late June 1949, Porter wrote his final examinations. In all, he sat nine: principles of economics, applied economics, economic history of England and the great powers since 1815, comparative social institutions, social philosophy, (sociological) theory and methods, psychology, social institutions, and French and Italian translation.[132] Porter passed the lot and graduated with a perfectly respectable but not stellar second class standing.[133]

With the pressure off, Porter treated himself to some time visiting family and friends in London, Oxford, and Wales. Soon, however, he would be off on an overseas journey. He had no job and no immediate prospects. Thus, when the Canadian Department of Veterans' Affairs urged him to 'at least visit Canada again,' presumably to survey employment prospects there, he felt obliged to do so.[134] He was ambivalent about the exercise, for he retained bitter memories of the years in Vancouver and had no desire to live in Canada.[135] However, as part of his demobilization package, the Canadian government had given him a one-way ticket to Vancouver, so he decided to do some travelling.[136] A side benefit of the trip, he reasoned, was that he could use the opportunity to do some freelance writing for British publications in the hope of securing a reporting job when he returned to London.[137]

4 Canada and Carleton College, 1939–1963

One of the first places Porter stopped on his trip across Canada was Ottawa. While there, he contacted Paul Fox.[1] Fox had left the LSE in 1948, dissertation unfinished, to assume a position in the Department of Political Science at Ottawa's tiny Carleton College.[2] The two friends met for lunch at the Ottawa train station, across Rideau Street from the Chateau Laurier hotel. In the course of their conversation, Fox discovered that Porter was without a job. Carleton's political science department had lost its only other member and Fox, desperate to find a replacement, offered Porter a position as a lecturer.[3] 'I said to John: "Why don't you stay here and lecture in political science? I am sure you can do it because you have done a lot of political science with your sociology in London."'[4] The offer took Porter off guard. He had never considered the possibility of an academic career and still harboured a desire to return to journalism.[5] As well, he was reticent because he had been away from his native country for more than a decade and had little knowledge of either Canadian political institutions or the current political scene.[6] Undeterred, Fox pressured him – as did Bob and Mary Anne Phillips, also in Ottawa – and he agreed to mull over the possibility. During the short time Porter had to decide, recalled Phillips, he 'agonized' about what to do and very nearly declined the offer.[7] However, the combined encouragement of Fox and the Phillipses won him over. In the current situation of formal hiring procedures and demands to publish, it seems remarkable that one of the most successful careers in the history of Canadian social science could have begun in such a serendipitous manner. But such informal hiring procedures were common – and not just in sociology. Fox recalls that 'it was the way academia operated in those days. Somebody offered you a job (for whatever reason) and you took it

… There was no tenure, no contract, no procedure for promotion. Just a job in a certain category.'[8] So, as the heat and humidity of late summer Ottawa faded into autumn, John Porter's plan for a leisurely trip across Canada ended abruptly.

He had to get ready for the back-to-school rituals – only this time, he would be the one at the front of the classroom. He did not have much time to be nervous, for the school year started shortly thereafter and the grind of lecture preparation, the bane of the novice professor, was soon upon him. Fortunately, he did not have to worry about research productivity since Carleton was still very much a teaching enterprise and the scholarly productivity of its faculty a secondary issue. Indeed, in 1949, Carleton was still a fledgling institution in every sense of the term.

The Birth of Carleton College, 1942–1949

Carleton College was in its seventh year of operation when Porter joined the staff in political science. According to Blair Neatby and Don McEown, chroniclers of the life and times of Carleton University, it had opened in September 1942 with a limited slate of evening classes and the mandate to provide two years of non-sectarian, English-language university education for career-minded civil servants and veterans.[9] The driving force behind the establishment of the college was seventy-seven-year-old Dr Henry Marshall Tory, a native of Guysborough, Nova Scotia. Tory, a mathematician and physicist, had received his formal education at McGill University and Wesleyan College and taught at McGill from 1893 to 1903.[10] Not long after receiving his doctoral degree, Tory began to pursue an outstanding career as a founder of postsecondary educational institutions. He helped to establish McGill University College of British Columbia, and then played a major role in the founding of the University of Alberta in 1907, becoming its first president.[11] For the next two decades, he oversaw its growth as it became a full-fledged university.[12] As well, in the midst of this daunting challenge, he took a leave of absence from Alberta to oversee the organization of the Canadian Army's Khaki College, an institution devised to provide accredited, university-level instruction to Canadian Forces personnel overseas during World War I. By the time Tory undertook the task of helping to found Carleton College in 1942, then, he had an impressive list of credentials and a wealth of experience on which to draw.[13]

Tory received assistance in his efforts to get Carleton up and running from the local chapter of the YMCA. In 1938, a committee of the Ottawa Y headed by Hugh Keenleyside had done some preliminary work looking into the prospects for an English-language, non-Catholic university.[14] The only local university, the University of Ottawa, was a French-language institution presided over by the Oblate Order of the Roman Catholic Church. It had an English-language affiliate, St Patrick's College, but many Ottawans thought that the city needed a non-denominational institution of higher learning.[15] Certainly, advance publicity for the new college stressed its secular character: 'There would be no religious instruction ... and no religious tests for professors or students ... [N]on-denominational was almost a code word for non-Catholic.'[16] The YMCA-based group became moribund with the declaration of war in 1939 but following a hiatus of about two years, Tory, Keenleyside and others revived it. It took a year to drum up sufficient community and financial support, but they eventually established the Ottawa Association for the Advancement of Learning, from which Carleton College – Ottawa's 'sundown college' – eventually emerged in the fall of 1942.[17]

One of the easiest parts of Tory's job in 1942 was the recruitment of instructors. Wartime obligations in the civil service had brought professors to Ottawa from all over Canada and many were eager to resume teaching. Early on, all students and faculty save Dr Tory were part time. Professors were paid the princely stipend of $2.50 per hour and Tory worked for nothing.[18] Indeed, Tory worked tirelessly at all manner of jobs to ensure the success of the little college, as historian James Gibson, an early recruit to Carleton's faculty, reveals:

> The office in which [Tory] worked had two doors. He sat at one desk as registrar and if the forms were complete he would say: 'Would you mind paying your fees to the bursar, next door on the left?' And he would then move from this chair over to one on his left so that the student with his chequebook would confront the same person acting as bursar. A part of the story was that the original receipts were kept in a cigar box. I can verify that this was true.[19]

Despite the somewhat makeshift nature of the operation, students got their money's worth. Over half the instructors held a PhD and most of the rest held a master's degree.[20] Yet not all were academics. Wilfrid Eggleton, a prominent newspaperman and Canada's chief censor during the war, headed the journalism department, and E.R. Steadman, a retired senior air force officer, headed engineering.[21] Early on, the college operated in the evenings out of rented classrooms in Ottawa's High School of Commerce and some local church basements, offering not only regular, university-credit courses but also preparation courses for those without proper credentials to enter university.[22] Since most students were teachers or civil servants trying to get credits toward a degree,[23] the question of the academic acceptability of Carleton's courses at other universities was paramount. Tory solved this problem by writing to the presidents of many Canadian universities and personally asking them 'to recognize in advance any credits which the new college would award.'[24]

From the outset, the college was a clear, if small-scale, success. When the first slate of classes was proposed for the fall of 1942, some voiced concern that they might not reach their budget-balancing target of 100 registrations. They need not have worried; over 700 students signed up.[25] But as Neatby and McEown point out, over the next decade, Carleton grew only very slowly and experienced numerous growing pains, including a lack of public profile and little in the way of political support:

> In the early years many Ottawa citizens may not even have been aware that Carleton existed. The story is told of a student coming to Ottawa in 1947 to enrol at Carleton and hailing a cab at the train station, only to discover that the cab driver had never heard of the college ... Nor did the college have a place on the agenda of civic politicians. City politics was dominated in those years by the problems of expanding services to meet the needs of a burgeoning federal government, and was the battleground of the feisty Charlotte Whitton on the one side and the developers on the other. Neither side had any reason to court Carleton. The isolation of the college was all the more complete because there were no prominent college alumni to defend its interests. Those associated with Carleton were left largely to themselves.[26]

Financial resources and space were particularly pressing problems. Prior to 1949–50, Carleton was a private college and thus received no grant money from the provincial government. It had to survive on tuition fees and private donations alone. Tuition funds were relatively easy to come by between 1942 and 1949 because of the large number of veterans who enrolled, but once they cleared the system, Carleton found it difficult to maintain and increase enrolments.[27] Two fundraising campaigns were helpful but only marginally, a clear indication that Carleton College was not high on the priority list of Ottawa philanthropists.[28] In fact, though the situation improved in 1949–50, when the provincial government provided $65,000 in grant money, Carleton's future remained uncertain until 1952.[29]

Inadequate space was a persistent problem throughout the period. Rented quarters in local high schools and churches had served the purpose during the early years, but the question of a permanent home soon became paramount, especially once Tory decided to turn Carleton into a full-time institution by offering day courses and admitting full-time students. The opportunity came when the veterans returned from Europe; the federal government wanted to avoid the unemployment problems that had plagued veterans after World War I, and decided to expand postsecondary schooling as part of their coping strategy.[30] To this end, parliament passed the Veterans Rehabilitation Act. The Act was a blessing for the college – and the university system more generally – because it not only paid some of the tuition and living costs for returning soldiers but also offered grants to universities for registering them. With this newfound largesse in place, enrolment at Canada's universities grew rapidly. Enrolment more than doubled between 1944–5 and 1947–8 – from 38,500 to 79,000, including 29,600 veterans.[31] Carleton took advantage of this opportunity and in the autumn of 1946 declared itself a full-time operation. Immediately, the need for a proper facility became a priority.[32]

Once they made the decision to obtain a proper permanent site, Tory and the others set to work, soon finding what they were looking for: the former Ottawa Ladies' College on First Avenue would fit the bill. Located in the Glebe, a mature residential area about a mile south of Parliament Hill and just north of Lansdowne Park, the building had been used by the Department of National Defence during the war. Carleton's Board of Governors discovered that it might be declared surplus and petitioned the minister to make it available. He refused. At that point, H.S. Southam, a key figure on Carleton's board, stepped in. In a clear illustration of a point Porter would later make about elites having direct personal access to one another, Southam spoke to C.D. Howe. Shortly thereafter, Carleton obtained the site.[33]

For the next five years, the college's enrolment grew slowly; by 1951, it had 484 full-time students and overall enrolment of 1,363.[34] But as enrolments grew, so too did the need for facilities. Carleton responded by purchasing three houses in the area – one to act as a student union building and two others to serve as office buildings – and by adding a 200-seat library to the original structure.[35] The library improved research and studying facilities immensely and, as a side benefit, provided a venue for first-rate concerts and public lectures. James Gibson recalled one occasion on which six justices of the Supreme Court came to hear a public lecture by the constitutional scholar Frank Scott.[36] But soon even these expanded facilities did not suffice and, in 1952, the college began looking for a truly permanent home. Five years earlier, in 1947, board member H.S. Southam, his brother Wilson Southam, and Col. C.M. Edwards had donated a parcel of land to the college.[37] Carleton now bought the balance of the acreage – located between the Rideau River and the Rideau Canal – thereby guaranteeing a site for its future growth.[38] By its tenth anniversary, then, Carleton College was well established as a liberal arts college; it had a staff of forty-two professors, an annual budget of almost $400,000, a provincial charter that recognized its academic legitimacy – including the right to grant degrees – and land on which to establish a permanent campus.[39]

The scope of its operations would soon expand well beyond these bounds. In 1954, the board began making plans to move the college to the new site.[40] In the summer of 1958, with a student body that now included 750 full-time students and a complement of nearly 100 faculty members Carleton moved to its current site on the Rideau River.[41] By this time, it had become Carleton University.[42]

Much happened to Porter during this formative period in the Glebe. Personal and scholarly experiences occasioned significant changes in his academic and political views, and it was here that he began to write *The Vertical Mosaic*. He watched first hand as Canadians tried to negotiate the new postwar world and built a career documenting and assessing their efforts.

The Wider Political and Economic Context: Canada 1939–1963

Canada and World War II

When Porter left Canada in 1937, the country had been mired in a deep depression. Beginning in 1939, however, Allied demands for war materiel precipitated a massive second industrial revolution in Canada, propelling the country to a previously unimaginable stature: the fourth most powerful industrial and trading nation in the world.[43] At the same time, farmers doubled the production of agricultural goods.[44] The result was impressive; between 1939 and 1945 Canada's GNP more than doubled.[45] As well, Big Labour and Big Capital transformed themselves, and the dramatis personae of Porter's *The Vertical Mosaic* – the members of Canada's various elites – consolidated their positions. During the early stages of the war, as more and more workers went off to become soldiers, unemployment disappeared. In fact, workers came to be in short supply and as a consequence organized labour became a powerful economic and political force, willing and able to stand toe to toe with Canada's capitalist class. Labour–capital relations became increasingly fractious, and the federal government had to rethink its largely pro-capital industrial relations policies.[46] By the time the war wound down, changes were in the offing.

But changes in labour–capital relations were only part of the story. Dramatic political changes were likewise imminent. The successful use of centralized government power during the war, in particular the management of the wartime economy, shifted popular opinion in an interventionist direction and, in a related development, the pro-labour CCF, which had been unable to garner even 10 per cent of the federal vote between 1935 and 1940, became a legitimate electoral threat.[47] In 1944, the CCF formed the Saskatchewan government after narrowly missing in Ontario and British Columbia a year earlier. Feeling pressured, the Liberals began to move in an interventionist direction, looking ever more favourably on the principles of the New Liberalism to which Porter had been exposed at the LSE: specifically, Keynesianism and an expanded set of social welfare measures. Mackenzie King, ever the reticent reformer, had to be convinced, but by 1939 had grudgingly agreed to budget for a Keynesian-inspired 'stimulative deficit.'[48] Keynesian policy involved more than just deficit budgeting, however, and King was forced to commit his government to greater involvement in the economy and increased spending on social security. Over the course of the war, annual federal spending on social security increased rapidly, from $78 million to $284 million.[49] This trend continued into the postwar period. So powerful was the memory of the Depression that many Canadians feared it would return. Such fears proved unfounded. From the late 1940s to the mid-1960s, Canada experienced the most sustained period of rapid economic growth in its history.[50] Between the end of World War II and 1963, Canada's GNP increased nearly fourfold.[51] This rapid growth transformed the social, political, and economic make-up of the country. An image of Canada as an egalitarian land of opportunity came to dominate the political-intellectual landscape and created the backdrop against which John Porter painted his soon-to-be-famous image of Canada as a vertical mosaic.

Reconstruction and Recovery: Canada 1945–1963

There were six stimuli to economic growth in postwar Canada: the release of pent-up consumer demand (especially for housing), the Korean War, massive federal government expenditures on transportation infrastructure, expanded spending on social security, rapid population growth, and a wholesale movement of foreign (especially American) capital into the Canadian economy.

Consumer spending, which had been kept under a tight rein during the war, grew exponentially. Returning soldiers – over a quarter million of them in Europe and the Far East – brought their demobilization money and benefits with them.[52] Similarly, the many workers who had earned good wages during the war and then dutifully bought millions of dollars in war bonds suddenly converted their savings into folding money and headed for the stores. The demand they created, when combined with greater than expected demand from Europe, first stabilized and then fuelled Canada's postwar economy.

The Korean War had a similarly stimulative effect. Between 1950 and 1953 the federal government invested over $5 billion to increase the size of the Armed Forces from 90,000 to 148,000 and to modernize and upgrade their equipment.[53]

Other government expenditures increased rapidly as well, helping to prevent an anticipated postwar decline in industrial production and consolidating wartime gains. Especially important were three massive infrastructure projects: the Trans-Canada Highway, the St Lawrence Seaway, and the Trans-Canada Pipeline. That they were undertaken as government-sponsored projects demonstrates the shift that had taken place in government thinking – and public expectations – regarding direct involvement in the economy.

The Canadian economy was changing fundamentally. Wartime increases in manufacturing continued, accompanied by a shift toward the service sector and away from agriculture and resource extraction.[54] As well, Canada became an urban nation. In 1941, just over half of Canadians lived in urban areas; by 1961, seven in ten did.[55] Two major causes of this urban growth were the high birth rate and large-scale immigration, which together caused Canada's population to increase from

14 million in 1951 to 18 million in 1961.[56] The federal government had restricted immigration during the war, but during the decade and a half afterward 2 million immigrants entered the country.[57] As Porter later noted in *The Vertical Mosaic*, the vast majority came from Europe (about a third from the United Kingdom) because discriminatory immigration policy then favoured immigrants from traditional sources.[58]

The rapid expansion of the Canadian economy between 1945 and 1965 was, of course, a good news story. Unemployment remained low, incomes went up, and most Canadians experienced an improved standard of living.[59] However, serious problems remained. Porter focused on these problems – sharp class, ethnic, and regional differences in economic well-being – in *The Vertical Mosaic*. For example, the bottom fifth of Canadians received just over 4 per cent of all earned income each year during the 1950s, while the top fifth received over 40 per cent.[60] Redistribution of income via taxes and transfer payments changed little. Wealth was even more unevenly distributed. Using dividend income as a rough measure of wealth, the data indicate that in 1950 the top 20 per cent of Canadians received nearly 80 per cent of all dividend income. The gap probably widened during the 1950s.[61] Most troubling of all, even in the allegedly affluent 1950s, over one-quarter of non-farm families, including 1.7 million children, remained below the poverty line.[62]

Women, the labour movement, and progressive intellectuals responded to the problems of gender, class, ethnic, and regional inequality by pressing for the development of a comprehensive welfare state. As I mentioned above, these demands, which had begun to take effect during the war, pushed the mainstream political parties reluctantly toward Keynesianism and the welfare state, but King and the Liberals remained unconvinced and especially reluctant to antagonize the business community. As well, King had to deal with the problem of Canada's rapidly increasing national debt.[63] In King's view, welfare state measures could come only slowly and piecemeal.[64]

Aspects of Canadian economic growth came with other costs. From the beginning of white settlement, the economy had relied heavily on foreign capital, a trend that intensified after World War II. American multinationals made massive direct investments in Canadian resources, resource extraction companies, and branch plants, and by the early 1960s they exerted considerable control over the Canadian economy.[65] Many Canadians responded with alarm. In combination with other developments – the crisis of confidence spawned by the Liberals' handling of the Trans-Canada Pipeline Bill, the end of the Duplessis era in Quebec, and the establishment of the federal New Democratic Party (NDP) – there soon came to be a new dynamic on the Canadian political and economic scene.

In 1958, the Conservatives, led by populist Western lawyer John Diefenbaker, took advantage, riding a wave of anti-American, anti-Liberal Canadian nationalism to what was then the biggest electoral majority in the history of Canadian politics: 208 of 265 seats in the federal parliament.[66] Diefenbaker's time in the sun was brief.

Unfortunately for the Conservatives, they came to office just as the international economic and political scene changed dramatically. Beginning in the late 1950s, Canada had to compete for markets with a rejuvenated Europe and a new economic power, Asia. Simultaneously, Canada's postwar boom ground to a temporary halt. The massive stimulus to economic growth provided by postwar infrastructure megaprojects such as the Trans-Canada Highway came to an end, the demand produced by the Korean War dried up, annual immigration declined by nearly half, and the baby boom ended.[67] As well, a huge proportion of Canada's wartime debt came due. The decision to refinance it was costly, driving up interest rates and slowing economic growth. At the same time, a capital shortage developed, a consequence in part of Canadian capitalists choosing to invest large amounts abroad rather than at home.[68] The Conservatives struggled to cope, but the pace of Canada's economic growth declined substantially.[69]

These economic troubles notwithstanding, and despite a promise to balance the budget, Diefenbaker pursued an essentially liberal set of policy measures, in particular by increasing government involvement in the economy and expanding the welfare state. Diefenbaker's tenure did not represent a substantial change in government philosophy or action from when the Liberals were in office. In fact, he was without doubt more liberal than his own party, even in some ways more left wing than many members of the Liberal Party.

Of particular interest to Porter, Diefenbaker poured an enormous amount of money into education. In 1955, the federal government had spent $57 million on education. Six years later, that figure reached $161 million.[70] This was a reflection of a changed view of education in Canada, one important to various of Porter's research and political activities over the years, beginning with his essays in *Social Purpose for Canada* in 1961 and ending with the McInnis Lectures in 1977. Until the 1960s, education was seen in strictly economic terms: a 'factor contributing to economic growth and ... raised living standards.' In the early 1960s, however, in part following the principles of New Liberalism, which were coming to the fore in Canadian political thinking, it came to be seen in a new light, as a vehicle for creating equality of opportunity.[71] The problem for Diefenbaker was that all this spending at a time when the economy was in recession led to a rapid growth in the annual deficit, from $196 million in the budget year 1958, when he took office, to $948 million for 1963.[72]

During the 1958 election campaign, Diefenbaker presented himself as a representative of 'the average Canadian.' And, while his anti-American nationalism and populism earned him the respect and support of many Canadians, his domestic and foreign policy decisions eventually led to a divided party and a divided country. In the election of 1962 the Conservatives were returned to power but with a minority government, and a year later they were ousted from office by the Liberals, who formed a minority government of their own.[73] The Liberal hold on power was precarious but strong enough to endure a few difficult years in the mid-1960s before first Lester Pearson and then Pierre Trudeau firmly reconsolidated Liberal dominance in parliament.

It was in the expansive and rapidly changing economic, social, and political environment of the 1950s and early 1960s that Porter wrote *The Vertical Mosaic*. The book reflects some of the optimism of the era – buying into the expansionary rhetoric of postcapitalism – but challenges it by pointing to the sobering reality of class, ethnic, and other barriers to social equality and democratic practice that remained during this period of rapid economic growth.

5 The Genesis of *The Vertical Mosaic*, 1949–1958

The MacOdrum Years, 1949–1955

Porter's first years in Ottawa were trying. He struggled to establish himself at Carleton but with limited success and satisfaction. Indeed, by the mid-1950s he contemplated leaving academia altogether. Part of the problem was his relationship with Carleton's second president, Murdoch Maxwell MacOdrum.

MacOdrum had assumed the presidency when Henry Tory died unexpectedly in the winter term of 1947.[1] MacOdrum's family, from Marion Bridge, Cape Breton, was religious and conservative – his father had been the moderator of the General Assembly of the Presbyterian Church of Canada – and the son embraced the values of his parents. After earning a PhD in English literature from the University of Glasgow in 1927, he taught for five years at Dalhousie and Queen's before attending McGill to study theology. After graduating in 1935, he assumed a ministry in Sydney, Nova Scotia. He left the ministry in 1939, shortly after war broke out and, after spending time in the private sector and with the National War Finance Committee, became Tory's executive assistant. He was promoted to vice-president in 1946 and, on Tory's death in 1947, succeeded him as president.[2]

MacOdrum holds an uncertain place in Carleton's history. For one thing, faculty members differ greatly in their assessments of his personality and manner. Some claim that he was 'well liked by the faculty,' whereas others remember him as a loner, a man with a 'moody' and 'uncertain' personality who did not have an 'easy social manner' and had no close friends on the faculty or the board.[3] They also dispute his legacy as a leader. Accounts uniformly portray him as a careful administrator and an effective 'broker' between the board and the faculty, but many of his contemporaries recall that he possessed few true leadership skills. Neatby and McEown are in the latter camp. They claim that 'leadership in financial matters came from prominent members of the board, [while] leadership in academic matters came from some of the young professors.'[4] Even if true, this does not diminish MacOdrum's contribution, for his administrative skills played a crucial role during a very shaky period in the college's development. 'There wasn't a year [from 1945 to 1952] when you couldn't look at Carleton and say it was all going to close down,' said McEown. MacOdrum 'may not have been the most dynamic, brilliant leader ... but [he helped Carleton] when survival was really quite a critical thing in the exercise.'[5] Paul Fox's recollection is similar to McEown's; MacOdrum was not particularly well liked, but faculty 'respected [him] for what he did as a managerial president.'[6]

Porter and MacOdrum did not get along. There were three sources of friction: academic, personal, and professional. The academic problem was that the president was a traditionalist who, according to Paul Fox, regarded the newfangled discipline of sociology as 'a lot of nonsense.'[7] Not only was it academically suspect but it appeared politically subversive as well. Phillips recalls that while MacOdrum tolerated the liberal and leftist political beliefs held by many of the faculty at the new college, he saw Porter as more radical than most.[8] It probably did not help that, according to Phillips at least, Porter would start the first lecture in each of his courses with the warning to students that he was a socialist and an agnostic and that they should bear this in mind when they listened to his lectures.[9] These scholarly differences then came to have personal consequences. 'John and MacOdrum were antithetical,' said Fox. 'MacOdrum was a Presbyterian minister and he saw John as a free-thinking, iconoclastic bohemian ... He did not take to John as a person – and the feeling was reciprocated.'[10]

The professional friction between them grew out of MacOdrum's refusal to grant Porter a permanent teaching position on the grounds that he possessed neither a graduate degree nor a major publication.[11] This became increasingly important as Carleton began the transition from community college to university, a shift that caused a bitter and protracted debate on campus. On the one side were those led by E.F. 'Ted' Sheffield, the registrar, who wanted to retain Carleton's focus on adult education.[12] On the other were the academically oriented young turks who wanted to make Carleton into a real university.[13] Sheffield and his allies – 'people who had been high school teachers and had moved up to [be] university lecturers ... [who] were quite happy' with the status quo – were sufficiently powerful that the community college orientation remained in place for a long time.[14] Eventually, however, after a 'sustained, vigorous and all-encompassing battle' that was 'fought in every corner of the campus,' the credentialed scholars, led by the social scientists, achieved their goal.[15] Had they not, said political scientist Kenneth McRae, many would have left:

> Those of us who came from the world outside – Oxford for myself or London for John – had serious doubts about whether Carleton College was the place to be ... Finances were very precarious [and] salaries ... were not great. But the real thing was that the library was so modest it could never be thought of as a research library ... [B]eing in a terribly small college among people who had limited intellectual horizons ... was a ... cultural shock.[16]

Ironically, given MacOdrum's reputation as a weak academic leader, it was he who struck one of the decisive blows in favour of the pro-university group. In the early years, Scott Gordon said, leaders of the pro-university faction believed that MacOdrum depended too much on Sheffield's advice.[17] Interestingly, however, Gordon recalls that eventually MacOdrum 'specifically instructed Sheffield to stick to his job as registrar and leave academic policy to teaching faculty.'[18] MacOdrum's directive did not resolve the issue immediately, of course, but it did help those who in the early 1950s were struggling to shift Carleton's policies and practices to match those of a full-fledged university.

As the shift gathered momentum, the quality of Carleton's teaching staff and the stringency of its academic standards assumed greater significance. Though colleagues recall that Porter did not become publicly involved in the debate, he made it clear that he wanted Carleton to become a real university.[19] Ironically, in adopting this perspective, Porter put himself at risk. As Blair Neatby pointed out, in order for Carleton to be perceived as 'academically respectable,' it would have to have faculty members 'who were as good as professors at any other institution.' This meant that they needed either a doctorate or a solid publication record.[20] Porter had neither. Thus, as the transition got underway, Porter's future looked ominous; he risked being found wanting by the very criteria of excellence he championed. And it wasn't just that he lacked credentials. According to Scott Gordon, he wondered whether he deserved to be on staff: 'John was still not sure that he belonged on a university faculty among others who had advanced degrees while he had none.'[21] James Gibson said much the same thing: 'It was always a touchy situation. Even after his appointment had been confirmed, he wasn't necessarily a fixture at Carleton, and I think that was unfortunate ... I did what I could to encourage him ... and the people in political science in particular reinforced that, [but] I'm not sure it answered lingering doubts in his own mind.'[22]

So precarious did Porter feel his position to be that, according to Fox, for the first several years at Carleton, Porter 'lived with the expectation that he would be fired.'[23] And with some good reason. According to Neatby and McEown, he survived only 'because his colleagues respected him as a scholar and rallied to his support.'[24] Indeed, Gibson reported that 'the stiffest academic contest' he faced during his early years as dean was the confirmation of Porter's appointment as Carleton's first sociologist.[25]

While Porter's testy relationship with the president, coupled with his anxiety over his job situation, often made him moody, sometimes even sullen, these were only two of several factors that came close to ending his academic career before it really began. [26]

Porter did not like Ottawa. It was small, with a population of just 150,000, and had a staid, conservative, small-town ambience.[27] Despite its status as a centre of government and tourism, it remained a transportation centre and lumber town, and the atmosphere in the city core reflected that reality. A substantial portion of the downtown near the Chateau Laurier and the Rideau Canal was taken up with a sprawling, unsightly tangle of railway tracks, while just a few hundred yards up the Ottawa River, the E.B. Eddy lumber mill spewed smoke and chemicals. In 1937, Prime Minister Mackenzie King had hired a European town planner, Parisian Jacques Greber, to redesign part of the city centre near the parliament buildings, but World War II had prevented him from executing any of the plans.[28] When the war ended, Greber returned to Ottawa to finish his master plan, but when Porter arrived in 1949 the Liberals had only just begun to implement it, razing and rebuilding slum areas in the downtown, establishing a green belt around the city, building an expressway through the heart of the city, relocating the railway station, and so forth.[29] But even with such growth and development, 1950s Ottawa was still a far cry from London, with its population of over 8 million and the many cultural facilities and amenities that made it one of the world's great cities. Paul Fox, who had also lived in London, recalled that Porter had great difficulty adjusting to life in Canada's capital: 'Nothing doing on Sundays. No movies (except film clubs), no sports (not that John Porter would have been interested in them), no TV, no Sunday papers (unless you went to the Chateau Laurier and bought the Sunday New York *Times*, which cost a dollar), nothing. The big amusement would be to go over to another faculty member's house and have tea or supper and talk.' John was by nature quiet, reserved, and somewhat moody, Fox said, but living in Ottawa made him even more so.[30] Marion Porter, too, recalled her husband's dismay at the lack of cultural life in Ottawa. He loved theatre and the arts, she said, and had enjoyed the street and pub life of London. His new hometown just could not compete. 'Ottawa was strange and somewhat second-rate to him,' she observed. The city's Little Theatre and the Canadian Repertory Theatre could not compare with the great theatres of London, and Ottawa's new cocktail lounges, which Marion and her friends judged to be 'civilized and sophisticated,' could not hold a candle to the pubs of England.[31] Pauline Jewett recalled that Porter was actually quite scornful of Canadian cities. He wanted to live somewhere, she said, where 'you could buy a newspaper at four o'clock in the morning.' She recalled that even the Group of Seven came in for opprobrium; he thought it 'typically Canadian' that they painted 'landscapes rather than people.'[32]

After living briefly in Hull, which he mistakenly thought would be more interesting than 'parochial' Ottawa, Porter was pleased to find a 'modest but attractive second-floor flat' in an old house on Delaware Street, just a brisk twenty-minute walk to Carleton through the tree-lined streets of the Glebe.[33] An added benefit was that it was about the same distance from Delaware Street northward along the stately walkway bordering the Rideau Canal to the University of Ottawa, Union Station, the Chateau Laurier, and the Old Byward Market. In Ottawa, it was probably as close as he could come to living in one of the older residential areas of downtown London near the Thames, Whitehall, and Fleet Street. Porter became attached to the Glebe and lived there throughout his time in Ottawa.

Adjusting to life in small-town Ottawa was not his only problem. His teaching load, though standard at Carleton, was demanding: three or four courses per term, nine to twelve teaching hours per week, plus whatever seminars he arranged.[34] His inaugural year was especially draining, as he had to make up for his relative lack of background in political science by doing extra preparatory work, though here the notes he had taken in Laski's and MacRae's classes at the LSE came in handy. Moreover, as befitted someone recently graduated from the politically lively LSE, Porter participated in some of the student-run political activities on campus. On one occasion, for example, he addressed the Carleton College CCF Club.[35] He had administrative responsibilities as well. As a new institution, Carleton generated what Scott Gordon referred to as 'an endless chain of problems' regarding policy, procedures, and planning, and Porter and his colleagues had to spend hours in committee meetings trying to solve or obviate such difficulties. This could be challenging because they often operated without benefit of either precedent or – until the community college/university struggle was decided – any 'clear view of what [Carleton] should try to become.'[36] So Porter's first years were hectic and he was under lots of pressure. However, as Neatby and McEown point out, he was just one of many young faculty members in the same position:

> Most of [John's] young colleagues shared with him the stresses of beginning an academic career. They had new courses to design, the constant pressure of preparing yet another lecture for the next day and, for most of them, the added pressure of having to find time to work on the as yet unfinished doctoral thesis. This was also often a formative period in their personal lives, with marriage, a mortgage, and children.[37]

His financial situation was worrisome as well. Salaries at Carleton were low and he had to be extremely frugal.[38] In 1949, his lecturer-rank salary was only $2,400 and had increased to only $4,300 when, in 1955, he was finally granted a three-year appointment as an assistant professor.[39] By this time, he had two young children. 'We were very, very poor, really,' said Marion Porter, 'because university salaries were very low.'[40] Like many of his colleagues, he had to take on freelance writing assignments in the summer to supplement his academic salary. For example, in 1950 and 1953 he returned to the Historical Section to work for Colonel Stacey.[41] 'Everybody [at Carleton] tried to earn a little extra money doing whatever he could,' said Paul Fox. 'I can remember thinking that Porter was lucky to have got the job with the Historical Section. I'm sure it paid more than the rest of us could earn.'[42] The problem for Porter was that this extra work made it difficult to mount a meaningful attempt at research, as he explained to Dean Gibson: 'My own research has been delayed because during two summers I have had to take remunerative employment ... All this work remains anonymous, of course, but I mention it because I feel that working for Col. Stacey has been an important part of my academic training, and has done much to give me high standards of research.'[43]

Despite these difficulties, factors came into play that kept him tied to Ottawa and Carleton. Especially important was the positive environment at the college. It was a small place, said David Farr, where faculty and students got to know one another:

> We had a very good, creative relationship with the students [because] our purposes were very similar. They wanted a degree from this new, fledgling college to be respected, and we wanted to make our careers at a place which would become respected. [As well] ... the students were highly motivated, the veterans particularly, and we had some extremely capable students. We met them ... in every sort of circumstance. After all, at the beginning, we were in one building. We ate together. We fraternized together. It was a very close relationship.[44]

Significant, too, was the intellectual and social relationship he forged with his colleagues. While it irked Porter that for the first few years he had to share an office, the situation had its benefits. Above all, it kept him in close daily contact with a cadre of fine scholars: Paul Fox, Don Rowat, Scott Gordon, David Farr, and James Gibson as well as Ted English and Tom Brewis and, slightly later, Pauline Jewett. Together, they provided him with a helpful point of intellectual reference as he tried to orient himself to Canadian political life.[45] Originally he shared an office with two colleagues but eventually got a small, private office in a house at 291 First Street that Carleton had purchased to provide additional accommodation for its social scientists. Even after this welcome development he continued to reap the benefits of the close scholarly and personal relationships he had forged earlier, however.[46] Working in close quarters spawned a good deal of fruitful intellectual interplay that ignored disciplinary boundaries, and discussions that could only have started in shared office accommodation would often spill over into the hallways and then into the dingy basement cafeteria where, sometimes joined by students, they would engage in extended informal seminars over coffee or lunch.[47] Eventually, many in the social science cadre became close friends. Paul Fox recalls it as one of the best periods of his life: 'We were friends, learning, working, socializing together. In and out of one another's apartments – no one had a home. Poor, but we didn't know anything else in those days.'[48] It was not

idyllic, of course. People often disagreed over scholarly and administrative matters – the debate over the future of the college most fundamental among them – but the little group of social scientists created an
interesting, exciting, and promising atmosphere that Porter enjoyed.[49]
The camaraderie boosted his sometimes flagging morale and helped to
make up for the spartan conditions prevailing during Carleton's early
years.

As time passed, Porter came to realize that while Ottawa was not
the most sophisticated or exciting place to live, it did have its benefits.
National political issues, always front and centre in the local papers,
sparked daily debates and discussions among his colleagues. As well,
he had first-hand access to the politicians and bureaucrats whose decisions shaped the country. Kenneth McRae recalls that the Carleton
social scientists were 'plugged into the Ottawa Political Economy Association which was the local branch of the Canadian Political Science
Association,' allowing them to rub shoulders with important government figures. Certainly, he said, 'you couldn't be in a better vantage
point for seeing policy formation.'[50] Such personal contact later proved
useful for Porter when he began to gather data on the political and bureaucratic elites for *The Vertical Mosaic* – though the results of meetings
with key public figures were not always expected. Don Rowat recalls
making an appointment to consult one of the justices of the Supreme
Court after the publishers of one of the Ottawa papers had fired its editor, apparently for his unacceptable political views: 'We wanted to see
what [the justice's] reaction was… [and] to get his advice on what we
might do about it as young scholars and academics.' He recalled being
floored by the response. The justice had no knowledge of the case and,
thus, no advice for them. He surprised them even further by saying
that 'he never read the newspapers.' He didn't bother, he said, because
he didn't think it worthwhile. Not only were they 'repetitive,' but they
'gave you the wrong kinds of news.'[51]

Porter took advantage of his Ottawa location and over time built a
network of contacts in the federal civil service. Frank Jones recalled
that throughout his career, John 'always seemed to know people who
were in the high levels of the bureaucracy.'[52] This was especially true
later, when he became more prominent at Carleton and counted among
his friends and acquaintances many senior Ottawa politicians and bureaucrats – Bernard and Sylvia Ostry, Morris Miller, Tom Kent, Pierre
Trudeau – but was also the case during the early years, thanks in part
to his friend Bob Phillips.

Living in Ottawa, the centre of Liberal-dominated Canadian politics, and teaching at Carleton within a close-knit group of liberal-minded colleagues helped to confirm the New Liberal scholarly and political views Porter had brought with him from England.[53] Porter's birth in 1921 had coincided with the beginning of an often shaky yet tenacious half-century of Liberal dominance in federal politics. Over Porter's lifetime, the Liberals held power for forty-seven out of fifty-eight years. And while an individualistic variant of liberalism dominated Canadian political philosophy and practice for the first half of the century, increasingly after World War II Canadians came to share a basic faith in the political and economic expediency, if not the humane wisdom, of mixed private–public enterprise, increased government intervention in the economy, and the expansion of the welfare state. Porter's own New Liberal political attachments and sociological ideas, while rooted in his upbringing in England and his training at LSE, received strong reinforcement in postwar Canada. In particular, the intellectual environment at Carleton further cemented these beliefs. Most of his university friends shared a set of liberal intellectual/political assumptions – humanism, rationalism, progressivism – much like those he had learned from his mentors at the LSE. This helped solidify the political beliefs he had brought with him from England and put him in step with Canada's increasingly New Liberal political climate.

Although all these factors cemented his ties to Ottawa and Carleton, nothing was as important in this respect as a development in his personal life. After separating from Elizabeth Stalker, Porter had been involved with a number of women, but nothing lasting had come of these relationships. This changed in the fall of 1949, when he met Marion Ruth Lyons, a high school mathematics teacher, at a dinner party at the home of mutual friends Peter and Valerie Johnson. The relationship blossomed quickly and they soon decided to marry. First, however, John had to obtain a divorce from Elizabeth. The process was complicated and slow in part because John was living in Canada, and eventually, he had to travel to London to finalize the arrangements.[54] The divorce decree finally came through in September 1951.[55]

John and Marion were already living together but – somewhat curiously, according to their friends – wanted to formalize their union via a church service. It was an odd circumstance, as Porter's friend and wedding guest, Bob Phillips, recalled. 'With Jack's wildly flapping antireligious banners' so apparent, he said, many people 'wondered why on earth they were both so determined to become churched.' Whatever the reason, they pressed ahead, canvassing various Ottawa churches for a suitable ceremony: 'The important thing to Jack was that God should not intrude in the service, and it should be as close to nothing as legal niceties would allow.' The winner of the 'minimum commitment derby' was the nearby Unitarian Church, just up the street. The ceremony could not have been more simple or brief: no guests, just two witnesses. 'We were bidden to come at seven-thirty for a post-ceremony celebration,' Phillips recalled, 'but when we arrived promptly with our rare bottle of champagne, they had not yet left the house. They half ran down the street, briefly paused at the church, and returned well content before Mary Anne and I had finished our shared bottle of beer. We never enjoyed a wedding more.'[56]

The marriage and subsequent birth of their children – Charles Anthony in 1953 and Ann Veronica in 1955 – provided John with a solid emotional home base and seems to have changed his outlook on life for the better. Though recollections vary somewhat by place and time, colleagues, family and friends from the period recall that during the last couple of years at the LSE and the first couple of years at Carleton, he was often unhappy. Paul Fox described him as pessimistic, even 'defeatist,' – 'an angry young man ... with a chip on his shoulder,' who felt that 'the class system was against him.'[57] John Grist, Porter's sometime university roommate and long-time friend, and James Gibson, his colleague at Carleton, also recall an edge to Porter's personality at the time. In reference to his days at the LSE, Grist said, 'I think [John] was angry with himself and the world ... He was angry about the class system in England ... very much in a personal sense.'[58] Gibson's memory focused more on Porter's reserve: 'His voice suggested to me ... that there was something "turned in from the edges"; not impolite, not uncivil, but sort of self-contained ... I think he had a feeling he had to maintain a sort of outer defence lest his own private world should be arbitrarily invaded from outside.'[59]

But other colleagues, notably those from his days at Carleton rather than the LSE, remember Porter differently. According to Scott Gordon, for example, Porter was certainly a social critic but not the disgruntled soul that Fox and Grist made him out to be: 'I spent a lot of time with John, and I certainly do not recall him as having "a chip on his shoulder" or being angry. On the contrary, I recall him as invariably even-tempered, even when strongly critical of Canadian society and politics. Moreover, I think this is reflected in the style of *The Vertical Mosaic* itself.'[60] Kenneth McRae said something similar: 'I was soon aware that

John could be playful, wistful, whimsical, a deft conversationalist, and often was – even while remaining an unswerving social critic.'[61] Phillips seconded McRae's interpretation. 'There's no denying Jack's cheerful (and sometimes not so cheerful) cynicism,' he said, 'but I share the view of your commentator [McRae] that our mutual good friend Paul Fox sometimes may have been a little too negative judging it.'[62] Whatever feelings of alienation or cynicism Porter harboured, they apparently dissipated once he married and became a family man. As Pauline Jewett remarked, his marriage and the birth of the children acted as catalysts, helping him to adopt a more optimistic outlook.[63]

Sociology at Carleton: Early Days

As Porter's inaugural year drew to a close, Fox, as chair of political science, faced a dilemma. Porter had admirably filled the gap created when Frank McKinnon left the department the previous summer. But Porter was not a political scientist and since others in the academic job market had degrees in the discipline, it would be difficult to defend his reappointment. The social scientists wanted to keep him, however, and decided to attempt to persuade MacOdrum to hire Porter to establish a sociology program. This proved difficult because of Porter's problematic personal and professional relationship with MacOdrum, but eventually lobbying efforts by Paul Fox and Scott Gordon succeeded, and a relieved Porter switched into sociology.[64]

Though this made Porter the first full-time appointment in sociology, he did not teach the first sociology course at Carleton. Enid Charles and Nathan Keyfitz had taught demography and statistics, respectively, between 1946 and 1948, and June Helm MacNeish had taught introductory sociology beginning in 1949.[65] Helm, an anthropologist, was an American citizen, then working on her MA. She had come to Canada with her husband, R.S. MacNeish, an archaeologist at what was then the National Museum of Canada. Responding in part to a student petition for a course in sociology, the president had offered her the opportunity to teach an introductory course on a trial basis. About eighty students enrolled, indicating that the subject would be a promising addition to the college curriculum.[66] In the fall of 1950, Porter assumed this responsibility and began to set up a full slate of sociology courses.

Not surprisingly, it took a while to establish the discipline firmly, in part because for the first seven years Porter was the only full-time, permanent appointment. Gradually, however, he put together his own modest slate of courses – 'Urban Sociology,' 'Introductory Sociology,' 'Theories and Methods of Sociology,' 'The Sociology of the Primary Group,' 'Social Psychology,' and 'Tutorial in Sociology' (on the LSE model) – supplemented by offerings from part-time appointments Bernard Blishen and Frank Jones.[67] Concurrently, June Helm developed the anthropology side of the curriculum.[68] The result was that by 1955–6 the calendar listed over a dozen sociology and anthropology courses. The situation improved even further in 1956 when Porter received permission to hire Muni Frumhartz, a Canadian then teaching at Hunter College, New York, to fill a second permanent, full-time position in the department.[69]

Student response to Porter's early teaching efforts was not what he hoped. Enrolment in his courses was often low, and Marion and the Phillipses had to encourage him to stick with it.[70] Sociology was new, and it may be that students perhaps saw it as less marketable than history or political science. As well, John was not the best lecturer. According to Ian Campbell, his delivery was straightforward but rather dull.[71] He was better, said Campbell – interesting and frank – during the 'free and easy exchange' of seminars, where he excelled at evoking student participation.[72] Another problem was that he often assigned low grades and many students dropped out.[73] He was not alone in this regard; high failure rates, high dropout rates, and low class averages were common in the early years at Carleton.[74] According to Kenneth McRae, the faculty disagreed on the question of academic standards. Those oriented to adult education were fairly liberal with marks, while Porter, Fox, Gordon, McRae, and others who considered themselves academics, marked according to stringent scholarly criteria. 'We were thinking basically of a first-rate college on the model of Queen's a hundred years earlier,' said McRae.[75]

Though Porter did not experience as much success in the classroom as he would have liked, students appreciated that he was conscientious and approachable. And he tried to establish personal connections with them outside the classroom as well. J.M. Davies, a student in a summer class taught by Porter in the early 1950s, recalls an evening when 'we all went to Professor Porter's house for a party ... just before we wrote the final exam.' Even though it was a first-year course, she said, 'everyone fit in the living room.'[76] That Porter used his faculty position to serve social purposes, as a mission of sorts, is evident as well in a story recounted by Arnold Ages, then a Carleton student working for the summer in northern Ontario:

My tent-mate ... was a congenial engineering student from Queen's who was a fine fellow and easy to get along with. However, he had one fault: he believed that all stereotypes of Jews, Blacks, Catholics, etc. were, despite exceptions, essentially correct. After one month of vigorous debate with him I wrote a note to Prof. Porter – whom I knew by reputation – to ask if he could recommend some titles that I could share with my colleague to persuade him that racial and religious stereotypes were wrong. Apparently Prof. Porter saw my letter as a challenge because within a week I received a lengthy response from him in which he expatiated at length not only on the falsity of stereotypes but on the immorality of basing character judgements on such notions.[77]

Porter's Early Courses

The archival materials indicate that in his first year Porter taught at least six or seven political science courses, including introductory political science and comparative politics.[78] His lecture notes, compiled over the year, run to hundreds of pages. They are a complete clutter, often undated, and sometimes difficult even to assign to one course or another, for he appears to have shifted materials from course to course as needed. An overview of the notes suggests that he held a broad, balanced conception of the discipline. For example, he began 'Introduction to Political Science' by asking whether or not the discipline was a science (it wasn't) and then went on to explain that for him it had two faces: political science proper – the ethically neutral study of the structure and dynamics of political institutions – and political philosophy, the ethically charged study of authority, obligation, and the limits of freedom and coercion in human society. His notes for 'Comparative Politics' dealt at length with citizenship, elections, federalism, political parties, and the like, focusing in particular on Canada and its comparators, Great Britain and the United States.[79]

When Porter switched into sociology in 1950, he once again had to construct all of his courses from scratch. As with his political science lecture notes, the Porter papers contain several files, hundreds of pages in all, variously titled, of materials suitable for teaching a wide range of courses: introductory sociology, theory, methods, primary groups, and so forth. Most of the material for 'Introductory Sociology' is standard: basic concepts, relations between sociology and other disciplines, bread-and-butter methodological issues, and the like. He did, however, introduce his students to topics such as the evolution of property and citizenship (Marshall) and the psychology of morals and religion (Ginsberg). The sources he cited in the lectures included both classical and contemporary scholars – Talcott Parsons, Robert Merton, Robert MacIver, Morris Ginsberg, L.T. Hobhouse, T.H. Marshall, John Dewey, William James, Sigmund Freud, and Jean Piaget – and ranged over philosophy, sociology, anthropology, and other disciplines.[80]

The notes for 'Theory and Methods' are likewise a hodgepodge, but they reveal that he had a broad and sophisticated conception of sociology as a theoretically informed and rigorously empirical discipline, though not a science per se. He portrayed the discipline as perspectival rather than cumulative, claiming that it built on different intellectual traditions: Weber and the German idealists, Durkheim and the French positivists, and Spencer and the British utilitarians. He distinguished it from presociological theorizing (Thomas Aquinas, St Augustine) on the grounds that it employed an empirical and inductive (rather than philosophical and deductive) method, and argued that its goal was to produce systematic and holistic explanatory theories. In drawing this distinction, he argued that some theorists, Comte and Marx, for example, were 'philosophers of history,' concerned in part with predicting future events, rather than sociologists. With the exception of Thorstein Veblen – and here probably echoing the views of his teachers at the LSE – he presented to his students the idea that the major theorists were European rather than North American. He acknowledged that Parsons' structural functionalism was the dominant theory of the time, but made it clear that he was not a Parsonian himself and as well criticized the work of the Chicago School, which he saw as outdated, atheoretical, and overly empirical.[81]

The Genesis of *The Vertical Mosaic*

As Porter tried to carve out a spot for sociology at Carleton, he had to deal with substantial pressure from MacOdrum because he lacked a graduate degree. As early as his second year in Ottawa, the president warned him that if he wanted to pursue an academic career at Carleton, he had either to pursue a graduate degree or to publish a major work. Discussing the incident years later, Marion recalled that John did not want to return to school. Instead, he 'decided to accept MacOdrum's challenge to publish a significant work.'[82]

In the summer of 1952 he took the first steps in that direction. He and Marion travelled to England, where Porter consulted Morris Ginsberg regarding possible research projects. The meeting turned out to be a career maker. At the time, Porter was teaching both 'Sociology of the Primary Group' and 'Social Psychology' and involved with Frank Jones, Nathan Keyfitz, and Wally Lambert in a reading group that focused on small groups research.[83] Perhaps as a consequence, the first project he proposed to Ginsberg was in this area.[84] Ginsberg was not impressed. He thought the subject matter 'trivial' and suggested that Porter undertake a more substantial study: something on 'class and power in Canada.'[85] According to Marion Porter, her husband was clearly predisposed to such a project for, since his arrival in Canada, he had been 'staggered' by the degree to which Canadians apparently believed that theirs was a classless society.[86] Nonetheless, despite being attracted to the idea, Porter recalls that he initially balked at Ginsberg's suggestion: 'I pointed out that it was not easy to obtain the necessary data in Canada. I doubted, working solo, that a good job could be done in less than ten years, and since I was interested in an academic career it was a long time to work on a thesis.'[87] Ginsberg did not buy his objection. 'He was a distinguished scholar in the old tradition,' said Porter, and he thought that 'if a study was worthwhile, it did not matter … if it took a long time.'[88]

Porter mulled it over and decided to follow Ginsberg's advice. A year later, in the spring of 1953, he began his labours in earnest, fully aware of the potential historical significance of the project. Years later he confessed that at this early stage he fantasized, 'with some foolhardiness and no little arrogance,' that he might write a grand 'interpretation of Canada as a modern democracy' in the tradition of Lord Bryce or Alexis de Tocqueville.[89] But as the grind of data gathering got underway, the enormity of such a task soon sank in. It took him nearly three years in the Library of Parliament (1952–4) just to pull together the information he needed to discuss the structure of property ownership in Canada and to get a conceptual grasp on the factual materials he was collecting.[90] Chastened, he put aside his grandiose plans and turned to refining his theoretical framework and analysing his empirical data.

It is ironic, given his life-long, stated preference for data over theory, that it was his theoretical labours that were first to bear fruit. On 3 June 1955, at the annual meeting of the Canadian Political Science Association at the University of Toronto, Porter delivered 'Elite Groups: A Scheme for the Study of Power in Canada.'[91] In this paper, which constituted the skeleton of his discussion of power in *The Vertical Mosaic*, he proposed a 'plural elite' model of the structure and dynamics of power in Canada.[92] The model was eclectic and multifaceted, incorporating elements of Parsonian and anthropological functionalism, classical elite theory as developed by Gaetano Mosca and Vilfredo Pareto, George Homans' exchange theory, some Freudian ideas on human nature, and Weber's approach to social stratification. As Porter conceived of them, modern industrial societies like Canada were best understood as complex, multilayered systems comprising a set of mutually interdependent and integrated subsystems, each of which performed a function for the maintenance of society as a whole. There were five subsystems: the economic, the political, the administrative, the defensive, and the ideological.[93] Each had a powerful elite, and social order was best understood as the outcome of struggles and accommodations among these somewhat overlapping elites. In Western societies, he argued, following Raymond Aron, 'elite groups are separate and compete for power, with the result that control tends toward an equilibrium of compromise.'[94] Not only did elites hold more or less undisputed power within their respective institutional subsystems but they recruited from their own economically privileged kin group and social circles. In adopting such an approach, Porter placed himself squarely in the tradition of those who adopted the mainstream 'power and stratification' approach to the study of social inequality in modern capitalist societies.

The 'Elite Groups' paper was a hit at the meetings and marked him as someone to watch.[95] Pauline Jewett recalled that as she sat listening to his presentation, she could not help but think his work was light years ahead of what others in sociology and political science were doing at the time.[96] And Jewett was not alone in her assessment, for a week or two after he gave the paper, Porter received a letter from publisher John Gray of the Macmillan Press. Porter, said Gray, was now a 'marked man,' someone from whom great things were expected.[97] Porter revised the paper over the summer and it appeared later that year in the November 1955 edition of the *Canadian Journal of Economics and Political Science*.

Not long after, his data-gathering efforts bore fruit as well. As early models for this aspect of his study he used H. Campion's *Public and Private Property in Great Britain* and A.A. Berle and G.C. Means' analysis of economic power in the United States, *The Modern Corporation and Private Property*. The Campion book analysed trends that showed property distribution in England to be only slightly more equal in 1936 than in 1911. Porter hoped to replicate for Canada the 'basic macrodata relevant to economic stratification' that Campion had gathered for England.[98]

Equally important was Berle and Means' work on the so-called 'managerial revolution' in the United States.[99] Porter wanted to determine the degree to which their findings held up in Canada. Years later, he recalled being shocked to discover that both fields of enquiry – property ownership and the managerial revolution – had lain fallow in Canada, largely ignored by the country's economists. This lack of interest, he argued, constituted a telling reflection of the Canadian value system, and raised a key question in Porter's mind. Canadians proclaimed that they valued the principle of social equality, he said. However, he noted that 'the roots of inequality in the economic system had never been examined.' How, then, could Canadians honestly make such a claim?[100] As he began to examine this fundamental question, he discovered that he had a lot of spadework to do because Canadian law afforded privately owned Canadian companies an unusual degree of anonymity and protection. They had to make only 'minimal disclosures' about their operations. This made it difficult for him to gather the data he needed in order to identify Canada's 'dominant' corporations; determine who sat on their boards of directors; and document interlocking directorships between dominant corporations.[101] Only by dint of weeks of searching through 'annual industry reports of the Dominion Bureau of Statistics, details of company reports ... in *The Financial Post Corporation Service, Moody's Industrials, The Stock Exchange Year Book,* and various directories of directors and reports of commissions of inquiry' was he able to assemble the data he needed.[102] Nonetheless, by the spring of 1956, 'Concentration of Economic Power and the Economic Elite in Canada' appeared in the *Canadian Journal of Economics and Political Science.*

Porter drew on the materials from these two papers to construct novel courses at Carleton. Beginning in the fall of 1954, he offered Canadian sociology's first course devoted to the analysis of social inequality. Along with a second new course he offered that same year, 'The Sociology of Political Power,' students were treated to a challenging new interpretation of Canadian society and a sneak preview of *The Vertical Mosaic.*[103] Although the course descriptions are mundane by current standards, at the time they constituted a tremendous novelty.[104] No Canadian university then offered a course entitled 'Social Inequality,' 'Social Stratification,' or the like.[105] With a few noteworthy exceptions, Canadian social scientists had paid relatively little attention to social class and power (see chapter 7).

As he tentatively worked his way through these materials, he plugged away at a third, related project: a study of the origins and social backgrounds of the economic elite that he had written about in 'Concentration of Economic Power.' It was, in some respects, a more difficult area of investigation than the other two, and at first he struggled to develop a practical and effective methodology. He considered using a mailed questionnaire similar to that employed by F.W. Taussig and C.S. Joslyn in their well-known 1932 study, *American Business Leaders,* but quickly ruled out this option. Powerful businessmen were unlikely to complete a questionnaire; they would see it as a violation of their privacy.[106] A low response rate would create a biased sample in which, he reasoned, the lesser members of the elite would be overrepresented. He likewise ruled out a massive program of face-to-face interviews, partly because he had little money, limited time, and no staff.[107] Also, however, he knew from preliminary interviews that they were of limited value: 'Elites found it as difficult to analyse their positions, either as individuals or collectively, as did members of other groups. Most had never been trained in systematic thinking about society, and were rarely moved to think about their role in the global scheme of things.'[108] In the end, he opted to employ secondary sources, most notably 'standard biographical dictionaries of the *Who's Who* type,' newspaper clippings, and articles in popular magazines and specialized trade journals.[109] In fact, Porter's papers contain only two sets of sketchy interview notes. Sometime in 1957, Porter spoke with Joseph Jeffrey, a lawyer and a member of a number of corporate boards: London Life and the Toronto-Dominion Bank, among others. Porter took with him to the interview a scrap of paper with about a dozen questions scrawled on it.[110] Afterward, from memory, he produced a one-page summary of the highlights of Jeffrey's responses. A key excerpt is as follows:

Thought that about 80% of directors earn about 10% of fees. Agreed with Masson that many directors useless to a corporation, and take fees dishonestly. Spoke about need for sense of responsibility of directors to their corporations. Thought they were on boards 1/ because they hold stock and cannot be held off board, or 2/ they will be useful to corporations as customers or suppliers ... J also felt responsible for his honorific jobs; i.e., London Hospital ... Liberal in politics – thought S. Smith was best thing conservative government had done.

Example of informality of elites – had lunch with Wally McCutcheon in Ottawa – discussed nasty combines case. (This is an e.g. of access to each other) ... General feeling that these men form a community. Refer to each other by first name.[111]

The other interview concerned a conversation with a senior executive at Consolidated Toronto Development Corporation who had been president of the Canadian Mortgage and Housing Corporation.[112]

Porter first reported his data on the social background and origins of the economic elite at a research colloquium at the University of Toronto in March 1956. Beginning in the early 1950s, S.D. Clark had organized an annual two-day conference to provide Canadian sociologists with a venue other than the meetings of the Canadian Political Science Association to present their research findings. Each year Clark invited an American or British 'star' to headline the event. Among those to give the keynote paper had been Talcott Parsons and Morris Ginsberg.[113] In 1956, the iconoclastic C. Wright Mills was the main attraction. It is an indication of Porter's growing stature in the discipline that he was chosen to be the featured Canadian. Among those in attendance was McMaster sociologist Frank Jones. Jones recalls that Mills, who gave a preview of his forthcoming work, *The Power Elite*, was very interested in Porter's work on Canadian elites.[114] Porter's correspondence reveals that the two met briefly and exchanged ideas at the conference, but 'didn't have the chance to get together for several hours of talk about their mutual problems' as they had apparently hoped.[115] Such a meeting would have been interesting, given their different personal styles and intellectual approaches. In the complacent and conservative sociological establishment of the 1950s in the United States, the ebullient Mills stood out as a scholarly maverick, an abrasive critic of American society and its mainstream sociology. He had developed a following among progressive and radical intellectuals by writing a series of insightful, controversial books that fulminated against what he regarded as the system-stabilizing ideology and research practices of the American sociological establishment. By contrast, Porter was reserved and traditional. He respected Mills' work and shared some of his views of class and power in modern liberal democracies, but was sceptical of Mills' somewhat conspiratorial conception of the structure and dynamics of power in the United States.[116] Moreover, he was convinced that the Canadian situation differed considerably. Porter doubtless realized that he gained considerable status in the eyes of his Canadian colleagues by sharing the stage with Mills but, according to Muni Frumhartz, did not want to be identified with 'Millsian sociology.'[117] He revised his conference presentation over the following months and it subsequently appeared in the August 1957 edition of the *Canadian Journal of Economics and Political Science* as 'The Economic Elite and the Social Structure in Canada.'

This trio of articles saved Porter's career at Carleton. Three years earlier, he had broached the subject of his future at the college in a letter to the dean, James Gibson. At that point, he had been on staff for five years without a promotion or benefit of a multiyear contract:

> I pointed out that I had completed five years at Carleton and since I had received no recognition in the way of promotion I thought the time had come to assess my future here. Promotion per se does not concern me, but since it is the way in which the College indicates that it is satisfied with one's work, I must assume that I have not been satisfactory ... The response of the faculty in general and the social sciences in particular has been very encouraging, but I am concerned about the response of the College itself. I am assuming that the College is interested in the subject matter, but not interested in me.[118]

By the time MacOdrum did the annual evaluations in the spring of 1955, however, Porter had produced the 'Elite Groups' paper. Presumably, based on this evidence, plus two papers and a book review he had published in *Canadian Forum* and evidence of progress on the other two papers on elites, MacOdrum offered him a three-year appointment as an assistant professor.[119] But there was a catch. For the first time, MacOdrum issued a formal written ultimatum:

> I think we should have an understanding about tenure. My proposal is that you may, if you wish, remain on staff in the rank of Assistant Professor for not more than three years, 1955–56, 1956–57, 1957–58, unless, within that three-year period you should proceed to a doctoral degree from an approved university, or in some other way make such a contribution to research in the field of sociology that I would feel justified in extending your term.[120]

MacOdrum was wise to offer Porter some hope of a permanent position, for other universities then establishing sociology programs saw Porter as an attractive prospect and were trying to recruit him.[121]

In the end, for several personal and professional reasons, Porter decided to stay at Carleton. Most important, Ottawa and Carleton had come to be home. His family was settled and he had close friends both in and out of the academy, in particular Bob and Mary Anne Phillips. Porter and Phillips had renewed their wartime friendship when Porter arrived from England in 1949 to discover that both Bob and Mary Anne were teaching part time at Carleton. The Porters and the Phillipses lived next door to one another in the Glebe for many years and Phillips remained his closest friend for the rest of his life.[122] The Porters had many other friends at Carleton as well: Munro and May Beattie, Pauline Jewett, Norm Fenn, Muni and Dvora Frumhartz, Bruce and Connie McFarlane, and Frank and Anita Vallee. Originally work-related contacts, these friendships spilled over from the campus, first to private parties in each other's homes and, later, for some of them, to a cottage community north of Ottawa near Renfrew.[123]

Starting in 1955, just four weeks after Ann's birth, the family spent three months each summer at a cottage on Constant Lake.[124] Initially, they rented, but in 1956 the owner of the tract of land on which 'their' cottage was located decided to sell. None of the families could afford to buy the whole property – ten cottages, 287 acres – but in the summer of 1957 they arranged to buy it as a collective.[125] According to Jewett, Porter was originally opposed to owning a cottage on the grounds it would make him too much the 'country gentleman,' but he soon relented and was later pleased to have done so.[126] The cottage came to be extremely important to him, a haven that provided much sustenance: time with family and friends and a private place to work uninterrupted.

Marion recalled that John wrote a great deal of *The Vertical Mosaic* at the cottage. In the late 1950s and early 1960s, he filled his summer days at the lake with work on the book – all morning and early afternoon – but in the late afternoon spent time with the children.[127] 'The cottage was very important to the family,' recalled his daughter Ann, who remembers these summers – and her father – with great fondness. He was 'warm and caring,' she said, 'a great dad.'[128] Tony expressed similar feelings. He noted that while he and his father had drifted apart when Tony was a teenager, he retained 'enormous affection and positive feelings' toward his father. The more difficult teenage years, he said, were 'just a phase.'[129] In the evening family friends, mostly academics, would gather to relax and talk shop around a bonfire while children played and roasted marshmallows. The Porters' most frequent visitor and closest family friend at the lake was Pauline Jewett: 'Often in the evenings, about ten o'clock, I would grab a beer or two out of my fridge and go down the hill, through the trees to the Porter cottage and we would chat for an hour, hour and a half ... Sometimes it would go on longer than that if we really got going on something, about his work primarily, but about my work, too.'[130]

John and Pauline enjoyed a close relationship. They shared many left-of-centre political beliefs as well as a faith in the potential of education to create equality of opportunity and the need for a strong central government to oversee a generous and effective welfare state. However, there were differences: on federalism (John referred to it as 'this hallowed nonsense'), nationalism, multiculturalism, and Quebec. Jewett's biographer, Judith McKenzie, has argued that Pauline 'embraced the idea of a cultural mosaic, ... strongly supported Quebec's position to be seen as a distinct society, ... [and] was an ardent Canadian nationalist.'[131] Porter was critical of all these notions. He regarded the United States as a model society of sorts, more egalitarian, meritocratic, and assimilationist than Canada and able to provide more people with a postsecondary education. In the mid-1960s, he made this clear to a newspaper reporter:

> In my optimistic moments, and I don't have many of them, I think the best thing for Canada would be greater Americanization – the more American values we get the more we can become genuinely North American. This idea horrifies many Canadians. They feel there's something wonderful, something to be proud about, in *not* being American. I cannot understand it.[132]

This is not to say he was devoid of nationalist sentiment, as Larry Glassford, his student in a Canadian studies seminar at Carleton attests:

> My most vivid memory of [John Porter] relates not to an academic topic, but the famous 1972 hockey series between Canada and the Soviets. The eighth and deciding game was to be played at the ... same time as our weekly seminar. With the apparently grudging approval of Professor Porter, a TV set was duly brought into the seminar room, and we all settled back to view the climactic game ... As the match seesawed back and forth, Dr. Porter became increasingly involved ... When Paul Henderson fired the winning goal, Professor Porter let loose with a war whoop as loud as any in the room. Then, realizing where he was, he looked about rather sheepishly, and settled back into his chair to endure the game's final seconds in strained silence. I do not remember the scheduled topic of our seminar that day. I will never forget the obvious pride in Canada which Carleton's noted sociologist, John Porter, exuded that September day, back in 1972.[133]

He was equally suspicious of multiculturalism and Quebec nationalism. Multiculturalism emphasized group loyalties and characteristics and focused on collective rather than individual rights, and Quebec nationalism served only to weaken the central state.[134] By contrast, he said, his loyalties were to 'North American values as exemplified by the American values of altruism and equality.' Change required 'a strong central government,' and he lamented the 'increasing fragmentation and impotence' of the state and the lack of interest in higher education, especially higher education, in Canada. In his view, these three factors – strong central government, education, and North American values – were 'the key to it all, the secret to developing a strong sense of Canada.'[135]

So close were Porter and Jewett that McKenzie has suggested John was Pauline's intellectual mentor.[136] This reading of their relationship does not ring true. No doubt they spent a great deal of time discussing the Canadian political and social scene. I agree with Ann Porter, though, that Pauline 'was very much her own person and ... very much an equal' in the relationship.[137] On this score, perhaps confidante or sounding board would be more appropriate descriptions.

Porter's ability to purchase a cottage and devote himself to full-time research in the summer suggests that the family's financial situation had improved. No longer did he find it necessary to take on contract writing jobs such as those he had undertaken for Colonel Stacey. John Meisel and S.D. Clark were instrumental here. They discovered that Porter was spending the summer terms carrying out mundane tasks like painting his house because he could not afford to pay for the work to be done. Concerned that he was wasting his time, they arranged for him to receive a modest stipend from the Social Science Research Council.[138] The money could not have come at a better time. Inspired by the appearance of the 'Elite Groups' paper in the *Canadian Journal of Economics and Political Science,* and with the added peace of mind his three-year contract had given him, he could intensify his research efforts.

Administrative changes at Carleton also contributed to Porter's decision to stay in Ottawa. MacOdrum died suddenly in August 1955 and the dean, James Gibson, again took over as acting president. Gibson had supported Porter's candidacy for a faculty position, and this may have helped to put Porter at ease. Gibson assured Porter that he could remain an assistant professor after the end of his three-year term, though there was no guarantee of tenure.[139]

Carleton Gets a New President: The Bissell Interlude, 1956–1958

In the summer of 1956, James Coyne, chair of Carleton's Board of Governors, announced that Claude Thomas Bissell, the young vice-president of the University of Toronto, would be the university's next president.[140] Coyne and C.J. McKenzie had recruited Bissell with the endorsement and encouragement of Sidney Smith, then president of the University of Toronto. Smith regarded Bissell as his likely successor and saw a period of seasoning at Carleton as a good experience for his protégé.[141]

Born in 1916 in Meaford, at the southern tip of Georgian Bay, Bissell received his high school education at Runnymede Collegiate in Toronto. A brilliant student, he graduated at sixteen and earned a BA and an MA at the University of Toronto before going to Cornell for his PhD. After a year lecturing in Cornell's English department and a year teaching at the University of Toronto, he enlisted in the Canadian Army.[142] He served in the infantry as a member of the Argyll and Sutherland Highlanders, and, like Porter, was part of the Canadian force that took part in the Allied invasion of Sicily and Italy. Indeed, like Porter, he served part of his time as an intelligence officer and was demobilized as a captain.[143] He then taught briefly at Khaki College in London before returning once again to the University of Toronto. There he taught English and served as dean in residence at University College before becoming an assistant to Sidney Smith, the university president, in 1948. In 1952, Smith named him vice-president.[144] He became president of Carleton four years later.

Bissell's tenure at Carleton was brief but eventful. MacOdrum had been leery of the prospect of moving to the new campus – perhaps, said McEown, because it was 'beyond his competence' – but 'Bissell welcomed the project with open arms.' He enjoyed fundraising and 'had ambitions for the place.' 'Instead of the board dragging the president along,' said McEown, 'it was the president dragging the board along.'[145] Bissell's primary goal was to complete Carleton's metamorphosis into a 'real' university.[146] In his memoirs, *Halfway up Parnassus,* he writes that he took advantage of what he described as 'a freedom from constraint' not possible at older universities to complete the task. His specific goals were to 'bring Carleton as quickly as possible into the mainstream [of the Canadian university community]; to raise salaries so that they were comparable with other institutions; to emphasize the basic disciplines;

... and to develop Carleton's responsibilities in the national capital.'[147]

Bissell realized that in order to carry out this agenda he needed strong community backing, so two of his priorities became community relations and fundraising.[148] He was fortunate that his time as president coincided with an especially important development in the history of Canada's universities. Not long after he took office, the federal government announced a decision to double its grants to universities and establish a $50 million fund to assist them with capital building costs related to the humanities and social sciences.[149] The Ontario government tagged along. The province had not foreseen that its few universities would be unable to cope with the rising demand for university education and had not provided them with appropriate support. Beginning in 1955, however, during Gibson's time in the president's office and for the two years of Bissell's tenure, the province came through with about a million dollars in funding each year.[150]

Despite this show of support from the federal and provincial governments, the City of Ottawa remained unhelpful. During the Tory and MacOdrum years, Carleton had received continuous support from the local business community. Municipal politicians were a different matter. The mayor of Ottawa for much of the 1950s was the fiery and acerbic Charlotte Whitton, a fiscal conservative who ran a 'barebones' municipal operation. Whitton made it clear that she regarded Carleton as a cultural frill that did not figure in her budget plans.[151] On two occasions she angered the Carleton community by attempting to block the university's efforts to move to its new site. She forced a delay in government approval of Carleton's plans to buy the Rideau River site and then refused to have the city cover the costs of extending sewer and water mains to the campus.[152] This delayed the start of the construction of the new campus until 1957.[153]

Bissell tried to improve Carleton's financial situation further by speaking to local groups and by aggressively soliciting money from wealthy benefactors – and with some success. 'Within a few months of my arrival I had completed my stint in the church basement league of oratory and was moving on to school and hotel ballrooms,' he said. He then moved on to the national stage to plead his case with chartered banks, national foundations, and the like. His memoirs convey his enthusiasm:

[We] conducted [the financial campaign] ... in a cheerfully amateurish way without any professional advice. In November 1956, Jack Mackenzie,

Senator [Norman] Paterson, and I set out in the senator's sturdy but aging Rolls Royce for Montreal ... to consult J.W. McConnell, wealthy business-man and philanthropist, about the secrets of money-raising. McConnell, a genial man with the elegance of a matinee idol ... talked discursively about money-raising, and then without any overt prompting, volunteered a contribution of $25,000. We were all so elated by this, even the senator, who had privately pledged $500,000, that we retired in high spirits to a neighbouring hotel, and, martinis in hand, hailed the certain success of the campaign.[154]

With the aid of other notables, including Kenneth Greene, an Ottawa businessman, and Brooke Claxton, a former minister in Mackenzie King's cabinet, Bissell's campaign raised over $1 million, 'a large sum in those days, especially for a small institution.'[155] Neatby and McEown surmise that the success of Bissell's campaign was a big factor in help-ing prime the pump for Carleton to receive financial support from the provincial government.[156] At the same time, Bissell tried to augment Carleton's visibility and reputation in the national university commu-nity by offering salaries that would attract and retain top-ranking schol-ars. His presidential report of 1956–7 indicates that he had succeeded; the university boasted one of the best salary scales on the continent.[157]

Porter consolidated his position during the Bissell years, and Bissell was not the only one to notice. Canadian academics and the popular media had begun to draw attention to his work. In 1957, for example, University of Toronto economist C.A. Ashley published a critique of Porter's article 'The Concentration of Economic Power and the Eco-nomic Elite in Canada' in the *Canadian Journal of Economics and Politi-cal Science*.[158] And in 1958 the CBC asked Porter to act as an adviser for an hour-long segment of the program *Explorations* during which six members of the economic elite were being interviewed. Some months later, Porter wrote to his friend, UBC sociologist Kaspar Naegele, com-menting on the benefits of the collaboration: 'I have since acquired the complete transcripts,' he wrote, 'and since I was in on the planning of the program, I obtained some interesting insights.'[159] Newspapers, too, occasionally reported his findings on Canada's wealthy businessmen and other elites.[160] This attention not only helped his budding reputa-tion but also provided much food for thought. 'I am glad I have pub-lished the articles in the way that I have,' he wrote to Naegele, 'because they have brought forth some interesting comments from a variety of sources.'[161]

But it wasn't just his data that scholars found interesting. He attracted attention as well because of his political views. It was clear that Porter's purpose in describing the structure of social inequality in Canada was not purely academic. As a New Liberal, he regarded inequality not just as a phenomenon to be studied but as a social problem to be fixed. As time passed, he increasingly challenged the view commonly held in Canada that the country was a democratic and classless society. It was neither, he asserted, and until Canadians discarded this myth they would be unable to undertake the societal changes necessary to make equality – even equality of opportunity – a reality. But in the mid-1950s, this was a tough sell. Marion Porter recalled that she and John spent many hours with academics such as Pauline Jewett and Paul Fox discussing the problem: 'They had all worked during the summers when they were at university and believed that they had put themselves through college. They thought that if they could do it, anybody could.'[162]

Nonetheless, despite some resistance to his ideas, he persevered – and for good reason. The three papers he had published in the *Canadian Journal of Economics and Political Science* had clearly cast doubt on the proposition that Canada was an egalitarian, democratic nation. They showed that a very small group of men – the economic elite – owned or controlled Canada's economic resources and possessed an enormous amount of power as a consequence. Moreover, they constituted an essentially self-recruiting cadre drawn almost exclusively from the upper reaches of the class structure.

As Porter put the finishing touches on these materials and prepared to knit them together for his book on class and power in Canada, he realized that he needed more data and a broader framework. Specifically, in order to assess the relative degree of power the economic elite possessed vis-à-vis other elites and the rest of Canadian society, and to draw the wider conclusions he wanted to make regarding the nation's structure of class and power, he needed to gather information on other elites. He could understand the relations between the structure of corporate power and Canada's class structure only if he could supplement his data on the ownership and control of the nation's productive resources with complementary data about the more general distribution of income, 'life chances' (especially educational opportunities), and so forth. In short, he realized that he needed to incorporate his findings regarding economic power and the economic elite into an analysis of class, power, and elites more broadly conceived. As he did so, his earlier desire to write a comprehensive, Tocquevillian analysis of Canada as a modern democracy came to seem less fantastic and he began to consider how to carry it off:

> While I was working on the analysis of economic power, I gradually re-
> gained my enthusiasm for undertaking a much more extensive investiga-
> tion into the entire range of power and stratification in Canada and for
> treating the two, not as isolated segments or aspects of social life, but as
> integrated in a total social system ... [So] as the study of elite groups was
> taking form, I turned increasingly to the problem of articulating the elite
> structure with the wider stratification system.[163]

His search for sources of information on elites other than the economic quickly proved fruitful and, in late 1956, he began two other
studies. One focused on Canada's political elite, the other on its bureaucratic elite. The former proceeded slowly, however, and other than
a brief opinion piece in *Canadian Forum* ('Political Parties and the Political Career'), the results did not appear until *The Vertical Mosaic* came
out. His work on the bureaucratic elite advanced much more quickly,
and he soon produced a short opinion piece – again published in *Canadian Forum* – and a scholarly article, 'Higher Public Servants and the
Bureaucratic Elite in Canada.' The latter analysed Canada's federal bureaucracy in terms of the degree to which it matched up to a 'model'
bureaucracy and discussed the social origins and characteristics of the
nation's bureaucratic elite. Porter argued that it was useful to characterize bureaucracies in terms of three ideal-typical continua: rational-
ized/non-rationalized, rivalled/unrivalled, and open/closed. On the
first count, Porter claimed that Canada's federal civil service was not
rationalized; political patronage too frequently interfered with the selection procedure and prevented qualified technical experts from holding the top posts. On the second point, he argued that the federal civil
service was essentially 'unrivalled'; it enjoyed a 'quasi-monopoly' on
technical expertise in a number of fields because there were no private
sector experts to provide an independent check. Finally, he said, it was
quite 'closed' in terms of recruitment patterns; members were overwhelmingly middle class and Anglo-Saxon. This article drew the critical attention of his Carleton colleague political scientist Don Rowat,
who challenged some of Porter's ideas about the bureaucratic elite in
the pages of the *Canadian Journal of Economics and Political Science*.[164]

By 1958, then, Porter's research program was well underway and,
once again, he had begun to think about undertaking a comprehensive

analysis of the structure and dynamics of class and power in Canada. His work had earned him the prospect of a permanent position at Carleton and garnered him a good deal of attention in Canada's small sociology community. Just as this took place, the Canadian government decided to make a massive investment in the nation's postsecondary education system. Porter, Carleton, and the discipline of sociology would reap great benefits.

6 Crafting a Classic, 1958–1965

The Dunton Era Begins

A new era began at Carleton in May 1958, when Claude Bissell's whirlwind stay in Ottawa came to an abrupt and early end and he departed to assume the presidency of the University of Toronto. Once again, James Gibson fulfilled the president's obligations while the university sought a replacement[1] and, once again, Chancellor C.J. McKenzie played a key role in the search process. One day, while lunching at the Rideau Club, he struck up a conversation with 'Davey' Dunton, then chairman of the Board of Governors of the Canadian Broadcasting Corporation. During the course of the meal, Dunton confided in McKenzie that he was looking for a job. He was certain that the new Conservative government headed by John Diefenbaker would soon replace him as head of the CBC. McKenzie seized the opportunity to discuss the prospect of the presidency with Dunton, who expressed interest. McKenzie then approached the search committee and the board about offering his friend the job.[2] A few months later, the board announced its decision: Carleton's fourth president would be Arnold Davidson Dunton.

Dunton was born in Montreal in 1912, the son of Robert Dunton, a lawyer, and Elizabeth Davidson. An exceptional student, he completed his secondary school education at the High School of Montreal and Lower Canada College by age fifteen.[3] Too young to attend university in Canada, he travelled and studied abroad for four years.[4] On his return, he took a job as a reporter for the *Montreal Star* and soon thereafter became editor of its sister publication, the *Saturday Standard*.[5] Beginning in 1942, he served as a member of the Wartime Information Board and at war's end became chairman of the Board of Governors of the

CBC, a post he held for thirteen years.[6] Remarkably, when Dunton assumed the presidency of Carleton University in 1958, he did not hold a university degree. Such were the possibilities for an intelligent, well-connected man with experience in the 1950s.

During his fourteen-year tenure at Carleton, Dunton became a larger than life figure who earned the respect of almost everyone on campus. Wise and humane, with a broad and liberal outlook on life, he had a keen sense of the role of the university in the modern world. He possessed excellent interpersonal skills, and used the stature and contacts he had built during his years at the CBC to advance Carleton's interests. 'Dunton,' said economist Gilles Paquet, 'was a bigger man than most people I have met in my life, a man of extraordinary talents: ... a diplomat, a schemer, a wheeler-dealer, ... a very smooth person ... able to stickhandle things because of his moral authority.'[7] His personal style was relaxed and egalitarian. As Kenneth McRae put it, he was 'open and friendly to everyone, from freshmen to visiting potentates.' Perfectly comfortable in the rarefied atmosphere of the Rideau Club and other exclusive haunts of the Ottawa mandarinate, he was equally at home with students and 'usually lunched in the Loeb cafeteria, often sitting with undergraduates.'[8] This personal openness was matched by intellectual openness and flexibility. 'Never wedded to any particular intellectual system,' said McEown, Dunton was 'responsive to new ideas.'[9] But there was more to him than flexibility, openness, and charm. An exceptionally intelligent and pragmatic leader, Dunton believed that university administration should be kept simple so that the institution could respond to circumstances in a nimble way. He never appointed vice-presidents and for years kept the university budget in his head.[10] As well, instead of working from a detailed agenda for Carleton, he relied on an implicit general philosophy of the proper nature and role of the university in modern liberal society as a guide. This combination of simplicity, flexibility, and pragmatism gave him the capacity to act unilaterally when the occasion arose, free to pursue Carleton's best interests.[11] And, according to McEown, he did all of this without being heavy-handed, managing situations indirectly by stacking committees and structuring choices rather than by telling people what to do.[12] As Kenneth McRae put it, he chose to 'steer' Carleton rather than 'rule' it.[13]

Whatever his tactics, Dunton was a potent force, so powerful and well known in the early years, said McEown, that 'in many ways, he *was* Carleton.'[14] This power of personality, combined with a mandarin's skill set and formidable contacts allowed him not only to advance Carleton's interests, but also to become a major figure in the Canadian university system. He came to have 'a much stronger influence in national and provincial university affairs than his institution would warrant,' said McEown, because of his contacts and insider knowledge. The other presidents soon realized that 'he knew how governments worked, ... where the risks were, and what was likely to happen.'[15]

Porter had great respect for the president – Gibson referred to Dunton as 'a companion spirit of John Porter' – and over the years they developed a warm professional relationship.[16] Indeed, the informal environment Dunton created may even have contributed to Porter's success as an academic. Certainly, as Porter's star waxed, Dunton supported him, and Porter took advantage of the opportunity to build a remarkable career. The key was the massive expansion of the Canadian university system in the 1960s and, as part of that expansion, the growth and development of Canadian sociology. Only in the context of such growth could Porter have forged such a distinguished and visible career.

Beginning in the late 1950s, and especially through the 1960s, Canada's university system assumed a much more prominent profile in the nation's institutional fabric than it had ever enjoyed. As late as 1961, only about half of Canadians finished high school and less than 10 per cent attended university.[17] Canada had only about forty universities in 1958 and most were small, despite having been in operation for many years.[18] Full-time enrolments totalled less than 80,000 across the country, and by far the greatest number of students came from the upper reaches of the class structure.[19] Everything changed in the early 1960s, however, when the first of the baby boom generation reached university age. The parents of the boomers came to believe that education, especially a university education, would create opportunities for their children that the Depression and World War II had denied to them and their parents. Also abroad in Canadian society was the idea that the expansion and democratisation of higher education would create a better-educated workforce that would allow Canada to be economically competitive on the international stage.[20] The result? By the mid-1960s about three-quarters of Canadian students completed high school and the percentage pursuing higher education nearly doubled to 10 per cent.[21] To accommodate these increases – full-time undergraduate enrolment reached 206,000 by 1965 – governments built new universities at an unprecedented rate: ten in just a decade, bringing the total to more than fifty.[22] Full-time graduate enrolment more than kept pace, increasing from 3,400 in 1955–6 to 17,200 in 1965–6.[23] The number of faculty grew rapidly as well, from 6,000 to over 14,000 during the same period.[24] Across the country, the budget for university education increased sevenfold to nearly $7 billion.[25]

Growth at Carleton reflected these trends. During the first five years of Dunton's tenure, 1958–63, enrolment more than doubled from 2,200 to 5,000, and its full-time faculty complement increased from 66 to 131.[26] The sociology program also grew rapidly. As late as 1957–8, English-language Canadian universities had only three dozen full-time sociology faculty, but by 1963–4 that had increased to 115.[27] In this regard, Carleton was unusual, one of a handful of places – Alberta, UBC, McGill, and Toronto were the others – with more than one or two full-time faculty appointments. By the end of the 1964–5 academic year, Carleton had five: Bruce McFarlane, Peter Pineo, and Donald Whyte had joined Porter and Frumhartz. The program boasted about forty majors and many times that number took sociology as an option.[28]

A Rising Star, 1958–1965

Porter served as the department's first chair from 1953–4 to 1959–60, but the associated administrative responsibilities did not detract from his research productivity.[29] Even during the confusion and extra work occasioned by the move to the new campus, Porter moved forward on his three major projects: a reader on Canadian society, his chapter for *Social Purpose for Canada,* and the manuscript of 'Elites, Power and Social Class in Canada,' the working title for what became *The Vertical Mosaic.* In the autumn of 1958, his work on the book manuscript received a major boost when he received a substantial grant from the newly formed Canada Council, founded in 1957 to oversee the activities of the Social Science Research Council of Canada (SSRCC).

From 1940 to the late 1950s the SSRCC had been the sole national organization responsible for promoting the interests and administering the common affairs of the social sciences in Canada. Ironically, given its nationalist mandate, the its budget came not from the Canadian federal government but from two American philanthropic foundations, the Rockefeller Foundation and the Carnegie Foundation both of which withdrew their support in 1957. At this point, yet another American philanthropic organization, the Ford Foundation, stepped in, offering to 'underwrit[e] the general program of the Social Sciences Research Council of Canada' on an interim basis while the SSRCC made the adjustment to the newly formed Canada Council. The Ford Foundation was generous and resources available for research increased dramatically during the transition. This allowed the SSRCC to sponsor a slate of large-scale, long-term research projects, a decision from which Porter benefited immediately.[30]

The first major endeavour approved by the SSRCC Research and Policy Planning Committee was a series of book-length studies gathered under the general title 'The Structure of Power: Decision-Making in Canada.' The series was directed and edited by a committee made up of S.D. Clark, G.A. Elliott, the Reverend N. Mailloux and, serving as chair, John Meisel of Queen's University, one of Canada's pre-eminent political scientists. The purpose was to examine 'the manner and setting in which important decisions are made in Canada in fields affecting the general public.'[31]

Meisel regarded Porter's work as highly significant and in late summer of 1958 approached him about taking part in the venture.[32] Pleased and flattered, Porter seized the opportunity, submitting a formal outline of his research program in mid-September, including a request for almost $10,000 to pay for research assistance, travel costs, and replacement salary.[33] About two weeks later, he received word that his proposal had been approved.[34] For the first time, 'Elites, Power and Social Class' was on a firm financial footing.

Just as Porter received this news, two other research opportunities came his way. Both turned out to be useful to the book project.

About a year earlier, Porter had decided, in collaboration with Frank Jones, Bernard Blishen, and Kaspar Naegele, to look into the prospect of compiling a new, fully Canadian sociology reader.[35] The only existing Canadian sociology textbook, written by Carl Dawson and Warner Gettys of McGill University in 1929, had long since fallen out of favour. Rooted in the human ecology approach developed at the University of Chicago by Robert Park in the early twentieth century, it had become dated, even though revised editions (1935, 1948) had incorporated progressively more aspects of the functionalist theory that had come to dominate American and Canadian sociology.[36] Moreover, even after three iterations and twenty years, it contained very little information about Canada and by the late 1950s, most Canadian sociologists wanted to teach from Canadian materials.[37] Porter and his collaborators hoped to tap into this market.

They began the project in the late summer of 1957 by hiring a graduate student to do a preliminary survey of the literature to see if in fact there was sufficient material to produce a reader.[38] Once they confirmed there was, they pressed ahead.[39] The first job was to prepare a short list of prospective materials. After finishing a review of the materials in his assigned areas – political sociology, social class, and social change – Porter wrote to Naegele disheartened. The pool of possible selections, he said, was very small: 'I am afraid that compared to yours and Bern's [my list] is rather short ... [P]olitical sociology, social class, and social change have scarcely been worked at in Canada. As it is, several of my suggestions are contributions of political scientists rather than sociologists.'[40] Eventually, they published five of Porter's selections: an article by Yves de Jocas and Guy Rocher on intergenerational occupational mobility in Quebec, an excerpt from Everett Hughes' classic monograph *French Canada in Transition*, Blishen's groundbreaking article on the construction and use of an occupational class scale, John Robbins' work examining relations between home life, family background, and IQ among school children, and Porter's own article, 'The Economic Elite and the Social Structure in Canada.'[41]

The book took three years to put together, but when *Canadian Society* appeared in 1961 it was an impressive volume of 622 pages. Naegele wrote an introductory essay and the book reprinted thirty-six selections. Classics such as Everett Hughes' *French Canada in Transition* were juxtaposed with more recent work, all reproduced with the aim of making Canadian materials more readily available for Canadian professors and their students. For the most part, they succeeded. Reviews were generally positive, praising them for bringing together scattered Canadian materials 'on a wide variety of sociological themes,' and drawing attention to the work of the most recent generation of Canadian sociologists.[42] But astute reviewers noted flaws as well. *Canadian Society*, Fred Elkin wrote, was too theoretically and methodologically eclectic.[43] Quebec sociologist Gérard Dion focused on a different problem. In a French-language review in *Relations Industrielles*, he expressed the view that many of the selections they had reprinted were dated.[44] Perhaps one thing the collection revealed above all else was how much basic research still needed to be done on Canadian society.

Despite these shortcomings, *Canadian Society* turned out to be a substantial and useful contribution and sold well – more than 10,000 copies over four editions from 1961 to 1971.[45] It might have done even better, but unlike a true text, it did not offer a systematic overview of concepts, theories, methods, and substantive areas. As well, because of its length it was expensive. Nonetheless, until the late 1960s it often served as a course text and, more often still, as a source of supplementary reading for courses in introductory sociology and Canadian society.[46] For their part, the editors were pleasantly surprised by the book's reception. Commenting thirty years later, Bernard Blishen thought its success said a lot about the undeveloped state of the discipline in Canada at the time.[47]

The second project with which Porter was involved at the time, other than his book, was also a collaboration. In late January 1958 a who's who of Canadian social democratic and left-liberal intellectuals and politicians – among them David Lewis, Stanley Knowles, Pierre Elliott Trudeau, Eugene Forsey, Frank Scott, H. Scott Gordon, Harold Winch, and Russell Bell – gathered at Woodsworth House in Ottawa to discuss a research project. Partly on the basis of his rising stature as a scholar, and partly on the basis of his reputation as a progressive critic of Canadian society, Porter received an invitation.[48] The undertaking they met to consider was an updating of the 1935 LSR classic, *Social Planning for Canada*.[49]

The impetus and the funding for the book came from the Boag Foundation. The foundation's namesake, Allan Boag, had immigrated to Canada from Scotland in 1894. A successful businessman, he had stipulated in his will that all of his considerable estate be used to establish a trust that would sponsor projects designed to further socialist and working-class politics and education in Canada. In 1958, the directors of the foundation, the first of its kind in Canada, decided to make $20,000 of the trust available for research and publication. Unsure how to proceed, they contacted Stuart Jamieson, a professor of economics at UBC, who they knew to be a sympathetic student of Canada's labour movement. Jamieson suggested they update *Social Planning for Canada*. The directors liked the idea and authorized Jamieson to proceed.[50]

Prior to the meeting in Montreal, Jamieson assembled a tentative outline, based in part on *Social Planning for Canada*, and over the course of the day the group reviewed his prospectus, made preliminary matches of chapters and scholars, and chose an editor and an editorial board.[51] Despite his expertise in the area, they did not ask Porter to write the section 'Growth of Corporate Concentration and Power.' Rather, he and George Grube of the University of Toronto were pencilled in to write a chapter on education.[52]

Over the following year and a half, more scholars and politicians became involved in the project, attending sessions and acting as advisers.[53] Writing assignments changed and personnel were added and dropped as the need arose. Most prominent among the new contributors was conservative philosopher George Grant, who produced a compelling chapter entitled 'An Ethic of Community.'[54] For his part, Porter eventually assumed sole responsibility for two chapters, the one on education he had originally been assigned and, on the basis of a last-minute request from newly chosen editor Michael Oliver, a polemical think piece that was to discuss the problematic relationship between the exercise of power and the need for freedom in modern industrial society.[55] This second essay, 'Power and Freedom in Canadian Democracy,' is by far the more interesting and famous of the two. Wallace Clement has gone so far as to argue that it is Porter's strongest piece save for *The Vertical Mosaic*.[56] Marion Porter recalls that her husband had a great deal of fun writing it because he felt 'free to write a free-wheeling essay,' unencumbered by the usual limitations imposed by scholarly precision.[57] The essay, which eventually came to constitute the basis of the concluding chapter of *The Vertical Mosaic*, contains a number of social democratic arguments in favour of selective socialization of Canada's means of production and the expansion of industrial democracy (see chapter 8). He finished it over the first part of the summer and it appeared alongside 'Social Class and Education,' the chapter on education, when the Boag book came out in April 1961.

Naturally, when *Social Purpose for Canada* first appeared, it evoked comparisons with its 1935 precursor, which was deservedly famous for being the first detailed analysis of the structure of Canadian society from a social democratic point of view. The fact that the Boag book came out at about the same time as the founding of the New Democratic Party was not coincidental and did not go unnoticed. Forty years later, Michael Oliver claimed that it was inappropriate to connect *Social Purpose for Canada* and the founding of the NDP in the same way that the earlier volume, *Social Planning for Canada*, had been linked to the establishment of the CCF.[58] The contributors to *Social Purpose for Canada*, he said, 'were not writing the platform for a new party. None of us knew at that stage it was even being planned ... [These] things were in the air, but ... we had no idea we were writing *for* it.'[59] However, there is much evidence to the contrary. Perhaps most significantly, some of those involved in the project, including Frank Scott and Oliver himself, were actively engaged in the effort to fashion the NDP from the organizational and symbolic pieces of the CCF.[60] Indeed, at an early meeting of the group, Jack Weldon, also involved in organizing the New Party, as it was then called, explicitly drew the links between the *Social Pur-*

pose for Canada volume and the founding of the NDP.[61] Finally, letters in Porter's papers in Library and Archives Canada regarding the new volume invite him to meetings and seminars organized by the New Party. For example, in July 1959 he was invited to attend a meeting of the Canadian Labour Congress/Co-operative Commonwealth Federation (CLC/CCF) National Joint Committee[62] and a year later he accepted an invitation from Stanley Knowles, then MP for Winnipeg North Centre, on behalf of the National Committee for the New Party, to participate in a session entitled 'Socialism and Socialist Techniques in the 1960s.'[63]

Whatever its direct or indirect connection to the New Party, *Social Purpose for Canada* marked an important milestone in the history of social democratic scholarship in Canada. As Oliver pointed out in the preface, 'works of social criticism had been rare'[64] since *Social Planning for Canada* was published in the mid-1930s. *Social Purpose for Canada* was intended to remedy that situation. Oliver and his colleagues expressed the hope that the updated materials would serve as a powerful and authoritative rallying point for democratic socialists in Canada. That said, Oliver acknowledged in his preface to the Boag book that since the publication of *Social Planning for Canada* twenty-five years earlier, social democrats – at least those involved in the new volume – had changed both their 'diagnoses' of Canada's problems and the 'remedies' they proposed.[65] J.S. Woodsworth had described the 1935 volume as the 'first comprehensive treatise on [the] Canadian economy from a socialist point of view.'[66] It came out in the throes of the Depression and, quite understandably, had been highly critical of capitalism. Taking the LSR's Regina Manifesto as its guide, the authors of the 1935 volume had indicted mid-Depression capitalism as 'unjust and inhuman, economically wasteful, and a standing threat to peace and democratic government.' They hoped to 'substitute a planned and socialized economy for the existing chaotic individualism' that drove Canada's capitalist economy and looked for a political-economic transformation that would produce in Canada nothing less than the 'eliminat[ion of] the domination of one class by another' and the implementation of 'economic equality among all men.' To achieve their goal, the authors of *Social Planning for Canada* had proposed a wide-ranging program of social transformation, including the public ownership of some utilities, the nationalization of banks, the development of agricultural co-operatives, and a comprehensive slate of social legislation, including public medicine.[67]

According to editor Michael Oliver, the contributors to the 1961 volume assumed a more limited mandate and proposed a more modest set of goals: 'We want[ed] to distinguish ourselves from the conclusions of *Social Planning for Canada* ... because we were much more Keynesian in our thinking than *Social Planning* had ever been.' In early meetings, he said, they had decided that 'public ownership of the banks was unnecessary, ... and that the problem of ownership ... had been exaggerated in earlier socialist literature.' The group was 'much more interested in the possibility of using various kinds of planning that had democratic roots, of using fiscal policy, monetary policy.' Sounding much like the British New Liberals, they argued that 'the welfare state as it had developed had the ability ... to stop the great peaks and troughs of capitalism through Keynesian policy.' Mostly, he said, they tried 'to spell out this new understanding that you could not do away with capitalism.' Instead, you had to 'modify' it, 'civilize' it, and 'control' it. For the contributors to *Social Purpose for Canada,* said Oliver, 'the market was not an area of sin. It was a convenient economic device which could go along with public ownership and would have ... a big part *with* public ownership in whatever kind of society or economy would evolve.'[68] In this regard, *Social Purpose for Canada* was very similar not only to the New Liberalism but also to the principles of the nascent NDP, which, as Laurier Lapierre later pointed out, 'rejected thoroughgoing socialism and nationalization, [but] was dedicated to full employment, effective economic planning, a national investment board, job retraining and relocation, public and cooperative ownership of utilities and national resources, more effective control over the Canadian economy through the curtailment and supervision of foreign ownership, free education, and a national labour code.'[69]

As might be expected, *Social Purpose for Canada* received mixed reviews. In academic circles, it provoked a generally positive response. University of Toronto political scientist Alex Brady wrote two brief reviews, both of which were generally complimentary, praising the new volume as 'easily superior' to its predecessor.[70] James Corry, Brady's colleague, followed suit, but singled out Porter and Grant as contributors who had done 'some serious thinking on the deeper issues' because they had developed a conception of the social good that involved more than high personal incomes. He was especially pleased that their conceptions of the social good involved opportunities for Canadians to participate creatively in national decision making.[71] Economist Ian Drummond focused almost exclusively on the contributions of the economists – Jack Weldon, Gideon Rosenbluth, Scott Gordon, Albert Breton, Meyer Brownstone, and Stuart Jamieson – providing a mixed assessment of their respective and collective views of the problems of a socialist economy.[72] In an especially lively and extended review, historian Frank Underhill praised *Social Purpose for Canada* as an improvement on the 1935 book to which he had contributed. He was highly critical of their failure to address the question of the viability of a left-wing party in an age of relative affluence but singled out Grant, Porter, Compton, and 'Adam Greene' (a pseudonym) for their exemplary contributions: 'They are not concerned with improving the functioning of our economic machine or the quality of our economic output, but with the quality of the life that is lived in Canada.' For his part, said Underhill, Porter had successfully shown 'how the concentration of power in our community undermines all our democratic myths ... and how unequal opportunities for education deprive our society of too much potential creative human ability.'[73] The popular business press also took note, though predictably, the volume was given a rough ride. A particularly sarcastic and dyspeptic review in the *Business Quarterly* by J.R. Winter, for example, noted that since the collection was clearly 'published to mark the founding of the New Democratic Party,' and its purpose was 'to provide a guiding light for those pioneers trudging along the poorly illumined path of social reform,' it constituted a 'dubious beginning' for worthwhile scholarship. Winter despaired that such books would 'be read and prove to be influential.' The highest praise he could muster for the social and political chapters was that 'reading them would not likely cause any lasting harm.'[74]

While working on the *Canadian Society* reader and completing his two chapters for *Social Purpose for Canada*, Porter soldiered on with the basic research for his increasingly hefty book manuscript, including a study of Canada's labour elite, the fourth of the five elites he intended to cover. Preliminary research that started in 1958 revealed that biographical and career-line data were not available for the labour elite because they did not have the high profile of other elites. However, as many Canadian workers belonged to unions, and unions had power, Porter knew that labour leaders would have to be taken into account. Fortunately, some of the key union-based labour leaders in Canada knew Porter's work on corporate concentration and the economic elite and wanted to help him study their own leadership. In Quebec, one of his colleagues in *Social Purpose for Canada*, Pierre Trudeau, knew many figures in the labour movement and helped Porter put together a list of contacts to get his study off the ground.[75]

Porter began by identifying 'the leading officials, elected and appointed, of the forty-two unions with over 10,000 members in Canada.'[76] This group he designated the labour elite. Subsequent consultations with officials from the CLC, the Confédération des Sydicats Nationaux (CSN), some leading trade unions, and some senior bureaucrats in the Canada Department of Labour led him to supplement the original list with key figures from smaller unions.[77] He then developed and pre-tested two questionnaires, one English, one French, and mailed them to approximately 500 officials in October 1958.[78] Accompanying the six-page survey was a letter of introduction and endorsement co-signed by Fernand Jolicoeur, director of education for the CSN, and Claude Jodoin, president of the CLC.

He supplemented these survey data with information he had gath-ered at the 'Round Table on Man and Industry,' convened in autumn 1956 under the auspices of the University of Toronto's School of Social Work. The high-blown purpose of the round table was to examine 'the impact on human well-being of a rapidly evolving industrialization' and, since numerous high-ranking business, government, and aca-demic figures took part, it could have been interesting.[79] However, the reports produced by the various groups amounted to little more than business-oriented boosterism and planning exercises. Porter attended in hopes of meeting members of various elites.[80] The Porter papers contain evidence of his success at using the sessions to his advantage; he arranged interviews with Gower Markle, director of education and welfare for the United Steelworkers of America, and D.F. Hamilton, secretary-treasurer of the Ontario Federation of Labour.[81]

Though Porter coded the data on the labour elite over the summer of 1959, he did not complete the analysis until over two years later.[82] Originally, he intended to publish a separate article on the findings but never did so; they were not made public until they appeared in *The Vertical Mosaic*.[83]

Just as he got his study of labour elites underway in late 1958, Porter submitted a tentative outline of his book to Meisel. Though the manu-script would not be completed for another five years, the outline was beginning to look much like the final version: introductory chapters on each of class and power; a chapter dealing with the history of immigra-tion and the contemporary social structure of Canada (its 'ethnic, occu-pational, educational and income distribution'); a chapter detailing the historical emergence of classes in Canada; six chapters on elites, includ-ing one on their 'fusion and separation'; and two concluding chapters, one on 'social class and educational opportunity' and the other on 'social mobility, power, and democratic ideals.'[84] He continued to refine the various parts of the manuscript over the next two years and in 1961, initiated two new pieces of the study: a chapter describing 'the structure and control of [Canada's] mass media' – newspapers, TV, radio – and another examining Canada's 'ideological elite,' scholars, writers, and religious leaders whose pronouncements about Canadian cultural, economic and political events contoured the way most people thought about their society.[85] The former study complemented his work on the economic elite. As could have been predicted, he discovered that some of the mass media complexes in Canada constituted major corporations in themselves and that there was some overlap between the economic and media elites. This part of the manuscript, which focused on ideological elites, was important. Part of the power of elites stemmed from their capacity to use the institutions of organized religion, formal education, and popular culture to influence how the public understood day-to-day political, social, and economic events. Here the business orientation of the media elite was telling.

Looking back at Porter's efforts with the benefit of a half-century of hindsight, one cannot but marvel at the staggering workload associated with these multiple projects. Working mostly on his own and while teaching full time, he was slowly cobbling together a comprehensive outline of the structure of class and power of an entire country. Not only that, but it looked very much as though he would meet the prospective 1962 deadline he had chosen years earlier – though he did report to Meisel in the fall of 1961 that he was working 'damned hard' to do so.[86] The academic year 1961–2 turned out to be particularly productive because he was awarded a Canada Council Senior Research Fellowship and was able to work full time on the manuscript all year.[87] He took full advantage and by the end of winter term had completed nine chapters. This progress buoyed his spirits considerably, and in late April 1962, he wrote to Meisel expressing confidence that he could finish the remaining chapters by autumn – 'providing I don't go crackers without a holiday.' Indeed, for the first time he asked Meisel about the logistics of publishing his study. He informed Meisel that commercial publishers had approached him but that he had put them off, doubting they would be willing to publish his work because it was too scholarly and quantitative. He acknowledged that his book should appear in the SSRCC-sponsored series but expressed reservations about publishing with an academic press because he thought they would be slow, so slow that he would be forced to incorporate the data from the 1961

Census into his manuscript – a considerable task that he did not want to have to undertake if he could avoid it.[88] Meisel responded a week later, reminding him that the decision-making series had the right of first refusal on the manuscript because the SSRCC had funded the project. As well, Meisel listed several reasons why in this instance an academic press would likely publish just as quickly as a commercial one. In a conciliatory gesture to his impatient young colleague and friend, Meisel said that at the end of the summer Porter could submit to him 'such parts [of the manuscript] as are more or less ready' and that he would then determine if the manuscript should be sent to a second reader.[89]

With this short-term deadline in mind, Porter increased the intensity of his effort and in August was able to send Meisel the first ten chapters. He then waited anxiously for Meisel's judgment while working on the remaining three. Three months later, he was upset to learn that Meisel, struggling under an enormous workload of his own, had been able to read only twenty pages of the manuscript and would be unable to finish the task until after the turn of the New Year.[90] But Porter would soon have more to worry about than his unread manuscript.

On 22 January 1963, he suffered a crushing setback – a massive heart attack. He was only forty-one years old and tried to stay healthy by following a regular program of exercise and walking to and from work as often as practicable.[91] However, he smoked heavily, worked Herculean hours, and had a driven, intense personality. The attack nearly killed him. He was in Calgary when it occurred. As editor of the newly established *Canadian Review of Sociology and Anthropology,* he had come from Ottawa to confer with Harry Zentner, the convenor of the *Review's* editorial board.[92] While there, he agreed to give a guest lecture in Zentner's class. During his presentation, he experienced a mild heart attack. Not understanding the symptoms, and not appreciating the gravity of the situation, he shrugged it off and finished the lecture. Later that evening, after returning to his hotel room, he suffered a second, near-fatal attack. He was barely able to phone Zentner, who came to the hotel and rushed him to the hospital. On the way, Porter lost consciousness. He survived, but was very ill and had to remain in Calgary General Hospital for nearly a month.[93]

After learning about the attack from Zentner, and hoping to relieve her husband's concerns about the book, Marion tried to get some closure on the manuscript before she left to join him in Calgary. She contacted their friend, Bernard Ostry, then associate secretary-treasurer of the SSRCC, and asked him to put pressure on Meisel to finish reading the manuscript.[94] As well, she wrote to Meisel directly, enclosing two chapters John had finished just before leaving for Calgary and urging him to hurry the book along:

> I would appreciate it very much if you could read the book, express an opinion, and arrange a publisher. As you can imagine, the book is the culmination of ten years of hard work for John and it is something he feels intensely concerned about. It would be a great load off his mind if he knew that publication was in sight ... I'm sure I don't have to impress on you the urgency of this. You have written books and you know how deeply involved with them one becomes.[95]

In his reply, Meisel expressed concern about Porter's health and was pleased to be able to tell her that he had nearly finished reading the ten chapters John had sent previously. While he described the materials as 'tremendously important and exciting,' he declined to provide a detailed assessment until he had read the final chapters. As well, he explained that it was pointless to try to make arrangements with a publisher until the draft was completed. That said, he also told her that he expected to finalize publication arrangements for the entire series with the University of Toronto Press the following week. How quickly the book would appear after Porter finished the manuscript would depend not just on the publication process at the press but also on the extensiveness of the revisions requested by readers.[96] Ostry wrote with similarly cautionary advice. The book would eventually appear, he told her, but not until after an inevitably long and sometimes frustrating process that was not likely to conclude for many months.[97]

When Marion arrived in Calgary and told John what had transpired with Meisel and Ostry, she was surprised to find that he 'was not the least bit interested.' He was just trying to get well, she said, and 'didn't even want to think about *The Vertical Mosaic*.'[98] Back in Kingston, Meisel finished reading the manuscript, minus the yet-to-be-written last chapter, and in early February sent Marion his reactions: 'I have now finished reading the available manuscript ... I am greatly impressed by it. I like not only the wealth of evidence collected in it, but also the fact that John has taken a [political] position which gives the whole narrative a vigour and urgency rarely found in the writings of Canadian academics.' He noted that he had some concerns – all relatively minor save for its length – and informed her that despite his best efforts he had not yet finalized a contract with the University of Toronto Press for the decision-making series.[99]

By late February, John had recovered sufficiently that the Porters could return to Ottawa and as the winter of 1962–3 ebbed, John convalesced. In early spring, he resumed work on *The Vertical Mosaic* but overdid it and, in May, experienced a second heart attack. It was less severe than the first but enough to force him to spend more time in the hospital.[100] Meisel found out and wrote to him, trying to convince him to worry less about the release date of the book. Even a difference of several months, said Meisel, would not make a difference: 'The book is certain to be a classic ... It is going to be of lasting value ... [T]he important thing is your health and in the long run your ability to carry on this work even further.'[101] Porter did not recover sufficiently to resume his former pace of work until summer's end, so it was not until the autumn of 1963 that he could submit the completed manuscript to Meisel and the University of Toronto Press. In preparing the revised manuscript, Porter had a second reviewer's comments to bear in mind. In the spring of 1963, Meisel had asked S.D. Clark to read the draft.

Clark's reading of the manuscript differed radically from Meisel's. Indeed, his review was sufficiently negative that it raised the possibility Porter would have to undertake extensive, fundamental revisions.[102] He began by pronouncing the book 'too long' and arguing that the two parts of the manuscript did not hang together:

> What John has done is write (though in neither case finish) two books ...
> In John's mind what is said about elites may seem closely related to what
> is said about social stratification. But to the reader there seems no relation-
> ship between the two. There are a few incidental references back but they
> have the appearance of having been added. Nothing that is said about
> elites depends on what is said about social stratification. As it stands now,
> certainly, I see no reason for putting the two sections together in one book.

Despite this negative assessment, Clark noted that he liked the first part of the manuscript and thought it nearly ready for publication: 'I have to confess to a much greater interest in and liking for the study on social stratification. I think John has here the substance of a very excellent sociological study ... It would be a must for ... any course in Canadian society.' However, unlike Meisel, who liked Porter's leftist political critique of Canadian capitalism and democracy, Clark was leery of Porter's 'strong socialist bias.' He acknowledged that Porter's critique of the social class–educational opportunity nexus constituted a welcome 'indictment of Canadian society and in particular ... the Canadian educational system' but regarded Porter's value-laden analysis as problematic. Despite these reservations, he then embarked on a raiding mission, trying to get Porter and Meisel to publish the first half of the manuscript in a series he was editing for the University of Toronto Press. The stratification study 'would not fit into your decision-making series,' he wrote to Meisel, 'but would put the sociology series on the map ... I would be prepared to accept it as part of this series with very little in the way of changes if John was reluctant to spend more time on it.'[103]

By comparison, Clark was not impressed with the second part of the book – the elite studies chapters. He had two concerns. One problem was his personal view of what constituted the appropriate subject matter of sociology. He confessed that Porter's study of Canada's elites was not his 'cup of tea,' in part because he considered it 'less strictly a sociological study' than the first section. His second criticism was even more damning. In his view, the second part of the manuscript was little more than 'a very long essay on Canadian society,' many of the claims in which were only weakly substantiated by the data. He argued that while the first seven chapters, on stratification, were somewhat 'speculative,' he nonetheless found them persuasive because they were based on 'an impressive body of data.' Not so the second half of the manuscript. Here, Clark charged, 'the empirical data is not very convincing.' His verdict? 'I think John can make his reputation as a sociologist with the study on stratification; not on this study.'[104] 'When John turns to elites,' Clark said, 'he lets himself go ... [W]hat is said goes far beyond the data.'[105] And once again Clark expressed a dislike for Porter's choice of a value-laden style of analysis. In the discussion of elites, he argued, Porter's 'socialist bias gives way to an NDP bias.'[106] It is fortunate that Meisel did not give undue weight to Clark's assessment. Had Clark been the editor of the decision-making series, *The Vertical Mosaic* might never have got into print in its now iconic form. In any case, however much Clark's preliminary assessment differed from the response Porter's book would soon provoke in Canada's social science community, it is worth noting that he did highlight the significance of Porter's value stance and he did surmise correctly that the book would be politically controversial: 'There has been nothing written in the social sciences in Canada as provocative as this study. It must not be judged as a work of scientific sociology. If it is, it will never get published ... It is a brave piece and one which is certainly not going to go unnoticed.'[107]

The only other person to read the entire manuscript before the University of Toronto Press took it in hand was Scott Gordon. Gordon, too, appreciated the provocative nature of the manuscript, but came to a very different conclusion from Clark regarding the merits of the book. 'I was a-bed with a slipped disc when [John] gave me the manuscript,' he said. 'I recall his coming to see me a few days later. I said to him: "John, you have not settled anything by this work." His face fell in disappointment, and then I added: "But you sure have *started* something!" I was rewarded with the broadest smile I had ever observed him to make.'[108]

In the end, Porter and Meisel ignored much of Clark's assessment. They briefly considered breaking the manuscript into two volumes, but soon rejected the prospect, deciding that Porter could handle any shortcomings with carefully targeted revisions.[109] Frances Halpenny, editor at the University of Toronto Press, played a pivotal role in this decision. Like Meisel, she thought the two parts of the book held together sufficiently to constitute a unity and did not see the manuscript as overly long.[110]

It was an enormous relief to have the draft finished and submitted, and Porter was well pleased when he received Meisel's highly positive response. Meisel did not regard the draft as flawless, but clearly saw it as a tremendous accomplishment: 'This is a monumental piece of work which is really first-class … It not only documents a great many things, but also takes a line which I think makes it much more exciting reading.'[111] The two parts needed to be better integrated and the final chapter needed to be strengthened, he said, but, otherwise, it needed only minor revisions. Talking retrospectively, three decades later, Meisel recalled that his very strong impression at the time was that John had 'run out of steam.' For the book to have maximum impact, he said, Porter needed to spend some time writing a 'big synthetic piece.' If he didn't, Meisel thought he would be 'short-changing himself.' He had written something that Meisel considered to be 'a really major work, but [had not] … in the end tied it together well enough … It was too fragmented; it was too much like … a series of papers. He had this grand design, but … too much energy [had gone] into each piece and not enough into the synthetic elements in it.'[112] Porter agreed and began the final round of revisions.

But all did not go well. Porter could be short-tempered and impatient – Blair Neatby referred to him as 'prickly' – and these features of his personality came to the fore more than once during the review and production process.[113] He first became angry when the Press took what he considered an inordinately long time to decide if they were going to publish the book. He then grew impatient at the slowness of the publication process, frustrated by the delay because he regarded the book as politically topical. He believed it had something important to say regarding 'debates which are going on about the nature of Canadian society' and wanted to be part of those debates. 'It would be absurd,' he wrote in late November 1963, 'if it were to lie around for a long period of time, as so many manuscripts obviously do, at the University of Toronto Press.'[114] Reflecting on these events many years later, Marion echoed her husband's view; the Press seemed to have no appreciation of the book's timeliness: 'They did not regard it as more topical or pressing than a history of the Ming dynasty.'[115] So frustrated did Porter become that at one point he threatened to publish the book elsewhere and, once again, Meisel had to intervene to smooth things over with the Press.[116] Then, as the rewriting process neared completion, Porter got into yet another disagreement, this time with Halpenny. She firmly believed that Porter would not be able to get the revisions done in time for the fall 1964 release date he desired and recommended spring 1965.[117] He got angry, but Halpenny turned out to be prescient. In order for the book to appear in the fall, Porter had to finish the revisions by February 1964. He could not do it.[118] In fact, he did not finish them until April 1964. Once they were done, Meisel re-read the manuscript. He wrote Porter with his reaction: 'This is, beyond question, one of the most important books to have been written in this country in a very long time. I cannot wait to see it all finished and congratulate you most warmly on what is a major achievement.'[119]

Interestingly, it was not until just a few months before the book went to press that Porter settled on a title. Over the years, he had referred to the manuscript by a variety of titles, including 'Class and Power in Canada: An Analysis of Social Structure.' However, in October 1964, Marion, Meisel and others persuaded him to opt for its now-iconic title, *The Vertical Mosaic.*[120]

7 *The Vertical Mosaic*: Canada as a Flawed Democracy

When *The Vertical Mosaic* came out, Porter presented it – and scholars and the media treated it – as if it were the first comprehensive snapshot of Canada's national structure of class and power. In one sense, that was true. No one had written anything as ambitious. Here was a detailed empirical portrait of long-standing class inequalities, combined with a rich description of the nation's highly unequal structure of power, all incorporated within a scathing, politically charged critique of the country's self-congratulatory image of itself as ethnically diverse, middle-class, egalitarian, and democratic.

Porter was well aware of the centrality to Canada of its complex ethnic make-up. His research had revealed significant, long-standing differences in the relative status of the English- and French-speaking populations of Canada, as well as between these two charter groups and other racial and ethnic groups. Indeed, they provided the idea for the book's title, *The Vertical Mosaic*. But while granting that ethnic politics, especially between French-speaking Quebeckers and the rest of the country, had long been among the most obvious centripetal forces in Canadian history, he assigned analytical priority to the phenomena of class and power. It was around these themes, not ethnicity, that he structured his book. He began by examining Canada's class structure.

History of the Study of Class in Canada, pre-1965

Porter knew that over the years French- and English-language scholars had examined aspects of social inequality in Canada, but he claimed that Canadian academics had largely ignored the study of social class. 'The idea of class differences,' he wrote, 'has scarcely entered into the stream of Canadian academic writing.'[1] In his view two factors, one ideological, one structural, explained this serious oversight. Historically, he argued, most Canadians had accepted the liberal ideological claim that 'their society ... has no classes.' They believed that 'Canadians are all relatively equal in their possessions, in the amount of money they earn, and in the opportunities which they ... have to get on in the world.'[2] Canadian intellectuals were not immune. They, too, had bought in to this persistent 'image' of Canada. They knew that some people were rich and some poor but, as most had come from the middle class, they tended to generalize from their own life experiences, 'projecting' a middle-class image of the country into their descriptions and analyses of Canadian society.[3]

Given the prevalence of this egalitarian self-image, and that *The Vertical Mosaic* came out during a two-decade-long economic boom, it is easy to understand why Porter's book had such a tremendous impact. Not only did it fill a perceived gap in the social scientific literature about Canada but it challenged this middle-class image in highly politicized language intended to provoke debate about equality, one of the values that Canadians allegedly held dear. Porter excused 'ordinary Canadians' for buying in to liberal ideological pronouncements about equality of opportunity, but he had no such patience for intellectuals. They should have known better and the book was meant to constitute a stinging critique of the country's scholarly conventional wisdom about itself.

The charge that Canadian social scientists had ignored the phenomena of class and power was generally accurate. Prior to 1965, the English-language Canadian scholarly community had paid very little attention to class, certainly less than its importance warranted.[4] But the area was not the complete blind spot Porter claimed. As early as the 1890s, members of the English-language Canadian intellectual community – sociologists, historians, economists, journalists, social activists, some university based, some outside the academy – had documented class inequalities and analysed class relations, often in considerable detail.[5] Curiously, given the thoroughness of his research, Porter either did not know about or chose to ignore all but a few of these studies, especially those written before 1950. And he often mentioned the post-1950 ones only in passing.

It is understandable, if unfortunate, that Porter did not make much use of at least some of these pre-1950s studies, for many of them provided data at the community level about objective dimensions or indicators of class inequality: lifestyle, expenditure patterns, housing, and so forth. Given the paucity of community-level studies done between 1950 and 1965, they might reasonably have been put to more good use than they were.[6] That said, not much was lost as a consequence. In the grand scheme of things, with one exception, none of the pre-1950 studies would have altered either his presentation of the materials or his findings about class in Canada in the mid-1960s.

The exception is Leonard Marsh's *Canadians In and Out of Work*, published 1940, a major but largely unappreciated study of Canada's national class structure that predates *The Vertical Mosaic* by over two decades.[7] Marsh was an economist/sociologist who, like Porter, studied at the LSE. While there, he came under the influence of Fabianism and other socialist and left-liberal doctrines, including the New Liberalism. During the late 1920s, he worked with H. Llewellyn Smith and William Beveridge on the *New Survey of London Life and Labour*, published 1930.[8] In 1930, newly minted MA in hand, he was hired as the research director of the McGill Social Science Research Project and, after settling in, became deeply involved in the League for Social Reconstruction. He soon made a name for himself and with other prominent Fabians contributed to *Social Planning for Canada* in 1935.[9] He is widely known and respected as the author of the 1943 *Report on Social Security for Canada*, the foundation of much of Canada's welfare state.[10] However, his contributions in the field of social security and the welfare state have overshadowed another of his major accomplishments: *Canadians In and Out of Work*.

The first purpose of the volume, researched during the Depression, was to describe the unemployment situation across Canada. From the outset, Marsh realized that the 1931 Census data on 'vocational levels' that he was using to describe patterns of employment and unemployment could be drawn on to outline in bold strokes the character of Canada's national class structure.[11] Marsh began his analysis by outlining the occupational structure of Canada according to 'skill' and 'status' levels, arguing there were eleven 'occupational status classes,' ranging from proprietary-managerial at the top to unskilled labour at the bottom (with two 'parallel' categories for farmers and farm labourers).[12] After outlining regional variations in these occupational class divisions, he outlined the 'ethnic base' of Canada's population, and – foreshadowing Porter directly – employed the term 'the Canadian mosaic' to describe the overlap between class and ethnic inequalities.[13] He concluded that in Canada 'economic class differences' were at least as obtrusive as 'racio-cultural' differences and described Canada as a place where 'class lines have hardened and mobility has dwindled.'[14]

The most noteworthy parts of the book – at least in terms of their potential relevance to Porter's project – dealt with income distribution and social classes. Like Porter a quarter-century later, Marsh reported that the 'average Canadian' was not as well off as people generally believed. Just over half of non-farm families were able to attain the minimum living income 'from the earnings of the breadwinner alone.' They needed the income earned by other family members to stay above subsistence.[15] Farm families, which made up one-third of the population, were no better off. Using American data as a proxy, Marsh suggested that nearly half of Canada's farmers would have a revenue insufficient for a reasonable living standard. Indeed, at least one in five had 'no certainty of a bare living income.'[16] To conclude his analysis, Marsh grouped Canadians into four major social classes: the 'well-to-do,' the 'middle classes,' the 'working classes,' and 'farm classes.'[17] The well-to-do comprised a very small group of especially wealthy families that wielded 'social and economic influence' as well as 'power ... in the spheres of production and finance, law and politics, [and] economic and social regulation' out of all proportion to its size.[18] The middle class was smaller than people assumed. On the basis of income and standard of living, Marsh argued, only about 25 per cent of Canadian families could be reasonably so designated.[19] Most Canadian families fell into either the working classes (43 per cent) or the farming classes (31 per cent), and many of those lived in poverty – or close to it.[20]

Like *The Vertical Mosaic* a generation later, *Canadians In and Out of Work* reported extensive empirical data that decimated the image of Canada as a classless or middle-class society.[21] Four decades later, in assessing the contribution his book had made, Marsh wrote that *Canadians In and Out of Work* clearly 'anticipat[ed] ... The Vertical Mosaic.' Indeed, as far as he was concerned, it was a pathbreaking effort, 'the first comprehensive presentation of income, employment and educational differences – in effect the social class structure – worked out quantitatively for Canada.'[22] Though Marsh does not make the point, it is worth noting that it was methodologically innovative as well. Unlike the American approach to class, which focused on *community-level* status rankings based on the *subjective* assessments of residents, Marsh employed *objective* quantitative data about *national* patterns of class structure (income, occupation, and educational opportunity). In this regard, it presaged Porter's work by a quarter-century and deserves more credit than it has heretofore received. That said, Marsh's book is no match for *The Vertical Mosaic*. Its treatment of class themes was less comprehensive and nuanced, and it lacked a detailed discussion of elites and power. As a consequence, it also lacked the rich, provocative discussion of the class-power dynamic that made *The Vertical Mosaic* such a noteworthy volume. Nonetheless, for its time, *Canadians In and Out of Work* marked a remarkable advance in the study of class in Canadian sociology. Indeed, in some respects Marsh's book, not Porter's, constitutes the first study of Canada's national class structure. As historian Michiel Horn put it, 'Contrary to what some uninformed people still think, John Porter *did not* pioneer the scholarly study of social class in this country.'[23] Leonard Marsh did.

Curiously, Porter failed to draw on it in *The Vertical Mosaic*, even though he knew about it.[24] This is unfortunate for Marsh's volume contains data about many aspects of structured inequality in the 1930s that would have proved useful as a point of historical comparison for his analysis of class structure in the 1960s.

As interesting as a lot of the pre-1950 literature was, Porter focused almost all his attention on later materials. The bulk of it came from government agencies: the Dominion Bureau of Statistics, the Department of Revenue, the Department of Labour, and so on. He drew his picture of Canada's class structure in this way, using statistics regarding income and various objective measures of lifestyle provided by government agencies, for three reasons. First, he had available to him no other sources of detailed, contemporary data about the objective structure of classes in Canada. Second, this statistical approach was then dominant in mainstream American sociology and he was eager to generate some comparative data and to attract the attention of key players in American sociology. Third, no studies using subjective methods had been done in Canada. In particular, the Canadian literature lacked studies of community class structure and as Porter knew well, no one had yet carried out a national-level study of the subjective rankings of occupational prestige.[25] Porter regarded this last-mentioned lacuna as especially unfortunate.[26] Such studies had been carried out in several countries, including England and the United States, and had proved extremely useful as an indicator of people's collective, subjective sense of the national structure of class in their respective countries. Especially noteworthy was that there appeared to be tremendous consistency in occupational rankings across countries. Porter and his colleague Peter Pineo would fill this gap in the Canadian sociological literature by 1967, but at the time Porter prepared his account of Canada's class structure in *The Vertical Mosaic* the only other major piece of related research Porter had to draw on was a study by his friend, Bernard Blishen, 'The Construction and Use of an Occupational Class Scale.' That work provided another objective index of Canada's class structure. Some years earlier, Blishen had developed a scale for ranking occupations using two objective measures: average years of education and average income. He created a combined score from these two measures and then used it to place 343 occupations into seven rank-order categories. His findings, reported in 1958, revealed a very strong correlation between these rankings and those produced by the method of subjective occupational prestige rankings employed by the National Opinion Research Center in Chicago.[27]

Porter on Class: Shattering the Middle-Class Myth

Part 1 of *The Vertical Mosaic* – six chapters – dealt with the structure of class. Here Porter outlined his theoretical conception of class, provided a historical and conceptual analysis of immigration and emigration, and documented the respective positions in the occupational structure of Canada's various ethnic groups. As well, he examined the distribution of rewards and opportunities in Canada using five variables: income and wealth, lifestyle, occupational stratification, educational attainment, and educational opportunity.

Income and Wealth Stratification

In looking at social class, Porter distinguished between income and wealth. Income refers to annual individual earnings, and wealth refers to individual total financial resources (property, stock, and so forth). For the first, he used the Department of National Revenue's taxation statistics on the incomes of individual Canadians. He realized this was not an optimal strategy for assigning people to social classes – family incomes would have been a better measure – but concluded that 'the profile of class derived from tax statistics ... is not likely to be very far wrong.'[28] These data revealed that – then as now – income was very unequally distributed and that the statistical middle majority of the population was much less affluent than suggested by the country's image of itself as a middle-class nation. Porter specified $8,000 as the dividing line between the 'real middle class' and everyone else below.

Less than 4 per cent of taxpayers made that much. In fact, in 1955, 75 per cent of individuals with taxable incomes made less than half that: $4,000.[29]

Porter complemented his discussion of earned income with an analysis of unearned income from investments, trust funds, and the like. This not only gave a better sense of total annual income but also offered a glimpse of the distribution of wealth, which is, of course, a much better indicator of class inequality than annual earned income. His data revealed that, as he put it, Canada was not the home of 'people's capitalism.' It had neither 'a large middle-level investing class' nor a 'fragmented system of stock ownership.'[30] Indeed, wealth in the form of capital rested in very few hands and thus most unearned income went to a very small group of 2,380 Canadians – 'the very rich or ... their representatives'[31] – all with incomes over $50,000.[32] This group, which made up only one one-hundredth of 1 per cent of Canadians, nonetheless 'received one-quarter of all the dividend income taken in by Canadian residents.'[33] Overall, Porter wrote, 'the very rich are a very small group' and 'there is a big gap, as far as money income is concerned, between the very rich and the moderately rich.'[34]

Porter supplemented his analysis of taxation data with information drawn from three surveys done by the Dominion Bureau of Statistics in the mid-to-late 1950s. The first examined the incomes of non-farm families, the second analysed expenditure patterns of families living in large urban centres and having incomes between $2,000 and $6,500 per year, and the third documented the distribution of income among non-farm individuals.[35] All three provided supplementary data about amounts and sources of income and types of housing and essentially confirmed Porter's other findings.

Patterns and Styles of Living

It is widely understood that income and wealth are the two major influences on lifestyle or standard of living. Porter's examination of the distribution of 'consumer durables'[36] and the availability of 'education, ... health services, family privacy, and leisure' revealed that only about one in ten Canadian families could afford what most people regarded as the 'standard package' that constituted a middle-class lifestyle.[37] In making this claim, he was aware that most Canadians owned many consumer items and basic amenities. For example, 'more than 90 per cent of households had electric refrigerators and radios; more than 80 per cent had electric washers, telephones, and television sets; and 75 per cent had automobiles and vacuum cleaners.'[38] As well, about three-quarters of Canadian families lived in separate, as opposed to shared, dwellings, and about 90 per cent of these dwellings had 'modern conveniences, such as hot and cold water piped inside, flush toilets, and baths or showers.'[39] One conspicuous element of this standard package was the automobile. At the time, just over half of Canadian families and unattached individuals owned a car.[40] Beyond this, however, Porter argued that 'in the mid-twentieth century ... such simple criteria as adequate calorific intake, a place of shelter, and sufficient clothing for warmth are not satisfactory to establish the boundary of the underprivileged.'[41] Nor did the possession of such amenities say anything about their condition – so that, for example, housing could be crowded, substandard, unsafe, and so forth. Beyond this clutch of possessions, he stated, 'the standard package begins to thin out' because patterns and styles of living were determined by income and wealth.[42]

As part of his discussion of class lifestyles, in particular when he articulated what he described as a fundamental difference between the statistical 'middle majority' of Canadian society and the 'real middle class,' he distinguished between them not just on the basis of 'the ownership of gadgetry' but also on the basis of what he referred to as 'the consumption of a different set of values.'[43] The term 'values,' as he used it, had two unspecified but interrelated meanings. In the one instance, Porter used the term 'values' to signify that the 'real' middle class had more discriminating taste or *held* different values. By extension, however, he also meant that the real middle class *consumed* both different and 'better' commodities ('values,' in that sense).

On this count, the statistical middle majority missed out because of a complex interdependence between low income and what he regarded as a lack of cultural sophistication. Different consumption patterns came about, Porter argued, not just because people *held* different values but also because they had different financial abilities to *realize* them. In his view, the children of the true middle class were 'exposed much more than children in classes below them to the general cultural heritage of their society. They will be in better health ... they will be sent to nursery school ... they will be encouraged to participate in Cubs, Boy Scouts and the Y.M.C.A. (or the feminine counterparts) ... [and] they will be sent to the academic high school rather than the commercial or technical one ... These children most probably will go to university.'[44] Porter tied this cultural definition of the real middle class to his statistically constructed income classes by arguing that only the former could afford to live this way:

> To provide this pattern of living, centred in a separate dwelling and administered by a mother who does not work outside of the home for pay, and to provide it during the child-rearing years would require an income far above the average. It is doubtful that without the aid of gifts or inheritance that it could be achieved on less than $8,000 a year – an income level which in the middle 1950's included at the most no more than about 10 per cent of Canadian families.[45]

Certainly, families with incomes less than $4,000 – namely 54 per cent of all Canadian families in 1955 – could not begin to afford this way of life. For Porter, the fact that only one in ten Canadian families could afford a middle-class lifestyle discredited the 'myth of affluence' that pervaded Canadian culture. Clearly revealing his New Liberal beliefs, he concluded his discussion of wealth and income by arguing that the market would never solve this problem on its own. Only if government used its power to redistribute income could it come to pass; there was no market-based 'built-in equalizing force [that would act] as a natural law' to do so as a matter of course.[46]

Occupational Stratification

Porter began his discussion of the occupational class structure by disputing the accuracy of a lingering and nostalgic image many Canadians held of their country as a rural, frontier society. However accurate it might once have been, he said, by the mid-twentieth century, it did not remotely reflect the reality of Canadian life. Most Canadians now lived in cities and worked not as farmers, miners, loggers, or fishers but in factories, offices, and stores. This change was evident in the shape of the occupational class structure. In the early part of the century, it had resembled a 'pyramid' because most Canadians worked in unskilled or semi-skilled manual occupations. By 1960, however, the unskilled base of the occupational pyramid had contracted and the middle levels had widened as the economy produced more white-collar, non-manual, service-sector jobs with the result that the pyramid had become a 'beehive' shape.[47] As the primary sector of the economy shrank and the secondary and tertiary sectors grew, the technical demands of many jobs changed, partly as a consequence of developments in workplace technology.[48] By 1960, over 20 per cent of Canada's workforce – mostly blue-collar but some white-collar as well – toiled in jobs affected by what Porter referred to as 'downward structural mobility.' Their jobs had less occupational status, less job security, and fewer prospects for upward mobility than the equivalent job of a quarter- or half-century earlier.[49] Jobs that retained or developed high occupational status were characterized by high educational requirements. Returning to a theme he had discussed with relation to lifestyle, Porter noted that 'high class position as measured by occupation' influenced one's capacity and desire to partake of the finer things in life. People with little education not only worked at less prestigious jobs and earned less money than educated people but, as a consequence, could not enjoy the 'cultural achievements of ... society' to the same degree as those who were better educated and wealthier.[50] This situation, Porter argued strongly, needed to be redressed. To do so would require a much greater societal investment in accessible postsecondary education.

Educational Stratification/Attainment

Porter began his analysis of the distribution of educational attainment by lamenting the general lack of formal education held by most Canadians. The Canadian population had been poorly educated when the country entered the post-World War II industrial boom, he said, and a decade and a half later the figures had not improved much.[51] Only one in ten Canadian males aged sixteen to sixty-five had some postsecondary education and nearly half had only elementary school education.[52] This was unfortunate and alarming because the link between education and occupation – then as now – was clear. The more education one had, the better the occupational prospects. A similar relationship existed between educational attainment and income. The longer people stayed in school, the more money they were likely to make once they entered the job market.[53] Porter hammered the point home by again drawing on Blishen's research.[54] He compared the profile of the class structure he had generated based on taxation statistics with the profile generated by Blishen's seven hierarchical occupational rankings based on education and income and found them similar.[55] He did so in order to show that unlike in an earlier period, when a man could go from bank teller to president, most Canadians would not be able to overcome an inadequate education through work experience. The idea that someone could do so was nothing more than a 'persistent myth.'[56] Hard work might allow a person to achieve some measure of upward mobility, but the distance most individuals would travel up the class structure was limited.[57]

It was not just educational *attainment* that was important. Porter noted that even if individuals attained different levels of education, and these translated into different occupations that received substantially different incomes, this need not doom those born into the lower echelons of the Canadian class structure – *if* they had an equal *opportunity* to get a good education.

Educational Opportunity

Porter believed above all that it was the class-based structure of educational opportunity in Canada that prevented it from becoming a modern and democratic industrial nation. He devoted a chapter of *The Vertical Mosaic* to a discussion of the reciprocal effects of industrialization, class structure, education, and egalitarian ideology. His claim was straightforward: 'Educational systems and industrialization have grown together,' and affect each other, and Canada's economic progress was being severely hampered by the generally low level of education its citizens had achieved.[58] Low educational attainment resulted, in turn, from class-based differences in educational opportunity. Far too few children from lower-class families went far enough in school.

Two interrelated sets of factors – one social, the other psychological – were to blame. On the social, or structural, side, he argued, income, wealth, family size, gender, religion, and ethnicity constituted formidable barriers to equal educational opportunity for those at the lower levels of the stratification system.[59] These structural barriers produced psychological barriers. Like his contemporary, American anthropologist Oscar Lewis, Porter claimed there existed a 'culture of poverty' that created intergenerational inequalities in educational attainment.[60] More specifically, he argued that those living in economically impoverished environments often exhibited an indifference to education.[61] Certainly, this is what the data in *The Vertical Mosaic* showed. In 1961, only about 60 per cent of children fifteen to nineteen years old were still in school.[62] Dropout rates for high school students were highest among those at the bottom of Blishen's occupational scale (65 per cent) and lowest for those at the top (29 per cent).[63] This then manifested itself in the make-up of the university population. Children from higher income and occupational categories were much more likely to get to university.[64] Using Blishen's seven-level occupational class scale and the 1951 census data, Porter showed that while only one in eight male heads of family had an occupation in one of the two highest-ranked categories, nearly half of university students came from these groups. By contrast, four in ten male heads of family had an occupation in one of the two lowest-ranked categories, but only one in nine university students came from such families.[65] These differences, Porter stated firmly, were produced by social factors, not genetic ones:

> Economic and social factors set the boundaries within which, at the psychological level, values and attitudes are formed. These values and attitudes become transmitted from generation to generation and help preserve the various social milieux of class ... The lower-class family does not value education so highly because in part it is a privilege beyond their horizons of opportunity, and at the same time, lacking education themselves, they fail to appreciate its value and to encourage their children.[66]

As well as documenting the clear class bias in educational attainment, he pointed to the yawning gap between Canada's liberal meritocratic ideology and the reality of educational opportunity. 'The egalitarian ideology,' according to which individuals 'move through the hierarchy of skill classes according to their inclinations and abilities' was comforting to the successful but was nothing more than a cruel illusion.[67] The structure of class – inequalities of income and wealth, related in turn to differences in religion, ethnicity, region, and so on – produced huge disparities in educational opportunity.

As an alternative to the existing, inequitable, class-based system, he proposed a more meritocratic model. Access to education should be determined not by capacity to pay (class background) but by ability. Such a system would have two benefits. First, establishing a meritocracy would contribute to 'the democratic ideal' by providing all individuals with an equal opportunity to 'develop their talents and make their contribution to the social good.' 'Now, more than ever,' he urged, 'education means opportunity.' Second, a meritocracy would have societal benefits. The occupational structure would reflect a more rational allocation of ability, Porter asserted, because the best people would rise to the top regardless of their class background:[68]

> No society in the modern period can afford to ignore the ability which lies in the lower social strata. Whatever may be said about average intelligence

and social class the fact remains that in absolute numbers there is more of the highly intelligent in lower classes than in the higher. If the principles of efficiency and equality are to be upheld, Canada must be prepared to put a great deal more money into education and educational research than it has up to the 1960's ... Without such policies, intergenerational continuity of class will remain [and] mobility deprivation will continue.[69]

Class and Ethnicity

Porter devoted an entire chapter of *The Vertical Mosaic* to the relationship between class and ethnicity. He began by describing Canada as a country with two 'charter groups' – French and British – who, since before Confederation, had been unequal.[70] This was true in two senses. The British charter group (English, Scottish, Irish) had always been larger than the French. In 1961, the figures were 44 per cent and 30 per cent of the Canadian population, respectively. Those from non-charter ethnic backgrounds made up the rest.[71] Here, then, was one of the origins of Porter's about-to-be-famous phrase: Canada as a 'vertical mosaic.'[72] But it was not just that the unequal ethnic *composition* of Canada's population had remained relatively stable over the period 1901–61 but also that their *respective positions* in the nation's class structure – 'the vertical arrangement of Canada's mosaic' – had changed little.[73] Porter discussed this in terms of what he referred to as 'structural assimilation,' i.e., the degree to which ethnic groups had been able to integrate themselves into the various institutional structures of society. If complete structural assimilation had occurred, he said, then 'ethnic origin [would not be a] relevant attribute in the allocation of people to positions in the social system or in the distribution of rights.'[74] Members of an ethnic group would be found scattered through the social structure, including the occupational and class structures, in direct proportion to their numbers. If 5 per cent of Canadians were teachers, then 5 per cent of any ethnic group would be teachers. If 8 per cent of Canadians were middle class, then 8 per cent of any ethnic group would be middle class.[75] But Porter's data showed no such thing. He had no data about the distribution of income by ethnicity, but he did have data on occupational stratification. They revealed that the ethnic tiles in the Canadian mosaic had been stacked one on top of another in a clear hierarchy – and then more or less glued into place. From 1931 to 1961, Canadians of British origin (along with Jews) clustered closer to the top of the hierarchy. Other ethnic groups were scattered along the hierarchy, northern Europeans (Germans, Scandinavians, Dutch) and French closer to the top and southern and eastern Europeans (Italians, Poles, Ukrainians) closer to the bottom. Asians and Native Canadians were at the bottom.[76] Citing Blishen's findings, Porter noted, 'The proportion of British in each class generally increases from the lowest to the highest class whereas the reverse is true for the French. The Jewish group follows a pattern similar to that of the British whereas all other origins follow the French pattern.'[77]

In Porter's view, this long-standing rank ordering of ethnic groups was a consequence of a 'reciprocal relationship between ethnicity and social class.' The dominant British ethnic group had initially appropriated the topmost occupations for itself and forced other ethnic groups to struggle to gain access to less preferred positions. Subordinate ethnic groups were forced to accept this assignment of occupational roles and opportunities and the hierarchy slowly calcified. When the government allowed immigrants into the country, they usually had to accept a low 'entrance status,' allowing them access only to less preferred occupations. Like other immigrant groups that had preceded them, they were subject to intense pressure to assimilate to the dominant anglophone culture. Immigrant groups might improve on their entrance status over time, sometimes by forcing more recent immigrants to assume their former occupational niche, but some immigrant groups became locked in positions near the bottom of the occupational class hierarchy.[78] The vertical mosaic crystallized.

Porter's Theory of Class

Porter was incensed, though not surprised, by what he found. Indeed, he had set out with a political goal in mind. According to his New Liberal views, Canada could and should be more egalitarian and democratic, but this could happen only if class barriers to equality of opportunity were eliminated. The first step in removing these impediments was to prove beyond any doubt that such barriers existed. *The Vertical Mosaic* achieved this purpose admirably, presenting systematic, compelling evidence about various aspects of class inequality showing unequivocally that Canada was not the egalitarian, middle-class society it thought itself to be. Porter then drew on this body of data to develop a political-theoretical critique of class inequality in Canada.

The political-theoretical framework he developed came mostly from mainstream American sociology. He did not abandon his European roots, as his references to Weber, Durkheim, Freud, and the elite theorists make clear, and he certainly did not abandon his Hobhousian New Liberal views, but at this point in his career, the language he used – postcapitalism, postindustrialism, the end of ideology, functionalism – reflected more than anything else the conventional wisdom of mainstream American sociology. A particularly important figure was Harvard sociologist Daniel Bell.

According to Bell and others, the type of capitalism excoriated by Marx in the nineteenth century had long since disappeared, superseded by 'postcapitalism,'[79] a society in which the means of production remained in private hands but 'structural changes' restricted the economic, social, and political power of the capitalist class.[80] A new class of managers and technocrats, rather than owners, now controlled the production process at the level of the individual firm.[81] More generally, technical experts of various kinds combined with owners to hold the reins of economic power at the level of the national economy. In a major shift since the nineteenth century, the primary source of power in postcapitalist society was no longer capital but various of forms of expertise or knowledge, technical or scientific knowledge in particular. The state took on an expanded role as well, using the technical expertise of the new 'knowledge society' to plan and coordinate economic and other activities and to develop and implement labour and welfare state legislation intended to improve home and working life for everyone.[82]

In Bell's version of the theory, postcapitalism was tied to 'postindustrialism.' According to this theory, the economy was no longer based on industrial production. Instead, the heart of the economy rested in the service sector, where the bulk of the workforce – most working in business and government – was engaged in semi-skilled and skilled labour, often using advanced technology. In part because of the increasingly central role of technology, the division of labour had become more complicated. These two changes had combined to transform the shape of the occupational structure from a pyramid to a beehive, as I noted above.[83] But it was not just the *shape* of the class structure that had changed; the very *nature* of the economic classes that walked the streets of modern industrial societies had been transformed.

The working class had become increasingly differentiated and stratified, a technical/managerial class had grown in size and influence, and societal institutions – government, the civil service, the educational system, the mass media, unions – had become more specialized and autonomous, developing distinctive sources of power and authority that they used to carry out their specialized functions.[84] Porter realized that capital was 'a smaller and probably more cohesive group – an elite within the private sector of the economy' with better administrative means of command at its disposal than ever, and that the managerial revolution had proceeded less far in Canada.[85] Nonetheless, he held fast to the broad claims of the postcapitalist and postindustrial arguments. Early in *The Vertical Mosaic*, he stated bluntly that the capitalism Marx had written about had 'passed out of existence.'[86] Citizens of Western liberal democracies now lived in a 'post-Marxian industrial world' with all the features of a postcapitalist society. Canada was a good example.

The theoretical conception of class Porter employed in *The Vertical Mosaic* derived from this postindustrial, postcapitalist snapshot of the new economy, and the methodological approach he used reflected, in turn, that theoretical choice. If capitalism in the Marxist sense had passed out of existence, so too had the 'real' classes of Marx's analysis. In Marx's view, classes had been constituted in and through their relationship to the means of production. In Porter's view, this conception of class was long out of date: 'In the nineteenth century it may have been the case that two groups classified by the criterion of owning or not owning property were sociological groups, but in the present day such classes are statistical categories and nothing more.'[87] Porter conceded that the new postcapitalist economic system continued to exhibit a degree of class inequality, but classes were purely nominal entities 'artificially created by social investigators' using *objective* criteria such as income, occupation, property ownership and education and *subjective* measures such as 'class reputation' and 'occupational prestige.'[88] This theoretical and methodological approach, typical of American *stratification* research of the time, drew at least part of its inspiration from the work of Max Weber.[89] Following Weber's logic, Porter argued that classes had their origins in 'economic processes and economic differences' and that economic classes based on income, education, lifestyle, and so forth were 'primary determinants' of individuals' 'life chances.'[90] And again drawing on Weber, Porter supplemented his discussion of economic class inequality with a discussion of the nature and role of status 'communities' in Canada, especially among elites, and analysed the structure of power using control of institutions and political 'parties' (in Weber's sense) as a central feature of the book.

The classes Porter created by the use of this Weberian theoretical-methodological approach differed from those described in Marxist political economy in another regard. Following the logic of Bell's theory about 'the end of ideology,' Porter argued that classes, or at least the working class, lacked 'a sense of identity,' 'common values and traditions,' and 'awareness of unity and common purpose.'[91] For the upper and middle classes this was not especially significant; they were generally well off and thus satisfied with the status quo. But for the working class, which might have benefited from a greater sense of collective fate, purpose, and identity, the result was consequential, even tragic. In the new, postcapitalist world, it had become too differentiated, too apathetic, too disorganized, and too bound to the interests of employers to develop any sense of collective identity or to engage in revolutionary ideological or political activity.[92] The class struggle had limped to a halt.

The one fly in the ointment in Porter's description was the wealthiest members of the owning class, for its situation less obviously contradicted Marx's argument. According to American postcapitalist theorists, ownership and management functions had become separated to some degree during the managerial revolution.[93] The owner-managers who constituted the 'bourgeois class of Marxian theory' had been replaced by 'professional and salaried managers' who ran 'the internal machinery of ... modern corporations.'[94] However, Porter's data revealed that in Canada capital had not gone through this process of 'decomposition.'[95] In fact, just the opposite; economic power had become more concentrated over the course of the twentieth century and managers had not usurped the power of owners.[96] For reasons peculiar to the Canadian case, Porter said, its economic elite was more powerful than those in other countries.[97] Nonetheless, he maintained that concurrent changes in other institutions had prevented capital from becoming a 'master class' in Marx's sense of the term.[98] Most important – and here his analysis of class in the first part of the book began to slide into his analysis of power in the second – he argued that the major institutional subsystems of modern society had become increasingly differentiated and functionally specialized. As part of this process, each had developed institutionally discrete sources of power and spheres of influence that enabled them to maintain their autonomy in the face of corporate power. Leaders of the corporate world had to share power with leaders of other institutional sectors.[99] In Canada, conflict occurred not between a powerful bourgeoisie and a powerless proletariat – the 'ins' and 'outs' of classical Marxist theory – but among elites, all of whom were numbered among the ins.[100]

Porter on Power

Elites Rule

Porter's treatment of class was detailed, but more detailed still was his analysis of power, which took up two-thirds of the text. The analysis employed two complementary strategies, one focused at the societal level, the other concerned with power held by influential individuals.

At the societal level, he was interested in the distribution of power across the various institutional subsystems that constituted Canadian society. There were four: the economic, the political, the bureaucratic or administrative, and the ideological. Together, they made up the 'total social system.'[101] Each subsystem could be identified by its functionally differentiated role, a special task that, if accomplished properly, allowed Canadian society to operate relatively smoothly while generally meeting the needs of the population as a whole. Each subsystem was made up of a number of bureaucratically structured institutions and had its own 'species' and degree of power, which it used to achieve its particular goals.[102] Subsystems sometimes cooperated and sometimes fought with one another as they pursued their respective goals. Some conflicts – as between the economic and labour elites within the economic subsystem – were fundamental, ongoing, and potentially disruptive of the system. Other conflicts – as between bureaucratic and political subsystems and their respective elites – were episodic, unlikely to threaten the system as constituted.

Porter augmented this analysis by examining the distribution of power among individuals. He defined power as 'the recognized right to make effective decisions on behalf of a group of people.'[103] In his view, those who possessed that right in modern, postindustrial societies were 'elites,' the individuals who filled the topmost positions in the key institutions that made up the various societal subsystems. Thus, the political subsystem had its political elite and so forth. The economic subsystem was unique in that it had two conflicting elites: those who controlled Canada's major corporations – the economic elite – and those who headed the country's major unions – the labour elite. These elites possessed both the right to control decision-making processes within key societal institutions and the capacity to 'mobilize' the power/resources of that institution or subsystem. While this often generated conflict and created problems, it was part of the logic of the system and thus unavoidable. Supplementary problems were created, however, when the elites exploited their positions of institutional power and responsibility to advance their personal interests.

For each subsystem, Porter undertook a two-part analysis. He began by describing the general structure and functioning of the subsystem in question, paying particular attention to questions of internal and external power relations. He then examined the backgrounds and characteristics of the individuals who occupied the elite roles at the top of each subsystem. In part through this examination of the social backgrounds and characteristics of elites, Porter was able to link his analysis of power back to his analysis of class and tie the two together.

The History of the Study of Power in Canada, pre-1965

Prior to the appearance of *The Vertical Mosaic*, Canadian historians, sociologists, economists, and political scientists had done little empirical research on the *national* structure of power in Canada. Political scientists had written treatises on the formal or official structure and procedures of government, such as R. Macgregor Dawson's *Democratic Government in Canada* and Norman Ward's *Government in Canada*.[104] Frank Scott, among others, had done important work on federalism, rights, and the Constitution.[105] C.B. Macpherson had earned a stellar international reputation as an expert on the historical development of liberal political theory, and scholars from a variety of disciplines had written about Canadian political culture, especially liberalism, nationalism, and regional political cultures and power struggles (Quebec, the Maritimes, the West). In addition, historians and political scientists had written biographies of prime ministers and other major political figures and completed numerous studies of political parties, pressure groups, and social movements.[106] John Meisel had initiated what came to be known as the 'behavioural revolution' in Canadian political science with his pathbreaking studies of election survey data.[107] Harold Innis, Arthur Lower, and Donald Creighton, among others, had earned a central place in Canadian political economy and economic history circles for their insights into the social, economic, and political consequences of the country's focus on the exploitation of staples.[108] Economists and others had done research in related areas: the interplay of government and private corporations vis-à-vis economic development, case studies of specific companies or industries, the process of capital formation, patterns of corporate concentration, and so forth.[109] Labour historians had focused some attention on the development of the capitalist labour market, subsequent struggles between labour and capital, the history of the labour movement and unions, and so on.[110]

Porter had framed his problem differently. He was interested in the national structure and dynamics of power in Canada in the mid-twentieth century – relations between institutional subsystems. The method he chose – a 'positional' style of analysis that focused on the elites who filled the 'command posts' at the top of powerful institutions – reduced greatly the utility of most extant published research.[111] Either it dealt with events long past or did not deal directly and in detail with the national structure of power. Certainly, none of it employed a methodology like the one he had chosen. Thus, he had to construct much of his data from scratch. The work paid off, however, for the results were impressive. His empirical description and theoretical analysis of power turned out to be novel, convincing, fruitful, and influential – just like his work on class.

The Concentration of Economic Power and the Economic Elite

Porter began his analysis of the economic elite by identifying 183 'dominant corporations' in the non-financial sectors of the economy.[112] He found complete data for 170 of them. He then defined the 'economic elite' as those who held directorships in these dominant corporations and/or one of Canada's major financial institutions (nine chartered banks and ten insurance companies). He justified this strategy – targeting individual members of the elite – by arguing that directors 'hold the ultimate power' within individual firms and 'collectively ... preside over all major segments of the corporate world.' He noted that they were tied together 'in an extensive interlocking network [and] are the ultimate decision-makers and co-ordinators within the private sector of the economy.' As well, he said, they operate at the points of intersection between the economic and political systems, representing 'the interests of corporate power.' In fact, said Porter, it was the economic elite, not the political elite (government) that planned the economy, 'and they resent bitterly the thought that anyone else should do the planning.'[113]

His research, like that of others before him, found that Canada's dominant corporations held tremendous economic power.[114] They accounted for about half of manufacturing output, nearly two-thirds of metal production, two-thirds of privately generated hydro-electric power, nine-tenths of rail transportation, and so on.[115] As for the economic elite itself, Porter reported that a mere '907 individuals ... shared between them ... 81 per cent of the directorships in the dominant corporations as well as ... 58 per cent of the directorships in the nine chartered banks and ... 58 per cent of [those] in the life insurance companies.' Because of the importance of banks to the economy, he added 78 bank directors who were not on the boards of directors of dominant corporations, and to that group a handful of men from corporations not designated as dominant. In total, 985 men – only 80 per cent of whom were born in Canada – made up the economic elite.[116] Porter was able to gather complete data on 760 of those he described as the most powerful.[117] He described their class origins, educational backgrounds, ethnicity, religious affiliation, career patterns, political party affiliations, and voluntary association memberships. The analysis revealed that, unlike other classes in Canadian society, the economic elite came close to constituting 'a sociological group rather than a statistical class.'[118]

Most came from a privileged class background. Nearly one-quarter 'directly inherited their position from near kin.' When he added those 'whose fathers were in elite groups other than the economic,' 'those whose wives came from elite families,' and those whose fathers operated 'substantial businesses' not in the designated dominant corporations, he brought the total of those 'who started out at or near the top of the class system' to nearly four in ten. When he included those who had attended private school and those whose fathers had high occupational rankings or an advanced education, he discovered that more than eight in ten Canadian-born members of the economic elite came from the 'middle class or higher.'[119]

Formal education played a noteworthy part in their background and preparation for a life of privilege. Over one-third had attended a private secondary school and almost two-thirds had completed some form of postsecondary education.[120] As well, their career paths revealed special treatment and advantages. The data revealed a 'high degree of internal recruitment as indicated by family continuity within the management of particular corporations, or family continuity on the boards of directors.'[121] Nearly a third either directly inherited a position in the economic elite or obtained one through family connections.[122] By contrast, only one in twelve had been an 'independent entrepreneur' who had started from scratch to build up a firm large enough to be considered nationally dominant.[123] More than three-fifths had a professional or financial background.[124]

The economic elite differed substantially from the rest of the Canadian population in two other respects: ethnicity and religious affiliation.

Canada's two 'founding peoples' – as the language of the time went – had fared very differently. I noted above that English Canadians made up only 44 per cent of the population. However, they constituted 90 per cent of the economic elite. French Canadians made up 30 per cent of the Canadian population but formed just 7 per cent of the economic elite. 'It is clear,' Porter reported tersely, 'that preference for recruitment to the economic elite is for English-speaking people of British origin.'[125] Religion, to a large extent, followed ethnicity; about 60 per cent of the economic elite were Protestant and 10 per cent Catholic at a time when 44 per cent of the population was Protestant and 43 per cent was Catholic.[126] An examination of the uppermost 100 members of the elite revealed that these patterns of exclusive class origin and educational background were 'even more marked' within this group.[127]

In considering the significance of his findings, Porter concluded that, beyond question, the economic elite possessed more 'consciousness of kind' and more social ties to one another than any other class grouping in Canada. Even when not directly related, members of the economic elite either knew one another or knew about one another in a way and to a degree that members of other classes did not. Moreover, their common socialization experiences had created a strong common world view – one shared over drinks at private clubs, articulated on the boards of various trade associations and commissions, and reflected in their choice of political parties and voluntary association memberships.[128] Nor did their sense of connectedness stop at the doors of Canada's boardrooms. They had strong ties to other elites, the most important of which was the ideological elite.

The Ideological System and the Ideological Elite

According to Porter, Canada's ideological system had three components: the mass media, higher learning, and the clergy. In some cases, the mass media constituted large-scale businesses in their own right. Higher learning and the clergy did not, however, so he discussed each group separately. By far the most powerful of the three was the mass media.

The Mass Media

Porter's research revealed that most English-language mass media enterprises in Canada – television, radio, newspapers – were privately owned by a relatively small number of very wealthy families. Those who owned them were members of Canada's 'upper class.'[129] Three chains – Southam, Sifton, and Thomson – accounted for one-quarter of all daily English-language newspaper circulation in Canada. A slightly larger group of chains, including these three, accounted for almost 87 per cent.[130] The pattern of ownership of English-language periodicals was similar. When Porter investigated the corporate holdings of the eleven privately owned English-language 'major mass media complexes,' he discovered that many of the individuals who owned or controlled them were members of the economic elite.[131] This meant there was substantial overlap between the two elites. Even when they were not members of the economic elite, it was common for there to be close class and family ties between the media elite and members of the economic elite.

The situation vis-à-vis the structure and control of the French-language mass media was in some respects similar. For example, he found that half of all French-language dailies accounted for approximately 90 per cent of all French-language daily circulation.[132] Unlike in English Canada, however, there were no substantial newspaper chains, though there were some links between newspapers and radio stations.[133] Porter provided few details about the social backgrounds of the owners of the French-language press other than to note that all were French speaking.[134]

As he considered the implications of these findings, he came to the conclusion that such ownership patterns created a major political problem. This small group of privileged families could express their political, economic, and social views to huge audiences in a way that others could not. This had obvious political implications. In a system in which media elites were 'devoted to the norms of corporate enterprise and profit-making,' Porter argued, they often made sense of the news in a way that served the interests of Canada's economic elite, identifying the corporate view of what was good with 'the common good.'[135] 'The ideological orientation that results from the existing pattern of ownership is conservative, supporting the *status quo* over a wide range of social and economic policy,' he asserted, arguing that the mass-circulation newspapers in Canada were 'instruments of an established social class.'[136] This tendency was exacerbated when owners 'hand-picked' ideologically suitable editors or engaged in direct editorial intervention.[137] Meddling inevitably led in a conservative, business-oriented direction.

The social origins of the media elite resembled those of the economic elite. For example, 'The controlling interest in the major newspaper complexes ... is in the hands of families or individuals with two or three generations of wealth behind them.'[138] Not surprisingly, he wrote, 'a large portion of the men who control the major newspapers ... are graduates of private schools, ... belong to the same exclusive metropolitan clubs, ... [and attended] ... university.' Rather stunningly, he found that all of them belonged to the British charter group.[139]

Intellectual and Religious Elites

The mass media component of the ideological elite was the one most clearly connected to, and indeed to some degree part of, the economic elite. Thus, in Porter's estimation, they were the most powerful segment of the ideological elite. The other components of the ideological elite – the intellectual and religious elites – were less influential and came from further down the class structure. Nonetheless, Porter found that they shared important social characteristics with one another and the mass media elites and, most important, played a similar ideological role.

Porter's analysis of the backgrounds and characteristics of Canada's intellectual elite, what he referred to as its 'clerisy of the higher learning,' focused on the membership of the Royal Society of Canada, the nation's most prestigious body of intellectuals.[140] Unlike the mass media elite, many of whom were wealthy or super-wealthy businessmen, both part of and well connected to the economic elite, the 500-plus members of the intellectual elite were well-off professionals: writers, university professors, research scientists. In an attempt to understand their political impact, Porter paid particular attention to the social characteristics and backgrounds of the 169 intellectual elites who played ideological roles: those who were social scientists and humanists rather than those who were natural scientists.[141] Over two-thirds were born in Canada and nearly all belonged to one of the two charter groups.[142] In the English-language group, all but one had a university degree.[143] More than 80 per cent of English-language members were university professors, of whom the largest group came from the University of Toronto, and about 60 per cent had a PhD.[144] By contrast, fewer than one in three of the French-language intellectuals were university professors, and far fewer held PhD degrees. Nearly as many worked either in government or as journalists or authors.[145] Most French-language intellectuals were

Roman Catholic, whereas four of five English-language intellectuals who indicated an affiliation were Protestant.[146] Most of the French-language intellectuals had attended classical colleges and then gone on to one of Laval, Université de Montréal, or the Université de Paris. By contrast, more than half of the English-language group had attended the University of Toronto, with Oxford, Cambridge, and Chicago preferred destinations for graduate training.[147] Few in either group indicated formal political party affiliations.[148] The English-language group seemed to come from middle-class backgrounds.[149] He reported no data on the question for French-language intellectuals.

Porter's analysis of Canada's religious elites involved the study of fifty-seven men who held positions in the Roman Catholic Church as bishops, archbishops, or cardinals and twenty-six with equivalent positions in the Anglican Church of Canada.[150] Only one in three of the Anglican bishops had been born in Canada, all were English-speaking, and nearly all came from middle-class rather than elite backgrounds. Nearly all the Roman Catholic religious elite were native born and two-thirds were French speaking.[151] Similarly, neither of the religious elites formally participated in a major way in other institutional systems and neither was well linked to other elites.[152]

More important than the social backgrounds and class positions of the intellectual and religious elites was their ideological role. Porter began by noting that churches and their elites held 'a crucial place in the structure of power,' but with societally negative consequences.[153] When 'interwoven with ethnicity and social class,' he wrote, religion had been and continued to be 'the most significant divisive element in Canadian society.' In his view, churches created – and then thrived on – differences over social issues, education most important among them. And while Porter was all in favour of 'dynamic dialogue' on political and social issues, he charged that the dialogue spawned by the churches always seemed 'esoteric and out of date.'[154] It was true that religious elites entered into coalitions and conflicts with other elites, he said, but the issues they raised did nothing to contribute to a progressive discussion of the existing social structure.[155] He directed a similar criticism at the rest of the intellectual elite.

Particularly in English Canada, he found that the ideological impact of Canada's most prestigious professors resembled that of the conservative mass media. 'With few exceptions,' he remarked, 'their attitudes and values are conventional.'[156] Humanities scholars in particular were more traditional – and therefore more conservative – than their counterparts in empirical disciplines such as sociology.[157] Painting the lot of them with a broad brush, he condemned them for having allowed higher learning to become 'depoliticized.' Few involved themselves in political debates or offered social criticism that would contribute to progressive, 'dynamic dialogue' on key political and social issues.[158] There had been little dynamism in the Canadian political system, he claimed, but even less in Canadian intellectual life: 'From the mass media to the halls of higher learning, the clerisy is firmly entrenched. Neither Canadian newspapers, churches, nor universities have harboured social critics in any large number.'[159] Indeed, just the opposite was the case; intellectuals had done their best to 'mute' social criticism. In this regard, he complained, Canada was unlike almost any other country in the Western world.[160] This had dire political implications. Had the political elite initiated and maintained a healthy dialogue about fundamental political principles, this would not have been a problem, but such was not the case. Political elites and the political system tended likewise to play a system-stabilizing role.

The Political System and the Political Elite

In the political elite, Porter included 'federal cabinet ministers ..., provincial premiers ..., justices of the Supreme Court of Canada, presidents of the Exchequer Court, and ... provincial chief justices who held office [from 1940–1960].'[161]

As a backdrop to understanding politics and the role of the political elite, he claimed it was crucial to appreciate that, unlike the United States, Canada did not have a 'resounding charter myth' and thus no absolute, utopian standard against which it could measure social progress.[162] Nor were its major political parties sufficiently polarized – right and left – to engender a 'creative politics.' Instead, political elites of all stripes fretted continually about 'national unity,' an 'obsession' that produced a stable economy but boring politics incapable of changing the social structure with respect to major social goals or values.[163] Porter charged that aside from national unity, Canada's political elites had never had any genuine goals other than to maintain 'a high level of employment and a respectable rate of economic growth' – precisely the goals of the economic elite.[164] This convergence of ideals and goals between the economic and political elites explains Porter's finding that very few members of the economic elite entered politics.[165] They did not need to.

More generally, Porter said, Canada had a poorly developed political culture. Political leaders were weak and most Canadians were not politically engaged. The newness of universal suffrage, the low levels of educational attainment ('too low to allow intelligent participation'), and the lack of a politicized labour movement were all factors.[166] Most politicians came from the middle class and depended on the corporate world 'to keep their political parties in funds.'[167] No surprise that the economic elite did not feel threatened by the holders of political power or the mainstream, brokerage politics they practised: 'Neither the corporate elite, nor the very wealthy, have much to fear from ... middle class politicians. It is more likely that the politicians hold the corporate elite in awe.' [168] Also important in this transitional period prior to the widespread acceptance and institutionalization of the principles of Keynesianism and the welfare state – the New Liberalism – was that political elites shared with economic elites a belief in the philosophy of laissez-faire. 'The political system has been incapable of generating its own power,' said Porter, because it had adopted the view 'that that government is best which governs least.' This laissez-faire ideology, expressly denied 'the social benefit of power,' thus playing into the hands of wealthy members of the economic elite.[169]

On other indicators, the political elite resembled other elites: nine in ten were Canadian born, three-quarters were British, three in ten had attended private secondary schools, nearly nine in ten had a university education (higher than for any other elite), and two out of three were Protestant.[170]

Political elites were not the only ones charged with the responsibility of running the country. Also important were the senior bureaucrats in the federal civil service, who implemented government policy. Porter referred to this group as the bureaucratic elite.

The Federal Bureaucracy and the Bureaucratic Elite

Porter defined the bureaucratic elite as '243 senior officials of the federal government departments, agencies and Crown corporations.'[171] His analysis was based on the 83 per cent for whom he was able to obtain detailed information. Like the political elite, the bureaucratic elite was neither directly dominated by the economic elite nor much connected to it.[172] This was significant because as a permanent, independent structure, not subject to political appointments, the bureaucracy could, and sometimes did, act from 'a position of relative autonomy within the overall structure of power.'[173]

Drawing on Weber's ideal type of bureaucracy, Porter argued that the power of the federal civil service was rooted in its specialized function, its distinct career system, and its professional norms. The progressive rationalization of the modern world, concomitant with the expansion of capitalism, meant that in Canada as elsewhere, experts – people with 'technical' knowledge – had come to dominate government bureaucracies.[174] Their power came from knowledge. Their capacity for independent, countervailing power was at its maximum when the bureaucracy was fully rationalized, had a monopoly of experts, and recruited from all classes. In this situation, political parties (government or opposition) would be unable to 'rival' the bureaucracy.[175]

In the Canadian case, the conditions for bureaucratic independence and unrivalled technical expertise had never been fully realized. The federal civil service never became fully rationalized and did not have a monopoly of experts. Corporations and political parties routinely employed their own intellectual hired guns to advance their interests and points of view. As for broad-based recruitment, Porter's data showed that fewer than one in five of the bureaucratic elite came from either an elite or 'upper class' family. Nearly nine in ten came from 'middle class or higher' backgrounds, so that while the federal bureaucracy was not the 'exclusive preserve' of the upper classes, it was not the 'broad avenue of upward mobility' that Weber's model suggested it should be.[176] Moreover, shared socialization and occupational experiences led this select group to be highly cohesive, holding values similar to those of political and economic elites.[177] This was to be expected, as they had come from similar backgrounds. Like the political elite then, the bureaucratic elite constituted no threat to the economic elite. They did not act at the behest of the economic elite, but since their job was to carry out government policy, which was intended to stabilize the economy, they often acted on behalf of or in the interests of the economic elite.[178] If they possessed the capacity to act as a powerful countervailing force to the economic elite, they seldom felt compelled to do so. In fact, Porter claimed that such close ties existed among the upper echelons of these three groups that they constituted a 'minor power elite' that ruled over 'a penumbral area of power' in senior decision-making circles.[179]

Those with a British background monopolized the bureaucratic elite, making up over 80 per cent of its membership; French Canadians filled only 13 per cent of the top posts. Other ethnic groups scarcely registered.[180] Of those that stated a religious affiliation, two-thirds were Protestant and just over one-fifth were Catholic.[181]

Organized Labour and the Labour Elite

Porter's analysis of organized labour and the labour elite began from the proposition that they were bound in a directly, if often covertly, adversarial relationship with Canada's most powerful elite – the economic.[182] This put them in a difficult position, for they possessed fewer resources than their adversaries and operated in a largely hostile ideological and economic climate within which 'the whole weight of institution and habit [was] against them.' 'The ideology of property ownership pervades the entire institutional system,' Porter said. 'John Dewey's modification of the Cartesian principle, "I think, therefore I am" to "I own, therefore I am" applies particularly to the North American way of life. Ownership has become the very principle of existence.'[183] So strong was liberal ideology that most Canadians regarded the interests of capital and the national interest as one and the same. By contrast, they viewed the activities of organized labour as detrimental to those of the country as a whole. In fact, Porter noted a distinct asymmetry in the way Canadians treated unions on the one hand and the economic elite on the other. They judged the actions of union members and their leaders by the criterion of social responsibility, i.e., in terms of their willingness to operate within the system-as-constituted and, in particular, their reticence to use the 'weapon' of the strike. Corporate elites, Porter noted, were not held to the same standard: 'When corporations close down factories ... or administer prices, these acts are not judged in terms of social responsibility but rather in terms of the logic of the system.'[184]

In sum, then, the labour elite differed from other elites in two ways. First, they wielded less power. Organized labour had succeeded in setting some limits on the power that stemmed from property ownership but had been unable to challenge the prevailing liberal orthodoxy regarding the appropriateness of private ownership and control of the means of production. In fact, rather than contesting the principle of ownership, Canada's unions had adopted the ideology and practice of 'market unionism,' bargaining for better wages by using the threat to strike as a last resort.[185] While this had provided unionized workers with a relatively high standard of living, it had weakened their legal and ideological capacity to challenge the system. This structural problem – they were enmeshed in a system that tended to act in the interests of capital – was exacerbated by two other factors that rendered their leadership, the labour elite, less powerful than other elites. The labour movement itself was splintered.[186] This in turn reduced their capacity to challenge the power held by other elites.[187] As well, however, labour leaders simply were not well tied in to the overall elite system. Labour's interests and goals often conflicted with those of other elites, with the result that Canada's English-language labour elite constituted an 'out-group.' It differed drastically from other elites on all counts. Most obviously, its members came from lower down the class scale. Half had fathers who had worked in manual occupations, one in five came from lower middle-class, non-manual occupational backgrounds, and a further one in seven came from a farm background. Only 10 per cent came from middle-class backgrounds.[188] Their educational backgrounds were likewise different. Only one in six had finished secondary school and only one in twenty held a university degree.[189] They came from a much wider ethnic and religious background as well. Though they did not mirror Canada's ethnic and religious mix exactly – only one in six had a non-charter group background, and there were few Catholics among them – they reflected it more closely than other elites.[190]

In many respects, the leadership of the Quebec-based Confédération des Syndicats Nationaux (CSN) resembled the leadership of the English-speaking unions. However, unlike the English-language union movement, which included many foreign-born members, the CSN was a culturally homogeneous 'indigenous movement.' All but one of its sixty-nine leaders were born in Quebec and all were Roman Catholic.[191] They were somewhat better educated than their English-language counterparts, but there was a bipolar distribution of education among them: one in three had only elementary school education, but over one-quarter had graduated from university or one of the classical *colleges* (three times as many as their English-language counterparts).[192] Like members of the English-language labour elite, about half came from families in which the father had engaged in manual labour.[193]

Porter presented extensive and illuminating data about each of Canada's elites and the institutional subsystems within which they operated. However, to appreciate fully his image of the distribution of power in Canada, it is necessary to understand his view of how elites wielded power within and across institutional subsystems. This requires an understanding of his theoretical conception of power and an appreciation of his account of the relationship between the structure of class outlined in Part 1 of the book and the structure of power outlined in Part 2.

Porter's Theoretical Approach to Power

I noted above that Porter defined power in terms of 'the recognized right to make effective decisions on behalf of a group of people.' For Porter, power was both inevitable – a 'social necessity' – and functional; it existed in all societies because of a 'general social need for order.'[194] Without it, he claimed that there would be nothing but a 'disorganized mass of human beings.'[195] Such a conception of power was unusual for the time. Unlike most scholars, he did not make a distinction between power and authority, arguing that while social order emerged out of a struggle among groups for social control, there was no difference between 'raw power,' power maintained through the use of overt coercion, and 'authority,' legitimate power that people willingly obey. In his view, there were no objective criteria for distinguishing between them. Throughout history, he said, people had willingly obeyed rulers who, to an outsider, would appear to be tyrants.[196]

He situated this definition of power within a complex , eclectic theoretical framework that employed three layers. Some aspects of his framework, such as his theory of human nature, were rooted in the *psychological* level of analysis. Other aspects, such as his account of the influence of bureaucracy, were focused on the *institutional* level of analysis. Finally, still other aspects of the framework, that is, functionalism and postcapitalism, operated at the *societal* level.

Human Nature

Porter's conception of human nature drew on a range of sources: liberal political economy, Hobbes, Freud, and the elite theorists. He began with a proposition from liberal political economy: 'The desire to possess and to own may be an almost inherent disposition of human beings. It certainly has been given strong reinforcement by the institution of property.'[197] In a similar way, he drew on Hobbes. Though he saw Hobbes' hypothetical state of nature as an 'anthropological absurdity,' he agreed with the Hobbesian proposition (stated by Freud and the elite theorists as well) that humans were by nature seekers after power.[198] Citing Freud, he wrote,

> Men are not gentle, friendly creatures, wishing for love, who simply defend themselves if they are attacked ... [A] powerful measure of desire for aggression has to be reckoned as a part of their instinctual endowment ... That men are divided into leaders and the led is but another manifestation

of their inborn and irremediable inequality. The second class constitutes the vast majority; they need a high command to make decisions for them, to which decisions they can usually bow without demur.[199]

Following Hobbes, he argued that for a perpetual and chaotic 'war of each against all' to be avoided, government was necessary. The problem was that humans were born with unequal mental and physical capacities, with the result that those with greater capacities inevitably came to positions of power. They then used this power for selfish ends. At this point, Porter's theory shifted its focus from the influence of human nature to the influence of formal organization. The elite theory of Pareto, Mosca, and Michels provided the link.

The Institutional Origins of Power

I have just noted that elite theorists held a conception of human nature according to which people were innately self-interested seekers after power. To this notion, they added the idea that some people, a very small number, were naturally superior to others and, thus, constituted a natural elite, destined to rule. Historically, such elites had used various means to establish and maintain control. Elites did 'circulate' over time (replacing one another), but the 'mass' had never held power – and never would. There is something of this logic in the penultimate paragraph of *The Vertical Mosaic,* where Porter seems to concur with Mosca and Pareto that rigid mass–elite distinctions were inevitable and that power would always be wielded by a small minority. 'Canada is probably not unlike other western industrial nations in relying heavily on its elite groups to make major decisions and to determine the shape and direction of its development,' he wrote. 'If power and decision-making must always rest with elite groups, there can at least be open recruitment from all classes into the elites.'[200] Porter supplemented this analysis with the ideas of twentieth-century elite theorist Robert Michels, finding wisdom in his aphorism 'Who says organization, says oligarchy':

> The organizational factors which created oligarchy lay in the need of the masses to give up control to a small number of persons who had administrative competence and technical specialization. The experts could be either leaders themselves or persons whom the leaders hired – the permanent officials of organizations. The larger the organization, the more experts there were and the more power they acquired. The increase in the

power of the leader was directly proportional with the extension of organization.[201]

Porter drew on Weber to complete his discussion on this point. He reviewed Weber's description of modern bureaucracies and suggested that as most institutional subsystems were made up of large, bureaucratized organizations, control over bureaucracies had become the primary means of social control in modern societies.[202]

The last pieces of his theory of power were derived from functionalism and the theory of postcapitalism, factors that operated at the level of the 'total social system.'

The Societal Origins of Power

The most obviously functionalist elements of Porter's approach were his definition of power, described above, which conflated power and authority, and his image of society as a functional system with a systemic goal and a systemic need for power to realize those goals. As Porter described it in *The Vertical Mosaic*, then, society was a 'total social system' comprising a number of separate but related and relatively autonomous subsystems, each of which had been created by 'as a means of getting certain essential tasks accomplished.'[203] In fact, and here he reverted to the standard functionalist tautology, the societal need to ensure the completion and coordination of tasks gave rise to power: 'Subsystems perform essential social functions. All of them must be directed and co-ordinated. It is this need for direction and co-ordination which gives rise to power.'[204] Subsystems sometimes had conflicting goals, but society as a whole used the political subsystem to achieve its 'major goals and values,' if any.[205]

Institutional differentiation and specialization (the growth in power of the government and the federal bureaucracy) spread power throughout the system.[206] For Porter, the power of any institution or subsystem was based on its control over institutional resources and, most significantly in a knowledge society, on its institutionally specific form of knowledge.[207]

Class and Power Together: Canada Is No Democracy

At various junctures in the book, but especially as he pondered relations among elites, Porter considered how this model applied to Canada. At the most general level, he concluded that no institutional subsystem could dominate any other subsystem and its elite.[208] In his view, all-out competition for system domination seldom occurred, if ever.[209] Instead, groups found themselves operating within a shifting but stable balance of 'countervailing' powers.[210] Elites had somewhat conflicting interests and occasionally encroached on one another's territory, sometimes even engaging in open conflict. But they also understood and honoured a set of agreed-upon 'ground rules by which power [was] exercised' which created in turn a 'confraternity of power in which the various institutional leaders share[d] attitudes and values.'[211] This produced the boring, centrist politics characteristic of Canadian society. The elites did not thus constitute a 'conspiratorial coalition.' Rather, they moderated their claims, 'accommodating' one another to the degree sufficient to maintain a 'floating equilibrium of compromise.'[212] This capacity to accommodate one another allowed competing elites to coordinate their activities sufficiently to create a 'national power structure' capable of satisfying the need for overall co-ordination and direction of the social system.[213] Despite the existence of factors leading toward elite coordination – the small size of elite groups, their common socialization experiences, increasing internal complexity within institutions, increasing complexity of external relations, inter-elite agreement on the legal ground rules for competition, and agreement on the 'givenness' of the capitalist institutional framework – Canada's elites constituted, for Porter, neither Marx's ruling class nor Mills' power elite.[214] On this point, it is interesting to compare his conclusions about this group in *The Vertical Mosaic* with the conclusions he drew a decade later in a review of Peter Newman's *The Canadian Establishment,* a volume that reported on some of the more gossip-worthy aspects of the lives of Canada's wealthiest businessmen. In that review, 'The Vertical Power Trip,' Porter was quite blunt, and radical, in his assessment of the men C.D. Howe had recruited to run Canada's economy during the war. After the war, Porter charged, their activities at the command posts of Canadian capitalism had made them 'as close to a ruling class as anything Canada has seen.'[215]

Though he hedged his arguments about the unity and power of elites, he was unequivocal in arguing that Canada was a very long way from being a 'thoroughgoing democracy.'[216] He argued that nothing of the sort was the case. Indeed, in his discussion of the Canadian political system, he seemed pessimistic about even the *possibility* that a large and differentiated society such as Canada could have the collective goals, 'shared social purpose,' and 'collective participation in achieving social ends' that would make it a democracy. Certainly, he said, in Canada such a system was 'a long way from emerging.'[217] He was pessimistic on a second crucial point as well. Though elites had not achieved the total degree of control necessary to constitute either a ruling class or power elite, he claimed that they sat largely uncontested and unaccountable at the 'command posts' of the institutional bureaucracies making the decisions that affected the public at large.[218] The legitimacy of their control was rooted in a broad, if vague, basis of popular support provided by pervasive 'Western' values: Christianity, capitalism, nationalism.[219] They used these to their advantage and were kept in line not by the citizenry at large but by one another: 'Power tends toward an equilibrium of competing elites. The checks and balances that are everywhere considered desirable do not come from control by the masses or from the membership of the corporate bodies which elites represent.'[220] Elites kept each other in line.

He regarded this as a 'democracy' problem in three senses. First, elites were not under popular control. Second, they used their power not just to achieve systemic and subsystemic goals but also to gain personal advantages and rewards. Third, the inter-elite conflict they generated led to a degree of inefficiency in the system. The interplay between the power structure and the class system compounded this inefficiency. According to liberal ideology, elites were to be recruited on a meritocratic basis from the population as a whole. However, the Canadian data showed that most came from the upper reaches of the class structure. Canada's steeply hierarchical structure of material rewards – the class system – regarded by Porter as an essential inducement for the meritorious to assume society's most responsible positions, acted, lamentably, as a barrier to equality of opportunity. An Anglo-Saxon charter group sat at the top of the class and power structures and ruled in their 'private' and collective group interest while simultaneously recruiting their progeny and social equals as future elites.

In the concluding paragraphs of the book, Porter criticized the systemic inefficiency this created and decried the limitations to democracy created by unequal reward structures and ascriptive, non-meritocratic recruitment procedures. But he was only selectively critical of the system. The disharmony among competing elites was not entirely debilitating, he argued, because there was sufficient general agreement on systemic values and goals that Canada 'worked' most of the time. Likewise, though countervailing elites created a degree of inefficiency, they also acted as a structural check on totalitarianism. No elite – not even the powerful economic elite – was able to master any or all of the others.

Finally, though Porter despaired of the limitations to societal development and rationality created by inegalitarian structures of class and power, and regretted the limitations they placed on individual social mobility, he also saw these difficulties as largely unavoidable given human nature, the logic of formal bureaucratic organization, and societal needs for order and task completion.

The following chapter, which surveys the critical response to Porter's magnum opus over his lifetime, provides a critique of his interconnected theories of class, power, and democracy.

8 Critical Response to *The Vertical Mosaic*

> Canada has ... taken the book as a moral tract, as a call of all true democrats to action. That a book so laden with facts, presented in charts and tables, so long and so expensive, should capture the imagination of so sober a country ... is a great and deserved compliment to its author.

So wrote the distinguished American sociologist and pioneer of Canadian sociology, Everett Hughes, a year after *The Vertical Mosaic* appeared.[1] Remarkably, despite its scholarly character and imposing heft, *The Vertical Mosaic* generated a major response in the popular press. Even before it appeared on bookstore shelves in the spring of 1965, it began to draw media attention. As early as 1963 Porter had received enquiries from both *Canadian Business* and *Executive* magazines about the possibility of serializing the book in anticipation of its imminent release.[2] He declined these offers, but did benefit from some other high-profile prepublication media exposure.

In 1964, just as *The Vertical Mosaic* went into production, the CBC caught wind of it. Frank McGee, host of *The Sixties*, a popular national social affairs program, produced a two-part series, *Paths to Power*, highlighting Porter's research on elites. On these programs, hosted by McGee, deputy ministers David Sim, David Golden, and James Roberts joined the chairman of the Canadian National Railway, N.R. Crump, and the principal of Upper Canada College, the Reverend Dr. C.W. Sowby, in commenting on aspects of the social and economic backgrounds of Canada's elites.[3] Porter appeared on camera, providing contextual information regarding their discussions. Wearing a dark suit, his short hair neatly trimmed, he looked and sounded every bit the mainstream professional. But there was no denying the radical nature of his comments.[4]

Media attention quickly intensified after the book was released. Canadian newspapers and news magazines gave the book highly laudatory reviews, and Porter became something of a celebrity.[5] NDP member of parliament and political journalist Douglas Fisher, who knew Porter and discussed the book with him on a number of occasions after it came out, reviewed it in the *Toronto Telegram* under the heading 'Corridors of Power: Secret and Ubiquitous.' Like others who had reviewed it, he noted that *The Vertical Mosaic* was going to become and remain well known – in some ways *despite* itself:

> A price of $15 puts a book beyond the buying habit of most of us. When the book is serious, long, complex and written without much literary grace or effort to popularize the arguments, it is unlikely to become a best-seller. Despite these omens for an unsensational future, John Porter's *The Vertical Mosaic* ... seems certain to be as important as any work published in Canada this decade.

Describing Porter as 'a somewhat dour, square-set man of middle years' with the sort of character and personality unlikely 'to make many concessions to those who are ignorant of the disciplines of his subject,' Fisher also made it clear that his friend was a 'radically inclined' man, much to be admired. He had written a book with a purpose. He had identified the mysterious 'they' who made the major decisions in Canada – often in their own rather than the public interest – and also suggested what needed to be done to make these powerful people accountable. Only in this way, said Fisher, would Canada become 'a more classless and more democratic society.'[6]

In a very unusual development, Tommy Douglas, the leader of the federal NDP, also reviewed *The Vertical Mosaic*. Douglas' article, published in the *Globe and Mail*, was even more laudatory than Fisher's. He described Porter's book as a 'masterly and incisive work' that promised to be 'a valuable source-book' for anyone 'seeking to understand Canadian society.' In his view, it was an especially important must read for politicians and other Canadian citizens who feared that their country was without a strong national identity and lacked the features that would make it a truly 'dynamic democracy.' Douglas' review appeared early in June, one month to the day after *The Vertical Mosaic* was released. In it, tongue firmly in cheek, Douglas poked fun at those graduation speakers who, at 'about this time of year, ... hold forth on the theme of Canada as "a land of equal opportunity for all."' The NDP leader warned such speakers to avoid *The Vertical Mosaic* if they wanted to 'preserve their illusions.' Douglas was particularly interested in the connections Porter drew between national identity and dynamic democracy. He agreed that Canadian culture lacked a longstanding 'clash of conflicting ideologies.' Instead, he said, politicians, in their desire to maintain national unity, had historically stressed 'administrative competence rather than creative leadership.' This had prevented the development of a polarized, left–right political culture at the national level that might have produced the degree and kind of political dynamism necessary to generate, in turn, 'the elusive national unity we seek.'[7]

Fisher and Douglas were not alone in drawing the public's attention to Porter's book. *Toronto Daily Star* reporter David Cobb interviewed him and wrote a feature on his work, as did James Bannerman from *Maclean's*, Kildare Dobbs in *Saturday Night*, and William Kilbourn from *Executive* business magazine.[8] He even made it into the Canadian edition of *Time* magazine. There, in an article entitled 'The Retarded Democracy,' *Time*'s editors heralded Porter as Canada's ranking 'establishmentologist' and focused particular attention on his claim that Canada was not a 'thoroughgoing democracy.' *The Vertical Mosaic* was 'bulky' and 'scarcely light reading,' *Time* reported, but 'in an era when Canada ... behave[s] most of the time as if it were on a psychiatrist's couch, ... the *Mosaic* seems certain to become one of the most hotly discussed books in years.'[9] Bannerman and Dobbs were especially interested in the book's critique of the morality of Canada's structure of class and power. Writing in *Maclean's*, Bannerman noted, 'We Canadians tend to think of our country as a land of opportunity for everybody, free of rigid class distinctions, where an impressive number of citizens can afford an abundant way of life.' But, said Bannerman, Porter's book, 'based on scrupulously authenticated facts that must be accepted whether you like them or not,' showed that image to be 'embarrassingly wrong.'[10] Dobbs' article in *Saturday Night* said something similar. *The Vertical Mosaic*, he wrote, systematically demolished 'almost every social illusion we've ever cherished.' Far from 'the egalitarian society most Canadians imagine it to be,' Porter's book showed Canada to be 'a depressingly rigid plutocracy with the WASPs firmly in command.'[11] And though Dobbs poked a bit of fun at *The Vertical Mosaic* for being 'a hippopotamus ... to read' because of its style – 'a vast, relentlessly documented compendium of facts, figures, definitions and statistical tables' – he drew flattering conclusions about the book's author.[12] The man behind the book, Dobbs wrote, surely 'reads the *Globe and Mail*, occasionally permits himself a scholarly chuckle, and has to make an effort to suffer fools.' Like Bannerman and others, Dobbs was particularly impressed with Porter's moral stand: '[He's] managed to be both objective and controversial ... Objective because so much of what he says seems irrefutable, rooted in facts and figures,... but controversial because he ...draws conclusions [and] ... acknowledges bias.' Porter, Dobbs nodded approvingly, was 'biased in favour of liberty and equality.'[13] William Kilbourn was equally impressed: 'If ever a serious piece of academic research deserves to be a best-seller,' he wrote, '*The Vertical Mosaic* is it.' He reviewed Porter's findings for his business readers and noted that while they might well be sceptical about some of Porter's conclusions, it was scarcely possible to ignore his claims. And, somewhat surprisingly for an economist writing in a magazine geared to business executives, he approvingly highlighted Porter's New Liberal view that progress could not be measured 'solely in terms of GNP ... real wages, ... [and] ownership of automobiles and appliances.' In a more ideal society, Kilbourn concluded, Canadians would have to gauge progress using such indices as 'the quality of our leadership ... [the state of] pollution ... and achievements in education, science, ideas, and the arts.'[14]

Not everyone in the business community was so impressed. Quite predictably, a *Financial Post* reviewer disparaged the book as 'political pamphleteering' and claimed that Porter was wrong about many things – certainly about the locus of power in Canada. Politicians and business managers, not boards of directors of banks and corporations, had the upper hand.[15] From a very different corner of Canadian society, A.C. Forrest, writing in the *United Church Observer*, was greatly troubled by Porter's analysis of the place of religion in the Canadian power structure. He quarrelled with Porter's treatment of the role of organized religion in the country on the grounds that his data were 'fragmentary,' his knowledge of religion limited, and his attitude toward religion dismissive and condescending. In his estimation, Porter's treatment of the senior Anglican clergy was simply inadequate.[16]

Media attention did not end with this flurry of immediate postpublication reviews. In 1968, a full three years after *The Vertical Mosaic* first appeared, *Maclean's* did a follow-up interview.[17] Questions focused mainly on the findings of *The Vertical Mosaic* and for the most part Porter's responses stuck to the data reported there. The interviewer did manage to pry a few novel titbits from him, however, mainly regarding the policy implications of his arguments about inequality and education. When prodded, Porter told the journalist that he favoured a universal program of free university education – without a means test – as a way of encouraging students from low-income backgrounds to go to university (and to choose honours and professional programs once there). This would constitute a first step toward removing the class bias in education because it would make financial resources irrelevant in people's educational and career choices.[18] As well, he argued that while the state should continue to fund anti-poverty programs, manpower training schemes, and programs to establish basic income levels, educational reforms should take precedence.[19] Finally, he spoke in cautious but favourable terms about a number of measures that he thought would aggressively redistribute wealth: a truly progressive taxation system and policies that would close tax loopholes which allowed capital gains for the wealthy.[20]

In 2000, thirty-five years after *The Vertical Mosaic* originally appeared on Canada's cultural landscape, I asked veteran political columnist Robert Fulford, long-time editor of *Saturday Night,* why the book had such an influence in journalistic circles at the time. 'With his book,' Fulford answered, 'we first began to think about the nature of the leadership class, not only its ethnic background but its abilities and its duties … [B]efore Porter, we accepted [this situation] as it was; we might hate it or we might love it, but we regarded it as unchangeable, automatic, as if God had put it there … [A]fter Porter, we tended to think more critically and speculatively about it.'[21] According to Fulford, the essential argument in the book came to be part of the political journalist's everyday stock of knowledge: 'Journalists I knew [talked] about what he said and [took] it seriously, adding it to their store of knowledge and … assumptions. To borrow Galbraith's favourite term: pre-1965, his thesis was an idea many individuals held in different and individual ways … [Porter's] book turned it into the conventional wisdom.'[22]

While Porter welcomed this media attention, as a scholar he was far more concerned about the response his book would generate among his academic colleagues. In January, 1965, just as the work went to print, he wrote to Meisel on exactly this point: 'I am, of course, looking forward very much to its publication. Many people have asked me about it and I now have fears that they will be expecting too much. In any case, we can only wait and see.'[23]

He need not have worried. Academic reviewers from Canada, the United States, and England, most of them sociologists and political scientists, responded in an overwhelmingly positive way.[24] Of the two dozen academic reviews that appeared in the first year and a half, nearly all argued that *The Vertical Mosaic* was a groundbreaking accomplishment, a benchmark study sure to be an inspiration to researchers for years to come.

Typical of the first blush response by Canadian sociologists was a review written by Porter's friend and colleague, Bernard Blishen. Writing in the *Queen's Quarterly*, Blishen referred to Porter's book as 'a milestone in Canadian sociological analysis,' an outstanding interpretive analysis of a total society that would 'set a standard for others to follow.'[25] The prominent British sociologist Tom Bottomore, who was then at Simon Fraser University, penned two reviews, each echoing Blishen's assessment. The first review, published in the *Canadian Journal of Economics and Political Science*, referred to *The Vertical Mosaic* as 'an outstanding achievement,' a 'massive and thorough account of social class and power in Canada.'[26] In the second review, printed in the *Journal of Commonwealth Political Studies*, he praised *The Vertical Mosaic* for being 'one of the very few successful attempts to depict the class structure of a whole society.' So successful was it, said Bottomore, that it was 'likely to remain, for a long time, the point of departure for all Canadian sociologists working in this field.'[27] Aileen Ross, sociology professor at McGill, was equally complimentary. Writing in the *McGill Journal of Education*, she welcomed Porter's volume as 'the first factual study' to explore 'the broad sweep of Canadian society.' Not only did it collate 'thousands of bits of information that add up to the total picture' of Canadian society, she said, but it did so in a way that would help them to 'translate information into action' – action specifically intended to make Canada a more egalitarian country.[28] From Université Laval, Gérald Fortin wrote that in demolishing a number of assumptions Canadians collectively held about their society, *The Vertical Mosaic* acted not only as a 'douche froide de réalisme' but also provided Canadian sociologists with 'un socle solide et extrêmement bien construit' from which to examine further their society and its assumptions.[29]

Most Canadian political scientists, French- and English-language alike, expressed similar admiration. Don Smilley, from the University of British Columbia, argued that *The Vertical Mosaic* was 'a monumental work,' a 'major event in the retarded development of Canadian social science' that would make 'our understanding of Canadian society immeasurably richer.' He expressed admiration for Porter's intellectual honesty and willingness to make 'political commitments' as a 'social critic.' Picking up on a controversial theme close to Porter's heart, he argued that the most important part of his analysis was its focus on class as 'a source of norms by which to evaluate the political system,' replacing the traditional focus on 'cultural duality, ... nation-building and national unity.'[30] University of Toronto political scientist Martin Robin, like Bottomore, wrote two reviews. In the first, published in the *American Political Science Review,* he noted that Porter's picture of Canada was not 'the happy portrait of a horizontal mosaic of diverse groups relatively equal in status and power' with which most Canadians identified but a dismal sketch of a nation fractured by class and ethnic inequalities. Porter made it very clear that Canada was far from being a 'fully developed democracy.' However, while it was no 'pluralist utopia,' neither was it run, as the Marxists would have it, by a ruling-class 'cabal.'[31] In the second review, Robin focused on education. Writing in the *University of Toronto Quarterly,* he argued that *The Vertical Mosaic* had 'immediately been recognized as an important contribution to Canadian sociology,' likely to become 'a classic of its kind.'[32]

Jacques Dofny, a political scientist from the Université de Montréal, was more critical. Focusing on Quebec more than most of the other reviewers, he expressed serious reservations about Porter's theoretical and methodological preferences, arguing that they produced impoverished and partial accounts of both class relations and French–English relations in Canada. Nonetheless, despite these concerns, he said Porter's effort deserved to be commended. *The Vertical Mosaic* constituted 'a monument of precision and sobriety' that had few sociological comparators in Europe or the United States.[33]

In a letter written a quarter-century after *The Vertical Mosaic* first appeared, Queen's University political scientist Hugh Thorburn tried to evoke the environment in Canadian political science at the time: a setting within which Porter's book received almost universal approval from his colleagues. One factor operating in Porter's favour, he said, was that the book 'could very well have been written as a treatise in political science,' and so for political scientists, *The Vertical Mosaic* was an easy and familiar read. But the intellectual context was important as well. The Canadian social science community was then very small and there were no clear divisions between disciplines. At Queen's, for example, 'political science and sociology were ... one and the same department ... until 1970.' Partly as a consequence, Thorburn recalled, it was common, indeed expected, that scholars would read outside their own discipline. And in this particular case, the push to read the book was irresistible. Such was the salience of *The Vertical Mosaic* – those in the discipline saw it as a pioneering work – that any political scientist who did not read it would have been regarded as negligent: 'Everybody felt obliged to become familiar with what it had to say.'[34]

While Canadian commentators were generally fulsome in their praise, a vocal minority on the left and right of the political spectrum did not share in the collective enthusiasm. For those on the left, many of them members of Canada's small community of academic Marxists, Porter's findings were no surprise. As McGill's Gad Horowitz put it in a review in *Canadian Dimension*, 'Porter brings together great masses of evidence which show just how undemocratic and inegalitarian our society is. But we knew that all along; Porter confirms it for us.'[35] Similarly, in *Marxism Today*, an unnamed reviewer praised Porter's data on the structure of class and power in Canada and underscored a point related to the one Horowitz had made: the evidence Porter marshalled to 'polemicize' *against* Marxism actually provided 'material in its support.'[36] Philip Resnick, writing in *Our Generation*, added his voice to the chorus. Porter's empirical documentation, he noted, 'filled important lacunae which traditional scholarship had left untouched,' allowing him to contradict the widely held conventional pluralist conception of power. Also important was Porter's decision to take a principled political position against the unequal and apparently hidebound structure of class and power. Opting to be openly political instead of falsely objective, said Resnick, Porter introduced into Canadian social science 'excitement and controversy which had been largely lacking.'[37]

That said, Resnick and other leftist scholars thought Porter's analysis fell short. With Gad Horowitz, Resnick argued that Porter's work could not constitute the basis for a radical politics in the country because his decision to ignore more recent and sophisticated forms of Marxism greatly enfeebled his theoretical and methodological strategy and compromised his entire analysis: 'Instead of seeking a theory of Canadian society in which objective and subjective definitions of class [were] correlated, and deductions derived from ideology and interest,' and instead of drawing 'dialectically' on such Marxist concepts as 'exploitation' and 'totality' to get an historically accurate, multidimensional picture of Canadian society, Resnick argued, Porter had adopted the trappings of mainstream empirical sociology.[38] Thus he produced only a 'taxonomy' of Canadian society rather than an accurate and useful theoretical understanding of it.[39] As well, in keeping with his views as a liberal sociologist and 'radical democrat,' Resnick said, Porter had downplayed the possibility of radical social change in Canada.[40] Where Resnick left off, Gad Horowitz picked up, fleshing out the argument

Tommy Douglas had made about Canada lacking polarized political ideologies and thus failing to develop a truly national identity.[41] Writing in *The Marxist Quarterly*, Emil Bjarnason made many of these same points. Like the others, he noted that none of the data in *The Vertical Mosaic* were 'new or startling' to Marxists, and he complained that Porter refused to draw sufficiently radical conclusions about the 'dominion of the propertied class' over Canadian society. Nonetheless, he acknowledged that *The Vertical Mosaic* was a 'valuable and interesting' book that provided the Canadian working class with 'scholarly verification of what it has always felt in its bones to be true.'[42]

Reactions from the conservative end of the political spectrum were far more negative and vitriolic. Conservative Canadian political commentators, academic and lay alike, responded with denial and criticism. Queen's University historian Arthur Lower wrote a particularly nasty and dismissive review that began by denying Porter's primary claim. 'If there is one statement we are apt *not* to hear,' Lower claimed, 'it is that "Canadians are all relatively equal" … How can a writer begin his book with such a statement and expect to be taken seriously?'[43] Lower had many misgivings about the book, but the most serious could be traced to the book's disciplinary lineage. Simply put, *The Vertical Mosaic* was 'sociological' and therefore flawed by definition. Among its faults, Lower charged, were the following. First, Porter's book reduced reality to statistical categories. Second, its alleged philosophical approach was repugnant, 'an economic determinism of the most absolute kind' that 'left little room for human free will.' Third, it was written in abhorrent 'sociologese' that belaboured the obvious. Fourth, and worst of all, said Lower, it did not take history sufficiently into account. 'I wish sociologists would take a little interest in … time,' he wrote. 'That might make them more respectful toward their betters, the historians.'[44]

Academics were not the only ones to respond to *The Vertical Mosaic*. The book enjoyed brisk sales in the trade market and Porter received many letters from friends and critics; some were eager to congratulate him for his efforts, others keen to challenge his various claims.

One especially gratifying note came from Davidson Dunton, then en route to Europe. 'One of the great advantages of crossing the Atlantic by ship,' Dunton wrote, 'was that I had a chance to read *The Vertical Mosaic* without any involuntary interruptions. It is all that I thought it would be – and more still. To my layman's mind it is probably the greatest single contribution yet made to an understanding of Canadian society.' Dunton closed the note by wishing his newly famous professor a 'relaxing summer basking in solid praise for a big job superbly done.'[45] Quebec scholar Guy Rocher was also laudatory. In a letter written in late 1966 from Harvard, Rocher noted that Harvard's library copy of *The Vertical Mosaic* had already been heavily underlined and annotated and then said,

C'est pour moi un devoir ... de vous féliciter pour ce travail. Grâce à un travail patient et méticuleux, vous avez su accumuler un matériel abondant, riche, varié; vous avez su ordonner tout ce matériel de façon simple, claire et précise ... Bref, votre lire restera longtemps comme une des plus importantes contributions canadiennes à la sociologie empirique et à la sociologie du pouvoir, un modèle de recherche bien conduite, bien structuré.[46]

A civil service friend, Court Bond, was even more effusive in his praise: 'For anyone wanting to understand his country, [*The Vertical Mosaic*] is a must. It is Canada's *Das Kapital* in terms of importance.'[47]

But not all letters were so friendly. Ramsay Cook, editor of the *Canadian Historical Review,* in the context of a generally complimentary note, claimed that *The Vertical Mosaic* was flawed. Porter, Cook charged, had on occasion oversimplified or even falsified historical events.[48] Porter took great exception to Cook's claim, of course, and in a subsequent letter Cook tried to mend fences: 'If I used the word "falsify," and I don't remember doing so,' he wrote, 'I apologise. I thought I said "simplify," though I may be wrong. And that is what I meant – since you had to compress a lot of history ... you inevitably simplified in places ... But I certainly did not mean any falsification of evidence. I hope you will accept this explanation.'[49]

Porter's book drew the ire of conservative readers in the general population as well. Evelyn Purvis Earle, from Gananoque, a small town on the St Lawrence River east of Kingston, wrote to Porter to take issue – in a polite but somewhat condescending way – with his conception of who constituted the true elites of Canadian society. 'As ... a Canadian whose people arrived here in the 1700's and the early 1800's,' she asked, 'I am wondering how many generations Canadian you yourself might be. Will you please tell me?' Earle was looking, of course, for status distinctions of the kind that Lloyd Warner had studied in the United States: 'We of the old U.E.L. and pre-Loyalist stock do not consider that the acquisition of money alone qualifies a family to be considered the elite. Indeed we do not consider such a term desirable. We simply say "of good family." Many of those [who] use the not-too-well-informed term "the elite" came of very ordinary stock indeed, but they reaped the benefits of the labour of those of the old families who prepared the country for them.' She concluded with an invitation: 'My view of the social structure of Canada is somewhat different from those who glorify those with millions. Should you be in Gananoque drop in for tea and I will explain.'[50]

The wealthy and powerful industrialist E.P. Taylor didn't invite Porter to tea but, according to Frank Vallee, when a television interviewer cited *The Vertical Mosaic* and asked Taylor about the power of the economic elite in Canada and his place in that hierarchy, Taylor, then head of the Canadian Brewing Company and later head of Argus Corporation, dismissively trivialized the question. 'I don't have any power,' he said, 'I am run by my wife.'[51]

The Vertical Mosaic drew considerable attention outside Canada as well, especially among sociologists and political economists in England and the United States. Writing from England, T.H. Marshall, Porter's former tutor at the LSE, wrote a highly respectful review in the *Canadian Review of Sociology and Anthropology,* praising Porter for his comprehensive and synthetic treatment of the 'total Canadian polis,' broadly defined. Porter's book had limitations, he wrote, but constituted a worthy and welcome addition to the literature on class, which in Marshall's estimation had been overconcerned with issues of status.[52] Richard Chapman, a political scientist at the University of Liverpool, wrote in similarly laudatory terms, referring to *The Vertical Mosaic* as 'an outstanding work of scholarship' that 'should now be required reading for anyone who wishes to know about Canadian society.'[53] Thirty years later, LSE sociologist Donald MacRae recalled that while *The Vertical Mosaic* received less attention in the United Kingdom than the United States – because in his view such findings were 'old hat' in class-bound Great Britain – it was seen to be sufficiently important that a number of British sociologists convened a seminar to discuss it.[54] And Porter's good friend Bob McKenzie, a Canadian staff member at LSE to whom Porter had sent a copy of *The Vertical Mosaic,* added his congratulations as well: 'I consider it a magnificent piece of work and only regret that it has not been more widely reviewed in this country.'[55]

The Vertical Mosaic generated an even more favourable and consequential response in the United States. Perhaps the most enthusiastic review, published in the prestigious *American Sociological Review,* came from Irving Louis Horowitz.[56] 'Only the informal prohibition against adjectival excess prevents me from beginning this review ... with

Ethel, John, Eileen, and Arthur Porter, Vancouver, BC, c. 1926. Alan had not yet been born. Photographer unknown, Eileen (Porter) Jones personal papers.

John Porter with Beattie MacLean, his friend and former high school teacher, Wrexham, North Wales, spring 1945. Photographer unknown, Eileen (Porter) Jones personal papers.

Captain John Porter, Seaforth Highlanders of Canada, Canadian Army Historical Section, London, England, 1946. Photographer unknown, Eileen (Porter) Jones personal papers.

John Porter and Elizabeth Stalker, London, England, c. 1946.
Photographer unknown, Fiona (Porter) Ellen personal papers.

Elizabeth (Stalker) Porter and Fiona Porter, Prestatyn, North Wales, 1950.
Photographer unknown, Fiona (Porter) Ellen personal papers.

John and Marion Porter, Constant Lake, near Renfrew, Ontario, August 1956. Photographer unknown, Ann Porter personal papers.

John, Ann, Tony, and Marion Porter, London, England, c. 1961. Photographer unknown, Ann Porter personal papers.

Marion Porter at a friend's cottage, Ontario, c. 1970. Photographer unknown, Ann Porter personal papers.

John Porter, Carleton University, Ottawa, c. 1968. Photographer Colin Jones, CUA, Public Relations and Information Services, Series: Former Employees, 1958– 87, box PINFO-40, file Porter, John, 1961–79, part 1.

raves,' he wrote. In Horowitz's estimation, Porter's book was destined to be '*the* sociological study of present-day Canada, … a basic reference work on Canadian social structure for some time to come.' Porter did nothing theoretically innovative, Horowitz said, but his use of established theory in political sociology was 'virtually unparalleled.' Porter had found a way to 'use the strengths of "classical" sociological theories without being used by their weaknesses.'[57] Horowitz was not alone among American sociologists in his admiration for Porter's volume. Jack Seeley wrote a similarly complimentary review in the other flagship US sociology journal, the *American Journal of Sociology*. 'Everything about [Porter's] book – except perhaps the price – is praiseworthy,' he began. He then went on to describe *The Vertical Mosaic* as a 'politically and morally relevant volume' that disproved central elements of Canada's collective self-understanding and raised troubling questions with which the country and its elites would have to deal if they wanted to create a better society.[58]

While these favourable reviews in high-profile journals indicated clearly that Porter had made a splash south of the border, the true esteem in which the book was held in the United States did not become fully apparent until the 1966 annual meeting of the American Sociological Association. There it was announced that *The Vertical Mosaic* would receive the Robert M. MacIver Prize, awarded annually to the best sociology book published the previous year.[59] According to Marion, John had no idea his book was even under consideration. At the time, the family was in Geneva, where John had taken a position as a visiting scholar at the Labour Studies Institute of the International Labour Organization (see chapter 10). He became aware that it was in the running only because his Carleton colleagues Peter Pineo and Bruce McFarlane had heard a rumour. When Pineo heard the news, he phoned Porter to let him know, and rushed to him an ASA membership application form.[60] Fred Elkin of York University, who attended the meeting that year, was witness to the shock occasioned among American sociologists by the announcement that the prize would go to a Canadian for a book written about Canada. A couple of weeks after returning from the meeting, he wrote to Porter with a first-person account: 'Outside of the committee members it seemed that few people were aware of you or the book. People were asking: "Who is John Porter? Where is Carleton? What is the book about?"' Elkin said that he hoped that the award would 'serve to educate … sociologists in the United States' about Canada and the quality of Canadian sociology. Unfortunately for

174 Measuring the Mosaic

Porter, the University of Toronto Press was as surprised as anybody and had no copies of the book on hand for people to purchase.[61]

The MacIver Prize propelled Porter's career to a new level, providing him with the status and visibility necessary to get a foothold in the big leagues of American sociology. Already known to some of the major figures in the discipline in the United States, the award cemented his position. Indeed, within a couple of years, he and Bernard Blishen had sufficient profile to be able to call on the expertise and status of key figures such as William Sewell of Wisconsin and Ralph Turner of UCLA to help them get the funding they needed to carry out an important, large-scale project on educational aspirations and achievement in Canada (see chapter 11).

I noted above that *The Vertical Mosaic* provoked a response in the popular press. Against all odds, it became a commercial success despite a prohibitive fifteen-dollar price tag, equivalent to nearly $100 now.[62] Indeed, the initial printing of 1,500 hardcover copies sold out within three weeks.[63] This was a welcome 'I told you so' moment for Porter, who, according to Bruce McFarlane, had been furious when he heard of the small original run that the University of Toronto Press planned. Mc-Farlane recalled Porter's exact words: 'They must think it is a book on placer mining in Alberta or something.'[64] By late December, a second printing had sold out and a third was ordered. As early as November, *The Vertical Mosaic* had reached the *Montreal Star*'s best-seller list, unprecedented for a Canadian scholarly book.[65]

Encouraged by such lively sales, the University of Toronto Press proposed a paperback version that would sell for $3.95. Once again, Porter objected, this time because he thought the royalties were inadequate. Earlier, he had been very upset to learn he would receive only 90 cents of the $15.00 the Press charged for the hardback. When he was offered a 5 per cent royalty on the paperback version – 20 cents per book – he again complained. Such a proposal, he fumed, was 'preposterous.'[66] Even after the assistant director of the Press, Eleanor Harman, explained that the book was a break even proposition, that the Press and the Social Science Research Council were simply recovering their costs for producing and distributing the paperback, Porter balked.[67] Further letters and a face-to-face meeting failed to resolve the impasse until finally, in mid-January, Porter produced a successful counterproposal: he would receive 10 per cent on a book repriced to $4.50.[68] The decision to produce the paperback version in time for the 1966–7 academic year was a good one. Carrying the relatively modest price tag of $4.50, professors could reasonably require students to buy it as a course text, and across the country *The Vertical Mosaic* became de rigueur reading in a wide range of university social science courses. As a direct consequence, Porter soon became the most visible figure in Canadian sociology. He also made a bit of money. The first year alone, even before the paperback version figured into sales, he earned in excess of $4,000 in royalties – a tidy sum in those days.[69]

As I noted in chapter 7, it is relatively easy to understand the positive response generated by *The Vertical Mosaic*. The volume had clear scholarly relevance and merit, carefully documenting central aspects of Canadian society with comprehensive data, useful theory, and an ideologically provocative critique. As well, Porter's timing was impeccable, if unintentional. *The Vertical Mosaic* came out just as programs in sociology, political science, and Canadian studies were expanding at an exponential rate in Canadian universities.[70] As Alan Hedley and Rennie Warburton point out, Porter's tome was a natural choice for Canadian sociologists then looking for source books for a wide variety of graduate and undergraduate courses. Their research showed that fourteen of twenty departments offering 'Canadian society' courses in 1971 used *The Vertical Mosaic* as a textbook. In fact, they claim that both *The Vertical Mosaic* and *Canadian Society*, the reader that Porter had edited ten years earlier, actually had a good deal to do with the establishment of Canadian society courses in Canadian universities.[71] Nor did it hurt that *The Vertical Mosaic* came out during the mid-1960s, at a time when both the general public and the federal government were deeply interested in the country's national identity. American economic and cultural imperialism was on the rise and ever-increasing expressions of 'ethnic identity' in Canada, especially in the form of Quebec nationalism, made many Canadians uneasy. Porter's book rode this wave of interest in Canadian identity. In many ways, *The Vertical Mosaic* both created and reflected the sociological spirit of the time. The result, as Harvey Rich put it, was that Porter's book experienced a 'spectacularly successful [academic] career' for over a decade.[72]

To agree with Rich is not to accept another of his claims, that in the decade after it first appeared, the work enjoyed 'a near immunity from criticism.'[73] Quite the opposite was true. From the outset, scholars from different disciplines, sporting a variety of scholarly and ideological badges, acknowledged the significance of Porter's accomplishment but were quite eager to take issue with nearly every aspect of *The Vertical Mosaic*.

Empirical/Substantive Problems

Critics generally regarded Porter's empirical documentation as the strongest element of the book.[74] Indeed, it is a testament to the meticulousness of Porter's scholarship that despite many tough-minded critiques written during the first few years, his empirical data went generally unchallenged – until the early-middle 1970s, really.[75] This was particularly impressive, as Stephen Longstaff has noted, because Porter had been forced to construct the book 'out of the scantiest of available materials.'[76] Obviously, his colleagues felt that he had done his homework well.

However, critics from both ends of the political spectrum argued that Porter had not provided sufficient evidence for at least some of his claims and failed to deal adequately with some important issues. For instance, I mentioned above the complaint of Queen's University historian Arthur Lower about Porter's claim that most Canadians saw their society as classless. Lower's colleague at Queen's, political scientist Edwin Black, agreed, noting that Porter used this claim as a straw man that he could easily demolish. 'As a literary device,' said Black, 'the straw man is sometimes useful, but social scientists should provide some evidence for social images that they assert are both persistent and ubiquitous. None is given.'[77] Black is right; Porter should have provided some evidence for this central assertion and it is puzzling that no sociologist challenged Porter on this claim.

How could this happen? Why did he use this device or make this claim without providing detailed evidence? And why did no sociologist take him to task for not doing so? As for his assertion, we can only surmise that it was a consequence of his casual observations of Canadian society based on reading newspapers, watching television, and assessing the popular culture of the time. Recall that none of the reviews in Canadian news magazines denied the existence of the egalitarian myth that Porter used as the starting point for his analysis. The second puzzle – that neither sociologists nor journalists challenged his unsubstantiated assertion about the existence of a conventional belief in the generally middle-class character of Canadian society – may provide a partial answer to the first. It is possible that there was a widespread belief or myth to this effect, albeit as yet undocumented, so no one regarded the claim as problematic. Canadian data gathered just after the publication of *The Vertical Mosaic* by Porter and Pineo in the 'Occupational Prestige' study and by McMaster PhD student John Goyder in his own study provide evidence in support of his claim, albeit not in its entirety.[78] Porter and Pineo found that about 62 per cent of Canadians placed themselves in the middle class or upper middle class, while the comparable figure in the Goyder study was 60 per cent. Thirty per cent of those in the Porter and Pineo study and 34 per cent in the Goyder study placed themselves in the working class. In neither study did more than 4 per cent combined place themselves in the upper or lower classes.[79] So it seems clear that around this time most Canadians saw themselves as middle class. Porter's sense of people's collective self-evaluation of their class positions was quite astute.

On a second point of criticism, Black wanted Porter both to provide conclusive evidence that elites possessed group consciousness and coherence and to show (via case studies of key decisions) that they had successfully exercised power.[80] On this issue and others, Black claimed that a great deal of research would be necessary 'before the yawning fissures in our knowledge [could] be bridged ... [and] a number of Porter's important propositions ... accepted.' 'Without that support,' Black said, '*The Vertical Mosaic* exhibits far too many faults in design and workmanship ... to be transferred to tablets of stone.'[81]

A particularly salient issue that received insufficient attention from Porter according to many critics was the influence of American economic and cultural domination. In the mid-1960s, social scientists were very sensitive to the fact that American corporations held a great deal of power in key sectors of the Canadian economy. This gave them considerable indirect influence over the Canadian government. Foreign capitalists made decisions that had a tremendous impact on the nation's overall economic development while sometimes exacerbating problems of regionalism and ethnic conflict by creating unequal economic opportunities among various peoples and geographic areas. This was of great concern to scholars and citizens alike because Americans held this power without being accountable to Canadians and their elected political leaders. As Harvey Rich put it some years later, the empirical realities of 'the asymmetrical power relations between Canada and the United States [and] the implications of the extent of foreign, largely American, economic domination' should have been built into Porter's conceptual scheme. Their absence was equivalent to 'presenting Hamlet without the prince.'[82]

Other significant omissions mentioned repeatedly when the book first appeared included Porter's failure to pay sufficient attention to regionalism in general, and the Quiet Revolution in Quebec in particular.[83] As well, and very curiously by today's standards, almost nothing was said about Porter's failure to deal with gender inequality. Published feminist criticism was not common in the late 1960s, in part because the small number of women scholars in sociology had not been able to make gender issues into a central concern in the discipline. I suspect that, for the time, Porter was no more or less attendant to 'women's issues' and feminist concerns than most male sociologists. Not until the late 1970s did feminist scholars produce a concerted, well publicized, and effective critique of 'malestream' scholarship.[84]

Theoretical/Conceptual Problems

Most criticisms of Porter's conceptual framework centred on his post-capitalist theoretical definition of class, though some commentators expressed related concerns about his concept of power. According to Porter's formulation, classes were no more than nominal groups: arbitrary statistical aggregates. Critics praised Porter's decision to try to capture the national structure of class, regarding it as clearly superior to American studies of status at the community level, but Marxists in particular argued that he lost some of the benefits that accrued to societal-level analysis by 'divorc[ing] class from its historical context' and positioning it in 'a statistical, as opposed to the real world.'[85] Having denied the reality of classes, they said, they became purely nominal entities, portrayed in necessarily static and ahistorical terms (i.e., changing patterns of income distribution or shifts in occupational structure).[86]

This theoretical/methodological choice had political implications. Radical critics acknowledged that Porter favoured the establishment of a more egalitarian society but balked at his decision to treat Canada's long-standing tradition of system-stabilizing brokerage politics as inevitable and were suspicious of the reformist brand of liberal policy science his work represented. Certainly, they did not share his faith in the ameliorative potential of education. More radical changes were necessary and possible, they said, via class struggle.[87] As proof of the validity of their claim that real classes existed in Canada, they pointed to Porter's own evidence, noting quite correctly that he sometimes ignored his own definition of classes as purely objective, statistical entities. For example, in his discussion of what the 'real' middle class *was* like and what a ruling class *would be* like, Porter sometimes made reference to criteria – subjective definitions of class and class consciousness – that suggested classes were real rather than nominal entities.

Critics paid much less attention to his conceptualization of power. Somewhat curiously, for the first few years, commentators largely ignored Porter's refusal to distinguish conceptually between power and authority.[88] Instead, many centred on his use of the plural elites model, making various claims about the degree to which his empirical evidence might be used to make the claim that Canada had a ruling class.[89] Others focused on his use of a Weberian notion of power, according to which *individuals* held power. Marxists in particular saw it as necessary to examine power at the structural level, tying the analysis of power to the analysis of class in a different way from that which Porter attempted.

At the time, there was little discussion of Porter's conception of ethnicity. Thirty years after *The Vertical Mosaic* appeared, however, sociologist Jean Burnet reminisced that at the time she thought there were three flaws in Porter's handling of these materials. First, he didn't distinguish between ethnicity and culture: 'When he wrote that culture was a myth, he thought he was saying that ethnicity is something that could be discarded.' In Burnet's view, this was wrong. 'One can see,' she said, 'that ethnicity [was] important to many, many people ... [O]ne cannot say that it [was] disappearing or becoming a myth ... after World War II.' Second, ethnicity was then and is still a socially constructed category, not an objective, ascribed social characteristic: 'I was very uneasy about the ... lack of symbolic interactionist basis in what Porter wrote ... To someone who had studied with Blumer and Hughes ... this just wasn't adequate at all.' And third, his statistics were based on 'the racial or ethnic origins statistics from the census and he [didn't] point out the limitations.' It was important to understand, Burnet cautioned, that people could redefine their ethnic origin 'every time the census person [came] around.'[90]

Methodological Problems

Methodological critiques of *The Vertical Mosaic* focused on three issues: Porter's operationalizations of class and power; his failure to adopt an explicitly comparative approach; and his decision to reject value freedom.

Marxists believe that classes are sets of historical relations between real groups of people whose interests, values, and identities are best understood in terms of their collective and respective relationships in and through the means of production. At the time, Marxists naturally supplemented their critique of Porter's theoretical definition of class by condemning his methodological decision to operationalize classes as nominalist groups of individuals who shared nothing more than similar incomes, educations, occupations, and the like.[91]

Equally unsatisfactory for critics from a wide variety of backgrounds was Porter's use of the positional method for studying power. This technique – examining elite positions rather than performing a decisional or reputational analysis – forced him to assume that there was a direct correlation between formal power (holding a position at the top of a bureaucratic hierarchy) and actual power.[92] This was a sore point for Edwin Black, for instance. In Black's view, Porter's discussion of power failed to distinguish between the *potential* capacity to realize one's goals and 'the actual having of one's way.'[93] Marxists took issue with yet another aspect of the positional method: it focused on individuals. This tied into their critique of his conceptualization of class. Focusing on individuals prevented Porter from examining power relations between real classes at the structural or societal level over time.[94]

A second methodological problem with *The Vertical Mosaic*, according to some critics, concerned Porter's failure to make a systematic comparative analysis, for clearly he had Great Britain and the United States in mind as comparators.[95] Porter himself acknowledged this shortcoming in a letter to Christopher Beattie, written two years after the book appeared: 'The book lacks a comparative perspective. My original plans called for a comparative chapter. But time and resources did not permit. Since then I have become much more interested in comparative work.'[96] Years later, Dennis Forcese claimed (despite Porter's mea culpa) that the charge was actually inaccurate. In Forcese's estimation, Porter 'implicitly or explicitly contrasted Canadian society and its flaws to the American in all his work,' and on most counts found Canada woefully lacking.[97] Again the letter to Beattie is revealing, for there Porter notes that he thinks it possible to use macrodata to show that the United States is more 'democratic' than Canada.[98]

A third methodological issue raised by many scholars was Porter's decision as a New Liberal to forego the so-called value freedom of mainstream, scientific sociology and to judge Canadian society as morally defective: far too unequal, unnecessarily undemocratic, and ideologically dishonest. Some commentators – journalists like John Bannerman, politicians like Tommy Douglas – regarded Porter's willingness to make such judgments as a breath of fresh air: invigorating, provocative, necessary. Only such pronouncements, they said, would produce the kind of open and creative political dialogue that had heretofore been lacking. John Meisel spoke to this issue in his foreword to *The Vertical Mosaic*: 'Professor Porter's study ... departs from a long-standing tradition in Canadian academic circles concerning the degree to which a scholarly work can be simultaneously respectable and polemical. It has been the custom (breached by only a handful of hardy souls) to assume that to be polemical and objective at one and the same time is impossible ... A sense of commitment, of *engagement*, has, in short, been a sign of scholarly impurity.' Meisel went on to note that he certainly did not see Porter's work as compromised in any way by his sense of moral engagement. *The Vertical Mosaic*, 'is outstanding both in the indefatigable meticulousness and ingenuity with which it documents its argument and in the clarity with which it articulates and defines its assumptions and values.'[99]

But other scholars from the right and left of the political spectrum disagreed. For some, like Edwin Black, the decision to mix description and moral assessment was unacceptable in and of itself. Worse, this mistake was compounded by another: not only had Porter made (faulty) moral judgments about the exercise of power in Canada, but he had done so on the basis of inadequate data. 'Serious students of government and politics cannot accept John Porter's pioneering study without close methodological examination,' wrote Black. 'The reader must always bear in mind the mixture in John Porter of social reformer and sociologist; the one often gets the better of the other. While the real picture of Canada's socio-political structure might be somewhat as the author paints it, artistic licence is evident, and the reality is considerably more complex.'[100] At the other end of the ideological continuum, Marxist scholars took an entirely different tack on Porter's decision to mix description, analysis, and moral judgment. From their perspective, a value-laden stance was perfectly acceptable, part of standard practice. Their complaint, the direct opposite of Black's, was that Porter had not gone far enough. Resnick, writing in *Our Generation*, referred to Porter as a 'radical democrat,' sometimes a 'straight liberal,' and claimed that a Marxist, using the same data 'would go much further, showing how the ... class structure of Canada infuses its control over the whole society.'[101] Half a decade later, Marxist James Heap made the same claim, that Porter's data begged for a more radical interpretation. However, he took an extra step, claiming that Porter had argued in bad faith.

The author of *The Vertical Mosaic* should be labelled value inconsistent, conceptually confused, and 'theoretically innocent' ... His questionable 'innocence' consists of a lack of any foundation for his analysis of class, the use of a narrow, faulty foundation for his analysis of power, and the loose employment of a democratic elitist context. Taken together, these multiple problems suggest something more than simply 'theoretical innocence.' They suggest the presence of an overarching strategy. A strategy of respectability.[102]

Few on the left shared Heap's view. More common were the sentiments expressed years later by Wallace Clement, Porter's student and a prominent figure in the then-nascent radical political economy tradition. *The Vertical Mosaic* might be flawed, Clement said, but it was no liberal whitewash. Speaking from personal experience, Clement defended his mentor who, he said, 'never hesitated to be polemical.' 'Any esteem Porter sought was for the quality of the work done, not by doctoring his conclusions to please the powerful. His "restraint" and "tentativeness" were confined to the strength of the conclusions which he could draw from the quality of the data available. When data warranted, he did not hesitate to draw a "radical" conclusion.'[103]

In sum, critics of all stripes claimed that Porter's choice of theoretical perspectives on class and power, combined with unfortunate methodological choices, prevented him from painting a thorough, historically accurate picture of the structure of class and power in Canada. They disagreed as well over his decision to offer a moral critique of Canada *and* the specifics of the critique he offered.

In my estimation, Porter's choice of the stratification approach to class and the positional approach to the study of power made sense. As a first-time examination of the structure of class and power in Canada, his work had to sketch the broad outlines of the structure of each before he could fill in details about how they worked. In chapter 1 of *The Vertical Mosaic* he made it clear that there was more to class than occupational structure, income categories, and lifestyle. He knew classes were 'real' in some measure and acknowledged this to be the case. Similarly, in chapter 17, Porter described a number of instances of elite conflict (a form of decisional analysis) as a way of fleshing out his purely positional analysis of power. For these reasons and others, Michael Ornstein commented many years later that Porter actually had quite a bit in common with the class theorists, certainly more than they allowed. In particular, Ornstein attached considerable significance to Porter's decision to follow his analysis of the economic elite with an analysis of the labour elite. That Porter analytically privileged capital and labour indicated – despite appearances to the contrary – that he actually held a *relational* conception of power, making his work 'more in keeping with class than elite theory.'[104]

While Porter's analyses of class and power had their respective shortcomings and provoked a great deal of further research and debate over the next ten years or so, they were important not just in and of themselves but because they had an impact on his discussion of the degree to which Canada was – or might become – a true democracy.

Democracy

In discussing Porter's conception of democracy in *The Vertical Mosaic*, published in 1965, it is useful to compare it to the conception he outlined in 'Power and Freedom in Canadian Democracy,' published in 1961.[105] They are not only notably different but also highlight many of the chief points on which critics focused in responding to *The Vertical Mosaic*.

In the 1961 piece, Porter expressed social democratic views. He claimed that elites had usurped societal power and decision-making capacity by gaining control over the 'machinery' and ideology of institutional bureaucracies. 'Each ... corporation is bureaucratically organized,' he said, under the 'effective command' of 'a small group of senior officers and directors.' These officers possess 'power': the capacity 'to direct the affairs of other people.' They use this power to force those in subordinate positions to adopt an 'attitude of obedience.' This allows elites to achieve their goals. Subordinates who wish to get ahead in the bureaucratic system – or want even just some measure of security – have to be 'docile' because they do not have property rights.[106] Porter did not claim that elites created this morality, but rather that they drew on it to maintain their advantage within 'the exploitative, predatory and restrictive' institutions that constituted capitalist society.[107] In so doing, he asserted, they negatively influenced the personal lives of many Canadians while simultaneously denying the population at large any meaningful control over the nation's collective life.

Porter wanted to deal with these problems through a set of social democratic remedies: public ownership of selected industries, the decentralization of production, and the expansion of industrial democracy. These changes would break the control of the rich and powerful over the Canadian economy and loosen their stranglehold over what he referred to as 'society's creative potential.'[108] With other changes, they would go a long way toward replacing Canada's purely formal *political* democracy with a more egalitarian *economic* democracy.

In framing these arguments, Porter cautioned that state intervention in many areas of social life was necessary but that the growth of bureaucracy, with its tendency to create new possibilities for personal power wielding, had to be closely monitored. It could not be eliminated – bureaucratic rationality was a necessary part of modern life – but it was crucial to make a concerted attempt to control it via informed state intervention, especially via public ownership of key industries. Plutocrats could not be left free to use bureaucracy to their personal advantage.[109] 'The case for public ownership to produce more material things may be weak,' Porter wrote, 'but the case for it as a means of allowing social participation and the humanizing of bureaucracy may be overwhelming.'[110] For Porter, state ownership or public control should be combined with a rethinking of the importance of efficiency and profit.[111] Central planning, decentralized production, and worker satisfaction were far more crucial: 'We must move towards some system of industrial democracy.' Since 'large productive units' were incompatible with 'worker participation,' in his view, planning should aim to decentralize production.[112]

These societal goals could be accomplished gradually, using the educational system and the mass media. In combination, they could create a more humane and rational citizenry, including, in particular, enlightened leaders.[113] The creation of such a citizenry was possible, according to Porter, because there was 'no such thing as a rigid psychological structure called human nature.' Instead, he argued, there were 'social *natures* in the sense that the prevailing psychological dispositions are socially created.' He believed it possible 'to create a society in which the prevailing personality is marked by humanitarianism and rationality.' '[W]hile such a goal may be far distant,' he said, 'it is the goal we must keep in mind.'[114]

Taken together, these arguments indicate that, in 1961, Porter was a social democrat: 'The answer surely lies in the desirability of social participation in defining and achieving goals, in the release of the potential for a creative life shared with others, governed not through competitiveness and authoritarianism but through co-operation.'[115] Certainly, this is how he saw the piece in retrospect. In the 1979 introduction to the reprint of 'Power and Freedom' in *The Measure of Canadian Society*, he noted that at the time it was written he regarded it as a 'critical and prescriptive, if not programmatic [contribution] to social democratic theory.'[116]

By 1965, he seems to have rethought some of these ideas. The most obvious change was his revised view of the character and potential of Canada's economic system. In 1965, he concluded that the postcapitalist economy had altered the exploitative tendencies of its nineteenth-century forebear so markedly that no shift to socialism was necessary. In both works, Porter worried about the harmful effects of an increasing concentration of power, growing bureaucracy, and structured social inequality, but whereas in 1961 he was optimistic that these tendencies could be monitored and controlled, by 1965 much of his optimism had evaporated. He no longer advocated the moral necessity or economic rationality of a fundamental transformation of the economy. Gone were his recommendations about public ownership, decentralization, and industrial democracy. Gone, too, were his comments about the benefits to be gained from the creation of a new, humanely rational, and enlightened citizenry. In fact, he seemed ready to accept a much compromised economic and political democracy in Canada. Stressing the inevitability and functional necessity of power differentials, and playing up the Hobbesian side of human nature, he suggested that the most rational social policy Canada could follow would be to establish a *liberal democratic elitism*. 'Canada,' he wrote near the end of *The Vertical Mosaic*, 'is probably not unlike other Western industrial nations in relying heavily on its elite groups to make major decisions and to determine the shape and direction of its development.' He thought it unlikely that 'widespread participation' could or would develop. He concluded that 'if power and decision-making ... always [had to] rest with elite groups,' then the best that could be hoped for was 'open recruitment from all classes into the elites.'[117]

In this context, education would no longer serve as a transformative agency charged with the creation of a new, enlightened citizenry. Instead, it was to act as a sorting mechanism, ensuring that individual initiative and societal rationality were served to the greatest degree possible by selecting the most able and ambitious members of society for the system's most demanding and responsible positions. To date, he claimed, the Canadian educational system had failed in this endeavour. In this respect, he charged, the country lagged behind other twentieth-century democracies, especially the United States.[118]

Many of his leftist critics regarded Porter's view of Canada's democratic potential with alarm. Menno Boldt, a sociologist from Trent University, issued a detailed critique of this part of Porter's argument. Reflecting the prevailing spirit on the left at the time, he focused on Porter's idea that 'the average Canadian' was inert, apathetic, and materialistic. In *The Vertical Mosaic*, Boldt wrote, Porter had issued a moral indictment of Canadians, claiming that they tended to exhibit three serious character flaws. First, the average Canadian was more interested in satisfying an appetite for 'American-style consumer goods' than in preserving 'the nation's economic and political autonomy.'[119] Second, Canadians were allegedly 'undisturbed by the inequalities in their society.' Third, although they possessed 'the economic, technological and social resources to achieve a more equitable distribution of life opportunities,' Canadians had not tried to reach that goal.[120] Porter, Boldt charged, was 'optimistic about the *possibility* of intervention but pessimistic about man's *determination* to intervene.'[121] Among the most important of the negative conclusions Porter adopted was that Canada had no 'charter myth' against which social progress might be measured, no 'utopian image of the future' that might give its citizens a reason 'to sacrifice material well-being for more worthy social objectives such as economic and political autonomy.'[122] Porter could and should have understood that trends toward bureaucratization and oligarchy were tendencies rather than certainties, Boldt concluded, and could and should have suggested how to counteract them. As well, he could and should have expressed faith in the intelligence and humanity of Canada's citizenry, thereby promoting the emancipatory possibilities of democracy.[123] In sum, he should have used his influence to urge Canadians to strive for the creation of a more progressive (read social democratic) Canada.

Writing in 1971, a full six years after the release of *The Vertical Mosaic*, Boldt might have noted that Porter's research and political activities in the interim suggested he had not in fact given up on the average Canadian. While deeply concerned about the prospect of democracy in Canada, he spent a good portion of his post-*Mosaic* academic career as a New Liberal 'practical intellectual,' gathering further data related to Canadian social problems, working as an advocate of egalitarianism, especially equality of educational opportunity, and suggesting policy solutions. No person who was engaged in such activity could truly have given up on his fellow citizens.

Boldt was also incorrect to say that Porter had no utopian goal toward which Canadians could or should strive. I discuss these issues at length in the afterword, but note for now that Porter's conception of Canada's best possible future – its utopian goal – combined two sets of New Liberal ideas: Hobhouse's principle of social development, that 'a community develops as it grows in scale, efficiency, freedom and mutuality'; and related ideas about the nature of citizenship and democracy drawn from Hobhouse, T.H. Marshall, and C.B. Macpherson.[124] He did not explicitly use these terms in *The Vertical Mosaic*, but he certainly demanded that something be done to make the country more egalitarian and democratic than it was.

As we shall see in subsequent chapters, following the publication of *The Vertical Mosaic*, Porter slowly drifted back toward the Hobhousian, social democratic end of the political spectrum. This suggests there is another way to look at the apparent change in his views between 1961 and 1965. That is, the different conclusions in the two works can be explained in part by the fact he wrote them for two different audiences and purposes and thus in two different styles. The 'Power and Freedom' essay constituted an unequivocal indictment of 'the system.' His colleagues in the *Social Purpose for Canada* venture were a company of left-liberals and social democrats. The group had a clear mandate from the Boag Foundation to foster socialist ideas and a pragmatic political agenda tied in some way to the founding of the NDP. In these circumstances, Porter threw some of his scholarly reserve to the wind and assuming the mantle of Hobhouse's 'engaged intellectual,' wrote a provocative opinion piece that revealed his New Liberal social democratic political principles.

Why did he back away from these views in *The Vertical Mosaic*? It is possible, indeed likely, that between 1961 and 1965 he temporarily changed his mind on some issues. T.S. Eliot has written that 'the great poet, in writing himself, writes his time.'[125] *The Vertical Mosaic* was written in the middle of a long-term growth phase in the Canadian economy in the middle of a North American sociological community taken up with postindustrialism and Daniel Bell's end-of-ideology ideology. Porter had rejected Marxism before leaving the LSE and was suspicious of Soviet communism. He had been a Labour supporter and had converted to Hobhouse's liberal socialism while in England, but by the mid-1960s had come to be convinced of the rationality of the postcapitalist transformation of the economy, impressed by the humane character of Canada's expanding welfare state and confident of the ameliorative potential of education. In these circumstances, it is not surprising that Porter played up the liberal side of Hobhouse's liberal socialism. His orientation to the data on class, power, and education in *The Vertical Mosaic* reflects the spirit of the times. In *From Culture to Power*, Robert Brym notes that Porter was like S.D. Clark and Seymour Martin Lipset, who around this time abandoned socialist ideas, opting instead for key ideas and approaches from American mainstream sociology: functionalism, postcapitalism, modernization theory, end-of-ideology theory, and so forth.[126] Like other sociologists, they were drawn into the orbit of mainstream American sociology. Gad Horowitz noted this shift as well but characterized it as a partial, temporary, and practical adaptation to circumstances rather than a change in fundamental beliefs. 'Porter is no mere liberal,' he wrote, 'He is a socialist.' He had not abandoned socialist goals such as 'equality of condition, public control of the economy [and the] meaningful participation of masses of people in the making of important social decisions.' However, nationalization and central planning had not worked, inequality seemed 'inevitable,' and democracy appeared to be a 'utopian dream.' Therefore, Horowitz said, 'Porter the socialist ... retreats a few steps to solid ground and assumes the role of Porter the sociologist ... [He] mutes his own radicalism.'[127]

Horowitz's interpretation makes a good deal of sense. Porter wrote 'Power and Freedom' as a polemic and among political colleagues who probably encouraged him to draw the strongest possible leftist conclusions in his analysis. By contrast, he wrote *The Vertical Mosaic* for his academic colleagues, partly with the intention of securing his future at Carleton. This might well predispose him to be more cautious, to come to more conservative conclusions. I think that in his heart of hearts Porter remained more radical than *The Vertical Mosaic* lets on. I do not think that in four years he would have completely abandoned his optimism about the possibilities for social democracy in Canada. But as a sociologist he could not overlook his findings – whatever his personal preferences and hopes as a citizen. The data indicated that more pessimistic conclusions were perhaps warranted. Thus, in *The Vertical Mosaic* and for about a decade thereafter, under the influence of American sociology and perhaps convinced of the possibilities of a more meritocratic liberal democracy with a growing welfare state, he hesitated to embrace too radical political beliefs. I expect that during this period he was not entirely sure in which direction Canadian society would move – what possibilities might remain open and viable for a more just and egalitarian society. Certainly, as his remarks in the 1968 *Maclean's* interview make clear, he had not become a card-carrying liberal. This created tension between his public pronouncements and private beliefs.

Moreover, as the chapters to follow show, the conclusions he reached in *The Vertical Mosaic* were actually tentative and temporary. During the decade following its publication there appeared a huge volume of research on issues of class, power, ethnicity, and democracy, some of it his own, much of it inspired by *The Vertical Mosaic*. As he considered the political implications of this wealth of information, he vacillated and then slowly shifted leftward, in the direction of the beliefs he had expressed in the 'Power and Freedom' essay. He never accepted the idea that it was enough simply to 'renounce ... capitalist modes of production' in order to create the best of all realistically possible social worlds, but within ten years of the publication of *The Vertical Mosaic*, seemed once again to have moved to the socialist side of Hobhouse's liberal socialist definition.[128]

Conclusion

When *The Vertical Mosaic* came out, the data it reported provided a background against which many elements of Canadian social, political, and economic life made sense. As well, the data and analyses opened up an enormous range of possibilities for further scholarship. New subjects could be explored more confidently and old ones looked at in a different light because of *The Vertical Mosaic*. So deep and widespread was its influence that it came close to being paradigmatic in the fully Kuhnian sense of that term, serving as a proximate exemplar for many of Canada's sociologists. As W.E. Mann put it, Porter provided the 'received wisdom' about trends in Canadian society 'as seen from the liberal perspective.'[129] And the effect was lasting. University of Toronto sociologist Robert Brym has pointed out that the work set the style, standards, and agenda for much of Canadian sociology for the next decade.[130] Apparently, this did not come as a surprise to Porter. According to Douglas Fisher, about a year after the book came out, the two of them discussed its impact. 'I mentioned he wasn't getting the hurrahs and national discussion created a decade before by Hilda Neatby's *So Little for the Mind.*' Porter, said Fisher, was unconcerned: 'He didn't have any envy of that bestseller. He thought the *Mosaic* would have a longer effective life both as a basis for continuing critical analysis and as a standard textbook for undergraduate courses.'[131]

Before turning to the events of the post-*Mosaic* decade in Canadian sociology, it is appropriate to comment at least briefly on the current relevance of *The Vertical Mosaic*. Clearly, the book no longer sets the agenda or style of Canadian sociology. Nonetheless, it holds a certain pride of place in the canon. This is not because of the data there reported; that information is now of historical interest only. Instead, it remains important for two other reasons: the *agenda* it set – to study class, power, and ethnicity from the point of view of a morally engaged macrosociologist – and the *imagery* it employed. While there have been tremendous changes in Canadian society in the past four decades, one fundamental feature remains unaltered. Canada is in many respects no more egalitarian now than it was then, and class and ethnicity still constitute two fundamental bases of that inequality. Thus, the inequities of class, ethnicity, and power that Porter addressed so ably in *The Vertical Mosaic* remain as central and contentious as ever, both within the academic community and in Canadian society at large. In 1965, Porter made the wise and lucky decision to describe the intersection of class, power, and ethnicity in Canada as a 'vertical mosaic.' Without question, the image became one of the best known and most insightful ever used to describe the social structure of Canada, easily competing with others such as the 'two solitudes/deux nations' of Hugh McLennan, Arthur Lower, and Everett Hughes, the 'British fragment' thesis of Louis Hartz, or the image of Canadians as 'hewers of wood and drawers of water' taken from the Bible.[132] In terms of ethnicity, class, and power, the mosaic, if not the vertical mosaic, remains a an iconic metaphor to which current Canadian social scientists turn in their attempts to understand changes in the character and quality of their national life.

9 Canadian Society and Canadian Sociology in the 1960s and '70s

The 1960s and '70s were eventful. Scientists made fundamental advances in nuclear energy, genetics, and computer technology that transformed almost every aspect of daily life. As well, the geopolitical map of the world changed dramatically as the Vietnam War, the Cuban Revolution, the Cultural Revolution in China, ongoing conflict in the Middle East, and struggles of national liberation in the Third World reconfigured political, economic, religious, racial, and ethnic tensions around the globe, leaving a sense of foreboding that political-economic stability was nowhere in sight. Particularly ominous was the escalation of the Cold War, an uneasy standoff between the world's great Communist powers – the USSR, East Germany, and China – and the rest of the Western world, most notably the United States. The most frightening aspect of this confrontation, which cast a threatening pall over the globe for nearly two decades, was a grotesque nuclear arms race between the United States and the USSR.

The United States played a central role in many of these scenarios. Despite serious problems at home – racial inequality and conflict, protests against the Vietnam War, and so on – the White House saw the spread of communism as the chief threat of the era and throughout the period presumed to act as the self-appointed guardian of the 'Free World,' repeatedly placing an American presence in the way of Communist expansion in Eastern Europe (Germany) and the Far East (Korea, Vietnam). As well, the United States intervened in the domestic politics of several countries – Indonesia, Chile, Nicaragua – allegedly to prevent Communist governments from coming to power and, not coincidentally, creating an environment receptive to American foreign investment. These repeated incursions, often bitterly resented by local populations, produced a great deal of anti-American sentiment around the globe.

The Sociopolitical Landscape

Canada was deeply influenced by the social, political, and economic turbulence produced by the Cold War, American economic and cultural imperialism, and various international protest movements: the Native rights movement, the women's movement, the anti-poverty movement, and the student/youth movement. And it had home-grown problems as well: the provincial rights movement and Quebec separatism among them. To cope, Canadian politicians employed two tactics. On the international front, they tried to implement a foreign policy somewhat independent of American influence. At home, they adopted an increasingly interventionist New Liberal philosophy, attempting to come to grips with various disputes, inequalities, and injustices by using the power of the federal state.

In chapter 4, I described the events of John Diefenbaker's rocky tenure as prime minister from 1957 to 1963. In 1963, the Liberals wrested power from Diefenbaker's Conservatives and then remained in power, first under Lester Pearson (1963–8) and later under Pierre Trudeau (1968–79), for the next decade and a half. During their respective times in office, Pearson and Trudeau instituted wide-ranging political and social reforms, including an unprecedented expansion of the welfare state. Until 1972, this proved a relatively easy task because the last echoes of the postwar boom provided them with the substantial fiscal resources they needed. In 1973, the Canadian economy entered an extended period of decline, however, in part because of a worldwide economic recession. The egalitarianism and generosity of the 1960s waned, and the last vestiges of the spirit of New Liberal reconstructive optimism that had helped to build Canada's increasingly comprehensive welfare state played themselves out. Shadows remained in Trudeau's call for a 'just society,' and the federal government remained interventionist on many fronts, but after 1973 Keynesianism was called into question and monetarism changed government's approach to social policy.

In the context of these developments, John Porter carved out the post-*Mosaic* phase of his career. His scholarly and political interests and activities during the period grew out of an attempt to understand the impact of class on the dynamics of educational and occupational opportunity in Canada. The political orientation he adopted, the theoretical and methodological tools and strategies he used to undertake his research, and the conclusions to which his research led – all of which changed over time – were much influenced by the demographic, social, economic, and political events of the period. I begin with a quick look at basic demographic and economic developments.

Many of the demographic trends from the immediate postwar period continued through the 1960s and beyond. Canada's population grew quickly, rising to 24.3 million in 1981, an increase of a third in just two decades.[1] A good portion of this increase came via immigration. The federal government abandoned its preference for Northern European immigrants, establishing a policy favouring skilled workers regardless of their national origin, and the racial and ethnic mix of Canadian society broadened quickly.[2] Population growth was accompanied by continued urbanization; by 1981, three of four Canadians lived in urban areas and nearly half lived in one of Canada's ten largest metropolitan census areas.[3]

The postwar pattern of rapid economic growth continued as well, though with substantial inconsistencies and fluctuations. Between 1963 and 1979, Canada's GDP more than doubled to 418 billion dollars, though in two distinct phases.[4] By far the best part of the period was the decade 1963–72. After that, the long postwar boom shuddered quickly to a halt. The GDP continued to rise, living standards continued to improve, and the size of the employed labour force continued to grow, but inflation and unemployment increased precipitously and the deficit became a debilitating problem.[5]

Other key changes in the Canadian economy included a continued shift from the primary and secondary sectors into the service sector and a related shift toward more skilled jobs.[6] Union membership grew rapidly as well. In 1961, 23 per cent of Canada's workforce was unionized; by 1981, that figure had grown to 30 per cent.[7] And organized labour flexed its muscles as it grew. The powerful Canadian Labour Congress (CLC) entered into a relationship of 'sympathetic independence' with the fledgling NDP, and though the endorsement never manifested itself in a huge number of new votes for the party, during the 1960s, at least, the labour movement became more militant.[8]

At the same time, women entered the paid workforce in record numbers. In 1961, fewer than one in three worked outside the home for pay. By 1981, that number had grown to one in two and women made up 40 per cent of the workforce.[9] This had a profound, long-term influence, though the effects were spread unevenly across the country and through the class structure as labour market segmentation developed and women were ghettoized into less desirable, poorly paid occupations, particularly in the service sector.[10] Despite this, they had more economic power and freedom than before. These gains were augmented when they began to stay in school longer and to use the birth control pill on a widespread basis. Birth rates dropped and families became smaller.[11] Taken together, these developments changed both the gender dynamics of Canadian families and the structure and workings of the country's formal and domestic economies. Marriage rates declined, divorce rates went up, and a new ideology of gender equality manifested itself in changed expectations, norms, and power relations within the family and the workplace.[12] By 1967, the National Council of Women and other women's organizations pressed successfully for the appointment of a Royal Commission on the Status of Women. When the Commission report was released in 1970, it had a major positive impact on the women's movement and feminist causes across the country.[13]

The long-term effects of these postwar demographic and economic trends had special salience during Pearson's time in office. In the mid-1960s, rapid economic growth meant that the Liberals had money to spend – revenues increased by 75 per cent during the period – and spend it they did.[14] Though they were cautious about expanding the welfare state too rapidly, public sentiment favoured various progressive and egalitarian social policies, and combined with persistent pressure from the NDP (which held the balance of power in parliament), forced them to expand many social programs and to institute others.[15] Indeed, the 1960s was probably the high water mark of interventionist New Liberalism in Canada. Certainly, during Pearson's time as prime minister, the scale of operations of the federal government, especially in the realm of social policy, increased to a new order of magnitude. In particular, widespread popular demand for a society in which more, if not all, Canadians could benefit from the postwar boom focused attention on education as a key to personal opportunity and national growth. As a result, and of special interest to John Porter, governments poured unprecedented amounts of money into postsecondary education.

But the picture was not entirely positive. Growth was sporadic and uneven across sectors of the economy and regions of the country and, as always, some Canadians benefited more than others. Data on the distribution of income illustrate the point. Between 1961 and 1969, the percentage of annual earned income that went to the top fifth of wage and salary earners in Canada remained just below 40 per cent, while the share that went to the bottom fifth remained just below 7 per cent, a five- or sixfold difference which remained constant throughout the 1950s and '60s.[16] And levels of class inequality were greater even than this, for these data do not take into account investment income (which tends to go to the top 10 per cent of Canadians) or wealth (the ownership of capital and other assets), both of which were far more unevenly distributed than earned income. In 1969, one Statistics Canada study found that the top 10 per cent of Canadian families owned 40 per cent of the country's wealth.[17] Data on poverty are equally revealing. Although many welfare state measures were put in place to help the disadvantaged, a 1969 report written by a Senate committee investigating poverty concluded that approximately 5 million Canadians, about one in four, lived at or below the poverty line.[18] Aboriginals, visible minorities, the aged, and women (especially single mothers and elderly women) were especially vulnerable to unemployment, low incomes, and poverty. Regional inequalities likewise continued to be problematic.[19]

Toward the end of the decade, American domination of the Canadian economy, a point Porter discussed at length in *The Vertical Mosaic,* increasingly became a point of contention. By the late 1960s, the two economies were highly integrated; 60 to 70 per cent of Canada's import/export trade was carried on with its neighbour to the south.[20] While this degree of *integration* was worrisome to some, far more troublesome was growing US *control* of the Canadian economy. By the end of the decade, as US corporations increased their degree of ownership or control to almost 30 per cent of all non-financial assets in the Canadian economy, economic nationalists became increasingly restive.[21] By 1970 most Canadians (80 per cent according to one poll) wanted the federal government to reduce the degree of American control over the Canadian economy.[22] Not everyone was as pessimistic as well-known McMaster University philosopher George Grant, who argued in *Lament for a Nation* that Canada's nationhood had been irretrievably lost, but many Canadians worried about the country's status as an independent nation.[23]

All of these trends continued during Trudeau's time in office. He made public noises about what he referred to as 'the just society' and pushed through a legislative agenda that finalized Medicare, improved the unemployment insurance scheme, and increased pensions.[24] However, after 1973 he was hamstrung by the recession.[25] He tried to fight it with a monetarist 'tight money' policy and wage and price controls, but with discouraging results: increased unemployment, wage increases below the level of inflation, and higher interest rates, all of which contributed to a massive increase in the annual deficit.[26] His efforts to rectify the problem of American ownership of the Canadian economy, particularly in the energy sector, had some positive results, but the measures he used were unpopular in corporate circles.[27] He angered not only many members of the Canadian business community – who had no qualms about a highly integrated continental economy – but also many American capitalists, who then looked elsewhere for a place to invest their money.

As well, Trudeau also had to struggle to keep Quebec in Confederation. The dilemma surfaced while Pearson was in office, in the early years of the Quiet Revolution during the era of Premier Jean Lesage. Quebec's goal of 'rattrapage' – catching up with the rest of North America – was only part of a larger social movement. This 'projet de société' involved not only economic modernization and a general secularization of education, hospitals, and social services but also nationalism ('maîtres chez nous'), and, for some, separatism.[28] The Quiet Revolution became very noisy indeed.[29] The stakes grew ever larger over the next few years as Quebec nationalism grew and separatism became more popular. The separatist issue reached its highest level of salience in 1976, when the Parti Québécois won a majority government in Quebec. The win did not signal a clear victory for the separatist project, of course, for the PQ was home to a wide range of groups whose interests had been poorly served by Robert Bourassa's Liberals.[30] Nonetheless, leader René Lévesque kept up the nationalist rhetoric, publicly proclaiming the establishment of an independent Quebec as his primary goal, though exactly how his concept of 'sovereignty association' might work was never made entirely clear. He saw his home province as one of two equal nations within the Canadian state and demanded that the Constitution be amended to give Quebec the special status and powers that would recognize that interpretation. Most of English Canada did not want to grant either special status or special powers and, like Pearson before him, Trudeau resisted. A champion of individual rights rather than the collective rights demanded by Lévesque, Trudeau tried to find a way to allow Quebec to keep its French-language culture while basing a unified Canadian state on an expanded set of universal individual freedoms and rights. The outcome of the struggle, which did not come to a head until after Porter's death, was the famous sovereignty association referendum of May 1980 that saw Quebec voters reject the separatist option offered to them by a relatively narrow margin of 60 to 40 per cent.[31]

There is one last signal feature of the 1960s, the youth movement, that I have not yet discussed. I have left it to the end because it is the best way to draw this general discussion of 1960s and '70s back to John Porter and his place in the history of Canadian sociology.

As Doug Owram points out in his history of the baby boom generation, *Born at the Right Time,* and as Cyril Levitt makes clear in *Children of Privilege: Student Revolt in the Sixties,* the youth movement was just one aspect of a wide-ranging, anti-authoritarian, anti-traditionalist movement that became prominent in Western culture in the 1960s. And while many of the changes were manifested in the area of popular culture – music, fashion, sexual behaviour – other long-standing institutions, practices, and values were profoundly altered or bulldozed out of the way by youth culture. The changes started immediately. In the late 1940s and early '50s, when the 'boomers' were infants and young children, new, more permissive and democratic theories and practices of childcare came into prominence.[32] Then, as the boomers came of school age, governments expanded and liberalized the primary education system to accommodate them.[33] The same thing happened when they entered high school. The system expanded rapidly to make room, and as more of them decided to stay in school they helped create the phenomenon of teenage culture, a sort of extended adolescence.[34] During the 1950s, this 'culture of the teenager,' as Owram refers to it, was relatively tame.[35] But by the mid-to-late 1960s, under the influence of the New Left, the leading edge of the baby boom became intellectualized and politicized and created an adversarial counterculture that constituted a wide-ranging critique of the authority system of Western society.[36]

The counterculture had a huge impact on the university system. As the 1960s got underway, Canadian universities were in many respects little different from their 1920s progenitors: traditional, bureaucratic, elitist, and authoritarian. In the late 1960s, when suddenly they became an intellectual, social, and political home away from home for an unprecedented number of young adults, many of whom were influenced by the counterculture, something had to give. Soon, the universities had been transformed, becoming more progressive, open, and flexible.[37] Universities became the venues where fundamental societal disputes often took place as student leaders and their followers struggled to transform 'the system,' displace 'the establishment,' and institute what student radicals regarded as a more humane and authentic form of society.

Some of the power of the younger generation to transform Canadian universities – and Canadian society more generally – can be explained by demographic factors. By the mid-1960s over half of Canada's population was less than twenty-one years of age.[38] As a group, they were used to being accommodated. When they passed through the first stages of their collective life cycle, they changed the family, the school system, and popular culture. As they aged, they presumed the process would continue. In addition, as Levitt has noted, they were an affluent group with the time and money to go to university. Once there, the university provided them with an environment that encouraged considerable freedom of thought, a place to pause, reflect, and, for some, condemn 'the system' their parents and grandparents had wrought.[39] Ironically, it was the university, the object of their criticism, that exposed them to a range of radical intellectual perspectives – the ideas of the New Left, Marx, critical theory – which they used to frame a more sophisticated critique of technocracy, sexism, racism, and class inequality than they could or would have developed otherwise.

But many of the changes occurring in the university system in the period had little to do with youth culture and power per se. There is no doubt that as the boomers passed through high school and entered university they changed the structure, philosophy, and practices of these institutions. They demanded reforms – more accessibility, choice, relevance, and control – and were eventually accommodated. However, some of the struggles they waged were easy to win because, as I noted above, for reasons of their own, the federal government, the provincial governments, and the business community had already placed the universities on their respective agendas. In the early 1960s the federal Liberals and a number of provincial governments decided it was crucial to use the postsecondary education system to train 'human capital' to drive economic growth in what they understood to be the new postindustrial society. The Canadian business community generally shared this view.[40]

At the same time, in the context of growing economic opportunities and creeping credentialism, parents began to hold postsecondary education in high regard and pushed universities to accept more students. The outcome? Governments across the country funded a massive and unprecedented expansion of the postsecondary education system and more students ended up in university than ever before. Once in university, they pursued their progressive sociopolitical agenda and, to a degree, succeeded. They forced the system (the universities in particular and society in general) to change to suit their preferences. But many other stakeholders and social forces played a part as well.[41]

Porter, the New Liberalism and Postsecondary Education

To understand why John Porter investigated some social issues rather than others, employed some theoretical-methodological perspectives rather than others, and, finally, why he decided to move from pure scholarship into policy-related research and then academic administration, it is necessary to supplement our understanding of the general economic, social and political environment in Canada during the 1960s and '70s I have just described, with an appreciation of the university milieu in which he worked.

The student movement itself was not one of Porter's first interests or concerns, but two questions integral to the debate about the role of education in society captured his scholarly attention: Who gets to university and why? And what role does education play in the dynamics of upward mobility in Canada? During the fifteen years following the completion of *The Vertical Mosaic* – a period that coincided with the expansion of the postsecondary educational system and the rise and fall of the student movement – nothing attracted as much of his time and effort as these questions. He did spend some time examining the brain drain, but it was questions of access to education and the nexus of class, gender, education, and occupational status that inspired *Towards 2000, Does Money Matter? Stations and Callings,* and *Ascription and Achievement,* the major publications of his post-*Mosaic* career.

Porter was not alone in his efforts to understand these relationships. Among the thousands of scholars whom Canadian universities hired during the period were hundreds of sociologists. Most were young and politically aware. Many had been part of the student movement – as well as other causes – but now, somewhat ironically, they were in the front lines facing their student successors. Not surprisingly, many of them turned their scholarly attention inward, so to speak, and began to examine critically the role of education, especially university education, in Canadian society. Like their counterparts in the United States and elsewhere, and partly under the influence of Porter's work, they tried to unravel the knot of social relations that connected class structure, gender, race, ethnicity, and the like with the structure of the educational system, the occupational division of labour, and patterns of social status and mobility. One question that engaged many of them was whether Canada's educational and occupational systems were meritocratic, i.e., places where those with ability could get ahead, regardless of their social background.

Porter was a key figure in these and other related areas of research in Canada, but unlike some of his colleagues, he took a direct hand in applied policy research that touched on university-related issues. At the same time, he became involved in senior administration at Carleton. He took up these interrelated tasks, I think, because he wanted to make postsecondary education accessible to as many motivated and capable students as possible, regardless of their social background. In his view, the university itself could be used as a political instrument in his New Liberal quest to make society more rational, egalitarian, and just. If researchers could refute the myth that it was not the best and the brightest who moved from high school to the universities but those from well-off middle- and upper-class families, then this finding could be used to put pressure on politicians and bureaucrats. Working with others, he could use these data to force the university system and society more generally to live up to the meritocratic ideology their members espoused. The task was particularly pressing and promising in the 1960s and early '70s; the system was growing rapidly and thus affecting an ever larger number of young people. Given the strength of the reformist, New Liberal ideology of the period, the system might – indeed should – be open to an egalitarian plea for an educational system based on merit and effort rather than class privilege. I noted above that the Canadian universities and Canadian sociology in particular grew rapidly during the 1960s. The details are as follows.

Canadian Sociology in the 1960s and '70s

Developments in the Canadian University System

During the period, Canadian universities in general and Canadian sociology in particular went through two distinct phases. The first phase lasted from 1960 to 1973, as universities enjoyed an unprecedented time in the sun. Public faith in higher education was strong and led to a massive increase in government spending. Old universities were expanded and new ones built. In 1960, Canada had thirty-eight universities, which survived on a combined budget of $262 million. Ten years later, there were forty-nine universities and their combined budget had grown nearly sixfold, to $1.6 billion.[42] Full-time undergraduate enrolment doubled between 1962 and 1971, to 287,000.[43] Graduate education grew even more quickly; enrolments nearly quadrupled, to 36,000.[44] Growth in Ontario was especially dramatic. In 1960, Ontario universities registered 32,000 full-time students. By 1970, that figure reached 121,000.[45] Rapid growth in the size of the student population forced universities across the country to hire legions of new faculty. In 1961, there were 8,800 university teachers in Canada, 2,900 of whom were in Ontario. By 1971, there were nearly 28,000, of whom 11,000 were in Ontario.[46] Porter was much heartened by these developments and, reflecting the individualist spirit of the times, stressed the meritocratic component of Hobhouse's liberal socialism that he held dear.

By the late 1960s, however, public and political support for higher education had dropped precipitously and government spending on universities came to be seen in some corners not as a profitable and beneficial economic investment but as a social cost, a factor that caused inflation and thus inhibited rather than contributed to economic growth and recovery.[47]

The turning point came in the early 1970s. The economy continued to worsen and both levels of government decided to cut funding to the universities.[48] In Ontario, the cuts were modest, but because student numbers continued to grow the province's universities, including Carleton, 'sustained the largest decline in real operating income per student' in the country.[49] Funding shortfalls created substantial political conflict between the universities and the government, but there was little the universities could do.[50] To cope, they put a freeze on new construction, trimmed operating budgets, and tried to reduce their faculty complements (despite continued enrolment increases). For its part, Ontario's professoriate became disenchanted with traditional university labour relations practices and, by the end of the 1980s, the faculty at seven Ontario universities, about 30 per cent of those in the province, had unionized.[51]

Developments in Canadian Sociology

GROWTH

Sociology was popular with the boomers, a generation interested in societal issues. Seeing an opportunity, the small Canadian sociology community of the 1960s took advantage of the financial resources, administrative flexibility, and intellectual openness of the period to expand the discipline. By the early 1970s, it had put into place the institutional infrastructure necessary to establish sociology as a fully fledged professional-academic presence: a large professoriate, independent administrative departments, an extensive network of undergraduate and graduate programs, access to substantial research funding (via the Canada Council), a national professional association (the Canadian Sociology and Anthropology Association), and a scholarly journal (the *Canadian Review of Sociology and Anthropology*). Both the CSAA and the *CRSA* played major roles in the 1960s and '70s, acting as venues for vitriolic debates over Canadianization, the rise of feminism, the development of Marxism and political economy, and the role of the CSAA as a scholarly professional and political organization.

Porter played a central role in these developments. In 1954, he joined one of two informal sociology chapters of the Canadian Political Science Association, the discipline's parent organization, operating out of Ottawa. In 1957, the two chapters succeeded in being formally recognized by the CPSA. So rapidly did the number of sociologists and anthropologists in the CPSA grow in the 1960s that Porter and some of his senior colleagues began to pursue the prospect of an independent professional organization and a new journal dedicated to their field. As early as 1961, Porter and the rest of the chapter's executive committee – Jean Burnet, Nathan Keyfitz, John Meisel, Guy Rocher, Aileen Ross, and Marc-Adelard Tremblay – held formal talks with their parent organization. The following year, they succeeded in establishing their journal and, as I noted in chapter 6, Porter was elected its first editor. Just a month later, however, he had to relinquish the position after suffering a massive heart attack. Two and a half years later, with assistance from Bruce McFarlane, Chuck Hobart, Jacques Brazeau and, most important, Rex Lucas, the editorial board of the *CRSA*, acting as a provisional executive, succeeded in completing the establishment of the CSAA, an independent professional organization for sociology and anthropology.[52]

Their success in establishing the discipline was greatly aided and abetted by a number of scholarly successes. One of these landmarks was *The Vertical Mosaic*, of course, but three royal commissions – Bilingualism and Biculturalism, Health Care, and the Status of Women – also played a role. In a fashion similar to the McGill Social Science Research Project and the Frontiers of Settlement Project of an earlier era, the commissions not only provided sociologists with a wonderful research opportunity but also allowed them to demonstrate their skills and thus legitimate the discipline as they worked alongside their colleagues in the more established social science and humanities disciplines.[53]

From 1960–1 to 1971–2, the number of full-time faculty teaching sociology in Canadian universities increased fourteenfold, from 61 to 829, while the number of sociology programs, courses, and students increased commensurately.[54] According to Vladislav Tomovic, in 1960–1 sociology was taught at thirty-one English-language universities, sixteen of which had independent departments of sociology.[55] By 1970–1, sociology was taught at forty English-language universities, about one-quarter of which had independent sociology departments.[56] Growth in graduate programs was just as dramatic. Whereas in 1960–1 only McGill, Toronto, and UBC had graduate programs in sociology and only McGill and Toronto offered the PhD, by 1969–70 there were twenty-three such programs, including twelve offering the PhD.[57]

Coincident with the growth in graduate education was an increased emphasis on research. This manifested itself in many ways. Increasingly, universities expected new faculty either to have the PhD or to be well into a PhD program.[58] As well, research productivity came to be a priority during the deliberations of hiring and tenure and promotion committees.[59] The demand to publish put pressure on existing publication outlets and contributed to the establishment of the founding of the *CRSA*.[60] Research funding grew as well. In 1964–5, the Canada Council awarded just $203,000 for research to all the humanities and social science disciplines combined. By 1968–9, that figure had grown to $378,000 for sociology alone.[61]

Although academics such as Porter were pleased with the speedy expansion of the university system in the 1960s, the rapidity of growth created serious problems. Nowhere was this more evident than in sociology, where the processes of growth, institutionalization, specialization, and professionalization spawned a set of divisive, long-term, and foundational debates. Sociologists teaching at Canadian universities maintained sufficient disciplinary cohesiveness during the early 1960s to be able to create a space for themselves in the Canadian academy, often in the face of opposition from traditional social science and humanities disciplines, but there was strife within the new community. Theoretical and political infighting among mainstreamers on the one hand and radicals (Marxists, feminists, political economists) on the other, combined with methodological squabbling over if and whether sociology could or should be a science balkanized the sociology community. Much of this quibbling took place within the confines of yet a third foundational debate: whether Canadian sociology had benefited or suffered from being 'Americanized' and if it needed to be rescued by being 'Canadianized.'

THE CANADIANIZATION DEBATE

Canadian universities produced only one sociology PhD between 1957 and 1964 and only nineteen during the entire decade of the 1960s.[62] As late as 1973–4, the system had produced just thirty-one sociology PhDs.[63] As a result, Canadian departments had to hire faculty from other countries, and throughout the fast-growth phase of the 1960s they recruited heavily from Britain, Australia, and especially the United States. The result? By 1971–2, only one in three of those teaching sociology in Canadian universities outside Quebec were Canadian citizens and by 1973–4, more than three-quarters of those holding PhDs and teaching in Canadian departments of sociology had earned their degrees outside the country.[64] The shortfall in PhDs meant that universities had to hire many people who did not have a doctoral degree. This later created major concerns about the quality of such faculty members, for many never finished their degrees. As well, many of those hired were Americans, with the result that courses had a great deal of American content. As late as 1972–3, a study revealed that only 25 per cent of required texts in undergraduate sociology courses were written by Canadian authors, and in graduate courses the corresponding figure was below 10 per cent.[65]

The domestic response to the Americanization of the Canadian university system was spirited and Carleton was at the centre of the storm, though Porter and the sociology department generally stayed on the sidelines. In 1969, two professors in Carleton's English department, Robin Mathews and James Steele, published *The Struggle for Canadian Universities*, a nationalist polemic that demanded the adoption of measures to Canadianize the nation's universities. Their book touched a nerve and the issue became a cause célèbre.[66] The Association of Universities and Colleges of Canada appointed a commission chaired by T.H.B. Symons to address the issue. Symons' report, *To Know Ourselves*, along with the Mathews and Steele book and other like-motivated volumes, generated a good deal of nationalistic sentiment.[67] Students became restive and a large part of the professoriate galvanized around the importance of hiring Canadians, teaching Canadian curriculum, and doing research on Canadian issues.[68] In an era of growing Canadian nationalism – sometimes manifested as anti-Americanism – the hiring of Americans and the use of American materials smacked of academic cultural imperialism.[69]

In sociology, the widespread disquietude generated by the situation manifested itself in the guise of a nationalistic Canadian sociology movement.[70] Sociology had the highest percentage of American nationals of any discipline, so the debate was especially fierce, divisive, and extended. For their part, Canadian nationalists regarded a 'sociology *about* Canada' done using the theoretical and methodological tools of scientific (read American) sociology as inappropriate. They argued for the necessity of a distinctively Canadian sociology that would examine the unique history, social structure, and dynamics of Canadian society.[71] Opponents of Canadianization, John Porter among them, argued the opposite. The pursuit of scientific knowledge, they countered, could not be fettered by nationalistic and parochial concerns. In their view, 'American sociology had traveled furthest down [the scientific] path' and therefore constituted the 'gold standard.'[72]

The upshot of the acrimony over the Canadianization of sociology, much of it played out in the committees and annual meetings of the CSAA and the pages of the *CRSA* and the *Canadian Journal of Sociology*, was a victory for the nationalists.[73] Canadian sociology became more Canadian as departments of sociology established preferential hiring practices that favoured Canadians, there was an increase in the production of Canadian texts, and curricula were revamped to focus more on Canadian issues.[74] But the victory was not complete. Even after the Canadian House of Commons passed legislation that allegedly forced universities to hire Canadians preferentially, the tendency to hire Americans persisted.[75] As a consequence, much Canadian and American sociology remained more or less indistinguishable. As Toronto sociologist Lorne Tepperman put it, summarizing an idea expressed five years earlier by Nathan Keyfitz, 'No distinction could be drawn between American and English-Canadian sociology: not in topic, style, ... content ... [or] quality.'[76]

The situation became even more difficult when cutbacks in university funding arrived in the early 1970s. The timing was terrible. Recently established and expanded graduate programs in sociology had just started to produce significant numbers of MAs and PhDs. In 1974–5, for example, Canadian sociology departments produced 184 MA graduates and 39 PhD graduates.[77] From 1972 to 1979, Canadian sociology departments graduated 295 PhDs and the floodgates were about to open because of the large number of PhD students in program across the country.[78] Just as departments began to produce home-grown PhDs in sufficient numbers to redress the balance in the national origins of sociology faculty across the country, the market seemed to be drying up.[79] Fortunately, however, sociology continued to expand, albeit much more slowly. In 1972–3, there were 720 sociologists with appointments in Canadian universities; by 1977–8, there were 909. Two-thirds were Canadian citizens.[80]

The impact of these disciplinary changes – growth, institutionalization, professionalization – combined with the politicization of the universities in general and the discipline of sociology in particular to influence the situation in Porter's home department at Carleton.

THE SITUATION AT CARLETON

I noted in chapter 6 that in 1964–5 the Carleton sociology department had seven full-time faculty members (five of whom were sociologists) and that by 1972–3, just eight years later, its full-time faculty complement had mushroomed to thirty-eight, of whom more than two-thirds were sociologists.[81] And student numbers continued to grow. During the three years from 1968–9 to 1970–1, enrolment in undergraduate arts programs climbed by 15 to 20 per cent per year.[82] Sociology seemed to get at least its share.Bruce McFarlane recalled that the number of sociology majors ballooned from less than forty in the mid-1960s to more than 400 a decade later.[83] Of course, undergraduates were not the whole story. Enrolment in arts graduate programs increased by a similar proportion and sociology did better than the norm, growing from thirty-nine in 1969–70 to fifty-two in 1970–1.[84]

Here Porter played a particularly significant role, helping to get the department's new PhD program off to a good start. The program was approved in 1969 under the leadership of Frank Vallee, then chair of the department.[85] The Carleton program had produced its first MA in 1964 and then ten more between 1965 and 1969. Porter was not much involved until the 1970s, however, when he supervised three MAs (Hugh Armstrong, Wallace Clement, Hugh McRoberts) and sat as a member of four other MA committees. His real contribution came at the PhD level. Between 1973 and 1978, the department produced twelve PhDs. Porter supervised six: Maria Barrados, Wallace Clement, Sid Gilbert, Graham Knight, Hugh McRoberts, and Dennis Olsen.[86] Clement in particular came to be a high-profile scholar. Indeed, during this period Carleton sociology had an outstanding reputation within Canada – Whyte referred to it as the department's golden age – and Porter had a great deal to do with this state of affairs.[87] According to Clement, other scholars such as Bruce McFarlane, Frank Vallee, Zbigniew Jordan, Dennis Forcese, and John Harp were important and made the department a first-tier choice for prospective PhD students, competing equally with places like the LSE and the University of Chicago, but Porter was 'the centerpiece' and 'drawing card.'[88]

The department stopped growing in 1972–3 and then remained in stasis to the end of the decade, while simultaneously increasing the number of female faculty.[89] In 1964–5, Carleton had no female faculty; by 1972–3 it had six: Monica Boyd, Bonnie Erickson, Florence Hughes, Valda Morlan, Gertrud Neuwirth, and Caryll Wells.[90] But there were no courses on women or women's issues per se.[91]

Curiously, Canadianization was not as significant an issue in the Carleton department as it was in sociology departments elsewhere, in part because until 1965 almost all Carleton's faculty were Canadians. John Hofley recalls that when he was hired there in 1966 only one of nine full-time faculty members was American. Eight were Canadians who had done their undergraduate degrees in Canada and then gone outside the country for the PhD.[92] By 1972–3, the situation had changed and more than half of the thirty-eight faculty members in the department were non-Canadians, but this was still better than the national average.[93]

Porter's view on Canadianization is telling, for it illustrates both his deep connection to American sociology of the time and his ambivalence about questions of Canadian nationalism. For one thing, he held meritocratic views about the utility of ideas and arguments: a good idea was a good idea regardless of the nationality of the person presenting it. So he was not a scholarly nationalist. If anything, he saw American society and its sociology as models to emulate, and wanted to make Canadian sociology more like American, not less. He appreciated that Canada had some unique economic, social, and political features and wanted to develop a Canadian sociology in the sense of sociology *about* Canada. In his view, Canadian social scientists knew far too little about their country and he saw it as part of his mission to gather such data. But he believed that the ultimate purpose of a sociology about Canada was to develop the kind of quantitative, comparative sociology best represented by the scientific sociology prominent in the United States.

Conclusion

During the postwar period Canadian sociology matured. It grew, institutionalized, diversified, and became more sophisticated. As Canadian sociologists built the infrastructure of the discipline, they applied many theoretical approaches and techniques of research and statistical analysis that had been developed in Europe and the United States. A considerable degree of theoretical, methodological, and substantive specialization became the norm. Until the late 1960s, this specialization did not create a problem because the discipline remained centred on a comfortable consensus created by the essentially liberal and sexist functionalism that had constituted the theoretical mainstream of North American sociology for about two decades. However, with the re-emergence of Marxism, the rise to prominence of feminism, the development of the new radical political economy, and the efflorescence of 'interpretive' or 'constructionist' approaches to the discipline, the consensus broke down. The discipline became not only more sophisticated and complex but also deeply politicized and confrontational.

The Canadianization debate illustrates the messiness of the situation. When Canadian sociologists objected to the American takeover of the discipline in their country, their criticisms painted with the same brush American Marxists and American mainstreamers. In any other accounting, these two groups would *never* have been lumped together. Likewise, Canadian and American mainstreamers crossed national lines and joined forces to square off against Marxists and the new radical political economists. Feminists, the third group, were perhaps most confrontational and splintered of all. They became embroiled in debates with the other groups – justly condemning them for sexism – but at the same time debated heatedly among themselves about the relative utility of liberal, radical, socialist, and other forms of feminism.[94]

Nor did these gender, national, and theoretical differences exhaust the list of fault lines that ran through the discipline. There were generational and methodological divisions as well. Most of the Marxists, feminists, and political economists were younger, Canadian, and nationalist. They were not shy about criticizing what they regarded as the generally conservative practices of their usually older American colleagues. For the young Canadian PhD student or faculty member interested in Marxism, political economy, or feminism and partial to historical or other qualitative methodologies, one of the enemies of the era was the older, usually male, mainstream, American or American-trained number cruncher. Departments and the discipline as a whole became fractured, disputatious, and highly political. As Lorne Tepperman described the situation, 'Many sociology departments appear to be stratified like rock beds, with one ideological layer sitting on top of another. The unfortunate congruence of rank and intellectual style has served to limit the sharing of ideas between age-cohorts. Worse, it has promoted and rationalized conflict in sociology departments during the period of greatest growth in Canadian universities.'[95]

These developments had profound consequences. By the late 1970s, the small, relatively cohesive national community of a few score mainstream sociologists who had formed the discipline in 1960 had become one group among many, absorbed into a new disciplinary community comprising competing, confrontational, quarrelling clusters of various sizes with a combined population nearly a thousand strong.

John Porter's research interests grew in part out of the political, social, and economic trends and events of his time and in part from the scholarly puzzles that fascinated the sociologists of his era. The societal trends and events that interested him were often international in reach and he was attuned to – in fact, driven by – a desire to be part of debates that had developed in sociology around the world, and especially in mainstream American sociology. For example, *The Vertical Mosaic* and his early essays reflected an interest in elites, class, and power that was widespread in mainstream British and American sociology in the 1950s and early '60s. Likewise, when he took up themes of social mobility, access to education, and equality of opportunity in the late 1960s and early '70s, he was following the lead of international scholars, primarily Americans. His intention in replicating for Canada a number of pieces of American survey research on occupational status, educational attainment, and social mobility was to push Canadian sociology along the same path as the American discipline. Nonetheless, Canada remained his chief concern and he was never completely drawn into the orbit of American sociology. During the second half of the 1970s, he developed considerable respect for the ideas of a handful of radicals, most notably American Marxist Harry Braverman and Canadian New Liberal political philosopher C.B. Macpherson. As well, he came under the influence of the new political economy approach that had captured the imagination of some of his own graduate students, Wallace Clement and Dennis Olsen in particular. Porter was much influenced by the creative tension generated by these opposing currents in American and Canadian sociology and it showed in the kinds of scholarly work he carried out and the political and sociological conclusions he drew.

But his efforts were not driven by academic puzzles and internecine struggles alone. He was an engaged and politically aware intellectual who was genuinely interested in the societal problems and political issues that these perspectives were intended to address. In my analysis of his later career, I reveal details of his ideas about key issues of the time: inequality, opportunity, education, mobility, and the like (see chapter 10 onward). In addition, I examine the influence of the changed university environment from the mid-1970s on, which constituted the political, economic, and scholarly context in which he developed his understanding of these issues.

My analysis in the afterword uses as its organizing principle the idea that Porter exemplified the scholarly political approach of the New Liberal 'practical intellectual.' Given his reputation and strong political beliefs, some might find it surprising that Porter did not become a public intellectual. From time to time he commented in the popular media on Canadian social, political, and economic life, but chose not to divert his attention from an essentially scholarly, rather than more popular and publicly political, consideration of the major issues of Western industrial nations and mainstream Western sociology: democracy, equality, power, education, opportunity. Why? For one thing, he was not personally attracted to the hurly burly of daily politics. Moreover, he already had a full plate: an ambitious program of research, substantial duties as a supervisor and mentor of graduate students, and increasing responsibilities as an academic administrator. More important, in these applied, practical activities – research, teaching, policy work, academic administration – he demonstrated *his sense* of how to be a practical and engaged intellectual. It was not necessary to become a public intellectual or to enter politics. I believe that in this regard Porter was following in the tradition of New Liberalism to which he had been exposed and converted at the LSE in the late 1940s. Later I outline in detail the ideas of New Liberalism and try to understand Porter's activities in this light.

But the story of the second part of John Porter's career rightfully begins with an account of the years 1966–9, a peripatetic period during which he reaped the rewards of *The Vertical Mosaic* and consolidated his position as one of the premier social scientists in Canada.

10 Geneva, Ottawa, and Toronto, 1966–1969

The attention generated by *The Vertical Mosaic* brought numerous opportunities Porter's way, providing a huge boost to his career. His reputation soon grew to formidable proportions and he came to be regarded as one of Canada's foremost social scientists. It is interesting, given these developments, that Porter originally had no idea his book would create such a stir. Three years after the book appeared, he answered a letter from American sociologist Wendell Bell at Yale University by confessing that it had 'been received in Canada in a way which I never foresaw.'[1] This helps to explain a noticeable increase in his self-confidence after the book came out. According to Porter's colleagues at Carleton, the success of *The Vertical Mosaic* had a major positive impact on his self-image. Muni Frumhartz recalled that afterward John developed a sense that he could make a major intellectual contribution to Canadian sociology, something 'he may have doubted very much previously.'[2] Frank Vallee's recollection was much the same. At first shocked, said Vallee, Porter soon 'got used to the idea that [*The Vertical Mosaic*] was a great work' and began to think and behave accordingly.[3] The response provoked by *The Vertical Mosaic*, especially the MacIver Prize, affirmed that his work was on the right track and he could reasonably aspire to undertake equally ambitious, high-profile studies in the future. And he seized the opportunity. Drawing on his newly augmented reputation, he secured funding for two large-scale research projects – a study of the educational and career aspirations of Ontario high school students and a national study of occupational mobility – that allowed him to follow up on central themes of *The Vertical Mosaic*.[4] These studies further enhanced his stature in the North American sociological community, which in turn had a positive impact at Carleton and in Canadian sociology more generally.

At Carleton, his soaring reputation began to draw talented graduate students to the department and helped make it one of the best – and best known – in the country. Queen's University sociologist Roberta Hamilton was a student at Carleton in the early 1960s and took Porter's 'Power and Stratification' class. She recalls her PhD thesis supervisor, Hubert Guindon, telling her a story years later. Apparently, Porter once asked Guindon if the Carleton sociology department was 'the best in the country.' Guindon replied, 'It is when you're there, John.'[5] But his contributions to Carleton went beyond those of a purely scholarly nature. He had already begun to develop a reputation as an able administrator, having served as director of the social science division of the Faculty of Arts from 1963 to 1966 and thereafter held a series of important department- and university-level committee memberships. Almost inexorably, his skills and expertise led him toward senior administration, a role he assumed with a flourish when, in 1977, he became vice-president academic.

And his influence extended well beyond Carleton. As an expert on postsecondary education, he became a university and disciplinary statesman with ties and responsibilities at the provincial and national levels of scholarship and university politicking. At the provincial level, he was for several years a member and then chair of the research and planning subcommittee of the Committee of Presidents of Ontario Universities and a member of that organization's Committee on the Ontario University System.[6] At the national level, he served first as a member of the academic panel of Canada Council and subsequently as a member of the executive committee of the Social Sciences Research Council of Canada.[7]

As important and meaningful as these contributions were, they pale beside his contributions to the scholarly development of Canadian sociology. Pineo has convincingly argued that Porter's decision to follow *The Vertical Mosaic* with three large-scale, survey-based studies of occupational prestige, educational opportunity, and social mobility had a truly transformative impact on the dominant ethos and practice of the discipline in Canada.[8] They solidified the place of macrosociology at the core of the discipline and provided essential, basic data about Canadian society. That they replicated major U.S. studies, thereby facilitating Canada–U.S. comparative research, was a bonus.[9] In prosecuting such studies, said Pineo, Porter and his co-investigators, along with other like-minded sociologists such as Maurice Pinard, Raymond Breton, and Anthony Richmond, used mainstream American sociology, specifically of the type undertaken at Chicago's National Opinion Research Center (NORC) and Columbia's Bureau for Applied Social Research, as a model to which the Canadian discipline should aspire.

Each of these opportunities, projects, and tasks raised Porter's profile and boosted his self-confidence. But each came with a hefty price tag attached. They scattered and drained his energies and had a deleterious effect on his increasingly fragile health, which, in the long term, came to have drastic consequences. In the immediate aftermath of the resounding success of *The Vertical Mosaic* in the summer of 1965, however, he had no such worries.

The Occupational Prestige Study

As the afterglow of *The Vertical Mosaic* dimmed, Porter once again focused his attention on the Public Evaluation of Occupations project. Pineo, his partner in this endeavour, was a Canadian with a Chicago PhD who had come to Carleton in 1962 after two years at Chicago and three at McMaster.[10] The two shared interests in macrosociology and social stratification and developed a strong collegial relationship that eventually blossomed into collaboration on the occupational prestige project. In thinking back to the genesis of the project many years later, Pineo mused that it was in one sense 'strange' that Porter chose the subject matter. Unlike *The Vertical Mosaic*, he said, the scope of the occupational prestige project was 'specific and limited' and their anticipated findings were never in doubt. In fact, said Pineo, the topic was entirely 'unadventuresome.'[11] But they had good reasons for undertaking it nonetheless.

In 1964, they discovered that the U.S. National Science Foundation had awarded three American sociologists, Peter Rossi, William Hodge, and Paul Siegel, $150,000 to undertake a nationwide study of occupational prestige. The study, to be conducted out of NORC, was designed as a follow-up to a pioneering analysis of occupational prestige that Cecil North and Paul Hatt had conducted in 1947.[12] Porter and Pineo decided it was the perfect opportunity to do a parallel study in Canada. Not only would it help to kick start the survey research tradition in their home country and showcase their department but also, said Pineo, it would 'bring considerable credit' to those who carried it off.[13]

In their proposal to the SSRCC, Porter and Pineo noted that 'Canada is one of the few modern industrial societies in which basic research into the prestige of occupations has not been done.'[14] Were such a study carried out, they said, it would produce four benefits. First, it would illuminate aspects of class Porter had not been able to address in *The Vertical Mosaic*. 'Almost all social behaviour,' they wrote, 'varies with the position people occupy in the stratification system. The most important item in the allocation of individuals in the stratification system is occupation.' While they noted it was true that 'scales can be derived from the objective data of the census, ... these need to be judged in the light of popular evaluation which is the *subjective* dimension of occupational structure.'[15] Second, it would allow them to compare Canada with other advanced industrial nations and show that Canada had developed a 'central value system' just like those of other modern nations, the United States in particular. In fact, on this account, Pineo recalled that Porter regarded occupational prestige as 'a suitable proxy measure for the whole complex of beliefs thought of as industrial culture.' Were they to discover a strong correlation between U.S. rankings and Canadian rankings, as they expected, this would confirm that Canada was best understood not as a preindustrial, resource-producing economic backwater but as a modern industrial nation.[16] Third, they argued, the occupational prestige scale would provide 'a valuable research tool.' Pineo recalled that Porter was disdainful of the occupation codes used by the Census Division of Statistics Canada, in one paper referring to them as 'absurd' three times and 'indefensible' twice. He intended to use the data from the occupational prestige study to pressure Statistics Canada into revising their coding system.[17] Unfortunately, though he got his wish, the scale that they developed to replace it was equally flawed. Porter and Pineo intended to use a scale developed by Blishen in 1951 as a suitable coding system in place of the Census scheme, but in the process of carrying out their study, they 'inadvertently created a competitive coding system.'[18] This system, which became known as the Porter–Pineo scale, was soon in use by other researchers. Fourth, and finally, the project would have practical utility. As a scholar interested in applied, socially relevant sociology, Porter noted that their data would be helpful to 'those concerned with recruitment to occupations, vocational guidance, [and] the representation of professional associations.'[19]

The advantages of undertaking the study coincident with the U.S. study were numerous. In particular, as the costs associated with the preparation and pretesting of questionnaires would be greatly reduced, the Canadian study could be completed much more cheaply and efficiently than would otherwise be the case.[20] Porter and Pineo realized that the American questionnaire would have to be adapted for Canadian use but were confident that with the help of their American colleagues this could be accomplished without much trouble.[21]

Despite the high-profile nature of their study, Pineo and Porter could not get all the money they needed from SSRCC. In the end, they had to sell their project many times over, rewriting their small proposal repeatedly, in each instance to 'slant it towards the interests of whatever agency [they] happened to be approaching.' Pineo also emphasized, however, that what they were really selling was Porter's reputation. Almost all their attempts to raise research funds involved face-to-face meetings but due to Porter's status in Ottawa civil service circles, 'doors opened easily.' 'In sending a small grant,' Pineo recalls, 'one government department wrote "for one of your stature, no contract is necessary."' Reflecting a decade and a half later, Pineo voiced the opinion that 'only someone with Porter's contacts and reputation, coupled with the convenience of his actually being in Ottawa, could have put together the financing package for the scheme at the time.'[22]

That Pineo and Porter had to struggle to obtain the funds for such a landmark study illustrates the underdeveloped state of the survey research approach in Canada at the time. They were forced to make the rounds from agency to agency, cap in hand, looking for funds, while their American counterparts had a bagful of money and the support of the large, well-funded NORC at Chicago.[23] Canada had no such facilities, in part because 'crucial gatekeepers' such as the press and politicians were highly sceptical about the worth of survey research. In such an atmosphere, wrote Pineo, Porter's decision to prosecute a national prestige study was a bold one: 'My immediate reaction was to marvel at his audacity. The problems to be anticipated were so numerous that I realized it was pointless to single out any one for discussion and I simply said "okay."'[24]

Once Pineo and Porter had the money, they prepared the questionnaire and engaged a private market research firm, Canadian Facts, to do the fieldwork.[25] The research design called for a national sample of 900 interviews, but the interviewers achieved only a very low 50 per cent completion rate, well below that reached by American college-based survey centres. Efforts to improve it were moderately successful, producing a 65 per cent rate.[26] Only later did Pineo and Porter learn that lower completion rates were common in Canada.[27] And there were two other difficulties. After they had the completed questionnaires in hand, they discovered that Carleton lacked the proper computer facilities to process the data. Fortunately, they were able to gain access to computing equipment at the City of Ottawa.[28] Also troublesome was that the Royal Commission on Bilingualism and Biculturalism initially refused to release some of their own data to them because they had gathered it as part of a contract research study they had done for the Commission.[29] In this regard, Pineo and Porter were not alone. Years later, Pineo recalled that the Commission 'irritated many contractors by reneging on commitments to publish studies while simultaneously denying rights to publish independently.' Persistent negotiating paid off, however, and the Commission eventually released their data.[30]

Despite these impediments and delays, by May 1966, they had calculated their preliminary findings. The outcome was a remarkable and gratifying 0.98 correlation with the American findings reported by Rossi, Hodge, and Siegel. The finding for French Canada – a 0.95 correlation – was particularly noteworthy, for it indicated that modernity had won out in Quebec. In that regard, they claimed, Quebec was just like the rest of Canada. 'Porter [had] risked the criticism of being unadventuresome in the choice of topics,' noted Pineo, but he had 'gained conclusiveness.' They hoped that this would help allay the scepticism of gatekeepers – funding agencies in particular – that doubted the accuracy and worthiness of survey-style research. This was important for two reasons. First, Porter envisaged the prestige study as just one of a series that would provide data for Canada–U.S. comparisons.[31] Second, he hoped to create an opening for other Canadian sociologists to do similar work. His goal was not to be working alone on this type of research but to be part of the leading edge of an era of survey research in Canada.[32] But it was not to be. Despite a promising start, the survey research tradition never flourished north of the 49th parallel in the same way it did in the United States.[33]

A month later, Pineo and Porter reported their findings at the meetings of the Canadian Learned Societies in Sherbrooke while simultaneously pursuing the possibility of joint comparative work with the NORC group.[34] The prospective Canada–U.S. collaboration never came to fruition, but Porter and Pineo pressed ahead with analysis of the Canadian data, intending to produce a book from the survey. That project, too, foundered and even the final draft of their joint publication, 'Public Evaluation of Occupations,' took much longer to complete than they had expected.[35] It remained unfinished when, in mid-summer of 1966, the Porters left to spend a year in Geneva.

The Geneva Interlude, 1966–1967

Not long after publishing *The Vertical Mosaic,* Porter applied to become a visiting research fellow at the Institute for Labour Studies of the International Labour Organization (ILO) in Geneva. The Economics and Research Branch of the Canada Department of Labour sponsored the fellowship, under the guidance of Deputy Minister of Labour George Haythorne. The institute itself was jointly funded by the two countries and directed by a Canadian, Robert Cox.[36] Porter wanted to do some comparative research on factors affecting 'the supply of skilled and professional manpower in highly developed industrial societies' and, as well, on the movement of highly educated workers from less developed countries to more developed ones in search of good jobs at salaries higher than those available in their home nations.[37] This latter phenomenon, known colloquially as the brain drain, had interested Porter for some time.[38]

Porter's application was successful and the family left for Switzerland in July 1966. They travelled first to Wales to visit John's mother and sister and then to London to look up old friends. Not until late August did they arrive in Geneva. John immediately set up his office at the institute on Route de Lausanne and began work. He took only three major breaks from his daily routine at the institute during the months he was there. Early in November, he travelled to Paris to visit the Organization for Economic Cooperation and Development, where he hoped to track down data sources for the brain drain project and make connections with other scholars working on the problem. A trip to London, taken later the same month, became necessary because the ILO library proved to be deficient.[39] As well, and quite surprising to him, the resources at the University of Geneva were equally inadequate.[40] He knew he would find the materials he needed in the familiar confines of the LSE library. A third trip took him home to Canada in April to give a paper at a conference sponsored by Canada's secretary of state.[41]

As might be expected, the Porters loved their year in Europe. They thought Geneva 'frightfully expensive' and not terribly interesting, but found it to be a splendid base of operations.[42] The family travelled most weekends and over the winter 'spent more weekends than not' in France or Italy.[43] At Christmas, they returned to Pilgrim's Way in Wrexham to spend the holiday with Eileen and Ethel and at Easter again headed for Italy.[44] As well, during the last few weeks of their stay, they quickly visited Austria, Germany, France, Yugoslavia, and Hungary.[45]

Ann Porter recalled the year as a wonderful family experience.[46] Tony had similar memories; his father really enjoyed their sojourn in Geneva, and Europe, said Tony, was 'a fantastic place to be' as a family.[47]

While Porter found the year at the institute personally enjoyable and academically useful, he did express some disappointment. The facilities were fine – indeed, he had been given a 'splendid' office – but staff members had not introduced him to other institute researchers who shared his interests and as a result he found it was not 'as good a place to engage with potential colleagues ... as he had expected.' He complained that he felt isolated the entire time, never made to feel entirely welcome in the institute's activities.[48] He also remarked in a letter to Pineo that it had been 'rather disappointing' in terms of work he had hoped to accomplish.[49]

Few people would have referred to his year's work that way. In the autumn of 1966, just after arriving in Geneva, he and Pineo put the finishing touches on 'French–English Differences in the Evaluation of Occupation, Industries, Ethnicities and Religions in the Montreal Metropolitan Area,' their contribution to the Royal Commission on Bilingualism and Biculturalism.[50] They also completed the final version of 'Occupational Prestige in Canada,' and it appeared shortly after in the *CRSA*.[51] As well, they finished a study they had undertaken for the Department of Manpower and Immigration.[52] And Porter did much else besides. 'Canadian Character in the Twentieth Century' appeared in the *Annals of the American Academy of Political and Social Science*, 'Some Observations on Comparative Studies' came out in the *Bulletin* of the Institute for Labour Studies, and 'The Human Community' appeared in J.M.S. Careless and R. Craig Brown's *The Canadians, 1867–1967*. In addition, he completed two articles dealing with class-related inequalities in Canadian education – 'Class Bias of Canadian Education' and 'Inequalities in Education' – and two articles on the brain drain: 'The Future of Upward Mobility' and 'Why the Shortage of Highly Qualified Manpower?'.

What's more, he completed a brief monograph entitled *Canadian Social Structure: A Statistical Profile*. This slim volume was essentially a compendium of tables organized into chapters dealing with various key elements of Canadian social organization: demographics, the economy, immigration, education, deviant behaviour, leisure, and the like.[53] He introduced each section with a brief commentary, highlighting what he regarded as the most noteworthy features of the data. Perhaps the most revealing part of the volume is the introduction, entitled 'Working with Statistics.' Porter opened it with a rhetorical flourish. 'Statistical tables are like skeletons,' he said. 'Perhaps that is the reason so many people view them with awe.' In the balance of the introduction, he proceeded to demonstrate the utility of macrosociological statistical data, arguing that they allowed people to understand the structure and dynamics of complex, large-scale social systems, in particular nation-states, as they evolve. He explained how such data were gathered and illustrated how data of this type, when presented in tabular form, could lead to fruitful hypotheses and research questions. He acknowledged that such research had limitations – 'Just as our knowledge of bodily structures would be limited if investigation were confined to skeletons, our knowledge of human society would be very inadequate if we did not extend inquiry beyond basic statistical materials'[54] – but remained adamant that macrosociological statistical data were the best point of departure for social analysis:

> Peoples and places have been described in prose, poetry and song. They have been written about by travelers, essayists, journalists, historians and politicians. Societies can also be described by statistics. Statistics are not the easiest way to learn about a country, but they are likely to provide a more accurate picture and are, therefore, of prime importance to the serious student of society ...
>
> Tables ... represent an initial ordering of the facts about a large-scale social system.[55]

The clear impression one gets from the introduction and Porter's commentary on the tables is that this is his métier. This is where he feels at home and this is where, from his perspective, good sociology begins. Indeed, it is illustrative of his orientation to sociology that he never wrote a separate monograph about theory parallel to this little compendium of tables. In keeping with the spirit of one of his own 'Porterisms' – 'Where confronted with a choice between theory and data, choose data' – he produced *Canadian Social Structure*.[56]

The Vertical Mosaic continued to reap rewards even while the Porters were in Geneva. As an alumnus of the LSE, he knew he could submit a major published work to the University of London for a doctoral degree. So, soon after *The Vertical Mosaic* appeared, he shipped it off to the LSE for review. The decision was favourable, of course, and on 14 September 1966 he received the DSc (Econ.) from his alma mater.[57] By coincidence, *The Vertical Mosaic* garnered the MacIver Prize the same week.

While the time in Europe was exciting and interesting because of the research projects he undertook, the travelling he did, and the honours he received, a made-in-Canada development created far more drama. Soon after arriving at the institute, Porter received a telephone call from S.D. Clark. Would he be interested in a position in the sociology department at the University of Toronto?[58] Over the years, Porter had received many enquiries from various universities in Canada and the United States, including some that offered him an entrée into senior academic administration, but he had always turned them down. Clark's offer intrigued him, however, and after mulling it over for about six weeks, he accepted.[59] Clark was pleased; in the face of competition from other rapidly growing Canadian departments of sociology, he was trying to reinforce Toronto's position as the top department in the country and had been engaged in a highly successful recruiting drive. He had already attracted well-known theorist Lewis Feuer from Berkeley and prominent historical sociologist Charles Tilly from Harvard. But he understood that to be the best department in Canada, he needed to have Porter on his faculty roster. 'What more can I say than that I am delighted?' wrote Clark. 'Your coming to Toronto will make a great difference to us. I feel, now, that we are well over the hump.'[60]

Soon, however, Porter's appointment became caught up in university politics. He had an obligation to spend a year at Carleton following his sabbatical and wanted to keep his decision a secret until September 1967, when he would return to Ottawa.[61] For his part, Clark wanted Porter to inform Carleton of his decision immediately, otherwise word might leak out and upstage their formal announcement of the appointment. 'Besides,' wrote Clark, 'our president may decide, out of courtesy, that he should inform your president. I agree with you it is important that you should be the first to inform Carleton. From this end, the appointment becomes official, and a matter of public knowledge, once the Board of Governors acts.'[62] But Porter did not see it as appropriate to inform Dunton this far in advance; he wanted to wait until after he returned to Ottawa. This refusal created a protocol problem, sparked some clandestine negotiations with Clark, and eventually set off a bidding war between Toronto's president, Claude Bissell, and Carleton's president, Davidson Dunton.

When Porter balked, Clark and Bissell had a new problem to solve: they had to make it look as if their raid on the Carleton sociology department was not a fait accompli. 'I [had] lunch with the president yesterday,' Clark said, 'and found him very anxious that we should not steal you from Carleton in a way that would damage our relations with that university ... He is, of course, enthusiastic about your coming here. The concern is wholly with how it is done.' More specifically, Clark wrote, 'He wants ... to pay Dunton the courtesy of asking his permission before making our offer ... Bissell has no thought the appointment should not be proceeded with, only that it should not appear as a high-handed act on our part.'[63] In a follow-up letter, written a week later, he continued on the same theme: 'Can we pretend that no approach has yet been made to you about a possible move to Toronto? I had lunch again today with the president. He is going to phone or write Dunton warning him that we are interested in you and may be approaching you about a possible appointment at Toronto 1968 [sic]. After that, I can approach you. You can indicate interest, but the matter can be let ride for the next two or three months.'[64]

But only part of Bissell's eagerness resulted from the considerations of courtesy. Another reason to inform Dunton immediately was the release of the Spinks Report, a study formally entitled 'Report of the Committee on University Affairs and the Committee of Presidents of Provincially-Assisted Universities of the Commission to Study the Development of Graduate Programs in Ontario Universities,' commissioned by Ontario's Committee on University Affairs.[65] As I noted in chapter 9, graduate studies had grown rapidly in Ontario in the 1960s, but without any system-wide planning or quality control. And as the Spinks committee soon discovered, in the absence of a provincial regulatory body all fourteen universities, even new ones such as York and Waterloo, had considered themselves 'free to declare their own objectives and to develop their own [graduate] programs without regard or reference to their neighbours or the needs of the Province.'[66] As a consequence, many departments initiated graduate programs or expanded existing ones, even at the doctoral level, without concern about duplication. This was worrisome, according to the Spinks Report, because many universities had neither the faculty expertise nor the financial resources to run top-notch graduate programs.[67]

After surveying the situation, the Spinks committee made four major recommendations. One in particular, that the government establish a Provincial University of Ontario modelled on the state universities of California and New York, was highly controversial. According to this plan, 'all existing and future publicly supported institutions' in the province would be 'constituent members of the Provincial University' and would retain substantial autonomy. However, the Provincial University – and the University of Toronto expected to be so designated – would be responsible for approving new graduate programs and monitoring the quality of existing ones in order to prevent 'unrestricted competition and ill-advised expansion.'[68] In this context, Porter's move from Carleton to Toronto would carry considerable symbolic weight. Hence Bissell's desire to have Porter act quickly, as Clark explained to him in a letter: 'The recommendation about your appointment arrived on [Bissell's] desk just at the time when the Spinks Report hit the front pages of the newspapers, with the talk about one university centred in Toronto, and certification of PhD work at the different Ontario universities. This university does have to avoid giving the appearance that it is prepared to buy up all the good people at the other Ontario universities.' Clark continued, 'As soon as I hear from the president ... I shall write you, going through the motions of "feeling you out" about a move to Toronto. But I trust that, on your side, as well as mine, the matter can be considered settled, apart from the little game that is being played.'[69] In other words, Toronto wanted to make it clear that the offer to Porter preceded the appearance of the Spinks Report.

As the fall and early winter of 1966–7 came and went, Porter continued to assure Clark he expected to move to Toronto, in part because he felt he could 'make a better contribution in a larger university.'[70] But at the end of January, when Bissell contacted Dunton to inform him about Toronto's 'intentions,' the situation altered dramatically. Dunton was not about to lose one of his star scholars without a fight. Immediately following his conversation with Bissell, he contacted Porter, asking him to hold off on any decision until Carleton could make a counter-offer. On 1 February, he wrote to Porter to make Carleton's case. He offered to match Toronto's salary offer, and arranged for Carleton's dean of arts, Gordon Merrill, to negotiate a reduced teaching load and other benefits. In addition, he noted that Carleton was trying to launch a doctoral program in sociology and would soon make a number of appointments to bolster the department. Moreover, in response to Porter's claim that he thought he could make a greater contribution at a bigger university, Dunton proposed to appoint him associate dean of graduate studies for arts and to make him Carleton's representative on an important new interuniversity provincial planning committee:

> In summary my plea is this: we offer you, to the greatest extent in our power, the teaching and research you wish; your contribution to sociology would be very great from here; and we need you badly to help make

Carleton the significant university in senior work and research that it can become. Knowledge that you are leaving would discourage a number of people; your staying would immensely stimulate others to good work, and help attract exciting people.[71]

A letter from Merrill arrived soon after, offering an excellent teaching and research situation that involved a reduced teaching load and the services of a full-time research assistant. He reiterated Dunton's argument:

> We are at a particularly crucial stage in our development in social science at Carleton, about to occupy facilities that are second to none in Canada for teaching and research. It is my personal opinion that you have a better opportunity to make an impact upon Canadian university life in all of its aspects through Carleton than through the University of Toronto.[72]

For the next two weeks, Porter agonized over the situation, writing letters to Merrill and Dunton that detailed his reasons for leaving Carleton but also suggesting by their general tone that he was not as decided about going to Toronto as he had earlier intimated.[73] To Merrill, he replied, 'The difficulty of choosing is so great that I have been solving the problem by repressing all thoughts about it.' 'There is no doubt,' he wrote, 'that the President's letter and yours have stopped me in my tracks ... I had hoped to slip away quietly.' In the letter he candidly weighed the two offers. Carleton was now offering a reduced teaching load and he knew that Carleton was 'more generous [than Toronto] in the matter of research funds, assistants and secretaries.' As well, he acknowledged that 'the physical conditions of work would be superior at Carleton.' But, he said, Toronto held several attractions, such as an already-established PhD program. He also revealed that he intended 'to get some students together and begin a series of studies on urban working class life. The Toronto industrial area would suit that purpose much better.' Finally, he noted that both Toronto and York had made 'some very good appointments,' with the consequence that the city of Toronto now had 'a fair concentration of sociological talent.' 'The business of deciding,' he went on, 'is very painful.' He concluded the letter by deferring his decision: 'Perhaps I should not decide at this time and at this distance, but leave it until I get back and I can have a closer look at both Toronto and Carleton, and so make a more reasonable judgment.'[74]

As the situation unfolded, it occurred to Porter that, if he stayed at Carleton, his status as a research professor might offend other members of the sociology department.[75] He wrote to McFarlane, the chair, to enquire.[76] McFarlane's reply was blunt. He had not canvassed the other members of the department, he said, but he doubted there would be any resentment: 'Rather I think it would be viewed as recognition for a job well done ... One of the best things that can happen in the department, for some members, at least, is that published research, articles, books, etc. *do* bring differential rewards within the University; that is, that the rewards are limited not only to public acclaim. Hopefully, it will act as a prod.' McFarlane pulled out all the stops in his attempt to get his friend to stay: 'As you can well imagine, John, your departure would be regarded as a terrible blow by every member of the department. It is true that "coffee-time" conversations have frequently centred around the topic "I wonder where John is receiving offers from this year?" ... I do hope, and here I'm certain that everyone in the department joins me, that we are able to coax you to stay by offering you optimum conditions for your research, as well as your other interests in higher education.'[77] In his letter, McFarlane let Porter know that others in the department – Vallee, Whyte, Pineo, and himself – had declined offers from other universities. This was a subtle way of informing Porter that his colleagues had all decided to stay and build the Carleton department, in part, perhaps, because John was there. Twenty years later, McFarlane reminisced that in private he also spoke more directly to John about his negative impressions of the University of Toronto:

I had taught at Toronto, so when John came by [to discuss the Toronto offer] I said: 'John, it's not going to be your atmosphere ... The arrogance will just cripple you.' 'Oh no,' he said, 'I know Del and I know Jim Giffen and I know ...' And I said: 'Well, I know them too. And I still like them, but I found it a very arrogant place right through the whole institution, one department to the other, right across the board.'[78]

As a result of these interventions by his Carleton colleagues, by early March Porter had all but decided to stay in Ottawa. 'The generosity and warmth of the response from Carleton has forced me to reconsider my position,' he wrote in a letter to Clark:

I knew this would happen and that was why I felt that I could slip away quietly after I got back there. After pondering all this for a few weeks I am coming increasingly to feel that I should stay at Carleton. The decision is an agonizing one since the alternatives are very attractive. Moreover, I will never be able to tell which was the right one![79]

With the matter still in doubt, Porter returned to Ottawa.

The Final Year in Ottawa, 1967–1968

The fall of 1967 was noteworthy for Porter not just because he was contemplating a move to Toronto. A second long distance telephone call from an unexpected source brought another major change in his life. Just after the Porters returned to Ottawa, John received a surprise telephone call from his first wife, Elizabeth. Unbeknown to John, in 1955, Elizabeth and Fiona had moved to the United States, living briefly in New Orleans before settling in Richmond, Virginia. Elizabeth had struggled as a single mother and had moved to America in order to escape what she saw as very poor prospects in England. She had returned to school – to Oxford, to earn credentials in orthoptics – and then, after writing some letters to American physicians, moved to the United States. After working for a year at a hospital in New Orleans, she was offered the opportunity to start an orthoptics clinic at the Medical College of Virginia and moved to Richmond to stay.[80] She had paid Fiona's tuition at private schools and had started her on a college career, but all was not well. She had a sensitive question for her former husband: Was he willing to enter into a relationship with his daughter? Fiona, now a young woman, wanted to get to know her father. Growing up in a single-parent family, and going to school within a traditional community and social circle in which such a situation was very unusual, she had come to feel very uncomfortable about not knowing her father.[81] He agreed to exchange letters with her.[82]

The situation must have been a difficult one for everyone involved. John and Elizabeth had separated on very poor terms. Both were quite bitter at the time and, according to Peter Cole, John had suffered a bout of extreme depression after the break-up.[83] There had been no contact between them after they divorced in 1951 and John had neither provided any child support nor attempted to see Fiona in the interim. He had seen her only once, for a few minutes just after she was born. For her part, Elizabeth had remained single and still harboured ill feelings toward John. According to Fiona, her mother had received poor legal advice about the prospect of 'forcing' John to provide child support and as a single parent had struggled to make a living for the two of them.[84] On his side, John had remarried and forged a new life. Quite understandably, Fiona wanted and needed a relationship with her father, but John now had another life and family which put him in a very awkward position. It was not an easy or positive situation for any of them.

Nonetheless, John wrote to Fiona in late September 1967. In the letter, he offered an explanation for his decision not to try to contact her over the years and apologized for whatever unhappiness she had experienced as a result of his silence:

> I have often thought about you and the kind of person you have grown to be. It is true that I have never translated these thoughts into any attempts to establish contacts with you. In part because it would have seemed an intrusion, ... in part for the selfish reason that I feared having a daughter over whom I could have no influence, without endless strife ... Nor would it have been particularly happy for you or your mother ... I do want to say with all sincerity that if my silence has been the source of unhappiness for you, I am very sorry.

That he seems unsure about how to deal with his emotions and hers is revealed by a number of things, including the brevity of the letter – less than two typed, single-spaced pages – and his rather impersonal choice of words in closing: 'All good wishes.'[85] They corresponded regularly over the next few months, but usually with some delay on his part. His extremely busy work and travel schedule always constituted a barrier.[86] They did not meet until May 1968.

While this was going on, Porter vacillated on the question of moving to Toronto. Not until mid-November 1967, after a visit to Toronto in early October and a full year after Clark made his original overture, did he formally accept the Toronto offer.[87] This made the last few months in Ottawa a bit awkward, but he remained productive, cleaning up a number of projects left over from his time in Geneva and, with Blishen, undertaking the background work necessary to launch another large-scale survey, this time concerning the educational aspirations (and patterns of attainment) of Ontario high school students. The project grew in part out of his interests in *The Vertical Mosaic* and in part out of then current public and government interest in education.

As I remarked in chapter 9, equality of access to postsecondary education had by the late 1960s become a hot-button issue. Many people regarded equality of educational opportunity as central to their vision of Canada as a fair and rational society. If a student's class of origin acted as a barrier to his or her chance to pursue a university education, then this was neither fair to the individual nor rational for society as a whole. Every able student deprived of the opportunity to realize his or her full intellectual capacity represented a net loss to Canada's potential. The Committee of Presidents of the Universities of Ontario (CPUO) had for some time convened a research and planning subcommittee, and both Porter and Blishen were members. The subcommittee was deeply interested in the issue and believed that policy makers lacked an understanding of the psychological factors that prevented lower-class students from going to university. Moreover, they were well aware that prominent American sociologists such as William Sewell and James Coleman were then undertaking research on this issue. However, while the subcommittee was sympathetic, it lacked financial resources, so Porter and Blishen decided to pursue the issue outside the committee structure. In August 1968, just before the Porter family moved to Toronto, they began to prepare a funding proposal.

The Toronto Interlude, 1968–1969: A Drama in One Act

New beginnings are always exciting and Porter went to Toronto in the fall of 1968 with high expectations. He was now in a large and storied department with over thirty faculty members, including some of the best-known figures in Canadian sociology.[88] He was already on friendly personal terms with a number of them and by virtue of his reputation received a respectful welcome at the university. Particularly exciting for him was that for the first time he had access to a large group of doctoral students. When the department first became independent of political economy in 1963, it had only five PhD students, but by 1968 that figure had already mushroomed to fifty-five.[89]

John and Marion chose a home on Walker Avenue in an older part of the downtown off Yonge Street, a few blocks north of Bloor, near the Summerhill subway station. They were close by Hunt's Bakery – so near you could smell the bread baking – and close enough to the university that John could walk to work each day.[90] But not all the signs were good. The sociology department was housed in the Borden building, a somewhat dilapidated former dairy on Spadina Avenue just north of College Street and, according to S.D. Clark, John considered the accommodations woefully substandard. Indeed, Clark recalled that John said he 'hated' the Borden building and interpreted the department's accommodations as an indicator of sociology's low status at the university.[91] Wallace Clement remembers he discussed the situation with Porter years later. Accustomed to much better circumstances at Carleton, and to having an 'in' with the senior administrators, Clement said, Porter decided to lobby for more suitable lodgings. After ferreting out data on funds expended per student in various departments indicating that sociology was at the bottom of the list, he went to see the dean and the president. Did they have any plans to change sociology's dismal place in their scheme of things? A blunt and unequivocal 'no' was the answer. They regarded sociology primarily as a service teaching department. Upset, Porter discussed the issue with Clark but found him unwilling to challenge either the dean or the president on the issue.[92] This immediately soured him on the department to the point that, according to Clement, he decided – even before meeting his first class – that coming to Toronto had been a mistake. He did not expect to stay.[93]

This was not the only disappointment he experienced on arriving. At Carleton, he had enjoyed the benefits of relatively small classes and the services of teaching assistants who did much of the marking. At Toronto, the students were very good – 'much more challenging' than those at Carleton – but his classes were large and he had an enormous amount of grading to do.[94] Far more important, he quickly became disappointed and frustrated over his official relationship with Clark. Porter respected Clark and when he decided to go to Toronto must have assumed that as a senior scholar with experience as a senior administrator he would have considerable influence in the department. At Carleton, he had chaired the Department of Sociology for a number of years and had served as director of the social sciences division of the Faculty of Arts, the modern-day equivalent of an associate dean, and was well connected to both the Social Sciences Research Council of Canada and the CPUO.[95] Moreover, just after arriving at Toronto, his stature was further cemented with his election to the Royal Society of Canada.[96] Much to his surprise, none of this brought the recognition and clout he expected.

This was in part a consequence of Toronto's traditional headship system of departmental governance and in part a consequence of Clark's personal style of leadership. Clark, the first head of the sociology department, had been appointed to the post five years earlier by Vincent Bladen, the dean of the Faculty of Arts and Science, when Bladen hived sociology off from political economy as an independent department.

According to university policy and norms, Clark had the right to rule as a top-down decision maker – and he did so, entirely comfortable in the role. And according to Charles Tilly, his colleagues were publicly satisfied with the situation. Certainly, Tilly said, he 'didn't notice dissidence among the old-timers' and recalled 'no struggle for control of the department' underway when he left for Stanford in the summer of 1968: 'We saw [Clark] as running the department on his own terms, assuming the prerogatives of founder and senior Canadian scholar.'[97] During his tenure as head, Clark had followed the practice of seeking advice from a small group of trusted senior advisers – Tilly, Jim Giffen, Jean Burnet, and Oswald Hall – if he felt so inclined, but he also insisted that all decisions were his alone. He knew he was ultimately accountable only to the dean and was quite prepared to act unilaterally.[98] As a consequence, he sometimes presented colleagues with policy and hiring decisions that were his own preferences. Ironically, Clark had hired Porter in just such a manner – on his own initiative without consulting anyone.[99] And he would at times overstep the bounds of his authority by being petty and inflexible about relatively trivial matters of departmental life. Years later, Jean Burnet recalled one such instance: 'Leo Zakuta went in one Sunday and painted his office door green because he was so oppressed by the greyness in the Borden Building. Del Clark ordered him to get it repainted.' Zakuta refused and said that 'if it was repainted, he would come back and paint it … again.' Burnet described the incident as 'one of the many interesting feuds of the late 1960s.'[100]

Earlier in the decade, Clark's management style had not been a major issue. As faculty ranks swelled with junior appointments in the second half of the 1960s, however, many of his young colleagues began to chafe under this top-down style of departmental stewardship. A substantial number had come from graduate schools in the United States, where they had taken part in student protests over the Vietnam War, the struggle for black power, women's liberation, and university governance. Once in Canada, many of them not only continued their activism but also refused to accept the type of non-collegial power Clark was accustomed to wielding.[101] As Jim Giffen wrote, 'The student-power movement and the simultaneous push among faculty for a greater role in decision-making, pandemic in California, reached the frozen north while Del Clark was still chairman.'[102] According to William Michelson, a faculty member at the time, Clark responded to pressure from some of his departmental colleagues by creating departmental committees that would make some significant decisions. However, while this constituted a significant change from his earlier modus operandi, it did not placate everyone, Porter included, because Clark insisted on hand-picking the committees rather than allowing them to be elected by faculty. At a department meeting subsequent to the change in policy, three faculty members – Michelson, Porter, and Norman Bell – tabled a proposal that departmental committees be elected. To everyone's surprise, Clark responded by 'announcing his resignation as chair.' In a retrospective account written forty years later, Michelson wanted to stress that those making the motion had not foreseen such an outcome and, like all members of the department present, were 'stunned' by Clark's announcement. They had no intention, Michelson emphasized, of pushing Clark out of the chair, believing that he was prepared 'to be flexible (to a point)' and preside over a more democratically administered department.[103]

Whatever Clark's intentions at the time, his own recollection of these events, related three and a half decades later, indicates that he might have been less flexible than Michelson's account suggests. When I interviewed him about the episode, he recalled clearly and immediately that 'friction' had developed between Porter and him over Clark's resistance to being more inclusive and collegial about departmental governance. At the time, Clark said, he believed that in order to provide leadership as the chair, he needed 'the power to do things.' Had he adopted the collegial and democratic administrative practices people wanted, his power would have been too greatly compromised.[104] Accounts of the episode are thus somewhat at odds, and certainly the situation at the time was murky. It would be reasonable to agree with Michelson's claim that technically Clark resigned rather than being pushed out, but Irving Zeitlin's claim that Clark was 'effectively deposed' also makes sense.[105] Either way, Clark's days as head were probably numbered in any event. The power of the pro-democracy movement in Canadian universities – and certainly in the sociology department at the University of Toronto – was far too strong for anyone to resist for long.

When Clark stepped aside, James Giffen replaced him. The job must have been nearly impossible to carry out, for the next few years of the department's administrative history constitute among the most unusual experiments in departmental governance ever undertaken in a Canadian university. After much internal wrangling among various departmental constituencies – graduate students, undergraduate students, various subgroups of faculty – they agreed on a 'constitution' by which the department came to be organized as a participatory democracy. For some years thereafter, the department's business was carried out by an assembly, under the chair, and a set of committees with student parity that provided non-binding advice to the chair.[106] The experiment eventually came to an end during Lorna Marsden's time as chair, but while they were in effect the constitution, the assembly, and related administrative bric-a-brac made for lively, sometimes confrontational departmental politics. But an unfortunate side effect was to compromise the status and credibility of the department in the eyes of the university's central administration.[107]

When Porter joined the department in the fall of 1968, then, it had low status in the university and was housed in substandard accommodations. Not a good start. And things immediately got worse. Even before the ultimate clash with Clark, he butted heads with him over questions related to departmental governance. However reasonable and principled Clark's tactics and views were by some standards, they were unacceptable to Porter. He had come to Toronto expecting to have a role in the department befitting his status and experience as a senior scholar, and became frustrated when the opportunity was denied him. In the end, the two men could not negotiate a working arrangement. And obviously, Porter was not alone; broader dissatisfaction with Clark's style set in motion the events that produced the departmental assembly and the balkanization and disarray that went with it. And these were not Porter's only disappointments. As early as November, he wrote to Fiona that he found the university a 'very bureaucratic and tradition-bound' place, 'at times enormously frustrating.'[108] McMaster sociologist Frank Jones remembers talking with John about his problems in adjusting to life in the Toronto department, in particular the administrative formality and bureaucratic ethos of the university more generally – not to speak of the relative lack of status and influence he experienced at his new place of work. Porter had discovered, said Jones, that Toronto was 'a large bureaucracy.' In order to get something as seemingly simple as extra secretarial assistance, 'you had to go through some kind of machinery.' Porter found this extremely frustrating, said Jones, because at Carleton he could 'walk into the president's office, or vice-president's office, and … get things.' There he had enjoyed 'very high status' and been 'quite influential.' At Toronto, plain and simple, he had little status and little influence.[109]

That he found the university's general culture not to his liking should not have come as a surprise. During his year as a research associate at Toronto, in 1961, he had spoken to the university's Commission on University Government in bluntly critical terms about exactly this problem. 'Any university values highly the principle of colleagueship,' he said. In such circumstances, 'administrators are somewhat of an anomaly. And the greater the status and prestige they enjoy, 'the greater does their position appear to be anomalous.' Nor did the problem stop there. The more bureaucratic the university became, the more broadly it 'spread a culture of status and hierarchy,' antithetical to the principle of 'equality of colleagueship.' This 'culture of status and hierarchy,' he charged, was 'particularly in evidence at the University of Toronto':

> It begins with the Calendar where the administrators with all their rank and title come tumbling out when the first pages are opened. Vice-Presidents, Provosts, Vice-Provosts, Executive Assistants, Directors, Assistant Directors (Acting) in a curious protocol take precedence over any of the scholars, leaving the impression that the main purpose of the university is to administer itself ... Administration there must be for a large organization such as at this university, but one wonders if it must be as bureaucratized, ... authoritarian and ... status yielding as it is.[110]

Apparently, the University of Toronto had not changed much in the interim.

At a New Year's Eve party at the Blishen household in Peterborough that year, Porter revealed his dissatisfaction to Bruce McFarlane.[111] Once back in Ottawa, McFarlane happily relayed the news to Davidson Dunton and Frank Vallee, then chair of the department. The three made a pact to get Porter back to Carleton by any means necessary. 'At the time,' Vallee recalled, '"democracy" was in the air and you had to consult with everybody – the students and the faculty and the junior and the senior. And I said: "Screw that. If we can get John Porter back here, I am not going to consult with anybody."'[112] So Vallee approached Porter unofficially, Dunton contributed presidential prerogative, and between them they lured Porter back to Carleton. It was not a hard sell.

In a letter written to a colleague in mid-summer, he summarized his experience at Toronto: 'We enjoyed Toronto very much as a place to live but, as you no doubt will have gathered, I found the university rather impossible.'[113] Early in the winter term of 1969, Porter submitted his letter of resignation to Clark and in early July the Porters returned once again to Ottawa.

11 Measuring Educational Opportunity, 1970–1979

Porter came to Carleton under very different circumstances the second time around. In 1949, he had travelled to Canada footloose and unhappy after having irrevocably split with his young wife, leaving their newborn daughter in her care. He had no firm career plan, job, or money. He fell into a teaching position at Carleton entirely by accident, accepting the job with no idea he would find a calling as a university professor. Over the course of the two decades since that fateful lunch meeting with Paul Fox, everything had changed.

Certainly, Ottawa was different. Its population had increased substantially, and its economy had diversified. Most important, it had become a true political centre: a city 'devoted mainly to the business of government.'[1] Carleton, too, had transformed itself. In 1949, it had been a small institution oriented to adult education, housed in cramped, makeshift quarters in the Glebe. Two decades later it had become a full-fledged university with numerous modern buildings on an attractive, sprawling new campus in the city's south end. Its Department of Sociology and Anthropology had come to be one of the best – and best-known – in the country. This was due in no small part to Porter himself. After a shaky beginning, he had become an academic star whose research was helping to redefine the sociology of his generation in Canada. The study of class and power had moved to centre stage in Canadian sociology – thanks in considerable measure to *The Vertical Mosaic* – and scores of sociologists across the country were engrossed in the study of various forms of inequality.

At the same time, his personal life had stabilized. He had remarried and he and his second wife, Marion, had two teenaged children: Tony and Ann. His stature as one of Carleton's marquee professors meant that his salary had grown considerably, and the family was now able to afford a spacious new home on Powell Avenue at the posh north end of the Glebe, just a few blocks from Carleton's original site on First Avenue. No longer an outsider to Carleton or Ottawa, he had many friends and acquaintances at the university and among senior bureaucrats in the civil service. After two decades, life in Canada was good.

Beginning in the late summer of 1969, as he resettled at Carleton, he undertook three other large-scale collaborative projects: *Towards 2000, Stations and Callings,* and *Ascription and Achievement.* These would define much of his post-*Mosaic* career. None was as massive in scope as *The Vertical Mosaic* and none had anything like an equivalent influence, but taken together they contributed greatly to the theoretical and methodological Americanization and maturation of Canadian sociology at a time when in other respects the discipline was moving in another direction. This put Porter's work in a nodal and controversial position in the discipline.

His first months back at Carleton in the autumn of 1969 were eventful. While still in Toronto, he and Bernard Blishen had done substantial background work on the aspirations study. In November 1968 they had applied to Canada Council for a large grant-in-aid. The Council had been receptive to the proposal but wanted them to do some exploratory work first.[2] They complied, submitting a more modest proposal, and in August 1969 the Council awarded them $18,000 for preliminary research.[3] So it was with the encouraging prospect of a major new collaborative project under his arm that Porter returned to Carleton.

The aspirations study that Porter and Blishen had in mind would require a grant unprecedented by Canadian standards – approximately $170,000.[4] To ensure the best proposal possible, they decided to hold a planning seminar and invited a handful of North America's highest-profile specialists to the event. Among those who accepted were, from the United States, A.O. Haller and William Sewell (Wisconsin), S.T. Boocock (Johns Hopkins), E.Q. Campbell (Vanderbilt), B.C. Rosen (Cornell), and Ralph Turner (UCLA); and from Canada, Raymond Breton (Toronto) and Guy Rocher (Université de Montréal).[5] Twenty additional professors and government officials such as Jan Loubser, Frank Vallee, Hubert Guindon, and Sylvia Ostry attended as observers. While Porter and Blishen specifically requested that their invitees come prepared to discuss the formal proposal and the draft questionnaire, they encouraged them not to feel constrained by this narrow frame of reference.[6] They wanted expert commentary on a wide range of relevant issues:

'the general state of research in this field, some of the major problems, ... new directions that research might take,... the relevance of this kind of research to educational policy, ... [and] the possibilities of comparative analysis.'[7]

Their guests did not disappoint. The discussion at the planning session, held 20 February 1970, was wide ranging and, interestingly, produced a greater degree of self-criticism from their American colleagues than Porter and Blishen had probably expected. They urged Porter and Blishen not to be concerned about replicating the American study precisely for the purposes of comparison. In their view, many of the benchmark American studies were flawed because the instruments employed had been ineffective, inapplicable, or outdated. The Americans urged Porter and Blishen to develop a questionnaire that would accurately measure the Canadian situation. They could consider Canada–U.S. comparisons afterwards.[8] Likewise, though the Americans recommended building policy-relevant questions into the research design, they warned Porter and Blishen not to attempt to use the data to develop policies and institutional practices that slavishly copied 'the U.S. experience.'[9] Canada was too far behind the United States in terms of economic development and the overall educational level of its population for such a strategy to work. The Americans expected that the study would expose the 'elitist' character of Canadian education – i.e., that social class background was a far more important determinant of educational opportunity than in the United States – and advised them to formulate sociologically sophisticated policy questions (and thus produce policy-relevant data) so that they could join economists in devising policy solutions to the problems of educational access that the study would unearth.[10] However, they reminded their hosts that it would be important to decide what kind of societal outcome they desired. Did they want to get as many people as possible into the postsecondary educational system (and thereby upgrade the entire labour force) or to identify the brightest individuals and target them for advanced education?[11] Unexpectedly, they argued that Canadians should not try to create a meritocratic, postindustrial society based on the U.S. model because in their estimation American society had 'clearly failed in many respects.' As E.Q. Campbell of Vanderbilt put it, the day's discussion with his Canadian colleagues reminded him of conversations he had had in Latin America in similar circumstances. 'They would like to be like us,' he said, 'and we keep telling them it's not all that nice where we are.' Like the Latin Americans, he claimed, the Canadians did not appreciate this.[12]

In all, the transcript of the day's discussion is fascinating, not only because it captures experienced researchers bluntly acknowledging the difficulties, weaknesses, and drawbacks of their research and openly discussing the political ramifications of their work but also because it shows clearly that Porter and Blishen were serious about soliciting feedback. The session was not a pro forma exercise. They wanted advice about every aspect of the study: goals, design, research techniques, sampling, variables, and so on. And they got what they asked for. Indeed, if Blishen's closing remarks are to be taken at face value, they seemed somewhat shell shocked. He thanked the group and then added, 'We now have to ... *see if in fact the study continues.*'[13]

They did decide to press on, of course, but before finalizing their proposal, travelled to Scotland and England to consult European experts.[14] While there, they obtained copies of questionnaires intended for purposes similar to their own.[15] On their return, Porter and Blishen recrafted the proposal and, in mid-May, submitted it to the Canada Council.[16] Three months later, they received the good news that the funding had been approved in principle.[17] It remained only to get precise estimates for the survey fieldwork portion of the project. They tendered it to three groups, including two private firms, but chose the survey centre at York University because they expected it would deliver the highest quality return.[18]

So, as the familiar routine of campus life pulsed into motion in the fall of 1970, Porter carried more than his usual heavy workload: the educational aspirations study was now a reality; *Towards 2000*, now nearing completion, still required his attention; and he had substantial duties on various senior-level committees at Carleton.[19] And there was more to come. During the term, he agreed to join a task force created by the American Sociological Association (ASA) to investigate a politically explosive situation in the Department of Politics, Sociology, and Anthropology (PSA) at Simon Fraser University.[20]

Since its founding in 1965, SFU had developed a reputation as a politically fractious place. It advertised itself as a progressive, even radical, institution and from its earliest days many of its faculty and students were active in left-wing political causes. The causes at the centre of the PSA dispute, referred to by Hugh Johnston as 'probably the most notorious conflict on a Canadian university campus, then or since,' were academic freedom, democratization, and university governance, in particular the question of who had the right to set and enforce standards of due process for faculty appointments (renewal, tenure, and promotion).[21] The struggle was not an isolated incident. It took place in the context of a series of ongoing, interrelated disputes, crises, and power plays that had defined SFU campus culture since its founding – and in a broader national context within which similar disputes simmered away on various Canadian university campuses. Porter had only just left behind a similarly confused and difficult situation at Toronto.

At the heart of the SFU struggle was its unusual structure and culture of governance. The university had been established in great haste and in a very unorthodox manner. It had therefore institutionalized an atypical governing structure and had employed highly unusual administrative operating procedures, made particularly problematic by the unacceptably invasive involvement of the university's founder and first chancellor, Gordon Shrum. SFU's first president, Patrick McTaggart-Cowan, ran a centralized administrative shop that many faculty members and students did not regard as appropriate. An enquiry into SFU operations by the Canadian Association of University Teachers (CAUT) in early 1968, just three years after it opened, had concluded that there was a serious problem of 'undemocratic distribution of power' involving the president, the system of appointed, permanent department heads, the chancellor, and the Board of Governors, the last of which had meddled inappropriately in the academic affairs of the university.[22] CAUT judged these governance problems to be sufficiently serious that it instituted a formal censure of SFU that was not lifted until about six months later.[23] McTaggart-Cowan stepped down, his place taken by Kenneth Strand.

The situation in the PSA department grew in part out of these long-standing disputes over university governance. The department was more politically radical than others at SFU and often at the centre of campus unrest. The crisis that the ASA asked Porter and his colleagues to investigate came about when eight of the departmental teaching staff – all self-professed radicals – came up for contractual renewal. As a group, they were highly politicized and concern had been expressed about the nature and quality of their teaching, their scholarly production, and their political activities in the classroom. Some at SFU thought that they had gone too far down the path of pedagogical experimentation, to the point at which academic standards had been lowered. Others expressed concern that some of the eight had not finished their PhDs and had not published. As well, some at the university thought they had democratized departmental governance to an excessive degree, allowing students to have a say in matters that were beyond their capacity to judge. Some even accused the eight of violating university norms on political tolerance and academic freedom by demanding ideological conformity from PSA students and colleagues. Nonetheless, the eight had the support of a large contingent of similarly radical, politicized students and were seen by some faculty members as fighting for foundational principles of university life: academic freedom, transparent governance, and administrative democratization.

As Hugh Johnston describes it in *Radical Campus: Making Simon Fraser University,* a mixture of administrative bungling, inadequate and unclear policies and procedures of university governance, and a fractious political culture among faculty and students bent on democratizing the university created a protracted, messy, and public struggle for control of the institution between its various stakeholders: the chancellor, the Board of Governors, two presidents, one of whom was fired during the process, faculty members, the faculty association, and students. In the end, all eight faculty members were forced to leave the university. In response, in November 1971, CAUT officially censured SFU a second time, urging prospective faculty members to boycott the university.[24] The censure was not lifted until 1977.[25]

In the early stages of the dispute, one of the eight faculty members involved, Kathleen Gough Aberle, an American citizen, filed a complaint with the ASA regarding 'academic freedom and due process,' the first time a faculty member had registered a such a complaint against a Canadian university.[26] It created a political problem. If the ASA were to investigate, it would be intruding into the jurisdiction of the Canadian Sociology and Anthropology Association (CSAA). The ASA therefore asked the CSAA to investigate, but the Canadian organization demurred. It did not want to act until the CAUT Academic Freedom and Tenure Committee had completed its enquiry. The ASA decided to carry out an independent investigation, deeming expeditious action necessary to 'inform its members who might be interested about the situation there.'[27] The ASA asked Porter to join Richard Flacks of the University of California and Edward Gross of the University of Washington on its committee of enquiry. That they did so says something about Porter's growing stature in the United States. That he agreed says something about his respect for the American sociological community of the time.

The committee visited SFU twice, once in February 1970 and then again in May.[28] By late July, Porter, who had agreed to be spokesperson for the committee, had drafted a report.[29] He sent copies to Flacks and

Gross and, with their consent, to three other parties whom the committee decided would be able to assess its factual accuracy.[30] This decision to show the report to only some of the participants in the dispute drew a nasty letter from Peter Rossi, secretary of the ASA. Rossi chastised Porter for circulating the report in this selective way.[31] Porter replied with a caustic note of his own and angrily resigned from the committee.[32] Immediately, Gross, Flacks, and others urged him to reconsider. Were he to withdraw at this late stage, they said, it would undermine the legitimacy of the report.[33] After an exchange of professionally polite letters of reconciliation with Rossi, he agreed to rejoin the committee.[34] Its members submitted the final report in mid-September of 1970.[35]

A month later, Porter had a second heart attack, this one much more serious than the one he had suffered seven years earlier. He did not leave hospital until late November, and then only to spend several weeks recuperating at home. As late as the Christmas holidays of that year, he remained unable to work more than a couple of hours a day, and his capacity for work would be greatly impaired for the rest of his life.[36] In the aftermath of his first heart attack in 1963, Porter had quit smoking and adopted a healthier lifestyle – walking to and from work when feasible, watching his diet, and the like.[37] However, after the publication of *The Vertical Mosaic*, fame beckoned. He received more and more invitations to travel and speak. Wanting to seize the opportunity to talk about his work, to urge changes to public policy, and to promote his views of sociology, he accepted more of these invitations than he should have and found himself busier than ever – despite medical advice cautioning him against such a heavy load of work and travel.[38] In the fall of 1970, he paid the price for his enthusiasm and ambition.

That autumn, while convalescing at home, he was cheered by news from the Canada Council that he and Blishen had received $168,000 to carry out the 'Survey of Ontario Student Aspirations' (SOSA).[39] Over the next few months, with Blishen doing the lion's share of the work, they hammered out draft after draft of a suitable questionnaire and by March it was ready. Fieldwork began in May and in late June, just as Porter recovered sufficiently from his illness to resume full-time work, the survey research centre at York University reported that it was complete. By autumn, they had finished coding the data.[40]

The timing of Porter's return to full-time work proved propitious. In addition to being able to contribute more fully to the SOSA project, he was able to serve as the front man for *Towards 2000* when it came out that summer. He had chaired the committee and had been deeply involved in the writing of the report until forced to withdraw due to his heart attack.

Towards 2000: The Future of Post-Secondary Education in Ontario was a group effort undertaken by the eleven-person research subcommittee of the Committee of Presidents of the Universities of Ontario (CPUO).[41] For years, the CPUO had done much of the planning of university-level postsecondary education in Ontario. The purpose of *Towards 2000* was to influence the Wright Commission, a body established by William Davis, Ontario's minister of education, under orders from Premier John Robarts. The mandate of the Wright Commission was to examine all aspects of postsecondary education in the province with the aim of providing advice to the government about educational policy, philosophy, and spending at a time when politicians and the general public were beginning to have doubts about the value of the province's enormous investment in postsecondary education.[42]

For their part, the authors of *Towards 2000* reviewed the entire postsecondary education sector – not just the universities – with the goal of providing policy recommendations that would be seen as 'responsible' and 'practical' in the light of two factors: an expected increase in government involvement in the funding and operation of postsecondary education, and expected changes in taxpayer demands on universities and community colleges. The authors were well aware that the days of rapid, unfettered, and unquestioned growth were over, but they were eager to counter the alarmism and negativity then surfacing over the rapidly rising cost of postsecondary education in Ontario.[43]

Towards 2000 was the first major policy document that Porter helped to prepare and, as Frank Vallee pointed out some years later, it exemplified a particular – what I would call New Liberal – aspect of Porter's intellectual style:

> One can see in John Porter's works something that those who knew him would confirm: he had little time for arguments about the distinction between pure and applied social science research, or about the virtues of one theoretical system compared to others, or about the role of the scholar in relation to social policy. The dovetailing of scientific rigour, scholarly analysis, and relevance to policy is exemplified in ... *Towards 2000*.[44]

The document was a group effort, however, and thus must be regarded as only generally illustrative of or in tune with Porter's views, rather than a direct expression of them. Yet in tone and content *Towards*

2000 could easily have been written by Porter. Certainly, its themes and arguments bear considerable resemblance to those in *Does Money Matter?* and *Stations and Callings,* which he wrote jointly with Marion Porter and Bernard Blishen.

The committee wrote *Towards 2000* with a keen sense of context, especially regarding what they saw as Canada's transformation from an industrial society to a postindustrial one. Following Daniel Bell, Porter and his colleagues argued that postindustrial society was a service-based economy 'organized around knowledge': in particular, 'theoretical, abstract knowledge.' This type of knowledge would be the new basis of 'innovation' and 'power.' In this emerging society, there was a need for 'planning and forecasting' of social change and development. However, unlike industrial society, in which the industrial ownership class had done the planning and forecasting, in postindustrial society governments would undertake these tasks. Indeed, governments would have to solve many of the problems left over from the industrial era. Given the centrality of knowledge (rather than property) to the emerging postindustrial society, its dominant institutions would be universities, industrial laboratories, and research corporations. As well, there would be a new leadership group. Those wielding power would be the technocrats: scientists, engineers, mathematicians, economists and, something new at the time, 'the creators and consumers of computer technology.'[45]

The balance of the book was comprehensive, containing chapters on the historical development of Ontario's system of postsecondary education, changing enrolment patterns, the respective organizational features and roles of the government and non-government agencies then responsible for the province's postsecondary educational system, and so forth. One chapter of special interest to Porter examined the thorny issue of the accessibility of postsecondary education.

Their chapter on the new professoriate is worth discussing briefly because it reveals the committee's political-philosophical orientation to education as well as its willingness to promote radical change within the system. Here as elsewhere, the watchword was flexibility. They were keenly aware that the time-honoured roles of the university – the dissemination, preservation, and advancement of knowledge – were under scrutiny, if not outright attack. With students demanding that the academy play a more public and vocal role as a critic of social conditions and public policies, they were convinced that the university had to become more flexible about questions of admissions, programs, and governance.[46] As well, the traditional role of the professoriate had to change, in their view substantially. They argued for the abolition of the traditional concept of tenure, arguing that it was 'an unusual privilege' (seen by some outside the university as an 'absurdity') in the 1970s.[47] In its place, they proposed the use of collective bargaining to guarantee the retention of the distinctive features of academic employment: academic freedom, responsible self-government, collegial work relationships, and the like.[48] They proposed as well the reduction of subdisciplinary specialization, an increase in organizational fluidity, the periodic retraining of professors, and early retirement for selected faculty. Finally, they advocated the adoption of a new tripartite division of duties among faculty; some should concentrate exclusively on teaching, others on research, while others would retain the traditional role of the professor-scholar.[49] Such measures would improve the economic efficiency of the universities while preventing professorial obsolescence and redundancy in an era of accelerating change.[50]

For Porter, what was perhaps the central chapter dealt with one of the committee's bedrock principles: 'accessible hierarchy.' In terms of accessibility, they argued that as a matter of principle, student access should be based on competence, not ability to pay.[51] However, they wanted to retain a hierarchical system of generalist and specialist programs (similar to the idea of pass and honours programs). This would make postsecondary education available to a broad range of interested and qualified students, regardless of their economic means, while preserving a special place for those who were particularly gifted. A radical policy recommendation growing out of this idea was that colleges of applied arts and technology, or CAATs, rather than universities would be the point of entry for general degree work in the arts and sciences as well as for technical training. Universities would cede this responsibility to the CAATs in return for being allowed to focus on specialist (honours) training of undergraduates, graduate training, professional programs, and research.[52] As well, the committee insisted that the system should become more flexible, in particular by allowing students greater freedom to move from CAATs to universities. In their estimation, the system should become a seamless web – 'a series of linked continua ... [with] no dead-end streets' – so that students could move from program to program within institutions or from institution to institution as their interests and capacities developed.[53]

The committee made many specific policy recommendations with respect to the various levels and types of postsecondary education –

undergraduate, professional, and graduate – and tackled as well the challenging question of the financial support of university research, in particular by governments.[54] The last third of the book deals with the role of the federal government in funding university research, infrastructure, and student aid. Some of the key recommendations were just as radical as those made with regard to the abolition of tenure, the integration of the universities and the CAATs, and so on. For example, beginning from a 'first principle' that the federal government should increase its involvement in (and funding of) postsecondary education, on the grounds that education and research served the *national* interest and contributed to the development of a *national* culture, the committee members proposed the establishment of a national university. Moreover, they argued that the federal government should assume responsibility for all graduate postsecondary education, using the logic that education was as important or more important than other competing claims for tax dollars and that the federal government had both the right under the BNA Act and the means, via its ability to tax, to institute such a plan.[55] At the very least, they pushed the federal government to provide greatly increased funding for research, infrastructure, and student aid and urged it to develop a strong national science policy.

Towards 2000 provoked a mixed response, as might be expected when so many interest groups with different agendas had a stake in the issue. One particularly significant negative response came from the committee representing the presidents of Ontario's colleges of applied arts and technology. They feared that under the proposed new system, the CAATs would lose their distinct identity. The CAATs had been conceived as venues in which students with an applied and practical bent could obtain a technical education in a setting intended exclusively for that purpose. The community college presidents realized that some status and cachet might accrue to the CAATs if they became part of the university system, but worried that under the existing proposal their students would become second-class citizens in their own institutions. They were not opposed to greater integration of the two systems, but considered that this could be accomplished 'without combining [the] physical, academic, advising, or administrative structures' of the CAATs and the universities.[56]

Towards 2000 did not generate much attention in the popular press outside Toronto, but journalists there provided generally favourable feedback.[57] They regarded the report's factual assessment of the situation and many of its predictions as accurate but expressed concern about some of the trends described in the report, in particular the committee's apparent acceptance of the drift to technocracy, with attendant possibilities for rule by an intellectual elite.[58]

Reaction in the academic press was similarly limited – and also more critical. For example, Denis Smith, writing in the *Journal of Canadian Studies*, regarded the volume as seriously flawed. In his view, the authors had bought too readily into the idea that postindustrial society was not only more or less inevitable but also good. Many of the authors' policy recommendations seemed to him wise and humane, and could 'be defended on the individualist ground that they would encourage men freely to nurture their abilities and interests,' but he also charged that they made no attempt to consider the negative effects that a hierarchical, regimented, and centralized postindustrial society would have on both the individual citizen and on the educational system.[59]

There is no way to determine what, if any, impact *Towards 2000* had on the analysis and recommendations put forth in the report of the Wright Commission. We do know, however, that when the commission issued its draft report, Porter was not impressed. He regarded its aims as questionable and its conclusions flawed. In its rush to make education accessible, he said, it advocated a downgrading of standards. As well, it was vague in its articulation of the respective functions that the three parts of the postsecondary educational system (universities, community colleges, and the Open University) were to play.[60]

Whatever the merits, faults, and impact of *Towards 2000*, it signalled a shift in Porter's research emphasis. Beginning from an interest in the workings of class and power, he had come to be fascinated by the more specific question of the dynamics of educational and occupational attainment in Canada as they were influenced by class structure. This shift in focus was accompanied by a shift in style: he had clearly become more committed to practical, policy-relevant research.

During the late 1960s and early 1970s, Porter continued to ask a fundamental question that he had addressed in *The Vertical Mosaic*: how do you make Canada a just and rational society? Consistently during the late 1960s and early 1970s his answer was essentially a meritocratic liberal one. The United States constituted a model for Canada to emulate; it was more modern, industrialized, progressive, individualistic, and meritocratic than his own country. So while he never accepted uncritically the superiority of US society – he harboured strong misgivings about the inequalities of condition and opportunity generated by American capitalism – he did seem to believe that the institutionalization of maximal equality of opportunity via education constituted the most direct and realistic way of making Canada into a just, rational, and democratic nation. To adhere to such a proposition it was necessary to believe that real equality of opportunity – not just a purely formal or legal form of equality of opportunity – could be created via the educational system. The conventional wisdom in Canada held that the educational system was sufficiently open and meritocratic that Canadian children benefited from relatively equal opportunities to get ahead whatever their class, ethnic, or gender background. Porter knew this to be nonsense: the school system did more to reinforce and reproduce the class structure than break it down.[61] Still, he retained the view that education remained the key to a more just and egalitarian society. Data showed that for most people only a university education could provide an entrée into the world of material and cultural rewards that accrued to those at the top of the occupational structure. Porter believed that by careful planning and appropriate public policy, the educational system *could* be made a realistic destination for many more intellectually qualified people than was the case. Only in this way would barriers to upward mobility be reduced and Canada be made more just and democratic. And there was an additional benefit: Canadian society could become more rational. The existence of class barriers that denied equality of educational opportunity meant that Canada was unable to make full use of all its human resources. Funding and policy initiatives could drastically reduce this irrationality.

Herein lay the roots of Porter's interest in the relationship between educational opportunity and social mobility. Like his earlier major works, Porter's final major study, *Ascription and Achievement*, constituted a part of his long odyssey to document the nature of the problem of inequality of opportunity in Canada and to assess the feasibility of his preferred solution – individual social mobility – in helping to create a nation in which democracy, social justice, and societal rationality prevailed.

It was important to Porter's career that he undertook at least part of his exploration of the self-contradictory nature of education – it was, after all, both a conduit and a barrier to opportunity – under the auspices of the CPUO. In the late 1960s and early '70s radical critics of postsecondary education abounded, but they tended to be outsiders to the structure of power. By contrast, Porter's membership on the research subcommittee of the CPUO gave him the opportunity to interact on a long-term basis with a group of senior and accomplished insiders, each a mover and shaker in the field of university–government relations. While writing *Towards 2000*, he learned the culture of senior university brainstorming and politicking and as chair of the committee came to be seen as – and to see himself as – an insider. Simultaneously, of course, he became even more visible as a senior disciplinary and university statesman, a position he came increasingly to assume, enjoy, and desire in the decade to follow.

With *Towards 2000* completed, Porter could now turn his full attention to other research. First on his agenda was the 'Survey of Ontario Student Aspirations,' the SOSA study.[62] Its purpose was to ascertain students' hopes and plans about postsecondary education and to identify the social factors that contoured such hopes and plans. Were bright children from lower-class backgrounds less likely to aspire to university than their middle- and upper-class counterparts? Were there gender, ethnic, rural–urban or other differences? Did lower-class students have high aspirations but lack parental support or the financial means to go on to postsecondary education, or both? Did parents from lower-class families have different attitudes toward education from those in higher classes? Detailed, reliable data bearing on these and related questions would allow informed discussion to replace the speculation and ideological musings that often dominated the highly charged debates about this subject in Canada. American and British researchers had done major studies of the problem, but in Canada only Raymond Breton had gathered roughly equivalent Canadian data.[63]

To answer these questions, Porter and Blishen constructed a seventy-five-item questionnaire, which they administered to over 8,500 students from 405 classes in 355 schools across Ontario.[64] Although their most pressing concern was to determine the relationship between social class and educational aspirations, the questionnaire was comprehensive, focusing on the relationships between a phalanx of independent, or causal, variables (among others, class, parental education, sex, mental ability, self-concept of ability, attitude to school work, school program, school performance) and four dependent, or outcome, variables (educational aspirations and expectations, occupational aspirations and expectations).[65] As subjects, Porter and Blishen chose students in Grades 8, 10, and 12 on the grounds that these grades marked the key decision-making years in a student's career: Grade 8 because at that point the student decides what kind of high school to attend and the courses to take; Grade 10 because many students are then old enough to leave school; and Grade 12 because at that point students must decide whether to continue to postsecondary education.[66] 'If the chances of children of different social classes are shown to be unequal,' they reckoned, 'the loaded dice are thrown at these branching points.'[67] In addition to filling out the questionnaire, each student completed a test of 'self-concept of ability' and a 'culture-fair' intelligence test (used in conjunction with grades) as a measure of mental ability.[68] Finally, since they thought that students' aspirations were framed by their home environment, Porter and Blishen interviewed a subsample of nearly 3,000 parents (1,000 within each grade cohort) as well.[69]

The data from this massive study became available in the autumn of 1971, and over the winter and spring terms they carried out some preliminary data analysis.[70] It soon became apparent that the findings were complex and would take considerable time to unravel. At the same time, however, some transparent data patterns emerged regarding who did and did not go on to postsecondary education as well as some obvious indicators of the key factors that allowed some to enjoy a university education and prevented others from doing so. Porter and Blishen wanted to make this information public, so they decided to write a preliminary, policy-oriented report. The more scholarly analysis could wait while they produced a document that spoke directly to the accessibility issues then in the public eye.[71]

The policy-oriented volume, *Does Money Matter? Prospects for Higher Education*, came out in 1973, published by the Institute for Behavioural Research at York University.[72] Accounts of the history of this manuscript and the subsequent manuscript of *Stations and Callings* are at odds. For her part, Marion remembered that in the aftermath of his heart attack in 1968, John had considered abandoning the project. Once Blishen promised to assume the major responsibility for completing the work, however, John decided to stay on. At that point, she says, Blishen left for England and she 'replaced BB as JP's collaborator.' As she tells the tale, the original idea had been that she would write a brief report on the data about financing a university education.[73] However, once immersed in the materials, she decided to undertake a more comprehensive analysis, focusing on practical, policy-relevant issues. This work was published as *Does Money Matter?* in 1973.[74] This account seems to explain why the first-named author of the 1973 version of *Does Money Matter?* is Marion Porter. By her recollection, it was largely the result of her efforts: 'That book is mine entirely ... John read it and made a couple of suggestions, but basically it's mine, and that's why John insisted that my name should go first – to make it clear I was the major author.'[75] Marion had long worked with and for her husband as a research assistant but until then had never received much public acknowledgement of her efforts. With *Does Money Matter?* her contribution became more independent and publicly visible. It was the furthest Marion had stepped out of her husband's academic shadow.

But Marion's account has been disputed. Blishen and two of the four graduate students involved in the project – Maria Barrados and Hugh McRoberts – provided rather different stories.[76] These disagreements made it difficult to determine exactly who was responsible for particular aspects of the completed volumes.[77] Whatever the respective merits of these accounts, a particularly noteworthy difference between the original and final versions of the SOSA study is that the first-named author of the final version of the study, *Stations and Callings,* is John Porter. Marion Porter and Bernard Blishen are listed as co-authors, in that order. According to Blishen, the four graduate students involved in the production of *Stations and Callings* – Barrados, McRoberts, Sid Gilbert, and Susan Russell – should have been given more recognition for their work.[78]

Whatever the relative veracity of the origin accounts, the three volumes (two editions of *Does Money Matter?* and *Stations and Callings*) contain an incredible volume of data. These data are particularly front and centre in *Does Money Matter?* which is in both versions largely atheoretical. All three volumes are data-centric throughout, but the volumes contain numerous polemical passages that reveal the authors' 'left-liberal' political beliefs. None of the three had patience for liberal banalities about the existence of equality of condition and opportunity in Canada; their analyses of the SOSA data cut quickly to the heart of this issue. There was, they said, a clear tension between the existence of an obdurate class structure in Canada and the naïve, widespread belief in the existence of equality of opportunity. A good deal of the analysis in *Does Money Matter?* (both versions) was intended to contribute to the debate then raging about who should get to go to university and who should pay for it. In their view, such difficulties and debates were inevitable because Canadian society and its dominant ideology were based on two contradictory principles: inequality of condition and equality of opportunity.

The SOSA data reveal that class-based differences in lifestyle, life experiences, and financial resources created huge differences in opportunities for those from different class backgrounds. Porter, Porter, and Blishen knew from extant data that most of Canada's university students in 1970 came from the upper end of the class structure, not so much because they were superior pupils but because they could afford the cost. The push for increased state funding of universities with the intention of promoting accessibility through the provision of practical and fair student assistance programs constituted a public recognition of the need to reduce the financial barriers to postsecondary education for lower-class students. However, Blishen and the Porters knew that simply offering money to graduating senior high school students would not solve the problem; by the time they graduated, it was already too late for the vast majority of lower-class students. Such students would not put in the effort to achieve the marks necessary to get into university or community college until they could see postsecondary education as a realistic goal. In short, they had see that it was sensible to *aspire* to a post-secondary education. Existing evidence demonstrated that students from the lower class had significantly lower educational aspirations and expectations from early on in their school careers. Why? According to Porter, Porter, and Blishen, partly because of a realistic lowering of expectations. Lower-class children and their parents generally regarded postsecondary education, especially university education, as beyond their financial means and adjusted their goals accordingly. In the view of Porter, Porter, and Blishen, it was necessary to document these financial difficulties and weigh them against other factors that prevented most lower-class high school students from going on to university or community college. An important competing explanation for why relatively few lower-class children went to university was that lower-class 'culture' got in the way. According to this theory, lower-class parents did not value education and therefore did not create the physical and emotional environment at home necessary for children to aspire to attend university or community college. This 'failure,' so the story went, meant that lower-class children did not try as hard and did more poorly. Exacerbating this problem were two others. Lower-class parents chose not to save money for their children's education and, likewise, working- and lower-class children chose not to delay financial gratification for the duration of a postsecondary education. They chose to work rather than to attend university or community college. One purpose of the SOSA study was to put this explanation to the test.

From the outset, Blishen and the Porters rejected the purely meritocratic approach to equality of educational opportunity – access for only the most intellectually gifted – in favour of universal accessibility, i.e., access to post-secondary education for all who wanted it and could benefit from it, as indicated by meeting minimum qualifications.[79] They were well aware that, formally at least, the Ontario government had adopted the principle of universal access. However, Porter, Porter, and Blishen claimed that this was mostly political posturing. Government policies – taxation, redistribution, student aid – indicated that the Ontario government was not really committed to creating the equality of condition necessary to produce true equality of opportunity. The accusation by Porter, Porter, and Blishen was blunt: 'They seek merely to give the shadow of universal accessibility without the substance. Their creators must be naïve about social affairs if they believe these contrivances can serve the principle of equality. They are providing patchwork for a society devoted to inequality.'[80] Insofar as the government supported the principle of universal accessibility, they said, it was rooted in a practical rationale, not a sense of moral obligation. The government wanted and needed well-educated workers for the new, knowledge-based postindustrial society. In the past, the Canadian educational system had been unable to produce enough highly skilled workers and the government had found it necessary to bring them in via immigration.[81] Self-sufficiency would better serve their purposes. Hence, they adopted of the language of accessibility and pushed to expand the postsecondary educational system.

One major problem, of course, was cost. The more accessible the system, the greater the expense. But as Paul Axelrod pointed out, governments and taxpayers had two other concerns. First, existing data showed that most university students came from middle- or upper-class backgrounds, so they were already a privileged group. Second, once they graduated, they would enjoy the rewards of their good fortune as exclusively private, personal benefits. The children of most of the working-class people who shelled out tax dollars to pay for universities would never get to university or enjoy those same benefits. Quite rightly, people were much concerned about the justice of this situation. Why should working-class people pay taxes to send already privileged middle-class children to university?[82] The SOSA data revealed the existence of class, gender, and other differences in educational expectations, aspirations, and achievements in Ontario and Porter, Porter, and Blishen tried to identify those factors, concentrating in particular on the financial circumstances that prevented the principle of universal accessibility from being realized in practice. They wanted to find a way to get as many qualified and motivated working-class students as possible into institutions of postsecondary education.

Porter, Porter, and Blishen treated educational aspirations as an outcome (dependent) variable and assessed how this outcome was influenced by seven variable sets as causes (independent and/or intervening variables).[83] The findings were entirely predictable from the results of previous studies. That is, for Grade 8, 10, and 12 students alike, there was a linear relationship between social class and educational aspirations and expectations.[84] The higher the social class, the higher the aspirations and the greater the expectations.

Overall, 30 to 40 per cent of all students (boys and girls) at each grade level expressed a desire to go to university – and only slightly fewer expected to go.[85] There were nonetheless great differences by grade and among class categories. For example, more than six in ten Grade 12 students (boys and girls) from the highest class category (SES I) wanted to go to university, while only three in ten from the lowest class category (SES VI) wanted to do so.[86] Likewise, twice as many Grade 10 and 12 students from SES I than from SES VI *wanted* to graduate from high school, and more than twice as many *expected* to graduate.[87] By contrast, twice as many Grade 12 students in SES VI as SES I expected to enter the permanent labour force immediately upon leaving high school.[88] These aspirations and expectations manifested themselves right at the beginning of secondary student careers, when they made their choice of academic programs and sealed their prospective fates. SES I students were much more likely to choose academic streams.[89] Choices and desires were related to students' own conceptions of their intellectual ability.[90] However, the data for Grade 12 students showed that at every level of mental ability lower-class boys were less likely than upper-class boys to aspire to a university education.[91]

The data on female students were even more dismal. Overall, girls at all grade levels were less likely than boys to aspire to some kind of postsecondary education.[92] Likewise, regardless of their grade level and school achievement, girls were less likely to expect to go to university than boys. This pattern held even for girls of high mental ability.[93] These gender differences were intensified by class. Six of ten girls from SES I backgrounds wanted to go to university; only one in five girls from SES VI did.[94] As Porter, Porter, and Blishen put it, 'Clearly, it was the girls of high mental ability at the lower end of the class system who constituted the greatest loss of potentially able students from the educational stream.'[95]

Throughout the discussion, Porter, Porter, and Blishen returned to the question of money, repeatedly making the claim that for children of the lower class, financial considerations placed limits on their aspirations and lowered their expectations. Despite these discouraging findings, the authors took heart in the notion that small gains were better than none and so, after writing what they referred to as their 'exposé' of the unmistakable links running from class and gender through aspirations and expectations to inequality of educational opportunity, they concluded the book with policy suggestions designed to redistribute education-related costs and opportunities more equitably across the class structure.[96]

Their suggestions were based on two premises. First, the data indicated that the 'culture of poverty' explanation had to be taken seriously. The problem was not that lower-class students and parents placed less value on education than their upper-class counterparts but that they had lower aspirations and expectations, a lower self-concept of educational and occupational ability, and insufficient cultural and financial resources to overcome class barriers to high aspirations and achievement.[97] 'Lower social class background creates a socio-cultural climate that can be inhospitable to educational achievement and aspirations. Its effects are all the more intractable because they come early in an individual's life.'[98] The root of these problems was class inequality:

> Family finances must be a factor in the limited educational horizons of lower class youth. This is not to say that the so-called ... cultural factors are non-existent or do not play a part. We felt, however, that to over-emphasize them is to forget that social class is the structure of inequality and deprivation, and that the absence of family resources helps to create attitudes and prospects of limited life chances, so that the cultural factors become adaptations to the inequality of the society. To state, as some have, that money does not matter because of the attitudes and values which mediate, seems deliberately to be avoiding steps to make education more accessible.[99]

Blishen and the Porters concluded, then, that postsecondary education, especially university education, was expensive, not something that lower-class children – even bright, high achieving ones – expected to be able to enjoy. So they lowered their aspirations and expectations to a 'reasonable' or 'realistic' level. If they did look beyond secondary school, they tended to select academic programs that would get them into community college or land them a job rather than prepare them for university.

This led Porter, Porter, and Blishen to a second justification for proposing policy changes. Not only did such barriers deny many highly capable and deserving lower-class students the opportunity to realize themselves more fully and enjoy the economic and cultural benefits of a higher education and a better job but, said the authors, they indicated that two foundational liberal principles – equity and accessibility – were being violated. To deny equality of opportunity to a large proportion of the population constituted a moral travesty and a colossal waste of human resources. While a higher percentage of upper-class students than lower-class students achieved high scores on mental ability tests, the absolute number of highly intelligent students in the lower classes dwarfed the number of highly intelligent students from the upper classes.[100] Test scores revealed that nearly half of the most intelligent students in Grade 12 came from the two lowest SES categories. In a postindustrial society based on the production of knowledge, it was foolish to allow the potential contribution of the majority of highly intelligent people to go essentially untapped. On grounds of consistency, moral rectitude, and societal rationality then, it made sense to undertake policy measures to increase the number of lower-class children who would get into university and community college. Porter, Porter, and Blishen offered a number of policy recommendations to this end.

They prefaced these with the blunt disclaimer that no amount of tinkering with the educational system would solve the problem of inequality of educational opportunity. They emphasized strongly that the Ontario public should not allow itself to be deceived in this regard. No matter how many times politicians and bureaucrats uttered unctuous assurances to the contrary, the data showed that Canada's highly inegalitarian class structure prevented the existence of anything more than a bare modicum of equality of educational opportunity. That said, the authors also acknowledged that Canadians generally regarded unequal rewards as both proper and inevitable and that therefore a significant shift in the direction of equality of condition – and thus real equality of opportunity – was at best a remote possibility. Despite this built-in limitation on economic policy, they suggested reducing income differentials across occupations and establishing a more steeply progressive tax system. They considered briefly the options of free tuition and student maintenance grants, essentially, salaries for going to school, and indicated that they would like to see postsecondary education regarded as a right of students as independent adults, rather than as a right held by parents to educate their children. But they were aware that such radical, progressive options were unrealistic in the context of an inegalitarian society such as Canada.[101]

The most important of the solutions they offered to the problem of inequality of access was, ironically, to make university education more expensive. They advocated a large increase in tuition fees, roughly in line with the real costs of a university education, but twinned this notion with the idea that governments should provide a generous system of student grants geared to parental income. This proposal, they argued, had four strengths: 1) it would make postsecondary education, especially university education, more accessible to lower-class children; 2) it would make the prospect of university *appear more accessible* because lower-class parents and students would know well in advance that loans and grants would be available; 3) those who could afford to pay more for tuition would pay more; and this would 4) provide funds for the operation of the system and broaden opportunities for those from less privileged backgrounds.[102]

Stations and Callings came out in 1982, nearly a decade after the first edition of *Does Money Matter?* It differed from the two versions of *Does Money Matter?* on only five major counts. First, it focused more on sex (what would now be referred to as gender) as a causal variable. Otherwise, the analysis of each of the independent variables was simply more detailed. Second, Porter, Porter, and Blishen incorporated a discussion of *occupational* choices into the analysis. That is, they talked not just about educational aspirations and expectations but about occupational aspirations and expectations. Third, they included chapters on other groups, including Ontario's French-language students, and chapters reporting the results of two follow-up studies from the original sample.[103] Fourth, they assessed the respective and combined influence of their complement of independent variables via a path analysis model first reported in the 1979 version of *Does Money Matter?*[104] As in *Does Money Matter?* they concluded that social class worked 'through' other variables to produce different and unequal levels of educational aspirations and attainment across the class structure.[105] Fifth, and finally, as I mentioned above, *Stations and Callings* was more theoretical. The original version of *Does Money Matter?* was a data-reporting piece and a call for policy changes. *Stations and Callings*, intended for a professional sociological audience, incorporated a full chapter on theory. This chapter demonstrated two things: Porter's attitude toward theory and theorizing; and, the degree to which he had come to see American mainstream sociology as a point of reference.[106]

Only thirteen of the 300 pages were given over to theory, and in that chapter only four pages were reserved for what the authors refer to as 'broad and discursive theorizing' about social structure, socialization, personality, and the like.[107] Porter was not a devotee of theorizing per se, especially if it meant purely speculative and abstract argumentation. He was much more interested in and convinced by empirical data. This in part explains why the theorizing in *Stations and Callings* is closely tied to the elaboration of a mathematical theoretical model based on the work of the prominent American sociologist Hubert Blalock.[108] The point of the discursive theorizing was here made clear: it was employed to develop a set of concepts that could be translated via operationalization into a set of variables that could be quantified and then organized into a formal causal model.

The authors' reliance in this section of the chapter on Blalock is just one indicator among many of the degree to which mainstream American sociology had become at this point in his career Porter's theoretical and methodological point of reference. *Stations and Callings* was a replication of a high-profile American empirical study, and the interpretation of the data was framed in terms of theoretical perspectives then dominant in American sociology. Functionalism and postindustrialism provided the two basic elements of their macrosociology. As in *The Vertical Mosaic* and *Towards 2000*, Porter argued that Canada was a postindustrial nation comprising a complex of interdependent subsystems and institutions, each of which contributed to the maintenance of system equilibrium. The education subsystem was a crucial aspect of postindustrial society. 'Within the economy … there exists a division of labour … If the economy … is to operate at all effectively,' wrote Porter, 'people must want to fill the various positions. Educational and occupational aspirations are therefore essential for the continuance of the division of labour. Aspirations … are the motivational prerequisites for filling a complex structure of adult roles, particularly those of the work world.'[109] The mechanism by which people are prepared for their 'slots' in the economy (as in other institutions) is the process of socialization, begun at birth and continued throughout life.

From infancy through adolescence, individuals learn not only the roles of their intimate primary groups but also those of the wider society. They are prepared for adult life when, in time, roles in the world of work, of citizenship and political participation, of males and females, and of parenthood all await. All these roles are integrated into the major institutional systems of the society, that is, the economy, the political system, and the ideological systems of religion and culture. Thus socialization in early primary group experience should achieve objectives for both the individual and society as that individual's social character becomes moulded to social structure.[110]

It is this process – the process by which children come to have specific educational and occupational aspirations – for which Porter, Porter, and Blishen wanted to provide a theoretical account in *Stations and Callings*. The micro- and mesosociological theories they used to do so drew on the standard coin of the realm in mainstream American sociology and social psychology at the time: B.F. Skinner's behaviourism, George Homans' exchange theory, role theory, and above all the 'symbolic interactionism' of George Herbert Mead and Charles Horton Cooley.[111] They argued that children, who by nature 'seek to maximize gratification and minimize deprivation' (liberalism, behaviourism), learn from interactions with 'significant others' or 'companion role players' (symbolic interactionism, exchange theory, role theory) to conform to norms and rules in order to receive 'rewards' and escape 'punishments and deprivations' (liberalism, behaviourism). In the end, children learn to 'fit in' and satisfy their own needs while simultaneously filling 'roles' and serving functions (role theory, functionalism) that 'serve the total social system' (functionalism).[112] Their sense of self-worth comes from the evaluations offered them by others during the process of socialization: the self is a 'looking glass self,' at once emergent and social (symbolic interactionism).[113]

Porter, Porter, and Blishen concluded *Stations and Callings* by claiming that educational and occupational aspirations are socially determined by forces operating within families and inside schools in a way that usually favours those from privileged class backgrounds: 'In locating the roots of ambition and desire to learn in the interaction processes of the small primary groups which socialize the individual and mediate between him and the wider society, we can see how great the inequalities of chances to exploit opportunity are.'[114] Schools act not to liquefy the class structure but to crystallize it. Only if educational opportunities can be equalized – and be seen by everyone to be equalized – will it be possible to create a society in which children of equal ability have equal opportunities to succeed. Otherwise, children from the lower reaches of the class system will continue to be denied the possibility of realizing their potential, developing occupational goals commensurate with their gifts and abilities, and contributing fully to the rational operation of the social system. It was to this puzzle – the causes, patterns, and dynamics of social mobility – that Porter next turned his attention.

12 Measuring Social Mobility, 1970–1979

One dividend of Porter's post-*Mosaic* reputation, burnished even brighter by the MacIver Prize and his election to the Royal Society of Canada, was that he received many invitations to travel and lecture. An especially attractive offer came his way during the ill-fated year in Toronto. That autumn, he received a phone call from Seymour Martin Lipset, representing Harvard University. Lipset wanted to know, on behalf of his colleagues, if Porter would be interested in spending a year in Cambridge, Massachusetts, as the visiting professor of Canadian studies on the Mackenzie King endowment.[1] The invitation was a great honour, of course, and Porter accepted. But because of other commitments, in particular the two national surveys and the logistics of moving back to Ottawa from Toronto, he deferred taking it up until the academic year 1973–4.

Harvard had established the Canadian studies professorship in 1967. It was to be awarded to an outstanding sociologist, historian, political scientist, or student of literature. Responsibilities included teaching graduate and undergraduate courses for students at both Harvard and Radcliffe, and guest lectures and specialized consulting for faculty and graduate students. About 175 Canadian students enrolled at Harvard each year and many took Canada-related courses. Porter's predecessors in the chair included Claude Bissell, Ramsay Cook, Albert Breton, and Thomas Wilson.[2]

The Porters moved to Cambridge in July 1973 and settled into an on-campus apartment in Eliot House, a lovely spot overlooking the Charles River. At the corner of Memorial Drive and J.F. Kennedy Drive, Eliot House was just across the street from the JFK School of Government and a pleasant fifteen-minute walk through stately Harvard Yard to his office in William James Hall. According to Marion, John was excited about going to Harvard, for he regarded it as one of the most prestigious and influential universities in the world. In a letter to Blishen written part way through his stay there he quipped that Harvard 'defines the world's problems, conceptualizes them and, indeed, creates knowledge. As they said of old Benjamin Jowett: "[W]hat they do not know here is not knowledge."'[3]

Once there, Porter took advantage of the intellectual ambience, attending numerous scholarly and social events.[4] 'Harvard is a fabulous place,' he wrote to Wallace Clement. 'I met and listened to Archibald Cox last evening ... Everybody is very friendly [and] we have a rather exhausting social life.'[5] Similarly, he noted in a letter to Blishen that he felt 'great elation at being at Harvard' because 'so much is going on that it is unbelievable.' Between them, he wrote, Boston and Cambridge 'provide an intellectual and cultural environment which I am sure cannot be beaten anywhere':

> The other exciting thing about Harvard is the way in which we have been received by the whole department and others as well. There are interdepartmental seminars on all manner of problems, a departmental colloquium which is of a particularly high standard, and even at dinner parties of which there are many the drinking is moderate and the conversation is serious, witty and so forth.[6]

Porter fit into the sociology department so well and they were so impressed by him that according to Daniel Bell, then a member of the department, they approached him about staying on as a tenured professor, effectively becoming the permanent incumbent of the Mackenzie King chair. While the King professorship was the vehicle they planned to use to bring Porter into the department, Bell emphasized that they wanted him 'not just [as] a Canadian specialist' but 'because of his general competence as a sociologist.' When they approached Porter about the possibility of a permanent position, he was pleased and interested. But when he mentioned his health problems, the offer was withdrawn.[7]

While in Cambridge, Porter continued to receive honours from his Canadian colleagues. He was chosen unanimously to be an honorary president of the CSAA and awarded an honorary degree by McMaster University.[8] But the year at Harvard had its down side. Overwork triggered long-standing health problems. As he confessed in a letter to Blishen, 'I arrived here exhausted and was faced with giving two courses for which I had done no preparation. It has been very tough and has meant almost constant work. I finally had to go to the doctor and my blood pressure was the highest it had ever been.' So overburdened did he feel that he contemplated leaving at the end of the fall term: 'I have seriously thought of trying to get out of the next term, but I am sure there is no way I can without incredible embarrassment all around.'[9] Part of the problem was that, as usual, he had taken on too many responsibilities. They did not finish *Does Money Matter?* until mid-September and had only just begun serious work on *Stations and Callings*.[10] As well, the mobility project was just underway. Then, over the fall and winter, he dabbled with the draft of what would become *The Measure of Canadian Society* (then referred to as *The Canadian Condition*),[11] agreed to advise a provincial task force in Manitoba,[12] and gave a number of public talks, including 'The Pluralistic Society in a Modern State,' at the Liberal International, sponsored by the Liberal Party of Canada.[13]

He taught three undergraduate lecture courses at Harvard: 'Canadian Society,' 'Modern National Systems,' and 'The Canadian Future: Problems and Prospects.' He also had a graduate seminar, 'Analysis of Modern National Societies.' All the classes were very small, the undergraduate courses populated in the main by first- and second-year students, many of them Canadians.[14] Nonetheless, he found the workload 'irksome and heavy.'[15] It is not hard to see why. The introductory Canadian society course, for example, ranged widely, examining theoretical models, presenting basic demographic data, and reviewing materials on Canada's basic institutional structure – the economy, the polity, the educational system – while simultaneously debating various issues and problems: stratification, women, Quebec, and so forth. The reading list was massive: nineteen pages and over 350 sources.[16] The other courses exhibited similar breadth. Although he delayed final course preparation until he arrived in Cambridge, he did much more than necessary to prepare for first- and second-year-level courses, doubtless because he wanted to demonstrate to his new colleagues that he belonged at a world-class university. But he had another goal in mind as well. In a letter to R.I.K. Davidson, editor at the University of Toronto Press, written in 1972, just a year before heading to Harvard, he noted that he intended to use the materials as 'the basis of a new book on Canadian social and political institutions,' something more than a heavily revised version of *The Vertical Mosaic*.[17] As he put it in a letter to Wallace Clement, written two years later in the midst of his sojourn in Cambridge, 'I hope that what I am doing will ultimately develop into a macrosociology – although the payoff is far ahead.'[18]

That particular payoff never came, for he never produced a second magnum opus, but much of what he worked on had other benefits. For years, he had been trying to develop a theoretical and methodological approach useful for the prosecution of comparative, macrosociological research – settling on a proper unit of analysis, determining the most accurate indicators of social change, and so forth. Likewise, he followed closely the 'social indicators' work promoted by Sylvia Ostry at Statistics Canada and intended his work on education and mobility to provide data for comparative research. Other work was conceptual. While at Harvard, he pieced together working drafts of two theoretical essays: 'Macrosociology: Some Problems with the Nation State as the Unit of Analysis' and 'Towards a Macrosociology: Further Notes,' which he then used in successive iterations as discussion pieces in a doctoral seminar he taught at Carleton. These two essays are pivotal for understanding Porter's late-career interests and perspective. Neither was ever finished, but when taken together they indicate the direction his new macrosociology would take. In a related vein, he began drafting two essays that tied together his interests in education and social justice. These later appeared as the McInnis Lectures and were published in 1977.

On his return to Carleton from Harvard in the summer of 1974, he had to start worrying in earnest about another major new project. In 1972, while Marion was immersed in the preparation of the first draft of *Does Money Matter?* Porter and his colleagues Frank Jones and Peter Pineo had done some preliminary work for what they regarded as a third fundamental piece of survey research that needed to be done in Canada: a national study of social mobility. Again, the model they had in mind was a landmark American study, 'Occupational Change in a Generation,' undertaken by Peter Blau and O.D. Duncan.[19] Jones remembers visiting Porter at Carleton shortly after Blau and Duncan published two articles from their study and suggesting to him that they do a Canadian version of the Blau–Duncan study. Porter agreed and suggested that they bring Pineo into the project.[20] They had great reasons for undertaking such a study at that time. First, there was tremendous international interest in the phenomenon of social mobility. In 1954, David Glass of the London School of Economics had undertaken a national study of mobility in Great Britain and since that time similar studies had been undertaken or were underway in many Western nations.[21] Mobility studies were of great interest at the time because scholars regarded mobility as an index of the 'openness' of a particular society's class structure. Second, scholars across Western societies were optimistic that mobility data could be put to practical use by government policy makers. Third, Porter, Jones, and Pineo recognized the importance of getting a Canadian study completed so that Canadian sociologists could take part in the debate. In Canada, they noted, research on social mobility had been limited to 'a small national sample,' a study of mobility in Quebec, and a few studies of 'single occupations or certain classes of occupations.'[22] Fourth, according to their colleague, John Goyder, they were not unmindful that there was scholarly prestige to be derived from being the first Canadian scholars to undertake such a study. In Goyder's view, Porter had become 'very attuned to and concerned about what American sociologists thought about him and his work' and regarded the mobility study as a way of augmenting his profile within and links to the American sociological establishment.[23] Another co-investigator, Hugh McRoberts, denied any such motivations. Porter, he said, was 'pretty confident about his status as a scholar and ... [didn't feel] the need of others to validate that status.' Insofar as Porter wanted to model his sociology on American methods, said McRoberts, it was because he saw it as good sociology, not because he wanted the Americans' attention or approval. As he put it, Porter's sociology was American 'only in the sense of a commitment to data and a belief it was important to create repositories of data that would allow a better understanding of Canadian society.[24] Similarly, he said, Porter preferred American theoretical approaches to European ones because he regarded Canada and the United States as so similar that it made sense to use American theory to describe Canadian, really North American, society.[25]

Whatever the motivations and benefits of mounting the mobility study, the group appreciated that it would be a huge undertaking, much more ambitious than either the prestige study or the SOSA project, requiring a landmark grant from the Canada Council as well as generous cooperation from the Dominion Bureau of Statistics (DBS). They were a prestigious group in Canadian sociological circles, however, and doubtless believed they had the reputation and skills both to sell the proposal and to execute the project successfully once funds were in place.

For his part, Porter regarded the mobility study as a logical development from his work on class in *The Vertical Mosaic*, on prestige with Pineo, and on educational and occupational aspirations with Blishen and Marion Porter. According to Pineo, he had grand intentions, if not a grand plan of sorts, from the beginning: 'Both projects [the prestige study and the mobility study] had long-term goals. They, along with the study of high school students, were part of a programme of research that Porter envisaged. He wrote in the proposal for the 1964 [prestige] survey of a series of studies he intended to have done at Carleton "comparing Canada and the U.S.A."'[26] With Jones and Pineo, Porter was committed to the rapid development of sociology in Canada and regarded large-scale national surveys that would provide basic macro-data as central to that endeavour. Such surveys would serve two purposes: they would allow for cross-national comparisons, in particular with the United States, and simultaneously provide a 'data heritage' for Canadian social science.[27] Together, these two developments would help Canadian sociology to catch up to the cutting edge of American sociology.[28] This is not to say that Porter was entirely taken with American sociology. Dennis Olsen, one of Porter's PhD students at Carleton in the 1970s, recalls Porter's comments about the negative political effects of American sociology in the United States and abroad. As Olsen phrased it in his notes, Porter claimed that mainstream sociology was 'part and parcel of the dominant reality-construction machinery (social science) of the dominant nation state (U.S.),' and that Canadian intellectuals had been 'co-opted' by American graduate schools. Thus, said Porter, it was crucial for Canadian social scientists to 'start thinking in terms of developing a national social science, i.e., one in which the social scientists focus on the problems of Canada.' If they did not, he warned, then they would be 'vulnerable when it came to combating the myth-making colossus to the south.'[29]

To prepare for this massive project, Jones, Pineo, and Porter undertook a great deal of background work as time allowed over the next five years. They began in late 1967 by discussing the project with Sylvia Ostry, then at DBS, hoping to piggyback the mobility study on to one of its regular Labour Force Surveys. Working through Ostry, they nearly convinced the DBS to field the survey in 1969, but at the last minute senior officials quashed the plan.[30] According to Pineo, had it not been for Jones, who 'continued to work on questionnaire testing and pre-design' at McMaster in the hopes that DBS policies and practices would change, 'the project would probably have died.'[31] Over the next couple of years, however, Jones, Pineo, and two doctoral students, John Goyder and Vincent Keddie, undertook a pair of pilot studies at McMaster and, in March 1972, with these pilot studies near completion, the group again approached DBS (since renamed Statistics Canada).[32] Ostry had replaced Robert Coates as chief statistician and they knew her to be sympathetic to the mobility study.[33]

In part to persuade Statistics Canada of the importance of the survey, and in part to get feedback from important American scholars, the group organized a planning forum similar to the one Porter and Blishen had convened for *Stations and Callings*.[34] The list of invitees to the forum, which took place at Carleton in June 1972, included Ostry and Jenny Podoluk from Statistics Canada, key people from the Canada Council, and three young stars of American sociology: David Featherman and Robert Hauser, then in the midst of replicating the Blau-Duncan study, and Donald Treiman, an expert on occupational prestige and comparative research. Porter and Pineo presided, but the younger members of what they came to call the CARMAC research team were in attendance as well: McRoberts, one of Porter's PhD students at Carleton; Goyder, a junior faculty member at Waterloo Lutheran University (now Wilfrid Laurier University); and Monica Boyd, a junior faculty member at Carleton with a PhD from Duke.[35] Though Goyder was the only one then officially a member of the research team, McRoberts and Boyd were added soon after.[36] The meeting was a great success and, for several weeks thereafter, Porter and McRoberts maintained a steady stream of correspondence with the various government agencies involved.[37] Their efforts paid off. Five months later, Statistics Canada agreed to administer the mobility questionnaire (as a supplement to their monthly Labour Force Survey) and to code and edit the data.[38] For its part, Canada Council agreed to fund the study: a huge and unprecedented commitment of $225,000.[39] The council had put the proposal through the usual review process and received enthusiastic comments from the assessors.[40] A good summary of the general sense of their collective response is the following: 'The social relevance and practical importance of this research,' wrote the reviewer, 'are so self-evident as hardly to require comment.' The study promised 'to demonstrate the inequalities that exist ... [Such] evidence is necessary to persuade policy-makers of what needs to be done to move towards removing or mitigating [them].'[41]

For Porter and his colleagues, the welcome news from Canada Council and Statistics Canada represented the culmination of nearly five years of work. Having Statistics Canada field the survey had some drawbacks in terms of timing, the length of the questionnaire, and data confidentiality, but the trade-off was a good one.[42] They would obtain detailed, reliable data on 45,000 male and female members of the workforce, properly weighted both nationally and by province, all for a fraction of what it would cost to administer the questionnaire and analyse the data through a private-sector firm.[43]

After months of sometimes frantic work by the group, including extensive consultation with Statistics Canada to refine the questionnaire, they fielded the survey on schedule in July and, by autumn of 1973, the completed questionnaires had been returned to Statistics Canada.[44] An unanticipated delay then developed as Statistics Canada spent over a year and a half cleaning the data and negotiating suitable protocols on issues such as confidentiality.[45] This put them well behind schedule. According to their original timetable, the group had planned, quite unrealistically, to have completed the data analysis and write-up by December 1975.[46] As it turned out, these two tasks took nearly five years. They did not submit a draft of the book to the Social Science Federation of Canada until the end of February 1980.[47]

Their original goal had been to prepare a unified, multi-authored volume. However, when *Ascription and Achievement* finally appeared in 1985, it looked more like a collection of papers than a coherent book: a set of related chapters written around a theme sandwiched between a jointly written introduction and conclusion. Several factors combined to delay the completion and subvert the unity of the volume. First, as Goyder emphasized, people became fatigued. The enormity and complexity of the task of research design, questionnaire construction, and preliminary data analysis, which took three years, meant that the early stages of the study proceeded slowly, siphoning off crucial energy. The researchers were tired before the project really got underway.[48] Second, there was a vast database to be mined, and the analysis proceeded more slowly than they had hoped. Technical problems added to their difficulties. More than once they had to ask computer experts at Carleton to modify existing computer programs because they were unable to handle the 45,000 cases in the sample and produce the kinds of statistics required.[49]

Members of the research team mentioned other logistical, scholarly, and interpersonal problems as well. The researchers were centred at two universities separated by a full day's car travel. They remained in contact via telephone and met occasionally in Hamilton and Ottawa, but the distance separating the two groups – in those days before the Internet – slowed communication and eroded group cohesion.[50] While Jones denied that the collaboration was 'a continually feuding relationship,' evidence from interviews and correspondence suggests that tensions developed early, splitting the team into two groups, one at McMaster and one at Carleton.[51] Originally formed on the basis of spatial propinquity and frequency of interaction, the geographical basis for the split between the two groups was reinforced by scholarly differences, in particular regarding theoretical orientation and data analysis preferences. A further complicating factor, one that cut across the Carleton–McMaster divide, had to do with career contingencies. The principal investigators were evenly divided into two generations – Porter, Pineo, and Jones in one, Boyd, Goyder, and McRoberts in the other – at different stages in their careers and who thus had in mind somewhat conflicting agendas and timetables regarding the completion of the project.[52] Taken together, these difficulties caused the project to stall in the writing stage for a very long time. A tangible manifestation is the form the volume eventually assumed: a set of essays rather than a unified book.

The extent of Porter's ongoing, day-to-day involvement and interest in the project is difficult to ascertain and the subject of some disagreement among the participants. Early on, he was central, playing a key role in the negotiations with Statistics Canada and Canada Council. Indeed, according to Pineo, without his name and reputation, the project might never have materialized. He recalls going with Porter to one meeting at which the chief departmental official began by saying, 'Our consultant says John Porter is the best sociologist in Canada; give him anything he wants.'[53] Porter was deeply involved in other aspects of the upfront work as well, including drafting the proposal and the questionnaire, making decisions about data analysis strategies, and so forth.[54] Once this phase was over, the extent of his engagement is more difficult to judge, but it does seem that he gave it less attention than did the others.

Certainly, other responsibilities got in the way. To begin, after 1972, he had ongoing commitments to the SOSA project. As well, he spent the academic year 1973–4 at Harvard and, as I noted above, confessed to being overwhelmed with teaching responsibilities while he was there. Then, after a year back at Carleton in 1974–5, he left for a year-long sabbatical in Paris. There he got some information about the mobility study from McRoberts, but seems to have been only tangentially involved.[55] Most important of all, in July 1977 he became vice-president academic at Carleton and made it clear to the CARMAC group that his administrative duties would take precedence.[56] For a good portion of the time the group was most heavily involved in the task of data processing and analysis, then, he was occupied with other things. According to Goyder, Porter had from the outset regarded his role in the project as essentially entrepreneurial and as late as 1979, wrote to Goyder saying that he had always seen his function as minor because of his other obligations.[57] He was keen to see the project undertaken and willing to put in the effort to get it underway, but he saw the data analysis as the province of the others, in particular the three junior colleagues. Goyder recalled chatting with Porter about this issue one day while they waited for a taxi: 'I remember him saying very clearly: "This is for the young people to do."'[58] Boyd had much the same recollection of his interest and involvement. 'Very quickly,' she said, Porter 'backed away from doing major substantive analysis.' In fact, it was her opinion that, unlike the other investigators, he did not 'come in with a specific interest in various parts of the project.' She speculated that he regarded the data as important but 'was not totally enthralled with individualistic liberal [approaches]' and did not find the status attainment approach 'intellectually satisfying.'[59]

But Jones, Pineo, and McRoberts disagreed with this account. Pineo agreed that Porter initially intended his involvement to be strictly entrepreneurial but noted that he took part in all phases of the project and eventually committed himself to writing three pieces of the manuscript: an introduction, a chapter with Pineo on mobility patterns in minority ethnic groups, and a projected essay comparing mobility rates in different countries.[60] Jones made a similar claim: 'Porter undoubtedly had heavy pressures from his other commitments, but … had a continued interest and involvement in the project.'[61] McRoberts was particularly concerned to correct what he saw as a misinterpretation on Goyder's part of Porter's apparent lack of interest. Goyder recalled that as the project unfolded Porter slowly disengaged from it, in part because he began to think that it would not be the kind of grand and prestigious study that would constitute a suitable follow-up to *The Vertical Mosaic*. As well, said Goyder, Porter began to see the study as dated, out of step with current developments in the literature. 'He couldn't see any way that those mobility data were going to feed the new arguments and discussions.' As a result, Goyder speculated, Porter thought that the project wasn't going to have the major impact he originally thought it would. Perhaps, said Goyder, he might even have been 'struggling with the ghost of *The Vertical Mosaic*.'[62] McRoberts disagreed with this interpretation, arguing it was not 'disinterest' as much as overwork and ill-health that influenced Porter's involvement.[63] And there is some evidence to support McRoberts' claim. In a note to Bruce McFarlane prepared just before he went on sabbatical in 1975, Porter wrote that he felt 'far too over-committed with two major surveys' and other administrative and research responsibilities.[64] And his health *was* deteriorating. While in Paris in 1975–6, Porter had experienced a recurrence of his heart problems, and ever since his second heart attack had suffered from a reduced capacity for work.[65] McRoberts also disputed Goyder's claim about Porter's sense of the prestige the mobility study might command. In McRoberts' memory, the Carleton group 'had much lower expectations for how the volume would be received and for its "stand alone" importance than Goyder did. The groups shared the view that it was an important piece of work, ... an important piece of science.' However, McRoberts said, the Carleton group did not see it in the same light as the McMaster people did: '[W]e just weren't as enthusiastic about this thing as they were ... There had to be a volume. There had to be a milestone ... But ... none of us expected to get rich or famous on it.'[66]

Whatever the case, the mobility study dragged on and, as it did, Canadian and international sociology shifted away from the social mobility/status attainment model toward neo-Marxist approaches. The CARMAC project, while au courant in when it began, was by the mid-1980s out of step. As Goyder put it, 'We worked ourselves out of date ... An awful lot happened in social stratification theory between '75 and '85 – [all of the] neo-Marxist work, Eric Olin Wright and many others. The [mobility] paradigm had come under attack ... [P]eople in France were saying that mobility [was] a bourgeois problem, which wiped the whole study off the map in a way.'[67] At the same time, feminists of various theoretical-political orientations argued that the 'attainment' problem – or at least the way it had been framed and studied using measures and methods appropriate to the study of 'male' mobility/ status attainment – would not and could not properly address women's experience.[68]

As the study dragged on, tensions increased between the Carleton and McMaster groups. According to Boyd and Goyder, this was partly a function of structural problems. From the outset, said Boyd, the research was 'underfunded on the support side,' so that principal investigators did not get release time to get on with the research and there was insufficient money for computer time, research assistants, and the like.[69] This caused some skirmishing among the investigators. Compounding these problems was what Goyder referred to as the American orientation of the Carleton group versus the Canadian orientation of the McMaster group. In Goyder's view, Boyd's training had oriented her to an American reference group, and McRoberts was a strong proponent of the use of advanced data analysis techniques and formal modelling. Porter was sensitive to his reputation in American sociology. The American sociology of the time, perhaps best represented by the work of Boyd and McRoberts, was oriented to the use of the most sophisticated statistical techniques possible. By comparison, the McMaster group was less interested in employing these techniques, regarding them as inappropriate to the Canadian data and situation. 'It's not that one approach is better than another,' Goyder mused, 'but they [are] ... different ... Monica, I think, came to see the McMaster group as kind of backward and out of date and sort of stuck with old techniques. And at McMaster our study group ... felt that especially the two younger people, Hugh and Monica, were a little bit faddish on the latest thing that Hauser and Featherman did without really thinking about how this would apply to Canadian society.'[70]

But McRoberts argued, again, that there was nothing particularly American about the Carleton group's approach. Instead, it was a question of a commitment to use the most advanced data analysis techniques available to achieve a specific goal: to build a formal, mathematical model. This approach had its roots in the United States. 'If by "American" [they meant] the fact that at Carleton we were certainly committed to try to push the limit of models as theoretical tools to more closely reflect the theoretical constructs that we were trying to test, yes, we were "American,"' he argued. However, McRoberts also pointed out that 'properly used, every equation in a model is a theoretical sentence. And the model is only as good as the analogue between those theoretical sentences and your theory. That's the way we tried to do our theory.'[71] For his part, Jones rejected both the Canadian–American distinction and any claim that the McMaster group was not up to date with the latest statistical literature.[72]

This rancorous dispute fuelled a second Canadian–American/McMaster–Carleton disagreement. The Carleton group wanted the volume to contain a chapter that directly compared Canadian and American mobility patterns, thinking it would draw the attention of American scholars and allow the CARMAC group a direct entrée into ongoing international dialogue about issues of social mobility and status attainment.[73] By contrast, the McMaster group thought a comparative article should be published separately, leaving the *Ascription and Achievement* volume to focus exclusively on the Canadian situation.[74]

There were two additional points of disagreement. One concerned the publication of results, the other the question of how contributors to the volume were going to be listed on the book's cover.

Part of the original promise of the mobility project was that the participants would reap substantial rewards for taking part. For Porter, the volume would provide the final flourish on his academic career. However, he already had an excellent publication record and a well-established career, so more than some of the others he could afford to wait for the book to come out. That said, he was also very sensitive to the career dilemma facing his junior colleagues and addressed it in an early memo: 'I certainly think we should give more thought to the position of our younger colleagues, particularly as they put increasing portions of their time into the project. They are facing a very stiff career situation over the next decade. If their visibility is lost until our book is available that is not a very attractive situation for them.'[75] Jones and Pineo were in a situation similar to Porter's; both were well-established scholars who could afford a delay. Everyone hoped for an early appearance of the book, but Jones and Pineo preferred that the data first appear in the book. This meant prolonging the time between data gathering and publication, though Jones in particular was keen to see the book finished as quickly as possible.[76] A related point of disagreement concerned the publication of articles based on the mobility data before the release of the book. The group realized that the publication of too many findings from the survey prior to the release of the full analysis might lessen the splash the book would make and, in Jones' view, might 'delay ... the principal task.'[77] Pineo was especially concerned on this point; he thought that if people were allowed to publish from the data on their own, then this might 'jeopardize the completion of the book.'[78] In his view, this was a major problem because 'the relative size of the CARMAC grant required a book-length publication to justify it.'[79] Others disagreed, arguing that if they were allowed to publish from the data as they went along, they would put more effort into the book manuscript. Porter's view, expressed in a note to the group in 1973 was that some publishing of results was both common practice and beneficial. He predicted that the book was not likely to be out until 1977 or 1978 and, in his view, that was 'too long in holding off on publication.' He suggested that they pick 'a few key papers' they could publish to keep the project in the public eye, maintaining interest without detracting from the book.[80]

As time passed, the question became more disputatious. The group presented selected findings at conferences – to get out the word that they were working on the data – but could not work out a satisfactory publishing policy.[81] The matter eventually came to a head in 1976 when McRoberts submitted a paper to *Sociologie et Sociétés* based on the CARMAC data. He submitted it as a sole-authored piece, but it eventually came out – against his wishes – bearing the others' names as well.[82] In an interview, he recalled that he 'bitterly resented ... the other[s] claiming credit for what was clearly and unambiguously [his] sole intellectual product.'[83] Then, in 1978 Goyder, who had long since finished his chapter for the book, submitted a manuscript comparing patterns of male and female income attainment to the *Canadian Review of Sociology and Anthropology*. He saw this as a safe topic, not subject to the publication embargo, he said, because it dealt with data on income. The CARMAC group had collected data on income but did not intend to discuss them in the book.[84] Some of the principal investigators, however, regarded his submission as a breach of their prepublication agreement, and this led to a breakdown. Testy letters were exchanged and soon Boyd and McRoberts also broke the embargo against publishing articles ahead of the book.[85]

The result of these heated exchanges was further delay and at one point Goyder wrote a letter to those he thought were responsible for what he felt was unreasonable foot dragging. When Porter read the letter, he replied, admitting that he was partly responsible, but chastised his young colleague for trying to blame specific people for the slow progress of the book. 'You are a bold person,' he wrote, 'to attempt to apportion the responsibility for the state of the Carmac project. We are all to blame in some measure. It is certainly not a collaboration we can look back on with any professional pride.'[86]

In an ironic twist, one of the events leading to closure on the book seems to have been Porter's death. After he died in June 1979, Wallace Clement organized a plenary session of the CSAA meetings to celebrate and assess Porter's contributions to the Canadian discipline. These papers were then published in a special memorial edition of the *CRSA*, edited by Clement. John Jackson, editor of the *CRSA*, thought something by Porter should be included. 'Clement suggested that something from the Canadian National Mobility Study would be the most reasonable choice,' said Pineo, so a jointly authored paper from the mobility study was included.[87]

The final point of friction, again generational, reached a head after the book was submitted to the Social Science Federation of Canada in June 1980. At issue was whether the 'junior' scholars would receive equal billing on the cover with the senior scholars. There were two options. Either they could be acknowledged as full colleagues and listed as equal co-authors or they could be treated as very advanced research assistants and receive some kind of secondary billing and less than equal credit. As McRoberts recalled the situation, he and Boyd rejected the latter option outright: 'Once Monica was fully on board ... from that day forward, had anyone suggested anything other than an alphabetical listing, they'd have had a war on their hands.'[88] Pineo said that he did not remember any 'serious discussion' of a model that would list seniors first but recalled that he was opposed to a juniors first model.[89] Jones noted in some comments on a draft of this manuscript that he did not remember the issue as 'a big deal.'[90] In the end, they adopted the alphabetical 'equal credit' model that, perhaps ironically, put two of the juniors (Boyd and Goyder) first.

In their proposal to Canada Council the group had claimed that the project would answer some theoretical questions about social stratification. In particular, they argued that they would be able to check the relative degrees of structural and circulation mobility extant in Canadian society and to ascertain the processes by which mobility operated. To test this they proposed using as their theoretical point of reference Blau and Duncan's formal model of status attainment.[91] They also claimed that they might contribute to a more general theoretical understanding of social inequality, specifically with regard to the accuracy of functionalist theory. However, the completed manuscript contained little discussion of theory, with the exception of a review of some of the differences between the 'social mobility matrix approach' and the 'status attainment model.'[92] Porter briefly mentions some issues in the social stratification literature but concludes that their project cannot solve such problems. All it could do, he said, was to 'throw more light on the nature and consequences of social stratification.'[93] But as one of the reviewers of the original CARMAC proposal had observed years earlier, 'The few pages which deal with theoretical significance indicate perhaps that it is not a high priority of the researchers, and it would not be mine either.'[94] A similar sentiment was voiced by one of the reviewers of the completed manuscript:

Je crois que les auteurs, canadiens anglophones, ont voulu par leurs travaux comblé l'écart qui existait entre la sociologie canadienne anglaise et la sociologie américaine touchant le problème de la mobilité sociale ... Sur le plan empirique, l'objectif a été atteint ... Le survey conduit par Statistiques Canada constitue une banque de données importante. Sur le plan théorique, les contributions nous apparaissent mineures; notant cependant l'accent qu'on a accordé à la variable 'sexe' dans le processus de mobilité et d'accomplissement.[95]

In the end, it was not theoretical incantation but masses of data and statistical pyrotechnics that were the overwhelming features of the volume. As Peter Pineo bluntly put it, 'The key issue in the study was to determine if Canada was lagging the U.S. in providing chances for social mobility. The answer was "no," and it was not "indecisive."'[96] In addition, as one of the reviewers of the draft manuscript put it,

> There has been no other national examination of social mobility and status attainment [in Canada] ... Scholars in the field of social stratification have long awaited the appearance of this manuscript. It ... makes an original contribution in terms of increasing our understanding of Canadian society, and should be published as quickly as possible ... It represents some of the best application of statistical methods to social stratification in Canada.[97]

So the data were important, but not because the findings were a surprise. 'Just as the core result of the prestige study was fully anticipated,' said Pineo, 'so were many of the results of the mobility study expected. The correlation between the father's and son's occupational status in the Canadian study was .40, exactly what other high-quality studies of mobility had found. So, too, the correlation between educational and occupational attainment was the same in Canada and the United States at about .60.'[98]

Porter contributed two chapters to the final volume: the introduction, 'Canada: The Societal Context of Occupational Allocation,' and a chapter co-written with Peter Pineo, 'Ethnic Origin and Occupational Attainment.'[99]

The introductory chapter, drafted in 1977, is a thorough, sweeping, thoughtful, and empirically informed description and analysis of the social factors that relate to an understanding of the dynamics of occupational mobility. It begins with a description of an 'ideal' system of occupational selection and recruitment – open, merit-based, rational, efficient – but notes that past research indicated many features of a postindustrial society like Canada prevented such a 'model' system from operating as it should in the real world. Porter concluded his remarks by noting that in Canada in the 1970s there remained great inequality with respect to many of these factors. One of the chief purposes of the book was 'to determine the extent to which inequalities of origin inhibit equality of opportunity.'[100]

In weaving together these materials and convincingly using empirical data, the chapter is a piece of typical Porter, theoretically aware but attuned above all to data about major social trends and structural changes in Canadian society. There is little evidence of the influence of Marxism or political economy. This suggests that at his point in his career he was for all intents and purposes a mainstream sociologist oriented toward the then current building blocks of American sociology: modernization theory, postindustrialism, functionalism, and political liberalism, broadly defined. It is the kind of wide-ranging and integrative piece at which Porter excelled and, according to Boyd and Goyder, illustrated what he saw one aspect of his role to be. In part, he was an entrepreneur – an initiator of projects and a finder of funding. But he also saw himself as an éminence grise and 'big picture' analyst.[101] He liked broad vistas and big questions, and while he wanted any data he used to be reliable and valid, constructed by the best scholars and techniques possible, he was not interested in doing such fine-grained analysis himself. Instead, he set for himself the task of writing the piece that would orient readers to the social and sociological issues and developments that the book would address.

His second contribution to the volume, co-authored with Pineo, involved an analysis of mobility patterns among minority ethnic groups.[102] According to Pineo, the chapter was, in a sense, a direct critique of a basic claim that Porter had made in *The Vertical Mosaic*:

> Early in the 1970s I had become aware that I had the information necessary to demonstrate that the effects of ethnic status upon occupational status, contrary to the argument in *The Vertical Mosaic*, were actually quite weak. I began writing up the material and sent advance copies of everything to Porter. He reacted quite cheerfully to it all and ... volunteered that he would like to collaborate. He was similarly [unfazed] by material Monica Boyd prepared for one of her chapters ... Both these instances were striking examples of his capacity to respond to new evidence, and he said of both pieces of information that he would have written those parts of *The Vertical Mosaic* differently had they been available to him at the time.[103]

It is difficult to know how much significance should be attached to these two pieces of Porter's work. The ethnicity chapter can be considered at face value as an accurate reflection of his views, even though Pineo finished it, because it had been passed back and forth between them many times. Pineo knew Porter well. It is hard to imagine he did not take into account his friend's views when putting the finishing touches on the chapter. The situation with the introduction is different. Porter died before the final versions of the substantive chapters were completed and there is no discussion of them in the introduction. He had seen drafts of some of the materials, but it was Marion who edited the final version of 'his' chapter. As for the book as a whole, he was not around to put his final stamp on it, and the volume cannot be said to reflect his ideas in the way that *The Vertical Mosaic* obviously does. Indeed, it could never have been 'his' book in any case. Six powerful intellectuals contributed to the volume, and no one could have put an individual stamp on such a project.

That aside, and however we assess the significance Porter attached to the study, it was a signal accomplishment, a baseline national study of patterns of social mobility in Canada. Fifteen years after it appeared, it was chosen one of the seventeen most important works produced by English-language Canadian sociologists in the twentieth century.[104] Students of social mobility have drawn on the CARMAC data repeatedly over the years and one of the early General Social Surveys was largely dedicated to a replication of the CARMAC study for the 1980s.[105] But its substantive and methodological contributions reflect only part of its significance. Like the prestige study, Pineo said, the mobility study served the discipline in other ways: 'Both were consciously designed to stretch the existing infrastructure of sociology and the agencies surrounding the discipline.' In particular, Pineo argued, 'the cooperation between Statistics Canada and academia created a useful precedent.' He also noted that 'the large sum of money required for the [mobility] study ... had the aim of encouraging granting agencies to raise their sights,' while the size of the project simultaneously tested 'the adequacy of existing survey research facilities' and pushed 'Canadian universities to tolerate large-budget, on-campus research.' On a more local note, he said, Porter wanted the mobility study to serve graduate students at Carleton – and presumably elsewhere – by providing them 'with the option of using good survey data for their dissertations, a responsibility he felt keenly.'[106]

A final point: Porter's introductory essay illustrates what had been for some years his liberal individualist view of the best of all possible worlds, a world in which an individual's position in society would be based on merit and effort. An accessible educational system would sort students justly and rationally and then a just and rational occupational system would sort them into appropriate slots in the division of labour on the same basis.[107] But as Porter well knew by the late 1970s, that is *not* how either system worked. Class and other barriers to equal opportunity were too great and intractable. This created some ambivalence and tension in his work. As Boyd and others noted, he did not find this type of work intellectually satisfying. What are we to make of this? For an answer, it is necessary to look outside the bounds of this project. He had helped initiate it many years earlier, when he was more deeply affected by an individualist strain of liberal political theory. His introduction to *Ascription and Achievement* remained within the bounds of the liberal questions it had posed for itself, but some of the more ruminative essays he was working on at exactly the same time – the macrosociology essays and the McInnis Lectures, in particular – indicate that he was in the process of rethinking, if not *rejecting*, the liberal individualist vision of social justice and societal rationality that had for so long guided his work. He was returning to his Hobhousian liberal socialist roots.

13 The Shift into Academic Administration, 1977–1979

In 1977, John Porter made a major career shift away from scholarship into academic administration. The transition was somewhat abrupt. He had held administrative positions at Carleton years earlier – he was department chair from 1953 to 1960 and the director of Division II (the equivalent of an associate dean of social sciences) from 1963 to 1966 – but never gave any indication when he assumed these tasks that he had changed his self-definition.[1] Between 1966 and 1977, he never assumed an administrative role per se, limiting such activities to membership on department, university, provincial, and national planning committees and policy bodies.[2] His decision to change course can be understood only by appreciating the influence on him of a specific conjunction of circumstances: his sense of his moral obligation as a practical, engaged intellectual; a serious and growing crisis at Carleton; the stage he had reached in his scholarly career; and, his desire for a new challenge and the rewards that would come from meeting it.

Porter's research endeavours, in combination with his involvement with various provincial-level research and planning committees, had given him a deep appreciation of the broad national role of education, particularly the nature and role of the university in Canadian society. There was no questioning that postsecondary education had limits as an instrument of social change and social justice, but in his mind it remained the best available tool for surmounting the barriers to upward social mobility that faced working-class students. In the 1960s, when governments and the public seemed receptive to expanding the system, Porter had done a good deal of policy-relevant research highlighting the individual and societal benefits to be garnered by making the universities open to those from underprivileged backgrounds. In the

1970s, he continued to do so, even as cutbacks in government spending on postsecondary education put these advances at risk. He regarded it as part of his moral obligation as an engaged, practical intellectual to speak for the universities at a time when the system was under siege. This decision to act as a champion was sparked in part, said Pauline Jewett, by Porter's admiration for John Evans, president of the University of Toronto (1972–8). In the late 1960s, Evans and Porter served together on the committee that produced *Towards 2000*. Evans had impressed Porter in his role as the universities' advocate in their dealings with the provincial and federal governments.[3]

However, the more immediate impetus for Porter's decision to become a senior administrator was the fallout generated at Carleton by government funding cuts. When they were announced in the early 1970s, all the universities were hard hit.[4] Angst grew within the university community as the situation worsened and political conflict between the universities and the Ontario government intensified.[5] Carleton shared in the general climate of despair. On a grey day in the early winter of 1974, Porter wrote to his friend Bruce McFarlane, then in Paris on sabbatical, to express his disquiet: 'The university situation here goes from bad to worse, at least financially. So you are being spared the gloom.'[6] A trip to the annual meetings of the CSAA the following spring confirmed for him that neither Carleton nor the other Ontario universities were alone in this regard: 'I suspect Carleton is not much worse off than other places. The future of the academic career is bleak from all perspectives … We have had our day in the sun.'[7]

At Carleton, provincial funding cuts were not the only problem. Porter and many of his colleagues believed that the university's own policies and practices were at least partly responsible for many of the problems on campus.

From 1958 to 1972, Davidson Dunton held Carleton's highest office. He was well liked by his colleagues and staff and for most of his tenure was widely regarded as a wise and steady hand at the tiller. And he was – but he was lucky as well. For most of the period, the problems with which he had to deal were 'good' ones, the kind occasioned by headlong expansion: the campus mushroomed from three buildings to two dozen; its budget increased from about $4 million to over $27 million; its full-time faculty complement grew from 66 to 544; and its full-time undergraduate student body increased from 720 to 8,500.[8]

In 1971, a very different kind of problem arose. That autumn, after years of double-digit annual increases in student enrolments and equally large enrolment-based increases in provincial funding, Carleton's intake increased not by the 12 per cent projected, but by 2 per cent.[9] The university had spent money and hired faculty based on inaccurate projections. With low enrolments in 1971–2 *and* lower-than-expected enrolments suddenly predicted for years to come, Dunton faced a looming financial crisis. Other developments – a shift in public perception of the role of the university and continuing student radicalism – only exacerbated the problem. By the time he left office a year later, there were unmistakable signs of serious, impending trouble. And according to some observers, Dunton was partly at fault. James Downey, then dean of arts, and an admirer of Dunton, recalled that some senior university insiders felt that he had perhaps stayed too long, grown tired, and lost the degree of enthusiasm and drive necessary to plot Carleton's long-term course in a rapidly changing environment.[10] The most serious problem, in Downey's view, was that the university had hired faculty in larger numbers than was justified by the longer-term prospects for funding.[11] Put simply, Carleton had more faculty than it could afford and something would have to be done. It would not be easy, however, in part because Carleton lacked the necessary policies and procedures.

Issues related to dismissal of *incompetent* faculty had been raised as early as 1960, but not until 1969 did Carleton strike a Senate committee to develop formal procedures.[12] By the time the committee reported back in 1971, the situation had changed.[13] In a new environment of comparatively poor funding and prospective cutbacks, the issue of dismissal had become less an abstract prospect and more a concrete issue. Dunton was now talking about a projected shortfall in Carleton's enrolment that would create a deficit of $1.5 million.[14] And now on the table for the first time was what came to be known as the redundancy issue.[15] The Carleton University Academic Staff Association (CUASA) and the university administration would have to develop formal mechanisms to deal with the prospect of dismissing not only incompetent professors but perfectly competent faculty members associated with programs that the university might want to shut down for reasons of financial exigency.[16] The redundancy issue sounded an ominous note as the bells tolled the end of Dunton's term in office.

The Oliver Presidency, 1972–1978

If someone ever writes the successor volume to H. Blair Neatby and Donald McEown's *Creating Carleton*, they will have to assess Michael

Oliver's presidency. That will be no easy task, for Oliver faced enormous problems and there is much disagreement among colleagues over his role in creating, exacerbating, and solving them. Oliver's dean of graduate studies and research, economist Gilles Paquet, believed that he had inherited most of them.[17] However, the university vice-president of administration, Albert 'Ab' Larose, disagreed. Oliver, he said, 'inherited very little from Davey Dunton' and 'made his own problems,' or at least 'made them worse.'[18] Some of the story of Oliver's presidency and John Porter's role in those events, can be recounted in a straightforward way. The main events of the period – administrative changes, faculty unionization – are not in dispute. Likewise, the forces at play – financial problems, the redundancy issue – have been documented. However, the dramatis personae – Oliver, Downey, Paquet, Larose, David Brown (then director of institutional analysis and planning) – as well as key witnesses to the events – Tom Ryan, then dean of social sciences, Don McEown, then secretary to the Board of Governors – offer conflicting accounts of events and the roles of the individuals involved.[19]

Michael Kelway Oliver came to Carleton from McGill University where he had held the position of vice-president academic since 1967. Born in North Bay in 1925, the son of Gilbert Oliver, an Anglican clergyman, and Winifred Kelway, Oliver moved to Montreal as a child. After finishing secondary school, he enrolled at McGill only to have his undergraduate career interrupted by the war. He spent three years in the service, from 1943 to 1945, including continuous service in an antitank troop in northern Europe from the month after D-Day to VE Day, returning to McGill to finish his BA in economics and political science in 1948. After spending a year in Paris as a scholarship student at the École Politiques, he returned to Canada to teach at the University of New Brunswick (1950–1), at the same time completing an MA in political science at McGill. He spent the next five years at United College in Winnipeg, teaching full time while working on his PhD. He finished his doctorate in 1956 and returned to Quebec in 1958, teaching briefly at Laval University in Quebec City before joining the academic staff of his alma mater, McGill.[20]

When he returned to Quebec from Winnipeg, Oliver became involved in social democratic political activities. In 1958, while working toward the founding of the New Party, he took up the editorship of *Social Purpose for Canada* (see chapter 6), and three years later became the first national president of the NDP. As well, in 1960 he joined the editorial board of *Cité libre.* But he also continued to work as a scholar and in 1964 was appointed research director of the Royal Commission on Bilingualism and Biculturalism, co-chaired by Dunton and André Laurendeau. From this position he returned to McGill in 1967 as vice-president academic. He served five years in that capacity before coming to Carleton as president in September 1972.[21]

In a retrospective account of his years as president, Oliver stated that he had three priorities when he took office: to establish a more formal organizational structure at Carleton; to develop a better 'information base' about the university (and an improved capacity for generating and analysing that data); and to make the governance and administration of the university more transparent and collegial.[22] To achieve the first goal, he created two vice-presidencies – academic and administration – and appointed Ross Love and Ab Larose to these positions. Love, a physicist, had been recruited by Dunton in the late 1950s to oversee the expansion of the new campus and he had stayed on as director of planning through Dunton's time in office. Larose had served for several years as Carleton's bursar. In addition to making these appointments, Oliver initiated regular meetings with the deans, a practice not followed during the Dunton years, so they could exchange information and formulate policy. Finally, he made efforts to, in his words, 'involve Senate as fully as possible in the academic affairs of the university.' He did this by establishing two committees: the Academic Planning Committee of the Senate, and a Budget Review Committee made up of members of the Senate and Board of Governors. To realize the second goal, he conducted an audit of Carleton's information systems and instructed Love and Brown to develop a formula that would allow resources to be allocated across the university on a more rational and equitable basis.[23] He intended this rationalization and restructuring (including the development of information management systems) to promote his third goal, improving the transparency of administration. He hoped that if he presented the Carleton community with a frank assessment of its problems, faculty and staff would work cooperatively to solve them. To his dismay, he discovered that this strategy, which had worked at McGill, did not work at Carleton. Faculty and staff, he said, 'found [it] merely upsetting.'[24]

During the first couple of years, Oliver and the senior administrative team were necessarily preoccupied with Carleton's financial problems and while they succeeded in keeping the university solvent, it remained in a precarious position.[25] This raised the concern that tenured faculty members might have to be dismissed in order to balance the books.

The matter became particularly salient in the autumn of 1974, when the university declared the prospect of a $4 million deficit for the 1975–6 academic year and Oliver explicitly mentioned the possibility of reducing the academic staff. Though he insisted there were no plans to do so, to no one's surprise, faculty began to worry.[26] The ramifications of the redundancy issue soon led to an open discussion of the possibility of faculty unionization and by June 1975, CUASA had unionized.[27] The negotiation of the first collective agreement, handled for the university by Love, Larose, and Cliff Kelley, did not go well.[28] The discussions generated even further distrust and bad feelings and, according to some observers, by the end of the process, both Oliver and Love had lost the trust of the faculty.[29]

As tensions rose between Oliver and Carleton's faculty during the redundancy and unionization drama, he became embroiled in a second struggle. At issue were actions he took to rationalize Carleton's administrative structures and procedures, establish new institutional planning mechanisms, and implement management information systems. Some of the members of Carleton's senior administrative team did not agree with his view that existing policies and practices were deficient and therefore did not see the changes as necessary. Moreover, they objected to the rapidity with which Oliver moved and the means by which he tried to achieve his desired changes. A number of them became suspicious and distrustful when he turned increasingly to David Brown, his director of institutional analysis and planning, to achieve by speedy and roundabout means things he could not achieve through established procedures and channels.[30] According to Downey, the perception developed among some of the senior administrators that Oliver and Brown had more or less 'arrogated all of the responsibility for determining the course of the institution.'[31]

For his part, David Brown claimed that he and Oliver considered they had no choice but to act quickly. Moreover, he argued that their need for haste justified their choice of means. In particular, in order to be eligible to apply for two special grants from the Ontario government in the mid-1970s, they needed to produce some information requested by the Ministry of College and Universities – and quickly. Without the money, Carleton would be in deep trouble. Part of Oliver's strategy for getting the money, said Brown, required the modernization of Carleton's information management systems. It was here, said Brown, that Oliver 'used' him to achieve his objectives, sometimes against resistance, and in so doing put some noses out of joint in his senior management team.[32]

Whatever the merits of these respective accounts of redundancy, unionization, and the restructuring of Carleton's administrative apparatus – and the situation is certainly misty and complex – by 1977 it became clear that Oliver would not serve a second term as president. It was in this highly charged and difficult context – the immediate aftermath of the rancour brought on by unionization, dissension within the senior management team, and in the prelude to what everyone saw as Oliver's final days as president – that Porter assumed the office of vice-president academic.

Porter replaced Ross Love. When Dunton left in 1972 and Oliver took over, Love had taken the job of vice-president academic for a three-year term. When his term expired, his reappointment was not recommended.[33] According to McEown, some on the committee saw Love as the president's 'loyal servant' and wanted someone more independent.[34] A search committee was struck.

Porter's name surfaced during the search committee's discussions,[35] and Oliver approached him about the job. He knew Porter from their *Social Purpose for Canada* days and was well aware of John's high profile at Carleton. In fact, Oliver recalled that Porter had been among those mentioned for the presidency back in 1972 when Oliver himself took the job and that he had tried to entice Porter into administrative responsibilities at the time, but without success.[36] This time, however, following Oliver's overture, Porter allowed his name to stand as a candidate for the vice-presidency and, despite some opposition within the committee, was appointed in July 1977.[37] Doris Whitteker, Porter's secretary in the vice-president's office, remembered that the university's senior administration team was well pleased with Porter's appointment, regarding it as a coup to have such a well-known scholar in the position.[38] Surely, one of the most enjoyable letters of congratulation came from David Lewis, then affiliated with the Institute for Canadian Studies at Carleton:

My wife has always chided me for the fact that I never seem to notice events or happenings which concern individuals. She has always accused me of being interested in humanity only and left myself little time to be aware of its individual members ... I have always strenuously rejected this charge.

    She has been right, however, as proved by the fact that I have only just become aware of your appointment to the position of Vice-President (Academic) ... Since there are very few people in the academic world for whom

I have greater respect and regard, my delayed awareness was not the result of any lack of interest ... I do warmly congratulate you and even more those who had the sense to appoint you.[39]

Downey remembered that Porter was well aware of the university's many financial and administrative problems when he assumed office, and accepted the post on the clear understanding from Oliver that he would be allowed to 'get on with the business of running the university, ... taking charge of its academic mission and character,' while Oliver attended to other matters.[40] Tom Ryan, then dean of social science, and later vice-president academic, commented on John's resolve to do the vice-president's job unhindered by interference from Oliver: 'Porter certainly made the same point clear to me. In fact, at one point, he told me that he had rebuked Oliver for treading into the business of the vice-president academic. He said that he told Oliver which way it was to be – John would be in complete charge of the academic side or he was out of there.'[41] For his part, Oliver seemed to be preparing to leave. He had found a position as director of international development at the Association of Universities and Colleges of Canada [AUCC] and appeared to be disengaging from Carleton.[42] But the administrative situation during the last year of his tenure was messy and post hoc accounts differ over who was in charge. According to Downey and Neatby, Oliver was disengaging, so Porter was probably more important than Oliver in the day-to-day running of the university, but Paquet and Larose disagreed, claiming that Oliver and Brown continued to be in charge.[43]

Porter had to deal with a number of difficult situations during the year, some spawned in part by political machinations within the senior management group of the university. The most publicized incident involved Philip Uren, a faculty member in the Norman Paterson School of International Affairs and director of the Paterson Centre.[44] In the spring of 1978, Uren, in his capacity as director, made a research trip to South Africa at the invitation of the South African government, which sponsored and paid for his trip. While there, he presented himself as speaking for Carleton University in a way that, according to the Faculty Council of the Norman Paterson School, damaged its reputation. A sensitive and volatile situation developed. Uren's supporters argued that he was simply exercising his right to academic freedom. His critics countered that as the director of the Paterson Centre, an administrative position, he did not have the same degree of academic freedom to which he was entitled as an individual faculty member; he was expected to represent the consensus of his colleagues at the centre.[45] The Faculty Council passed a resolution censuring Uren and the committee responsible for managing the Paterson Centre met with him to express their concerns.[46] He was not asked or pressured to resign from his administrative position by the university, but feeling that he had lost the confidence of his colleagues in the School, he submitted his resignation as director and resumed his regular faculty position.[47]

At the time, Oliver was away from the university and Porter, acting on his behalf, accepted Uren's resignation. A heated debate followed, both on campus and in the pages of the *Ottawa Journal*. Some people, including some members of Carleton's Board of Governors, thought that Uren had been denied his right to academic freedom. John tried to defuse the issue by writing a long letter to the editor of the *Journal* that explained the logic behind the university's decision, but the issue remained problematic.[48] According to McEown, some board members thought that Porter had acted precipitously in accepting Uren's resignation, perhaps even made the wrong choice.[49] Worse, recalled McEown, Porter was 'curt' and 'talked down' to the board at the meeting at which they discussed the controversy: 'He made some unnecessary enemies that day.'[50]

By far the most ambitious project Porter undertook during his year as vice-president was an administrative planning task. In early 1978, Oliver instructed him to undertake a study of Carleton's short-term prospects with an eye to devising a strategy that would allow the university to cope in the increasingly straitened financial circumstances with which they had to deal.[51] It would not be an easy job. At the time, said Downey, 'There was a sense of academic drift' at Carleton, that, 'combined with the sense the tide was going out for us financially and so on, made for a very unhappy place.'[52] Nonetheless, following his pattern of hard work, Porter immersed himself in the exercise and within a few months his committee produced 'Carleton University to 1982,' a document intended to provide both a vision for the university and a nuts-and-bolts plan. A benefit of the exercise for Porter was that it allowed him to get a firm grasp of the university's make-up and culture. The report on 'Carleton University to 1982' that he and his committee generated had two benefits: it offered solutions to a set of practical problems at the university, and it gave him the opportunity to put into practice some of his principles about education. As Downey put it, the report constituted an opportunity for John 'to provide strong leadership to an institution that in an academic sense had lost its way a bit.'

If 'Carleton University to 1982' was not 'the realization of John's *ideal* view of education,' he mused, it certainly revealed many of the general principles he had formulated regarding the proper nature and purpose of university education.[53]

Porter had proclaimed some of these principles in a memorandum written at the instigation of the presidential search committee that had chosen Oliver in 1972. In that memo he outlined four criteria he considered 'most important in judging the suitability of a candidate for the presidency of Carleton University': an appreciation of academic values, high stature as a scholar, capacity as an administrator and academic leader, and experience with and understanding of young people. He also listed the key academic values of a university: 'freedom of inquiry, a commitment to searching out the cause of things, the creation of a marketplace where ideas find their own value through free debate, and the bringing to bear of a "critical intelligence" by which the university examines itself and the society at large.'[54] He also stressed that university governance should be 'collegial' rather than 'hierarchical,' perhaps expecting that the former model would come increasingly under fire in the changed funding environment of the 1970s.[55]

These ideas underwrote 'Carleton University to 1982.' Porter began by talking about the university's own conception of its nature and purpose as an institution. In the difficult financial situation it faced, Porter argued, Carleton had to come to an understanding of its 'spirit' and 'mission' – an idea of the kind of university it wanted to become. Only then could restructuring be undertaken in a productive way.[56] Since at the time Carleton had no official, educational 'objectives,' 'philosophy,' or stated 'academic priorities,' Porter and his committee outlined a set of ideas to serve in their stead.[57]

The report argued that Carleton should aspire to be a national university of middle size with extensive offerings in the humanities, the sciences, and the social sciences. There would be advanced work in each, plus a selection of high-quality professional schools: engineering, journalism, and commerce.[58] The report reiterated that whatever the state of the economy, and whatever the financial priorities of the government of the day, a university education was a good 'investment' for individuals and societies alike.[59] It was a means by which individuals and societies could maximize their respective potential. Notably, the document contained no criticism of – and therefore a tacit acceptance of – Carleton's long-standing liberal admissions policy. Equality of opportunity, one of Porter's bedrock principles, would remain one of

Carleton's foundational values. At the same time, noting that Carleton attracted far fewer Ontario Scholar high-school graduates than Queen's or Toronto, he stressed the importance of excellence for faculty, staff, and students.[60] 'The danger, as we see it, is ... that we will not ... expect enough of ourselves as individuals and as an institution. And in expecting too little we may achieve too little.'[61]

Porter's concern that excellence be promoted and rewarded helps explain why a couple of years earlier – and in private – he had so bitterly criticized faculty unionization.[62] Years later, Sylvia Ostry recalled discussing it with him. He opposed the prospect of unionization, she said, because he thought it would 'eat at the very heart of the raison d'être for the academy.'[63] He made this very clear in an unsent memorandum he wrote on the subject: 'Unionization is ... incompatible with the free life that is supposed to go on in the house of intellect ... A body of unionized intellectuals is a contradiction in terms ... What I find difficult to see is a place for excellence.'[64] In 'Carleton University to 1982,' he supplemented these arguments. The adoption of largely seniority-based policies on pay, tenure, and the like would, he wrote, protect less productive faculty and make it difficult to reward and retain faculty members whose work was outstanding. Such policies would disadvantage Carleton by institutionalizing 'the tyranny of the mean.'[65] The *Report* hinted that some suspect faculty members had been awarded tenure too easily in the 1960s.[66] Porter feared that with a collective agreement in place, tenure, designed to protect the principle of freedom of enquiry, had become a job guarantee and might prevent the dismissal of unproductive members of the academic staff.[67] Bearing this in mind, the report challenged the faculty union to sign a long-term contract and requested that departments, faculties, and administrative divisions agree on terms for ridding the university of unproductive personnel and for allowing more central control of staffing 'in the interest of a more equitable and rational policy for the deployment of personnel.'[68] Some faculty and staff might have to be shuffled into new jobs for the university to survive.[69] Unproductive faculty would be rooted out and dismissed.[70]

One of the most interesting characteristics of the report is its moralizing tone. 'Carleton University to 1982' is not a dispassionate, clinical planning document phrased in the tedious bureaucratese characteristic of so many official reports. In it, members of the Carleton community are chided in the way that an adult might lecture a wayward teenager. In Porter's view, presumably shared by the committee, Carleton's malaise stemmed in large part from a loss of individual and collective self-esteem and nerve, combined with a lack of willingness to work for the common good of the institution. The report offered a pointed critique of deficiencies of attitude and behaviour – a lack of trust, discipline, direction, resolve, and effort – that stood in the way of Carleton's success. At the same time, however, Porter drew attention to the university's demonstrated strengths and real potential.[71] The general philosophy of the committee seemed to be that intelligent, constructive criticism, offered honestly, fairly, and in good faith, if taken seriously and acted upon with resolve, would allow the institution to adapt to its new environment.

'Carleton University to 1982' generated a mixed response. Oliver offered public praise for the document, referring to it in his farewell convocation address as 'a sober and confident assessment of the university's strengths and a compilation of proposals for effective future action.'[72] And officially, at least, it received high marks from Carleton's Senate and Board of Governors. A letter from the clerk of the Senate was 'loud in [its] praise of [the report's] conclusions,' which showed 'quality' and 'vision,'[73] while a letter from the board referred to the report as 'thorough, imaginative and clear.'[74]

But not everyone was impressed by either Porter or his report. Brown and Paquet were particularly critical. Brown focused on the fact that Porter's experience as an administrator at the time was 'extremely limited.' He believed that Porter had used the planning task as a means to educate himself on governance and administrative issues at the university and stressed that the report offered nothing new to the university's senior administration team.[75] Paquet, who had earlier been considered for the position of vice-president academic when Porter was offered the job, was even less impressed. He argued that the planning exercise was a diversion and claimed that Oliver had given Porter the task of writing the document as a way of keeping him busy while Oliver and Brown ran the university. Indeed, in Paquet's view, Porter 'had no real impact on the running of the place' during his tenure as vice-president and accused him of abrogating his responsibilities by failing to take a number of difficult decisions about running the university:

> I tried to persuade him that he should take action and be a real V-P; that he should not allow himself to be sent on a bloody wild goose chase. I became vehement at the committee meetings, saying: 'There are real decisions that have to be taken now that are very rough ...' The problem I had with Por-

ter was a mushiness, the fact that he was quite willing to escape the real responsibility of his job as the Academic VP.[76]

Downey challenged Paquet's account. He argued that Oliver saw the committee's work as important and claimed that Porter was far 'too smart and too knowing to be shunted off to the side' by being assigned a meaningless task.[77] Either way, the truly salient point is that for Paquet, who later served on the presidential search committee, Porter's actions during his year as vice-president academic rendered him unsuitable as a prospective president of the university.[78]

As Oliver's term went into its final stage in the autumn of 1978, Porter increasingly entertained the idea that he would like to be Carleton's next president. According to Downey, it is in this context that Porter's approach to 'Carleton University to 1982' may be best understood. Put simply, he 'seem[ed] to assume that he would be the next president,' said Downey. 'There was implicit in that exercise, and the way John went about it … that he would be [president] and we would be there to make his plan work.'[79] Downey thought it noteworthy that though the Report was the responsibility of a committee, Porter decided to write most of it himself. He drew on data prepared by others and sought advice in constructing the document, but saw the committee largely as a sounding board for his own ideas. At the same time, operating increasingly under the assumption that he was likely to be the next president, he treated the exercise as a kind of 'self-administered training program or seminar' for the committee.[80] Ab Larose recalled that during this period Porter spent hours doing 'homework,' familiarizing himself with the intricacies of university policies and issues with which he would have to deal if he became president: 'I talked to him a number of times about what would happen should [he become president] and so I had a sense he expected that to happen. Certainly that was his wish.'[81]

Oliver, too, thought Porter had the presidency in mind when he took the job of vice-president. And as events unfolded, he became increasingly certain that John would be his successor.[82] According to many on the senior administration team, this was quite apparent, and in an unwise breach of protocol, Oliver began to treat Porter as the president-designate even though he had not been chosen for the position.[83] For his part, in an uncharacteristic and unfortunate lapse of judgment, Porter accepted Oliver's assessment and began to behave accordingly. In the summer of 1978, for example, when the Constant Lake group debated the prospect of bringing in a telephone line, Porter argued strongly in favour of the proposition on the grounds that he was expecting to be named president later in the year.[84] Similarly, Tom Ryan remembered an evening he and his wife spent at the Porters' home with the Olivers: '[We] had returned to Porter's house after the deans' farewell dinner for Oliver. The topic of the presidency was raised … [and] in the course of the discussion, the Porters considered out loud if they should stay in their own home or move into the president's house after John assumed the role.'[85] So Porter not only *wanted* the presidency but also *expected* to get it. He was well aware that many in the local Carleton community regarded him as the university's logical and likely choice and may well have heard the rumours circulating at the time that the selection committee was poised to choose him.[86] And so his expectations grew.

I have mentioned the chief political and institutional factors that went into Porter's decision to seek the presidency – his general sense of obligation as an engaged, practical intellectual and his desire to help Carleton through a crisis – but there were scholarly and personal factors at work as well. At play were developments in the discipline of sociology, career contingencies, and personality variables.

Developments in Sociology

The large contingent of American sociologists imported to Canada to staff the departments of rapidly growing Canadian universities in the late 1960s and early 1970s brought with them the theoretical, methodological, and political approaches of American sociology. Many were mainstream liberal scholars. For their theory, like Porter, many of them relied on functionalism, modernization theory, postindustrial theory, end-of-ideology theory, and a heavy dose of Max Weber. And, again like Porter, those who did empirical research relied on the techniques of survey methodology. But many Americans who came to Canada, as well as some of the Europeans, stood clearly outside the box of mainstream sociology. They were of two types. One group comprised interpretive sociologists of various orientations: phenomenologists, symbolic interactionists, and ethnomethodologists. The other was a mixed group of feminists (of different theoretical and political inclinations), New Left and other Marxists, critical theorists and – a 'made in Canada' development – advocates of the so-called new political economy.

American New Left sociologists had developed a new appreciation for a revived and less economistic and deterministic Marxism than had characterized the Communist-dominated old left of the 1930s, '40s, and

'50s, and they fostered a rapid growth in Marxist scholarship in Canada. This 'new' Marxism, more academic than the older variant, was sometimes combined in an uneasy alliance with the sophisticated, if sometimes impenetrable, marxisant theorizing of the Frankfurt School of critical theory, in particular the writings of Herbert Marcuse and Jurgen Habermas, both of whom had become darlings of the American student left. In Canada, this burgeoning interest in Marxist approaches to class, economic development, and cultural domination was combined in a novel way with two other theoretical orientations: selected aspects of the staples thesis, the indigenous theoretical perspective developed by Harold Innis; and the work of Latin American dependency theorists such as A.G. Frank and F.H. Cardoso. Canadians also added into the mix some recent developments in working class and women's history, as well as a widely shared appreciation for the philosophical writings of the University of Toronto New Liberal political theorist C.B. Macpherson.

The phrase '*new* political economy' was used to differentiate the approach from the mainstream 'old political economy' that, under Innis' influence, had dominated Canadian economics in the 1930s and '40s. Though radically different, the two perspectives were deeply intertwined. Advocates of the new approach such as Mel Watkins, Gary Teeple, and Wallace Clement drew directly on two central pillars of the old political economy – the staples thesis and metropolis–hinterland relations – in constructing the new version. Initially formulated in the late 1960s, the new political economy changed rapidly, its devotees quickly broadening their interests to include the state, working-class politics, workplace relations, regionalism, and so on. As well, they drew on new theories of development and underdevelopment to determine more accurately Canada's place in the world capitalist system.[87] Finally, stinging under early and powerful critiques levelled at them by feminists – who justifiably accused the approach of being just as 'malestream' as the liberal social science it sought to unseat – they soon incorporated gender (the domestic economy, split labour markets, and so on) into what came to be a wide-ranging, powerful, and foundational challenge to exactly the kind of mainstream liberal scholarship that constituted Porter's stock-in-trade.

These developments were just nicely underway in the late 1970s – many of the most significant developments did not occur until the 1980s – but they nonetheless factored heavily into the choices Porter had to make about his scholarship and career in the mid-1970s. On the scholarly side, it is clear that Porter never became a part of the political economy network and never identified himself as a political economist. Nonetheless, he was very interested in it and, in my view, had much to do with its development – in both a general and specific sense. At the general level, I think that much of the new political economy in Canada emerged in part out of a critical dialogue with *The Vertical Mosaic*. A number of the people working within this new framework took up Porter's explicit and implicit claims about the structure and dynamics of class, power, elites, regionalism, the state, foreign ownership, and the like and, using *The Vertical Mosaic* as a take-off point, contributed to the development of the new political economy as a novel and compelling approach to the study of Canadian society and its place in the international capitalist system. Porter had to develop an equally compelling response in defence of his preferred alternative: mainstream quantitative macrosociology. But there is a more direct or particular sense in which Porter contributed to the development of political economy; that is, through his influence on a generation of students, especially at Carleton. Though he personally remained within the liberal tradition, he was sufficiently open as a scholar that he was able to inspire, guide and sponsor his leftist graduate students in their effort to create a new kind of macrosociology – historical, comparative, empirical, theoretically informed, progressive, morally laden, but social democratic rather than liberal in orientation.' Here, the career trajectory of Wallace Clement, perhaps his best-known student, is illustrative.

Clement came to Carleton in 1972 expressly to study with Porter. While completing his undergraduate degree in sociology at McMaster, Clement had become interested in *The Vertical Mosaic*. For his master's thesis, he decided to update and partially replicate the work, and in the fall of 1971 wrote to Porter to propose the project.[88] After an exchange of letters and a couple of meetings, Porter agreed to supervise his thesis.[89] The collaboration proved remarkably fruitful. Within two years, Clement had produced a massive thesis, eventually published as *The Canadian Corporate Elite* which, like *The Vertical Mosaic*, became an instant classic.[90] While Clement did not undertake a straightforward replication of the relevant sections of *The Vertical Mosaic* in his MA thesis, he was greatly influenced by the methodology and theoretical orientation of Porter's volume. Most important, like Porter, Clement used a positional form of analysis, identifying the top corporations in Canada and then gathering and reporting data on the social origins and characteristics of the individuals occupying these positions. These data indicated that the ethnic and class exclusiveness of the economic and media elites on which Porter had reported had increased. In addition to replicating this aspect of Porter's analysis, Clement took one step further. Unlike Porter, he combined data on the economic elite with data on the members of the ideological elite who held directorships in dominant media corporations – on the grounds that media enterprises were dominant corporations as well – and made the claim that together these two groups constituted a relatively unified 'corporate elite' that held both economic and ideological power in Canadian society. This led Clement to conclude, here moving in the direction of Marxism, that the group constituted a collectivity that shared many characteristics with the ruling class of Marx's analysis. This constituted a direct challenge to the 'plural elites' model Porter outlined in *The Vertical Mosaic*. As well, Clement paid more attention than had Porter to the role of the state in structuring and mediating relations among elites and between elites and other classes. In addition, he examined to a greater extent the impact of American penetration of the Canadian economy. He pursued the latter issue at great length in his PhD thesis, published as *Continental Corporate Power*, just two years later. Here he extended his analysis of the Canadian corporate elite to an analysis of links between it and the American economic elite as represented by directors and owners of American corporations doing business in Canada (i.e., American corporate directors living in Canada, Canadian directors working for American multinationals). Clement's two books, with Dennis Olsen's 1980 replication of Porter's study of the bureaucratic elite, *The State Elite*, constitute a direct and highly influential legacy of Porter's work.

But none of these volumes was political economy in the sense that today's new political economists, Clement included, would use the term. As I said, in the early elite studies, Clement and Olsen, like Porter, studied elites and power using a positional form of analysis. As Clement's work developed, however, he moved away from a focus on elites, access to elite positions, and classes as distributive categories and began to study classes as sets of historical, contested relations. That is, he began to address issues of class exploitation and conflict as they were manifested both within classes (the 'industrial fragment' versus the 'financial fragment') and, more important, between classes (the working class versus the capitalist class). In addition, along with others such as Leo Panitch, he began to tackle more carefully the thorny problem of the role of the state in capitalist society. Clement has discussed the dynamics of his personal shift into political economy in more than one semi-autobiographical overview of the development of the political economy approach in Canada.[91]

The work of Clement and Olsen had a deep impact on Porter, drawing his attention to the ideas of Marxist scholars such as Harry Braverman, author of *Labour and Monopoly Capital*, sparking his interest in the writings of C.B. Macpherson, and providing food for thought as he reconsidered and refined the new, value-laden macrosociology he had been working on since his year at Harvard.

These scholarly dilemmas and approaches had a direct bearing on Porter's career choices in the 1970s. In order to keep abreast of developments in radical scholarship, mainstream scholars such as Porter had to absorb a complex and rapidly growing new body of literature. In the mid-1970s, he did so by learning it alongside his graduate students. For example, in a reading course with Olsen in 1971–2, they read work by the Marxists Paul Baran and Paul Sweezy, A.K. Davis, Andre Gunder Frank, Antonio Gramsci, Leszek Kolakowski, Ernesto Laclau, Keri Levitt, Georg Lukacs, and Ralph Miliband.[92] And, of course, he worked closely with Clement and Olsen as they prepared their respective theses. In the process, he became familiar with key texts in the radical literature. And he did so with authentic interest. Both Clement and Olsen stressed that he did not read this material dismissively. As I noted above and illustrate in detail in chapter 15 and the afterword, Porter incorporated some of these ideas into his own writing, particularly his later essays on macrosociology, social justice, and democracy.

While he was truly interested in and influenced by some of these ideas, and supported graduate students as they used Marxist and other emerging radical perspectives to frame their work, however, he never became a Marxist or political economist.[93] Some comments he made in an article review around this time make this clear:

> Judged by the 'either/or' constraints of Marxian orthodoxy, I fall pretty clearly into the category of bourgeois analyst. I find the Marxian apparatus, particularly as it is employed in 'The Political Economy of ...,' intellectually uncongenial and empirically unrewarding. I grant without hesitation the fundamental character of economic relations and economic factors in social structure, but I would deny their universal primacy and I long ago abandoned any ideological commitment – if I ever had it – to the revolutionary finality of historical materialism ... It sounds to me like an old left vainly trying to revive or maintain the quasi-religious dogma of the inevitable revolution.[94]

Graham Knight, whose PhD thesis Porter supervised, recalls on this score that Porter was very familiar with Marxist approaches but simply not convinced by them. In Knight's view, Porter preferred the 'left Weberianism' of scholars such as Frank Parkin, author of the influential *Class Inequality and Political Order*, and thought in terms of the 'abatement' of class injustices and inequalities in liberal democracy rather than in terms of truly radical transformation of Canada's economic and political institutions.[95] Another of his PhD students in the 1970s, Maria Barrados, offered an explanation. First, she said, in her view, Porter was a logical positivist who regarded non-quantitative forms of sociology such as Marxism and political economy as marginal because they lacked the 'rigour' of quantitative mainstream sociology. 'All the work on stratification and labour force and education; it was all an effort to really understand what was going on, to try and *measure* it,' she asserted. 'John was engaged with Statistics Canada [on work dealing with] social indicators because this *mattered*.' Second, it mattered not just in a scientific sense but in a political sense as well. Politicians and policy makers would give credence to mainstream work but not to 'marginal' work done by radical scholars. 'He wasn't a big fan of Marxism,' she argued, because Marxists were not 'players' in the venues where government policy decisions were taken: 'If you look in terms of any of the issues that are debated in the country, [the Marxists] are not there. John Porter would have been there.'[96]

In the early 1970s, Porter's decision to remain within the bounds of liberal scholarship, studying issues such as educational aspirations and social mobility, was fateful. In the 1960s, *The Vertical Mosaic* had been seen as radical and path breaking. But by the mid-1970s, his work on education and mobility belonged clearly in the mainstream of sociology; by the radical standards of the time, it appeared politically conservative. This put him in an ambiguous position. He was famous, a living legend almost, and influential in some circles, but somewhat out of fashion among those on the cutting edge of the discipline. This sea change, which saw his visibility and status erode somewhat, took place at a critical juncture in Porter's life course as a scholar.

Career Contingencies and a Sense of Service

The president's job became open at a point in Porter's academic career when it made sense for him to step out of the role of senior scholar and into administration. For one thing, though only fifty-six in 1977, he had been in the academy since 1949, almost three decades. He had carried out a string of major projects and, in Frank Jones' view, they had left him somewhat drained. 'He may have been tired of doing research on the big studies,' said Jones. 'He often said to me: "I'll get involved in this and support it, but it's just to get money for graduate students and an opportunity for them to do research."'[97] A related factor, in my view, was the ghost of *The Vertical Mosaic*. When he produced his master-work in 1965 he was only forty-three. For the next decade, he turned his attention to questions of educational aspirations and attainment, occupational status, and social mobility. These were sociologically and politically significant issues, and he did important work, well recognized by the mainstream sociological establishment. But everything he did was judged in light of *The Vertical Mosaic* – and I think that to some degree in his own mind none of these projects ever quite measured up. In Jim Downey's view, this was consequential; to the end of his life, he said, John lived in the shadow of his early magnum opus. It may even have become a millstone of sorts.[98] Had he perhaps peaked too early, thereafter having to compete against himself – and not matching up? Certainly, as the 1970s unfolded he became less central in the discipline as a new wave of leftist scholarship took the foreground in Canadian sociology.

This is not to say that he opted for administration as an easy out. As Downey put it, Porter was not an older academic who was scared of the competition, did not want to retool, and switched into academic administration as a default.[99] Rather, his decisions first to become vice-president and then to let his name stand for the presidency were positive choices to move in a new direction. On this count, interestingly, Downey and sociologist John Myles came to different conclusions about the legacy of *The Vertical Mosaic*. Both thought that Porter had come to terms with the realization that he was not about to produce another *Vertical Mosaic*. Whereas Downey thought that this troubled him, however, Myles believed he was perfectly comfortable with the idea and that it explained his move into administration. Myles argued that in 1977 Porter was at a stage in his career when he likely began to ask himself the same questions that *all* academics ask themselves at a similar stage: Do I have another big book in me? Do I want to keep writing articles for scholarly journals? Is there another challenge?[100] Myles judged that Porter opted to pursue the new challenge of senior administration because he felt he could make a more meaningful contribution by becoming vice-president, and perhaps president, than by writing another book or pile of articles. He had already succeeded as a scholar. University administration provided another challenge. He could help 'rescue' Carleton, allowing him to prove himself by a different set of criteria.[101]

I think his self-imposed sense of obligation or service played a role here as well, just as it had throughout his career. He believed that university scholars had a personal and social responsibility to use their privileged position to contribute in an informed, rational way to public debates concerning socially and politically salient issues. Downey underlined this issue when he noted that John was an 'applied intellectual,' who believed deeply that 'the university was not an ivory tower':

> He had a strong view that our job was ... to think about real problems that confront real people and find ways of making our views known and our contributions known ... [H]e felt that there wasn't enough of that done by academics in Canada. We made a great fuss about the importance of academic freedom as a bulwark against capricious decisions and actions by government administrators, ... governors of universities, and so on. We talked a good game but ... didn't do a hell of a lot.[102]

John's daughter, Ann, said something similar. 'He saw himself as very engaged in the political issues of the day,' she said, and recalled that her home life was often punctuated by 'very vigorous discussions' of political issues: 'I don't think it's coincidental that Tony and I both ended up in political science because there was a sense [in our family] that politics mattered and [that we should be] engaged in the issues of the day.'[103] Her father, she said, tried 'to change the way things worked' by focusing his practical efforts on the educational system, particularly the universities, in an effort to make the university 'more open, ... more accessible.'[104] Tony agreed: 'I think when he got further into the administrative work ... [it] was consistent with his belief that education was really important for social mobility. So I think when he started getting involved in the planning of education ... I had the sense that he felt that was a part of his commitment to education – not just as an instructor, but because of its social implications.'[105]

From his earliest years at Carleton, this sense of service and practical engagement manifested itself in his harsh indictment of Canada's class and power structures and his criticism of the highly unequal system of mobility opportunities they created. Throughout his career, he saw his research as a kind of service to Canadian citizens: documenting the existence of the country's class structure, demonstrating the impact of an unequal system of mobility opportunities, and encouraging them to use the educational system to correct these faults. The same sense of service came into play in 1977 when Porter decided to take on the vice-presidency, and in 1978 when he allowed his name to stand for the presidency. He was a long-time citizen of Carleton, knew it well, had considerable research-based knowledge about university education, and some experience as an administrator. He had strong moral views about the proper place of higher education in a liberal democratic society and a keen desire to put his philosophy, knowledge, and experience to work in the service of 'his' university. So a very real part of his personal motivation was his sense of obligation as a New Liberal practical intellectual to work in the service of both the 'societal good' and an institution to which he had developed an extremely close and meaningful personal bond: Carleton University. As Ann put it, his decision was tied to 'his commitment to education and feeling that he could make a difference in the way the university was run.' He had 'a big commitment to universities in general,' and a particular 'fondness for Carleton' that contributed to this decision.[106] Porter's Carleton colleague, historian David Farr, summarized it as follows: 'He had been academic vice-president and I think he assumed that he would be asked to take over as the president. He had had a long association with Carleton and was one of [its] real builders ... I think he saw [the presidency] as a sort of culmination of the service he had provided to Carleton over many years. He was loyal and he saw this as something he could do better than anyone else.'[107]

Personality Variables

There were powerful personality forces at work when Porter decided to let his name stand for the presidency. When I asked Porter's colleagues, students, and friends what drove him in his various endeavours, in particular his decision to allow his name to stand for the presidency, I received a range of sometimes conflicting answers. All thought he sought the presidency in part because he was committed to helping his university out of a difficult situation. But some believed he had personal goals in mind as well. He was an ambitious man who was driven to demonstrate his competence and earn the status and other rewards that went along with such achievements. In short, the presidency of Carleton University was the final major target of Porter's ambition. Pauline

Jewett recalled that Porter greatly admired and respected accomplished and powerful people, indeed, felt an 'affinity' with them.[108] Bruce Mc-Farlane and Muni Frumhartz agreed. As McFarlane noted, 'John certainly admired people who got things done, even the business elite, ... though he at times disdained *what* they had done.'[109] Frumhartz concurred, but put a different spin on Porter's interest in elites:

> I don't think he ever really saw the fascination the power elite held for him, in almost personal terms. I think all the while he saw himself as 'outside' of that and therefore as a critic of this kind of society, certainly ... not as one who would in any way be captured by it ... Like other people with an interest in elites and power structures, he was sufficiently fascinated by it to ... want in some sense to be closer to these people.[110]

At one point, Frumhartz remarked, Porter received an invitation to a gathering of elites: 'There was no question he derived some pleasure from that. Now, perhaps it was some sort of perverse reaction, because he could then say to himself that he had in some sense "made it."'[111] Some of those who knew him extended this analysis to explain his shift into senior administration. They noted that he had enjoyed – some said needed – the recognition, status, and influence that came to him because of his academic accomplishments. Bernard Blishen made this claim directly and linked it to John's humble background:

> John, like me, always wanted, coming from a working-class background, always wanted recognition. We used to kid each other and Marion used to kid the two of us ... If John ever thought he was being ignored for what he had done, it didn't sit very well. He didn't suffer fools gladly and he didn't suffer flattery gladly; he just wanted the recognition he had earned. I mention this because at the end of his life he wanted to be a president. He talked about it ... He became ... academic vice president and I could see that he could really appreciate that life. Not that John ever boasted. No way. He was a very modest sort of person, but I could see inside he was very pleased to be given the vice-presidency – that was just the thing. The next step was the ultimate.[112]

Certainly Porter seemed quite comfortable wielding power in the various leadership positions he had held as a senior scholar and administrator.[113] Becoming president of Carleton University was the next and last logical step up the scholarly ladder. It would require tremendous commitment to meet the challenges involved, but would be a great accomplishment.

Certainly that was the view of the man Porter hoped to succeed, Michael Oliver. Perhaps speaking from his own experience, and here sounding much like John Myles, Oliver said that as a scholar you came to a stage at which you had reached your academic peak, where you had 'done [your] big books.' 'At this stage,' Oliver argued, 'you can always force yourself to do the kind of tough research that would maintain that scholarly air, [but] you also want to know about power, what wielding power is all about.' Porter had written his big books and had written a lot about power. Oliver had no reservations about interpreting Porter's interest in the presidency as evidence of a desire to be in a position of status and power:

> Having written a great deal about what should be done in various fields it would be ... fun to see what you can do now that you had some power ... Very few people that have the qualities that John had are also lacking in vanity. I think that he enjoyed being seen as a person of stature and importance ... [W]hile he had this on the academic side, it would be interesting to see whether he [could] build up the same kind of thing in another kind of role. The desire to be perceived as a leader – I think he probably had his share of it.[114]

Doris Whitteker, Porter's secretary in the vice-president's office at the time, remembered a conversation with Porter during which they discussed why he wanted the presidency. She recalled that he remarked, 'I really wanted to see if I could run something.'[115] More evidence for this interpretation came from S.D. Clark, who recalled meeting Porter at the Learned Societies conference in Saskatoon in the spring of 1979, just a few months after the completion of the presidential search at Carleton. During that conversation, said Clark, they discussed Porter's reasons for seeking the top job. Prominent, if not most prominent among them, said Clark, was power: 'What he said to me was that this was something that he *wanted*: to experience the kind of power that a president of a university had. And that came to me as a great surprise.'[116]

That Porter wanted Carleton's top job did not surprise his former doctoral student Maria Barrados. According to her, Porter wanted it for two reasons. First, being president would allow him to take control of Carleton and – to the extent such a thing was possible – bend it to his will. 'If you were going to do this kind of thing [i.e., university administration], why not do it from the top job?' In her view, he 'felt there were some real threats to the university and the university's excellence' and wanted to have the capacity to address them. Looked at from this angle, the decision to seek the presidency was 'eminently logical.' Second, Barrados noted that he had earned great respect within the academic . community for his scholarly work. The presidency would add to his list of accomplishments and thus the respect he would command. Part of his thinking, she asserted, was that it would be 'the way to get [the respect] he had in the academic world.'[117]

Paul Fox and Jim Downey agreed that Porter wanted the job in part so he could wield power and get things done but disagreed on the degree to which ego considerations were important in his decision. Downey argued that his colleague wanted to 'take a grip on an institution that was drifting, ... anxious, and nervous ... and give it some resolve.' And that, Downey acknowledged, was 'an exercise in will, ... an exercise in power.' At the same time, though, Downey downplayed any *search* for recognition or status on Porter's part, denying that he was prompted by 'vanity ambition.' 'I don't think John would have derived immense satisfaction from being president, but it was an opportunity for him to exercise a very strong will and in that sense it would have brought a lot of ego gratification.'[118] Fox disagreed. He remembered being 'amazed' when Porter decided to venture down the path toward senior university administration because he recalled Porter claiming early in his career that anybody who became an administrator did so only because they were 'losing it' as a scholar. When Porter changed his mind and pursued the presidency, Fox said, he did so not just because he wanted the power to accomplish some of his goals, to set Carleton on a more promising course, but also because he wanted the 'reassurance' and 'certification' that came from holding such an office.[119]

Fox's claim is bolstered by Porter's handling of his election to the Royal Society of Canada in 1968. In *The Vertical Mosaic,* Porter had criticized the members of 'his' reference group within the Royal Society, the members of Section II, on the grounds that they had abdicated their responsibility to act as social critics. He characterized them as a self-selecting group from a relatively privileged social background who were entirely content to be part of the mainstream clerisy, defending dominant values and institutions.[120] Once he received a nomination himself, however, he did not turn down the opportunity to become a member – and for two reasons. First, as Marion Porter recalled, he felt he had earned it. 'He certainly was not surprised' to learn that he had been elected and, moreover, 'he did not suffer from a sense of humility; ... he thought he was entitled to it.'[121] Second, if his colleagues' views are any indication, he liked the respect, status, and validation that went with it.

But many of Porter's friends, colleagues, and students had a difficult time reconciling their image of him with the portrait drawn in the paragraphs above. Among them was Maria Barrados. As I noted above, she had no doubt that her mentor was fully prepared to seek and use power, and she granted that he demanded respect, 'to be listened to, taken on board, and ... engaged.' But she denied vehemently that he was driven by egoism or status consciousness. 'You were saying that some [people] considered him [to be] driven by ego needs. I never really saw him that way ... I didn't see him as someone who ... wanted to ... achieve positions because they had social status associated with them.' Quite the opposite: 'He was not very impressed by people in positions of power ... They were really good friends of the Ostrys, ... Morris Miller, Pierre Trudeau ... [Y]ou could meet these people at their [home]. But [the Porters] weren't particularly taken by these kinds of contacts.'[122] Hugh McRoberts said the same thing: 'The John I knew ... had a pretty good ego, a pretty good sense of his self, who he was, and where he was going.' To be sure, McRoberts said, Porter saw the presidency as an honour, but he also realized it was an onerous task, a 'Faustian bargain.' McRoberts thought Porter sought the presidency not out of a need for status or recognition but out of a sense of duty. His main motivation was to 'try and turn around a situation at Carleton with which he and many of his colleagues were increasingly uncomfortable.'[123]

When I discussed this issue with Carleton historian David Farr, he expressed the view that *originally* his long-time friend and colleague was not driven by a need for recognition and status. Rather, 'It was something that happened to him as he made his name as an academic and he derived satisfaction from it.' But Farr also said – in his own words 'not unkindly' – that after his friend became 'an established and respected figure in sociology and the academic world generally,' he seemed to become 'very conscious of the position he had ... attained and took great satisfaction in it.' Thus, when from time to time Porter was invited to a prestigious gathering, at Rideau Hall, for example, 'he made a little more of it than some of us would have.' Perhaps, Farr said, this was one way 'that his early years might have affected him later.' 'He was ... very conscious of his own position and rather relished the opportunity he had to mix in circles that wouldn't be encountered by the ordinary academic.'[124] For his part, Tony Porter regarded his father as ambivalent about the status that came with being a senior administrator: 'He didn't want to run after the trappings of authority, but ... he took a lot of pride in the reception that *The Vertical Mosaic* got, so he valued recognition of his achievements ... I would imagine that he got some pleasure ... [and] satisfaction out of getting recognized for his administrative achievements as well.' It was Tony's view that his father moved up the ladder not because of his 'people management skills' but because of 'his contribution to the direction of Carleton ... He felt a lot of loyalty to Carleton, a lot of pride in it. And I think he liked getting recognized for his part in that.'[125] Kenneth McRae, too, was leery of the 'status-seeker' interpretation, claiming that it was Porter's 'ideal of service' or sense of 'noblesse oblige' above all else, that motivated him. 'He had been given a lot, and he wanted to give a lot in return,' said McRae. He remembered in particular a late-evening exchange between them on the bus ride home from work one very cold winter evening a year or two before John died. 'I said something about: "Oh, you're working late tonight." We were both tired..., and he said: "But you find inner reserves ... and you keep going."' This led McRae to the conclusion that Porter was not personally ambitious: 'I would have said more that if the demand [were] there, he would try to meet it.'[126]

Monica Boyd's contribution to the debate was different again. She argued that any attempt to capture his feelings and intentions, to divine his motivations on this issue and others, was probably fruitless. In her view, Porter had an 'infinitely subterranean' personality, impossible to fathom in any definitive way.[127] Perhaps. Certainly, it is difficult to assign respective weight to all the claims and counter-claims about what motivated John Porter to seek the presidency. But there can be no doubt that a sense of duty and loyalty, a search for new challenges and accomplishments, and a desire for status, influence, recognition, and validation must be factored in to the equation. Subsequent events show that he paid a high personal price for his loyalty, his desire to serve, and his ambition.

The Presidency Denied

The selection committee considered nearly a hundred candidates for the position of president of Carleton University and, in late September 1978, announced their choice. To everyone's surprise, Dr William Beckel, then president of the University of Lethbridge in Alberta, was given the nod.

Beckel, born in Kingston, Ontario, in 1926, had attended Queen's University, graduating in 1949 with a BA in biology. He went on to the State University of Iowa for a zoology degree (MA 1953) and received his PhD in entomology from Cornell University in 1955. After working briefly for the Canadian Department of Agriculture, he had moved to the University of Toronto in 1956. There he became deeply involved in administration, first as dean of science (1964) and, later, as dean of Scarborough College (1965–8). In 1968, he moved to Alberta where he served briefly as vice-president academic and finance before becoming president of the University of Lethbridge. He had taught, supervised a series of productive research laboratories, published, and so on, but what was decisive during the selection process was his extensive administrative experience.[128] He had been a central figure at Scarborough College of the University of Toronto during its founding and early years, and had been involved in the earliest stages of the establishment of the University of Lethbridge. As well, he had served as a member of the Board of Directors of the Association of Universities and Colleges of Canada (1967) and chair of the Council of Western Canadian University Presidents (1974).[129] According to McEown, there was a general feeling among observers to the process that the board and the presidential search committee regarded Beckel as someone who would be a good business manager: 'They were persuaded that what the university needed was a good housekeeper, an administrator to clean up the mess and try and get control of whatever the union negotiations had wrought.'[130] Remarks by Paquet, a member of the search committee, add weight to McEown's impression. He recalled that the committee was much impressed by Beckel's reputation as a hard-nosed administrator: 'Beckel was a man who had been able to show extreme firmness in making tough decisions. That impressed the committee.'[131] Though no one mentioned it, Beckel was an outsider with no connection to Carleton. He would have had no inside enemies, a factor that may have worked in his favour.

For his part, Porter was widely respected for his accomplishments as a scholar. Sylvia Ostry, then a member of Carleton's Board of Governors, recalled that one of the key things Porter had going for him as a presidential candidate was the tremendous intellectual stature he would have brought to the office.[132] As well, he was well known across the university, and evidence suggests that he was the clear local favourite. Certainly, that was McFarlane's recollection. In his view, there was 'no question' that most people wanted John to be president.[133] Downey concurred: 'I was unaware of any serious opposition anywhere on campus, by faculty or staff, to John's candidacy for president. I think the community would have been quite happy had he been chosen.'[134] A reporter from the *Ottawa Journal* got the same sense. 'Talk around campus,' he wrote, 'had Porter ... heavily favoured to replace retiring president Michael Oliver.[135] Jean Teron, a member of the selection committee, chosen from the Board of Governors, said much the same thing: 'John Porter was certainly the darling of the campus, had the experience, had the ability to speak. He would have been in my view the favourite.'[136] A clear indication of the degree to which locals expected Porter to be chosen was their response at the meeting of Senate at which Beckel's appointment was announced. A professor who attended the meeting recalled that Senate's collective first response to the announcement was 'stunned disbelief' that they had not chosen John Porter.[137]

The letters of support Porter received after being denied the presidency provide another indication that many on the Carleton campus regarded him as a model scholar and senior administrator who had done a top-notch job as vice-president and should have been chosen to succeed Oliver. They praise him for having shown 'wisdom' and 'integrity' as well as academic and intellectual 'leadership' and 'vision.' They mention, too, his personal 'commitment' and 'energy' and describe his handling of the vice-presidential role as 'balanced' and 'rational.' These letters convey the strong sense that people at Carleton were disturbed about the university's general health and regarded Porter as the most suitable person to lead the institution out of its difficult situation.[138]

But Gilles Paquet and Carl Amberg, both members of the search committee, expressed a second view, a discordant minority perspective on Porter's relative popularity. They claimed that support for Porter was much less widespread than Downey, McFarlane, and the others suggested. According to Paquet, Carleton was 'split right down the middle' and Amberg challenged McFarlane's claim, saying he had 'vastly exaggerated' the support for Porter.[139]

Whatever his popularity on campus, Porter's candidacy was hampered by significant deficiencies. Most important, in comparison with Beckel he lacked administrative experience.[140] He had been vice-president just a year and his only previous administrative experience, as associate dean, lay more than a decade in the past. While the letters cited above suggest that he was regarded as a strong and valuable vice-president academic – Jean Teron recollected that people on campus generally thought he had done 'an absolutely excellent job'[141] – it was Downey's view that this might actually have worked against him. The committee may have assumed Porter was already in the proper job for him: a prominent scholar running the academic affairs of the university.[142]

Porter's case had other deficiencies. If widely respected and apparently the local favourite, he was not universally liked. According to his colleague Dennis Forcese, Porter had a reputation among some people at Carleton for being 'uncompromising' and 'insufficiently pragmatic.'[143] As Downey phrased it, Porter was often more 'decisive' than 'persuasive.'[144] I noted above that Paquet claimed Porter did little of substance while vice-president academic. Others disagreed, claiming that it was precisely because he *was* active, because he *did* initiate the process of restructuring Carleton, that he lost some support. Most important in this regard, McEown thought, were initiatives he undertook 'to put some order in the academic side of the house.' 'All right,' he said, 'we've got a bunch of problems. Let's take them one at a time and start sorting them out.' The measures Porter employed to do so did not endear him to some of his colleagues. For example, it was clear from 'Carleton University to 1982' that he intended to be 'far more strict with personnel decisions on the academic side' than had previously been the case. This put him into potential conflict with faculty members who were threatened by such promises.[145] Likewise, 'he began to look at the malaise of the university's programs,' said McEown, and threatened to overturn some administrative and academic apple carts in the process of fixing them. Again, this doubtless generated some angst and antagonism.[146] Finally, said McFarlane, 'John felt that there were a number of incompetents in university administration and he hoped to weed them out.'[147]

Supplementary to these problems were somewhat adversarial relationships Porter developed with the Board of Governors on the one hand and his former rival for the position of vice-president academic, Gilles Paquet, on the other. Porter's problematic relationship with the board stemmed from two sources. One was his political reputation. According to Downey, some of the business people on the board were uncomfortable with what they perceived as Porter's socialist political leanings.[148] These leanings, he thought, might have created a connection in their eyes between Porter and Michael Oliver, who was also a socialist.[149] According to McEown, the board did not trust Oliver's judgment. Given that Oliver had treated Porter as the president-designate, this might have worked against him. If Oliver wanted Porter, then the board did not. And Porter's dealings with the board had not been entirely positive, as his handling of the Uren affair illustrated: 'To the extent that the board had any experience with John, he tended to be abrupt with them, and not prepared to explain why things were being done, especially in areas where he didn't think the board had any business.'[150] Downey said much the same thing: 'John had not always behaved in the most politic way in the handling of issues at the level of the board ... [He] *could* give the appearance on occasions of being somewhat intemperate and inflexible. That wasn't the essential character of the man, but he wasn't always at his best in a situation where politics and diplomacy had to be carefully practised.'[151]

Porter also had a difficult relationship with prominent economist Gilles Paquet, a key member of the search committee. According to rumours that circulated at the time, Paquet scuttled Porter's bid for the presidency, but both Paquet and McEown deny it.[152] Paquet readily admitted that his relationship with Porter was 'cold,' and he acknowledged that he did not support Porter's candidacy in the committee.[153] However, he argued that the issue was professional, not personal. As I noted above, in Paquet's view, Porter's tenure as vice-president academic had been a failure because he was more concerned about holding the position, about being an 'icon,' than about administering the university. Moreover, he said, Porter's sense of what Carleton should strive to become was too retrospective, too tied to a 'romantic' image of 'when it was great on First Avenue' in the Glebe. And Paquet claimed that he was not alone among committee members in having reservations about Porter's suitability for the job. Right from the outset, he said, Porter's prospects were slim, in part because he did not have the 'profile' that the committee was looking for: 'My sense is that if one had been brutal about applying the criteria that we had determined, ... I'm not sure he would have made ... the short list.' The only reason Porter got an interview, Paquet argued, was that he was an inside candidate with an obvious interest in the job. 'It had become quite clear that we could not *not* interview him ... In any of these situations, there is a minimum of civility, a minimum of deference you have to have for the insider candidate who is in the obvious position and ... interested in the job.'[154] Moreover, said Paquet, the lack of fit between Porter's curriculum vitae and the job profile was not the committee's only concern. While Porter had an obvious plan to restructure the university – 'Carleton University to 1982' – Paquet recalled Porter's presentation to the search committee as unimpressive: 'He didn't try to persuade us that he had a view of where the place should go. Here's a man who had been ... for years designing what Carleton should be ... And you say: "Where are we going? What are you going to do with this place?"' His response? "Terribly aloof. Terribly unclear. Terribly evasive."'[155] But Jean Teron, another member of the committee, had no recollection of evasiveness on Porter's part.[156]

There were two additional concerns, however. First, according to both Teron and Paquet, John did not appear physically vigorous enough to handle the job: 'The search committee held [a very lengthy interview] with John ... It must have been six or seven hours all together. John appeared exhausted by the end of it ... We were very conscious of the kind of energy the president [must] have, and we sensed that if he was exhausted getting through that one day, what did that mean about his long-term energy levels?'[157] Second, Paquet thought that even if Porter did have a plan to undertake major changes, he would lack not just the strength to carry it out but also the nerve; he was a 'diminished' man physically and too tied to the people and practices of the old Carleton to turn the place upside down, should it be necessary. In fact, said Paquet, much of Porter's plan and talk of change was pure rhetoric:

> After years where Dunton made all the right decisions that pushed Carleton always a bit higher, [Oliver's term] had been a period of floundering in which Carleton had lost an immense amount of credibility ... [The committee] felt they needed a very decisive person who could take the school one step further ... The problem was that ['Carleton University to 1982'] was rhetoric ... At the time, there was too much mortgage in Porter's connection, [his] friendliness with all of these people. He would not have been able to do this. He certainly did not convey to the selection committee any sense of willingness to do that.[158]

It is difficult to get a sense of the specific political and programmatic differences that distinguished between Porter's vision for Carleton and whatever alternative Paquet and like-minded colleagues held. According to Ryan and Downey, there were no large groups on campus who argued or organized in favour of or against Porter's candidacy.[159] Moreover, Tom Ryan speculated that any issues about Porter that faculty might have discussed would have had 'zero influence on the search committee.' Certainly, he said, faculty members were unlikely to object to Porter's plans as outlined in the 'Carleton University to 1982' document because few of them would have read it.[160] My own sense is that Paquet, Beckel, and the board wanted to institute a more corporate style of administration and focus in particular on financial issues, while Porter was willing to be tough but wanted to use more traditional scholarly criteria for making decisions rather than just financial ones. It is difficult to believe, after Porter's stand on the Uren incident and his willingness to talk tough with the Board of Governors while vice-president, that he would have hesitated to stick by his plan and principles once president.

Whatever the reasons for their collective decision, Paquet claimed that the selection committee had so many reservations about Porter's appropriateness that when it came time to discuss his candidacy, the discussion was brief:

> We were looking for a variety of things and on many, many of those things
> – the fact of [Porter's] health, the fact of his administrative experience, the
> fact of his unwillingness to be 'hands on' and forceful when he had been
> VP – all of these things and many, many others led to the decision ... It was
> *not* an agonizing debate. It was a debate where unanimously people came
> to that decision, and quickly.[161]

Teron recalled that the key thing swaying the committee was Porter's apparent lack of physical stamina. She did not note any of the issues Paquet mentions here.[162]

According to McEown, who was there when Porter was informed of the committee's decision, John's immediate reaction to the announcement was extreme 'shock and disappointment.' 'He couldn't understand what had gone wrong or what had happened.'[163] According to Tom Ryan, one of the secretaries in the president's office recalled that 'Porter was so upset, visibly shaken and shaking [when he got the news] that she worried he was going to have a heart attack immediately.'[164]

Porter's response is understandable. It was an unexpected and devastating personal insult. All the signs had indicated that he would be appointed. He expected to get the job. As well, he was a proud man, not used to failure. But he had been rejected by 'his' university, an institution to which he had developed a deep personal attachment, to which he had demonstrated great loyalty, and for which he had made great sacrifices. Though he subsequently claimed that he harboured 'no bitterness' about the committee's decision, he immediately resigned, refusing to stay on as vice-president and assume the role of president in the interregnum between Oliver's leave taking and Beckel's arrival.[165] The reasons he gave in his public statement were logical and compelling:

> Over the last year, I have worked very hard to create an atmosphere around Carleton which would enable it better to face the very difficult times which lie ahead for this and all universities. I have initiated organizational changes and planned others which I thought would help us mobilize our very great strengths ... I had the feeling that there was some approval for what I was doing which might have been confirmed by my being given the full presidential role. When I was informed of the outcome of the presidential search, and at the same time asked if I would be president *pro tempore*, I declined, because in the forthcoming year of hard choices it seemed to me improper to pursue policies or make decisions knowing someone other than I would have to live with them; or equally unsatisfactory, I could make no choices at all.[166]

Despite his public utterances, it seems he felt very bitter and disappointed, for a number of reasons. First, as Hugh McRoberts, pointed out, Porter 'saw the selection – I'll make this my attribution, because John was too gracious to say it – particularly of a man who was so obviously his intellectual inferior, as a clear vote of non-confidence on the part of the governors of the university.'[167] Porter once discussed this issue with Doris Whitteker. She recalled that he said he would not have minded so much if the appointment had been given to someone with 'significant academic credentials, someone of great prominence.' What bothered him was that they had chosen someone who, in his view, was 'untried' and 'unknown,' just not of the 'same calibre.'[168] Blair Neatby recalled a similar conversation: 'John ... said that if [David] Golden had been appointed, he wouldn't have been miffed because it would have been a choice of a sound administrator. What miffed him was somebody with mediocre academic pretensions was chosen.'[169] McEown observed Porter's apparent lack of respect for the new president quite directly: 'One of the [things] I had to organize was Dr. Beckel's first visit to the campus ... I arranged a meeting between Porter and Beckel. My distinct impression from the meeting I had with John to make those arrangements is that he had little respect for Dr. Beckel.'[170] Beckel's recollection of this meeting focused not on the degree of respect Porter showed him but on the great disappointment Porter felt at not having been chosen: 'I met Professor Porter only once: when Don McEown arranged a meeting the day of the announcement of my Presidency … I asked, even begged him to stay on as Vice-President Academic, stating that I and the University needed him. He flatly refused. I was surprised at how small he seemed to be for such a big man and how sad and beaten he appeared.'[171]

It is logical that Porter did not want to remain as vice-president or assume the presidency on an interim basis. He was not prepared to suffer what he considered to be the indignity of serving as a lame duck president for half a year: 'It is not clear to me what plans or goals the Board of Governors might have for the university. I did not wish to spend the best part of a year in pursuit of unknown goals or in a temporary capacity. There are others who are competent to assume this role until the arrival of the new president.'[172] Rather than publicly denounce Beckel, however, he focused on what he saw as the flawed process by which Beckel had been chosen. He indicated as much on three occasions. The first was a relatively mild public statement, published in *This Week at Carleton*. 'Because most are reluctant to say so,' he wrote, 'I feel forced to observe that we have all been caught up in unsatisfactory and questionable selection procedures which require no public accountability for decisions taken, even though Carleton is a public institution.'[173] The second was in his confidential letter of resignation to Oliver, where he was less politic: 'My final note, since no one else seems prepared to say it, is that in my opinion the University's procedures for presidential selection are, for a public institution, both bizarre and irresponsible.'[174] The third was in a private conversation with Bruce McFarlane. According to McFarlane, Porter 'was hurt because of what he saw as the incompetence of those making the presidential decision. He didn't think that they fully had the future of the university as a major *research* institution at heart.'[175]

Porter made his feelings public in another venue as well. Here the issue was Paquet's refusal to support him during the deliberations of the presidential search committee. He believed that Paquet had scuttled his bid for the presidency and, in a testy exchange shortly afterward, turned on Paquet. Downey recalled the incident clearly:

The meeting where John confronted Gilles Paquet was the last meeting (in the fall of 1978) of the Committee on Carleton to 1982. John had made the revisions we had agreed upon previously and we were meeting to wrap

up our work. In the meantime, since we had last met, the presidential selection committee ... had announced its choice.

Just before the meeting John came to my Dean of Arts office ... to tell me
what he proposed to do at the meeting, which was to confront Gilles with
the question of why he had been supportive of the presidential choice
made when we on the 1982 committee had worked so hard to design a
strategy for Carleton over the next three years that would require the team
represented by our committee to execute. Instead, an outsider, and from
all reports not a very impressive one, was to be brought in who had no
knowledge of Carleton, and it looked like our plan would be still-born. I
honestly cannot remember whether, in the meeting, John said he would
resign, but he indicated to me that this was his intention in this pre-meet-
ing visit.

It happened pretty much as John had said it would. Though there was
high-voltage tension in the air from the beginning, John proceeded, as
chair, to deal with the changes he had made and to get our agreement
that this was the document we could all endorse. Then, with controlled
but visible anger, he confronted Gilles. Gilles, as I remember, responded
defensively and calmly, trying to make the argument that the selection
committee had acted in what it felt was the best interest of Carleton, and
that there was no reason to think the plan of our committee couldn't be implemented if the present team stayed in place (with John as VP Academic)
... The rest of us listened, I think without comment. The storm didn't last
long; the meeting was soon over. But we all knew Carleton was in for a
serious rupture.[176]

Paquet's account of this meeting was essentially the same except he
claimed that Porter, using extremely 'intemperate' language, chastised
him for preventing him from getting the presidency. 'A week after the
decision had been announced,' said Paquet, 'he harangued me in public in anger, saying, "I was owed that position. What have you done to
me?"'[177] Others at the meeting do not remember Porter making that
claim, though they noted that he had expected the appointment.[178]

It was not long before the rupture that Downey predicted took place.
The choice of Beckel rather than Porter created what Downey referred
to as a 'right royal mess' on campus, exacerbated by Porter's negative
reaction to the decision.[179] McEown and Downey recalled that some
objections to Beckel's appointment were raised at the 'lively' meeting
of the Board of Governors at which the presidential search committee
recommended Beckel's appointment.[180] As well, as soon as the decision

was announced, a minor firestorm of letters and petitions objecting to it was unleashed. According to McFarlane, '95 per cent of the university' thought that Porter should have been named president.[181] When it didn't happen, people responded with shock, disappointment, and anger. As one professor remarked, there was 'a feeling of deep sadness [that] John Porter was not named. He is a scholar, a man who has been here for a long time, the kind of man to lead us through a difficult period. We are very afraid that he will now resign and this would be a tragedy.'[182] More than two dozen letters of support came in to Porter's office from all over the campus: from staff as well as faculty, scholars senior and junior, men and women alike. As well, petitions were signed and sent, letters to the editor of *This Week at Carleton* penned and published.[183] There was even some coverage in the local Ottawa papers.[184] But the search committee and the Board of Governors held firm, of course, and Beckel's appointment was soon confirmed. Ironically, it was Downey, Porter's colleague and friend, who, with his 'blessing,' stepped in from his position as dean of arts to assume the dual portfolio of president *pro tempore* and vice-president academic before Beckel's arrival on campus.[185]

If the short-term effect on Porter of being denied the presidency is obvious, the longer-term effect is not. According to some of John's colleagues and friends, he was disappointed, hurt, and bitter about the snub but sufficiently resilient to recover quickly. By this account, he returned to his former life as a scholar without suffering a lasting or too-grievous blow to his pride or sense of self. This was Bernard Ostry's view. According to him, Porter felt the rebuke especially keenly because it was 'a public hurt,' but did not suffer any long-lasting effects.[186] McFarlane, McRoberts, Downey, Farr, McRae, and Whitteker concurred. As McFarlane put it, Porter was both 'disappointed' about the committee's choice and 'bitter' about the way the selection process had been carried out but also 'a pretty strong person ... [who] had gone through a lot ... He could take a lot and he was quite philosophical about a lot of things.'[187] Similarly, McRoberts noted that Porter's failure to become president 'cut very, very deep' but added that John had a very strong sense of self and so quickly moved on.[188] One of the ways he dealt with the disappointment, said Downey, was to refuse to recognize the legitimacy of the committee's decision. He never accepted the decision as a 'valid judgment on him' and coped by simply getting on with his life. 'John's will to put things behind him operated to his benefit' and he pushed the failed bid for the presidency into the past:

I think he came to terms with it ... When I saw him, we didn't spend time stirring old coals ... He didn't change his views, but he didn't persist in revisiting them either. Was he happy? Probably not at that stage ... He had been less than fulfilled in his ambition to be an academic administrator toward the end of his life and perhaps though he was doing some interesting thinking and writing of essays, [he was] still living in the shadow of *The Vertical Mosaic*. You know, I don't think he was a particularly happy person, but John would not have felt it necessary to visit that on others. He would just have got on with things – which is what he was doing.[189]

Farr said something similar: 'He and Marion were hurt, no doubt about it. Marion was more bitter openly about particular individuals who had been close to Michael Oliver, advisers whom she felt had worked against John. But I never heard John make these assertions.'[190] Kenneth McRae went so far as to argue that by the following spring, Porter had come to terms with the decision. McRae and the Porters had breakfast together at the Learneds, he recalled, and by McRae's account, John was 'sprightly' and 'light-hearted' – 'absolutely at peace with the world in general.'[191] Doris Whitteker, too, felt that Porter had been deeply hurt but soon 'moved on.' In her view, Marion was more angry than John. She was 'very ambitious' for her husband to be president, said Whitteker, and shocked and disappointed by the committee's decision.[192] For his part, John's friend Bernard Ostry went so far as to claim that Porter was able to let it go because he was ambivalent about both the job and his own worthiness for the position.[193] No one else offered this interpretation.

Porter's close friends Pauline Jewett and Bob Phillips expressed a very different view. They claimed that the hurt was more consequential than others allowed because, in their opinion, John very much wanted the recognition, status, and validation the presidency would provide. Moreover, he wanted to use his ideas and will to help take Carleton through tough times. When the presidency was withheld, he was not just angry and disappointed, not just offended and hurt, but deeply and irrevocably shaken. He had been a loyal and hard-working servant of Carleton throughout his career, and his university had betrayed him. Perhaps this idea is what Pauline Jewett had in mind when she said John died not of a heart attack but of a broken heart.[194] Bob Phillips provided a more nuanced analysis but came to much the same conclusion. By 1978, he said, his long-time friend had developed 'a driving desire to be the president of Carleton University.' The presidency 'mattered terribly' to his best friend because it was a final sign of 'complete acceptance.' 'It kind of went back to his beginnings; it was something he really wanted to have.' 'Here was where he wanted to make his final mark – as the president of the university ... One can put it in terms of a contribution one can make, or one can put it in terms of satisfaction from enjoying the post. Whichever it was, perhaps there is a fine line between them.' Phillips recalled that while the search committee was active, he and his wife met John and Marion for dinner at least once a month. On each occasion, he said, John would give them, 'in tremendous detail ... a week-by-week, blow-by-blow account' of the machinations of the search, as best he knew them. The prospect of becoming president, 'simply dominated [John's] life, his health, his mental health.' So important was it to Porter that when the office was denied him, Phillips suspected that it actually hastened John's death.[195]

The second interpretation is tempting. Were it true, it would read like the final chapter in a classical tragedy: boy from lower-class background and broken family struggles through class barriers, the adversity of war, a failed marriage, and other early travails to create a happy family life and become an academic star. Sadly and ironically, while his ambition and drive produce one success after another, he sets the stage for his own downfall by setting his goals one step too high. In the end, he suffers the disappointment and indignity of failing to achieve his ultimate goal. Perhaps – but I am not sure.

As I noted above, Monica Boyd cautioned that John Porter was an extremely complex individual whose feelings were difficult to read. Like her, I believe his motivations for throwing his hat in the ring and his response to the failed bid reflect that complexity. As well, it makes sense that in the months following the announcement of Beckel's appointment his discussions of the incident with various people would generate different readings of his feelings and views, partly because he felt different about it at different times and partly because they would have to try to divine his response from his generally controlled and reserved demeanour. Either way, I have no doubt that it constituted one of the defining moments of John Porter's life. For all the successes he had enjoyed and for all the honours he had earned, it does seem that his last goal eluded him – and in a cruel and unfortunate way. He had spent almost his entire academic career at Carleton University and had developed an understandably deep personal attachment to the institution. He had been loyal to it, saving the abortive year in Toronto, despite many offers to leave. He believed he understood what was necessary to get his beloved university out of a difficult situation and had prepared himself for the job. He was doubtless aware that he was the local favourite to become president, and Oliver had for some time treated him as the president-designate. When the unexpected came to pass, he could not help but feel a sense of profound shock and betrayal. Typically, however, he kept most of his feelings inside. He flared up in the immediate aftermath of the decision, clearly angry, hurt, and disappointed, perhaps even feeling betrayed. It seems that, as with past ventures, he had presumed he would achieve his goal, make his mark, and receive appropriate rewards – here, perhaps, a final validation. But if that is true, he was denied his final accolade and had to pay a steep price.

In any case, he left the vice-president's office as soon as he could.

14 Marion Porter, John Porter's Intellectual Partner

As John Porter's biographer, I first became aware that Marion Porter had played a significant role in her husband's research efforts when I began to find snippets of her handwriting in the background notes and rough drafts of various chapters of *The Vertical Mosaic*. It appeared that she had drafted paragraphs, pages even, of the rough manuscript. I knew that she had been involved in the writing of *Does Money Matter?* and *Stations and Callings* because she was officially named as a co-author. But I had no idea she had been involved in other projects. As the evidence mounted, I attended more carefully to the issue of her intellectual relationship with her husband and the nature and extent of her contribution. To do this, I needed to get a sense of her personal and scholarly background. But I was apprehensive. The first time I interviewed Marion about her husband's life and work, I had asked her about her own background. She had politely but very firmly declined to offer any personal details: 'My story is at least as difficult as John's. I talk about it to friends, but I don't think I really want to [make it public].'[1]

This created a dilemma. I wanted to acknowledge and assess Marion Porter's substantial contribution to John's – really, in some cases, their – work. She had played an integral part in his life as an intellectual and in this respect it was only proper for me to tell her story as it intersected with his. Moreover, as one of the lesser known women pioneers of Canadian sociology, her story deserved telling in its own right. Her career is noteworthy because she was unusual, if not unique, among her generation. She worked, sometimes on a more or less full-time basis, as an academic researcher in sociology although she had no formal training in the discipline, no advanced degree of any kind, and never held a university appointment. Other female sociology pioneers of her generation (i.e., those born 1917–29) such as Helen Abell, Jean Burnet, Kathleen Herman, Thelma McCormack, Grace Anderson, Eleanora Cebotarev, Helen Ralston, and Dorothy Smith carved out academic careers, but all had advanced degrees in sociology, most the PhD, and all did so from positions within academia, even if sometimes on the margins. Burnet and Smith became extremely well known, Smith in particular because of her contributions to 'feminist' theory.[2]

The key in Marion Porter's case, of course, is that she was a 'faculty wife,' married to one of Canada's best-known social scientists. Some unusual dynamics between Marion and John provided her with an opportunity to become involved in research to a much greater degree than other well-educated faculty wives of her generation. There are lots of anecdotal accounts about generations of women who contributed to – and were *expected* to contribute to – their husbands' academic careers by providing 'wifely help,' performing the duties of an unpaid research assistant, typist, clerk, editor, and the like. Marion Porter did all these things while furthering her husband's career by entertaining colleagues and contributing to university activities, as other wives did.[3] In addition, like other women, she did a disproportionate amount of the domestic labour – maintaining the family home, caring for children, and so forth – while her husband focused on building his academic career. Marion's life, like the lives of many academic wives, illustrates some aspects of Dorothy Smith's claims in *Conceptual Practices of Power* about the gendered nature of the 'textual relations of ruling' as one aspect of the 'relations of ruling.'[4]

It says something about Marion and John Porter as individuals, about their relationship, and about the period during which they lived – a time of major changes in gender relations – that Marion was able to move at least partly beyond the role of faculty wife to become John's intellectual partner. Later, I unpack what the term 'intellectual partner' means because Marion, John, their friends, and their colleagues used it to describe her role but interpreted it in very different ways.

Once I made the decision to tell Marion's story as part of John's, I wrote to inform her. I asked if she was willing to make the necessary elements of her life story public and to itemize for me her contributions to John's work. I told her that one way or another I felt obliged to address the issue. Her cooperation would be helpful, but I was going to proceed without it if necessary. After a month's delay, during which she consulted her children, she wrote to tell her story, at least in short compass, and to describe her contribution to the writing.[5]

Subsequently, a few years after this exchange of letters with Marion, some details of her life surfaced in Rosemary Sullivan's biography of Gwendolyn MacEwen, *Shadow Maker*.[6] MacEwen, one of Canada's best-known poets, was Marion's foster cousin.[7] When Gwendolyn was a child and Marion a teenager, they had lived in the same house, though with different families. In her efforts to understand Gwendolyn MacEwen's life story, Sullivan had interviewed Marion and Marion's half-sister, Dora Lyons.[8] During that interview and in related correspondence thereafter, Marion made public some elements of her background that she had not revealed in her interview with me. Some of the 'secrets' revealed in *Shadow Maker* were quite shocking and only increased my respect for the life that Marion built for herself against incredible odds. I have incorporated some of Sullivan's materials into the account below.

A Difficult Childhood

The autobiographical letter that Marion Porter wrote to me in the late fall of 1991 is a brave and straightforward one that speaks with dignity and insight about a tragic childhood and youth far more difficult than her husband's. The story begins with her mother, Winnifred Harvey:

> Actually, I know very little about my origins. I have no idea who my father was. My mother, Winnifred Harvey, grew up in a respectable farming family near Uxbridge, Ontario. I have a picture of her as a young woman – quite beautiful, refined, well-dressed. She must have gone to Toronto in the early 1920s. My birth certificate gives my birth as August 27, 1922, with my name, Harvey. I also have a picture of myself at about one year old – also looking well-dressed and healthy.
>
> My mother at some time married William Lyons, an American from a wealthy New York family who had left home to join the Canadian Army at age 17 to fight in the First World War. My half-sister, Dora, was born in March 1925. I thought until I was 14 years old that William Lyons was my father and although he never adopted me I was known as Marion Lyons until I married.
>
> My mother was a battered wife. I have vivid memories of brutal scenes. When I was five years old, she cracked. She was taken to the mental hospital at Whitby Ontario and I never saw her again and heard nothing about her. Lyons put Dora and me in the care of the Protestant Children's Homes. We spent the next few years in a variety of foster homes. In 1931,

we were placed with the Martins on Keele Street. This became a permanent foster home.[9]

Life with Margaret and Charlie Martin was an improvement on the placements in temporary foster homes but far from idyllic. Marion noted that her childhood was 'always full of anxiety' even after she and her sister moved in with the Martins.[10] Marion and her sister were always well cared for, but 'Aunty' Margaret never gave them the affection they needed and craved. 'Once, desperate for approval, [Marion] complained that Margaret cared more for Gwen and Carol [her nieces] than for her and Dora. Margaret replied coldly but honestly: "Blood is thicker than water" – and then added: "I know I'm not loving. I'm very strict, but I'm fair."'[11] The sad truth was that Marion's foster mother was a distant and stern woman, a respectable, teetotalling, God-fearing Christian, as Marion described her, who took in the Lyons girls only because she was paid to do so by the Protestant Children's Homes.[12] Life was not easy for the Martins, a family Marion characterized as 'the respectable poor,' and, according to Marion, Charlie and Margaret decided to become foster parents only in order to buy the big house they lived in at 38 Keele Street, in the west end of Toronto. So, while the Martins provided Marion and Dora with some domestic stability – Margaret never threatened to turn them out – their foster home was emotionally barren. Their living arrangements tell the tale. Charlie and Margaret lived on the first floor. Margaret's sister, Elsie, and her husband, Alick MacEwen, and their two children, Gwendolyn and Carol, lived on the second. Marion and Dora lived separately on the third. As well, Margaret, a deeply religious woman who held to a very conservative Victorian Protestant morality, did not hesitate to demean and reproach Marion over her 'shameful' background. 'Considering my origin,' Aunty said, 'I was lucky to live in a comfortable house and to have enough to eat.' Not only that, but Margaret 'constantly told me that I was ugly and later it was a great surprise to me to find out that I was fairly attractive.'[13]

In 1936, when Marion was fourteen, William Lyons reappeared and tried to claim Marion and Dora. Dora, then twelve, had no alternative but to go with him; she was his daughter.[14] But Marion was shocked to learn that she had a choice: William Lyons was not her biological father and had never legally adopted her. She did not have to go and decided to stay with the Martins.[15] The stress of this situation – the decision to live separately from her half-sister, the discovery that she was not only a foster child with a mother in an institution for the mentally ill but a child born out of wedlock with no knowledge of her father's identity – must have been profound for someone so young:

> When I made a friend I wondered about how many of my shameful se-
> crets I should reveal. The fact that I was a foster child. That was bad but
> not the worst. Worse was that my mother was in a mental hospital. The
> very worst, which I'm sure I never revealed, was that I didn't know who
> my father was, that I was a bastard. So for years I carried around a heavy
> burden of shame and guilt which Aunty certainly did nothing to dispel.[16]

There is no doubt that the disorienting and hurtful dynamics at 38 Keele Street made it a difficult, dysfunctional place to grow up. None-theless, in comparing her own childhood to that of her foster cousin Gwendolyn MacEwen, Marion assessed her situation as follows: 'In many ways, our life [hers and Dora's] was more stable [than Carol's and Gwendolyn's], ... yet in other ways, we were rejected too. It was a crazy life for all of us.'[17]

Off to University

Despite her feelings of loneliness and anxiety, Marion was an excel-lent student, sufficiently accomplished that her teachers at Humberside Collegiate and her social worker decided that she should go to univer-sity – the first child from the Protestant Children's Homes to be given this opportunity. Marion had never contemplated such a prospect: 'At that time, incredibly, I didn't even know what a university was or that there was one just off Bloor Street, down which I had many, many times travelled by street car.'[18] Her lack of awareness was what could be expected. At that time, young women from working-class families simply did not go to university. The economic difficulties were all but insurmountable and gender discrimination was clear. No one expected a working-class girl to have the mettle to compete successfully in sec-ondary school, let alone university. For the few who could, a logic of diminished, 'realistic' expectations was in place. Certainly this was the case with the young Marion Lyons. Marion recalls that her aunt was quite impressed by her school performance and gave her 'one enduring gift,' – 'a belief in her own intellect' – but 'her highest goal for me was to attend Normal School and teach in a public school.'[19]

In September 1940, Marion enrolled at Victoria College of the University of Toronto, a remarkable accomplishment: 'Two young girls who lived at 38 Keele Street [Marion and Gwendolyn] somehow received the message that they could save themselves with their minds … Given [Marion's] personal history, she was astonishingly brave and determined.'[20] Marion enrolled at Victoria on the understanding that the funds had been provided by the Imperial Order Daughters of the Empire. In truth, half her tuition had been paid anonymously by one of her high school teachers. She did well at Victoria and by 1943 was ready to graduate. Then, just prior to the end of her final term, she received a letter from her anonymous benefactor: 'He wrote [telling] me of his contribution, suggesting that he would like to go to my graduation, and asking me to send him the same amount of money for three years so that he could help another deserving girl attend university.' Marion was 'shocked and mortified' by this revelation and request. She determined that 'no one else should have that embarrassing experience,' denied his request, and made other arrangements: 'I found out the girl's name and deposited the money for her tuition at Simcoe Hall for three years. This remained an anonymous contribution.'[21]

Early Years: Teaching, Marriage, Family

Marion Lyons' experience at the University of Toronto was invaluable, providing her with the tools to lift herself out of the working-class milieu in which she had lived into the social and occupational world of the middle class. She became a secondary school teacher and for four years taught full time during the school year at Bradford Collegiate (1943–6) and Lindsay Collegiate Institute (1946–7) while taking summer courses at the Ontario College of Education in Toronto. In 1947, she moved to Ottawa, where she got a job teaching mathematics and physical education at the High School of Commerce. The move proved fateful. One of her colleagues at the high school, Val Johnson, was married to Peter Johnson, one of John Porter's friends from Army days. John and Marion met at a dinner party at the Johnson home in 1949. Their relationship blossomed quickly and two years later they married.

For the next two years, Marion continued teaching, but when Tony was born in 1953, she assumed the role of full-time mother. Ann was born two years later. After a couple of years as a homemaker, Marion began to grow restless. She had not lost her desire for a career and began taking courses at Carleton. She would probably have resumed teaching in the late 1950s except she had developed epilepsy, the result of a fall from a bicycle during a trip to England in 1951. It was not until 1963 that the epilepsy was under control and she was able to return to teaching – this time at Ridgemont High School in Ottawa's south end, not far from their home in the Glebe.[22]

During these early years, John was an involved father who, somewhat atypically for the period, did a good deal to look after Tony and Ann: changing diapers, walking the floor with them in the middle of the night if they were ill, and so on. Nonetheless, if on this account he was more enlightened than many men of his generation, he remained a traditionalist. He left Marion to run the house and care for Tony and Ann. Marion pointed out that he was 'not an emancipated man' and, in that regard at least, entirely 'typical of men of his era.'[23] And he later acknowledged this. In a conversation with a young family friend just a year or two before he died, he observed that like most men of his generation he had been a 'male chauvinist,' who saw the gendered division of labour in essentially unproblematic terms.[24] This may have had some implications for his relationship with Tony and Ann. Both recalled their father with great respect and love, but at least one family friend said that he got the impression Porter's relations with them were sometimes difficult, especially during their teenage years.[25]

Wifely Help: The Early Phase of the Intellectual Partnership

Sometime in the late 1950s, Marion became involved in her husband's research, gathering data and historical information, creating statistical tables, and reading early versions of chapters of *The Vertical Mosaic*. She enjoyed the intellectual challenge immensely and became thoroughly familiar with the draft of *The Vertical Mosaic*. So comfortable was she with the manuscript that when John suffered his first heart attack on his trip to Calgary in 1963, she offered to draft the last chapter in her husband's stead. 'I have gathered most of the material together and we have discussed it,' she wrote.[26] Meisel declined her offer but acknowledged Marion's commitment to the project in his reply: 'I think that John has a tremendously important and exciting work here (and you do too – I know that you have been deeply involved in it as well).'[27] When the book finally appeared in May 1965, it was a source of pride and satisfaction for both of them. In the preface, John acknowledged her major contribution: 'My greatest debt is to my wife, Marion, who helped with research into historical and statistical materials. She read and criticized the manuscript at all stages. Discussions with her have forced me to clarify many of the ideas which have been introduced into the book, and to abandon others which have not appeared.'[28]

Just prior to the release of *The Vertical Mosaic*, about the same time as John was recovering from his first heart attack, Marion returned to teaching full time. She enjoyed the job and found the hours convenient in terms of childcare. But John, she said, did not like the new status quo. He had become accustomed to daily consultations with her about his research and missed her input. They discussed the matter frequently over the next year or so, and when the opportunity arose for John to go to Geneva for the 1966–7 academic year, she agreed to resign from teaching on the condition she be allowed to contribute more fully to his research projects. After they returned from Europe, Marion took courses in calculus and statistics at Carleton and the University of Toronto both to upgrade her skills as 'a prospective maths teacher' and 'to help John with statistics in the surveys he was becoming involved in.'[29] As well, she forced him to make good on his promise to let her assume a bigger role in his work.[30] Slowly, their intellectual relationship changed. At first just a part-time research assistant, within a few years she became a full collaborator and co-author.

The transition occurred, really, beginning in 1968, when she helped write 'The Democratization of the Canadian Universities and the Need for a National System,' a paper intended for the American journal *Minerva*.[31] She recalled twenty years later that the *Minerva* article, which appeared under John's name in July 1970, was really a joint effort: 'At John's suggestion, I did all the research and outlined the article. I was happy at the time to be involved without any recognition. Later, John felt remorse that he had not included a reference to my work in a footnote. In fact, realistically I should have been named as co-author.'[32] Marion enjoyed working with her husband but yearned for a more fulfilling and independent challenge for her skills and career ambitions. Thus, when in 1971 Bernard Ostry offered her a position in the Department of the Secretary of State, she accepted. By this time, Tony and Ann were well into their teenage years and not in need of constant supervision at home. She was keen to resume her independent professional career.

She recalled being 'elated' with her new job. Once again, she was part of what she referred to as 'the real world' of the paid labour force. And again, in the beginning, John was supportive. He could see how much she enjoyed her job, she said, and 'felt badly' about having deprived her of working for so many years.[33] Soon, however, he began to protest.

He had continued his habit of working at home in the mornings and had got used to having Marion around to discuss his work. Now that she was working full time for the civil service, this was not possible, and he didn't like it: 'He got to depend on me to discuss things with [him] ... He discussed things more with me than anyone else; there's no doubt about that. But here I was working. He at first felt guilty; then he started to grumble, grumble, grumble.'[34] Eventually, they struck a deal. She would quit her job after a year on condition that he would allow her to share more fully in his work. And so it was done. She regretted having to tell Ostry she was leaving, but she had a perfectly legitimate excuse. John had been offered the Mackenzie King Chair at Harvard and she believed Ostry would understand that she could not deny him such a wonderful opportunity.[35]

Full-Time Collaborator and Co-Author

If Marion's career as John's full-time collaborator began with the article in *Minerva*, it was cemented when she became involved in the student aspirations study, described in chapter 11. When John and Bernard Blishen received the data from the SOSA study in the fall of 1971, they decided that they should as quickly as possible produce a policy-oriented document that could have an immediate impact on ongoing debates about educational opportunity. With this in mind, Marion said, they asked her to write up the materials related to student financial problems. Soon, she decided to undertake a full-scale analysis of the data and with their help and guidance quickly produced *Does Money Matter?* In recognition of her efforts, she received top billing as first author. They then turned their attention to a more detailed examination of the data that eventually resulted in *Stations and Callings*. John and Bernard took a more directive role in this more scholarly analysis, but Marion continued to play a major role, authoring or co-authoring eight of the sixteen chapters in the original manuscript.[36] When John died with the book still unfinished, she assumed the major responsibility for carrying it through the final stages of production.[37] 'Methuen agreed to publish it,' she recalled, but wanted them to undertake 'major reductions and elimination.' She carried out the bulk of this task: 'I prepared the manuscript for publication.' According to Marion, John had previously decided that 'the authors should be listed as JP, MP, and BB [and while] Bernard was probably not too happy about this, ... [he] did not demur.'[38]

By the mid-1970s, then, Marion Porter had developed considerable skills as a researcher, writer, and data analyst. She had come to see herself – and be seen by others, including John – as his intellectual partner. But she built an independent career as well.

Final Years

In 1977, Marion became involved in the Canadian Research Institute for the Advancement of Women (CRIAW).[39] An activist-scholarly organization, CRIAW had been founded in 1976 as part of and in consequence of the great political and intellectual ferment generated by the women's movement in Canada in the late 1960s and early '70s.[40] Marion became involved in the organization through Pauline Jewett, CRIAW's first president. In 1978, Jewett successfully applied for a small, three-month start-up grant from the women's program within the Secretary of State to move CRIAW from the 'kitchen table' stage of its development to the next level of organization.[41] Pauline chose Marion to take on this task. Over the next couple of years, Marion worked with CRIAW's membership and Board of Directors to strengthen the organization. She left in 1980 and, in recognition of her contribution, CRIAW established an annual research award: the Marion Porter Prize, given for 'the most significant feminist research article to appear in a journal or anthology.'[42]

John died during Marion's time at CRIAW. Afterward, her personal and academic life changed immediately and markedly. Though she remained actively involved in research – she contributed to a memorial issue of the *Canadian Review of Sociology and Anthropology* devoted to her husband's lifetime contribution to the discipline and worked with Judah Matras at Carleton as a research associate – she lost touch with many of their mutual scholar-colleague friends.[43] Indeed, she became an outsider to the community of scholars to which her husband had been central and with which she had been involved for years. Marion believed this was because other members of the group misunderstood her contributions as John's intellectual partner.[44] Years later, Carleton historian Naomi Griffiths remarked that at least one part of Marion's experience was quite typical: 'The common experience of the widows of professional men in particular and many widows in general [is that] socially their life immediately shrinks.'[45]

Not until 1982 did Marion begin a major new undertaking. That autumn, Marion returned to university as an MA student in the women's studies program within the Institute for Canadian Studies at Carleton.[46]

According to her daughter, Ann, she did so in part to fill her time and in part to use her abundant energy in an intellectually satisfying way.[47] Her son, Tony, felt she had additional motivation:

> She'd been in a kind of an unusual position of being able to engage ideas and academic work at a very high level but not to have the credential. It worked very well when my father was alive, but I think when she was considering her options after he died ... it raised all kinds of questions about what she was going to do ... Doing the MA was probably a combination of getting a kind of certification for herself that she hadn't had, sort of reinforcing in [an] independent way her academic merit ... She needed something that would be rewarding, that would continue to involve her in academic things ... and an MA is a ... structured way to do that ... I think it was probably a kind of validation, something that she could shoot for and achieve.[48]

As part of her program, under the supervision of Naomi Griffiths, Marion wrote a thesis, 'The Church and the Status of Women in Quebec,' which dealt with the oppression of women in Quebec during the early middle part of the twentieth century.[49]

While enrolled as an MA student, she undertook some other projects. She collaborated with Joan Gullen, a local women's activist, to produce a chapter for a 1984 volume edited by Jill Vickers that dealt with the sexism manifest in the so-called spouse-in-the-house legislation that threatened to make criminals out of single mothers who lived with a male friend while at the same time receiving welfare benefits.[50] As well, in 1985, she contributed an entry to *The Canadian Encyclopedia* that dealt with educational opportunity, finishing this project about the same time that she helped tidy up part of John's contribution to *Ascription and Achievement*. Finally, that same year, she returned to the Department of the Secretary of State to work as a research analyst for Maria Barrados in the Education Support Branch.[51] There she remained for two years, leaving in 1987.

At that point, she struck out on an entirely new path, travelling half way around the world to X'ian province in China, where she taught English as a second language at the Institute of Mechanical Engineering at Jiaotong University.[52] She returned to Canada in 1988, again taking up residence in her spacious eleventh-floor apartment on Laurier Avenue, close to the Rideau Canal and the National Arts Centre in downtown Ottawa. Now sixty-six, Marion went into quasi-retirement. She kept politically and intellectually active by working as a citizen adviser with the Ottawa Board of Education and as a community representative on the editorial board of the *Ottawa Citizen*, but spent increasing amounts of time with her grandchildren.[53] According to Ann, the grandchildren helped provide a focus for her after John's death and 'got her out of herself a bit,' providing 'a bit of happiness' for her that the family 'had not seen for a while.'[54]

Eventually, Marion discovered she had cancer. She underwent surgery in 1995, but the procedure was only partially successful and despite additional treatments her condition worsened. On 8 September 1996, at the age of seventy-four, she died.

A Politics of Gender and Knowledge

In a paper on the early female pioneers of Canadian sociology, Margrit Eichler notes that these women experienced considerable institutional sexism in the various universities at which they worked while also having to deal with the structured gender inequalities and discrimination that characterized wider civil society of the period. Most remained unmarried or became single again after being married. Few had children. As a group, they did more than their share of the domestic labour in their respective families.[55] And they had to deal with scholarly sexism as well. As Dorothy Smith points out in *Conceptual Practices of Power*, until the 1970s sociology paid little attention to women's lives and employed theoretical and methodological approaches that did not construct or capture women's life experiences in a way that made sense to them.[56] Much of this is relevant to understanding John and Marion Porter's intellectual partnership. I noted above that Marion regarded herself as John's intellectual partner. Their colleagues and friends used the same term but meant very different things. One observer argued that in the years immediately following John's death, Marion felt she should be seen as John's intellectual and scholarly *equal* and full partner, a true academic colleague. Indeed, Marion claimed to be just like Beatrice Webb, even to the point of drawing the specific comparison.[57] In the eyes of most of their friends and academic colleagues, however, this was an overstatement.[58] Monica Boyd's characterization of their relationship is a more typical assessment:

> By the time [Marion] reached her forties and fifties, she [saw] herself as a helpmate to John. She collaborated with him on some of those educational

studies and ... began to believe she had a certain expertise in those areas. So I think her influence was substantial, largely as a supportive helpmate ... She would most certainly have listened to him ... and she *would* argue with him ... She would probably have edited his work, and she would have argued with him about how he was interpreting things.

'But,' Boyd added, 'it would not have been the same kind of relationship that [he] would have had with a colleague.'[59] McRoberts, Barrados, and Oliver concurred. In McRoberts' words,

There was no doubt that intellectually they saw each other very much as partners. John valued Marion ... as, in a sense, the anvil on which he hammered out his ideas. She was not in awe of him and challenged him. And she had a good mind in her own right. That challenge and exchange was important to John. In fact, that was a lot of John's style. John – I don't want to use [the word] 'used' because it implies an exploitation, and it wasn't; it was in every sense an equal partnership, but John – 'used' other people as anvils to hammer out ideas.[60]

Barrados, too, recognized that John and Marion had 'a really close ... supportive relationship,' and knew that Marion had done 'a lot of work and slogging for John,' but considered Marion to be the assistant and John clearly the intellectual leader.[61] Michael Oliver likewise acknowledged that there was 'a huge area in which Marion [had] ... a very big influence' on John, particularly as 'a sounding board for his ideas,' but with the others agreed that John was the driving intellectual force in the pair – and for two reasons. First, his training and position had provided him with a much greater reservoir of knowledge. Second, their intellects differed. In Oliver's estimation, John was, quite simply, 'brilliant': 'I always ... want[ed] to hear what he had to say because it was usually something that was just a little bit different from what everybody else was saying ... [H]e had that kind of spark which really great social scientists ... have.'[62]

I should note that some scholars who read early drafts of this chapter questioned the wisdom of my efforts to define clearly the nature of the intellectual partnership forged by John and Marion Porter. In particular, Naomi Griffiths, Marion's MA thesis supervisor, and Queen's University sociologist, Roberta Hamilton, regarded the question as unfair and inappropriate. In any such analysis, they said, Marion was bound to seem the junior partner: 'At the time that they lived,' said Griffiths, 'the society in which they lived did a great deal to structure the way in which they would pursue their intellectual interests: whether Marion might have demonstrated an "equal" creativity to John's had she lived … in different circumstances it is impossible to say.'[63] Focusing on a different issue, Hamilton, drawing on the work of French philosopher Michelle LeDoeuff, argued that it would have been very difficult for Marion to demonstrate the same degree of creativity as John because she had only 'mediated access' to sociology – through John, rather than directly via formal training and an academic position.[64] Both felt that the important thing to note was Marion's contribution: 'She was an active and intelligent partner to a very considerable scholar, a scholar who found her attitude to his work stimulating, her criticism of it useful and her research in aid of it invaluable.'[65]

For her part, Marion thought the question perfectly reasonable, but when I asked her to specify what she meant when she said the two of them were intellectual partners, she had some difficulty. She clearly saw herself as John's equal, at least in the day-to-day process of doing research. But she found it harder to articulate her sense of her overall contribution:

> It is hard for me to evaluate my overall contribution to John's work. Obviously, I was not a Beatrice Webb … But I was [certainly] much more than a research assistant … John was quite obviously much more original and creative. I often thought and said that John got the ideas and I was very good at building the infrastructure for them – at supplying the arguments that would result in his conclusions.[66]

However we decide the issue – and whether it is even appropriate to question the exact nature of their intellectual partnership – it is clear that John and Marion were a scholarly team and for the period in which they lived their union was very unusual. John's marriage to Marion constituted a turning point in his life. She provided him with a solid, traditional home base, both literal and figurative, from which to work. His early family life had been unsettled and his first marriage a disaster. He needed the certainty that a stable marriage provided and, by all accounts, his relationship with Marion was intellectually and emotionally satisfying. The marriage was no less important to Marion. As a young woman, she had been emotionally and intellectually insecure. She recalled in her letter that 'going into the pass course at middle-class Victoria College did nothing to increase my self-concept. Until I met

John, my greatest concern was to get along, to fit in, to smile, to hide my shameful secrets.'[67] John helped change this. As their daughter, Ann, observed, her father 'introduced [Marion] to a whole world she had never experienced before ... [P]art of why they got together was they both came from quite broken households ... Survived the Depression. Working class. And my father, through the university ... got out of it ... [I]n taking her out of that background, he was obviously very important to her.'[68] Marion and John were in that sense kindred spirits.

Their emotional bond matured and became both an intellectual bond and enduring partnership and, as time passed, both developed as intellectuals. John was clearly a gifted, creative, and devoted professional scholar who enjoyed great success. Marion contributed to this success and enjoyed and benefited from his growing reputation. However, following a pattern typical in their generation, *his* work and career remained the focal point of their joint efforts. On more than one occasion, he pressured her to give up paid work to help him with his scholarly career. She consented but demanded to be as fully included as possible. And he acceded, so that she was a part of his work, certainly much more than other spouses who provided 'wifely help' to their academic husbands. While both enjoyed and benefited from these arrangements, he clearly benefited more than she, at least in terms of receiving recognition for his intellectual work. That said, it is also true opportunities came her way which would never otherwise have arisen. For example, she was presented with the chance to write *Does Money Matter?* an opportunity that would not normally have been given to someone with her qualifications. At other times, however, the relationship was less beneficial. Though she achieved a measure of scholarly success on her own, her husband became an academic star and she basked in ever increasing amounts of *reflected* glory. While there were some benefits, the situation later created a problem. Some of her success was a direct result of and dependent on doors he had opened for her. She ended up living in the shadow of her husband's reputation and was never perceived by other scholars as John's full and equal partner. After he died, many of the doors that he had opened soon shut.

During the decade from John's death in 1979 to 1988, when Marion retired, she lived an interesting, engaged, and active life. Moreover, she carved out a brief career as an independent intellectual. Understandably, given the professional and personal closeness of her relationship with John, she was depressed for a long time after he died. It did not help that she lived outside the mainstream of academia – she never held an academic job – and without benefit of the kind of ongoing employment that she might have expected in light of her connections to well-known academics and her credentials as a published scholar.

But part of the problem was that however much John had regarded Marion as his intellectual partner and treated her as an equal, their division of labour was a relatively traditional gendered one. He was respectful and supportive of her efforts as his collaborator, indeed, sought her help. In Monica Boyd's view, 'there will be debate as to how much she really was his partner in intellectual things as well as the extent to which she was a researcher independent of him, of his stature. I think she did see herself as his co-equal.' And this happened in part because this was 'very much a part of John Porter's personality': 'He could easily have diminished her and he never did ... [H]e allowed her to develop in this way, was supportive of her thinking of herself in this way.'[69] However, right from the beginning she remained in a secondary role and I'm not sure *he* ever moved beyond seeing Marion as working for and with him *in support of his* career.

This was in part a consequence of his traditional view of gender relations. Marion recalled reading Simone de Beauvoir's *The Second Sex* and Betty Friedan's *The Feminine Mystique* in the early 1960s and being deeply affected by them.[70] She encouraged John to read these works and he did, but when they discussed the ideas that de Beauvoir and Friedan presented, she was disappointed and frustrated to discover that he was 'not terribly interested.'[71] 'In looking back,' she wrote, 'I sometimes think that John opened doors for me and then closed them. Although more enlightened than most men of his generation, he shared their belief that a woman's role was to support the man in her life.'[72] Thus, while their relationship allowed her more freedom than was typical for her generation, she remained tied to many of the expectations of a relatively traditional gender role, the role of the 'incorporated wife.'[73] Ann Porter thought that her mother experienced considerable internal turmoil as a consequence:

> I think it was always a kind of internal conflict for her. On the one hand, she saw an important role as wife and mother, but on the other hand was never really satisfied ... She used to pose to me as the daughter: 'You have to make a choice. Do you want to be a career person or a stay-at-home person?'... For me, being presented with the choice at fifteen or sixteen,

I'd say, 'Oh, I want to have a career.' And then she'd be a little put out because, after all, she had spent … a large part [of her life] being a wife and mother. So I think she felt conflicted ideas about that.[74]

This is not to say Marion simply accepted John's traditional views on gender relations. She educated and pushed him – and with some success. It is not clear that John ever adopted feminism, either as a cause or as a matter-of-course way of thinking in the sense that it became common in the 1970s and after, but Maria Barrados, for one, argued that he was very supportive of her as a female student and proactively feminist in his relations with her:

He was very, very supportive. I was … a battler on many issues and he would always encourage that. He made a point of making sure I met Pauline Jewett, for example, somebody he saw as a role model of what women could achieve. If I ever ran into difficulties and there was any sense of sexism, he would always – if I missed it, he would take me aside and say: 'Did you see that? You can't tolerate that.' So he was … probably ahead of his time in many respects … You never got the sense that you were any less value as a female than as a male.[75]

His daughter, Ann, was more equivocal. Her father, she said, was 'intellectually open' to feminism but not too keen to have it intrude into or affect his own family life:

He always encouraged me to be independent and intellectually involved. He didn't make any distinction between me and … my brother going to university. He was very much an egalitarian in that sense; i.e., with respect to the treatment of his children. But he was also a product of his time and so he had certain values and I think he liked my mother's support in the house. She was certainly the main person keeping the house.[76]

Marion was even less generous in her assessment of John's feminist sensibilities. Her husband, she said, was intellectually flexible and concerned with questions of justice and equality and in that sense concerned with the plight of women. However, he was not especially concerned with women or 'women's issues.'[77] It was Marion's position that however far John moved during his lifetime toward 'unlearning' or modifying his traditionalist views of gender roles and relations, he retained some sexist sensibilities. 'He never treated me or any other women as intellectually inferior because of her sex,' said Marion, but he did think 'a man's role was to be a provider and that a woman's place was in the home.'[78] In fact, she said, 'he was somewhat hostile to successful women, with the exception of Pauline Jewett [and] Sylvia Ostry.'[79]

Whatever the case, the bond between John and Marion was very strong despite the contradictions and tensions, and he was the most important person in her life until the day he died in June 1979. As Tony Porter phrased it,

> There's no question ... that she deeply loved him and saw their relationship ... along with our family relationship as the most important things in her life. She was extraordinarily proud of him and supportive of him and [while] I think part of her working with him was her desire to do something meaningful for herself ... it was also, in my mind, unquestionably that she just wanted to support him and help him in what he loved to do.[80]

Even after John died, he remained central to her. Friends and family alike recall that she had an extremely hard time dealing with her husband's death.[81] David Farr recalled that for years after John died, 'she talked about him continuously ... John was always in her mind.'[82] In 1987, I went to interview her for the first time at her apartment in downtown Ottawa. The first thing I noticed was a picture of her late husband. She had hung it just inside the entrance so that it would be the first thing anybody saw on entering her home. At one point during our interview, after nearly two hours of talk, I asked if she would like to take a break or finish the interview another day. She laughed. 'No,' she said, 'I'm not tired at all.' John, she said, was her favourite topic of conversation.[83]

Much more could be said about the layered and nuanced gender-related factors – societal, institutional, and interpersonal – that created the framework within which John and Marion Porter constructed an intellectual partnership within the broader partnership of their married life. My analysis here mentions only some of the historically and institutionally specific, sometimes obvious, often hidden, forces and factors that contoured the roles played by men and women in Canada from 1950 to 1980. John and Marion Porter created a partnership that reflected many of these forces and factors. Yet through her force of will and his flexibility, sometimes in spite of feminism and sometimes because of it, they created an intellectual partnership that produced for Marion

Porter a set of opportunities and a degree of recognition very unusual for the time in which they lived and worked together. In my view, John Porter, for all his talents, efforts, and drive, would never have achieved all that he did without Marion Porter's considerable contributions.

15 Second Thoughts: Ruminations on Social Justice

After the shock and deep disappointment of failing to get the presidency, Porter returned to the sociology department. His colleagues, recognizing the hurt he had experienced, did what they could to ease the transition. Monica Boyd and John Myles held a 'Welcome Back, John' party, a nice gesture, well received.[1] As well, for the first while, people spent extra time with him, reintegrating him back into the department and its business.[2] It didn't take long; he was quite happy to return to teaching and research, activities he referred to as 'things too long neglected.'[3]

Of course, he had by no means neglected scholarly work during his period as an administrator. Just before assuming the vice-presidency, he delivered the McInnis Lectures and with Monica Boyd prepared a paper for the International Sociological Association meetings in Dublin, Ireland.[4] While vice-president he helped to complete the SOSA project, wrote his introduction to the mobility book, and presented a couple of papers.[5]

On returning to the department in the late autumn of 1978 he took on other obligations, some quite unusual for him. In November, he agreed to act as a member of a Canada Council committee charged with selecting books for a French–English Book Kit Exchange Program.[6] His task was formidable: to choose the fifty best scholarly non-fiction books written in English by Canadian authors. The list he compiled included titles from history, political science, anthropology, literary criticism, economics, and sociology. Of particular interest was his selection of the top ten, regardless of discipline. His choices? Margaret Atwood's *Survival*, Donald Creighton's *Empire of the St. Lawrence* and *John A. Macdonald* (volume 1), Northrop Frye's *The Bush Garden*, George Grant's

Lament for a Nation, Harold Innis' *The Fur Trade in Canada,* Harry John-
son's *The Canadian Quandary,* Anthony Scott's *Natural Resources: The
Economics of Conservation,* F.R. Scott's *Essays on the Constitution,* and *The
Vertical Mosaic.* His top ten sociology list included a number of stan-
dards in addition to *The Vertical Mosaic*: S.D. Clark's *Church and Sect in
Canada* and *The Developing Canadian Community,* Wallace Clement's *The
Canadian Corporate Elite,* and Rex Lucas' *Minetown, Milltown, Railtown.*
But it contained some surprises as well: Ken Adachi's *The Enemy That
Never Was: A History of the Japanese Canadian,* Fred Elkin's *Rebels and Col-
leagues: Advertising and Social Change in French Canada,* Freda Hawkins'
Canada and Immigration: Public Policy and Public Concern, R.J. Joy's *Lan-
guages in Conflict,* and Myrna Kostash's *All of Baba's Children.*[7]
    In a related vein, he chaired a committee that selected the 1979 Gov-
ernor-General's Literary Awards for non-fiction.[8] According to Bruce
McFarlane, John relished this task because it gave him the opportunity
to read several works he had not previously found time to enjoy.[9] Ann
Porter noted that her mother read a great deal of literature, Canadian
and otherwise, throughout her life but that her father never read fic-
tional works, perhaps only two or three that she could remember – and
then only when he was convalescing.[10] Even when on vacation, Marion
said, her husband preferred physical activities, carpentry in particular,
to sitting under a tree with the latest piece of Can lit.[11]
    The Canada Council and the Governor-General's Literary Awards
were not the only organizations to draw on his expertise and influence.
In July 1978, he became chair of the awards committee of the Royal
Society of Canada and in February 1979 accepted an invitation from
Sylvia Ostry to take part in a conference on Canadian incomes sponsored by the Economic Council of Canada.[12] Around the same time,
he accepted an invitation from Amnesty International of Canada to become a 'national councillor.'[13] Nor did he withdraw entirely from the
Carleton scene, agreeing to serve on the Senate as a representative of
the Social Science Faculty Board.[14]
    That November he visited Fiona. They had kept in touch over the
years since being reunited in 1967 but had never developed a close relationship. John and Marion had spent a weekend with Fiona in the
spring of 1968, just a few months after they began to correspond. John
had to go to Duke to present the MacIver Lecture and arranged to
spend a few days with Fiona in Washington, along with Marion, while
he was there.[15] In what must have been a surreal experience for all of
them, they met for the first time at the airport in Washington. Recalling

the event four decades later, Fiona remembers how excited she felt in anticipation and how disappointed she was at her father's greeting – a handshake instead of a hug.[16] Fiona also visited the Porters during their year in Toronto, but afterward they kept in touch only by mail. In 1973, when Fiona married Harry Ellen, a physician, she invited John and Marion to the wedding. He declined the offer, citing work-related obligations. Not until the autumn of 1978, when Fiona and Harry had their first child, did John see her again. He paid them a visit in Jacksonville, Florida, and brought a toy for the baby.[17] It would be the last time father and daughter would see each other.

In January 1979, one of his final projects came to fruition, *Part-Time Studies and University Accessibility*, a collaborative study of 5,000 of Carleton's part-time students, undertaken with one of his graduate students, Elizabeth Humphreys. Little was known about the social backgrounds of part-time students at the time, but the prevailing orthodoxy held that most came from relatively modest social backgrounds and had been unable to attend university when they completed high school due to financial constraints. They were compelled to undertake university studies on a part-time basis later as a way of playing catch up. Their orientation was assumed to be instrumental; that is, they chose their courses with an eye to improving their job prospects.

The findings of the survey, commissioned by the Ministry of Colleges and Universities of Ontario, were surprising. Though some students fit the profile just described, a far greater proportion, about half, came from upper middle-class backgrounds. Fully 85 per cent were employed full time, most in professional, managerial, or administrative occupations, and half possessed a postsecondary degree or diploma. More than half were female and two-thirds were registered as non-degree students. About half stated they were taking courses for personal enrichment and, perhaps most unexpected, only one in eight said they were taking courses out of a desire for a better job. After digesting these unanticipated findings, Porter came to an equally startling conclusion: if part-time students were already a privileged economic group, drawn largely from professional and managerial occupations and an upper-middle-class income group, then they should pay higher fees and not be subsidized by the government. With Humphreys, who did most of the data collection and analysis, he delivered a paper on the findings at the annual meeting of the Learned Societies that June in Saskatoon.[18]

One of the most interesting episodes of the spring took place in mid-March. T.E.W. Nind, president of Trent University, wrote to Porter to ask if he was interested in being nominated to succeed him. While Porter's answer – an unequivocal 'yes' – led to a trip to Peterborough to meet the search committee in late May, it is difficult to know what to make of this episode.[19] There is no question that he regarded being the president of a university as a fitting final touch to his career, and Trent, a liberal arts university, would have been a perfect place to put his ideas about higher education into practice. But to leave Carleton? To leave Ottawa? Was he sufficiently angry and unsatisfied to pull up stakes and move to Peterborough? Did he really think he had the energy to take on the task? Marion thought he could not have been serious; he was simply not feeling well enough to pursue the prospect.[20]

Another project that reached the publication stage that spring was one of Porter's most important. Years earlier, in 1972–3, Porter had assembled a prospectus for a collection of his most significant 'reflective' essays. He had fiddled intermittently with the manuscript, originally titled *The Canadian Condition,* but nothing had come of his efforts.[21] Finally, in the autumn of 1978, he put together a roster of ten essays, wrote a brief prologue, and negotiated with Gage to have the volume published. He retitled the manuscript *The Measure of Canadian Society* and presented it to Bruce Conrod, editor at Gage, during the Learned Societies conference in Saskatoon in late spring 1979.[22] He was not in good health at the time and, according to Marion, had determined that this would be his last book. He told Marion that he would like to dedicate the volume to her. Reluctantly, she agreed.[23]

The Measure of Canadian Society is one of Porter's most significant works.[24] He regarded it as a showcase for some of his most important 'think pieces,' and taken together the essays demonstrate his scholarly and political orientation to the discipline, including in particular the principle that sociology should serve a moral purpose. The title and subtitle – *The Measure of Canadian Society: Education, Equality and Opportunity* – hint at his intentions. He meant the essays to constitute a *description* – or a 'measuring' – of Canadian society in that sense. As well, though, and this is not obvious in the title but clear in some of the essays, he also intended the notion of measuring to mean *an assessment of Canadian society against a specific moral standard.* He states this directly in the prologue: 'The major task of social science is to abstract from the confused flow of events perspectives which clarify and which permit some judgment about society in the light of moral principles.'[25] The volume unambiguously illustrates his view that the purpose of sociology is ultimately normative and prescriptive. For all his attachment to systematic empiricism, he did not see sociology as a purely descriptive or factual-analytical enterprise, a value-neutral endeavour on the model of the natural sciences. In fact, he rejected value neutrality and offered a specific social and moral standard against which Canadian society could and must be measured. He had been exposed to and had adopted this New Liberal standard during his student days at the LSE and had then used it as a moral compass throughout his career. Early works, in particular *The Vertical Mosaic* and the essays in *Social Purpose for Canada*, were enlivened by this moral sense. Clement referred to his work in *The Vertical Mosaic*, for example, as an 'indignant' moral critique of Canada's rigid structures of class and power.[26] Such structures were, in Porter's view, inimical to the values of social justice and rationality, preventing the nation from operating as a maximally open, meritocratic, and humane liberal democracy. These same sentiments appear repeatedly in *The Measure of Canadian Society*.

Perhaps the best exposition of this moral critique is found in his brief introduction to 'The Research Biography of *The Vertical Mosaic*.' There Porter notes that while studying at the LSE he had taken to heart Leonard Hobhouse's principle of social development, 'that a community develops as it grows in scale, efficiency, freedom and mutuality: efficiency toward an end, freedom and scope for individual thought, [and] mutuality in a service toward an end in which each participates.'[27] Fifteen years later, in 1979, his sense of the nature and lofty moral purpose of sociology had not changed. In *The Measure of Canadian Society*, he reprinted the research biography of *The Vertical Mosaic* and recalled the same moral standards, drawing in particular on the T.H. Marshall's concept of citizenship as a tool and a benchmark. 'I would like ... to work toward a macrosociology that is capable of both explanation and evaluation,' he wrote. 'We should be able to judge whether or not [society] is moving in the direction of human welfare ... The guiding judgmental principle ... for an evaluative sociology derives from the concept of citizenship as it has been developed by T.H. Marshall.'[28] So his view of sociology as empirically grounded, critical, and evaluative, his ideal of the rational good – a society should be characterized by growth, efficiency, freedom, and mutuality – and his indictment of Canada as an unequal, irrational, and undemocratic society that denied full citizenship to all its members remained unaltered during his career. The *means* to be used to realize these values and beliefs varied – he was sometimes more 'liberal' in outlook, sometimes more 'social democratic' – but the moral yardstick remained the same.

The essays in *The Measure of Canadian Society* that best reveal the details of his position are the McInnis Lectures: 'Education and Equality: The Failure of a Mission' and 'Education and the Just Society,' his last two major pieces of writing and those with which he chose to conclude *The Measure of Canadian Society*.[29] In the McInnis Lectures, Porter recanted his liberal individualist's faith in public education as a solution to the problem of inequality in modern liberal society. He began the first lecture with a blunt claim: 'If the question were asked which of the major social innovations of the twentieth century had most failed in its mission, a likely answer would be public education.'[30] Why? For two reasons: first, it had failed to create equality of opportunity; and, second, it had failed to produce a higher standard of living by increasing the number of well-paid, satisfying jobs and improving the efficiency and productivity of the economy.

Especially important to Porter was the debate over the role(s) that education played in modern Western democracies in addressing questions of social equality. How much equality – and of what type – *could* education create? How much equality – and of what type – *should* education create? In the first McInnis Lecture, Porter addressed a number of philosophical issues related to equality and inequality, concluding that equality must be a goal of the 'good society.'[31] But this was, of course, a complicated issue. The problem with specifying that equality should be a societal goal is that people are not equal by nature. Some are smarter, stronger than others. Moreover, one basic type of equality valued in liberal society – equality of opportunity – is largely nullified by the existence of inequality of condition or rewards.[32] This contradiction is seemingly irresolvable because in liberal society people are supposed to be free to compete, allegedly as equals, for unequal rewards. To find a best possible, if imperfect, solution to this dilemma, Porter reviewed the work of a number of philosophers and opted for the doctrine of 'fundamental egalitarianism' outlined by American philosopher John Rawls. In his influential 1971 book, *A Theory of Justice*, Rawls had argued that justice and equality had to be placed ahead of other values in ordering society. If inequalities were necessary, they were to be kept to a minimum and tolerated only if they acted in the interest of society's least privileged members: 'All social primary goods – liberty and opportunity, income and wealth, and the basis of self-respect – are to be distributed equally unless an unequal distribution of any or all of these goods is to the advantage of the least favored.'[33] Porter adopted this view, which involved a degree of redistribution of social resources in favour of the disadvantaged, because he thought it allowed for maximum social justice. He rejected other options that denied the equality principle on the grounds that he felt a 'visceral' attachment to the notion that equality was a fundamental human right.[34] In his view, humans understand how others less privileged than themselves feel. That empathetic understanding, he said, might explain 'the ultimate appeal of egalitarianism.' And he added succinctly, 'It has been for me, at least.'[35]

But it is essential to understand what Porter meant by equality. Like Rawls, Porter did not believe that thoroughgoing equality of condition was possible, wise, or even morally necessary. In his view, inequality of condition had to be minimized to the degree it interfered with societal efficiency and equality of opportunity. The latter was important because Porter, for all his attachment to equality, was, as McRoberts and others have noted, a meritocrat: 'He was clearly committed to a Canada with greater equality of opportunity, more egalitarian. But ultimately John was a meritocrat ... [He was] not afraid of elitism, provided [it was] based on merit.'[36] Two anecdotes, one from Bruce McFarlane, one from Pauline Jewett, confirm the two aspects of McRoberts' claim. McFarlane recalled the story of a young high school student, the Porters' newspaper boy, from an immigrant family recently arrived in Canada. Although he was a bright pupil, the school had shunted the young man into a non-academic stream of study because of his class and ethnic background. John took it upon himself to speak to the parents and then to act as the boy's advocate at school. The principal responded to the effect, 'Oh well, it really doesn't matter because the family wouldn't be able to afford to send him to university anyway ... It was probably the best place for a lot of the immigrants' children.' McFarlane recalled that Porter 'blew his top' and threatened to go to the Board of Education. The principal transferred the boy to the academic stream.[37] Pauline Jewett's anecdote reveals the obverse of Porter's commitment to equality. She recalled that when she became president of Simon Fraser University she insisted, as a feminist, on receiving 'the same salary as her male counterparts at universities of a similar size.' However, once in office, she refused the increase to which she was entitled in her second year and attempted to reduce the ratio of difference between the president's salary and the salary of the university's lowest-paid clerks and secretaries. Porter, she recalled, thought she was 'foolish' to have turned down money she had earned. Furthermore, she said, he told her that he would never have undertaken such a 'levelling project' as one of his goals.[38]

The other issue Porter took up in the first McInnis Lecture, after re-confirming his belief in the slippery and complicated principle of equality, was the veracity of the claim that public education could contribute to the creation of equality – in particular, equality of opportunity.[39] He claimed outright that he never believed it could create equality of condition. More important, though, on the question of whether public education could create equality of opportunity, he did a complete volte-face: 'I have always argued that education [is] the bridge between the deprived environments of the least privileged classes in any society and the opportunity presented by economic growth.'[40] However, after reviewing the sociological evidence bearing on the link between education and equality, he concluded that – on that count at least – the time, energy, and money that had been spent on public education had been wasted.[41] Never intended to produce equality of condition, public education had been touted as a vehicle for creating equality of opportunity in an allegedly meritocratic struggle for highly unequal rewards in modern industrial capitalist society. But it had failed.[42] Why? Because success in school was determined largely by class-based private resources, such as parental support, cultural enrichment, and an early positive learning environment that students brought with them to school from home.[43] And the schools were no help. They tended to reproduce the structure of economic inequality rather than break it down.[44] Not only that, but 'the less well-off contribute substantially in relation to their resources for educational services which they do not use ... [T]he present form of financing higher education contains substantial subsidies to the better-off in society.'[45]

In the second McInnis Lecture, 'Education and the Just Society,' he addressed three questions about the relationship between the structure of occupational opportunities created by industrialization and the expansion of public education. First, did industrialization provide an expanding set of occupational and mobility opportunities, as the conventional wisdom claimed? Second, what role did public education play in providing access to those opportunities for social mobility to members of the lower classes? Third, was access to educational opportunity 'essential to the just society'?

On the first question, Porter noted that the standard account of the impact of industrialization was that it created many new opportunities for social mobility by creating lots of new jobs requiring high levels of skill. However, basing his argument on Harry Braverman's work in *Labor and Monopoly Capital*, he claimed that this was nonsense. Industrialization created some new high-skill jobs, but they were few relative to the size of the labour force. In fact, the opposite tendency was dominant; over the course of the twentieth century, the evidence demonstrated that far more jobs were deskilled or 'degraded' than upgraded. Any apparent upgrading claimed by the proponents of industrialization was illusory, a statistical artefact of outdated census categories that did not take into account changes in the real content of many formerly skilled blue-collar and white-collar jobs.[46]

On the second question, he drew on the work of Ivar Berg in *The Great Training Robbery*. The degradation or deskilling of work had occurred simultaneously with a tremendous increase in credentialism and a corresponding increase in the general educational level of workers. Workers made sacrifices to acquire increased educational credentials but were then overqualified for the deskilled jobs they obtained. As a result, they neither received economic returns for the money they spent earning their credentials nor were rewarded with meaningful, satisfactory labour. Finally, since it cost money to earn credentials, money that members of the working class did not have, the process simply reinforced and recreated the existing class structure.[47]

Porter concluded the two lectures by addressing the third question, the one that consumed him during the entire post-*Mosaic* phase of his career. How can public education be transformed to serve the interests of equality and social justice? Here he drew on the writings of American Marxists such as Herbert Bowles and Samuel Gintis and radicals such as Ivan Illich, supplemented by the work of Canadian political philosopher C.B. Macpherson. Macpherson, like Porter a New Liberal, held some socialist ideas but wanted to rescue as much of the positive legacy of liberalism as possible.[48] Macpherson based much of his argument on a distinction between humans as 'consumers of utilities' and as 'possessors of capacities.' He regarded the first conception of human nature as limited and self-defeating, contributing to the obdurate inequities of condition and opportunity that Porter wanted to overcome. Following Macpherson, Porter argued that in order to make progress, the second conception of human nature would hold the key. If society could be structured so that humans could both individually and collectively develop and enjoy the full range of their capacities – the 'egalitarian maximization of powers' – then social justice and societal rationality would be served.[49] Public education was pivotal; it could not by itself solve problems of alienation at work or the unequal distribution of rewards, but it could create 'active citizens.'[50] Such citizens would actively seek these goals, using all the means at their disposal to create an 'authentic' democracy characterized by the maximum amount of realistically possible 'distributive justice' rather than a narrow, purely legal democracy characterized by large and unjustified inequities of condition and opportunity.[51]

It is easy to see in these lectures the basis for the claims made by liberals on the one side and social democrats on the other that Porter was one of their kin. On the one hand, like Macpherson, he wanted to rescue what he could of the 'good' (i.e., more social democratic) parts of liberalism. On the other, however, while convinced by some of the claims of the radicals, Marxists in particular, he was no Marxist. It was this flexibility and openness that allowed him to be a productive mentor to graduate students with a wide variety of political orientations as well as a thoughtful analyst of social issues for those in both the liberal and social democratic camps.

Around the time he delivered the McInnis Lectures he issued two other public pronouncements of his views on the relationship between education and equality: an interview with the York University student newspaper, *Excalibur,* and a convocation address at the University of Waterloo, delivered in late October 1977.

In the *Excalibur* interview, Porter reiterated points from the McInnis Lectures but touched directly on policy questions as well. He noted approvingly the 'very considerable' increase in postsecondary educational opportunities for low-income Canadians that had developed since the publication of *The Vertical Mosaic* a dozen years earlier but noted that postsecondary education remained less available in Canada than in the United States. As well, he said, postsecondary education continued to be overly focused on 'formal labour force preparation' and had 'failed to equalize opportunities in society.' The solution he proffered was to replace the principle of universality with means testing. 'If the welfare state has failed,' he said, it was because it had failed 'to redistribute social and economic benefits.' In particular, the middle class had taken advantage of the principle of universality to exploit publicly provided services like education and health care. This had subverted the whole purpose of the welfare state: 'If there are going to be publicly supplied services, then they should go to those people who genuinely need them. A good example is the student assistance plan, where students from better-off families should pay more ... I think that should be carried over to other aspects of the welfare state – means testing rather than universality.'[52]

The University of Waterloo convocation address made many of the same points about the failure of education to create equality of opportunity but again pointed to the personal and social relevance and value of education despite these shortcomings:

> The relevance of the contemporary university becomes evident if it has in any way contributed to your capacity to *measure the morality* of things in the modern world, ... if your education has enabled you to start asking the right questions. The privileges you will enjoy [as university graduates] ... place on you an obligation to use your talents for the good of others in your own country and abroad. Whether the new millennium is truly millennial or truly miserable, the demands for social justice and fairness in the distribution of the world's resources will be loud and clear.[53]

This convocation address turned out to be Porter's public swan song, and his words captured the gist of much that he had been thinking and writing over his career.

After delivering the manuscript of *The Measure of Canadian Society* in Saskatoon, John and Marion flew to Vancouver. It was in one sense an official trip; Porter had agreed to serve as the external examiner for a PhD thesis at Simon Fraser University.[54] But they were looking forward to visiting Tony, then living in San Francisco, and Ann, then living in Vancouver. They were to stay with Pauline Jewett, at the time in transition between academia and politics. A month earlier, she had been elected the member of parliament for New Westminster–Coquitlam and was in the process of disengaging herself from the role of SFU president. She lived in an apartment near the foot of Burnaby Mountain on which SFU was built. So there was a Porter family reunion of sorts and, for the first time since he was a child, Porter revisited many of the places of his youth. According to Marion, he took great delight in showing them where he had lived and attended school. He even raised the prospect of retiring to Vancouver.[55]

On 13 June, the final day of their visit, the family hiked up Garibaldi Mountain, north of Vancouver. John enjoyed it immensely, said Tony, in part because it gave the two of them an opportunity to have a long talk. They had not been in touch very much for a number of years and the occasion allowed them to reconnect and engage in some reconciliation. Jewett recalled that after they returned to her apartment, John said he was very tired and did not feel well. Later, despite feeling ill, he stayed up to chat with her after Marion had gone to bed. After some small talk, he said he hoped that she and Marion would remain friends if anything should happen to him.[56]

Perhaps he knew that he was quite ill. In the immediate aftermath of his first heart attack in 1963, he had stopped smoking and paid more attention to diet and exercise. After the second attack, he realized he had a serious problem and needed to address it. In a letter to Fiona apparently written in early 1971 he acknowledged that self-imposed overwork was the culprit and resolved to do something about it:

> Before I became ill last October I was going full tilt, doing so much all over the place. No doubt I got some satisfaction from it all, but the signs that I should slow down appeared well in advance ... I paid no heed. However, my recovery has been a steady one and all the indicators are good providing I do not go back to the ridiculous pace I was setting before. Consequently, I have been shedding a great number of responsibilities that I once thought important or rewarding, but which I now feel are very dispensable.[57]

He also changed other habits, walking back and forth to work when he could and having a bed installed in his office at the university so that he could rest if he felt ill or tired.[58] Friends and colleagues were aware of his health problems and made efforts to accommodate them. He appreciated this collective concern, said Marion, but in her estimation really made only modest concessions to his declining health.[59] Bob Phillips remembered that despite his professed intentions about cutting back on his workload after the second attack, he was soon back at full pace, carrying on as if he were not ill, taking on more work and travelling more than he should.[60] Maria Barrados went so far as to say that in the mid-1970s and after, in a sense, he was in denial: 'He didn't behave as if he was sick. He would every now and then say, "Oh, well, I better not do that. Not good for the ticker."'[61] But beyond that he tried not to let his health dictate what he would or would not do, especially in terms of his university responsibilities. Eventually, the strain began to show. A workaholic his entire career, increasingly he found he could not drive himself as he had in the past. Marion recalled that late in his career, he would excuse himself to go upstairs to work in his study after dinner, as had been his habit for many years. Ever more frequently as time passed, she would find him asleep on the bed instead of at work at his desk.[62]

There were more visible signs of diminished health as well. Through the 1960s and early 1970s, Porter had aged gracefully. Newspaper and magazine photographs and pictures from television programs show him to have filled out substantially from his Army days, and he carried about 170 pounds on his five-foot eleven-inch frame. Always clean shaven, he had a square-jawed, serious look, topped by dark, salt-and-pepper hair, combed back off his face. He favoured typically professorial clothes – slacks, a tweed jacket, and tie – supplemented by suits when necessary.[63] Although he was a strikingly handsome man, pictures from the late 1970s hint at the strain of occupying the vice-president's office. While still very good looking, he had greyed considerably and his face had become heavily lined. He became more jowly and had large bags under his dark eyes.

It would poetically apt to say that his life came full circle during the trip to Vancouver. Marion recalled that while they were in Saskatoon they had stayed at the Bessborough Hotel, just across the Saskatchewan River from the university. During their brief daily walks back and forth across the bridge, he would have to walk very slowly and stop frequently to catch his breath. In her view, at that point he really felt that 'his days were numbered.'[64] Nonetheless, during the week in Vancouver, he took the risk of going on the long hike up Mount Garibaldi. The following day, Marion and John flew back to Ottawa. Marion recalled that John complained he did not feel well and went to bed early. He never woke up. Some time during the night, he had a third major heart attack and died. He was just fifty-seven.

Marion was devastated. She called the children home and local friends rallied round. Bernard Ostry helped arrange a private memorial service for 18 June.[65] John's old friends, Bob Phillips, Munro Beattie, Frank Vallee, and Pauline Jewett read tributes. The day following, the *Ottawa Journal* noted his passing:

> It is almost a cliché, and certainly it is inadequate to say that John Porter was the founder of Canadian sociology. His influence went beyond his own discipline. *The Vertical Mosaic* made an impact far exceeding any merely scholarly work because Canadian society had never been examined before in such a systematic, penetrating way. It is a seminal work. If some of its conclusions and assumptions have been questioned in recent years, that is its own tribute to a work of great originality and, perhaps, even genius. John Porter showed the way. The distinguished scholar possessed also a humane intelligence and natural qualities of leadership. The combination is rare; it accounts in part for the shock and the outpouring

of tributes following his death, a reaction which transcended the university community. He led by the qualities of his own work and the sheer excellence of example. His loss is not only Carleton University's; it is his country's – which he helped to know itself.[66]

A week later, in the late morning of 25 June, John's spiritual and intellectual home, Carleton University, staged a public memorial service in his honour. Nearly 400 friends, colleagues, and students gathered in the sunny amphitheatre between Paterson Hall and the Alumni Theatre on the Carleton campus to celebrate his life and console his family. Bruce McFarlane, Hugh McRoberts, and Jim Downey offered tributes. All spoke of his exemplary qualities as a scholar, his commitment to his students, and his contributions as a citizen of his university and his country. Perhaps Davidson Dunton, who delivered the eulogy, best captured the spirit of their collective tribute:

For me, as for many, John Porter embodied an ideal for Carleton, for any university. He was devoted to students and to teaching, and he carried out brilliant, demanding research that brought new understanding of Canadian society. He personified rationality, that quality that is supposed to reign in universities. He was moved by strong feelings about society and injustices he saw in it, but his feelings never clouded the rigour of his analyses. When called upon, he was ready to serve his academic community, and serve with keen perception ... He was a master of his own discipline, but read widely in other fields ... and could talk well ... about things in [other] fields of interest. Gentleness went well with his great intellectual strength. In discussion, he did not obtrude. He would listen courteously to others; when his own remarks came they were succinct and quietly piercing ... John Porter was a wonderfully warm and sensitive human being. Many had an affection for him that matched their great respect ... For Carleton a very special light has gone out.[67]

These public offerings, in combination with condolences offered by colleagues and close friends, did much to support Marion, who struggled greatly with her husband's death for many years. She was pleased as well when Carleton University and the Canadian sociological community recognized John's contributions with lasting tributes. That autumn, Carleton established the John Porter Publication Grant and, in November 1981, renamed the Main Hall of the Carleton's University Centre 'Porter Hall' in his memory. Wallace Clement organized a special plenary session at the 1980 meetings of the CSAA devoted to a consideration of his mentor's pivotal contribution to Canadian sociology. The papers were subsequently published as a special memorial issue of the *CRSA*.[68] In addition, the CSAA, which had some years earlier made Porter an honorary president, established a book award in his name. Winners of the prize, first awarded in 1983, have included some of Canadian sociology's most prominent figures.[69]

Margaret Atwood once wrote that the Canadian national motto ought to be, 'Who does he think he is, anyway?' Many years ago, Robert Brym invoked Atwood's remark in relation to John Porter. Brym pointed out that – as of that date at any rate – there had been no 'second *Vertical Mosaic*.' In explaining and lamenting the fact, Brym mentioned a couple of factors that made the prospect daunting for anyone presumptuous enough to contemplate the idea. By far the most important, in Brym's view, was a failure of nerve or lack of ambition on the part of Canadian sociologists.[70] There is much sense in Brym's claim.

One thing that separates leaders such as John Porter from the majority of their colleagues is their breadth of vision and willingness and capacity to take on seemingly insurmountable tasks; in the case of *The Vertical Mosaic*, it was the intimidating job of describing and explaining the structure and dynamics of an entire nation-state. Porter noted in his retrospective account of the writing of his master work that 'grandiose fantasies' aside, he did not start out with the intention of writing a Tocquevillian study of Canada as a modern democracy.[71] The tale grew in the telling, however, and though he soon appreciated the enormity of the task he had set for himself, for the better part of a decade, he simply toiled away until the job was done.

After *The Vertical Mosaic* was published, he became a major public figure in Canadian sociology, in the broader Canadian social science community, and to some extent in Canadian society more generally. He did not set out to be a public figure, but became one anyway. In fact, he was a rather shy and private man, sometimes difficult to approach, hard to get to know well. Some said this was a result of a natural reserve. This was Sylvia Ostry's view: 'I don't think he was the sort of person who you knew very well. He was not easily approached ... He wasn't the sort of person you had long, intimate conversations with, unlike Pauline [Jewett], for example.'[72] Others had a different sense of the nature and roots his shyness and reserve, as Dennis Forcese indicates:

You will have heard that he was a shy man. I think that may be true. I have talked with former undergraduate students taught by John, or advised by him, and compared their impressions with my own as a junior colleague. Shy may be apt, but the reserve was seen by some as disinterest. I think the truth is probably somewhere in between, a blend; he was a reserved man, probably not as confident as his status would seem to have warranted, but amiable and supportive whenever his preoccupations permitted.[73]

Due to the demands of the scholar's lifestyle, Porter spent a great deal of time alone, working. This probably suited him well, being temperamentally something of a loner. This is not to say he was a recluse; many of his students, colleagues, and friends stressed that he could be a warm and gracious host and a deft and humorous conversationalist. As his good friend Bruce McFarlane put it, 'He was one who got a great deal of enjoyment out of life and had a quiet sense of humour ... [T]hose of us who had the opportunity to meet him in more personal surroundings also had the chance of seeing him as a gentle and proud father, attentive and loving husband and thoughtful and considerate friend.'[74] Certainly, this was the experience of his student Hugh McRoberts:

> He was unfailingly concerned for his students in a way which went well beyond his responsibilities as a professor. Marion and he often invited us into their home and to their cottage for times that were filled with both much laughter and their pleasure in wide-ranging and stimulating conversation. They made us feel increasingly to be not so much simply students, but to be an integral part of the community of scholars.[75]

Close friends remember as well, however, that even in his public roles, he seemed more comfortable with those he knew than with strangers, and was especially at home with intellectuals. It is my sense that he could never have followed his good friend Pauline Jewett into politics. The constant hurly-burly of public life would have made him uncomfortable. As Jewett herself noted, even in the familiar company of family and friends, 'he would frequently go off into thought ... you could almost see him retreat.' She claimed that he was easily bored with mundane conversation and somewhat uncomfortable chatting with those outside his regular circle of friends and intellectual colleagues.[76]

So, even after he was pushed into the academic limelight in 1965, he remained at heart a modest and private man, more at home in the relatively sedate and cerebral atmosphere of academia and university politics than elsewhere. Nonetheless, once in the public eye, he acquitted himself exceptionally well. He became a disciplinary eminence and assumed the mantle of university statesman and senior administrator. As successes followed one another, he became comfortable in these roles despite his apparent natural shyness and modesty.

What does this tell us? Clearly, a combination of factors led him, first, to be offered the opportunities that came his way and, then, to take on the challenges they entailed. The record shows that he accomplished a great deal as a consequence of the hard work, insight, and intellect he brought to bear on the social, political, scholarly and administrative issues, problems, and opportunities that cropped up during his career. But his accomplishments came about only because he was an ambitious man who repeatedly made a success of the opportunities he was offered.

No Canadian sociologist since has attempted to replicate or otherwise produce the equivalent of *The Vertical Mosaic*. Nor did Porter make a serious effort to do so, despite repeated invitations. As early as the spring of 1970 he fielded an enquiry from R.I.K. Davidson, editor at the University of Toronto Press:

> I have been giving thought to a revision and an up-dating of the book. I think the appropriate time would be when the 1971 census data become available. That would be around late 1972. Therefore, perhaps 1973 would be a realistic date for the revised edition. Of course, I am very pleased with the success of the book – something which was totally unexpected at the time it was written.[77]

He said much the same thing in 1977 in response to another enquiry from Davidson:

> I have of course given a good deal of thought to updating and revising *The Vertical Mosaic*. A few years ago I took a close look at what was involved and came to the conclusion that the book would have to be almost completely rewritten ... I concluded that it was a big job which would take me from my current research interests. The solution I think might be possible is a long introductory essay on trends in Canadian society since the time the book refers to ... At the moment I don't see how I can do that even for some time since I have numerous obligations to which I must give priority, among them the job of Vice-President (Academic) of Carleton which I begin soon ... Many people ask me if I am revising or updating the book

so I feel there is a good deal of interest. Perhaps I should give it a firm spot on my not too distant agenda. At the moment all I can say is I hope I can.[78]

Several scholars have carried out partial replications; Wallace Clement's *The Canadian Corporate Elite* is probably the most high-profile example.[79] As well, sociologists and political economists have filled in many of the lacunae in Porter's now-dated analysis, challenging or updating many of his theoretical and empirical claims. Some of these studies have demonstrated the kind of ambition Porter demonstrated in *The Vertical Mosaic*.[80] However, to date *The Vertical Mosaic* remains unique in the history of Canadian sociology.

Why might such a study fail to appeal to contemporary scholars? For one thing, it might actually be impossible to undertake a similar project. For all its considerable merits, Porter's magnum opus had many theoretical and methodological shortcomings and empirical gaps. Any contemporary scholar wanting to replicate the book while taking care of these deficiencies would have to possess immeasurably wider theoretical and methodological expertise and the capacity to winnow and organize an exponentially larger amount of empirical data than that with which Porter dealt. These materials would have to be made sense of in the context of a much more complicated national and international environment. It may be that there is too much for any single scholar, perhaps even a small group of scholars, to master.

That said, to explain Porter's decision to write *The Vertical Mosaic* exclusively on the basis of his idiosyncratic curiosity, nerve, or ambition would be naïve. In any historical period, societal and disciplinary factors create openings for certain kinds of research projects while others fail to come to mind or are discouraged if they do. There was something about Western industrial nations in the middle of the twentieth century that led sociologists from several countries – Raymond Aron in France, C. Wright Mills in the United States, Saul Encel in Australia, John Porter in Canada – to undertake in different ways elite-type studies of the national structure of class and power in their respective societies. There was something going on that we cannot explain by referring exclusively to Porter's personal nerve or ambition.

At the same time, we cannot ignore the role it must have played. John Porter was a man who thought in terms of the big picture and liked big challenges. He made big plans because it never occurred to him to make any other kind. His entire scholarly career provides evidence for this assertion. After completing *The Vertical Mosaic*, he decided that

Canadian sociology would benefit from the development of a survey research tradition modelled on that extant in the United States and set out to establish it, despite very great scepticism among the public, government agencies, and opinion makers. The occupational prestige study, the educational aspirations and attainment study, and the mobility study were the result. Their benefit was enormous; they provided essential, basic data about Canadian society and helped put into place the technical infrastructure and research culture necessary to develop the survey research tradition. Similarly, once he became involved in university administration, Porter did not hesitate to pursue the presidency of Carleton University. Ambition and grandness of vision and a sense of duty or service and obligation to his discipline, his university, and his country explain these decisions. Each time he was offered the opportunity to accept a challenge, to take a step up the academic ladder – as a scholar, an administrator, as a disciplinary and university spokesperson – he seized it. For all his natural reserve, modesty, and preference for privacy he chose to become a more public person.

Porter possessed substantial personal ambition and a steely resolve, to be sure, but these two aspects of his personality were always channelled through a deeply felt sense of public service and responsibility. He believed he had a duty and a mission as an engaged, practical intellectual to do what he could to improve his discipline, university, and country. His inspiration derived in large measure from the New Liberal view of social progress and the social good to which he had been exposed in the late 1940s at the LSE. It is to this idea that I turn next.

Afterword: Duty, Service, and Mission

In previous chapters I have written about the scholarly legacy John Porter left for generations of Canadian social scientists – sociologists in particular. Porter pushed Canadian sociology to become more international in orientation and comparative in method, and to use the most sophisticated quantitative methodological and statistical techniques available. In his view, this would allow Canadian sociologists to take part in international scholarly debates and provide high-quality data to inform progressive, humane policy decisions in Canada. In addition to his research legacy, I have also described his contributions as a mentor of graduate students, an administrator at Carleton, and a builder of the Canadian discipline. To conclude, I want to consider all of this together in order to place Porter in the intellectual history of Canadian sociology.

When I began the project, this did not seem a problematic issue. There was a widely accepted interpretation of his intellectual *formation* which stressed the influence on him of British Fabianism and a set of unspecified 'social democratic' political leanings that he picked up at the London School of Economics. Likewise, there was a standard interpretation of his later sociology according to which he looked increasingly to American theoretical perspectives and methodological practices for inspiration. But as I delved more deeply into his work, I found these interpretations partial and oversimplified. Most significantly, as I pointed out in chapter 3, the received interpretations have failed to appreciate the deep and permanent influence on him of the Hobhousian tradition of New Liberal politics and sociology that he encountered via Morris Ginsberg and others at the LSE. New Liberal ideas, much more than Fabianism, shaped his sense of the nature and purpose of sociology during his early years as an academic. And even after he became increasingly enmeshed in American sociological practices, they remained at the core of his scholarly and political world view. That he retained New Liberal views throughout his career helps us to understand some apparent shifts in his political perspective and some otherwise puzzling aspects of his sociological perspective. First, it helps to explain why he appeared to vacillate between liberal and social democratic political views and, second, why he adopted the stance of the engaged, practical intellectual, one who did sophisticated quantitative, policy-relevant research, without adopting the value-neutral position of the professional, scientific scholar.[1]

My analysis of Porter's place in the historical development of English-language Canadian sociology locates him in terms of two partially overlapping triangles: one geographic, one philosophical. In geographic terms, his work is simultaneously Canadian, American, and British. In this regard, he is typical of English-Canadian intellectuals in general and sociologists in particular. In *Society and Change*, Harry Hiller's very helpful biography of S.D. Clark, Hiller argues that English-language Canadian sociology developed in four stages: European transfer, environmental adaptation, disciplinary differentiation and specialization, and consolidation. The first, European transfer, began in the twilight years of the nineteenth century. During this period, sociology was one of many aspects of culture transferred from England to Canada. British sociology was institutionally and intellectually intertwined with philosophy, history, and economics and often tied to concerns about social 'betterment.' In Canada, this influence extended into the 1930s, especially at Toronto. At other universities, chiefly Protestant denominational colleges, the British influence was less important than that of the Social Gospel, another import from abroad (the United States, Germany, and Britain). From the early 1920s, however, during the period of environmental adaptation, some Canadian sociologists began to draw on American mainstream sociology: first and most notably, the Chicago School (1920s–1950s); later, functionalism and the survey research tradition. During this three-decade-long phase, Hiller notes, American sociology gradually supplanted British and other European conceptions of the discipline and became more scientific and less oriented to social betterment. Simultaneously, it developed a larger presence in the universities, although it remained marginal. Few universities offered sociology programs and the number of trained sociologists in the system remained small. Only during the 1960s, Hiller's stage of disciplinary differentiation and specialization, did sociology become fully institutionalized as an autonomous and substantial academic discipline. By that time, it was modelled largely on its American counterpart.[2]

Porter came to Canada near the end of the environmental adaptation phase and, like many Canadian sociologists who had gone abroad for training, was forced to come to terms with American scientific sociology. Interestingly, even though he had been trained in Britain, where American sociology was regarded with great suspicion, Porter soon adopted many elements of U.S. practice and became ever more embedded within the network of American sociology. Yet he did not abandon his New Liberal first principles. Though he pushed the Canadian discipline in the direction of American practice, he retained core aspects of New Liberal sociology. This created substantial tension not only within his own approach but also between his approach and other perspectives that became influential in the discipline during the 1960s and '70s.

One way of understanding these tensions is to locate Porter's work in terms of a second, intellectual, triangle. His theoretical and methodological approach is simultaneously scientific, philosophical, and in a very particular sense, practical.

In theoretical terms, Porter employed an eclectic approach that, from the 1950s to the mid-1970s, drew heavily on American perspectives (modernization theory, postindustrialism, and the end-of-ideology thesis) but was larded thoroughly with aspects of classical European theory (Freud, Durkheim, Weber, and the elite theorists) and, less obviously, the New Liberalism. As the 1970s wore on, however, he came increasingly under the influence of the new political economy, a made-in-Canada approach that incorporated staples theory, Marxism, theories of underdevelopment, and social democratic rather than liberal political philosophy. Porter's interweaving of elements from mainstream, liberal sociology and radical scholarship created some theoretical/philosophical tensions in his work, which were then augmented by complications that grew out of his choice of methodological approaches. At the time, many in the Canadian social science community, especially on the left, were nationalists who regarded scientific sociology as an instance of cultural imperialism. For them, 'science' as practised in North American sociology at the time was a euphemism for 'American.' But Porter was not an academic nationalist and rejected this negative view. Indeed, he held up the American survey research tradition and its scientific methodology as a standard of excellence to which the Canadian sociological community should aspire. To make the situation even more complex, he mixed into this essentially American mainstream methodological approach some core elements of British New

Liberalism, including, as I note in detail below, a rather unusual conception of sociology as a science.

Despite appearances, then, Porter's approach was highly unconventional, a complex theoretical-methodological amalgam, largely but not entirely congruent with mainstream, scientific sociology. Certainly, it is not easy to place it in one of the slots normally used to pigeonhole sociologists and their scholarly writing. The tension is most apparent where the corners of the second triangle meet: philosophy, science, and political practice. For much of his career Porter used an apparently conventional, American-style scientific sociological approach. However, it was always – or almost always – undergirded by New Liberal views about politics and methodology that differentiated it from mainstream sociology. Graham Knight, one of Porter's PhD students, recalls that when he came from England to do his graduate work at Carleton, he was struck by this rather unusual aspect of Porter's perspective. By contrast with the University of Kent, Knight said, he found the atmosphere at Carleton very 'American,' that is, 'professional' and 'quantitative.' In this environment, according to Knight, Porter stood out. Though his work was highly quantitative, he remained ambivalent about American sociology. There was no doubt he had a foot in the American camp, but he seemed a Fabian, by which Knight meant Porter had a strong sense of the *ethical* mission of sociology, especially vis-à-vis issues of class abatement. As well, Porter seemed more 'complex' than a typical 'professional sociologist.' He had a 'good, objective, scientific mind,' but 'seemed much more of an *intellectual*,' and Knight found this appealing.[3]

Part of the complexity of Porter's intellectual approach grew naturally from an inherent duality in New Liberalism, which is both a political perspective and a scholarly orientation. In political terms, it was a radical, interventionist form of liberal doctrine, referred to by Leonard Hobhouse as 'liberal socialism.' Introduced in Canada at the conclusion of the nineteenth century, it became increasingly influential in Canadian politics during the interwar period before becoming central, if not hegemonic, during the reconstruction era following World War II. In scholarly terms, New Liberal sociology distinguishes itself from mainstream sociology because it involves the adoption of a value-laden approach to intellectual activity. The social scientist is not a politically disinterested professional expert – the mainstream American conception of the sociologist – but an engaged, practical intellectual who should not, indeed can not, be morally neutral.[4] He or she is obliged by a sense of moral obligation or duty to work in the service of society by pursuing a liberal mission: specifically, by identifying an absolute standard of social progress, an objective conception of the collective social good, and working to realize that democratic goal in very practical, applied ways. This creates tension, if not a contradiction, in Porter's work. A proponent of American scientific sociology, his New Liberal sympathies forced him to reject the principle of value neutrality central to that approach. But he could do nothing else, for his sense of moral purpose was crucial to him. It provided the impetus for his research and gave personal meaning to his life's work, including his efforts at practical social reform.

A few words are in order regarding Porter's reformism and sense of moral purpose. To begin, I want to make it clear that his value commitment was not rooted in religious beliefs. There is a long history of religion-based movements of social and moral reformism in Canadian intellectual circles, many of which advocated the adoption of political values – equality, freedom, justice, and so forth – just like those cherished by Porter.[5] As well, in their pursuit of progressive ends, religious reformers often employed empirical, social scientific means similar to Porter's. The use of the social survey by Social Gospellers in the early twentieth century is a good example. There is even some similarity between the religious conception of the activist social reformer – think of J.S. Woodsworth – and the notion of the engaged, practical New Liberal intellectual. But as I mentioned in chapter 2, Porter was not a religious man. Indeed, he was an adamant atheist and his reformism was rooted entirely in secular, liberal conceptions of the good and of progress tied to notions such as equality, inclusiveness, justice, and democracy, operationalized in terms of citizenship rights. While Canadian secular reformism is a river fed by many streams dating back to the nineteenth century, and there is no doubt that Porter came under the influence of more than one such doctrine – Fabianism, Tawney's ethical socialism, the Marxism of Harold Laski, the general humanism of the Enlightenment as manifested in 'reconstructionist' sensibilities after World War II – the most important wellspring of reformist ideas for him was the New Liberalism.[6]

British New Liberalism: Sociology and the Engaged, Practical Intellectual, 1880–1930

The New Liberalism had its roots in England in the last years of the nineteenth century and the first years of the twentieth.[7] It was in part a challenge to the classical liberalism of the eighteenth century and in part a development from it. According to classical liberals, humans were by nature intelligent and adaptable. This made progress possible. As well, they were 'rational,' self-interested calculators of pleasure and pain who possessed a natural propensity to 'truck, barter, and exchange.'[8] Humans were also seekers after power with an insatiable desire to satisfy a set of emergent and ever-escalating needs. Bearing this conception of human nature in mind, classical liberals argued that society should be set up according to the doctrines of utilitarianism and laissez-faire. Utilitarianism, the greatest good for the greatest number, would be achieved by giving individuals a framework of legal rights, mostly to do with property. They would then compete as equals in an open, competitive marketplace, determining their own best interests (calculating pleasure and pain according to their own metric) and pursuing them as they saw fit. As they did so, they would simultaneously maximize their own happiness and unintentionally contribute (via the workings of the 'invisible hand') to the net maximization of happiness in society as a whole. The role of the laissez-faire state under this new social contract would be minimal; it would guarantee rights, enforce contracts, and carry out a small number of endeavours (such as building infrastructure and maintaining domestic and international security) that were not properly left to the market.

By the end of the nineteenth century, the historical record showed that the system did not work as the theory said it would. The list of problems was long. Many firms grew enormous and came to control massive resources, dominating entire sectors of the market and setting prices rather than taking what the market determined. In negotiations over wages and conditions of labour, firms and individual workers did not bargain as equals in anything other than a formal, legal sense. Capital held most of the cards. As well, capital internationalized its operations, moving production facilities to Third World countries where they hired cheap labour, further disadvantaging workers in the domestic labour market, for labour was not equally mobile. Finally, the highly unequal rewards that characterized capitalist economies created huge and long-standing inequalities of income and wealth. And, as the law allowed the intergenerational transfer of assets via inheritance, the privileges of wealth accumulated over time. People from affluent backgrounds entered the allegedly free and equal marketplace with overwhelming advantages.

Clearly, in the harsh struggle of the capitalist marketplace, the guarantee of equal legal rights would never create a truly free, equal, just, and rational society. Understanding this, progressive intellectuals and social reformers – Fabians, Christian socialists, Marxists, 'single taxers,' and the like – became increasingly vocal in their challenges to the wisdom and justice of classical liberal political economy. Many proposed changes, often quite radical. Among these critics was a cadre of liberal theorists including John Stuart Mill, John Hobson, Graham Wallas, and Leonard Hobhouse. Beginning in the second half of the nineteenth century, they developed what came to be known as radicalism or New Liberalism.

The New Liberals argued that it was necessary to reconceptualize basic principles such as equality, freedom, rights, and universality to make society more inclusive, rational, and egalitarian; in short, more truly liberal. They had no thought of doing away with the marketplace, private property, rights of contract, and so forth – they regarded them as 'progressive elements of the "individualistic society"'[9] and wanted to preserve them – but believed that laissez-faire capitalism had failed. Liberal principles could be realized in practice only if some of the rights and privileges of private property were reconstituted and a much more powerful interventionist – or 'positive' – state put into place. As Dennis and Halsey point out in English Ethical Socialism, far from being the foe of liberty, the state was regarded by Hobhouse and the New Liberals as 'one of the principal means of securing it.'[10] Only a strong positive state, they said, could constitute a means of collective or societal 'self-determination' sufficiently powerful to 'place economic laws under ethics.' In reframing their view of the state, the New Liberals denied any great discontinuity between their perspective and the classical doctrine, arguing that much of the new credo was actually immanent in the old; indeed, they saw themselves as completing leading liberal ideas rather than destroying them.[11]

Their description of New Liberalism was often phrased in the language of socialism. The writings of Leonard Hobhouse furnish a good example. He referred to his perspective as 'liberal socialism' and argued that the mixing of liberalism and socialism – individual rights and the market combined with increased state intervention and collectivism – was natural, practical, and necessary.[12] Social circumstances had changed and liberalism had to adjust. 'The ideas of Socialism,' he wrote, 'coincide with ideas to which Liberals are led when they seek to apply their principles of Liberty, Equality and the Common Good to the industrial life of our time.'[13] This combination of liberalism and socialism with the interventionist state at its core was, they said, the only way to free the possibilities of liberalism from the 'crippling class integument' that prevented it from realizing its full potential.[14]

The doctrine that New Liberals produced, which combined progressive impulses from various doctrines that inhabited the British left of the time – Fabianism, ethical socialism, guild socialism, the labour movement, and others – differed from classical liberalism on several counts.

First, the New Liberals held a different conception of human nature. Rather than take the utilitarian view of humans as naturally inert and reluctant to work (labour as pain), they claimed that people needed and wanted to express themselves through creative activity, including work (labour as pleasure). Likewise, they argued that people did not by nature possess insatiable, ever-escalating needs and did not desire ever greater amounts of power. They had come to be this way as a result of living in a market society. Once society had produced the possibility of a reasonable standard of living for everyone, they said, then the utilitarians' crippled and limited sense of human nature could be jettisoned. In turn, this would cast a new light on debates over human rights (including property rights and the right to work), the role of the positive state, the nature and possibility of progress, and so on.

Second, they argued that it was necessary to address what was referred to at the time as 'the social problem,' actually a clutch of interrelated problems – poverty, crime, poor housing, widespread unemployment – caused by the workings of the market. For society to be made more equal, especially in terms of equality of opportunity, reforms were necessary. By its own logic, they claimed, the marketplace created so much inequality of condition (via unequal rewards) that many citizens had only legal, rather than real, equality of opportunity. The so-called 'negative' rights and freedoms granted to citizens in the classical liberal model were a necessary but insufficient condition for the realization of the good society.[15] People should also be given a set of 'positive' citizenship rights that would create much more equality of opportunity.

Third, the New Liberals challenged the classical atomistic view that society was nothing more than an agglomeration of individuals and the related idea that the collective interest was nothing more than the sum of the interests of individual citizens. As John Allett notes, Jeremy Bentham and Adam Smith had claimed that 'the general happiness was merely the ... aggregate of each individual's happiness.' Hobhouse and

Hobson rejected this view. Society, they said, was an emergent 'organic' or 'harmonic' entity, a whole greater than the sum of its parts. Invoking the notion of the common good, they argued that the greatest happiness was both different from and greater than the sum of the separate and several happinesses of the individual members of society.[16] This notion, the common good, came to constitute the cornerstone of the New Liberal view of society and social progress more generally.[17] As Hobhouse put it, 'the mere reform of machinery,' i.e., the reorganization of the industrial system, would be 'worthless' unless accompanied by 'a change of spirit and feeling, ... a feeling for the common good, a readiness to forego personal advantage for the general gain, a recognition of mutual dependence.'[18] The New Liberals acknowledged that the concept of the common good limited individual rights, but in their estimation, individual rights *had* to be defined in terms of the common good. Put another way, individual rights had to contribute to the common good. At the same time, however, the concept of individual rights was broadened and reconstituted rather than diminished. In Hobhouse's words, liberty was 'not so much a right of the individual as a necessity of society.'[19] The introduction of the notion of the common good required, among other things, a reconceptualization of property rights. According to Hobson and Hobhouse, production was a cooperative enterprise that gave rise to societal property rights separate from and in addition to individual property rights. When people worked cooperatively in society their joint product was greater than what their separate and several efforts could have produced. This surplus, an economic reflection of the organic character of society, constituted what Hobson referred to as 'organic surplus value,' a form of public property that could be appropriated by the positive state for societal purposes.[20]

These two concepts – organic surplus value and public property rights – were central to the fourth way in which the New Liberals differed from their forebears. Classical liberals had argued that since all individuals had the same legal rights in the marketplace, they could reasonably be held accountable for their life situations, however dismal. Thus was poverty defined as a personal rather than a social problem. Seldom should the state redistribute wealth to help those in need.[21] New Liberals disagreed. They regarded poverty, like unemployment, as societal in origin, 'a national industrial disease requiring a national industrial remedy.'[22] The positive state had the right and duty to redistribute wealth to solve this and other problems, in this way promoting the *social* interest directly.[23] Anticipating John Maynard Keynes, Hobson in particular argued that the state should manage the economy, in part by using societal monetary resources (taxes on unearned income, for example) to help solve the problem of underconsumption that plagued capitalist economies and from time to time led to recessions and depressions.[24] This necessitated not only the distinction between *private* property and *societal* property described above but also the development of a social system that would simultaneously allow individuals to use their private property to develop their personal potential while allowing the state to 'interfere' with private property 'in the interests of the community.'[25] Private property was 'essential to the individual,' according to Hobhouse, and had to be protected. Equally important, however, was 'common property,' necessary for 'the expression and development of *social* life.'[26] Keynes later refined and expanded this and related aspects of Hobson's work greatly, combining them with his own ideas and publishing them as *A General Theory of Employment, Interest and Money*, one of the most influential books of the twentieth century.[27] In it, Keynes argued that the state could use fiscal and monetary policy as well as its collective resources to manage the economy and mitigate, if not prevent, the worst effects of the cyclical downturns to which modern capitalist economies seemed susceptible.

One aspect of managing the economy in the interest of the common good was to guarantee that all people enjoyed a basic standard of living. The New Liberals did not believe in a complete levelling of rewards, but they did push for basic standards that would ensure a healthy life: a minimum wage, adequate housing, and social assistance for those who were sick, old, unemployed, and the like.[28] Moreover, they insisted that these benefits be seen not as a dole but as part of a citizen's rights as a human being. 'Provision for the old age of the workman is not so much a matter of benevolence,' said Hobhouse, 'as of justice.'[29] As time passed, they extended the principle that the state had a duty to defend the freedom and interests of the disadvantaged very far indeed. Note, for example, Hobhouse's claim about relations between capitalists and workers: 'Freedom of choice is in all contracts a variable quantity … [W]here a whole class of men is permanently at a disadvantage in its bargains with another, for example, where one class is economically weaker, … the State has a right to intervene as arbitrator.'[30]

On a related point, the New Liberals argued that the positive state had a responsibility to maximize equality of opportunity. In keeping with their critique of the concept of negative rights, they argued that liberty could no longer mean 'the absence of restraint.' Instead, it had to mean 'the presence of opportunity.'[31] The positive state, said Herbert Samuel, was 'to provide the fullest opportunities for every person,' for only then would each citizen be able 'to attain the best and amplest development of his life.'[32] This was of utmost importance to Hobhouse who, following Aristotle, argued that only in this way could individuals learn to exercise 'rational self-control,' which would in turn allow them to promote the welfare of others from 'a sense of inner commitment.'[33] Thus would ideal citizens create and be created by an ideal community.[34] The crucial means to this end, and one of John Porter's interests throughout his career, was the extension of public education.[35]

Two additional principles completed the roster of New Liberal ideas: their view of progress and its relationship to intellectual activity, sociology in particular. Both had a great influence on John Porter. For the New Liberals, a rethinking of liberal philosophy and the establishment of the positive state would facilitate societal progress, which, by their reckoning, had stalled in the late nineteenth century. Hobhouse's view on the issue was typical. For him, progress was not just possible but probable.[36] The term he used to describe societal change in the direction of social improvement was 'orthogenic evolution,' that is, 'the gradual replacement of instinct by reason ... [bringing] all the experience of the race to bear in organizing the whole life of the race.'[37] The reference to evolution was intentional; much New Liberal thinking developed in a debate with Herbert Spencer's social Darwinism. For New Liberals, evolution in the Darwinian sense did not constitute progress; it was simply random variation in response to a changing natural environment. Evolution influenced all creatures but, according to Hobhouse and his colleagues, humans were unique in that they were capable of *orthogenic* evolution: they could use individual and collective reason to develop an increased societal self-consciousness or intelligence that they could then use to *suppress* 'the struggle for existence,' and substitute 'social cooperation' in its place.[38] Rational collective control of that struggle and the implementation of a morally just, cooperative, altruistic, and efficient social order – that is, the application of 'humanitarian principles to political affairs' – would provide the conditions necessary for the realization of individual and collective self-development: progress.[39]

The New Liberal Engaged and Practical Intellectual

The source of the societal intelligence that would inform or create social progress was social science, in particular, an historically specific New

Liberal conception of sociology.[40] Just as an individual could develop rational self-understanding and use this knowledge to put himself or herself under rational self-control, society could use sociology to develop a collective self-understanding that would allow people to set society aright.[41] In this regard, Hobhouse considered sociology to be a 'systematization of Humanity's self-consciousness' that included both sufficient social scientific knowledge to allow the best possible 'scientific adjustment of ... man to man' and a rational ethics, a set of objective moral principles that would, as Collini notes, provide a 'guarantee of right conduct.'[42]

It perhaps goes without saying, given this conflation of science and morals, that the New Liberal framing of sociology as scientific does not readily match up to any modern conception of the term. As Hobhouse scholar John Owen has pointed out, Hobhouse's sociology incorporates both rational humanitarianism and rational empiricism.[43] As rational humanitarians, Owen says, the New Liberals wanted to put value questions, especially issues of social justice, under careful logical and empirical scrutiny with the goal of identifying a set of objectively good moral principles and societal best practices. Clearly, modern sociologists would regard such an endeavour as non-scientific moralizing and philosophical speculation. As well, Owen says, Hobhouse wanted to combine the insights of the rationalist philosopher with those of the empiricist. The former would use a broadly conceived reason rather than 'just' science in the examination of social phenomena, whereas the latter would look to the facts of experience, again defined more broadly than science allows, for empirical data and theoretical generalizations.[44] Again, in adopting such a position, Hobhouse proclaimed himself an empiricist on grounds that would be unacceptable to present-day scientists.

Nor did the New Liberals adopt the standard scientific position on value neutrality. Properly practised, they argued, sociology is intrinsically and unavoidably moral, its purpose to identify and work toward 'the good.' As Hobhouse put it, 'We must have a philosophically thought-out standard of value, as a test by which we can appraise the different stages of evolution. In that sense ... ethics is necessary to sociology.'[45] Dennis and Halsey point out that Hobhouse believed it possible to identify 'a reasoned ethical basis for political reform.'[46] He regarded it as a 'duty' for the 'man or woman of reason' to act on those convictions:

> Because no one can be certain he is right, it does not follow that everybody's version of the empirical world is just as true as everybody else's,

and one ethical code just as valid as any other ... 'The duty of having convictions is correlative and supplementary to the duty of tolerance and openmindedness.'[47]

They believed, then, that there existed a set of objectively good moral criteria toward which sociology should work: the rational application of the principles of freedom, tempered with altruism and universal humanitarianism, would lead to cooperation, a sense of community, and social harmony. For his part, Hobhouse, the New Liberal who influenced Porter most, talked about four objective moral criteria of progress or measures of the good: scale, efficiency, freedom, and mutuality. These constituted, Hobhouse said, the basis of a 'rational ethics.'[48] By scale or scope, Hobhouse meant the size and extent of the community; the more people covered by the principles of rational ethics, the better. By efficiency, he meant the degree to which the community was able to meet its common goals, however they defined them at any given time, while bearing in mind the existence of an objectively real common good. At the heart of the common good were freedom and mutuality. By freedom, Hobhouse meant 'scope for thought, character and initiative on the part of members of the community,' and by mutuality he meant 'service of an end in which each who serves participates.'[49] This conception of the social good incorporated the ideas of freedom and restraint, individual rights, and community needs. Society could be judged as good only if 'the manifold social qualities of man [could] develop in harmony.' Any 'restraints' involved would have to be voluntary and self-imposed.[50] In sum:

> The most developed community would be that which effectively achieve[d] the most complete synthesis of the widest range of human activity, including within its membership the largest number of human beings, but in such wise as to rest most completely upon their free cooperation thus expressing the whole of their vital energies as far as these are capable of working together in harmony.[51]

Clearly, the New Liberal concept of sociology was very different from current versions. Rather than viewing sociology as an academic discipline, profession, or positivist social science, they regarded it as a vocation, a life's orientation that was really a duty and a calling, a mission.[52] It combined a form of moral, rational, and empirical understanding with a commitment to transformative practice; the sociologist could identify and should work toward a collective rationality and a sense of societal mutuality under the guidance of principles of universal humanitarianism and social justice. John Porter was deeply influenced by these New Liberal ideas, probably to a degree greater than other English-language Canadian sociologists of his era. But he did not introduce such ideas into Canadian sociology or Canadian social science more broadly. By the time Porter arrived in Ottawa in 1949, the doctrine had a long history in this country.

The New Liberalism in Canadian Academia and Politics, 1890s–1950s

Historians Barry Ferguson, A.B. McKillop, J.L. Granatstein, Ramsay Cook, and Doug Owram have shown that Canadian intellectuals, especially economists, drew ever more frequently on New Liberal ideas between the 1890s and the 1960s.[53] The developments occurred in three phases: pre–World War I, the interwar years, and World War II and the postwar reconstruction era.[54] During this seventy-year period, Owram argues, most Canadians came to share the notion that the positive state was a good thing: 'Nothing marked the first half of the twentieth century so much as this change in the nature and role of the state ... If the "rugged individualism" of Canada ... trumpeted about in Laurier's time had ever been a part of Canadian society, it was certainly replaced by a more complex web of government support systems by the end of the Second World War.'[55] This changed view of the positive state was accompanied by, indeed partly dependent on, a related change in the conception of intellectual practice, a good deal of which took its inspiration from the New Liberal conception of the engaged, practical intellectual. This latter shift, which occurred only slowly and against sustained scholarly resistance, involved a double transformation, i.e., a reconceptualization of the relationship between the university and society, and more particularly, a rethinking of the relationship between social scientists and politics, broadly defined. John Porter's place in the history of Canadian sociology is best understood when located in the context of this slow, halting and incomplete shift to an historically specific New Liberal conception of the role of the intellectual.

The first thing to note in undertaking this analysis is that the New Liberalism entered the mainstream of Canadian society and Canadian social science via political economy and economics, not sociology. So it is with the history of political economy that the story properly begins.

Before World War I

In *Remaking Liberalism,* Barry Ferguson argues that the earliest scholarly manifestations of the New Liberalism appeared in Canada during the 1890s in the writing and practical activities of well-known Queen's University political economist Adam Shortt. Shortt's successors at Queen's – O.D. Skelton, W.A. Mackintosh, and W. Clifford Clark – picked up where he left off. Over the first three decades of the twentieth century, Ferguson says, their writing and applied work in the federal civil service did much to provide the philosophical underpinnings and practical impetus for the establishment of the interventionist welfare state. Ferguson acknowledges that many other sources of social and moral reform, religious and secular, contributed to this development but maintains that New Liberalism was just as central to the process as the three other influences that Canadian scholars have generally identified as most important in the formation of the positive state: the Christian idealist philosophy of T.H. Green (as articulated by John Watson at Queen's), the Social Gospel and other forms of social Christianity or social evangelism (as espoused by the Protestant churches), and Fabianism (as advocated by the League for Social Reconstruction).[56]

The founding of the positive state did not occur in a vacuum. Between 1890 and 1930 a combination of economic, social, and political changes – industrialization, large-scale immigration, urbanization, World War I, the growth of scientific knowledge – transformed the nation and in concert with scholarly factors forced Canadian universities, and the discipline of political economy in particular, to reorient themselves.

Owram notes in *The Government Generation* that for much of the nineteenth century English-language universities had merged the classroom and the pulpit in an effort to preserve the status quo by producing cultured gentlemen, comfortable with the truth of God's word as revealed in the Bible.[57] The curriculum designed to achieve this goal included the physical sciences, classical political economy, Christian idealist moral philosophy, and theology.[58] The scientific and religious aspects of the curriculum were seen to be 'perfectly complementary' because the findings of science were thought to provide evidence of providential design.[59] However, the appearance in 1859 of Charles Darwin's *On the Origin of Species* threw a spanner in the works. Combined with the influence of the so-called higher criticism (philosophical and historical investigations of the authenticity of the Bible), Darwin's findings produced an era of intellectual uncertainty in much of English Canada and, according to some scholars, helped to precipitate a 'crisis of belief' among Protestants.[60]

In *The Regenerators*, Ramsay Cook notes that in their attempts to deal with this uncertainty some Protestant churches modified their doctrines in a way that, ironically, contributed to the secularization they were trying to fight. Rather than trying to defend orthodox theology regarding the absolute truth of the Bible, they opted for a 'modernist' liberal theology, a 'social gospel' focused on criticizing social inequalities and injustices and geared to 'social regeneration.' Their purpose was to make religion immediately relevant in the real world. Rather than focusing on personal salvation and life in the hereafter, they tried to keep believers in the fold by making the church a force for the creation of the kingdom of heaven on Earth. Their hope was that, if successful, they could stem the tide of secularization. The opposite occurred. By the time they were done, Cook claims, those who opted for modern liberal theology had turned Protestantism into 'a mere sociological instead of a religious doctrine,' replaced 'the kingdom of God on Earth' with 'the secular city,' and transformed the Christian social reformer into a 'secular social worker.'[61]

Darwin's work and the fallout from the crisis of belief had a huge impact in the universities as well. In English Canada, the religious aspects of the curriculum came under intense scrutiny and criticism. Slowly, science assumed pride of place. The shift was especially consequential in political economy, which during the nineteenth century had held it as self-evident that society, including the economy, was ruled by providential design. The elements of classical economics – the free market, the minimalist state, the laws of supply and demand – were, so it went, part of God's plan: immutable, divinely ordained pieces of a 'Christian political economy.' 'The laws of production and distribution of wealth,' wrote Goldwyn Smith, 'are the most beautiful and wonderful of the natural laws of God.'[62] The New Liberals, many of whom were influenced by modernist liberal theology, found this idea appalling. They shared the view that 'a Christian God would ... have devised a Christian political economy,' but argued that it would challenge rather than justify the injustices of capitalism that Smith regarded as natural, inevitable, and godly.[63] And while not all were followers of Henry George's *Progress and Poverty*, they all agreed with his argument, as framed by Cook, that 'social and economic arrangements were not forever sanctioned by divine or scientific laws beyond the power of man to change' but rather were entirely subject to human control.[64] Social salvation was possible. The means for attaining it included the empirical study of social conditions tied to a Christian ethic of sharing, a progressive program of social work, and state intervention in the economy.[65]

The new interventionist philosophy of the nature and role of the state arrived hitched in tandem to a new conception of the place of the academic in social and political affairs. Previously, professors had for the most part stayed behind the walls of the university community. If they commented on practical affairs, they usually interpreted them in terms of Christian morality and laissez-faire political economy. The best solution to the social problems attendant industrialization, they intoned, was the moral betterment of the individual: 'Moral guidance, not social scientific assessment, was ... the key to a better world.'[66] At the time, political economy was not regarded as a scientific discipline, and politicians consulted political economists only infrequently because they were not seen as appropriate sources of technical advice.[67] This changed toward the end of the nineteenth century. At Queen's, Shortt and Skelton, chafing under the extant ivory tower conception of their discipline, tried to promote political economy as a science. In their view, human society was ruled not by God's will, but by statistical probability, and they began to advocate in favour of a more professional and activist role for the scholar, one not based on Christian beliefs.[68] As might be expected, they experienced little early success in this endeavour. Not until after World War I did they make significant headway. World War I was pivotal to substantiating their claim because during the hostilities notions of community and common purpose, specifically as expressed in an acceptance of the idea that government should play a greater role in society, grew in popularity and importance. Many people had reservations about the cost to democracy of the growth of statism, but the importance of the task at hand swept aside their concerns. Indeed, before too long the federal government had instituted a business profits tax and income tax, nationalized two Canadian railways, begun to provide veterans' benefits, and invoked conscription and rationing, among other measures. As World War I drew to a close, then, Canada 'no longer even pretended to be a true laissez-faire state.'[69]

Note, again, that most of the influence of New Liberalism took place *outside* the universities. Academic sociology, which had only the most modest presence in English-language Canadian universities, remained largely inconsequential in these developments. Other than the events at Queen's, few developments took place except at a handful of Protestant

Church colleges such as Acadia, McMaster, Wesley College, and Mount Allison where the influence of the Social Gospel was strong.[70] And even in these venues, sociology remained a teaching subject. Research was not a priority and the political impact of lectures was probably minimal outside the classroom. The small amount of research carried out at this time was undertaken not by professors but by Social Gospellers operating outside the universities. Good examples are Herbert Brown Ames' *The City below the Hill*, J.S. Woodsworth's *My Neighbor* and *Strangers within Our Gates*, and social surveys such as those carried out by the Methodist and Presbyterian churches of Canada.[71]

Between the Wars

During the interwar years, New Liberal ideas gained stature only slowly, sometimes because of and sometimes, ironically enough, in spite of the ascension to power of Mackenzie King's Liberal Party. In *The Government Generation*, a study of intellectuals and the Canadian state from 1900 to 1945, Doug Owram argues, in concert with Ferguson and against Nancy Christie and Michael Gauvreau, that while some social scientists continued to cling to earlier idealist or religious conceptions of reform as a 'social passion' (the Social Gospel), the idea of a form of purely secular, ameliorative social science grew in popularity and influence.[72] The new social scientists treated social problems as societal rather than personal in origin and in need of secular rather than religious solutions. Economists in particular built the case that they were scientific experts able to solve such problems. Along with civil service mandarins and federal politicians, they came to agree on the essentials of an eclectic 'intellectual liberalism' – not yet tied to particular political party – that provided a moral and philosophical justification for the practical necessity of a managerialist, interventionist state.[73]

Among the factors that led to their success were the efforts of two scholars at Toronto. Joining Skelton and the new political economists at Queen's in their advocacy of New Liberal politics and scholarship were Robert MacIver and E.J. Urwick. MacIver, a political philosopher and sociologist, came to Toronto from Scotland to serve as head of the Department of Political Science in 1915, remaining in that post until 1927. He was succeeded by Urwick, who occupied the headship for a decade.[74] A.B. McKillop notes that MacIver had been central to the development of the New Liberalism in England and became equally important to the spread of such ideas in Canada.[75] In fact, according to Owram, while in Toronto, MacIver developed 'the most complete expression' of the new philosophy of the interventionist (or 'service') state yet to emerge from the Canadian academic community – *The Modern State*.[76] There, and more especially in *Elements of Social Science*, writes McKillop, he promoted a New Liberal conception of sociology. For MacIver, as for Hobhouse, sociology was an 'architectonic' or transcendent endeavour, part social philosophy and part science, which subsumed many of the other social science disciplines.[77] Its purpose was not just to measure but also to understand. 'There are things we cannot measure,' MacIver wrote, '[but whose] meaning is perfectly clear to us.'[78] Likewise, and here he challenged the American conception of sociology as a science, he argued that the discipline was intrinsically ethical.[79] And he tied his conception of the place of values in sociology to a New Liberal view of the practical utility of the discipline. Simple populism would not provide wise direction to government; this was best left to experts.[80] An interventionist state enlightened by social scientists constituted the best means to allow humans to realize their collective moral purpose: the creation of a just and progressive 'community.'[81] Deeply involved in social service and community work during his time in Toronto, MacIver taught in the Department of Social Service, worked with the Workers' Educational Association, and wrote as a 'champion of labour.' In 1919, he published *Labour in the Changing World*, which proposed a series of New Liberal pro-labour measures including a guaranteed minimum wage, decent workplace health and safety standards, unemployment insurance, and worker–management joint boards of control for industry.[82]

E.J. Urwick, also a political and social philosopher, came to Toronto from the LSE. He held a conception of the discipline in some respects quite similar to that of his predecessor and, like him, was greatly concerned with social service.[83] Indeed, according to McKillop and S.D. Clark, this social service orientation provided some of the impetus for the establishment of sociology at Toronto.[84]

As in the pre-war era, interventionist economists experienced much more success in the civil service than in the university. Many of the economist civil servants who advocated interventionist measures – Skelton, Mackintosh, W.C. Clark – began their careers in the university before moving into the federal civil service. Once there, they used their influence as government advisers to spread the wisdom of Keynesian economics and the interventionist state.[85] This group, referred to by Owram as Canada's 'reform elite,' comprised early members of

J.L. Granatstein's 'mandarinate,' a set of well-connected, progressive, secular, and highly educated individuals who shared interventionist views and the belief that the university had a key role to play in public affairs.[86] Building on advances made during World War I and the Depression, by the mid-1930s they had reached the inner councils of government and the civil service. Economists in particular became influential and by the time World War II broke out, economics had replaced religion as 'the keystone by which the intellectual community communicated with politicians and the public alike.'[87]

Until then, the Canadian public remained sceptical of interventionism and most economists espoused the wisdom of Alfred Marshall's neo-classical theory of equilibrium economics.[88] According to Granatstein, that would have remained the status quo if not for the efforts of the New Liberals who pushed the Liberal Party in an interventionist direction. 'Compare the Mackenzie King government of the 1920s to that of the war and postwar years,' he says. 'The first was cautious and careful, a small government devoted to laissez-faire. The second ... was the creator of a wartime government that was interventionist, centralist, forceful in social measures and on the world stage. What had changed? The times and the advisers.'[89]

The interventionist measures advocated by the newly influential mandarins had two purposes. First, most were economists, and they took it as a professional challenge to try to use their technical skills and practical reasoning to make the economy run smoothly. Second, and above all, they wanted to prevent another Depression. Drawing increasingly on Keynes, they applied a set of principles and practices that Granatstein refers to as 'free-enterprise Keynesianism' to promote economic well-being and efficiency while simultaneously achieving broad moral goals such as individual fulfilment and social justice, in particular 'the more equitable distribution of economic rewards and opportunities.'[90]

In combining these two types of logic – practical, technical, and expedient on the one hand, moral and humane on the other – the 'Queensmen' were advocating a novel, specifically New Liberal conception of the proper role of the social scientist. They claimed not to want to politicize the university or to become a scholarly political vanguard for any particular class in Canadian society, but Ferguson points out they did hold the view that they had both a mandate and an obligation to create a more just, rational, and broadly democratic society.[91] They saw themselves as experts engaged in a morally charged social scientific 'mission' intended 'to solve general problems and ... preserve democracy and capitalism through a commitment to justice as well as efficiency.'[92] And, as Owram stresses, unlike their religiously oriented nineteenth-century predecessors, they had come to define social well-being in terms of 'material standards of living' rather than in 'spiritual or moral terms.'[93]

According to Ferguson, this rethinking of the nature and purpose of political economy entailed a further redefinition of the political role of the university and the scholar. The university was to become a site of independent empirical investigation, theoretical analysis, and political discussion, the ultimate purpose of which was to shape the understanding of economic and social questions held by business, government, and the Canadian population at large. The university was to provide direction and the social scientist, in particular the political economist, would assume new power and status. As experts and professionals with critical, reformist beliefs and in possession of 'exclusive knowledge,' Ferguson writes, they were to devote themselves to public service, which, according to Granatstein, they saw not just as a 'duty' and a 'virtue' but a 'privilege.'[94] For the mandarinate, says Granatstein, public service had two aspects. They had a 'duty ... to serve the government of the day to the best of [their] ability, to provide ideas, advice, and the competent administration of policies that the government passed into law.'[95] As well, however, they had an obligation to serve the Canadian population by helping to preside over the 'humanization of capitalism.'[96]

On the first count, they were highly successful; generations of progressive liberal scholar/civil servants acted as 'intellectual garage-mechanics of Canadian capitalism,' providing eminently liberal 'practical' solutions to social and economic problems for a series of Liberal administrations.[97] But as I noted above, they saw themselves as more than liberal technocrats. Like their British progenitors Hobson, Hobhouse, and Wallas, and like Canadian pioneers of the New Liberalism such as Shortt, MacIver, and Urwick, the mid-century mandarins saw themselves as serving their country by developing a systematic and comprehensive moral critique of laissez-faire capitalism that would help provide humane, practical solutions to its most pressing problems.

They accomplished the latter goal in a way that reflected Canadian conditions. In England, advocates of New Liberalism had come from a variety of disciplinary backgrounds – sociology, philosophy, economics – and had often presented their arguments in a relatively abstract, philosophical form in specialized academic and lay journals. In Canada, by contrast, most New Liberals were economists who spread their views on Keynesianism and the welfare state through a series of policy and organizational measures that emanated from political organizations such as the League for Social Reconstruction and, more significantly, the offices of senior bureaucrats in Ottawa. So successful were they in this endeavour that, according to Owram at least, by the 1940s they were able to make the civil service the 'new pulpit' of the intelligentsia.[98] By contrast, little of this sort of thought emanated from the universities. As Porter pointed out in *The Vertical Mosaic*, influential individuals such as Harold Innis actually tried to dampen enthusiasm for the new interventionism. With many of his colleagues, Innis was leery of handing over too much power to a centralized state.[99] As well, with other traditional academics, he championed the long-held view that the university should remain oriented to pure, basic research. Truths would be slow to appear and he was sceptical about the wisdom of scholars trying to provide quick answers to policy questions. This was particularly the case when the 'science' in question was in a rudimentary state. Innis' final reservation was that such advice might be offered based on analysis that employed imported intellectual approaches not necessarily applicable in the Canadian context. Despite these misgivings and objections, and despite concerted efforts to curb the political activities of university-based intellectuals, many pressed ahead.[100]

For its part, sociology continued to play a minor role. The entire Canadian college and university community was small – between 2,500 and 3,000 faculty members in the 1930s – and the social science contingent numbered only about 150.[101] Fewer than twenty universities offered courses in sociology, and until well into the 1940s only about two dozen people taught the subject in English-language universities in any given year.[102] Few held appointments as sociologists. McGill was the first to establish an independent sociology department in 1925 and as late as 1939 its faculty complement remained at two: Carl A. Dawson and R.E.L. Faris.[103] At Toronto, the discipline remained under the umbrella of the Department of Political Economy and as late as 1939–40 had a teaching staff of four, none of whom had a PhD in sociology.[104] In fact, very little research has been done regarding the academic training and political beliefs of those who taught sociology during the pre–World War II era.[105] As far as we know, among them only Leonard Marsh seems to have been much influenced by the New Liberalism.

I noted above that Marsh was an LSE graduate who spent 1930–40 as research director of the large, Rockefeller-funded Social Science Research Project (SSRP) at McGill University. He is generally understood to have been a Fabian.[106] But he did not see himself as such; he recognized the influence of Fabianism on his work but described himself as equally influenced by New Liberals such as Hobhouse, Marshall, Tawney, and Keynes.[107] Their combined influence is apparent in *Canadians In and Out of Work* and *Social Planning for Canada*, both of which advocated a greatly increased role for the central state in managing the economy and providing social welfare, but most centrally in the *Report on Social Security for Canada*.[108] Marsh's report emerged out of his work in Ottawa as a member of King's Advisory Committee on Reconstruction and was based in part on a similar report prepared in England by Marsh's mentor, William Beveridge, in 1942.[109] Marsh's document advocated a series of measures (e.g., unemployment insurance, universal health care, old-age pensions) designed to humanize capitalism along New Liberal lines. Few of his recommendations were implemented in the 1940s, however, because King's Liberals ignored the report and then buried it.[110] Today it is regarded by many scholars as the basis of the modern welfare state in Canada.[111]

World War II and Postwar Reconstruction

It was not until the middle of World War II that New Liberal ideas began to come to full flower in Canada. As was the case a quarter-century earlier, war provided the impetus and the opportunity. The demands of the war effort caused or allowed Canadians to accept what they assumed would be a temporary enlargement of the role of government in their lives, and this precipitated a corresponding increase in the size and power of the federal civil service.[112] But even after wartime successes, it looked as if the interventionist trend might be stopped, in part because of King's reluctance to jettison classical liberalism.[113] An especially important stumbling block was C.D. Howe, who argued that intervention was unwise other than as a wartime strategy. Howe and his coterie of 'dollar-a-year' men, corporate executives Howe had seconded to manage Canada's economy during the war, were strongly averse to government interference in the peacetime economy. They wanted private enterprise to return to 'normal' operations as soon as possible.[114] But as historian William Kilbourn has argued, at the time, many people thought that the Great Depression had never really finished but had simply been absorbed into the war effort and would in peacetime return.[115] According to Scott Gordon, most Canadian and American economists had the same fear.[116] Various groups favouring interventionism pointed to the fact that the federal civil service and the government had done a good job of planning and managing during the war, and came to the conclusion that it made sense to continue it beyond the end of conflict.[117] In fact, according to Alvin Finkel, 'wartime surveys indicated that at least four in ten Canadians wanted extensive public ownership while twice that number wanted the federal government to institute a comprehensive national medical insurance plan.'[118] Clearly, a good portion of Canadians, including intellectuals, had 'abandoned earlier assumptions about rugged individualism in favour of greater state intervention.'[119]

Interventionist economists such as Mackintosh, Clark, Bryce, A.F.W. Plumptre, and Alex Skelton were deeply involved in this debate, of course, stressing the same themes and siding with the general populace against the proponents of laissez-faire. They did not use the term New Liberalism, but it certainly seems to have driven their collective enterprise. Seizing on the notion of 'reconstruction' as a fundamental rethinking and reconfiguring of the nature and role of the state, they argued, *contra* Howe, that it should not be defined narrowly as a brief postwar period of adjustment to business as usual. Rather, as Owram phrases it, they believed it should be taken as a permanent 'change from a traditional and outmoded laissez-faire capitalism to a new, more humane and more efficient era in which capitalism was subordinated to social needs.' The two most important means to this end were partly in place: a planned, mixed economy and a comprehensive program of social security measures that would achieve 'a high and stable level of national income' and boost public spending.[120] In their view, Keynesian economic theory had provided the technical capacity to manage the Canadian economy, and the war had been a 'practical laboratory of Keynesian theory.'[121] They had confidence that the newly reformed and enlarged civil service could oversee the appropriate measures.[122]

As well, they believed that they had solved the problems of objectivity and value neutrality which had bedevilled those who, during the first half of the century, wanted status as scientists along with the authority to make claims about the kinds of social policies that ought to be put into place. The British New Liberals had refused to adopt the principle of value freedom and declined to see their enterprise as scientific in the conventional sense of the term. MacIver and Urwick at

Toronto held a somewhat similar view. But the economists and political economists who institutionalized Keynesianism and other New Liberal ideas in Canada between the 1920s and the 1940s were not so inclined. As I noted above, most were economists who increasingly came to see economics as a science and themselves as scientific experts. Thus, it was difficult for them to reject the scientific principles of detachment and objectivity. Yet at the same time, many wished to transform Canadian society, to make it more egalitarian, just, rational, and democratic. They handled the issue of their engagement and advocacy by drawing on the ideology of professionalism that characterized mainstream economics at the time.[123] By this rendering, those who remained in the academy were autonomous intellectuals protected from government interference by the university. Those in the civil service saw themselves as sufficiently independent of business interests that they could engage themselves with broad social concerns without being constrained to offer narrowly technical or practical, business-friendly solutions to economic and social problems.[124] According to Owram, a model for many of them was O.D. Skelton, the scholar-turned-bureaucrat who believed that objective analysis and fact finding were the key tasks of the social scientist. One could work in either the university or the civil service, indeed move back and forth, without compromising the tenets of professionalism and detached involvement that went with interventionist academic beliefs and practices.[125]

This is not to say the New Liberals achieved all their goals after the war, or that, en masse, federal and provincial politicians conceded the proposition that civil service experts should plan and manage the economy. As Owram's account of the 1945–6 Dominion–Provincial Conference on Reconstruction makes clear, provincial governments were unwilling to modify the British North America Act to allow the federal government the kind of jurisdiction it needed to manage the economy in the way New Liberal economists preferred. As a consequence, says Owram, the positive state emerged in Canada 'not by means of a rational, efficient and bureaucratically dominated Dominion government but as a series of compromises between the demands of industrial society and the public on one hand and the realities of a federal constitution and regional divergence on the other.'[126]

Neither did the positive state emerge out of an abstract philosophical debate about liberal democracy among politicians, civil servants, academics, and citizens. To the degree that Canadian civil servants used the abstract principles of New Liberalism, it was not because they had decided to apply them after reading Mill or Green, Hobhouse or Hobson. Indeed, senior bureaucrats wanted to avoid philosophy and ideology and to fulfil their administrative goals by employing what they regarded as practical measures to solve day-to-day problems.[127]

Whatever the means by which the shift to the interventionist state occurred, a profound change had taken place in the relationship between the discipline of economics and the practices of government in less than fifty years. A half-century earlier, social scientists had been irrelevant to the planning and implementation of social and economic policy. By the time World War II wound down, Keynesian economists were central. Economics had become the 'most prestigious' social science discipline in Canada, and economists enjoyed a relationship with the state that allowed them to have substantial impact on the policy process.[128] So deep and widespread was this influence that Granatstein claims they essentially 'ruled in Ottawa.'[129] Many of these individuals showed up as members of Porter's 'bureaucratic elite' in The Vertical Mosaic and he knew some of them personally through his contacts at Carleton.

By comparison, the role of sociology remained minor. Hiller has argued that during 1945–60 Canadian sociology adapted to its North American environment, growing slowly and experiencing some internal turmoil as a consequence of a struggle between two conceptions of the discipline. At most anglophone universities, he writes, sociology remained under the influence of British historical and philosophical conceptions of the discipline, modified in some measure by the political economy orientation made popular by Canada's most powerful social scientist, Harold Innis, a harsh critic of American-style sociology. The other conception dominated at McGill University, where Carl Dawson and his colleagues kept alive the fading American tradition of human ecology.[130] As of 1945, less than twenty universities offered sociology courses and only about two dozen sociologists, some part-time, some full-time, held teaching positions. Only some held appointments as sociologists. And only Toronto and McGill, with four appointments each, had programs of any size.[131] As late as 1957, at a time when Canadian universities had 173 full-time economists, they had only 32 full-time appointments in sociology.[132]

This changed dramatically in the 1960s and 1970s. Economics continued to grow in both size and influence but sociology, after years of lagging behind, finally caught up – in size, if not influence.

Toward the 1960s and 1970s

By 1969–70, Canadian universities employed 762 economics professors, and 960 by 1976–7.[133] As well, more economists found a permanent home in the federal civil service. According to mandarin R.B. Bryce, by the late 1960s there were in excess of 200 economists in government.[134] The discipline's success hinged in large part on its vision of itself, shared by civil servants, as a true science characterized by a neoclassical theoretical paradigm and a mathematically sophisticated, allegedly value-neutral methodology and style.[135] This success allowed economists to continue the special relationship they had developed with the federal civil service in the glory days of mandarin rule in Ottawa.

For its part, sociology remained a markedly smaller disciplinary community until about two decades after the war. Not until 1962–3 did Canadian universities house more than 100 sociologists. Within a decade, however, the tally stood at 848.[136] As it gained disciplinary presence and matured by founding its own journal and professional association, it gained increased influence in the policy process, at least in the sense that it began to tap into the new interventionist social science infrastructure of royal commissions, policy advisory bodies, and government task forces. The first large-scale project in which sociologists played a relatively major part was the Royal Commission on Bilingualism and Biculturalism.[137]

But English-language sociology never became as central to the policy consultation process as economics. Even when influential mainstream sociologists like Porter adopted the trappings of science – survey methodology and sophisticated statistical techniques of data analysis – and thus garnered for themselves some stature among policy makers, economists continued to have far greater standing and clout. Even Porter, one of the country's most respected sociologists, experienced this kind of labelling and ranking. Though he was a member of some government research and policy bodies, he found their policy deliberations to be dominated by conservative professional economists opposed to fundamental changes to the Canadian economy or society more generally. He had 'tried serving on committees … but they seldom took his advice.'[138] So he decided to attempt to have an impact by other means: his research.

One reason for their relative lack of success was that, unlike economists, sociologists never did come to agree on a disciplinary paradigm. As I noted in chapter 13, during the 1960s and '70s sociology became increasingly balkanized as members of the discipline embraced and developed a variety of perspectives, some European, some American, some scientific, some not. Many were radicals – Marxists, feminists, and new political economists – who regarded Canadian society as deeply flawed and, like Porter, put social class in a place of central importance in their analysis of its problems. However analytically appropriate it might have been, this decision cost them legitimacy in government circles. Radicals did not receive the respect given to mainstreamers, especially economists. Put another way, social scientists had only 'conditional legitimacy'; the label of expert was reserved for those with mainstream views.[139] A further factor in the small degree of policy-related influence enjoyed by English-language sociologists was their inability to create or latch on to a social or political movement that would give them a power base from which to press for change.[140] Sociologists and political scientists offered social criticism and suggested alternative non-liberal forms of policy – they were no longer the 1950s 'clerisy' Porter critiqued in *The Vertical Mosaic* – but they remained university based and oriented, with little political influence outside the academy, 'overwhelmingly academic in orientation and remote from the centres of policymaking,' as Brooks and Gagnon phrase it.[141] The situation in Quebec was completely different. French-language intellectuals from a variety of social science backgrounds constituted part of the vanguard of the new secular and professional middle class (and other interests) that carried out the Quiet Revolution during the 1960s.[142]

Whatever the specific degree to which legislators and civil servants trusted sociologists as experts, Brooks and Gagnon argue that it did not matter much in any case. They claim that at no time was the influence of any of the social science disciplines very great, including during the golden era of the mandarins. Historically, they say, the general impact of the social sciences on policy in Canada has usually been indeterminate – 'minor' or 'oblique' at most.[143] Real power in the policy process rests with politicians and special interests.[144] I think we can suspend this assessment in the case of the New Liberal economists, especially for the postwar reconstruction period. As a consequence of unique circumstances – the small size of the civil service at the time, considerable direct access to senior politicians, the especially able people who formed the mandarinate – Skelton, Mackintosh, and their colleagues seem to have had a substantial impact. And they did so despite the fact that their ideas were quite progressive for the time. In this regard, they would seem to offer a counter-instance to the general rule framed by Brooks and Gagnon.

Brooks and Gagnon also assert that in Canada the influence of social scientists on policy is limited. Only economists, who are 'linked to the dominant segment of the capitalist class' and generally act as 'ideological spokespersons for the existing social order,' are drawn on as experts.[145] Why? Because they take the property and power relations of capitalist society as a given and offer narrowly 'practical' advice, tinkering with the system as constituted. This provides legitimacy to the system, a good example of the system-stabilizing function of 'contained dissent.'[146]

But again, in the case of the New Liberal economists, this judgment seems unfair, for they were not really within the mainstream until the 1940s and after. Especially during the early years, many of their ideas were regarded as radical. In that sense, then, they were not just the garage mechanics of capitalism, though they were that, but designers of what was seen at the time as a new kind of vehicle. Their goal was not to keep the old model of the economy and state on the road but to design a new kind of economy and state that could accomplish different tasks – and in very different ways – from those the designers of the original laissez-faire state had foreseen. New Liberal economists wanted to manage a capitalist, liberal economy to make it more productive, efficient, and stable but were convinced that this required a more humane and just division of wealth and opportunity. Efficiency and productivity without justice would foster instability and fail to meet new moral standards that highlighted equality of opportunity in a way that had not previously been the case. While the new model would not be so different from the old that it would be impossible to see the continuity of lineage – it remained a liberal capitalist form of society – it was not going to be Adam Smith's Model T, either. New Liberals did perform a legitimating function, finding a way simultaneously to alter the Canadian state and economy and to justify them by keeping the system more or less the same. But they changed the state beyond anything that nineteenth-century liberals would have recognized as an appropriate vehicle of state.

Whatever the accuracy of Brooks and Gagnon's claims in terms of the degree of influence social scientists had, it is ironic that sociology gained some access to and standing within the cadre of mainstream policy sciences just as the direct impact of the social sciences on social policy apparently declined with the end of the mandarin era. It was in the context of the maturation of sociology and the rise to a hegemonic position of interventionist liberalism that Porter came to Carleton. The way he fit in there and in Canadian sociology more broadly was in part a consequence of his training at the LSE. In what follows I review the influence on Porter of the ideas of British New Liberals L.T. Hobhouse, Morris Ginsberg, and T.H. Marshall. I briefly describe Porter's New Liberal research agenda before concluding with a discussion of where Porter and others like him fit in the intellectual development of Canadian sociology.

John Porter as a New Liberal

There were five connections between Hobhouse's scholarly-political orientation and Porter's: his training at the LSE; his pronouncements about his political allegiances; his choice of research subjects and issues; his value orientation; and his methodology.

Training at the LSE

At the LSE John Porter took a degree in economics and was thus exposed to Keynes' work, a central component of the New Liberal package of ideas. Keynes' economics, built in part on Hobson's, had by that time become a staple of Western economics. The specifically New Liberal *sociological* aspect of Porter's perspective came from his exposure to T.H. Marshall, R.H. Tawney, Harold Laski, Donald MacRae and, above all, Morris Ginsberg, Hobhouse's student, friend, and successor in the Martin White Chair in Sociology. Ginsberg was a leading New Liberal of his generation in England and through him Porter became much impressed by Hobhouse's scholarly political orientation.[147] In interviews, Donald MacRae, John Grist, and Pauline Jewett recalled this clearly, and Porter himself noted Ginsberg's (and, therefore Hobhouse's) influence in an interview with a student reporter at Carleton in March 1950.[148] And while he did not often cite sources in his introductory sociology lecture notes, Ginsberg and Hobhouse were among those on whom he drew most frequently in the 1950s.[149]

It is notable that in drawing so extensively on Ginsberg and Hobhouse, Porter was the odd man out in his student cohort. The three student-colleagues who commented on the issue – A.H. Halsey, Asher Tropp, and Anthony Richmond – claimed that many LSE sociology students shared Porter's liberal views and reconstructive optimism but that few, if any, were at all impressed with Ginsberg and Hobhouse. Tropp, for example, stated bluntly that Ginsberg engaged few students: 'Ginsberg was totally preoccupied with passing on the teachings of L.T. Hobhouse but had little influence on either his students or his colleagues.'[150] Richmond fleshed out Tropp's observation. Ginsberg was the LSE's main sociologist, he said, and a 'petty dictator' in this capacity. He set the examinations and demanded some regurgitation, so Porter probably paid close attention to Ginsberg's lectures and writing not because he saw them as having any great intrinsic merit but for practical reasons. To fail any of the numerous final examinations meant repeating the lot.[151] Halsey acknowledged that students generally recognized Ginsberg's obvious 'philosophical sophistication ... and knowledge of social history' but nonetheless regarded him as an advocate of an outdated and arid 'nostalgic rationalist humanitarianism.' 'Vigorous young men wanted a future as well as a past,' he asserted. 'Their politics assumed the practice of progress, and they were ready to believe in some English, Fabian, Labour-movement version of the idea of progress. Ginsberg's version would not do. They looked elsewhere in sociology for a theoretical answer.'[152] According to Tropp, their gaze fell on Jean Floud, T.H. Marshall, Edward Shils, and David Glass.[153]

Despite his student colleagues' collective rejection of Ginsberg's Hobhousian sociology, Porter was much impressed with Hobhouse's core notions, and drew on them not only at the beginning of his career but years later. In a reading course Porter did with Dennis Olsen on comparative macrosociology during the 1971–2 academic year, over two decades after leaving the LSE, he assigned three books by Ginsberg: *On Justice in Society, Nationalism: A Reappraisal,* and *The Idea of Progress: A Revaluation.*[154] Similarly, in his introduction to the reprinting of 'Ethnic Pluralism in Canadian Perspective' in *The Measure of Canadian Society,* written in 1978 or 1979, Porter twice referred in a positive way to Ginsberg and his Hobhousian concept of 'the unity of mankind.'[155] The best evidence, however, is Porter's own testimony. In 1970, in a piece about the preparation of *The Vertical Mosaic,* Porter wrote that 'as a consequence of studying sociology at the London School of Economics at that time, where importance was attached by Ginsberg and others to the work of L.T. Hobhouse,' he became much impressed with the essentials of Hobhouse's sociology. More specifically, he claimed,

I was attracted to Hobhouse's principle of social development, that a community develops as it grows in scale, efficiency, freedom, and mutuality:

efficiency toward an end, freedom and scope for thought, mutuality in a service toward an end in which each participates. "Social development corresponds in its concrete entirety to the requirements of rational ethics … Good is the principle of organic harmony in things." Hobhouse was a grand theorist of social evolution and he saw emerging in the process the principle of reason and progress. To [Hobhouse], the relationship between social values and social science was close. He was firmly convinced of the need for an empirical social science and believed one could be developed which was closely linked to ethical principles.[156]

Before examining philosophical first principles, methodology, and scholarly political values in greater detail, it is useful to note the following very general parallels and links between Hobhouse and Porter that grew directly out of Porter's years at the LSE.

The two shared a concern with philosophical issues, including the philosophy of science and knowledge, especially as these related to questions of methodology and the purpose and morality of social research. For Hobhouse and Ginsberg, philosophy and sociology were inseparable.[157] Though abstract philosophical argumentation about such issues was probably the aspect of Hobhouse's and Ginsberg's sociology that Porter found least engaging, he had worked out a clear personal position on such issues and always underlined their importance. It is true that early in his career he did not write much about philosophical questions, but this was typical of the generation of English-language sociologists with whom he worked. Most treated questions about ontology, epistemology, and methodology as answered and followed the tenets of systematic positivistic empiricism. Certainly Porter spent little time fretting over foundational issues; he spent his time gathering what he regarded as basic data about major features of Canadian society.[158]

Not until the end of his career did Porter revisit philosophical issues in any depth. Three things provoked his renewed interest. First, he developed a relationship with Zbigniew Jordan, a Polish émigré scholar with whom he co-taught a doctoral seminar in the sociology department. According to Hugh McRoberts, Jordan was 'a commanding intellectual presence in his own right' and an expert in philosophical matters. Porter and Jordan discussed these questions both in the seminar and informally outside of class.[159] Second, Porter's growing familiarity with the work of the Marxists and new political economists who raised thoughtful challenges to the basic underpinnings of liberal society and its (liberal) sociology, combined with the failure of education to transform Canadian society in the 1960s and '70s, forced him to rethink his philosophical presuppositions.[160] Third, late in his career, he tried to develop a methodology that would allow him to better study nation states and other sociologically meaningful units of analysis in a comparative, historical, empirical, macrosociological way. This required him to revisit a number of foundational philosophical issues in detail.[161]

This brings us to a second point of comparison between Hobhouse and Porter. Hobhouse's (and thus Ginsberg's) sociology was multidisciplinary in scope and evolutionary, comparative, synthetic, and macrosociological in character.[162] Porter did not see sociology in exactly these evolutionary terms, but his early lecture notes at Carleton College and the interdisciplinary sweep of his theoretical approach in the introduction to *The Vertical Mosaic* suggest that from the outset of his career he saw sociology as an *omnium gatherum* discipline. Pauline Jewett recalled this synthetic character of Ginsberg's sociology as a feature that Porter admired.[163] His career-long interest in comparative sociology, as well as remarks he made in unfinished, later macrosociology essays, and comments he made in the prologue to *The Measure of Canadian Society* indicate that he never ceased advocating a macrosociological, comparative, and synthetic view of the promise of the discipline.[164] Sociology, he said, should address questions of societal progress at the level of nation-states.[165]

This mention of progress raises a third point of similarity. Like Hobhouse and Ginsberg (and many European social thinkers of the twentieth century), Porter wanted to understand the interplay in human society of reason and unreason.[166] According to Philip Abrams, at the time Hobhouse formulated his conception of the nature and purpose of sociology, he felt the need for a philosophy – at once 'scientific,' moral, and political – that would 'demonstrate the *meaning* of history, ... unravel the structure of present social problems, and ... specify strategies of amelioration.'[167] Ginsberg, too, struggled with this question, and his moralistic sociology seems in part a response to the wars and Depression through which he lived, an effort to battle the 'flight from reason' in thought and action that characterized Western society during much of his adult life. There is something of this struggle with reason and its uses in Porter's writings as well. In his case, however, he did not have to fight a flight from reason but to determine and help to realize reason's full potential during the reconstructionist period after World War II, when liberal rationality and optimism held sway. In his view, sociology could help in this noble cause.

Frank Vallee, Porter's Carleton colleague, saw this as a central aspect of his friend's intellectual outlook. John, he said, 'seemed to be quite optimistic ... about ... working toward the "right solution." All liberal-minded people would see the truth ... People who had wrong-headed views ... [might not] change their minds, but their opinions wouldn't matter.' In Porter's view, said Vallee, social science was always discovering something new and if they kept doing so, 'eventually ... all *right-minded* persons would see' what needed to be done.[168]

This leads directly to the fourth view shared by Hobhouse, Ginsberg, and Porter: their conception of the uses to which sociology should be put. Like his British New Liberal mentors, Porter wanted to use sociology for 'practical' purposes. Hobhouse saw sociology as a tool to be used to construct and measure societal progress, and once defined sociologists as 'all who treat problems of social life in the scientific spirit.'[169] And as a concerned citizen, newspaper columnist, and academic, he followed through on this notion, working throughout his career as an engaged and practical reformer intent on contributing to the ultimate goal: 'the unity of mankind.'[170] Porter, too, believed that sociology should be practical: central to the public discussion of social issues, relevant to the formulation of public policy, and useful for the measurement of societal progress. Like Hobhouse, he worked throughout his career on research projects designed to provide policy-relevant information to educational and governmental decision makers. Maria Barrados stressed this in her 2004 John Porter memorial lecture. She talked about her mentor's belief that the explanations of social phenomena sociologists came up with 'should be given when and where they might have a practical effect on policy development and review.' In this regard, Barrados said, Porter's own work was exemplary, 'a model of how sociological research can, and should, come out of the classroom, out of the textbook, out of the lecture hall, into the world':

> What we learn from John Porter is that sociological research matters precisely because it evaluates situations that relate to real people, living in real societies ... John used to joke about how his students kept disappearing 'over there' – said pointing roughly in the direction of Parliament Hill. But I think he also liked knowing that our academic learning, and intellectual theories were being used, and moving with us into our work places.[171]

Yet Porter adopted this practical orientation without becoming a narrow policy analyst or liberal technician because he did not believe that capitalism and liberal democracy needed only to be tweaked. He held a Hobhousian vision of the good society – cohesive, consensual, egalitarian, based on generous citizenship rights – and shared the view that a comprehensive, philosophically sophisticated, empirically informed, social justice-oriented sociology could help reach that goal. In order for the kind of progress, social harmony, and societal rationality he had in mind to be realized, tinkering would not be enough. Capitalism and liberal democracy would have to be substantially restructured along New Liberal lines.

Stating His Political Perspective

Porter was a thoughtful and complex man, and this came through in the declarations of political faith he made over his career. There is no hiding that his statements show him to have vacillated in his beliefs. For example, in the prologue to *The Measure of Canadian Society*, written just weeks before he died, Porter stated categorically that he had been recruited early in his intellectual development to the 'liberal egalitarian position' and that he had maintained that outlook throughout his career.[172] But this should not be interpreted to mean he was always a classical liberal, for while he consistently believed in meritocracy, he did so within the bounds of broader liberal views that drew on Hobhouse's liberal socialist principles. And sometimes he was quite blunt about this. During Porter's early years as an instructor at Carleton College, he had a reputation as a radical and would begin the inaugural lecture in each of his courses with the following warning: 'I am a socialist and an agnostic, and I think you should know that.'[173] Likewise, in his 1979 introduction to 'Power and Freedom in Canadian Democracy,' he reminisced that at the time he wrote the essay, in 1960, he regarded it as a 'critical and prescriptive, if not programmatic [contribution] to *social democratic* theory.'[174]

There is nonetheless substance to Porter's description of himself as a liberal meritocrat. The fire of his socialist beliefs, which had been fanned at the LSE, burned brightly only until the early 1960s. At that point they seemed to flicker and all but die out.[175] Like many sociologists of his generation, he came to hold an optimistic view of the possibilities of the then expansionist Canadian economy and state, and became increasingly convinced of the descriptive and explanatory adequacy of modernization theory, the end-of-ideology thesis, and so forth – all of which were uncritical of the fundamentals of capitalism and liberal democracy.[176]

As I point out in detail below, however, after 1974 he began once again to champion a set of clearly social democratic principles.

These vacillations explain some of the difficulty in pigeonholing Porter as a liberal or a social democrat. But another part of the problem stems from fluid boundaries between liberalism in its two variants, and between New Liberalism and social democracy. As a New Liberal, he held views that combined elements of both forms of liberalism and overlapped with social democracy.

I described Porter's major research projects in great detail in the chapters above. In the paragraphs that follow I briefly outline their connections to the scholarly-political agenda of the New Liberalism.

Choosing Research Topics

Porter's choice of the class–education relation as a research subject has an obvious link to New Liberalism. During the long postwar boom, Porter, like many of his colleagues, thought that capitalism, for all its shortcomings, would continue to provide abundant opportunities for economic growth and social development. The power of capitalist modernity, in particular as manifest in the United States, would eventually do away with atavistic, collectivistic, anachronistic allegiances and rights, dissolve structures of social privilege, and produce a more liberal individualist (and democratic) Canada, characterized by equality of opportunity, especially educational opportunity.

This explains Porter's career-long fascination with class, education, and opportunity. After completing *The Vertical Mosaic*, which itself focused a good deal on education, he undertook policy-relevant research on aspects of labour force dynamics such as the shortage of highly qualified labour and the brain drain while also researching issues of access to and funding for secondary and postsecondary schooling in Ontario. He became a long-time member of the Research Committee of the Presidents of the Universities of Ontario and from this base became involved in policy-oriented advocacy for reform of the postsecondary education system, in particular in *Towards 2000*. He followed up with *Ascription and Achievement*, a policy-relevant analysis of the relation between educational attainment (as well as other independent variables) and social mobility. And finally, he tried to apply his philosophy of education and his research-based knowledge of the dynamics of the university system to his day-to-day activities as a senior administrator at Carleton.

Porter's style of research likewise shows that he belongs in the New Liberal tradition of engaged and practical scholarship and politics.

Though less the public intellectual than some of his New Liberal fore-bears and contemporaries, from the beginning of his time at Carleton, he focused on the class–education–opportunity nexus and tried to solve problems inherent to it. The means he chose were typically academic: undertaking and publishing policy-relevant research and taking part in relevant advisory and policy-oriented bodies. In choosing this style of engagement and practical activity, he did not readily fit the label of the public intellectual in the same sense as his friend Pauline Jewett, or his fellow LSE alumnus and acquaintance Pierre Trudeau, both of whom became politicians. Nor was he a public intellectual in the sense that Ottawa mandarins such as Louis Rasminsky or R.B. Bryce filled the role. He did present the results of his research in public media forums (radio, television, newspapers, and public lectures) and at gatherings of relevant professionals – social workers, teachers, advisers, and administrators – but never achieved or wanted the kind of public profile sought and enjoyed by media commentators of his era such as Frank Magee, Laurier Lapierre, Patrick Watson, or Claude Ryan.[177] However, though not a truly public intellectual, he was an engaged, practical one, a politically motivated scholar who through his research and other efforts within the sphere of academic and related advisory bodies contributed to the informed debate of crucial social, economic, and political issues.

There is a third, more unusual, and especially telling way in which Porter's research agenda and style place him in the New Liberal camp: his attempt to use sociology to conceptualize, measure, and pursue progress. He undertook this effort in an especially concerted way in a set of papers – some philosophical, some methodological, some published, some not – written near the end of his life.[178] He intended the ideas in some of them to be incorporated into a philosophical-methodological magnum opus he was working on at the time. The philosophical touchpoints on which he relied most heavily in these essays were the writings of Leonard Hobhouse, T.H. Marshall, C.B. Macpherson, and the American philosopher John Rawls.[179] His purpose was to develop a conception of the good society and describe sociology's contribution to realizing that goal.

Adopting New Liberal Values

In May 1977, with these concerns in mind, Porter delivered a lecture that dealt in short compass with his sense of the proper place of values in the construction of the good society. He began by arguing that the classical liberal conception of human nature, which stressed the naturalness and goodness of the pursuit of self-interest, could no longer be used to derive a conception of 'the good' around which to construct a social order. If pursuing one's own self-interest was all there was to it, he argued, then 'there would be no moral problems other than acting naturally.' However, humans had often acted badly in pursuit of their personal interests. People were thus faced with 'the problem of finding a morally supportable social order, a set of social arrangements through which human beings [could] cooperate for their mutual advantage.' Even if humans were naturally self-interested in some measure, human nature was flexible and progress had already occurred because societies had been able to develop 'morally approved institutional structures' that progressively suspended 'inherited dispositions' such as self-interest.[180]

In his search for an appropriate moral code, Porter rejected a return to traditional values. It was just such values that had created and legitimated the 'fetters' of inequality, privilege, power, and authority that modern societies had to overcome.[181] Religion in particular was useless as a guide because Western societies had become predominantly secular.[182] Western societies had to look to modern, secular, intrinsically liberal social values – in particular, liberty, justice, and equality – for their conception of the good. Those who he thought had produced the most useful ideas about these concepts were John Rawls (for his abstract definition of liberty and related principles of distributive justice and equality), C.B. Macpherson (for a conception of human nature on which to base notions of liberty, justice, and equality in the 'good society') and to T.H. Marshall (for an elaboration of these principles in the form of citizenship rights).

Porter liked Rawls' conception of liberty, outlined in *A Theory of Justice*, doubtless because it had a more socialistic character than classical liberal formulations. For Rawls, the social good was just as important as freedom and the pursuit of individual happiness. 'The principles of justice' developed by Rawls, said Porter, 'require that each person have an equal right to the most extensive basic liberty compatible with a similar liberty for others. Liberty can only be restricted for the sake of liberty. Liberty can only be lessened if it strengthens the total system of liberty shared by all, and a less than equal liberty must be acceptable to those with the lesser liberty.'[183] Rawls' principle of distributive justice followed a similar logic. Any unavoidable inequalities had to be arranged in order to provide 'the greatest benefit to the least advantaged.' For Rawls, Porter wrote approvingly, this principle of justice, along with liberty and equality of opportunity, 'are prior to efficiency or the utilitarianism which have been our guiding principles for so long and which make economists our priestly caste.'[184] Porter used this Rawlsian argument to make one of his favourite points about educational opportunity in the McInnis Lectures:

> Rawls ... points out that superior ability can be an essential asset in a highly productive economy and recognizes there is an efficiency problem in its use, which may require at the higher levels the allocation of unequal educational resources to the brightest because the least favored could benefit in the long run. He suggests that individual talents should be considered as social resources to be developed for the benefit of all, particularly the least favored. In the past we have too readily accepted the view that the accidents of genetic endowment and the effects ... of social investment in education at the higher levels should become personal capital for unlimited acquisition. Such a view scarcely has a place within a framework of social justice.[185]

While Porter wanted to come to the assistance of the disadvantaged, however, he wished to do so only via the means of universal, individual rights. He adamantly opposed what he regarded as the retrograde step of granting collective or group rights. However well intentioned, they were a step backward, toward atavism. He was aware that his view on the subject of collective rights was not a popular one in Canada, where multiculturalism was an official policy and relations between Quebec and the rest of Canada often hinged on some exceptionalist policy favouring different treatment for Quebec or for French-speaking Canadians as a group. As he put it in a CBC interview, ethnic leaders often 'despised' his views on the retention of strong ethnic ties among hyphenated Canadians.[186] However, he justified his position on the grounds that postindustrial societies were moving in the direction of one 'world culture' based on science and technology. The retention of cultural particularisms and traditional values, beliefs, and behaviours would prevent Canadians from fully taking part in that emerging new world.[187] 'It is important,' he said, 'that some of these historical cultures are perhaps left in museums or wherever it is we like to watch them. They are not cultures which we should actually live.'[188] Elsewhere, in defence of this particularly liberal conception of progress and the social good, he drew explicitly on Hobhouse – not once, but twice:

While there might be some psycho-social benefits to be derived from the return to [ethnic] community, the movement also contains dangers because it can generate hostilities as well as shift loyalties from the larger national entities. It runs counter to any emerging concept of *the unity of mankind* within a conceivable rational order and directed towards a common good, as Morris Ginsberg put it many years ago. Loyalties to the larger national systems are important because they are the principal instruments by which some measures of a stable international order can be maintained and humanity as a whole can be served. In the transnational order which has emerged since the Second World War, we have seen something of the sense of common purpose and obligation develop which makes the unity of mankind in a contracting world a much more attainable objective than earlier in history.[189]

In framing his view of the best of all possible worlds, Porter cited not just Hobhouse but also Hobhouse's New Liberal colleague, Graham Wallas: 'We need to know how the great society in Graham Wallas' sense can also be the good society.'[190] He fleshed out his Rawlsian conception of social justice by drawing on the ideas of C.B. Macpherson and T.H. Marshall.

He found Macpherson's conception of human nature, which I would describe as a New Liberal conception, especially helpful. Macpherson had done graduate work at the LSE in the 1930s and was influenced while there by Laski, Tawney, and Ginsberg.[191] Sounding much like Marx, his theory of human nature stressed that people possessed creative capacities that needed self-realization through rational, self-directed productive activity. In Porter's view, this conception of human nature constituted a helpful and promising basis on which to build a more just and democratic society: 'Macpherson has made the point that liberal theories of distributive justice ... are often cast in terms of this first aspect of humans as consumers of utilities: justice, that is, in terms of some equal or fair distribution. Thus we may say that justice is served when there is some redistribution to the less advantaged in terms of the consumption of things.' However, following Macpherson further still, Porter noted that the redistribution of utilities constituted only a partial answer to the problem of social justice. Why? Because redistribution served 'only one aspect ... of the dual nature of humans.' In order to truly fulfil the task of the liberal democratic society, Porter said, it was necessary to – in Macpherson's words – 'maximize each man's ability to use and develop his essentially human attributes or capacities.' Thus, he concluded, again quoting Macpherson, 'we must increasingly think of the good society in terms of the "egalitarian maximization of powers."'[192]

Expanding the powers of individuals to increase the social good meant expanding the liberal conception of rights. Porter pursued this issue by drawing on T.H. Marshall's writings on citizenship. He may have heard these famous lectures before they appeared in 1950 as *Citizenship and Social Class*, for Marshall had delivered them in 1949 at the LSE but however he encountered them, they had impressed him. Porter regarded Marshall's conception of expanded citizenship rights not just as the basis for a new, more just society but also as 'the guiding judgemental principle' for the kind of 'evaluative sociology'[193] he wanted to develop:

> The individual makes claims as a citizen, a status common to all members. T.H. Marshall has traced the development of citizenship rights and the manner in which they have served the process of class abatement ... They are essential also to the development of modern egalitarianism. First civil rights provided equality before the law, then political rights allowed participation in government, eventually social rights brought about education, health, and decent living standards and some measure of equality of condition.[194]

Porter's stress here on the idea that sociology should be judgmental and evaluative – ceaselessly pushing for a wider distribution of *societally responsible* individual rights – demonstrates his long-term allegiance to the New Liberal view that sociology should not, indeed could not, be value free:

> If we are not concerned with questions of value then sociology will return to that condition of aimless empiricism and laborious webs of theory spinning towards which recent criticism has been directed, or it will return to that condition where its hidden major premises are those of the status quo. The argument that values have no place in social scientific inquiry is in my view incorrect for the central question of that inquiry relates to the conditions and capacities that a society needs to move itself in the direction of the social good.[195]

Further, he said, the social scientist's freedom to pursue research – a societally granted privilege – carried with it the responsibility to use that freedom in the service of society, in particular, to assess and criticize the social order when it served particular rather than general interests. Twice in the last five years of his life he made this crystal clear. In the prologue to *The Measure of Canadian Society*, he stated bluntly that scholars had to choose sides in moral and political skirmishes. 'The major task of social science,' he said, 'is to abstract from the confused flow of events perspectives which clarify and which permit some judgment about society in the light of moral principles.'[196] Similarly, and even more emphatically, in rejecting the principle of value neutrality, he wrote the following:

> Although many would like to avoid the issue, social scientists have to choose sides and to fashion their work with a clear idea of what their values are. Some may think there is a neutral position on every issue of great social importance which can be analysed objectively, but that is the position of the bureaucrat rather than the intellectual, and almost always a position taken from a power base with a prior commitment to the status quo.[197]

But by what methodological normative means was one to judge? Surely, here was the most complex and divisive question of the lot. Porter answered it, again in ways that echoed Hobhouse directly, on more than one occasion late in life, but in greatest detail in the two unpublished, ruminative essays on macrosociology noted above. In my view, the most obvious indicator of the connection between Porter's work and the New Liberal conception of sociology and its interpretation of the good society is the cover page of the first macrosociology essay, 'Macrosociology: Some Problems with the Nation State as the Unit of Analysis,' which bears in full the Hobhouse quotation cited above: 'Social development corresponds in its concrete entirety to the requirements of rational ethics ... Good is the principle of organic harmony in things.'[198]

This conception of the good society constituted a career-long source of inspiration not only about the *purpose* of sociology but also about its *methodology*.

Framing a Value-Laden Methodology

In 'Macrosociology: Some Problems with the Nation-State as the Unit of Analysis,' Porter begins by stating that sociology should be grand in scale and synthetic; i.e., methodologically wholist. Here he had in mind the grand political economy and moral philosophy of the nineteenth century. Following up on the notion of grandness of scale he argued that, properly practised, sociology should be comparative in orientation and international in scope. While its basic unit of analysis was the nation-state, and though it had to take into account unique features of the development of national societies, it should study individual nation-states as examples of a wider type of society developing along a common path of development. 'What [might we] expect from a macrosociology?' he asked: 'It should be a general model and not one specifically created for a particular society. By general, I do not mean of universal applicability to all groups at all places ... Rather, there are a number of societies at different stages of social evolution which have a similarity of structure such that they may be viewed as a type or a species.'[199] Nor could individual nation states be understood in isolation: 'Any studies undertaken with the goal of ... *measuring the progress* of modern nations which ignore the interconnectedness between nations [are] bound to fall short of adequacy. Nations no less than men are not islands unto themselves, and it is the very relations which they enter into in the trans-national context that become constitutive of their national characteristics and dynamics.'[200]

Second, macrosociology should be as quantitatively sophisticated as possible.[201] In Porter's view, sociologists needed to develop empirical indicators of 'social development equivalent' to those employed by economists to describe economic development. He understood full well that post-Keynesian economics had its flaws, but thought its 'macro' focus and 'scientific' method (the gathering and analysis of quantitative data) constituted a good model for sociology to emulate.[202] 'Sociologists have not measured the nation's growth or performance in any respect,' he indicated. 'Unlike economics, there is not for sociology a bundle of concepts and measures about which there is substantial agreement.'[203] And make no mistake; by 'social development,' he meant progress in the New Liberal sense. In 'Towards a Macrosociology: Further Notes,' he described the purpose of his efforts in exactly such terms.

> The aim of this paper is ... to deal with the question of what is necessary to provide a macrosociology through which judgements can be made about whether a society ... is moving, developing or progressing in a direction which meets ethical criteria ... The central question then for macrosociology is can a modern national society be both great and good, and if so,

what would it look like and what capacities are necessary for it to move itself toward such a goal?[204]

And he regarded it as possible to measure progress in a sophisticated, mathematical way. In 1970, over twenty years after he left the LSE, he wrote,

> The present resurgence of interest in [macrosociology] may reflect a new concern of sociologists for the quality of social life and in the conditions of progress ... [T]he major problems of contemporary societies ... are the problems of achieving 'organic harmony' ... The macrosystem can be viewed as one in evolution, and the appropriate macrodata to trace out this evolution are to be found in time-series and ultimately expressed in complex mathematical models.[205]

One of the most important potential indices of progress was citizenship rights: 'Citizenship has evolved historically at different times and rates in western societies with the extension of legal, political and social rights. Social indicators can be developed to measure their distribution.'[206]

In the second macrosociology essay, 'Towards a Macrosociology: Further Notes,' he offered more details of his approach, listing a dozen common elements of industrialized society that he wanted to operationalize as variables and combine into a tentative model or 'explanation sketch' capable of describing and explaining the logic of modern industrial society. The goal was to see which of the independent variables were most important for predicting four variables he designated in the model as desired outcomes. The practical purpose? To provide 'societal guidance' about how to produce a maximally open, just and democratic society. The idea is captured in two excerpts:

> Certain common elements appear with sufficient frequency to suggest their being indispensable to a model of a national-state-society at a high level of industrialization, that is, a modern industrial society [MIS] ... The relevant data for any one society would constitute the sociography of that society ... [W]e could with comparable data for a set of MISs seek to develop a general theory or to make statements about how the components (variables) relate to each other in 'explaining' desirable outcomes ... designated as 'dependent' variables. From the ... list of components or common elements we might consider ... four as outcomes about which value

judgements are made. These 'variables' are the distributive system, the mobilization and consensus formation process ..., the evolution of citizenship, and the surrounding ecosystem. All of these can be examined with relationship to justice.[207]

Each of the components of the social system can be described and quantified ... Similarly the development of each component can be described over time since each will have their own histories as shown in the case of the evolution of rights ... [T]he model can be considered one of an evolving industrial society. In value terms the outcomes can be viewed as goals. The major social divisions are shown in ecological-demographic terms since they comprise the human population classified in ways which have social significance, but which change over time until finally the principle of equality has removed the social significance of any differentiating criteria that remain such as sex, colour and so on: all are citizens ... Eventually, perhaps, a common set of categories and measures can lead to a comparative macrosociology, a general theory of societal evolution and guidance, a return to the earlier concerns of 'political economy' which is a search for the conditions which might maximize social welfare.[208]

This stress on the idea of moral judgment in light of absolute (liberal) standards of social development makes clear the third essential feature of Porter's conception of macrosociology. In the last year of his life he wrote, 'I would like ... to work toward a macrosociology that is capable of both explanation *and* evaluation ... [W]e should be able on the one hand to understand ... how a society in its totality works and how it got to be where it is, and on the other hand we should be able to judge whether or not it is moving in the direction of maximizing human welfare.'[209] And it was not just that it was possible to judge. As I noted above, the sociologist had a moral obligation to have an explicit moral position, to make clear what that position was, and to defend it against other moral positions. As well, it was one's duty to try to move these values from the realm of the desirable – this is what should be – to the realm of the real:

I have always ... directed my energies and my inquiries into problems of immediate ... relevance to planning and trying to change society. I certainly don't consider myself to be one of those sociologists who withdraws into an ivory tower ... And the underlying value that has always guided me is ... individual equality.[210]

Like Hobhouse and the British New Liberals, then, Porter believed that one could and should use carefully gathered empirical data and objective moral standards to subject societies to a thorough moral assessment. Social development and moral progress were two sides of the same coin. Just as societies had developed to greater and lesser degrees in terms of economic growth and other sociographic measures, so, too, had they achieved varying levels or degrees of moral progress. 'Not all cultures have equal claims on our moral support. Some cultures treat human beings in profoundly inhuman ways,' he wrote. 'Our claim to the judgement of cultures is not put forward because we have created a perfect society, but because in the course of social evolution some principles of social life have emerged which are more morally supportable than others.' This meant that some 'outdated,' non-liberal cultures would *and should* disappear: 'Many of the historic cultures are irrelevant to our futures. Opportunity will go to those individuals who are future-oriented in an increasingly universalistic culture. Those oriented to the past are likely to lose out.'[211]

The process of evaluation was not to stop at the boundaries of individual nation-states. In keeping with the internationalist flavour of New Liberal thinking,[212] Porter argued in favour of restructuring the web of relations between have and have-not nations in a way that was morally defensible, drawing on a variation of Rawls' 'just savings principle':

> The productive capacity of most modern industrial societies rests on an exploitative relationship with the underdeveloped world ... So if our model has an evaluative concern as well as an explanatory one, it cannot ignore this important issue. Here one might think of some adaptation of Rawls' just savings principle, which holds that present generations should not exploit succeeding ones by squandering resources, or present generations should not be required to save for future generations at a sacrifice to their own welfare, with something of a just sharing principle. We would have to develop empirical indicators by which we could evaluate the nature and extent of a modern society's openness as an exploiter and openness to exploitation.[213]

Porter, the New Liberalism, and Postwar Canadian Sociology

In 'Provincials and Professionals: British Post-War Sociologists,' British sociologist A.H. Halsey offers a semi-autobiographical account of the personal backgrounds, political orientations, scholarly interests, and careers of one woman and a dozen men, himself included, who graduated from the LSE in the early 1950s and then, over the next decade and a half, went on to play a major role in the establishment of modern sociology in Great Britain. While Halsey's analysis makes no mention of the term 'the New Liberalism,' there is no mistaking the New Liberal nature of the views held by those whose lives and careers he describes. Halsey could as easily have been describing John Porter and his role in Canadian sociology, and might easily have identified Porter as part of his group, except that Halsey defined his cohort as having graduated in the early 1950s and as having contributed to the establishment of modern sociology in England. Porter graduated in 1949 and spent his career building sociology in Canada.

I do not claim here, as Halsey does regarding his own cohort, that Porter was part of a group of Canadians, trained at a particular institution (the LSE) and at a particular time (the late 1940s and early 1950s), who set out with the intention of establishing a particular form of ethical/scientific sociology in their home country. Instead, I draw on Halsey to lend weight to three related claims about John Porter, the New Liberalism, and the development of English-language sociology in Canada after World War II.

First, I want to claim that the personal backgrounds, academic training, political orientation, scholarly interests and sociological approach of Halsey and his colleagues are all but identical to that of John Porter. In a very real sense, it is fair to say that he was one of them or, at least, just like them. Second, and here my argument is more tenuous, I want to claim that Halsey and his cohort developed and then successfully institutionalized in England what seems to me a New Liberal form of sociology. Porter's New Liberal sociology was slightly different from theirs because of the greater influence of Ginsberg and Hobhouse, but theirs was virtually isomorphic with New Liberalism in its origins, methods, and agenda nonetheless. In helping to establish a form of New Liberal–inspired sociology in Canada after World War II, Porter unwittingly carried on a social scientific tradition begun in English Canada by Adam Shortt in the late nineteenth century. Third, and here my argument is more tenuous still, I want to use Halsey's description of the general, generational nature of the biographical and scholarly forces that created the cohort of New Liberal sociologists in Great Britain to speculate that the same thing happened in Canada. That is, I want to claim that Porter was just one of many English-language sociologists of his generation whose similar personal backgrounds (family, class, Depression, war, reconstruction, academic training) led them to develop a form of 'sociological expression of autobiographical experience' that I have referred to here as New Liberal sociology.[214] In this regard, at least some of those hired at Canadian universities in the 1940s and '50s, before the years of rapid expansion, were much like Halsey and his cohort in England. Porter was more classically New Liberal than most of his colleagues because of the unusually strong influence on him of Hobhouse. But with his colleagues and under the influence of the British, European, and American sociology of the time, he constructed and helped to institutionalize a New Liberal sociology – politically progressive, reformist, theoretically eclectic, and 'scientific' – designed to inform and influence public debate and government policy. Porter was better known than most, but they shared a common background, training, approach, and agenda.

The details of my three claims are as follows.

Porter's personal background is all but identical to those of the members of Halsey's group. Halsey and the cadre of (mostly) British postwar sociologists on whom he focuses were born between the two great wars.[215] They came not from the metropolitan professional and business class backgrounds typical of prewar generations of English university teachers but from families of the working- and lower-middle classes. Porter's circumstances, born in 1921, the son of an often un- or underemployed clerk whose family lived in poverty or near poverty for much of his childhood and adolescence, are a direct match. Similarly, Porter was a provincial: he came not from the metropolitan geographical and cultural axis of Oxford–London–Cambridge but from the hinterland. Indeed, Porter was doubly provincial: his parents came from Wales and he was born in a former colony. Despite his difficult circumstances at home, Porter was an excellent student who, had he lived in England, might well have won the scholarship, as so many of Halsey's cadre did, as a means of getting to university. The route Porter followed to the LSE – serving in the Armed Forces and using a veterans' benefits program to gain entry – was identical to that taken by many in Halsey's group.[216]

Nor do the similarities end there. Like Halsey and his colleagues, Porter received his early political socialization in England. His family was strongly pro-Labour and, like the British LSE sociologists, Porter doubtless rejoiced in July 1945, when Clement Attlee and the Labour Party were swept into office in Britain's first postwar election.

He entered the LSE in 1946, during the years of heady reconstructive optimism that followed the war and, like Halsey's cohort, immersed himself in the political ferment that was part of day-to-day education at the School. Together, they were exposed to the same mix of ideas, ideologies, and teachers – Shils, MacRae, Marshall, Glass, and the rest. As a group, they entered the LSE deeply influenced by their class backgrounds and the war. While there, they fashioned from pro-Labour and New Liberal pieces an activist orientation to scholarship, but none was drawn into formal electoral politics. Instead, they spent their careers as university teachers and researchers. Halsey and his British colleagues left Houghton Street for various provincial universities, where collectively they carried out a substantial and progressive slate of empirical research using a morally driven, scientific sociology that allowed them to document the inequities of modern-day England and exploit the reconstructive political atmosphere of the postwar period to push for what Halsey refers to as 'a free and socialist Britain.'[217] Porter, originally without any idea or intention of becoming an academic, left London for Canada and ended up pursuing the same agenda in his native land: the creation of a more open, egalitarian, and less class-bound society than the one into which he had been born.

Halsey and his colleagues examined the same social issues as Porter – class, status, education, opportunity – using a similar, morally inspired, empirically informed sociological approach. As Halsey put it, 'The emphasis was again on egalitarian analysis of social inequality, ... consciously carrying on the tradition of political arithmetic – marrying a value-laden choice of issue with objective method of data collection and analysis.'[218] Though highly critical of Britain's social structure, in particular the detrimental effects of its rigid class system, Halsey's colleagues never abandoned the left-liberal, social democratic orientation of the New Liberalism. They had no need for Marxism and no time for communism because neither was necessary. In Halsey's words, 'We were confident that the democratic institutions invented by the Victorian and Edwardian working class, the Unions, the Co-operative Societies and the Labour Party were the foundations of a New Jerusalem.' 'If their Party and their Attlee government lagged behind,' Halsey suggested, 'their idealistic impatience called for renewed radical persuasion ... Resolve, pressure, argument and firm insistence on democratic action would be repeatedly necessary over a long haul. But democracy and decency need never be abandoned.'[219] Much of the pressure and many of the compelling arguments necessary to initiate such changes would come from their own engaged, practical research. Halsey perhaps phrased it in more simple and prosaic terms than they might collectively have liked when he said that his sociologist colleagues saw themselves as members of an 'intellectual trade union' designed 'to solve [England's social] problems by the hypothetico-deductive method,' but they certainly would have shared the sentiment.[220]

Porter, like them, returned to the hinterland from which he had come and did his best to establish a similar kind of sociology there. Once recruited to the staff of Carleton College, he completed the process of academic socialization he had begun as a student at the LSE by learning to be a professor and scholar in the nation's political capital. His political and academic socialization occurred during the 1950s and '60s, a period when the New Liberalism gradually became hegemonic in Canadian political culture. Together, his training at the LSE and his immersion in Canadian political culture turned him into a New Liberal. He did not ignore aspects of European and, more important, American 'scientific' and 'professional' sociology, especially from the early 1960s to the early '70s, but even then he remained committed to a New Liberal conception of his *mission* as a scholar-citizen. It was his *duty* as an engaged, practical intellectual to engage in public *service* aimed at making Canada more truly and broadly democratic.

For a variety of personal and professional reasons, it seems that many of the sociologists of Porter's generation, those who made up the first postwar cohorts of Canadian sociologists, were much like him and, by extension, much like Halsey and his colleagues: eager to use sociology for progressive social reconstruction, whether they referred to themselves as New Liberals or not. Like Porter, and like their contemporaries in the British Isles, most were children and young adults during the Depression and many had served in the Armed Forces during World War II. All became adults and completed their postsecondary education during the immediate postwar period, when most Canadians wanted to define 'reconstruction' broadly rather than narrowly. Like many of their fellow citizens, they were convinced that the economy and the state should not revert to business as usual after the war. Unlike most citizens, however, they were privileged to attend university. Some even studied at the LSE.[221]

Their university training augmented the influence of popular political culture because they were trained at a time when British, American, and Canadian universities became increasingly influenced by liberal, interventionist, professional models of intellectual practice. As a consequence, they developed a faith in the ameliorative potential of professional social science, a sense that they could and should contribute as scholars and citizens to the building of a better postwar world. Sociology might not be a science like chemistry, and it might not allow for 'social engineering' in any narrow sense of that term, but it had the potential to transform purely ideological public debates over social issues into problems amenable to rational, even technical, solutions. This liberal belief in the practical and political purpose of sociology and the power of social science to contribute to social amelioration can be stated in the form of four propositions:

1 Knowledge about (and the explanation of) social issues ought to based on sound empirical studies.
2 Social scientific knowledge ought to be made available to the public so that they could engage in informed, reasoned debates about policy decisions.
3 Individual sociologists had the right and obligation as citizens and experts to take make policy recommendations based on their own values.
4 Empirical knowledge, informed debate, and wise policy decisions could create progress.[222]

Many sociologists of Porter's era donned the mantle of the morally committed, politically active citizen-scholar and, guided by these four propositions, conducted academic research, worked on royal commissions, contributed to policy discussions and the like. In all this, they were much like John Porter.

On one important count, however, many parted company with him. Most had been socialized in a Western intellectual community – the university – where, in the 1940s, '50s, and '60s, value freedom was integral to scholarly political activity. So, for them, sociology was both a science and a profession. Academic activity was scientific in a relatively straightforward sense of the term. The scholar had an obligation to pursue truth in an objective and disinterested manner. Scientific evidence so gathered could then be brought to bear in civil society, i.e., in the sphere of value choices, practical reason, and political activism. The problem was that if the social scientist expressed a value position – claimed that one value orientation was better or truer than another – and engaged in political activity, he or she had stepped outside the bounds of science. Having grown up in a reconstructionist, progressive liberal political culture, many probably believed that Canadian society could be made better and more democratic by pursuing a left-liberal, social democratic political agenda. But their desire to hold to scientific standards, according to which objectivity and value freedom had to be maintained, meant that most drew a line between science and philosophy, data and values, *is* and *ought*.

Porter *never accepted the principle of value freedom*. He agreed that the objective gathering of data using scientific approach was a crucial aspect of intellectual practice. Drawing specifically from the original British roots of the New Liberalism, however, he argued that sociology was both science (of a sort) and philosophy, both a means of gathering socially important knowledge and of putting it to practical, morally good use. As a part of this commitment, he rejected value neutrality and claimed that it was possible to use philosophical and sociological reasoning to identify *objective standards of moral worth* that could and should then be scientifically operationalized and used as a standard against which to measure progress. He drew on the New Liberal conception of the practical, engaged intellectual to claim that it was his duty and mission to define the good, pursue truth, and create and measure progress.

Conclusion

Perhaps it was the combination in Porter's work of Hobhouse's reform liberalism and normative scholarship, presented in the theoretical and scientific methodological style of American mainstream sociology, that gave his work such wide appeal in the broader North American sociological community. With the publication of *The Vertical Mosaic* he set a new standard for the discipline in Canada while simultaneously establishing his credentials as a social critic and offering an interpretation of Canadian society that meshed nicely with the dominant liberal reformist ideology of the period.

Subsequently, in collaboration with like-minded colleagues, he replicated a series of high-profile American studies of occupational prestige, educational aspirations, and social mobility using the large-scale survey research modus operandi increasingly favoured by Ottawa bureaucrats and federal politicians. This had two consequences. In Canada, it cemented his reputation as one of the country's premier sociologists, and his work came to constitute a model for many of his English-language colleagues As well, government and university consultative bodies came to regard him as an expert and offered him opportunities to take part as a scholarly adviser and researcher on various committees and research projects related to educational policy. Even radical Canadian scholars were impressed, thankful for his data on inequalities of power, class, opportunity, and the like, even if they didn't share what they regarded as his liberal political sensibilities. Among American sociologists, including those recently hired to staff rapidly expanding Canadian departments of sociology, Porter's work was seen as sophisticated and compelling, even if some probably balked at his left-liberal political beliefs. More than most Canadian sociologists, he was invited into the network of senior and prestigious scholars that constituted the American sociological establishment.

But in another sense Porter was marginal to all of these groups. He did not fit neatly into mainstream sociology, Canadian or American, because he was too much the critic. He did conduct some relatively narrow policy research designed to inform official 'tinkering with the system' – his work on educational opportunity is a good example – but he never limited himself to this role. Certainly, he never became a member of the clerisy as some other sociologists and political scientists did. In fact, at times, he was seen by some mainstream scholars as too radical. In part, as I have noted repeatedly, this was because he eschewed the value neutrality that for many liberals was a fundamental principle of professional sociology. And in part it was because he never stopped arguing that class was salient in people's daily lives, in terms not only of their living conditions but of the opportunities they would enjoy at school and in the work world. Then, as now, his complaints about the detrimental impact of obdurate, structured inequality of condition would be seen as inappropriate and inaccurate by liberal scholars who believe that, for all its weaknesses, Canada's opportunity structure is largely open. Certainly this was the case during the 1950s and '60s, when the economy was growing rapidly and people believed Canada to be a relatively equal land of opportunity for all. At the same time, though for very different reasons, Porter did not fit in with many of those on the political left: radical political economists, Marxists, and fellow travellers. Although they shared much of the social democratic side of Porter's political self, many were suspicious of the scientific, American research model he employed, wary of the American mainstream sociological company he kept, and dismissive of the meritocratic liberal political philosophy he adopted during the central portion of his career. For them he was insufficiently radical.

In the contested and fractious domain of politically engaged social science, this kind of mixed or uneven response is unavoidable. Certainly Porter occupied an uncertain position after Canadian sociology radicalized in the late 1960s. By the middle of the 1970s, whatever consensus had existed in the discipline had weakened substantially. Mainstream liberal sociological beliefs and practices were challenged by a variety of sociological and political perspectives that found problematic the functionalist sociology, narrowly applied empirical survey work, and piecemeal liberal policy science orientation that had served as the discipline's core. If for many in the Canadian social science community he was a model scholar – mature, knowledgeable, principled, engaged – for theoretical, methodological, and political hardliners from either end of the political spectrum he seemed a man out of time and place.

My own view is that his works stand as a testament to the scholar's life wisely lived. Inspired by a moral and political vision of the best of all realistically possible social worlds, he worked on a variety of fronts to achieve that goal. You might not share his theoretical and methodological preferences but would have to acknowledge that Porter could provide a sophisticated defence of their usefulness. You might not share his political beliefs, but there was no denying he held close to his heart a well thought out set of humane, progressive scholarly, moral, and political views. Certainly, you could easily have strong doubts about his optimism, highly guarded though it was, that progress was likely or possible. Finally, in our age of liberal relativity, you might protest his views on the possibility of defining and measuring progress. But you would be hard pressed to argue that he was wrong in his desire to be politically and intellectually engaged in the scholarly definition of and solution to the social problems that stand in the way of what Leonard Hobhouse would have referred to as a developing 'rational harmony' in Canadian society.

Notes

A Note about Citation

My personal correspondence is cited as in the following example: Shils to
RHH [Rick Helmes-Hayes], 27 July 1996. As well, several people provided
comments on iterations of some or all of the manuscript. These are cited according to the following format: Frank Jones comments, 12 June 2002. If no
possibility of ambiguity exists, only the surname is given.

Materials from personal papers are cited as follows: JAP to McFarlane, 22
August 1967, McFarlane personal papers. If personal papers are cited for two
or more people with the same surname, the full name is given.

I conducted all the interviews in person unless otherwise stated. If the same
person was interviewed more than once, the format is as follows: Jewett interview 1; Jewett interview 2. A complete list is provided in the bibliography.

For published sources cited only once in the text a full citation is provided
within the chapter. Published sources cited more often are given in abbreviated form in the endnotes. A full reference for each such source is provided in
the section of the bibliography entitled 'Selected Secondary Sources.'

Abbreviations

Archives

BLEPS, LSEA	British Library of Economic and Political Science, LSE Archives
Canada/Labour	Canada, Department of Labour, Economics and Research Branch
CU, ARC	Carleton University, Archives and Research Collections

CUA	Carleton University Archives
HUA	Harvard University Archives
LAC, DND, RDE	Library and Archives Canada, Department of National Defence, Regimental Documents Envelope
LAC, JPP	Library and Archives Canada, MG31, D104, John Porter Papers
QUA, JMP	Queen's University Archives, John Meisel Papers
UBCA	University of British Columbia Archives
UTARM, GMP	University of Toronto Archives and Records Management Services, Gwendolyn MacEwen Papers

Periodicals

Periodical titles that appear multiple times have been abbreviated as follows:

AAAPSS	*Annals of the American Academy of Political and Social Science*
AJS	*American Journal of Sociology*
AmS	*The American Sociologist*
APSR	*American Political Science Review*
AQ	*American Quarterly*
ASR	*American Sociological Review*
BJCS	*British Journal of Canadian Studies*
BJS	*British Journal of Sociology*
BQ	*The Business Quarterly*
CAUTB	*Canadian Association of University Teachers Bulletin*
CC	*Canadian Counsellor*
CD	*Canadian Dimension*
CF	*Canadian Forum*
CHR	*Canadian Historical Review*
CJEPS	*Canadian Journal of Economics and Political Science*
CJHE	*Canadian Journal of Higher Education*
CJP	*Canadian Journal of Psychology*
CJS	*Canadian Journal of Sociology*
CJSHE	*Canadian Journal for the Study of Higher Education*
CPA	*Canadian Public Administration*
CRS	*Cahiers de Recherches Sociographiques*
CRSA	*Canadian Review of Sociology and Anthropology*
CS	*Current Sociology*
FP	*Financial Post*
Hs/SH	*Histoire sociale/Social History*

IJCS	*International Journal of Comparative Sociology*
IJPCS	*International Journal of Politics, Culture, and Society*
JCPS	*Journal of Commonwealth Political Studies*
JCS	*Journal of Canadian Studies*
JHBS	*Journal of the History of Behavioral Sciences*
JP	*Journal of Politics*
LG	*Labour Gazette*
LSEQ	*LSE Quarterly*
MJE	*McGill Journal of Education*
MR	*Monthly Review*
OG	*Our Generation*
PI	*The Public Interest*
PON	*Public Opinion News*
PS	*Political Studies*
PSQ	*Political Science Quarterly*
QQ	*Queen's Quarterly*
RS	*Recherches Sociographiques*
SA	*Sociological Analysis*
SE	*Sociology of Education*
SF	*Social Forces*
SN	*Saturday Night*
S/S	*Society/Société*
SR	*Sociological Review*
TMQ	*The Marxist Quarterly*
TSQ	*The Sociological Quarterly*
TWAC	*This Week at Carleton*
UTQ	*University of Toronto Quarterly*
WPQ	*Western Political Quarterly*

Preface

1 LAC, JPP, vol. 9, no. 3, JAP to H. Leal (Dean, Osgoode Hall Law School), 7 September 1965.

2 Hiller and Langlois, 'The Most Important Books/Articles.' The publication- and sales-related data were provided by Virgil Duff, University of Toronto Press (Duff to RHH, 13 May 1997, 18 February 2004). *The Vertical Mosaic* also made the 2004 list of 'Canada's One Hundred Most Important Books' chosen by the *Literary Review of Canada*.

3 See Brym, with Fox, *From Culture to Power*, 92.

4 Gender inequality remains a problem as well, but Porter did not have

much to say about it in *The Vertical Mosaic* (see Armstrong, 'Missing Women,' in *Vertical Mosaic Revisited*, ed. Helmes-Hayes and Curtis).

5 Though I use the qualifier 'English-language' here, I am not certain it is warranted. French-language sociology in Canada has its own pantheon (Père Lévèsque, Jean-Charles Falardeau, and Hubert Guindon, among others), but Porter's contribution to Canada's *national* sociology seems greater. This is in part because French-language sociologists in Quebec have generally taken their home province – the *nation* of Quebec – as their unit of analysis. See Fournier, 'Quebec Sociology and Quebec Society: The Construction of a Collective Identity,' *CJS* 26, no. 3 (2001): 333–47, and Leroux, '"La nation" and the Quebec Sociological Tradition,' *CJS* 26, no. 3 (2001): 349–73.

6 See Pineo, 'Prestige and Mobility.'

7 See Hiller and Langlois, 'The Most Important Books/Articles.' Hiller and Langlois also report that three of the titles on the English-language list were authored or co-authored by Porter's students: Wallace Clement, *The Canadian Corporate Elite* (Toronto: McClelland and Stewart, 1975), Wallace Clement and John Myles, *Relations of Ruling: Class and Gender in Post-Industrial Societies* (Montreal and Buffalo: McGill-Queen's University Press, 1994), and Pat and Hugh Armstrong, *The Double Ghetto: Canadian Women and Their Segregated Work* (Toronto: McClelland and Stewart, 1978).

8 Forcese to RHH, 5 January 1989.

Introduction

1 Porter, *Vertical Mosaic*; Porter and Pineo, 'Occupational Prestige in Canada'; Porter et al., *Towards 2000*; Porter, Porter, and Blishen, *Stations and Callings*; Porter et al., *Ascription and Achievement*.

2 Other significant figures in the history of English-language Canadian sociology have been the subject of book-length studies. Deborah Harrison and Harry Hiller have written about S.D. Clark in D. Harrison, *The Limits of Liberalism: The Making of Canadian Sociology* (Montreal: Black Rose, 1981) and Hiller, *Society and Change*. Marlene Shore's account of the development of sociology at McGill University, *The Science of Social Redemption*, has much to say about Carl Dawson, and Leonard Hatfield has written about S.H. Prince at Dalhousie University in *Sammy the Prince: The Story of Samuel Henry Prince, One of Canada's Pioneering Sociologists* (Hantsport, NS: Lancelot, 1990). It is odd that there is no equivalent volume about John Porter, for in many respects he is more important than any of them. All were true disciplinary pioneers, of course, but Porter's work had much more wide-

spread and long-term influence on the discipline, in part because he wrote at a time when the Canadian university system was expanding and sociology was going through a phase of rapid growth. As significant as Clark and Dawson were – Prince much less so – the growth of the university in the 1950s and 1960s created a much larger audience for Porter's writings than any of the others enjoyed.

3 Porter suffered no false modesty about the importance of *The Vertical Mosaic*. He ranked it among the top ten Canadian scholarly non-fiction books ever written. LAC, JPP, vol. 5, no. 2, John Porter, 'List of 10."

4 W. Clement to JAP, 11 June 1976; JAP to Clement, 14 July 1976; Clement to JAP, 11 October 1976; JAP to Clement, 28 October 1976; and Clement to JAP, 2 November 1976, all Clement personal papers.

5 Porter, 'Power and Freedom in Canadian Democracy,' in *Social Purpose for Canada*, ed. Oliver, 27–56; Porter and Pineo, 'Occupational Prestige in Canada; Porter et al., *Towards 2000*; Porter, Porter, and Blishen, *Stations and Callings*; Porter et al., *Ascription and Achievement*; Porter, 'Education and Equality,' in Porter, *Measure of Canadian Society*, 242–62; and 'Education and the Just Society,' in ibid., 263–80. All citations to *Measure of Canadian Society* are to the first edition unless otherwise stated.

6 McFarlane interview.

1: Growing Up in Vancouver and London, 1921–1941

1 Unless otherwise indicated, the details in the paragraph that follows are from my interviews with Eileen Jones and Alan Porter.

2 The information about Arthur's parents is taken from British Columbia, Ministry of Health, Division of Vital Statistics, 'Verification of Marriage Particulars,' 14 March 1989. That Arthur was an orphan was related to me by both Alan Porter and Eileen Jones. According to Eileen, Arthur was unofficially adopted by Cornelius Porter and Annie Mayo (Eileen Jones interview). Arthur was under the impression that his biological parents were wealthy and spent a long time looking for them in hopes of getting money (Ann Porter interview).

3 *Henderson's*, 1912: 1,119; 1913: 1,205; and 1914: 1,157.

4 Arthur is not listed in the 1915 edition of *Henderson's* Vancouver city directory, which means he may have enlisted and left home by that time. The 1916 version of the directory lists him as living with his mother, the 'widow of C.E.' (847; see also 350), and describes him as being 'on active service' (847). He is not listed in the directory in 1917, 1918, or 1919.

5 Ibid., 1920: 868.

6 'Verification of Marriage Particulars,' 14 March 1989. The document lists her mother's name as 'FINK.' This should read 'TINK' (Eileen Jones interview).

7 Eileen Jones interview; see also Alan Porter interview.

8 *Henderson's Directory*, 1918: 470.

9 Ibid., 1918: 470 and 1919: 477; Eileen Jones interview.

10 Eileen Jones interview.

11 'Verification of Marriage Particulars,' 14 March 1989.

12 On the early history of Vancouver and British Columbia, see Hull, Soules, and Soules, *Vancouver's Past*; Roy, *Vancouver*; Macdonald, 'Population,' in *Historical Essays on British Columbia*, ed. Friesen and Ralston, 201–27; and Caves and Holton, 'Outline of the Economic History of British Columbia,' in ibid., 152–66.

13 Roy, *Vancouver*, 168, table 8 (see also Macdonald, 'Population' 214, table 7, and 215–16.

14 Hull, Soules, and Soules, *Vancouver's Past*, 70.

15 There are inconsistencies in the occupation Arthur claims for himself in the Vancouver city directories. He worked at Pemberton's from 1920 to 1926, moving from bookkeeper to clerk to accountant to clerk and then accountant again (*Henderson's*, 1920: 868; 1921: 957; 1922: 1,016; 1923: 1,091; 1924: 1,022; *Wrigley-Henderson Directory*, 1925: 1,086; 1926: 1,170). He worked at V.W. Odlum, another insurance and financial firm, from 1927 to 1930. During his first two years at Odlum, he lists himself as a bookkeeper; during the last two, as an accountant (*Wrigley-Henderson*, 1927: 1,221; 1928: 1,363; 1929: 1,530; 1930: 1,245). Given the family's very modest circumstances, no evidence that Arthur earned an accountant's papers, and John's recollection that his father 'did some clerical work,' it is likely that Arthur remained a clerk throughout his career.

16 *Henderson's*, 1920: 326, 868; 1921: 957; 1922: 1,016; and 1923: 1,091.

17 Ibid., 1924: 1,022; *Wrigley-Henderson*, 1925: 1,086; 1926: 1,170; 1927: 1,221; 1928: 1,363; 1929: 1,530; and 1930: 1,245.

18 Horn, *The Great Depression*, 3, 10; see also Brown, *When Freedom Was Lost*, 19.

19 On Bennett's ineffectual efforts, see Kenneth McNaught, 'The Thirties,' in *The Canadians 1867–1967*, part 1, ed. J.M.S. Careless and R. Craig Brown (Toronto: Macmillan, 1967), 242–51. Not until well after the Depression did Canada's federal government institute the modern welfare state.

20 Struthers, *'No Fault of Their Own,'* 216–19, appendix II; see also H. Blair Neatby, *The Politics of Chaos: Canada in the Thirties* (Toronto: Macmillan, 1972).

21 Hull, Soules, and Soules, *Vancouver's Past*, 79–80; see also Struthers, *'No Fault of Their Own,'* 1983.
22 M. Porter, 'John Porter,' 1.
23 Brown, *When Freedom Was Lost*, 27n11.
24 Kelly to RHH, 16 February 1989.
25 Canada, Dominion Bureau of Statistics, General Statistics Branch, *The Canada Yearbook 1937* (Ottawa: King's Printer, 1937), 801, table 10.
26 Struthers, *'No Fault of Their Own,'* 221, appendix IV.
27 Ibid.
28 Canada, *Canada Yearbook 1937*, 800, table 9.
29 Hull, Soules, and Soules, *Vancouver's Past*, 80.
30 Colombo, ed., *1994 Canadian Global Almanac*, 152, 'Federal Election Results, 1867–1988.'
31 On the founding of the CCF, see Horn, *League for Social Reconstruction*, and Oliver, ed., *Social Purpose for Canada*.
32   John's younger brother, Alan, knew little about his father, and John's elder sister, Eileen, was reluctant to make public that aspect of the family's history.
33 David Cobb, 'John Porter,' *Toronto Daily Star*, 31 December 1965.
34 Alan Porter interview.
35 Arthur does not appear in the *Wrigley-Henderson Directory* in 1931.
36 Ibid., 1932: 1,191; *Wrigley's*, 1933: 688; *Sun Directory*, 1934: 1,444; 1935: 1,329; and 1936: 1,044.
37 Unless otherwise noted, the information in this paragraph is taken from my interview with Eileen Jones.
38 Jewett interview 2. Ann Porter said her father seldom talked about his childhood (Ann Porter interview).
39 Eileen Jones interview.
40 Kelly to RHH, 16 February 1989; see also John Oliver High School, *South Vancouver's John Oliver High School: A Proud Record, 1912–1986* (Privately published, 1986).
41 'Grade Report,' John Oliver High School, Vancouver, 6 February 1989 (document provided by Principal J.W. Killeen).
42 John's mother expressed great pride in Porter's excellent marks. Marion later noted that Ethel 'adored' her eldest son (Marion Porter interview 1) and Pauline Jewett remarked that Ethel 'favoured' John, even 'worshipped' him. 'She just saw that he was going to be an absolutely first-class mind' (Jewett interview 1).
43 MacLean to RHH, 20 May 1990.
44 Marion Porter interview 1.

45 Eileen Jones interview.

46 M. Porter, 'John Porter.' Neither Eileen Jones nor Alan Porter mentioned it, but it appears from the Vancouver city directory that in 1934 and 1935, Arthur and Ethel may have lived separately for at least part of the time. In 1933, the directory, which had previously listed only the male head of the household and any other *employed* family members as residents at any given address – housewives and unemployed children did not appear – began to list the name of the wife in brackets following the husband's name. In neither 1934 nor 1935 is Ethel listed as living with Arthur (*Sun Directory*, 1934: 1,444; 1935: 1,329). In both 1933 and 1936, she is listed (*Wrigley's*, 1933: 688; *Sun Directory*, 1936: 1,044).

47 M. Porter, 'John Porter,' 1. Dennis Olsen claimed that in his youth Porter sold the Communist newspaper *The Daily Worker* (Olsen interview). Marion did not mention this and I suspect John's regular route was a mainstream Vancouver daily newspaper.

48 Eileen Jones interview.

49 M. Porter, 'John Porter,' 1.

50 Marion Porter once wrote – incorrectly – that John's family had been 'deported' to England (M. Porter, 'John Porter,' 1). She later retracted this statement (Marion Porter comments, 23 February 1993). In a different version of this story, related by Alan Porter, it was Arthur's girlfriend, a wealthy woman, who paid their fare from Canada to England (Alan Porter interview).

51 Eileen Jones interview.

52 Ibid.; see also Marion Porter interview 1.

53 Eileen Jones interview; Alan Porter interview; M. Porter, 'John Porter,' 1. The summer before the war started, Porter met a wealthy man named Geoffrey Gilby, who owned a yacht that was moored near Devon in the south of England. Gilby brought together boys from Borstal, the reform school, and boys from wealthy local families and took them for trips on his yacht, presumably in the hope of reforming the former through the influence of the latter. Porter lived on the yacht for the summer and helped him with this project (Eileen Jones interview).

54 Marion Porter interview 1.

55 JAP to MacLean, 28 October 1939, MacLean personal papers. This letter should in fact be dated 1940 because it was written during the Blitz, which began in August of 1940.

56 Eileen Jones interview; Alan Porter interview; Marion Porter interview 1.

57 Alan Porter interview; Marion Porter interview 1.

58 JAP to MacLean, 28 October 1939 [1940], MacLean personal papers; Eileen Jones interview.

59 Alan Porter interview; Eileen Jones interview.
60 Eileen Jones interview.
61 Marion Porter interview 1.
62 Marion Porter comments, 7–8 July 1987; Jewett interview 1; Marion Porter interview 1; Alan Porter interview; Eileen Jones interview.
63 John Porter was known to his birth family as 'Jack.' Many of his friends called him Jack as well.
64 LAC, JPP, vol. 1, no. 13, JAP to Ethel Porter, n.d. [1943]. He makes a similar comment in a letter at the end of the war. 'As far as Dad is concerned, I could not care less what happens to him' (LAC, JPP, vol. 1, no. 14, JAP to Ethel Porter, 20 June 1945).
65 Marion Porter interview 1. According to Ann Porter, John did not talk to Arthur during her lifetime.
66 Marion Porter interview 1; M. Porter, 'John Porter,' 1.
67 Jewett interview 2.
68 Fox interview.
69 M. Porter, 'John Porter,' 1. In the interview with a student reporter from *The Carleton* referred to above, Porter noted that he also worked for the *Daily Graphic* (CU, ARC, no author, 'Profile: John A. Porter,' *The Carleton* 5, no. 19 [21 March 1950]: 16–17). I could find no other reference to or record of this employment.
70 JAP to MacLean, 28 October 1939 [1940], MacLean personal papers.
71 Canada's prime minister, Mackenzie King, followed suit a week later (Stacey, *Canadian Army*, 1).
72 Ralph Barker, ed., *The RAF at War* (Alexandria, VA: Time-Life, 1981), 52, 56–8.
73 Mack and Humphries, *London at War*, 160–1.
74 Ibid., 59.
75 Ibid., 171. London was not the only city bombed during the war; over 30,000 British civilians from outside London died from German air attacks, 1940–5 (Stacey and Wilson, *Half-Million*, 44–5). Other sources on daily life in London and Britain more generally during the Blitz include Tom Harrison, *Living through the Blitz* (London: Collins, 1976); Philip Ziegler, *London at War 1939–1945* (New York: A.A. Knopf, 1995); Norman Longmate, *How We Lived Then: A History of Everyday Life during the Second World War* (London: Hutchinson, 1971); and *Front Line: The Official Story of the Civil Defence of Britain* (Toronto and Vancouver: J.M. Dent and Sons Canada, 1943).
76 JAP to MacLean, 28 October 1939 [1940], MacLean personal papers.
77 Ibid.
78 Eileen Jones interview; see also M. Porter, 'John Porter,' 1.

79 Eileen Jones interview; see also Porter's military record (LAC, DND, RDE, JAP, 'Report on Security Candidates, Intelligence Corps [Field Security Wing]').
80 Marion says the manuscript was called 'Blitzkrieg over London' (M. Porter, 'John Porter,' 1). The manuscript entitled 'London's Story' is available in LAC, JPP, vol. 1, no. 23.
81 Porter expressed his pride in a letter to MacLean: 'The magnificent courage of the Londoners will ever be remembered as an epic. Both men and women staunchly resist with all their power' (JAP to B. MacLean, 28 October 1939 [1940], MacLean personal papers).
82 Chapter 5, 'Transportation,' 11. There is a similar comment in the chapter on 'Evacuation,' 9.
83 Ibid., Chapter 6, 'Shelter Life,' 16.
84 LAC, DND, RDE, JAP, 'John Porter: Particulars of Service.'
85 Porter was by temperament and conviction a pacifist, but believed strongly that World War II was worth fighting (Marion Porter interview 1; see also Ann Porter interview).
86 JAP to B. MacLean, 28 October 1939 [1940], MacLean personal papers.
87 M. Porter, 'John Porter,' 2.

2: The Army Years, 1941–1946

1 Bothwell, Drummond, and English, *Canada 1900–1945*, 337; Douglas and Greenhous, *Out of the Shadows*, 287–8.
2 LAC, DND, RDE, JAP, 'Field Medical Card,' 25 May 1942.
3 Phillips interview.
4 'The unit [John] was in was a very small one [and] the two officers who were in charge of it ... became very good friends [with him]' (Marion Porter comments, 23 February 1993).
5 Re the preparedness of the Canadian Armed Forces, see Stacey, *Six Years of War*, ch. 1; see also Douglas and Greenhous, *Out of the Shadows*, 23–39 and Stacey, *Canadian Army*, 1–4. Re the size of Canada's Armed Forces by war's end, see Stacey, 'Through the Second World War,' in *The Canadians, 1867–1967*, part 1, ed. Careless and Brown, 285–8.
6 Re the Army, see Stacey, *Six Years of War*, 35–7; Douglas and Greenhous, *Out of the Shadows*, 26–8; and Granatstein and Morton, *Nation Forged in Fire*, 7. Re the Navy and Air Force, see ibid., 7, and Douglas and Greenhous, *Out of the Shadows*, 30–3, 33–7, respectively.
7 Stacey, *Six Years of War*, 53–5; see also Bothwell, Drummond, and English, *Canada 1900–1945*, 337, and Stacey and Wilson, *Half-Million*, 32.

8 Mowat, *Regiment*, 7.
9 Stacey, *Six Years of War*, 54, 72; see also Stacey, *Canadian Army*, 6.
10 Stacey, *Six Years of War*, 230–4; see also Stacey, *Canadian Army*, 7–8.
11 Stacey and Wilson, *Half-Million*, 33, x.
12 Mowat, *Regiment*, 17.
13 Roy, *Seaforth Highlanders*, 71.
14 Stacey and Wilson, *Half-Million*, 36.
15 Ash Vale and Aldershot, 'Aldershot's Canadians,' www.ash-vale.co.uk; see also Roy, *Seaforth Highlanders*, 72.
16 Barrie interview. Lieutenant Barrie was a drill instructor in the Canadian Army both in Canada and at Aldershot during World War II.
17 Ibid.
18 McAndrew, *Canadians and the Italian Campaign*, 16.
19 Roy, *Seaforth Highlanders*, 76.
20 Barrie interview.
21 Stacey, *Six Years of War*, 234–8; see also Stacey and Wilson, *Half-Million*, 10–13.
22 Stacey, *Six Years of War*, 296–9; see also Stacey, *Canadian Army*, 18–21.
23 Stacey and Wilson, *Half-Million*, 13, 14; see also Stacey, *Canadian Army*, 21–3.
24 LAC, DND, RDE, JAP, 'Canadian Active Service Force Attestation Paper.' Presumably he did his basic training between 24 February 1941, when he enlisted, and 5 May 1941, when they sent him for clerical and language training. Curiously, there are no entries for this period in either his 'Record of Service' or his 'Service and Casualty Form' (LAC, DND, RDE, JAP).
25 LAC, DND, RDE, JAP, 'Certificate of Medical Examination,' 1 February 1941.
26 Ibid., 'Service and Casualty Form,' entries 3 May 1941 and 9 August 1941; see also 'Certificate of Trade Proficiency,' Class III Shorthand Typist, 9 August 1941.
27 LAC, DND, RDE, JAP, 'Record of Service,' entries 5 August 1941 and 1 September 1941; 'Service and Casualty Form,' entries 5 August 1941 and 1 September 1941; London County Council Public Health Department, Northwestern Hospital Bed Card, entry 5 August 1941; and Ministry of Health, Emergency Medical Services Form, 5 August 1941.
28 Ibid., 'Record of Service,' entry 2 December 1941; see also 'Service and Casualty Form,' entry 1 December 1941.
29 Ibid., 'Record of Service,' entries 2 September 1941–1 December 1941; see also 'Service and Casualty Form,' entries 2 September 1941 and 1 December 1941.

30 Ibid., 'Record of Service,' entries 25 January 1942 and 31 January 1942; see also 'Service and Casualty Form,' entries 25 January 1942 and 31 January 1942; and course certificate from Canadian Corps Intelligence School, 31 January 1942.

31 Ibid., 'Record of Service,' entry 13 March 1942; see also 'Service and Casualty Form,' entry 13 March 1942; Ibid., 'Service and Casualty Form,' entries 15 April 1942 and 29 April 1942.

32 Ibid., 'Intelligence Corps, Field Security Wing, Report on Security Candidate: Porter, John Arthur,' 29 April 1942.

33 Ibid., 'Record of Service,' entry 9 May 1942; see also 'Service and Casualty Form,' entry 9 May 1942; see also Elliot, *Scarlet to Green*, 608–9, 630–1. Porter retained his unit affiliation with the Seaforths but became a member of the Canadian Intelligence Corps. Cooper remained Porter's commanding officer for most of the Mediterranean campaign (Ibid., 219–51, 630). Porter Cole was his commanding officer for part of the time as well (Porter Cole interview). He became good friends with both (Marion Porter comments, 23 February 1993).

34 Elliot, *Scarlet to Green*, 94.

35 Ibid., xvii–xviii.

36 Parts of the 1st Canadian Division were dispatched to take part in the defence of France in mid-June of 1940, but their engagement was brief and they soon withdrew back to Britain (Stacey, *Canadian Army*, 13–17).

37 Nicholson, *Canadians in Italy, 1943–1945*, 20–2; Stacey and Wilson, *Half-Million*, 16; and Stacey, *Canadian Army*, 44–7, 94. General A.G.L. Mc-Naughton, commander of the Canadian Army, delayed inserting Canadian troops into the order of battle because he wanted to keep the force together rather than have it parcelled out piecemeal to serve under other Allied commands. Eventually, political pressure in Canada and the needs of the supreme Allied command in Europe grew too great and they split the 1st Canadian Army (Stacey, 'Through the Second World War,' in *The Canadians, 1867–1967*, part 1, ed. Careless and Brown, 289–90; Douglas and Greenhous, *Out of the Shadows*, 131–2).

38 JAP to MacLean, 23 July 1941, MacLean personal papers.

39 His feelings of impatience and boredom are mentioned in LAC, JPP, vol. 1, no. 3, JAP to E. Porter, 9 February 1942. The quotation 'a doubt at a distance' is from his poem, 'After Ortona,' written 9 February 1944, ibid., vol. 1, no. 22.

40 Eileen Jones interview; and John Grist interview.

41 JAP to MacLean, 23 July 1941, MacLean personal papers.

42 Jewett interview 2.

43 Alan Porter interview.

44 Eileen Jones interview; Alan Porter interview; and Ann Porter interview; see also Marion Porter comments, 7–8 July 1987. The time he spent with the Bartholomews had a great impact (Ann Porter interview).

45 LAC, JPP, vol. 1, no. 13, JAP to E. Porter, 19 June 1943; also B. MacLean to RHH, 20 May 1990. In 1941, Porter submitted a composition to the Churchill Essay Competition, sponsored by the Canadian Legion Educational Services of the Canadian Army Overseas (LAC, JPP, vol. 1, no. 18, Director of Education, Canadian Legion Educational Services to JAP, dated 'in the field, 1941').

46 LAC, JPP, vol. 1, no. 13, JAP to E. Porter, 13 January [1942?].

47 John Grist interview.

48 Porter Cole interview.

49 Dodie Cole interview.

50 I noted in a draft of this manuscript that John's style seemed similar to that of World War I poets such as Wilfred Owen, Rupert Brooke, and Siegfried Sassoon. Marion Porter agreed, noting that John liked Sassoon's work and had emulated it (Marion Porter comments, 23 February 1993). Re World War I poetry, see Paul Fussell, *The Great War and Modern Memory* (New York and London: Oxford, 1975); and Cecil Boura, 'Poetry and the First World War,' in *In General and Particular* (1964, reprint Freeport, NY: Books for Libraries Press, 1972), 193–221. Re World War II poetry, see Kiedrych Rhys, ed., *Poems from the Forces* (London: George Routledge and Sons, 1941); Kiedrych Rhys, ed., *More Poems from the Forces* (London: George Routledge and Sons, 1943); and Jane and Walter Morgan, eds., *Soldier Poetry of the Second World War: An Anthology* (Oakville, ON: Mosaic Press, 1990).

51 Marion Porter told this story in an interview with Rosemary Sullivan, MacEwen's biographer (UTARM, GMP, Thomas Fisher Rare Book Room, Robarts Library, R. Sullivan interview of M. Porter, 4 February 1993). According to Marion, John was so impressed with MacEwen's work that he discussed with her the possibility that she come to Ottawa and stay with them while attending Carleton. By the time MacEwen 'should' have gone to university, however, she decided she was not interested in continuing her formal education.

52 MacEwen to RHH, 5 January 1987.

53 LAC, JPP, vol. 8, no. 19, John Porter, 'Speech to the 9th Ontario Universities Computing Conference,' 1978.

54 At the time, Porter held the poems dear enough to harbour them as keepsakes. Apparently, for the first few years of the war, he kept a diary that

contained among other things a great deal of poetry. He mailed the diary to his mother just before he left for Sicily in 1943. Years later, when his mother died (28 November 1971), Eileen found the diary among her personal effects. When she returned it to him, he burned it (Eileen Jones interview).

55 Marion Porter comments, 23 November 1993.

56 Porter's wartime poems (plus rough drafts and fragments) can be found in LAC, JPP, vol. 1, no. 22. There are two other poems in his papers, both written after the war and among the documents dealing with his divorce from his first wife, Elizabeth Stalker (vol. 1, no. 12).

57 JAP to B. MacLean, 10 November 1941, MacLean personal papers.

58 LAC, JPP, vol. 1, no. 13, JAP to E. Porter, 25 June 1943.

59 He makes the same point in 'Is This Our Harvest?' written in February 1943 (LAC, JPP, vol. 1, no. 22).

60 LAC, JPP, vol. 1, no. 22, 'Death's House,' written Boyne Regis, June 1942.

61 Ibid.

62 LAC, JPP, vol. 1, no. 22, 'Hospital Ship,' written Bristol, December 1942.

63 LAC, JPP, vol. 1, no. 22, 'Majella Moon,' n.d. Porter Cole's copy of this poem is dated 20 February 1944 (Porter Cole personal papers).

64 JAP to MacLean, 10 November 1941, MacLean personal papers.

65 By comparison, said Ann, her mother was an agnostic who thought it appropriate to expose her children to religious ideas (Ann Porter interview).

66 Porter wrote to his mother that 'many young women' had asked him for a copy of this poem. 'I rather feel,' he said, 'that somehow there might be a common message in it for all of us, and in the mood in which it was written I think I have captured the thoughts of many young men at a time when life is very tense and indefinite' (LAC, JPP, vol. 1, no. 13, JAP to E. Porter, 19 June 1943). It is likely that the poem was written in May 1943 because it appears on a typewritten sheet with other poems dating from that time (LAC, JPP, vol. 1, no. 22).

67 Charles Messenger, *The Chronological Atlas of World War 2* (New York: Macmillan, 1989), 116–19 and 126–31, respectively.

68 The United States had already engaged the Japanese in the South Pacific. However, early in their collaboration, Churchill and Roosevelt agreed it was imperative to defeat Germany first (McAndrew, *Canadians and the Italian Campaign*, 17–21).

69 Re Allied planning for the D-Day offensive, see Stacey, *Victory Campaign*, 3–27. On Canadian preparations, see ibid., 28–47. For a detailed account of the Canadian role in the Sicilian and Italian campaigns, see Nicholson, *Canadians in Italy*, 1956.

70 Stacey and Wilson, *Half-Million,* 18; McAndrew, *Canadians and the Italian Campaign,* 17.

71 On the tactical significance of Sicily and a discussion of the operational difficulties involved in mounting the campaign, see McAndrew, *Canadians and the Italian Campaign,* 20–4.

72 Stacey, *Six Years of War,* 108–9, 238–53.

73 Porter took courses at CMHQ in London from 24 June 1942 to 16 July 1942 and from 18 July 1942 to 12 August 1942. See LAC, DND, RDE, JAP, 'Record of Service,' entries 24 June 1942, 16 July 1942, 18 July 1942, and 12 August 1942; also 'Service and Casualty Form,' entries 24 June 1942, 16 July 1942, 18 July 1942, and 12 August 1942. For his promotion, see 'Record of Service,' entry 3 December 1942; also 'Service and Casualty Form,' entry 3 December 1942.

74 For his time in London see ibid., 'Record of Service,' entries 7 and 23 February 1943; also 'Service and Casualty Form,' entries 4 and 23 February 1943. His time at the 1st Division HQ is listed in 'Service and Casualty Form,' entries 23 February 1943–30 March 1943.

75 Roy, *Seaforth Highlanders,* 149–50; see also McAndrew, *Canadians and the Italian Campaign,* 24–5, 32, 35–6. Section title phrase from Mowat, *My Father's Son,* 5.

76 Nicholson, *Canadians in Italy,* 65–72. Porter did not disembark until 13 July, after the beachhead had been firmly established and the first wave of troops had moved well inland (LAC, DND, RDE, JAP, 'Statement of Service,' entry 13 July 1943; 'Service and Casualty Form,' entry 13 July 1943; see also Elliot, *Scarlet to Green,* 222). More troops took part in the invasion of Sicily than in the invasion of Normandy on D-Day, a year later (McAndrew, *Canadians and the Italian Campaign,* 32).

77 McAndrew, *Canadians and the Italian Campaign,* 35–44, quotation from 42.

78 Stacey, *Canadian Army,* 97–9.

79 During the first week, one of the biggest problems Canadian troops faced was the 1,000–1,500 Italian prisoners of war they captured each day as they moved north. See Divisional History, unit reports, cited McAndrew, *Canadians and the Italian Campaign,* 46. Regarding the other factors, see ibid., 44–5, and McDougall, 'War, a Narrative,' 87.

80 LAC, JPP, vol. 1, no. 13, JAP to E. Porter, 19 July 1943.

81 Stacey, *Canadian Army,* 100–5.

82 Quotation from Mowat, *My Father's Son,* 5. Stacey, *Canadian Army,* 106; for slightly different figures see Douglas and Greenhous, *Out of the Shadows,* 139.

83 Nicholson, *The Canadians in Italy,* 50–179. For a Canadian newspaper

account, see Daniel de Luce, 'Sicily Battle Comes to End after 38 Days,' *Globe and Mail* (Toronto), 18 August 1943, www.civilization.ca/cwm/ newspapers/operations/sicilianitalian_e.html.

84 His promotion is recorded in LAC, DND, RDE, JAP, 'Service and Casualty Form,' entry 3 August 1943.

85 Elliot, *Scarlet to Green*, 224.

86 Ibid., 225–6.

87 Field security sections normally arrived with a blacklist of local fascists, collaborators, and agents prepared for them by Army Intelligence (Elliot, *Scarlet to Green*, 222).

88 McAndrew, *Canadians and the Italian Campaign*, 106–7; and Elliot, *Scarlet to Green*, 243, 235, 223.

89 LAC, DND, RDE, JAP, 'Record of Service,' entries 3 September–3 November 1943; 'Service and Casualty Form,' 3 September 1943–2 November 1943; also 'Postings from O/S Casualty Lists,' 20 September 1943–4 October 1943. Porter wrote to his mother about this episode (LAC, JPP, vol. 1, no. 13, JAP to E. Porter, 21 September 1943, 24 September 1943, 2 October 1943, and 7 October 1943).

90 LAC, JPP, vol. 1, no. 13, JAP to E. Porter, n.d.

91 Re Canadian troop movement, see Elliot, *Scarlet to Green*, 229.

92 There is an interesting side story from this period. In early November, Porter lost a large portion of his equipment, including his personal effects, in a small town near Campobasso. These effects were returned to his mother with the accompanying note: 'The enclosed personal possessions, which appear to be those of your son, were among a soldier's kit and equipment, parts of which recently came into my charge. They seem to have been packed up but left behind in a small town in southern Italy, probably about two months ago. No evidence of the circumstances or clue to his name, unit or identity could be found except the address on your letter which I am returning ... May I offer my best wishes for his safety and return to you' (Capt. E. Elliott to E. Porter, 1 December 1943, Ann Porter personal papers).

93 Roy, *Seaforth Highlanders*, ch. 8; Nicholson, *The Official History*, 304–37. Porter wrote the initial draft of this chapter for the Nicholson volume. Re the assault on Ortona, see also Ralph Allen, *Ordeal by Fire: Canada, 1910–1945* (Toronto: Doubleday, 1961), 432–47; and McAndrew, *Canadians and the Italian Campaign*, 68–84.

94 Elliot, *Scarlet to Green*, 228–9.

95 Marion Porter interview 1.

96 LAC, JPP, vol. 1, no. 22. 'After Ortona' is the only one of Porter's war

poems to be published (see *Poems from Italy: Verses Written by Members of the Eighth Army in Sicily and Italy, July 1943–March 1944* (London: Harrap's, 1945), 77–8. It was one of 72 poems chosen from 596 entries submitted to a poetry competition organized by the Army Educational Corps (M. Porter to RHH, 19 February 1990). The only other poem Porter had published was 'Village Sunday Morning,' which appeared in the LSE student literary paper the *Clare Market Review* (summer 1947): 2.

97 I am indebted for this observation to military historian Geoffrey Hayes, my colleague at the University of Waterloo (Hayes to RHH, n.d. July 2002).

98 Marion Porter interview 1; see also Marion Porter comments, 23 February 1993.

99 Ann Porter interview.

100 Stacey, *Canadian Army*, 124–7.

101 The major parts of the 1st Canadian Corps were the 1st Canadian Division and the 5th Canadian Armoured Division (Hayes to RHH, n.d. July 2002).

102 LAC, DND, RDE, JAP, 'Record of Service,' entries 1 and 2 May 1944 and 4, 5, and 6 August 1944; also 'Service and Casualty Form,' entries 1 and 2 May 1944, and 4 and 5 August 1944.

103 See Douglas and Greenhous, *Out of the Shadows*, 149–55; Stacey, *Canadian Army*, 130–44; McDougall, 'War, a Narrative,' 92–100; Roy, *Seaforth Highlanders*, ch. 9.

104 Douglas and Greenhous, *Out of the Shadows*, 155.

105 The exception was a brief period spent in action near Florence (McAndrew, *Canadians and the Italian Campaign*, 114).

106 Elliot, *Scarlet to Green*, 236–40 passim.

107 It took nearly a year to bring the rest of Italy under Allied control (Stacey, *Canadian Army*, 146–67). Almost 92,000 Canadians served in the Italian theatre. More than a quarter became casualties, including 6,000 who were killed (ibid., 165).

108 Ibid., 158–64; see also Douglas and Greenhous, *Out of the Shadows*, 208–12.

109 LAC, DND, RDE, JAP, 'Service and Casualty Form,' entries 2–6 August and 6 September 1944.

110 Ibid., 'Service and Casualty Form,' entry 1 October 1944.

111 Hayes to RHH, n.d. July 2002.

112 LAC, DND, RDE, JAP, 'Record of Service,' entry 23 February 1945; also 'Service and Casualty Form,' entry 23 February 1945.

113 Ibid., 'Cadet Record Sheet, Royal Army Ordnance Corps and Royal Elec-

trical Mechanical Engineers, 206 Officer Cadet Training Unit,' 6 February 1945.

114 Phillips interview.

115 MacLean to RHH, 20 May 1990.

116 LAC, JPP, vol. 1, no. 19, Notebook. According to Marion Porter, John's friendship with R.A.J. (Bob) Phillips had some influence in this regard. Phillips, she said, 'was very interested in the Left – had many pamphlets and articles – and visited Lord Passfield [Sidney Webb]' (Marion Porter comments, 23 February 1993).

117 Clement interview 3.

118 LAC, JPP, vol. 1, no. 13, JAP to E. Porter, 19 June 1943.

119 Phillips interview. In a letter to his mother John asks her to get subscriptions to *New Statesman* and *Nation* (LAC, JPP, vol. 1, no. 13, JAP to E. Porter, 20 April 1945).

120 LAC, DND, RDE, JAP, 'Service and Casualty Form,' entry 5 April 1945. Dodie Cole recalls that Porter dropped into see Porter Cole in the Officer's Mess in Deventer in March or April of 1945 and then again later after Cole had been moved to The Hague (Dodie Cole interview).

121 The 1st Canadian Army was created by the joining of the 1st and 2nd Canadian Corps. It was an auspicious event, the first and only time during the war that the two corps would be united in battle under Canadian command (see Stacey, *Canadian Army*, 164–7; see also Stacey, *Victory Campaign*, 529–30).

122 Stacey, *Canadian Army*, 256–72.

123 Stacey and Wilson, *Half-Million*, 169.

124 LAC, DND, RDE, JAP, 'Service and Casualty Form,' entry 18 May 1945; see also LAC, JPP, vol. 1, no. 14, JAP to E. Porter, 18 July 1945.

125 Ibid., Porter, 'Service and Casualty Form,' entries for 9 April 1945–27 July 1945; see also JAP to E. Porter, 7 May and 3 June 1945.

126 Hayes to RHH, n.d. July 2002.

127 LAC, JPP, vol. 1, no. 14, JAP to E. Porter, 20 June 1945.

128 Ibid., JAP to E. Porter, 7 May 1945.

129 Ibid., JAP to E. Porter, 3 June 1945.

130 Ibid., JAP to E. Porter, 3 June and 12 July 1945.

131 P. Johnson to JAP, 1 June 1945, Ann Porter personal papers. In this letter, Johnson indicates that Porter has received his 'third pip,' i.e., that he has been promoted to captain. This is odd because Porter was not officially promoted to captain until much later, when he was working in the Historical Section in 1945–6.

132 LAC, JPP, vol. 1, no. 14, JAP to E. Porter, 3 June 1945.

133 Ibid., JAP to E. Porter, 7 May and 7 June 1945.

134 Ibid., JAP to E. Porter, 27 June 1945.
135 Ibid. JAP to E. Porter, 18 July and 20 August 1945; see also B. MacLean to JAP, 30 July 1945, Ann Porter personal papers.
136 LAC, JPP, vol. 1, no. 14, JAP to Ethel Porter, 20 June 1945.
137 LAC, DND, RDE, JAP, 'Service and Casualty Form,' entries 29 and 30 July 1945.
138 LAC, JPP, vol. 1, no. 14, JAP to E. Porter, 24 August 1945; see also M. Porter interview 1.
139 Ibid., JAP to E. Porter, 24 August 1945.
140 LAC, DND, RDE, JAP, 'Service and Casualty Form,' entry 30 August 1945 and 'Officer Record of Service.'
141 Ibid., 'Record of Service'; see also Eileen Jones interview.
142 M. Porter, 'John Porter,' 2.
143 LAC, JPP, vol. 1, no. 14, E. Porter to P. Johnson, 20 January 1946; see also E. Porter to P. Johnson, 18 October 1945.
144 About twenty of these letters remain. In them, Cole refers to other letters, indicating that he wrote to John nearly every day (P. Cole to JAP, February–July 1946, Ann Porter personal papers).
145 Tom [illegible] to JAP, 20 July 1946, Ann Porter personal papers.
146 LAC, JPP, vol. 1, no. 4, telegram, J.G. Jenkins to JAP, 18 September 1946.
147 LAC, DND, RDE, JAP, 'Canadian Army (Active), Certificate of Service,' 8 November 1946. Porter had been promoted to captain while in the Historical Section (ibid., 'Record of Service,' entry 23 August 1945; also 'Service and Casualty Form,' entry 23 August 1945).
148 Ann Porter interview.
149 Marion Porter recalled that on one occasion when Pauline Jewett was visiting the Porter family cottage, John broke off his reminiscences about the war because Jewett said she had already heard the story. Ann, said Marion, was upset at this because she said her father never talked about his experiences during the war (Marion Porter interview 1).
150 Ann Porter interview.
151 Helmes interview.
152 Tony Porter interview 1.
153 LAC, JPP, vol. 4, no. 26, 'Thoughts about Unionization of Faculty,' February 1975.
154 Hayes to RHH, n.d. July 2002.
155 See M. Porter, 'John Porter,' 2. Stacey comments on this in his autobiography, *A Date with History* (Ottawa: Deneau, 1983), 179.
156 LAC, DND, RDE, JAP, 'Canadian Active Service Force Overseas Last Pay Certificate.'
157 M. Porter to RHH, 25 November 1991.

158 M. Porter, 'John Porter,' 5.

159 Eileen Jones interview. Kenneth McRae made a similar point in a different way, suggesting that the war 'opened up a bigger part of the world for him, as it did for many others' (McRae interview 1).

3: The LSE Years, 1946–1949

1 Sections of this chapter are based on Helmes-Hayes, 'Hobhouse Twice Removed,' and Helmes-Hayes, 'J.A. Banks.'

2 See McKenzie, untitled, in *My LSE*, ed. Abse, 83–103, especially 88–9.

3 Porter, 'Research Biography,' in Coleman, Etzioni, and Porter, *Macrosociology*, 149–52. For Porter to equate his undergraduate years with a graduate education makes sense for three reasons. First, he went to the LSE as an adult. Second, he already possessed considerable research skills from his time at the Historical Section. Third, most of those with whom he spent his time while at the LSE were graduate students. See CU, ARC, no author, 'Profile: John A. Porter,' *The Carleton* 5, no. 19 (21 March 1950): 16–17.

4 W. Clement, 'Foreword,' in Porter, *Measure of Canadian Society*, xii.

5 See Caine, *Foundation of the LSE*. The most detailed account of the history of the LSE is Dahrendorf, *LSE*. He discusses the founding years on pp. 3–71.

6 Caine, *Foundation of the LSE*, 6–8.

7 Wilcox-Magill, 'Paradigms and Social Science,' in *Introduction to Sociology*, ed. Grayson, 11.

8 Dahrendorf, *LSE*, 16–19, 49; see in particular S. Webb to A. Robertson, 3 January 1903, cited p. 19.

9 Ibid., 43; see also 46–8. Hewins, the first director, was a Conservative.

10 Ibid., 21–5.

11 Ibid., 24.

12 LAC, JPP, vol. 1, no. 3, D.G. MacRae, 'LSE: Seventy-Five Years of the London School of Economics and Political Science: Some Personal Reflections,' 1971, 2.

13 C. Bermant, untitled, in *My LSE*, ed. Abse, 180; see also B. Crick, 'Civilising LSE,' in *LSE People, 1947–1953*, ed. Deborah Manley (London: LSE Alumni Group, 1987), 24–5.

14 Porter regarded the immediate postwar era as the School's 'most superb period' ('Research Biography,' in Coleman, Etzioni, and Porter, *Macrosociology*, 149).

15 Arthur Rucker, 'The Martin White Benefaction,' in *Inauguration of the Martin White Professorship of Sociology, University of London, December 17,*

1907 (London: John Murray, 1908), 3–4; see also Abrams, 'Origins of British Sociology,' in Abrams, *Origins of British Sociology,* 101–9 passim.

16 On Hobhouse's life, see J. Hobson, 'L.T. Hobhouse: A Memoir,' in J. Hobson and M. Ginsberg, *Leonard Trelawney Hobhouse: His Life and Works* (London: Allen and Unwin, 1931), 15–95; and Owen, *L.T. Hobhouse,* 7–20. In England, some scholars regard Hobhouse as an underappreciated giant in the field, equivalent in stature to Spencer, Toennies, Pareto, Durkheim, even Weber (see, for example, Fletcher, 'Introduction,' in J. Owen, *L.T. Hobhouse, Sociologist* (London: Nelson, 1974), x–xi; Owen, *L.T. Hobhouse,* 1–7; D.G. MacRae, *Weber* (London: Woburn, 1974), 85; MacRae interview; and Dahrendorf, *LSE,* 103–6.

17 Dahrendorf, *LSE,* 94–107.

18 Caine, 'Ginsberg at the LSE,' in *Science of Society,* ed. Fletcher, 31.

19 See Abrams, 'Origins of British Sociology,' 109–13, 129–32. On the belated development of sociology in Britain, see also H.P. Becker and H.E. Barnes, *Social Thought from Lore to Science,* vol. 3 (Gloucester, MA: Peter Smith, 1978), 793–814; and H. Maus, *A Short History of Sociology* (New York: Citadel, 1962), 44–51.

20 In 1942–3 Ginsberg was elected president of the Aristotelian Society and, in 1953, fellow of the British Academy. He retired in 1954 as professor emeritus in sociology after receiving honorary degrees from Glasgow and Nottingham Universities. A.H. Halsey, 'Ginsberg, Morris (1889–1970),' *Oxford Dictionary of National Biography* (London: Oxford, 2004), www.oxfordnb.com/view/article/33411.

21 MacRae argues that 'the history of the Sociology Department at LSE was for a very long time the history of sociology in the United Kingdom' (cited Dahrendorf, *LSE,* 380).

22 Dahrendorf, *LSE,* 376.

23 Henry Pelling, *Modern Britain 1885–1955,* 2nd ed. (London: Sphere, 1969), 170–98.

24 During the war, the LSE shifted its operations to the campus of Cambridge University (see Dahrendorf, *LSE,* 342–61). Re the return to Houghton Street, see 361–2.

25 Ibid., 372.

26 The full-time day student registration was nearly 1,500 in 1935–6, the highest number prior to the war. Enrolment dropped during the war but climbed quickly afterward, from a low of less than 500 in 1940–1 to 2000 in 1946–7 (BLEPS, LSEA, 'The Director's Report on the Work of the School for the Session 1944–45,' LSE *Calendar 1946–7,* 28; 'The Director's Report on the Work of the School for the Session 1945–46,' LSE *Calendar 1947–48,* 30).

27 Dahrendorf, *LSE*, 371; see also Robson to RHH, 1 November 1990.
28 On the student culture at the LSE during this period, see Dahrendorf, *LSE*, 389–93; and Ken Braidwood, 'Forty Years On,' in *LSE People*, ed. Manley, 36.
29 Dahrendorf, *LSE*, 389.
30 Richmond to RHH, 11 March 1988.
31 Comments by Braidwood, 'Forty Years On,' 36. In Chesworth's words: 'Up to 1951 ... [students] thought that Jerusalem was on its way,' if they would just put in the effort (Chesworth interview).
32 Porter, 'Research Biography,' in Coleman, Etzioni, and Porter, *Macrosociology*, 150; see also J.A. Banks, 'From Universal History to Historical Sociology,' *BJS*, LX, no. 4 (1989): 521–43; and John Grist interview.
33 See Robson to RHH, 1 November 1990; Gill Grist interview; and Chesworth interview.
34 Porter, 'Research Biography,' in Coleman, Etzioni, and Porter, *Macrosociology*, 150; see also Robson to RHH, 1 November 1990.
35 Robson to RHH, 1 November 1990.
36 There is some disagreement among my sources on this point. Some remember undergraduates as having been required to attend lectures.
37 Fox interview.
38 The mysterious workings of the courses and examinations at the LSE were explained to me by Paul Fox and Robert Fenn in interviews, and also by Anthony Richmond (Richmond to RHH, 11 March 1988; Richmond interview).
39 Richmond to RHH, 11 March 1988.
40 John Grist interview.
41 Porter's expertise in economics later earned him considerable stature among his social science colleagues in Canada (McFarlane interview). According to Norman Dennis, 'First-year economics was of a rather "Whig view of history" sort, from benighted mercantilism and then laissez-faire to the bright day of Keynes. (No question of Marxian economics!) We were rather dismissive of Hayek, presumably on the basis of hints from some of our teachers, but there were already plenty of economists around who would now be called "monetarists"' (Dennis to RHH, 1 August 1990).
42 BLEPS, LSEA, LSE *Calendar 1946–7*, 224.
43 See comments by Robert McKenzie (15), Jack Sheard (21), Enid Wistrich (28), and Leslie Young (29) in *LSE People*, ed. Manley. See also comments by B.K. Nehru (36–7), J.W.N. Watkins (78–9), Robert McKenzie (86–91 passim), Jacqueline Wheldon (135–7), and Bernard Crick (149–51) in *My LSE*, ed. Abse.

44 The interview can be found in CU, ARC, no author, 'Profile: John A. Porter,' *The Carleton* 5, no. 19 (21 March 1950): 16–17. MacDonald's remarks were attributed to her by Marion Porter (Marion Porter interview 1). There are no notes from Laski's lectures in Porter's student notes. However, when Porter was first hired at Carleton, he taught political science, not sociology, and one of his sets of Carleton College lectures deals with precisely the subject matter of Laski and Smellie's course (LAC, JPP, vol. 2, nos. 6–11). Based on the fit between the subject matter of the two courses and the fact that Porter transferred some of his other LSE student notes to his Carleton College lecture notes when he began teaching in 1949, we can reasonably surmise that Porter used Laski's lectures as the basis for his lectures at Carleton.

45 Marion Porter interview 1.

46 According to his daughter, Ann Porter, John was much more 'political' at the LSE than 'artsy' (Ann Porter interview). In interviews, both Marion Porter and Donald Chesworth remarked that he was more directly involved in politics than at any other time in his life. And there is other information as well. Like many LSE students, he attended meetings of the student Labour Society (M. Porter, 'John Porter,' 4) and with his friends John and Gill Grist attended a socialist youth organization conference in Holland (Marion Porter interview 1; Gill Grist interview). Marion recalls that he canvassed for Donald Chesworth against Anthony Eton in a national election (Marion Porter interview 1), but Chesworth has no recollection of this (Chesworth interview). Paul Fox claims that not too much should be read into Porter's 'radical' student activities because even at this time 'he was more interested in the theory of democratic socialism than its practice' (Fox interview).

47 The details in the balance of this paragraph come from my interview with Fiona Ellen and from Elizabeth's obituary: 'Elizabeth Edith Porter,' *Richmond Times Dispatch,* n.d. [c. late January 1991], Ellen personal papers.

48 Ellen interview.

49 Dodie Cole interview.

50 'Wren Officer's Marriage,' newspaper clipping, n.d., and 'Military Wedding Prestatyn,' newspaper clipping, n.d., Ellen personal papers.

51 For the story of the wedding and the robbery, see Dodie Cole interview. That the thefts took place was confirmed by Fiona Ellen in conversation after our formal interview, 10 November 2007.

52 Ellen interview.

53 Ibid.

54 According to Marion Porter, Elizabeth refused to do 'domestic' chores

such as washing John's clothing (Marion Porter interview 1). At the time, John held a traditional view of gender roles and this kind of disagreement probably created problems between them. Details of the break-up of their marriage from John's perspective can be found in letters Porter wrote to his lawyer in the course of applying for a divorce (LAC, JPP, vol. 1, no. 12, JAP to L. Bingham, 10 February 1951, attachment: 'Answers to Questions Set Out in Counsel's Opinion').

55 Fiona was born 20 April 1948 (Ellen interview).
56 Marion Porter interview 1.
57 Chesworth interview.
58 Fox interview.
59 MacRae interview.
60 Gill Grist interview; John Grist interview.
61 MacRae to RHH, 28 August 1987.
62 Shils to RHH, 28 July 1987 and 7 September 1987.
63 Ibid. In 1949, Shils wrote a letter of reference in support of Porter's application for a job in the Canadian Department of External Affairs. He wrote to his former pupil that Porter 'would do better to go into the Canadian Foreign Service than into sociology.' It is not clear whether this was a consequence of Shils' negative assessment of Porter's potential as a scholar or his view of the academic job market in Canada (LAC, JPP, vol. 1, no. 1, Shils to Personnel Officer, Department of External Affairs, 29 July 1949).
64 John Grist interview.
65 Fox interview. Eileen Jones, Porter's sister, agreed with this assessment (Eileen Jones interview).
66 M. Porter, 'John Porter,' 2.
67 BLEPS, LSEA, LSE *Calendar 1948–49*, 278, 275–6. In 1948, Shils' lectures from these two courses were published as *The Present State of American Sociology* (New York: Free Press, 1948).
68 Blishen felt that despite some 'antipathy' Porter had toward Shils, he had an impact on Porter (Blishen interview).
69 LAC, JPP, vol. 1, no. 30, Shils, 'Community Studies,' 21 October, no year indicated. Two out of the five *Yankee City* volumes are W.L. Warner and P.S. Lunt, *The Social Life of a Modern Community* (New Haven: Yale University Press, 1941); and W.L. Warner and P.S. Lunt, *The Status System of a Modern Community* (New Haven: Yale University Press, 1942).
70 Ibid. For example, they reviewed William Booth's *New Survey of London Life and Labour* (BLEPS, LSEA, LSE *Calendar 1948–9*, 278)
71 G.D. Mitchell, *A Hundred Years of Sociology* (London: Duckworth 1968), 223. Dahrendorf argues that Glass' *Social Mobility in Britain* 'established the

centrality of the study of social stratification [at LSE] for almost two decades' (Dahrendorf, *LSE*, 377).

72 BLEPS, LSEA, LSE *Calendar 1948–9*, 276. These sources are Campion,
Public and Private Property in Great Britain; Berle and Means, *The Modern
Corporation and Private Property*; Tawney, *The Acquisitive Society* (New York:
Harcourt, Brace, 1920); and T.H. Marshall, ed., *Social Stratification and Class
Conflict* (London: Le Playhouse Press, 1938).

73 Richmond to RHH, 11 March 1988. Glass' contribution to English sociology resembles Porter's contribution to the Canadian discipline (see John
Westergaard, 'In Memory of David Glass,' *Sociology* 13, no. 2 [1979]:
173–7).

74 Porter, 'Research Biography,' in Coleman, Etzioni, and Porter, *Macrosociology*, 150.

75 BLEPS, LSEA, LSE *Calendar 1948–9*, 275–6. The full references for these
sources are: G. Lundberg, *Social Research* (New York: Longmans Green,
1948); H. Cantril, *Gauging Public Opinion* (Princeton: Princeton University
Press, 1944); P.V. Young, *Scientific Social Surveys and Research* (New York:
Prentice-Hall, 1949); and G. Allport, *The Use of Personal Documents in Psychological Science,* Social Science Research Council Bulletin 49 (New York:
SSRC, 1942).

76 Halsey, 'Provincials and Professionals,' 58–9.

77 Richmond to RHH, 11 March 1988.

78 John Westergaard notes on this account that by 1950 theory teaching at
LSE 'had turned to the "holy trinity"' – Marx, Durkheim, and Weber – in
part as a consequence of Shils' influence 'and, at a larger remove, of the
Parsons of *The Structure of Social Action*' (Westergaard to RHH, 1 August
1990). Interest in Weber's work grew rapidly in the United States after the
publication in English of his major works. Parsons' discussion of Weber's
work in *The Structure of Social Action* (Glencoe, IL: Free Press, 1949) and
the publication of Gerth and Mills, eds., *From Max Weber,* also contributed.
Shils was at the time translating and editing Weber's *The Methodology of
the Social Sciences* (ed. and trans. E. Shils and H.A. Finch [Glencoe, IL: Free
Press, 1949]). Porter drew extensively on Weber's work and the work of
French Weberian, Raymond Aron, in *The Vertical Mosaic*. In fact, Aron's
essays on elites, which appeared in *BJS* in 1950, were originally delivered
as lectures at the LSE in 1948 or 1949. Porter may well have attended them
(see Aron, 'Social Structure and the Ruling Class'). Tawney and MacRae
were Weber scholars as well.

79 Dennis and Halsey, *English Ethical Socialism*, 149, 151; see also 242.

80 Chesworth interview. According to Blishen, Porter did attend some of

Tawney's lectures. 'He talked about Tawney sitting down at lectures and spilling cigarette ash' (Blishen interview).

81 Another figure who may have been important to Porter in a similar way, but did not join the LSE staff until the year Porter left, was Robert MacIver. MacIver was a key figure in the development of the New Liberalism (McKillop, *Matters of Mind*, 672n61) and played a significant role in bringing it to the University of Toronto (ibid., 498–505; see also my comments in the afterword). MacIver's book *Society* was an important 'required text' for sociology examinations even before he arrived at LSE (Richmond to RHH, 22 November 1988). Norman Dennis, who studied at the LSE beginning in autumn 1949, noted that he studied MacIver's text 'carefully' while there (Dennis to RHH, 1 August 1990).

82 Dennis and Halsey, *English Ethical Socialism*, 156–69.

83 BLEPS, LSEA, LSE *Calendar 1948–9*, 277.

84 LAC, JPP, vol. 1, no. 26, and BLEPS, LSEA, LSE *Calendar 1948–9*, 254. See MacIver, *Modern State*; Hobhouse, *Elements of Social Justice*; F.A. Hayek, *The Road to Serfdom* (Chicago: University of Chicago Press, 1944); E.F. Carritt, *Morals and Politics* (Oxford: Clarendon, 1935); and Laski, *Grammar of Politics*.

85 LAC, JPP, vol. 1, no. 26, Laski, 'Political and Social Theory,' Lecture 1, n.d.

86 Oliver, ed., *Social Purpose for Canada*; Porter, *Vertical Mosaic*; Porter, 'Education and Equality,' and 'Education and the Just Society,' in Porter, *Measure of Canadian Society*, 242–62 and 263–80.

87 The information that Marshall was Porter's tutor came from Bruce McFarlane (see Wallace Clement, 'Power, Ethnicity and Class,' in *Vertical Mosaic Revisited*, ed. Helmes-Hayes and Curtis, 55n13). Porter would have seen Marshall every two weeks during that time (A. Richmond comments at a session of the Canadian Sociology and Anthropology Association, 6 June 1988).

88 Re Marshall's admiration for Hobhouse, see Dennis and Halsey, *English Ethical Socialism*, 136. Marshall was appointed to the Martin White Chair in sociology in 1956 after Ginsberg stepped down.

89 Richmond to RHH, 11 March 1988.

90 BLEPS, LSEA, LSE *Calendar 1948–9*, 276–7. See Hobhouse, *Morals in Evolution I*; Ginsberg, *Sociology*; MacIver, *Society*; and A.M. Carr-Saunders and D. Caradog Jones, *A Survey of the Social Structure of England and Wales as Illustrated by Statistics* (London: Oxford, 1927).

91 LAC, JPP, vol. 1, no. 30, Marshall, 'Comparative Social Institutions,' n.d.

92 Dennis and Halsey, *English Ethical Socialism*, 124.

93 Porter, *Measure of Canadian Society*, 3. The idea, specifically drawn from Marshall's *Citizenship and Social Class* (1950), appeared often in Porter's work (e.g., Porter, 'Ethnic Pluralism in Canadian Perspective,' in Porter, *Measure of Canadian Society*, 128).

94 LAC, JPP, vol. 1, no. 30, lecture 8, 13 November.

95 Hobhouse makes the same argument (see Hobhouse, *Liberalism*, e.g., 46–8).

96 LAC, JPP, vol. 1, no. 30, lecture 15, 22 January. Lipset has pointed out that in Marshall's view class and citizenship stood in unequivocal and irremediable opposition ('Tom Marshall – Man of Wisdom,' *BJS* 24, no. 4 [1973]: 415–16). For a discussion of Marshall's notion of citizenship, see Dennis and Halsey, *English Ethical Socialism*, 140–8.

97 A. Richmond comments at a session of the CSAA, 6 June 1988.

98 Halsey, 'Provincials and Professionals,' 47; see also Dennis and Halsey, *English Ethical Socialism*, 136.

99 Dahrendorf, *LSE*, 378.

100 See the afterword for a detailed discussion of these ideas.

101 On the New Liberalism in general, see Clarke, *Liberals and Social Democrats*; Freeden, *New Liberalism*; and Allett, *New Liberalism*. Hobhouse plays a central role in all of these accounts. A work that deals in detail with Hobhouse's contributions is Collini, *Liberalism and Sociology*.

102 Westergaard to RHH, 1 August 1990. Basil Bernstein said something similar: 'I have no recollection whatever of welfare state liberalism on the model of L.T. Hobhouse as a reference for students I know or junior staff' (Bernstein to RHH, 6 August 1990).

103 Porter's notes refer to it as 'social psychology' (LAC, JPP, vol. 1, no. 25).

104 BLEPS, LSEA, LSE *Calendar 1948–9*, 275. References for these sources are: A.L. Bowley, *The Nature and Purpose of the Measurement of Social Phenomena* (London: P.S. King, 1915); B. Webb and S. Webb, *Methods of Social Study* (London: Longman's Green, 1932); Hobhouse, *Social Development*; MacIver, *Society*; and Pitirim Sorokin, *Contemporary Sociological Theories* (New York and London: Harper and Brothers, 1928).

105 LAC, JPP, vol. 1, no. 24, Ginsberg, 'Theories and Methods of Sociology,' 6 October 1948.

106 Porter took introductory logic from Popper and recalled the course as 'tremendously impressive' (LAC, JPP, vol. 1, no. 28, see Porter, 'Research Biography,' in Coleman, Etzioni, and Porter, *Macrosociology*, 149).

107 BLEPS, LSEA, LSE *Calendar 1948–9*, 281. References for these sources are: T.H. Green, *Lectures on the Principles of Political Obligation* (London:

Longman's Green, 1924); J.A. Hobson, *Wealth and Life: A Study in Values* (London: Macmillan's, 1929); Hobhouse, *Elements of Social Justice*; Laski, *Grammar of Politics*; and E. Urwick, *Social Good* (London: Methuen, 1927).

108 LAC, JPP, vol. 1, no. 24, Ginsberg, 'Social Philosophy,' lecture of 10 November, n.d.

109 See Wilcox-Magill, 'Paradigms and Social Science,' in *Introduction to Sociology*, ed. Grayson, 18–22. Others who have referred to Porter as a Fabian, or at least as having been influenced by the Fabians, include F. Vallee, 'Obituary: John Porter,' 14; Clement, 'John Porter and the Development of Sociology,' 584; and Forcese, 'Macro-sociology of John Porter,' 651, 653.

110 MacRae interview.

111 Shils to RHH, 21 June 1989. Part of the reason for the lack of sympathetic attention paid to the Webbs, Norman Dennis suggests, is that they had foolishly associated themselves with the Stalinist Marxism of the postrevolutionary Soviet Union by publishing *Soviet Communism: A New Civilization*, 'first with and then without the qualifying question mark' (Dennis to RHH, 1 August 1990).

112 Robson to RHH, 1 November 1990.

113 Westergaard to RHH, 1 August 1990. The political arithmetic tradition involved the collection and analysis of statistical data regarding population, the economy, and the like. It has a long history but gained particular prominence in the nineteenth century with the development of modern techniques of statistical analysis. The term 'Blue Book' refers to annual publications regarding such data produced by the government of the United Kingdom.

114 Porter, 'Research Biography,' in Coleman, Etzioni, and Porter, *Macrosociology*, 149.

115 Richmond to RHH, 20 June 1988.

116 Vallee interview.

117 Westergaard to RHH, 9 August 1994.

118 Dahrendorf, *LSE*, 405.

119 Owen to RHH, 23 June 1989.

120 MacRae interview.

121 Ibid.

122 Apparently there was little disciplinary specialization. Collegiality in the fullest sense of the term was, as MacRae phrased it, 'very great across departments.' Indeed, until after World War II, there were no departments as such at LSE (ibid.).

123 Vallee said that Porter often referred to Shaw and the Webbs (Vallee interview). Blishen disagreed: 'While [Porter] talked about Fabianism, ... he

didn't talk about the individuals involved ... and he didn't seem to give them the appreciation that he gave his tutors and the general milieu of the London School of Economics' (Blishen interview).

124 For a detailed discussion of the history and principles of Fabianism and the influence of Fabianism on Porter, see Helmes-Hayes, 'Hobhouse Twice Removed,' 1990.

125 Porter, 'Two Cheers for Mental Health,' 145.

126 Porter, 'Research Biography,' in Coleman, Etzioni, and Porter, *Macrosociology*, 149.

127 Fox interview.

128 Porter, *Measure of Canadian Society*, 164; see also LAC, JPP, vol. 8, no. 14, Porter, 'Some Limits to Self-Determination,' [1978], 1. Re the Fabians' view that progress would be relatively easy, see G.K. Lewis, 'Fabian Socialism: Some Aspects of Theory and Practice,' *JP* 14 (1952): 453.

129 Porter, *Vertical Mosaic*, 552–6. In the early 1970s in a discussion of sociological theorizing with Dennis Olsen, a PhD student, Porter said that he thought the reason people theorized was because they had 'some really deep-seated need (Freudian) ... to rationalize' (Olsen, Notes from Sociology 610–11, September 1971–April 1972, Olsen personal papers). See also Porter's review of *The Origins of Psycho-Analysis*, ed. Bonaparte, Freud, and Kris, 163–4.

130 Laski, quoted by Leonard Tivey, 'Years of Hope,' in *LSE People*, ed. Manley, 18.

131 Porter, 'Research Biography,' in Coleman, Etzioni, and Porter, *Macrosociology*, 151–2.

132 LAC, JPP, vol. 1, no. 4, William Carr-Saunders, Director of the LSE, 2 December 1949.

133 Ibid.

134 M. Porter, 'John Porter,' 1.

135 Ibid.

136 Fox to RHH, 8 March 1991.

137 M. Porter, 'John Porter,' 2.

4: Canada and Carleton College, 1939–1963

1 M. Porter, 'John Porter,' 2.

2 Fox to RHH, 8 March 1991.

3 M. Porter, 'John Porter,' 2; Fox interview; Marion Porter interview 1.

4 Fox to RHH, 8 March 1991. Fox recruited Bob Phillips to teach an evening course in Soviet Studies in the same way (Phillips to RHH, 14 March 2000).

5 CU, ARC, no author, 'Profile: John A. Porter,' *The Carleton* 5, no. 19 (21 March 1950): 17.

6 M. Porter, 'John Porter,' 2.

7 Phillips to RHH, 14 March 2000.

8 Fox to RHH, 8 March 1991; see also Gibson interview.

9 Neatby and McEown, *Creating Carleton*, 3–10 passim.

10 CU, ARC, gathering file: Tory, H.M. – Biographical Dossier: R.W. Boyle, 'Henry Marshall Tory,' *The New Trail* 5, no. 4 University of Alberta, October 1947, 189–91.

11 McGill University College of British Columbia was a branch college of McGill University of Montreal until it became part of UBC in 1915 (ibid., 191).

12 Ibid.

13 Regarding Tory, see E.A. Corbett, *H.M. Tory: Beloved Canadian* (Toronto: Ryerson Press, 1954). On his part in the founding of Carleton College, see pp. 185–98.

14 Keenleyside was then a member of the Department of External Affairs (Neatby and McEown, *Creating Carleton*, 4, 5). He later became an ambassador and United Nations official (www.library.ubc.ca/archives/tributes/tribk.html).

15 Gibson interview; Neatby and McEown, *Creating Carleton*, 3–10 passim.

16 Neatby and McEown, *History of Carleton University*, n.p. In *Creating Carleton*, Neatby and McEown relate the following story about the origins of Carleton's college crest: 'Some years later, when the Board of Governors had agreed on a motto for the new college ['Ours the Task Eternal'], H.S. Southam – one of the early supporters of the college, and chairman of the board – expressed his approval of the board's decision but commented in an aside that the real motto of the college had always been "To hell with the Pope"' (5).

17 The phrase 'sundown college' comes from Claude Bissell, Carleton's third president, 1956–8. In his view, Carleton succeeded by meeting the demand for evening courses created by federal civil servants (CU, ARC, gathering file: Bissell, C.T., C. Bissell, 'A Role for Carleton,' address delivered at his installation as 3rd President of Carleton College, 13 November 1956, 8).

18 Neatby and McEown, *Creating Carleton*, 7–9.

19 Gibson interview. Ian Campbell, a Carleton student of the period, told a similar story (Campbell interview 1).

20 Neatby and McEown, *Creating Carleton*, 14.

21 Fox to RHH, 8 March 1991.

22 Neatby and McEown, *Creating Carleton*, 14, 15, 21, 24–5.

23 Fox to RHH, 8 March 1991.

24 Neatby and McEown, *Creating Carleton*, 9; see 9–10 more generally. Before any classes were offered, Gibson said, Tory contacted authorities from twenty Canadian universities to guarantee that students who did the first two years of their arts degree at Carleton would be able to transfer these credits without penalty (Gibson interview). The letters can be found in CU, ARC, Board of Governors' fonds, BOG–01, file: 'Recognition of Carleton College by Other Institutions, 1942–1955.' Only McGill was slow to agree.

25 Neatby and McEown, *Creating Carleton*, 10. The figure of over 700 students is also given in CU, ARC, gathering file: Carleton University: Its History, D.A. George, 'A Report on Continuing Education and Related Matters at Carleton University.' A retrospective account of enrolment that appears in *President's Report 1955–1956* sets the figure at 779 (CUA, Office of the President fonds, Series: Annual Reports, James Gibson, 'A Retrospective Report 1942–1956,' *President's Report 1955–1956*, 8). However, the *Carleton College Calendar 1949–50*, gives the figure of 550.

26 Neatby and McEown, *Creating Carleton*, 48.

27 Ibid., 17, 37.

28 The two campaigns are described in ibid., 30–1 and 37–8, respectively.

29 Ibid., 36. In 1952, it received a one-time federal grant as well as increased ongoing funding from the provincial government. For an account of the college's financial difficulties 1945–52, see 34–9.

30 Ibid., 24–5.

31 See Peter Neary, 'Canadian Universities and Canadian Veterans of World War II,' in *The Veterans Charter and Post–World War II Canada*, ed. Peter Neary and J.L. Granatstein (Montreal and Kingston: McGill-Queen's University Press, 1988), 110–48; Harris, *History of Higher Education in Canada*, 456–7, and Neatby and McEown, *Creating Carleton*, 24.

32 Neatby and McEown, *Creating Carleton*, 25–7.

33 Ibid., 26–7.

34 Dorothy Zaluska, ed., 'Student Registrations, 1942–43 to 1995–96,' *Carleton University Data Book 1995–96* (Ottawa: Carleton University Graphic Services, May 1996), 24.

35 Neatby and McEown, *Creating Carleton*, 34, 36.

36 Gibson interview.

37 Neatby and McEown, *Creating Carleton*, 31.

38 Ibid., 81–4.

39 For an account of the struggle to get a provincial charter and degree-granting privileges, see ibid., 39–42.

40 CU, ARC, Buildings gathering file: *The Carleton,* souvenir edition, 15, no.
    14 (12 February 1960); see also Neatby and McEown, *Creating Carleton,* 86.
41 CU, ARC, gathering file: Dunton, A.D. – Biographical Dossier, D.M. Farr,
    'The Dunton Years, 1958–1972,' Carleton University Public Relations/In-
    formation Services with the assistance of the CBC, Ottawa, n.d., 7.
42 Carleton College became Carleton University in May 1957 when, at the
    instigation of Claude Bissell, the Ontario legislature amended the Carleton
    College charter (Neatby and McEown, *Creating Carleton,* 42).
43 Kenneth McNaught, *The Pelican History of Canada* (Harmondsworth, UK:
    Pelican, 1969), 272.
44 Colombo, ed., *1994 Canadian Global Almanac,* 204, 'Value of Canadian Agri-
    cultural Products.'
45 During the period, Canada's GNP grew from $5.7 billion to $11.8 billion,
    measured in current dollars. In constant (1949) dollars, the GNP grew from
    $9.5 billion to $15.6 billion, a 64 per cent increase (Canada, Dominion Bu-
    reau of Statistics, *Canada Year Book 1964–65,* 1009; 'Gross National Product,
    in Current and Constant 1949 Dollars, 1927–63').
46 See Stuart Jamieson, *Industrial Relations in Canada,* 2nd ed. (Toronto: Mac-
    millan, 1973), 90–9. King's Industrial Disputes Investigation Act, which
    served workers' interests poorly, remained the cornerstone of Canada's
    industrial relations policy until after World War II (Heron, *Canadian Labour
    Movement,* 75–81 passim; see also Jamieson, *Industrial Relations in Canada,*
    2nd ed., 121–5).
47 Palmer, *Working-Class Experience,* 267.
48 Vincent and Alice Massey were important during the 1930s in persuading
    King and the Liberal Party to adopt the goals and methods of intervention-
    ist liberalism. Vincent Massey was president of the Liberal Party at the
    time and continually pressed King to be more progressive. A significant
    event in this process was a 'summer school' for the Liberal Party Mas-
    sey organized, at which the ideas of New Liberalism were thoroughly
    aired and promoted with the intention of 'wean[ing] the Liberals from
    the laissez-faire traditions of the party to a new, more technocratic and
    interventionist view of government' (Owram, *Government Generation,* 189).
    Quotation from Morton, *1945,* 3.
49 Leacy, ed., *Historical Statistics of Canada,* series H19–34: 'Federal govern-
    ment budgetary expenditures, classified by function, 1867 to 1975 (millions
    of dollars).'
50 Scott Gordon claims that the Liberals were not responsible for this growth.
    They happened to be in office during a period when growth was a 'world-
    wide phenomenon' (Gordon to RHH, n.d. January 2002).

51 In current dollars, the GNP rose from $11.9 billion to $43 billion. In constant 1949 dollars the respective figures were: 1945, $15.6 billion, and 1962, $28.1 billion (Canada, Dominion Bureau of Statistics, *Canada Year Book 1965*, 1,009, table 'Gross National Product, in Current and Constant 1949 Dollars, 1927–63').

52 Morton, *1945*, 11.

53 See O.J. Firestone, *Canada's Economic Development 1867–1953*, Income and Wealth series 7 (London: Bowes and Bowes, 1958), 216; and Bothwell, Drummond, and English, *Canada since 1945*, 169.

54 Porter, *Vertical Mosaic*, 147–55.

55 McVey Jr. and Kalbach, *Canadian Population*, 149, table 6.1.

56 Ibid., 42, table 2.4.

57 W. Kalbach and W. McVey, Jr., *The Demographic Bases of Canadian Society* (Toronto: McGraw-Hill, 1971), 42; 43, table 2:1; 33, figure 2.1.

58 Peter Li, *The Making of Post-War Canada* (Toronto: Oxford University Press, 1996), 98–100; see also 163n2 and n3.

59 Between 1951 and 1961, the average income of families and unattached individuals increased from $3,619 to $4,815 in constant 1961 dollars (Hunter, *Class Tells*, 56).

60 Ibid., 56, table 5–2.

61 Ibid., 70, table 5–7.

62 Finkel, *Our Lives*, 9–10.

63 The national debt had held steady at $11,000 per person for the period 1945–54, but rose rapidly thereafter (Colombo, ed., *1994 Canadian Global Almanac*, 183, 'Per Capita National Debt, 1940–1992').

64 Finkel, *Our Lives*, 15–23.

65 See e.g., Walter L. Gordon, *Troubled Canada: The Need for New Domestic Policies* (Toronto: McClelland and Stewart, 1961), 83–97.

66 Colombo, ed., *1994 Canadian Global Almanac*, 153, 'Federal Election Results, 1867–1988.'

67 Norrie, Owram, and Emery, *History of the Canadian Economy*, 381–2. For immigration see Leacy, ed. *Historical Statistics of Canada*, 2nd ed., 1983, series A350: 'Immigrant Arrivals in Canada, 1852 to 1977.' For birth rates see McVey Jr. and Kalbach, *Canadian Population*, 270, table 9.2.

68 Peter Newman, *Renegade in Power: The Diefenbaker Years* (Toronto, McClelland and Stewart, 1973), 202.

69 Colombo, ed., *1994 Canadian Global Almanac*, 179, 'Canadian Gross Domestic Product.'

70 Husby, 'Education,' in *Canadian Economy*, ed. Bellan and Pope, 193, table 7.

71 Ibid., 184.

72 The average annual deficit during the period 1958–63 was $664 million (Colombo, ed., *1994 Canadian Global Almanac*, 183, 'Federal Government Annual Surplus or Deficit'). During the Conservatives' tenure in office, the cumulative debt grew from $18.4 billion to $24.8 billion (Canada, Dominion Bureau of Statistics, *Canada Year Book 1963–1964*, 989, table 13).

73 The Conservatives retained only 116 seats, the Liberals jumped to 99, Social Credit held 30, and the newly formed NDP had 19. After the 1963 election, the Liberals held 129 seats, the PCs 95, Social Credit 24, and the NDP 17 (Colombo, ed., *1994 Canadian Global Almanac*, 153, 'Federal Election Results, 1867–1988').

5: The Genesis of *The Vertical Mosaic*, 1949–1958

1 CU, ARC, no author, 'Doors Opened by Dr. Tory,' *The Carleton* 3, no. 20 (2 April 1948): 4; see also Neatby and McEown, *Creating Carleton*, 32.

2 This succession arrangement had been made when MacOdrum was hired (McEown interview; see also Neatby and McEown, *Creating Carleton*, 12–13). The material in this paragraph is taken from J. O'Meara, 'Carleton Vice-President a Man of Many Talents,' *The Carleton* 2, no. 5 (13 December 1946): 6; No author, 'Dr. Murdoch Maxwell MacOdrum Dies of Heart Attack,' *South Ottawa Gazette* 8, no. 6 (12 August 1955): 1–2; and No author, 'Death a Going Home,' *The Carleton* 11, no. 1 (26 September 1955): 2–3, all in CU, ARC, gathering file: MacOdrum, M.M. – Biographical Dossier.

3 Rowat interview; Neatby interview; McEown interview; Farr interview; see also Neatby and McEown, *Creating Carleton*, 32.

4 Neatby and McEown, *Creating Carleton*, 32; see also McEown interview. Faculty members have different views about leadership at the college. David Farr argues that senior scholars such as James Gibson acted as leaders (Farr interview), while Scott Gordon argues that department heads shouldered this responsibility (Gordon comments, n.d. January 2002). Gibson claims that the appointment of C.J. Mackenzie as chancellor in 1954 was a key development in terms of leadership: 'It bolstered the overall sense of academic direction; not in any interfering [sense], but in enlightened encouragement' (Gibson to RHH, n.d. January 2002).

5 McEown interview.

6 Fox to RHH, 9 January 2002.

7 Fox interview; see also Gibson interview; Phillips interview. Note also Blair Neatby's comment: 'I don't know about John's relations with MacOdrum, but MacOdrum certainly didn't think much of sociology as a discipline' (Neatby interview).

8 Phillips interview. For the time, Porter was quite critical of capitalism and liberal democracy (see MacLean to JAP, 16 July 1946 and P. Cole to JAP, 3 May 1954, Ann Porter personal papers).

9 Phillips interview.

10 Fox to RHH, 9 January 2002.

11 Neatby interview.

12 Neatby and McEown, *Creating Carleton*, 50.

13 For a description of this struggle, see Neatby and McEown, *Creating Carleton*, 43–60 and Fox to RHH, 9 January 2002.

14 McRae interview 1.

15 Fox to RHH, 9 January 2002; Neatby interview; McEown interview.

16 McRae interview 1.

17 Gordon comments, n.d. January 2002.

18 Ibid. Neatby and McEown claim that MacOdrum's support was less enthusiastic and directive than this (*Creating Carleton*, 56).

19 Neatby interview; Farr interview.

20 Neatby interview.

21 Gordon to RHH, 6 August 1987.

22 Gibson interview. Fox disagreed. He believed that Porter always possessed a core of self-confidence that simply took a while to mature: 'John had confidence in himself … [H]e always knew that he had something to say and those of us who knew him, of course, were convinced that he was a superior person … We gave him encouragement and support but it was a long, long process' (Fox interview).

23 Fox interview; see also Phillips interview.

24 Neatby and McEown, *Creating Carleton*, 45.

25 Gibson interview; also Gibson to RHH, 9 January 2002.

26 Fox to RHH, 8 March 1991.

27 See Charles Gordon, 'Our Times,' *Ottawa Citizen*, 9 January 2000, 1.

28 Woods, *Ottawa*, 192.

29 Ibid., 282–3.

30 Fox to RHH, 8 March 1991. Tony Porter said that his father had 'mixed feelings' about living in Ottawa. In the early years, before cultural amenities such as the National Arts Centre were built, he found that Ottawa lacked the 'excitement' of European cities. It was, however, an interesting place to live because of postwar developments in government and the civil service. Later, Tony said, his father 'ended up developing some very good friendships and having a network of people that made Ottawa a great place to be' (Tony Porter interview 2).

31 M. Porter to RHH, 25 November 1991. Frank Jones made the same com-

plaint: 1950s Ottawa was 'dreary and dull,' especially compared to the lively intellectual and social life at Harvard. There was little street life and only a handful of bars and restaurants. Even the private party circuit had its pitfalls: 'The city was essentially stratified by civil service levels. And if you were naïve, as we were, and invited people to a party from different levels, you wouldn't get any interaction at all because people each had their own place' (Frank Jones interview).

32 Jewett interview 2. Ann Porter commented that her father was very excited when they went to England in 1964 because they were going to be staying in London and he 'loved the big city' (Ann Porter interview).

33 Ann Porter interview; Phillips to RHH, 14 March 2000.

34 Neatby and McEown, *Creating Carleton,* 44. Kenneth McRae noted that the teaching load at Carleton was better than that in the Maritimes, where faculty members were expected to teach 12–15 hours per week, and at Toronto, where there were fewer teaching hours (7.5 per week) but many more students (700–800 per professor) (McRae to RHH, n.d. January 2002).

35 CU, ARC, no author, 'CCF Club,' *The Carleton* 5, no. 19 (21 March 1950): 19.

36 Gordon to RHH, 6 August 1987; also Fox to RHH, 8 March 1991. McRae remarked on this score that 'the early years may have had hardships in building upon no earlier precedents … but by 1955 I saw this as a marvellous opportunity, a *tabula rasa* waiting to be written on, a chance to innovate that was impossible at older places' (McRae to RHH, n.d. January 2002).

37 Neatby and McEown, *Creating Carleton,* 46.

38 Ibid., 56–57; see also McRae interview; Fox interview.

39 Marion Porter reported her husband's salary in comments on an early draft of this book (Marion Porter comments, 23 February 1993). Porter's salary in 1950–1 was $2,800 and for a number of years thereafter he received a raise of about $300 per annum (LAC, JPP, vol. 2, no. 1, MacOdrum to JAP, 18 April 1950, 17 May 1951, 15 May 1952, 20 May 1954, 20 May 1955, and J. Gibson to JAP, 17 May 1956).

40 Marion Porter interview 1.

41 LAC, DND, RDE, JAP, Department of National Defence Message Form, 31 May 1950 (4 May 1950–2 July 1950); and Memorandum HQ–TC–41645 (D Hist) 27 July 1953 (4 May 1953–7 August 1953). See also LAC, JPP, vol. 2, no. 1, JAP to Gibson, 30 August 1954.

42 Academic salaries were low across Canada (Fox to RHH, 8 March 1991). Carleton professors created a staff association early on and played a part in the 1953 founding of the Canadian Association of University Teachers (Neatby and McEown, *Creating Carleton,* 57–8; see also Fox to RHH, 9 Janu-

ary 2002). The minutes of the first meeting of the CUASA (18 November 1952) are reprinted in the *Carleton University Academic Staff Association Handbook*, 2002, 8). Two decades later, the members of CUASA would be among the first to create a faculty union in Ontario.

43 LAC, JPP, vol. 2, no. 1, JAP to Gibson, 30 August 1954.

44 Farr interview; see also McRae to RHH, n.d. January 2002, and Neatby and McEown, *Creating Carleton*, chs. 3 and 4.

45 Fox to RHH, 9 January 2002.

46 McRae comments, n.d. January 2002. Some of his problems, such as the fact that for years he had to share an office and had no phone, were relatively niggling. Indeed, such difficulties were often lessened, if not eliminated, via ingenuity, cooperation, and goodwill. Historian David Farr recalls the example of the arrival of economist Scott Gordon in 1948. Gordon was working part time on a government contract and needed to be in daily contact with his government colleagues: 'The university … was too poor to provide anybody but the president and the bursar … with telephone service. So Scott arranged to rent a phone and he very kindly allowed us to use it.' They did so by cutting a hole in the wall and passing the phone back and forth between one office and the other (Farr interview).

47 Fox to RHH, 8 March 1991.

48 Ibid. According to Phillips, the collegiality was not universal. He remembers 'morale' problems that led to some 'politicking and backbiting.' 'It was … far from the idealistic monastery on which Jack may have been willingly sold. The causes may have been partly the universal insecurity of people in a struggling institution with a shaky future, and partly the weak leadership of the college' (Phillips to RHH, 14 March 2000). Fox commented on Phillips' view as follows: 'I don't know what the "politicking and backbiting" to which Bob P [sic] refers was, except for the big battle over the future of the college. From my experience there was much less of both problems than one normally sees in most university faculties' (Fox to RHH, 9 January 2002).

49 Fox to RHH, 8 March 1991. Frank Jones confirmed that Porter felt a real sense of collegiality at Carleton in the early years (Frank Jones interview).

50 McRae interview 1.

51 Rowat interview.

52 Frank Jones interview.

53 On the generally shared liberal beliefs of Porter's colleagues, see Gibson interview.

54 Re Porter's divorce see the correspondence in LAC, JPP, vol. 1, no. 12.

55 *Decree Nisi Absolute* (Divorce), High Court of Justice, London, England, 12 September 1951, Ellen personal papers.
56 Phillips to RHH, 14 March 2000.
57 Fox interview; and Fox to RHH, 9 January 2002. Eileen Jones agreed with this assessment (Eileen Jones interview).
58 John Grist interview.
59 Gibson interview.
60 Gordon to RHH, n.d. January 2002.
61 McRae to RHH, n.d. January 2002.
62 Phillips to RHH, 14 March 2000.
63 Jewett interviews 1 and 2; see also John Grist interview; and Fox to RHH, 9 January 2002.
64 Fox interview; see also M. Porter, 'John Porter,' 2; and Fox to RHH, 8 March 1991.
65 McFarlane to RHH, 25 July 2002. June Helm was then June Helm Mac-Neish. She requested that I use her current professional name, June Helm.
66 Unless otherwise noted, the information in this paragraph is taken from Helm to RHH, 15 March 1991; see also CU, ARC, Naomi Bender, 'Profile: Mrs. MacNeish,' *The Carleton* 5, no. 8 (29 November 1949): 1, 3; and Phillips interview.
67 CU, ARC, *Carleton College Calendar,* 1950–1 to 1955–6; see 1954–5, 137.
68 See ibid., 1949–50 to 1953–4 and Helm to RHH, 15 March 1991.
69 Porter consulted S.D. Clark, Frank Jones, and Oswald Hall before first offering the job to Leo Zakuta, then Frumhartz, a Columbia PhD student (LAC, JPP, vol. 2, no. 1); see also Frumhartz interview.
70 Phillips interview.
71 Campbell interview 1.
72 Abbott interview. J.M. Davies made the same point about Porter's skill at provoking seminar discussion in the early years (Davies to RHH, 17 July 1991).
73 LAC, JPP, vol. 4, no. 23, Carleton University, Sociology Students, Marks, 1951–68.
74 Neatby and McEown, *Creating Carleton,* 56.
75 McRae interview 2.
76 Davies to RHH, 17 July 1991.
77 Ages to RHH, 18 July 1991. Porter's willingness to aid students that he did not know continued long after he became prominent (Morton Weinfeld, letter to the editor, *S/S* 6, no. 2 [1982]: n.p.).
78 Student marks for these courses can be found in LAC, JPP, vol. 4, no. 23. This number of courses seems high, beyond the standard level. Perhaps some of the files are misdated.

79 LAC, JPP, vol. 2, no. 6, 'Introduction to Political Science' and 'Relation between Social Sciences and Political Sciences,' 4; see vol. 2, nos. 6–11 (inclusive).

80 Ibid., vol. 2, nos. 2, 3, 4, 5, 13, 14, 17.

81 Ibid., vol. 2, no. 17.

82 There is no written warning in Porter's annual salary letters from MacOdrum during the first couple of years. However, in her biographical essay about John, Marion Porter states that MacOdrum issued him with an ultimatum before 1952 (M. Porter, 'John Porter,' 2–3). Perhaps it was a verbal warning. MacOdrum issued the first written ultimatum in May 1955, discussed below (LAC, JPP, vol. 2, no. 1, MacOdrum to JAP, 20 May 1955).

83 Frank Jones interview.

84 M. Porter, 'John Porter,' 3.

85 Ibid. In his autobiographical essay on the writing of *The Vertical Mosaic*, Porter does not mention that he proposed the small groups study. Instead, he suggests that he outlined to Ginsberg his 'interest both in Canada and in social stratification' (Porter, 'Research Biography,' in Coleman, Etzioni, and Porter, *Macrosociology*, 151).

86 M. Porter, 'John Porter,' 4.

87 Porter, 'Research Biography,' in Coleman, Etzioni, and Porter, *Macrosociology*, 151. Porter also described his choice of topics in a newspaper interview in 1965. 'When I decided on an academic career I got down to research. So it was a question of finding an area that interested me and that had been neglected in Canada ... I chose [the area of social class] because of an interest in the problems of equality, a somewhat forgotten idea' (Cobb, 'John Porter,' *Toronto Daily Star*, 31 December 1965).

88 Porter, 'Research Biography,' in Coleman, Etzioni, and Porter, *Macrosociology*, 151.

89 Ibid., 153.

90 Marion Porter comments, 7–8 July 1987.

91 LAC, JPP, vol. 6, no. 29, 'The Canadian Political Science Association 27th Annual Meeting Toronto 1955' (program).

92 Porter, 'Research Biography,' in Coleman, Etzioni, and Porter, *Macrosociology*, 160.

93 Both here and in *The Vertical Mosaic*, Porter dealt with two 'elites' from the economic subsystem: the business elite and the labour elite. He explained his reasons for excluding the military elite from *The Vertical Mosaic* in a letter to Mildred Schwartz: 'I did nothing about the military elite in my book, although I did collect extensive biographical data on them. I suppose the main reason I left them out was that the project had become so immense. Also I do not think that the military have been very important in

Canadian power structures' (LAC, JPP, vol. 9, no. 3, JAP to Schwartz, 5 April 1965).

94 Porter, 'Elite Groups,' 504.

95 Marion Porter comments, 7–8 July 1987.

96 Jewett interview 1.

97 LAC, JPP, vol. 2, no. 1, Gray to JAP, 10 June 1955.

98 Porter, 'Research Biography,' in Coleman, Etzioni, and Porter, *Macrosociology*, 154.

99 According to the theory of the managerial revolution, control of individual firms had been transferred from owners to managers because of the technical demands of modern factories. This was related to the 'technocratic revolution,' the control of the economy by managers, engineers, and scientists.

100 Porter, 'Research Biography,' in Coleman, Etzioni, and Porter, *Macrosociology*, 155.

101 Ibid.

102 Ibid., 156.

103 Abbott, Course notes: Sociology 368 (1956–7): 'Social Class and Stratification' and 'Sociology of Political Power,' Abbott personal papers. For other undergraduate course notes from the period, see LAC, JPP, vol. 4, no. 9 and no. 10. I also have copies of course notes from Porter's Sociology 370: 'Primary Groups' (1953–4) (Blois personal papers) and Sociology 368: 'Power and Stratification'(1960–1), and Sociology 210: 'Introduction to Sociology and Anthropology' (1959–60) (Shaw personal papers).

104 'Criteria of social class and social status. Relationships between social class and economic and political systems. Social mobility. Examination of various class and caste systems and their ideologies' (*Carleton College Calendar*, 1954–55, 137). 'An analysis of political power, institutions, and parties based on empirical studies of political elites. The relationships between political, economic, and social power. The psychology of social movements' (ibid.).

105 Terms such as social class, class, and inequality had appeared from time to time in course descriptions but not in course titles (e.g., UBC 1917–18, Western 1930–1, Toronto 1942–3, Saskatchewan 1948–9, Manitoba 1950–1). Not until 1954–5 did Carleton devote an entire course to the subject.

106 Porter, 'Research Biography,' in Coleman, Etzioni, and Porter, *Macrosociology*, 167.

107 Ibid., 168.

108 Ibid., 170.

109 Ibid., 168.

110 LAC, JPP, vol. 9, no. 16, 'Econ Elite: Questions for Interviewing.'
111 Ibid., 'Notes in Conversation with J. Jeffrey: Jeffrey and Jeffrey, London Life, Tor-Dom Bank, etc.'
112 Ibid., Notes in conversation with David Mansur. Porter also wrote a page of notes regarding his general impressions of the businessmen and union leaders who attended the Round Table (ibid., 'Impressions from Round Table').
113 Frank Jones interview.
114 Ibid.
115 LAC, JPP, vol. 2, no. 1, Mills to JAP, 6 March 1956. Mills was not the only student of elites with whom Porter compared notes. In 1960, Saul Encel, an Australian sociologist, came to Canada. He and Porter spent some time together and considered undertaking a comparative study of political leaders in Canada and Australia (LAC, JPP, vol. 6, no. 15; Encel to JAP, 24 December 1960 and 27 January 1961, JAP to Encel, 1 June 1961).
116 Mills, *Power Elite.*
117 Frumhartz interview.
118 LAC, JPP, vol. 2, no. 1, JAP to Gibson, 30 August 1954.
119 At that point, Porter's publications included 'Two Cheers for Mental Health'; 'Karl Mannheim'; a review of *The Origins of Psycho-Analysis,* ed. Bonaparte, Freud, and Kris; and a review of Henry, *The Role of Groups in World Reconstruction.*
120 LAC, JPP, vol. 2, no. 1, MacOdrum to JAP, 20 May 1955. On 18 June 1955, Porter replied to MacOdrum outlining his publication record (ibid., handwritten draft, JAP to MacOdrum, 18 June 1955). A week later, MacOdrum replied confirming his willingness to grant him a permanent reappointment based on published research rather than a formal degree (ibid., MacOdrum to JAP, 24 June 1955).
121 LAC, JPP, vol. 2, no. 1, JAP to MacOdrum [handwritten draft], 18 June 1955.
122 Phillips to RHH, 14 March 2000.
123 See McKenzie, *Pauline Jewett,* 43; Fox to RHH, 8 March 1991.
124 Marion Porter interview 1.
125 McKenzie, *Pauline Jewett,* 43.
126 Jewett interview 2. According to McKenzie's biography of Jewett, it was the other way around; i.e., Porter talked Jewett into joining the collective (ibid., 43–4).
127 Marion Porter interview 1.
128 Ann Porter interview.
129 Tony Porter interview 2.

130 Jewett interview 1.
131 McKenzie, *Pauline Jewett*, 145–6.
132 Cobb, 'John Porter,' *Toronto Daily Star*, 31 December 1965. Emphasis in original.
133 L. Glassford to RHH, 26 August 1991.
134 McKenzie, *Pauline Jewett*, 145–6.
135 Cobb, 'John Porter,' *Toronto Daily Star*, 31 December 1965.
136 McKenzie, *Pauline Jewett*, 144–7.
137 Ann Porter interview; Tony Porter interview 2.
138 Meisel interview.
139 LAC, JPP, vol. 2, no. 1, Gibson to JAP, 17 May 1956. Porter thanked him for this (ibid., JAP to Gibson, handwritten note, n.d.).
140 For an account of the somewhat contentious process by which Bissell was selected, see Neatby and McEown, *Creating Carleton*, 88–9.
141 McEown interview.
142 Clark, 'Evolution of an Administrator,' 36–40.
143 Ibid.; see also CU, ARC, gathering file: Bissell, C.T., C.V. Hotson, Press release, 1 February 1956.
144 Clark, 'Evolution of an Administrator,' 36–40. For details of Bissell's life, see the entry about him in *Who's Who in Canada, 1958–9* (Toronto: International Press, 1959), 25–6.
145 McEown interview.
146 McRae interview 1.
147 Bissell, *Halfway up Parnassus*, 35.
148 Coyne and McKenzie chose Bissell in part because they thought he would be able 'to convince governments and the public generally that Carleton College was a respectable academic institution [that] deserved their support' (Neatby and McEown, *Creating Carleton*, 88).
149 CUA, Office of the President fonds, Series: Annual Reports, *The President's Report 1956–1957*, 5–6.
150 Ibid., and CUA, Office of the President fonds, Series: Annual Reports, *The President's Report 1957–1958*, 7.
151 McRae interview 1.
152 At the time, the city considered using the land for a zoo rather than a university. After the decision had been made in Carleton's favour and the university was up and running, said Kenneth McRae, some people joked they got both (McRae interview 2).
153 Neatby and McEown, *Creating Carleton*, 85–6. Some of Whitton's behaviour can be explained by her dislike of the Southams, who often criticized her in the pages of the *Ottawa Journal*, which they owned (McEown in-

terview; see also Neatby and McEown, *Creating Carleton,* 85–6). Carleton got the last laugh on the issue of the sewer and water mains: 'As a sequel, two years later, when the city was extending Bronson Avenue over the Rideau River and needed a narrow strip of college land ... it discovered to its chagrin that it could not expropriate university property ... Carleton agreed to cede the land if the city would reimburse it for expenses incurred for the pumping station and the sewer line built under city property. Carleton received $65,000 – but did not endear itself to Charlotte Whitton in the process' (ibid., 86; see also McEown interview).

154 Bissell, *Halfway up Parnassus,* 34.
155 Ibid.; see also CUA, Office of the President fonds, Series: Annual Reports, *The President's Report 1956–1957,* 6–7.
156 Neatby and McEown, *Creating Carleton,* 90.
157 CUA, Office of the President fonds, Series: Annual Reports, *The President's Report 1956–1957,* 10; see also Neatby and McEown, *Creating Carleton,* 91.
158 C.A. Ashley, 'Concentration of Economic Power,' *CJEPS* 23, no. 1 (1957): 105–8.
159 LAC, JPP, vol. 3, no. 4, JAP to Naegele, 30 January 1959.
160 See, for example, the *Evening Journal* (Ottawa), 7 June 1955.
161 LAC, JPP, vol. 3, no. 4, JAP to Naegele, 30 January 1959. Porter also asked experts to comment on sections of the book as he worked on them. For instance, Joseph Jeffrey, a member of the economic elite who Porter had earlier interviewed, read the chapter on corporate concentration (ibid., vol. 9, no. 16, 'Notes in conversation with J. Jeffrey: Jeffrey and Jeffrey, London Life, Tor-Dom Bank, etc.'; see also Jeffrey to JAP, 15 November 1957 and JAP to Jeffrey, 20 November 1957). Wilfrid Kesterton, who founded the journalism program at Carleton, read the chapter on the media (Kesterton to RHH, 11 May 1991 and 20 May 1991 and attachment).
162 M. Porter, 'John Porter,' 4.
163 Porter 'Research Biography,' in Coleman, Etzioni, and Porter, *Macrosociology,* 157, 172.
164 D. Rowat, 'On John Porter's 'Bureaucratic Elite in Canada,' *CJEPS* 25, no. 2 (1959): 204–7. Porter and Rowat planned this exchange beforehand (Rowat interview).

6: Crafting a Classic, 1958–1965

1 Gibson said he was never seriously considered as a possible successor to Bissell: 'An emissary of the Board [of Governors] told me they didn't think I was tough enough' (Gibson interview; for a slightly different

account, see Neatby and McEown, *Creating Carleton*, 114). Scott Gordon recalled that 'there was a great deal of faculty opposition to James Gibson as president' (Gordon comments, n.d. January 2002).
2 McEown interview; see also Neatby and McEown, *Creating Carleton*, 114–15.
3 Other than where specifically noted, the details in this paragraph are taken from: 'A. Davidson Dunton, a brief curriculum vitae'; 'Former Head of CBC, Carleton Dies at 74,' *Ottawa Citizen* 9 February 1987, B2; 'A. Davidson Dunton 1912–1987: A true member of the company of Carleton,' *This Week* 8, no. 6 (12 February 1987): 1; 'The Dunton Years, 1958–72,' *The Carleton Alumneye* (Winter 1972): 7–9; and Arnold Davidson Dunton, Carleton University Public Relations/Information Services Project 166, 1987, all in CU, ARC, gathering file: Dunton, A.D. – Biographical Dossier.
4 'Dunton, Arnold Davidson,' in *Current Biography*, ed. Charles Moritz (New York: W.W. Wilson, 1959), 10–11.
5 Ibid.
6 Ibid., 11–12, and CU, ARC, Board of Governors, BOG–01, Series: Ceremonies, file: Mr. A.D. Dunton – Memorial Service, 'Arnold Davidson Dunton,' Fraser McDougall, 'For the Press,' n.p.
7 Paquet interview; see also McEown interview.
8 McRae to RHH, n.d. January 2002.
9 McEown interview.
10 Ibid., see also Neatby and McEown, *Creating Carleton*, 115–16.
11 McEown interview; see also Neatby interview; and Neatby and McEown, *Creating Carleton*, 117–18.
12 McEown interview.
13 McRae to RHH, n.d. January 2002.
14 McEown interview.
15 Ibid., see also Neatby and McEown, *Creating Carleton*, 119.
16 Gibson interview. In 1967, Porter pondered a move to the University of Toronto. Dunton wrote to him more than once, attempting to dissuade him. Porter commented on one of these letters: 'Dunton's [letter] was particularly warm and expressed the very keen hope that I would not leave. As I think I mentioned to you before, I have always liked him very much and I have never felt any strong desire to leave as long as he remained' (LAC, JPP, vol. 5, no. 27, JAP to S.D. Clark, 8 March 1967).
17 Porter, *Canadian Social Structure*, 114, table G2.
18 See Association of University and Colleges of Canada, 'Founding Year and Joining Year of Institutions,' www.aucc.ca/_pdf/english/aboutaucc/joinaucc_e.pdf.

19 Porter, *Vertical Mosaic,* 184, 186, tables 21–3.

20 Axelrod, *Scholars and Dollars,* 7–53.

21 Owram, *Born at the Right Time,* 140; Sheffield, 'Enrolment in Canadian Universities and Colleges,' 15, table 1.

22 Re enrolment figures, see Sheffield, 'Enrolment in Canadian Universities and Colleges,' 15, table 1. Re the number of universities in the mid-1960s, see Association of University and Colleges of Canada, 'Founding Year and Joining Year of Institutions.'

23 Sheffield, 'Enrolment in Canadian Universities and Colleges,' 17, table 4.

24 Leacy, ed., *Historical Statistics of Canada,* series W475–485: 'Full-time university teachers, Canada, and by province, selected years, 1920–1975.'

25 Ibid., series W519–532: 'Operating and capital expenditures of universities, by source of funds, Canada, selected years, 1920–1974.'

26 Full-time enrolment increased from 837 to 2,247 (CUA, Office of Budget Planning, *Carleton University Data Book 1995–1996,* ed. D. Zaluska, 'Student Registration Statistics, 1942–3 to 1995–96,' May 1996, 24). Regarding the faculty figure for 1958–9, see CUA, Office of the President fonds, Series: Annual Reports, *The President's Report 1958–1959,* 6, and regarding 1963–4, see ibid., *The President's Report 1963–1964,* 10.

27 Hiller, *Society and Change,* 23, table 3.

28 McFarlane interview.

29 CU, ARC, *Carleton University Calendars,* 1953–4 to 1960–1. See also CU, ARC, Tina Harvey, 'Administrative Summaries,' September 1995, 117.

30 Information about the history of the SSRCC is taken from Mabel F. Timlin, 'The Social Sciences in Canada: Retrospect and Potential,' in Mabel F. Timlin and Albert Faucher, *The Social Sciences in Canada/Les Sciences Sociales au Canada: Two Studies/Deux Études* (Ottawa: Social Sciences Research Council of Canada, 1968), 61–8.

31 QUA, JMP, box 28, file 638, J. Meisel, 'Studies in the Structure of Power: Decision-Making in Canada,' Application to the Canada Council for assistance to a project sponsored by the Social Science Research Council in Canada,' n.d. [1958], 1.

32 Ibid., box 30, file 734, Meisel to JAP, 23 July 1958.

33 Ibid., JAP to Meisel, 15 September 1958, and attachment.

34 For a letter written by Porter that refers to correspondence from Meisel giving him notice the grant had been approved, see ibid., JAP to Meisel, 8 October 1958.

35 It is difficult to discern who had the idea for *Canadian Society.* See the accounts in Frank Jones interview; Frank Jones comments, 12 June 2002; and correspondence in LAC, JPP, vol. 1, no. 5.

36 C.A. Dawson and W.E. Gettys, *Introduction to Sociology* (New York: Ronald, 1929, 1935, 1948).

37 See R. Helmes-Hayes, 'C.A. Dawson and W.E. Gettys' *An Introduction to Sociology* (1929): Canadian Sociology's First Textbook,' *CJS* 19, no. 4 (1994): 461–97; Frank Jones interview.

38 LAC, JPP, vol. 6, no. 33, F. Jones to JAP, 20 August 1957 and 16 June 1958.

39 Initially they intended the work to have a double return: it would produce not just a reader/text but also be the basis for a collaborative magnum opus on Canadian society (Blishen interview). However, work on the larger project never got underway and the *Canadian Society* reader took longer to put together than they had imagined. See also LAC, JPP, vol. 6, no. 33, Naegele to JAP, 20 December 1957, and 10 January 1958.

40 LAC, JPP, vol. 6, no. 33, JAP to Naegele [handwritten draft], 9 October 1958.

41 Porter et al., eds., *Canadian Society*, 1961.

42 E. Loosely, 'Book Review,' in *Continuous Learning* 1, no. 4 (1962): 221–2; F. Laviolette, 'Book Review,' *CJEPS* 28, no. 3 (1962): 442–4.

43 Elkin, 'Book Review,' 159.

44 G. Dion, 'Book Review,' *Rélations Industrielles* 18, no. 2 (1963): 285.

45 See Hiller and DiLuzio, 'Text and Context,' 497–500, especially 499.

46 Ibid. In the late 1960s, *Canadian Society* was supplanted by true textbooks. For a list, see ibid., 501, table 3. See also 500–3; and Jim Curtis to Harry Hiller, n.d., Curtis personal papers.

47 Blishen interview.

48 LAC, JPP, vol. 8, no. 12, Bell to JAP, 16 January 1958.

49 Regarding the LSR, see Horn, *League for Social Reconstruction*.

50 The materials in this paragraph are taken from LAC, JPP, vol. 8, no. 12, 'Meeting to Consider Research Projects to be Financed by the Boag Foundation,' 26 January 1958, 1–2.

51 They chose Jamieson as editor, Bell as assistant editor, and Scott, Trudeau, Forsey, Lewis, and George Grube as the editorial committee (ibid., 5). Jack Weldon and T. Shoyama were subsequently added to the committee (Oliver, 'Preface,' in *Social Purpose for Canada*, vi).

52 LAC, JPP, vol. 8, no. 12, 'Meeting to Consider Research Projects to be Financed by the Boag Foundation,' 26 January 1958, 4.

53 For example, Léon Dion, Fernand Dumont, and Gerard Pelletier came to the April 1959 meeting (LAC, JPP, vol. 8, no. 12, 'Conference Agenda: Boag Book on Canadian Social and Economic Policy,' 11–12 April 1959).

54 George Grant, 'An Ethic of Community,' in *Social Purpose for Canada*, ed. Oliver, 3–26.

55 Porter revised the education chapter two years later using material from the 1961 Census and DBS surveys to constitute the basis of chapter 6 of *The Vertical Mosaic*. Oliver stepped in as editor when Jamieson became ill. Oliver was well known to the other contributors, Scott and Trudeau in particular, and had connections to the French-language intellectual community that the others did not (Oliver interview).

56 Clement, 'Foreword,' in Porter, *Measure of Canadian Society*, 2nd ed., xii.

57 M. Porter to RHH, 1 April 1985.

58 Oliver, 'Preface,' in Oliver, ed., *Social Purpose for Canada*, vii.

59 Oliver interview.

60 Ibid. Others included Jack Weldon and Neil Compton.

61 LAC, JPP, vol. 8, no. 12, J. Weldon, 'On an Economic Program for Canada's New Political Party.'

62 Ibid., C. Hamilton (National Secretary of the CLC/CCF Joint Committee) to JAP, 16 July 1959.

63 Ibid., Knowles to JAP, 12 September 1960 and JAP to Knowles, 20 September 1960. John and Marion attended the founding convention of the NDP, Marion as the delegate from their Ottawa riding association. Ann Porter recalled that her parents voted NDP and always had NDP signs on their lawn during election campaigns but noted that only her mother canvassed for the party (Ann Porter interview).

64 Oliver, 'Preface,' in Oliver, ed., *Social Purpose for Canada*, v.

65 Ibid., vii.

66 J.S. Woodsworth, 'Foreword,' in Research Committee of the League for Social Reconstruction, *Social Planning for Canada* (Toronto: University of Toronto Press, 1935), vi.

67 Reproduced in F.R. Scott, L. Marsh, G. Spry, J. King Gordon, E. Forsey, and J.S. Parkinson, eds., 'An Introduction,' in Research Committee of the League for Social Reconstruction, *Social Planning for Canada*, rev. ed. (Toronto: University of Toronto Press, 1975), ix–xi.

68 Oliver interview.

69 Lapierre, 'The 1960s,' in *The Canadians 1867–1967*, ed. Careless and Brown, 351–2.

70 A. Brady, 'Social Studies,' in 'Letters in Canada,' *UTQ* 31, no. 4 (1962): 506–8; and A. Brady, 'A Political Scientist's View,' part 1 of 'Two Views of Social Purpose for Canada,' *CJEPS* 28, no. 2 (1962): 300–4.

71 J. Corry, 'Book Review,' *CPA* 5 (December 1962): 513–17; see also F. Underhill, 'New Canadian Frontier,' *QQ* 69, no. 2 (1962): 294–301.

72 Ian Drummond, 'An Economist's Comments,' part 2 of 'Two Views of *Social Purpose for Canada*,' *CJEPS* 28, no. 2 (1962): 304–6.

73 F.H. Underhill, 'New Canadian Frontier?' *QQ* 69, no. 2 (1962): 294–301. Quoted passages from 298.

74 J.R. Winter, 'Book Review,' *BQ* 30, no. 2 (1965): 90, 94.

75 Marion Porter interview 2.

76 Porter, 'Research Biography,' in Coleman, Etzioni, and Porter, *Macrosociology*, 163.

77 Ibid. For various versions of the mailing list, see LAC, JPP, vol. 20, nos. 5, 6, and 7.

78 For rough copies of the questionnaire, see ibid., vol. 20, nos. 5 and 7. The overall response rate was about 70 per cent (Porter, *Vertical Mosaic*, 601–3).

79 University of Waterloo, Dana Porter Library, Rare Book Room, *Proceedings: Round Table on Man and Industry*, 22–6 October 1956 (Toronto: University of Toronto School of Social Work, 1956).

80 Frank Jones interview.

81 LAC, JPP, vol. 9, no. 16, 'Some notes on talk with Gower Markle, USA,' and 'Notes on talk with B.F. Hamilton, Secretary-Treasurer, Ont Fed of Lab.'

82 QUA, JMP, box 30, file 734, Porter, 'Progress Report on "Elites, Power and Social Class in Canada,"' Autumn 1959; ibid., JAP, rough draft of 1960 Report to Meisel, n.d. [summer 1960]; JAP to Meisel, 1 June 1961 and 30 October 1961. There are handwritten tabulations of materials for the labour elite study in LAC, JPP, vol. 9, no. 13.

83 Ibid., JAP to Meisel, 15 September 1958, attachment: 'Further remarks on the attached outline.' Porter originally intended to publish the results separately as a way of thanking those in the labour movement who had helped him to gather the information.

84 Ibid., JAP to Meisel, 15 September 1958, 'Tentative Outline of Elites, Power and Social Class in Canada.'

85 Ibid., JAP to Meisel, 30 October 1961. Some of the rough notes and data for this section can be found in LAC, JPP, vol. 9, nos. 17 and 18.

86 QUA, JMP, box 30, file 734, JAP to Meisel, 30 October 1961.

87 J. Porter, curriculum vitae, Clement personal papers.

88 QUA, JMP, box 30, file 734, JAP to Meisel, 20 April 1962.

89 Ibid., Meisel to JAP, 27 April 1962.

90 LAC, JPP, vol. 9, no. 2, Meisel to JAP, 29 November 1962; see also Meisel interview.

91 Marion Porter comments, 23 February 1993.

92 Re Porter travelling to Calgary to confer with Zentner, see Marion Porter interview 1. Re Porter's selection as editor, see QUA, JMP, box 1, file 12, I Associations, CPSA, Soc/Anthro Chapter, R.L. James to Ian Whitaker, Sociology and Anthropology Chapter, CPSA, 18 December 1962.

93 Marion Porter interview 1. Jean Burnet assumed his responsibilities as editor and it was under her guidance that the first issue of the *Review* was published in 1964 (Burnet interview). Porter remained a member of the *CRSA* editorial board from 1963–8.

94 Marion Porter interview 1.

95 QUA, JMP, box 30, file 734, M. Porter to Meisel, 23 January 1963.

96 Ibid., Meisel to M. Porter, 28 January 1963.

97 LAC, JPP, vol.9, no. 2, B. Ostry to M. Porter, 13 February 1963.

98 Marion Porter interview 1.

99 QUA, JMP, box 30, file 734, Meisel to M. Porter, 10 February 1963.

100 Marion Porter comments, 7–8 July 1987.

101 LAC, JPP, vol. 9, no. 2, Meisel to JAP, 24 June 1963

102 Clark wrote two reviews: one of the ten-chapter version and another of the twelve-chapter version (i.e., minus the final chapter) (LAC, JPP, vol. 9, no. 2, Meisel to JAP, 9 November 1963, with two enclosures from Clark, n.d.).

103 LAC, JPP, vol. 9, no. 2, Clark enclosure 1 in Meisel to JAP, 9 November 1963.

104 Ibid., and Clark enclosure 2.

105 Ibid., Clark enclosure 2.

106 Ibid., Clark enclosure 1.

107 Ibid., Clark enclosure 2. Forty years later, I reminded Professor Clark about this review and asked him about his retrospective opinion of the incident. He acknowledged that his view of the book had been 'dead wrong' but correctly noted that he had been 'dead right' about the impact it was likely to have (Clark interview).

108 Gordon to RHH, 6 August 1987.

109 LAC, JPP, vol. 9, no. 2, JAP to C.A. Ashley, 23 October 1963 and Meisel to JAP, 9 November 1963.

110 Ibid., JAP to Meisel, 29 December 1963.

111 Meisel gave Porter forty-five typewritten pages of mostly minor editorial suggestions (ibid., vol. 9, no. 19, Meisel to JAP, n.d., enclosure: 'Porter manuscript').

112 Meisel interview. As well, said Meisel, Porter needed to incorporate the materials from the 1961 Census, as he had feared. Porter hired a research assistant to carry out this task (M. Porter to RHH, 1 April 1985).

113 Neatby interview.
114 LAC, JPP, vol. 9, no. 2, JAP to Meisel, 29 November 1963.
115 M. Porter to RHH, 1 April 1985.
116 LAC, JPP, vol. 9, no. 2, JAP to Meisel, 29 November 1963; see also Meisel to JAP, 3 December 1963.
117 Ibid., JAP to Meisel, 29 December 1963.
118 Ibid., JAP to Halpenny, 5 February 1964.
119 Ibid., Meisel to JAP, 5 May 1964.
120 Ibid., JAP to S. Wismer, 1 October 1964; see also Porter, *Vertical Mosaic*, xii–xiii; Meisel interview; and QUH, JMP, box 30, file 734, JAP to Meisel, 20 April 1962.

7: *The Vertical Mosaic,* Canada as a Flawed Democracy

1 Porter, *Vertical Mosaic*, 6.
2 Ibid., 3.
3 Ibid., 6.
4 On this point, see Brooks and Gagnon, *Social Scientists and Politics in Canada*, 81–2, including table 12.
5 On the treatment of class themes by Canadian social scientists prior to 1965, see my PhD dissertation, Helmes-Hayes, 'Images of Inequality.' Since then, I have written the following articles to refine, extend, or correct arguments made there: 'A Dualistic Vision'; 'The Image of Inequality in S.D. Clark's Writings'; 'Everett Hughes: Theorist of the Second Chicago School'; 'The Concept of Social Class: Everett Hughes' Contribution'; and with D. Wilcox-Magill, 'A Neglected Classic.' Many of these ideas are summarized in Helmes-Hayes, 'L'analyse des classes sociales.' Wallace Clement has made this same point re Canadian historians. Scholars such as Harold Innis and Donald Creighton did not often make class an explicit focus of their work, Clement argues, but they did 'in their own subtle way' provide 'evidence of class distortions' in Canadian history (W. Clement, 'Canadian Class Cleavages: An Assessment and Contribution,' in W. Clement, *Class, Power and Property: Essays on Canadian Society* [Toronto: Methuen, 1988], 135).
6 Two of the studies of 'community-level' lifestyle or standard of living that Porter mentions in *The Vertical Mosaic* are J. Seeley, A. Sim, and E. Loosely, *Crestwood Heights* (Toronto: University of Toronto Press, 1956); and W. Mann, 'The Social System of the Slum: The Lower Ward, Toronto,' in *Urbanism and the Changing Canadian City*, ed. S.D. Clark (Toronto: University of Toronto Press, 1961), 39–69.

7 See the discussion below, which is based in part on Helmes-Hayes and Wilcox-Magill, 'A Neglected Classic.'

8 H.L. Smith and W. Beveridge, *The New Survey of London Life and Labour,* vol. 1, *Forty Years of Change* (London: P.S. King and Sons, 1930).

9 Research Committee of the League for Social Reconstruction, *Social Planning for Canada* (Toronto: T. Nelson, 1935).

10 Marsh, *Social Security for Canada;* see also B. Kitchen 'The Marsh Report Revisited,' *JCS* 21, no. 2 (1986): 38–48. Marsh's report was to some extent modelled on W. Beveridge, 'Social Insurance and Allied Services Report,' presented to Parliament by command of His Majesty, November 1942.

11 Marsh, *Canadians In and Out of Work,* 2–4.

12 Ibid., 10, table 2.

13 Ibid., 129.

14 Ibid., 126.

15 Ibid., 198; see also 193 and 166, table 29.

16 Ibid., 175–7 and 197, respectively.

17 Ibid., 391, table 65; see also appendix A, 458–9, tables 2 and 3.

18 Ibid., 392; see 390–3 more generally.

19 Ibid., 198–9; see also 393–6, especially 396.

20 Ibid., 391 table 65.

21 Ibid., 377–404.

22 L. Marsh, untitled autobiographical essay, n.d., 13, 3, respectively, Wilcox-Magill personal papers.

23 M. Horn, 'Leonard Marsh and His Ideas, 1967–1982: Some Personal Recollections,' *JCS* 21, no. 2 (1986): 68, emphasis added; see also Horn, 'Leonard Marsh and the Coming of a Welfare State in Canada,' *HS/SH* 9 (1976): 199.

24 Basing her claim on an interview with Marsh, Shore argues in *Science of Social Redemption* (271) that Porter did not know about *Canadians In and Out of Work.* But he did. There is a scrap of paper with Marsh's name and the title of the book in Porter's handwriting in a file in the John Porter papers containing potential selections for the original edition of *Canadian Society* (LAC, JPP, vol. 20, no. 17).

25 Community class structure studies relied on the subjective perceptions held by community residents themselves. An example is W. Lloyd Warner and Paul S. Lunt, *The Social Life of a Modern Community* (New Haven, CT: Yale University Press, 1941).

26 Porter, *Vertical Mosaic,* 14. The only Canadian article on this subject was based on data from a small sample of the residents of Montreal and provided rankings for only twenty-five occupations (J. Tuckman, 'Social Status of Occupations in Canada,' *CJP* 1, no. 2 (1947): 71–4).

27 National Opinion Research Centre, 'Jobs and Occupations: A Popular Eval-
    uation,' *Opinion News* 9 (1947), cited Porter, *Vertical Mosaic,* 14n12. Porter
    also cites Blishen in ibid., 15, 160–3.
28 Porter, *Vertical Mosaic,* 105.
29 Ibid., 108, table 5. These findings concerned those who made enough to
    pay federal income tax. The figures for those making less than $2,000 and
    less than $4,000, respectively, rose to 37 per cent and 82 per cent when 'all
    returns' were considered (107, table 4).
30 Ibid., 118. The 'very rich' constituted an even smaller group (460 out of the
    2,380) with annual incomes over $100,000 (113).
31 Ibid., 118.
32 Ibid., 113.
33 Ibid.
34 Ibid., 114.
35 Canada, Dominion Bureau of Statistics, *Incomes, Liquid Assets and Indebt-
    edness of Non-Farm Families in Canada, 1955* (Ottawa: The Bureau, 1958);
    Dominion Bureau of Statistics, *City Family Expenditure, 1955* (Ottawa: The
    Bureau, 1958); and Canada, Dominion Bureau of Statistics, *Distribution of
    Non-Farm Incomes in Canada by Size, 1959,* (Ottawa: The Bureau, 1962), cited
    in Porter, *Vertical Mosaic,* 119–25, 130–1.
36 Porter, *Vertical Mosaic,* 125–6.
37 Ibid., 125–6, 129, 131–2.
38 Canada, Dominion Bureau of Statistics, *Household Facilities and Equipment,
    May, 1961* (Ottawa: The Bureau, 1961), cited in ibid., 130.
39 *Census of Canada, 1956,* cited in ibid., 131; *Household Facilities,* cited in ibid.
40 Porter, *Vertical Mosaic,* 130.
41 Ibid., 125.
42 Ibid., 131.
43 Ibid., 125, 126.
44 Ibid., 131.
45 Ibid., 131–2.
46 Ibid.
47 Ibid., 150–1.
48 Ibid., 152–4.
49 Ibid., 154–5.
50 Ibid., 155.
51 Ibid.; see also 156, figure 3.
52 Ibid.; see also 159, figure 6.
53 Ibid., 160. The Census revealed that the same patterns held for women.
    Data from a 1959 Dominion Bureau of Statistics survey also confirmed
    these results.

54 Blishen, 'Occupational Class Scale,' cited in Porter, *Vertical Mosaic*, 160–3.
55 Porter, *Vertical Mosaic*, 163, figure 8.
56 Ibid., 163.
57 Ibid., 163–4.
58 Ibid., 165.
59 Ibid., 168–79 passim.
60 Oscar Lewis, *La Vida: A Puerto Rican Family in the Culture of Poverty – San Juan and New York* (New York: Random House, 1966).
61 Porter, *Vertical Mosaic*, 172–3.
62 Ibid., 175, table 14.
63 Ibid., 180–3, including table 19.
64 Ibid., 183–91.
65 Ibid., 186, table 23.
66 Ibid., 195.
67 Ibid., 166.
68 Ibid., 167.
69 Ibid., 197–8.
70 Ibid., 60–1.
71 Ibid., 77, figure 1. The percentage of non-charter group Canadians grew over the course of the twentieth century, in part as a consequence of sometimes massive immigration, but, as of 1961, the high birth rate in Quebec and federal immigration policies favouring British immigrants had prevented other ethnic (and racial) groups from seriously challenging the long-standing status quo.
72 Porter claimed that the term 'Canadian mosaic' was first used by Victoria Hayward, an American writer, in describing the varied church architecture in Western Canada (*Vertical Mosaic*, 70n24).
73 Ibid., 82.
74 Ibid., 72.
75 As well, he noted that membership of society's topmost groups – elites – should also reflect the ethnic make-up of society (ibid., 74). Porter dealt with this index of assimilation in Part 2 of the book.
76 Regarding the shifts in the position of various ethnic groups over the period, see ibid., 83–98, summarized 87, table 1.
77 Ibid., 90, citing Blishen, 'Occupational Class Scale,' 524.
78 Ibid., 63–4.
79 See, for example, Daniel Bell, 'Notes on the Post-industrial Society (I),' *PI* 6 (Winter 1967): 24–35; and 'Notes on the Post Industrial Society II,' 6 (Spring 1967): 102–18 (Porter, *Vertical Mosaic*, 19–25). Porter uses postcapitalist theory to critique Marx's conception of class (*Vertical Mosaic*, 20–5). On the origins of postcapitalist theory and its multiple meanings in the

1950s, '60s, and '70s, see Howard Brick, 'Optimism of the Mind: Imagining Postindustrial Society in the 1960s and 1970s,' *AQ* 44, no. 3 (1992): 348–80.

80 Porter, *Vertical Mosaic*, 24.

81 Ibid., 21–2; see Berle and Means, *Modern Corporation*; and R. Dahrendorf, *Class and Class Conflict in Industrial Society* (Stanford: Stanford University Press, 1959).

82 Porter, 'Postindustrialism,' 1971.

83 Porter, *Vertical Mosaic*, 150–1.

84 Ibid., 20–5.

85 Ibid., 22–3, 255.

86 Ibid., 19, 20.

87 Ibid., 20.

88 Ibid., 9.

89 It is odd that Porter makes no mention of the 'Class, Status and Party' fragment from *Economy and Society* because he is clearly following Weber's general framework. See Gerth and Mills, eds., *From Max Weber*, 180–95; and Weber, *The Theory of Social and Economic Organization*, 424–9.

90 Porter, *Vertical Mosaic*, 28, 10, 11, respectively.

91 Ibid., 10.

92 Ibid., 25–8.

93 Ibid., 21–2. See Berle and Means, *Modern Corporation*.

94 Ibid., 21.

95 Ibid., 22.

96 Ibid., 22–4.

97 Ibid., 240–1.

98 Ibid., 23–5.

99 Ibid., 24–5.

100 Ibid., 27.

101 Ibid., 201. The ideological elite was made up of the media, education, and religious elites. He also mentioned the military elite but regarded its role as minor and did not include it in his analysis.

102 Ibid., 206.

103 Ibid., 201.

104 R. MacGregor Dawson, *Democratic Government in Canada* (Toronto: University of Toronto Press and Copp Clark, 1949); and N. Ward, *Government in Canada* (Toronto: Gage, 1960).

105 F.R. Scott, *The Canadian Constitution and Human Rights* (Toronto: Canadian Broadcasting Corporation, 1959); and F.R. Scott, *Civil Liberties and Cana-*

dian Federalism (Toronto: University of Toronto Press and Carleton University, 1959).

106 Macpherson, *Political Theory of Possessive Individualism*, 1962. On Canadian political culture, see, for example, F.H. Underhill, *In Search of Canadian Liberalism* (Toronto: Macmillan, 1960); Grant, 'An Ethic of Community,' in *Social Purpose for Canada*, ed. Oliver; and Canada, *The Massey Report*, Royal Commission on National Development in the Arts, Letters and Sciences (Ottawa: King's Printer, 1951). On regional cultures and power struggles, see Herbert Quinn, *The Union Nationale: A Study in Quebec Nationalism* (Toronto: University of Toronto Press, 1963); Hubert Guindon, 'Social Unrest, Social Class, and Quebec's Bureaucratic Revolution,' *QQ* 71, no. 2 (1964): 150–62; Marcel Rioux, *French-Canadian Society*, vol. 1, Carleton Library no. 18 (Toronto: McClelland and Stewart, 1964); S.B. Ryerson, *French Canada: A Study in Canadian Democracy* (Toronto: Progress, 1953). For biographies, see D.G. Creighton, *John A. Macdonald*, 2 vols. (Toronto: Macmillan, 1952 and 1955; and Kenneth McNaught, *A Prophet in Politics: A Biography of J. S. Woodsworth* (Toronto: University of Toronto Press, 1959). On political parties, pressure groups, and social movements, see, respectively: C.B. Macpherson, *Democracy in Alberta: The Theory and Practice of a Quasi-Party System* (Toronto: University of Toronto Press, 1953); John Irving, *The Social Credit Movement in Alberta* (Toronto: University of Toronto Press, 1959); W.L. Morton, *The Progressive Party in Canada* (Toronto: University of Toronto Press, 1950); Hugh G. Thorburn, 'Pressure Groups in Canadian Politics,' *CJEPS* 30 (1964): 157–74; S.M. Lipset, *Agrarian Socialism: The Co-operative Commonwealth Federation in Saskatchewan: A Study in Political Sociology* (Berkeley: University of California Press, 1950); C. Cleverdon, *The Woman Suffrage Movement in Canada* (Toronto: University of Toronto Press, 1950).

107 J. Meisel, ed., *Papers on the 1962 Election* (Toronto: University of Toronto Press, 1964).

108 H.A. Innis, *The Fur Trade in Canada* (Toronto: University of Toronto Press, 1930); H.A. Innis, *The Cod Fisheries: The History of an International Economy* (Toronto: University of Toronto Press, 1940); and H.A. Innis, *Essays in Canadian Economic History*, ed. M.Q. Innis (Toronto: University of Toronto Press, 1956); A.R.M. Lower, *The North American Assault on the Canadian Forest: A History of the Lumber Trade between Canada and the United States* (Toronto: Ryerson Press, 1938); and D.G. Creighton, *The Commercial Empire of the St. Lawrence, 1760–1850* (Toronto: Ryerson Press, 1937).

109 Regarding the interplay of government and private corporations, see for example Vernon Fowke, *The National Policy and the Wheat Economy*

(Toronto: University of Toronto Press, 1957); J.S. Galbraith, *The Hudson's Bay Company as an Imperial Factor, 1821–1869* (Toronto: University of Toronto Press, 1957). For case studies, see O.D. Main, *The Canadian Nickel Industry: A Study in Market Control and Public Policy* (Toronto: University of Toronto Press, 1955); and E.E. Rich, *The Hudson's Bay Company, 1670–1870*, 3 vols. (Toronto: McClelland and Stewart, 1960). For capital formation, see Kenneth Buckley, *Capital Formation in Canada, 1896–1930* (Toronto: University of Toronto Press, 1955). For patterns of corporation concentration, see for example W.H. McCollum, *Who Owns Canada?* (Regina: CCF Research Bureau, 1935); and Ashley, 'Concentration of Economic Power,' 105–8.

110 For development of the labour market see H.C. Pentland, 'The Role of Capital in Canadian Economic Development before 1875,' *CJEPS* 16, no. 3 (1950): 457–74; and H.C. Pentland, 'The Development of a Capitalist Labour Market in Canada,' *CJEPS* 25, no. 3 (1959): 450–61. For struggles between labour and capital, see, for example, Stuart Jamieson, *Industrial Relations in Canada* (Toronto: Macmillan, 1957); S. Jamieson and P. Gladstone, 'Unionism in the Fishing Industry of British Columbia,' *CJEPS* 16, no. 1 (1950): 146–71; D. Masters, *The Winnipeg General Strike* (Toronto: University of Toronto Press, 1950); P.E. Trudeau, *La grève de l'amiante* (Montreal: Éditions Cité libre, 1956); and H. Logan, *State Intervention and Assistance in Collective Bargaining: The Canadian Experience, 1943–1954* (Toronto: University of Toronto Press, 1956). For labour history, see H. Logan, *Trade Unions in Canada: Their Development and Functioning* (Toronto: Macmillan, 1948).

111 The positional style of analysis assumes that those who hold formal positions of power (here on boards of directors) actually wield effective power as a consequence. In the *reputational* style of analysis, the investigator asks people in the organization who really – rather than officially – holds power (an insider's approach). Another approach is to follow key decisions in an organization and find out who actually makes them (which might be different from what the official organizational chart would say).

112 Porter defined a dominant corporation as one with more than 500 employees (*Vertical Mosaic,* 233; see also the discussion in appendix II, 570–96).

113 Ibid., 255.

114 See Ashley, 'Concentration of Economic Power,' 105–8; I. Brecher and S.S. Reisman, *Canada-United States Economic Relations,* Royal Commission on Canada's Economic Prospects Studies, study no. 502 (Ottawa: Queen's Printer, 1957); and Rosenbluth, 'Concentration and Monopoly,' in *Social Purpose for Canada,* ed. Oliver, all cited Porter, *Vertical Mosaic,* 233–8. (See also the discussion in appendix II, 570–96)

115 Porter, *Vertical Mosaic*, 233.
116 Ibid., 234, 274, 275, table 27. For details, see 570–96, appendix II.
117 Ibid., 274. The 170 corporations actually had 1,613 directorships, but 256 were held by Americans and 53 by residents of the United Kingdom. Porter excluded these foreign-held directorships from his analysis.
118 Ibid., 304.
119 Ibid., 291–2, table 28.
120 Ibid., 284, 282–3.
121 Ibid., 274.
122 Ibid., 291.
123 Ibid., 275–6, table 27.
124 Ibid., 275; calculated from table 27.
125 Ibid., 287; see 285–7 more generally.
126 Ibid., 290, 289. For figures on religious affiliation of the Canadian population, Porter cited *Census of Canada 1951*, vol. 1, table 37 (*Vertical Mosaic*, 289n46).
127 Porter, *Vertical Mosaic*, 294–5. Re the criteria for being in the 'top 100,' see 295n56.
128 Re political party affiliations, voluntary association activities, and club memberships, see ibid., 296–308.
129 Ibid., 463, 483.
130 Ibid., 463.
131 These are the Southam Co. Ltd., Sifton-Bell (F.P. Publications Ltd.) and Sifton Group, Thomson Newspapers Ltd., Toronto Star Ltd., The Globe and Mail Ltd., Telegram Publishing Co., The Montreal Star Co. Ltd., Gazette Printing Co. Ltd., The Halifax Herald Ltd., Maclean-Hunter Publishing Co. Ltd., and Fengate Publishing Co. Ltd. (Porter, *Vertical Mosaic*, 472–81).
132 Ibid., 487.
133 Ibid., 487–8.
134 Ibid., 487.
135 See ibid., 467, 305.
136 Ibid., 484, 463.
137 Ibid., 484–7.
138 Ibid., 463.
139 Ibid., 483.
140 Ibid., 494.
141 Ibid., 496.
142 Ibid., 498, 501, 505. Porter had complete data for 88 of 104 members of the English-language elite and 55 of 65 of the French-language elite.

143 Ibid., 499.
144 Ibid., 497, 499, 500.
145 Ibid., 504.
146 Ibid., 506, 501.
147 Ibid., 506, 499.
148 Ibid., 506, 503.
149 Ibid., 502.
150 Ibid., 511–19. Porter had data on 57 of 63 Roman Catholic bishops and 26 of 29 Anglican bishops (514–15).
151 Ibid., 515–17.
152 Ibid., 517.
153 Ibid., 511.
154 Ibid.
155 Ibid., 513, 511, respectively.
156 Ibid., 500.
157 Ibid., 494–5.
158 Ibid., 503, 500.
159 Ibid., 494.
160 Ibid., 503–4. He singled out Harold Innis as the key figure who had engendered this depoliticization. As Michiel Horn has pointed out, however, prior to the 1960s, university boards of governors and politicians acted in ways that discouraged professors from engaging in political activities. See M. Horn, *Academic Freedom in Canada: A History* (Toronto: University of Toronto Press, 1999); see also M. Horn, 'Running for Office: Canadian Professors, Electoral Politics, and Institutional Reactions, 1887–1968,' in Paul Stortz and E. Lisa Panayotidis, eds., *Historical Identities: The Professoriate in Canada* (Toronto: University of Toronto Press, 2006), 63–83.
161 Porter, *Vertical Mosaic*, 386.
162 Ibid., 366. The concept of a charter myth that could provide a standard against which to measure social progress was important to Porter for, as a New Liberal, he believed such absolute criteria existed. (See the afterword, below.)
163 Ibid., 368–9.
164 Ibid., 417.
165 Ibid., 393–4.
166 Ibid., 371.
167 Ibid., 412.
168 Ibid., 394, 412.
169 Ibid., 371–2.
170 Ibid., 386–9.

171 Ibid., 433; see also appendix III, 597–613.

172 Ibid., 448.

173 Ibid., 456; see also 418, 422, 453.

174 Ibid., 419–20.

175 Ibid., 423–5.

176 Ibid., 445, 444. Porter's criteria for placing someone in the middle class were either (1) attendance at a private school and father's income, or (2) possession of a university education.

177 Ibid., 447–8.

178 Ibid., 456.

179 Ibid., 431. Here, of course, Porter is comparing his work to that of C. Wright Mills in *The Power Elite*.

180 Porter, *Vertical Mosaic*, 441–2.

181 Ibid., 443.

182 The labour elite comprised 275 individuals who responded to a questionnaire mailed by Porter to 394 individuals pre-selected as labour elite members. Included in the group were the leaders of large unions and large union locals, city labour councils, provincial labour federations, and the Canadian Labour Congress. They were divided into two groups: leaders of English-language Canadian and international unions; and leaders of French-language *syndicats* (see ibid., appendix III, 597–613).

183 Ibid., 311–12.

184 Ibid., 312.

185 Ibid., 314–18, 310–11.

186 Ibid., 314–36.

187 Ibid., 336.

188 Ibid., 343–6, including table 31.

189 Ibid., 341, table 30.

190 Ibid., 347–9.

191 Ibid., 361–2.

192 Ibid., 362.

193 Ibid., 363.

194 Ibid., 202

195 Ibid.

196 Ibid., 224–7.

197 Ibid., 312.

198 Ibid., 224.

199 Ibid., 555.

200 Ibid., 558.

201 Ibid., 554.

202 Ibid., 418–25 passim.
203 Ibid., 201.
204 Ibid., 202.
205 Ibid., 367.
206 Ibid., 24–5, 202.
207 Ibid., 221–4.
208 Ibid., 25.
209 Ibid., 208.
210 Ibid., 213, citing J.K. Galbraith, *American Capitalism: The Concept of Countervailing Power* (Boston: Houghton Mifflin, 1952).
211 Ibid., 522–3.
212 Ibid., 27, 523, 210.
213 Ibid., 209.
214 Ibid., 210–15, 303–8. Porter employed this logic to reject both the '"umpire" theory of the state,' according to which ultimate power belonged to the political elite, and the Marxist theory of the state, according to which 'the economic rather than the political system [was] the master' (ibid., 205–6).
215 Porter, 'The Vertical Power Trip,' 4.
216 Porter, *Vertical Mosaic*, 557.
217 Ibid., 372.
218 Ibid., 208, citing Mills, *Power Elite*, 4.
219 Ibid., 212.
220 Ibid., 214.

8: Critical Response to *The Vertical Mosaic*

1 Everett Hughes, 'Book Review: *The Vertical Mosaic*,' *AAAPSS* 366 (July 1966): 196.
2 LAC, JPP, vol. 9, no. 2, JAP to Meisel, 29 December 1963.
3 LAC, National Film, Television and Sound Archives, accession no. 8309 1914–1915 (83–194), CBC, *The Sixties*, 'Paths to Power: Parts I and II,' February 1 and 8, 1965. Years later, in 1973, in the aftermath of Wallace Clement's successful defence of his master's thesis – a partial replication and updating of Porter's work on the economic and media elites that would soon be published as *The Canadian Corporate Elite* – the CBC's Rob Parker produced a segment for the public affairs program *Up Canada* dealing with Clement's findings. In addition to Porter and Clement, Parker interviewed Joseph Jeffrey, chairman of London Life Insurance Company, and Michael Clifford Sifton, publisher and broadcaster (LAC, National Film,

Television and Sound Archives, vol. 1 7905 192 and vol. 4 7901 030, CBC, *Up Canada*, 'Corporate Elite/ Canada,' 27 November 1973).

4 CU, ARC, gathering file: Porter, John A., 'People at the Top,' *CBC Times*, Toronto, 23 January 1965. Porter had caught the attention of the popular press as early as 1955 when the *Ottawa Journal* interviewed him about his paper on the economic elite (see ibid., 'Porter Stands By Remark: Trying To Learn How Elite Chosen,' *Ottawa Journal*, 7 June 1955). Likewise, in July 1961, the *Toronto Telegram*, in a review of *Social Purpose for Canada*, accorded special attention to his essay 'Power and Freedom' (see ibid., 'Ottawa Sociologist: He'd Have Gov't Buy a Metro Daily,' *Toronto Telegram*, 22 July 1961).

5 See, for example, F. Poland, 'Power Race Faces Hurdles,' *Montreal Star*, 20 October 1965, n.p.; and ibid., 'Colour, Racial Bias Studied,' 22 October, 1965, n.p. See also R.J. Anderson, 'Decision Makers,' *Calgary Herald*, 26 June 1965; the North Battleford *News-Optimist*, 18 June 1965; and the Yorkton *Enterprise*, 18 August 1965.

6 Douglas Fisher, 'Corridors of Power: Secret and Ubiquitous,' *Toronto Telegram*, 9 June 1965, night edition, n.p.

7 T.C. Douglas, 'Masterly Study of Canadian Elites,' *Globe and Mail* (Toronto), 12 June 1965, 13. I asked Ottawa mandarins Sylvia Ostry and Bernard Ostry about the possibility that *The Vertical Mosaic* might have influenced federal politicians and senior civil servants when it came out. Sylvia Ostry replied that typically such people paid very little attention to academic work, though the situation was somewhat better under Trudeau and Michael Pitfield in the late 1960s and early 1970s (Sylvia Ostry interview). Bernard Ostry fleshed out this notion, adding a twist. The discussion of academic books in such circles was, he said, 'very rare,' but in a sense it did not matter: 'Those civil servants that were … liberal or left liberal would not have had any difficulty assimilating what *The Vertical Mosaic* said because they believed it before John wrote it' (Bernard Ostry interview).

8 David Cobb, 'John Porter,' *Toronto Daily Star*, 31 December 1965; Bannerman, 'Truth about Our Classless Society,' 47; Dobbs, 'Strains of Social Climbing,' 27; and Kilbourn, 'In Canada's Society, No Room at the Top?' 63–4.

9 No author, 'The Retarded Democracy,' *Time* 85, no. 24 (11 June 1965): 15–7.

10 Bannerman, 'Truth about Our Classless Society,' 47.

11 Dobbs, 'Strains of Social Climbing,' 27.

12 Ibid., 28.

13 Ibid., 28, 27.

14 Kilbourn, 'In Canada's Society, No Room at the Top?' 63–4.

15 J.B. McGeachy, 'It's Easy to Fall into Old Traps Looking for "Power" Sites in Canada,' *FP* 59, no. 51 (18 December 1965): 7.

16 A.C. Forrest, *United Church Observer*, 15 September 1965, 41–3. For similar latter-day critiques on the same and related issues, see the following by David Nock: 'Anglican Bishops and Indigeneity: John Porter revisited,' *Studies in Religion* 8, no. 1 (1979): 47–55; 'The Anglican Episcopate and Changing Conceptions of Canadian Identity,' *Canadian Review of Studies in Nationalism* 8, no. 1 (1981): 85–99; 'Patriotism and Patriarchs: Anglican Archbishops and Canadianization,' *Canadian Ethnic Studies*, vol. 14, no. 3 (1982): 79–94; and 'John Porter: The Unknown Functionalist,' *S/S* 12, no. 3 (1988): 12–22.

17 Marshall, '*Maclean's* Interviews John Porter,' 9, 51–4.

18 Ibid., 51. Within ten years, Porter reversed his views on means testing and support of the principle of universality (LAC, JPP, vol. 3, no. 1, Agnes Kruchio, '*Excalibur* interview,' *Excalibur*, York University, 10 February 1977, 13).

19 Marshall, '*Maclean's* Interviews John Porter,' 52.

20 Ibid., 53, 54.

21 Fulford to RHH, 2 February 2000.

22 Fulford to RHH, 3 February 2000.

23 LAC, JPP, vol. 9, no. 3, JAP to Meisel, 11 January 1965.

24 Scholars from a variety of disciplines expressed interest in the volume. Historian Margaret Prang from the University of British Columbia praised Porter's efforts and used the book to provoke her colleagues into filling some lacunae in the historical literature he had found ('Book Review,' *CHR* 47, no. 2 [1966]: 156–8). Queen's University historian A.R.M. Lower was, by contrast, completely dismissive of Porter's work ('Book Review,' 158–61; discussed below). Economist G.A. McEachern referred to *The Vertical Mosaic* as 'perhaps one of the most exhaustive and relevant analysis [sic] of the Canadian scene by any social scientist' ('Book Review,' *Canadian Journal of Agricultural Economics* 15, no. 1 [1967]: 145–6). Even scholars in philosophy and English literature paid it some attention (E. Mandel, 'Book Review,' *Dialogue* 4, no. 4 [1966]: 546–8; H. MacLennan, 'Two Books on Canada,' *The Tamarack Review* 37 [1965]: 90–7; and W. Young, 'Canadian Elites,' *Canadian Literature* 32 [1967]: 74–5).

25 Blishen, 'Social Structure in Canada,' 135, 130.

26 T.B. Bottomore, 'Review,' *CJEPS* 32, no. 4 (1966): 527–8.

27 T.B. Bottomore, 'Book Review,' *JCPS* 5, no. 3 (1967): 245–6.

28 Aileen Ross, 'Book Review,' *MJE* 1, no. 2 (1966): 131–3.

29 G. Fortin, 'Comte Rendu,' in *RS* 6, no. 2 (1965): 200–2. Curiously, *The Vertical Mosaic* was never translated into French.

30 D. Smilley, 'Book Review,' in *WPQ* 18, no. 4 (1965): 943–5.

31 Martin Robin, '*The Vertical Mosaic*: Reviewed,' *APSR* 60 (March 1966): 153–4. See also R. Chapman, 'Book Review,' *PS* 15 (1965): 132–4.

32 Martin Robin, 'Letters in Canada 1965,' Social Studies: Education, *UTQ* 35, no. 4 (1966): 487–91.

33 Dofny, 'Book Review,' 1967.

34 Thorburn to RHH, 24 April 1991.

35 Horowitz, 'Creative Politics,' 14.

36 'Editorial Comments,' *Marxism Today* 10, no. 3 (March 1965): 68. Nearly two decades later, Pat Marchak made a similar comment in an article situating *The Vertical Mosaic* within the historical development of the political economy tradition in Canada. 'The effects of working in isolation are evident in Porter's remarkable *Vertical Mosaic*,' she wrote, 'which provides the evidence of so much more than his analysis acknowledges' ('Canadian Political Economy,' *CRSA* 22, no. 5 [1985]: 674).

37 Resnick, '*The Vertical Mosaic* Revisited,' 134.

38 Ibid., 142.

39 Ibid., 135, 142.

40 Ibid., 141, 149–50.

41 Horowitz, 'Creative Politics.'

42 E. Bjarnason, 'Class and Elite in Canadian Society,' *TMQ* 16 (Winter 1966): 1,10.

43 Lower, 'Book Review,' 158, emphasis added. I discuss this observation below. Lower and Edwin Black seem to have been the only ones to criticize Porter on this count.

44 Ibid., 158–61.

45 LAC, JPP, vol. 9, no. 3, Dunton to JAP, 30 August 1965.

46 Ibid., vol. 1, no. 6, Rocher to JAP, 18 August 1966.

47 Ibid., vol. 9, no. 4, Bond to JAP, 6 October 1965.

48 Ibid., vol. 9, no. 3, Cook to JAP, n.d. [July] 1965.

49 There is no evidence in the Porter papers that he responded in writing to Cook, but it seems likely he did and that Cook was then forced to backpedal a bit in a second letter (Ibid., Cook to JAP, 29 July 1965).

50 LAC, JPP, vol. 3, no. 5, Earle to JAP, 31 May 1966. Ms Earle's comments are not those of a scholar, so her criticism is interesting for another reason. It demonstrates that, like many Canadians, she was not ignorant of the existence of class inequality but used a different set of criteria from Porter's for assessing who should be placed where on the social ladder.

51 This story was related to me by Frank Vallee, Porter's colleague (Vallee interview).

52 Marshall, 'Class and Power in Canada,' 215–17.

53 R. Chapman, 'Book Review,' *PS* 15 (1967): 132–4.
54 MacRae interview. By November 1965, *The Vertical Mosaic* was available in England, distributed by Oxford University Press. The University of Toronto Press tried unsuccessfully to get the French publisher Plon to distribute it in France (LAC, JPP, vol. 9, no. 4, R.M. Schoeffel [University of Toronto Press] to JAP, 23 November 1965). A brief and unsigned but positive review of the book appeared in *Revue français de science politique* 27, no. 6 (1967): 1,213.
55 LAC, JPP, vol. 1, no. 6, R. Mackenzie to JAP, 3 November 1966.
56 Frank Jones recalled that Horowitz gave a talk at McMaster just after *The Vertical Mosaic* came out. During a lunch following the presentation, Horowitz praised Porter's book highly, referring to it as the 'best sociological work I've read' (Frank Jones interview).
57 I.L. Horowitz, '*The Vertical Mosaic*: A Review,' *ASR* 31 (1966): 862–3.
58 J.R. Seeley, 'Review,' *AJS* 72, no. 3 (1966): 321–2; see also C.P. Wolf, 'Foreword,' in Coleman, Etzioni and Porter, *Macrosociology*, xix; and Longstaff, 'John Porter's *Vertical Mosaic*.'.
59 See LAC, JPP, vol. 1, no. 6, E. Volkart (Executive Officer, American Sociological Association) to JAP, 19 September 1966 for the official notification. Porter is the only Canadian author to win the MacIver Award.
60 Whyte to RHH, 1 February 2002. Pineo, Porter, and McFarlane were under the mistaken impression that only American Sociological Association members were eligible to receive the MacIver Award (LAC, JPP, vol. 1, no. 6, McFarlane to JAP, 13 September 1966).
61 LAC, JPP, vol. 1, no. 6, Elkin to JAP, 7 September 1966.
62 Bank of Canada, Rates and Statistics, Inflation Calculator, www.bankofcanada.ca/en/rates/inflation_calc.html.
63 LAC, JPP, vol. 9, no. 3, JAP to H. Leal (Dean, Osgoode Hall Law School), 7 September 1965.
64 McFarlane comments, 23 April 2002; see also McFarlane interview and Marion Porter interview 1.
65 LAC, JPP, vol. 9, no. 4, Fred Poland (Editorial Department) to JAP, 15 November 1965.
66 Ibid., Eleanor Harman to JAP, 6 December 1965; and JAP to Harman, 13 December 1965.
67 Ibid., Harman to JAP, 20 December 1965.
68 Ibid., JAP to Harman, 5 January 1966; JAP to Hilary Marshall, 13 January 1966; JAP to Marshall, 9 February 1966; and Marshall to JAP, 8 March 1966.
69 Ibid., Harold Bohne to JAP, 12 May 1966.

70 Helmes-Hayes and Wilcox-Magill, 'A Neglected Classic,' 94.

71 R. Alan Hedley and T. Rennie Warburton, 'The Role of National Courses in the Teaching and Development of Sociology: The Canadian Case,' *SR* 21 (1973): 306, 312–13, respectively.

72 Rich, '*The Vertical Mosaic* Revisited,' 15.

73 Ibid.

74 See, for example, Resnick, '*The Vertical Mosaic* Revisited,' 142.

75 Perhaps the first major challenge regarding the accuracy of Porter's data appeared in 1976 when Rich argued that Porter had inaccurately calculated rates of upward mobility into elites and higher occupational categories ('*The Vertical Mosaic* Revisited,' 21–2).

76 Longstaff, 'John Porter's *The Vertical Mosaic*,' 84–5.

77 Black, 'Fractured Mosaic,' 642.

78 Porter and Pineo, 'Occupational Prestige in Canada'; and Goyder, 'Subjective Social Class Identification.'

79 Porter and Pineo, 'Occupational Prestige in Canada,' cited in Goyder, 'Subjective Social Class Identification,' 30, table 2:1 and 40, table 2:3. These data refer to respondents' self-identification on a forced-choice question. On open-ended questions, respondents were much less likely to say that classes existed and/or that they thought of themselves as belonging to a class.

80 Black, 'Fractured Mosaic,' 644. On the second point, Porter did some of this in discussing relations between elites.

81 Ibid., 653.

82 Rich, '*The Vertical Mosaic* Revisited,' 25. For earlier examples, see Seeley, 'Review,' 322; Resnick, '*The Vertical Mosaic* Revisited,' 138, 143–4; and Longstaff, 'John Porter's *The Vertical Mosaic*,' 85.

83 Horowitz, 'Creative Politics'; Longstaff, 'John Porter's *The Vertical Mosaic*,' 84, 87; and Rich, '*Vertical Mosaic* Revisited,' 15. Porter defended himself on this count in a letter to Christopher Beattie, written after reading Longstaff's article. He claimed that in 1963, when he submitted the manuscript for review, events had not unfolded in a way that would allow him to comment authoritatively on developments in Quebec. Even as late as 1967, he was not sure how to read the data about Quebec (LAC, JPP, vol. 9, no. 5, JAP to C. Beattie, 8 November 1967).

84 For an insightful feminist commentary on *The Vertical Mosaic* written in the late 1990s, see Armstrong, 'Missing Women,' in *Vertical Mosaic Revisited*, ed. Helmes-Hayes and Curtis, 116–44.

85 Resnick, '*The Vertical Mosaic* Revisited,' 142; see also Dofny, 'Book Review,' 655–6; and Marshall, 'Class and Power in Canada,' 215.

86 Longstaff, 'John Porter's *The Vertical Mosaic*,' 87–8; see also Dofny, 'Book Review,' 655 and Bottomore, 'Review,' *CJEPS* 32, no. 4 (1966), 528.
87 Longstaff, 'John Porter's *The Vertical Mosaic*,' 88–9. According to Porter, the only real example of class struggle in Canada was the Winnipeg General Strike (*Vertical Mosaic*, 316).
88 Later commentators did, however (see, e.g., Heap, 'Conceptual, Theoretical and Ethical Problems,' in *Everybody's Canada*, ed. Heap, 123–30; and Black, 'Fractured Mosaic,' 644).
89 Marshall, 'Class and Power in Canada,' 218; and Resnick, '*The Vertical Mosaic* Revisited,' 143.
90 The quotations in this paragraph come from the Burnet interview.
91 Resnick, '*The Vertical Mosaic* Revisited,' 135, 142, 143; see also Marshall, 'Class and Power in Canada,' 218. Many of the new political economists elaborated on this critique at length. This relational and historical method has been developed to a great degree of sophistication (see, e.g., Clement and Myles, *Relations of Ruling*).
92 Marshall, 'Class and Power in Canada,' 219.
93 Black, 'Fractured Mosaic,' 644.
94 See, e.g., Resnick, '*The Vertical Mosaic* Revisited,' 142–3.
95 Longstaff, 'John Porter's *The Vertical Mosaic*,' 85; see also Bottomore, 'Review,' *CJEPS* 32, no. 4 (1966), 528; and Black, 'Fractured Mosaic,' 645–6.
96 LAC, JPP, vol. 9, no. 5, JAP to Beattie, 8 November 1967.
97 Forcese, 'Macro-sociology of John Porter,' 653.
98 LAC, JPP, vol. 9, no. 5, JAP to Beattie, 8 November 1967.
99 Meisel, 'Foreword,' in Porter, *Vertical Mosaic*, x.
100 Black, 'Fractured Mosaic,' 653.
101 Resnick, '*The Vertical Mosaic* Revisited,' 141–2, 143.
102 Heap, *Everybody's Canada*, 140.
103 Clement, 'John Porter and the Development of Sociology,' 586.
104 Michael Ornstein, 'Three Decades of Elite Research,' in *Vertical Mosaic Revisited*, ed. Helmes-Hayes and Curtis, 149.
105 Porter, 'Power and Freedom,' in *Social Purpose for Canada*, ed. Oliver.
106 Ibid., 27, 47.
107 Ibid., 38.
108 Ibid., 34.
109 Ibid., 38–44.
110 Ibid., 47.
111 Ibid., 54–6.
112 Ibid., 54.

113 Ibid., 50–2.

114 Ibid., 51, emphasis added.

115 Ibid., 35.

116 Porter, 'Introduction to "Power and Freedom,"' in Porter, *Measure of Canadian Society,* 208.

117 Porter, *Vertical Mosaic,* 558.

118 Ibid., 557–8.

119 Boldt, 'Images of Canada's Future' in *Sociology of the Future,* ed. Bell and Mau, 190.

120 Ibid., 191.

121 Ibid., 196, emphasis added.

122 Ibid., 200, 199.

123 Ibid., 202–7.

124 Porter, 'Research Biography,' in Coleman, Etzioni, and Porter, *Macrosociology,* 151–2.

125 T.S. Eliot, 'Shakespeare and the Stoicism of Seneca,' an address read before the Shakespeare Association, 18 March 1927 (reprinted Folcroft, PA: Folcroft Press, 1970), 15.

126 Brym, with Fox, *From Culture to Power,* 24–6. Regarding S.D. Clark, see D. Nock, '"Crushing the Power of Finance": The Socialist Prairie Roots of S.D. Clark,' *BJCS* 1, no. 1 (1986): 86–108. Regarding S.M. Lipset, see Randall Collins, *Three Sociological Traditions* (New York: Oxford, 1985), 104.

127 Horowitz, 'Creative Politics,' 14.

128 Porter, Introduction to 'Power and Freedom,' in Porter, *Measure of Canadian Society,* 208.

129 W.E. Mann, 'Review of J. Porter, *The Measure of Canadian Society* (1979),' *CJS* 6, no. 3 (1981): 389.

130 Brym, with Fox, *From Culture to Power,* 92.

131 Fisher to RHH, 7 December 2006.

132 The 'two solitudes/deux nations' images are found in Hugh MacLennan's *Two Solitudes* (Toronto: Macmillan, 1945); Arthur Lower's 'Two Ways of Life – the Primary Antithesis in Canadian History,' Canadian Historical Association *Report* (1943): 5–18; and Everett Hughes' *French Canada in Transition* (Chicago: University of Chicago Press, 1943). The 'fragment thesis' was developed in Louis Hartz, ed., *The Founding of New Societies* (New York: Harcourt, Brace and World, 1964). The famous phrase 'hewers of wood and drawers of water' comes from *the* Bible, Josh. 9:21 (AV). For a discussion of these and other images of Canadian society, see Helmes-Hayes and Curtis, 'Introduction,' in *Vertical Mosaic Revisited,* ed. Helmes-Hayes and Curtis, 11–15.

9: Canadian Society and Canadian Sociology in the 1960s and '70s

1 Colombo, ed., *1994 Canadian Global Almanac*, 42, 'Population of Provinces and Territories.'
2 Norrie and Owram, *History of the Canadian Economy*, 425; Alan Simmons, '"New Wave" Immigrants: Origin and Characteristics,' in S. Halli, F. Trovato, and L. Driedger, eds., *Ethnic Demography* (Ottawa: Carleton University Press, 1990), 141–59.
3 Colombo, ed., *1994 Canadian Global Almanac*, 46, 'Canadian Urban and Rural Population,' and 52–3, 'Population of Census Metropolitan Areas in Canada.'
4 Ibid., 179, 'Canadian Gross Domestic Product,' measured in constant 1986 dollars. Measured in 'current' (1994) dollars, the increase was from $48 billion to $276 billion.
5 Norrie and Owram, *History of the Canadian Economy*, 398–9, 408–22.
6 Li, *Making of Post-War Canada*, 48, table 3.3; and 151, table A3.
7 Colombo, ed., *1994 Canadian Almanac*, 201, 'Union Membership in Canada, 1961–93.'
8 Palmer, *Working Class Experience*, 272–3. Stuart Jamieson, *Industrial Relations in Canada*, 2nd ed. (Toronto: Macmillan, 1973), 94–9; and Heron, *Canadian Labour Movement*, 120–46.
9 Li, *Making of Post-War Canada*, 149, table A:1 and 152, table A:4, respectively; see also Roberts et al., eds., *Recent Social Trends*, 121, table 1.
10 Paul Phillips and Erin Phillips, *Women and Work: Inequality in the Labour Market* (Toronto: Lorimer, 1983), especially ch. 4; see also Pat Armstrong and Hugh Armstrong, *The Double Ghetto: Canadian Women and Their Segregated Work* (Toronto: McClelland and Stewart, 1978).
11 Roberts et al., eds., *Recent Social Trends*, 30, table 4; 130; 139, table 1; and 154, table 2.
12 Roberts et al., eds., *Recent Social Trends*, 126, table 8; and 127, table 9. Divorce laws were liberalized in the late 1960s, and provincial governments determined that women should receive half the property accumulated during a marriage (Granatstein et al., *20th Century Canada*, 394).
13 Canada, no author, *A Report of the Royal Commission on the Status of Women in Canada* (Ottawa: Information Canada, 1970).
14 Bothwell, Drummond, and English, *Canada since 1945*, 2nd ed., 306.
15 Finkel, *Our Lives*, 133–4. The Liberals were reticent, according to Finkel, because the 'free market' types in the party resisted the growth of the welfare state. As a result, the Liberals had to be pushed to produce such measures. Finkel notes that they introduced the bulk of their social programs during

the periods 1963–8 and 1972–4, when they had only a minority government (*Our Lives*, 130–45).

16 Adams et al., *Real Poverty Report*, 21, table 1.4.iii.

17 Porter, 'The Societal Context,' in Porter et al., *Ascription and Achievement*, 56. Note that these data would actually underestimate the degree of concentration of ownership of wealth. The very wealthiest Canadians – the Bronfmans, the Westons, and so forth – would not be likely to be included in these data.

18 Senate of Canada, Special Committee on Poverty, *Poverty in Canada* (Ottawa: Information Canada, 1971) 11; and 12, table 2. For a brief discussion of methods of calculating the poverty line, see ibid., 5–9, and Adams et al., *Real Poverty Report*, 8–16.

19 Re differences in per capita income reported by province, see Adams et al., *Real Poverty Report*, 59, table II.6.ii, and Norrie and Owram, *History of the Canadian Economy*, 433–5.

20 Colombo, ed., *1994 Canadian Global Almanac*, 218, 'Canadian Imports by Country,' and 219, 'Canadian Exports by Country.'

21 Marchak, *Ideological Perspectives on Canada*, 50. Especially problematic to economic nationalists was American control over the mining, petroleum, natural gas, and manufacturing sectors (Li, *Making of Post-War Canada*, 24–5, table 2:1; see also Finkel, *Our Lives*, 159–64). These trends continued through the 1970s (Marchak, *Ideological Perspectives on Canada*, 52, table 7).

22 Finkel, *Our Lives*, 168.

23 Grant, *Lament for a Nation*, 1965.

24 Finkel, *Our Lives*, 140–1; see also Norrie and Owram, *History of the Canadian Economy*, 431–3.

25 Norrie and Owram, *History of the Canadian Economy*, 437–48.

26 Ibid., 437–40; see also Finkel, *Our Lives*, 145–50, 284–7.

27 Finkel, *Our Lives*, 168–70.

28 Ibid., 176–88.

29 On the Quiet Revolution, see Kenneth McRoberts and Dennis Posgate, *Quebec: Social Change and Political Crisis*, rev. ed. (Toronto: McClelland and Stewart, 1980).

30 Finkel, *Our Lives*, 198–200.

31 Bothwell, Drummond, and English, *Canada since 1945*, 374–87. Just less than 50 per cent of francophones voted in favour of sovereignty association (see Finkel, *Our Lives*, 200–3). Regarding René Lévesque and the Parti Québécois, see Graham Fraser, *Parti Québécois: René Lévesque and the Parti Québécois in Power* (Toronto: Macmillan, 1984).

32 Owram, *Born at the Right Time*, 31–53.

33 Ibid., 111–35.
34 Ibid., 140.
35 Ibid., 145–6; see 145–58 more generally.
36 Ibid., 159–247.
37 Ibid., 175–83. Ironically, as universities became 'home' to an ever greater number of Canadian young adults, they forced the universities to abandon their traditional practice of acting *in loco parentis* (Johnston, *Radical Campus*, 136, 292).
38 Owram, *Born at the Right Time*, 309.
39 Levitt, *Children of Privilege*, 4.
40 Axelrod, *Scholars and Dollars*, 35–53. On the relationship between the development of capitalism and the growth of postsecondary education, see Levitt, *Children of Privilege*, 19–25.
41 Levitt, *Children of Privilege*, 22–36.
42 Leacy, ed., *Historical Statistics of Canada*, series W519–532: 'Operating and capital expenditures of Universities, by source of funds, Canada, selected years, 1920 to 1974'; and Association of Universities and Colleges of Canada, 'Founding Year and Joining Year of Institutions,' www.aucc.ca/_pdf/english/aboutaucc/joinaucc_e.pdf.
43 Leacy, ed., *Historical Statistics of Canada*, series W340–438: 'Full-time university enrolment, by sex, Canada, Canada, and by province, selected years 1920 to 1975.'
44 Ibid.
45 Ibid. According to *Towards 2000*, Ontario had 111,000 full-time university students in 1970–1 as opposed to just 29,000 only a decade before (Porter et al., *Towards 2000*, 48; for related data on the postsecondary system as a whole, see Porter, Porter, and Blishen, *Stations and Callings*, 22).
46 Leacy, ed., *Historical Statistics of Canada*, series W475–485: 'Full-time university teachers, Canada, and by province, selected years, 1920 to 1975.'
47 Axelrod, *Scholars and Dollars*, 141–78.
48 Ibid., 180–1 and the sources listed in 248n2; see also Hardy, *Politics of Collegiality*, 22.
49 Hardy, *Politics of Collegiality*, 26.
50 For a description of the Ontario case, see Axelrod, *Scholars and Dollars*, 158–78.
51 Ibid., 204, 205; for a general discussion, see 203–13.
52 On the founding of the CRSA and the CSAA, see Jones, 'Establishing the CSAA.'
53 Re the Royal Commission on Bilingualism and Biculturalism, see Hiller, *Society and Change*, 26; and Brooks and Gagnon, *Social Scientists and Politics*, 43–4, 97–8, 121.

54 Hiller, *Society and Change*, 23, table 3.

55 Tomovic, 'Sociology in Canada,' 20, table 1 and 50–1, table 4, respectively.

56 Connor and Curtis, *Sociology and Anthropology in Canada*, 78–9, table 3.

57 I went through the available calendars in the collection of Robarts Library at the University of Toronto in order to determine these figures. The collection is incomplete, however, so the data may be inaccurate. Certainly, though, there were very few places offering graduate education in sociology prior to 1960. See also Connor and Curtis, *Sociology and Anthropology in Canada*, 77, table 2.

58 See Zeitlin's reference to this issue regarding the Department of Sociology at the University of Toronto in Zeitlin, untitled, in *Forty Years*, ed. Helmes-Hayes, 63.

59 For an illustration of the novelty and influence of this development, see Johnston, *Radical Campus*, 98–100, 293–329 passim.

60 In 1975, Canadian sociologists established a second general journal, the *Canadian Journal of Sociology*.

61 Hiller, *Society and Change*, 26.

62 Ibid., 24, table 5; and 22, respectively.

63 Ibid., 32, table 7.

64 Grayson and Magill, *One Step Forward*, 18, table 2A. Hofley notes that Britain, France, and the United States had similar demographic situations to deal with but solved them without hiring foreign nationals. Australia followed the same path as Canada ('Canadianization,' in *Fragile Truths*, ed. Carroll et al., 110–11, 105–6). Many of those holding American or other foreign degrees were, of course, Canadians who had studied abroad.

65 John Redekop, 'Authors and Publishers: An Analysis of Textbook Selection in Canadian Departments of Political Science and Sociology,' *Canadian Journal of Political Science* 9, no. 1 (1976): 107–20.

66 For an insightful description of their efforts to make this a high-profile public and scholarly issue, see Cormier, *Canadianization Movement*; and Cormier, 'Nationalism, Activism.'

67 T.H.B. Symons, *To Know Ourselves: The Report of the Commission on Canadian Studies* (Ottawa: Association of Universities and Colleges of Canada, 1975).

68 Cormier, *Canadianization Movement*, and Hiller, *Society and Change*, 33–9.

69 Cormier, *Canadianization Movement*, and Hiller, *Society and Change*. For a discussion of how this form of colonization was bound to a patriarchal form of sociology, see Dorothy Smith, 'Remaking a Life, Remaking Sociology: Reflections of a Feminist,' in *Fragile Truths*, ed. Carroll et al., 125–34.

70 Cormier, *Canadianization Movement*, and 'Nationalism, Activism'; and Hiller, 'Canadian Sociology Movement.'

71 See Cormier, 'Nationalism, Activism,' 14–16 for a description of the basic

epistemological debate that draws in particular on two sources: Robert Brym, 'Trend Report: Anglo-Canadian Sociology,' *CS* 34, no. 1 (1986): entire issue; and Hiller, 'Canadian Sociology Movement.' Other excellent sources on the Canadianization issue in addition to Cormier, *Canadianization Movement,* are Grayson and Magill, *One Step Forward*; Michael O'Hearn, 'The Canadianization Debate,' in ibid., 154–70; Harry Hiller, 'Universality of Science and the Question of National Sociologies,' *AmS* 14 (1979): 124–35; and Hiller, 'Paradigmatic Shifts, Indigenization, and the Development of Sociology in Canada,' *JHBS* 16, no. 3 (1980): 263–74.

72 Helmes-Hayes, 'John Porter: Canada's Most Famous Sociologist,' 85–6.

73 See, for example, Gordon Inglis, 'Reflections on Not Being Sued,' in *Fragile Truths,* ed. Carroll et al. 57–63; Hofley, 'Canadianization,' in ibid., 103–22; Eleanor Maticka-Tyndale and Janice Drakich, 'Striking a Balance: Women Organizing for Change in the CSAA,' in ibid., 43–55; and Cormier, 'Nationalism, Activism,' 20–4.

74 Helmes-Hayes, 'John Porter: Canada's Most Famous Sociologist,' 85; re the success in Canadianizing sociology curricula, see Grayson and Magill, *One Step Forward,* 10–11.

75 Cormier, 'Nationalism, Activism,' 22–4; Grayson and Magill, *One Step Forward,* 19–22, 58–62.

76 Tepperman, 'Sociology in English-Speaking Canada,' 436; see N. Keyfitz, 'Sociology and Canadian Society,' in *Perspectives on the Social Sciences in Canada,* ed. T. Guinsberg and G. Reuben (Toronto: University of Toronto Press, 1973), 10–41.

77 Hiller, *Society and Change,* 32, table 7.

78 Grayson and Magill, *One Step Forward,* 55, table 1B; for enrolment figures to 1975–6, see Hiller, *Society and Change,* 33, table 8.

79 For projections about the meagre prospective job openings at the time, see Grayson and Magill, *One Step Forward,* 9.

80 Ibid., 16, table 1A.

81 Part of this growth occurred when Carleton absorbed seven faculty members from St. Pat's College (CU, ARC, *Carleton University Calendar,* 1972–3, 237).

82 CUA, Office of the President fonds, Series: Annual Reports, *The President's Report 1968–1969,* 9; *The University Report, Carleton University 1969–1970,* n.p.; and *The University Report, Carleton University 1970–1971,* 1.

83 McFarlane interview.

84 For arts graduate programs see CUA, Office of Budget Planning, *Carleton University Data Book 1995–1996,* ed. D. Zaluska, 'Student Registration Statistics, 1942–43 to 1995–96,' May 1996, 24. For sociology graduate programs

see Joel Nordenstrom (Department of Sociology Administrator, Carleton University) to RHH, 18 December 2003.

85 Whyte to RHH, 1 February 2002. Whyte notes further that 'the task of guiding the program through the initial assessment protocols, indeed, in setting up the protocols for Ontario universities, was aided in no small part by the efforts of John Harp and Al Steeves.'

86 I compiled these data on 18 November 2004 from the volumes stored in the Carleton University Department of Sociology and Anthropology collection of MA and PhD theses. To determine committee membership I referred to the acknowledgements and a sheet that the committee members signed when they approved a thesis.

87 Whyte to RHH, 1 February 2002.

88 Clement interview 3.

89 There were forty full-time faculty in 1978–9 (CU, ARC, *Carleton University Calendar,* 1978–9, 235).

90 For these figures, see CU, ARC, *Carleton University Calendars,* 1964–5 and 1973–4.

91 Toronto offered the first women's studies courses in Canada in 1970–1 (Johnston, *Radical Campus,* 249). Other universities followed suit over the next few years. For an account of developments at SFU, probably quite typical, see ibid., 249–54.

92 Hofley, 'Canadianization,' in *Fragile Truths,* ed. Carroll et al., 104.

93 I used CU, ARC, *Carleton University Calendars,* 1965–6 to 1972–3, to try to determine the nationality of the department's full-time teaching staff.

94 See, e.g., Heather Jon Maroney and Meg Luxton, 'Editors' Introduction,' in *Feminism and Political Economy,* ed. Maroney and Luxton, 1–3; and ibid., 'From Feminism and Political Economy to Feminist Political Economy,' 5–28.

95 Tepperman, 'Sociology in English-Speaking Canada,' 435.

10: Geneva, Ottawa, and Toronto, 1966–1969

1 LAC, JPP, vol. 3, no. 6, JAP to W. Bell, 30 May, 1968.

2 Frumhartz interview.

3 Vallee interview.

4 Porter, Porter, and Blishen, *Stations and Callings,* and Porter et al., *Ascription and Achievement,* respectively.

5 Hamilton comments, n.d. July 2006; Hamilton to RHH, 18 December 2006.

6 He remained chair of that committee until 1971. LAC, JPP, vol. 3, no. 8, D. Williams (Chair, CPUO) to JAP, 26 April 1971.

7 J. Porter, curriculum vitae, Clement personal papers.

8 Pineo, 'Prestige and Mobility.'

9 McRoberts noted that replication was important to Porter, who regarded it as crucial to the development of sociology as a credible empirical science in Canada: 'Part of what had to be done was replication. You couldn't always just go on and do new things' (McRoberts interview; see also Pineo, 'Prestige and Mobility,' 623–5).

10 For details of Pineo's academic background, see LAC, JPP, vol. 8, no. 3, 'Department of Sociology, Carleton University: A Proposal for Research on Public Evaluation of Occupations in Canada' [hereafter 'Public Evaluation of Occupations Proposal'], 9

11 Pineo, 'Prestige and Mobility,' 620.

12 LAC, JPP, vol. 8, no. 3, 'Public Evaluation of Occupations Proposal,' 1–3. The reference for the original study is C. North and P. Hatt, 'Jobs and Occupations: A Popular Evaluation,' *PON* 9 (September 1947): 3–13. The reference for the follow-up is R. Hodge, P. Siegel, and P. Rossi, 'Occupational Prestige in the United States, 1925–1963,' *AJS* 70, no. 3 (1964): 286–302.

13 Pineo, 'Prestige and Mobility,' 615.

14 LAC, JPP, vol. 8, no. 3, 'Public Evaluation of Occupations Proposal,' 1.

15 Ibid., 2–3, emphasis added.

16 Pineo, 'Prestige and Mobility,' 621.

17 Ibid.

18 Blishen, 'A Revised Socio-Economic Index'; Pineo, 'Prestige and Mobility,' 620–1.

19 LAC, JPP, vol. 8, no. 3, 'Public Evaluation of Occupations Proposal,' 2.

20 Ibid., 3.

21 Ibid.

22 Pineo, 'Prestige and Mobility,' 617. Eventually, they received money from the federal Department of Labour, the Canada Council, the Royal Commission on Bilingualism and Biculturalism, the McConnell Foundation, the SSRCC, and Carleton University (LAC, JPP, vol. 20, no. 1, 'Progress Report on Research Project on Public Evaluation of Occupations,' March 1965).

23 Pineo, 'Prestige and Mobility,' 616.

24 Ibid.

25 LAC, JPP, vol. 19, no. 15, JAP to O. Werfhorst (Canadian Facts), 1 April 1965.

26 Ibid., Pineo to T. Nosanchuk, 12 October 1965; and JAP to L. Gray (President, Canadian Facts), 9 December 1965.

27 Pineo to RHH, 21 February 2002.

28 LAC, JPP, vol. 19, no. 15, JAP to J. Lowther (City of Ottawa), 1 June 1965; and Lowther to JAP, 5 June 1965.

29 LAC, JPP, vol. 19, no. 15, JAP to Oswald Hall, 9 April 1966.

30 Pineo to RHH, 21 February 2002.

31 Pineo, 'Prestige and Mobility,' 615.

32 Ibid., 620.

33 Ibid., 625.

34 LAC, JPP, vol. 19, no. 15, JAP to Rossi, 17 May 1966 and Rossi to JAP, 31 May 1966; and vol. 16, no. 12, Pineo to JAP, n.d. (c. October 1967).

35 Drafts of chapters and other materials regarding the proposed volume, *The Canadian Status System,* can be found in LAC, JPP, vol. 6, no. 1; vol. 7, nos. 7, 8, 29, 30, 31, 32, 33; vol. 8, no. 2; vol. 16, nos. 7, 10, 11, 12, 13, 14, 15. The 'Proposed Outline for Monograph on Occupations Study' is in vol. 16, no. 13. They continued to work on the manuscript until 1971. Porter and Pineo co-authored two articles from this survey: 'Occupational Prestige in Canada' and, with Hugh McRoberts, 'The 1971 Census and the Socio-Economic Classification of Occupations.' Though the study never appeared in book form, it had a major impact, furnishing both a data set and a valuable research tool that Canadian sociologists drew on for years thereafter. See, for example, P. Pineo and J. Goyder, 'Social Class Identification of National Sub-groups,' in *Social Stratification: Canada,* ed. J.E. Curtis and W.G. Scott (Scarborough, ON: Prentice-Hall, 1973), 187–96; P. Pineo, 'Social Mobility in Canada: the Current Picture,' *Sociological Focus* 9, no. 2 (1976): 109–23; P. Pineo, 'Public Evaluations of the Social Standing of Industries and Firms,' *IJCS* 17, nos. 3 and 4 (1976): 226–41; P. Pineo, 'The Social Standing of Ethnic and Racial Groupings,' *CRSA* 14, no. 2 (1977): 147–57; J. Goyder and P. Pineo, 'The Accuracy of Self-Assessment of Social Status,' *CRSA* 14, no. 2, (1977): 235–46; and J. Goyder and P. Pineo, 'Social Class Identification,' in *Social Stratification: Canada,* 2nd ed., ed. J. Curtis and W. Scott (Scarborough, ON: Prentice-Hall, 1979), 431–47.

36 McFarlane comments, 23 April 2002.

37 LAC, JPP, vol. 16, no. 6, JAP to M. Abrams (Research Services Ltd., London, England), 28 September 1966; JAP to R. Lyons (International Institute for Educational Planning, Paris), 8 November 1966.

38 Porter, *Vertical Mosaic,* 44–8.

39 LAC, JPP, vol. 1, no. 6, JAP to G. Merrill, 7 December 1966.

40 Ibid., vol. 3, no. 6, JAP to A. Richmond, 16 December 1969.

41 Ibid., vol. 1, no. 7, M. Andrassy and I. Varjassy (Secretary of State) to JAP, 19 May 1967.

42 Ibid., vol. 3, no. 6, JAP to Richmond, 16 December 1969.

43 Chesworth interview; see also Ann Porter interview.
44 The trip to Wrexham was among the last times Porter saw his mother. She died in November, 1971 (E. Jones to RHH, 1 March 1990). LAC, JPP, vol. 1, no. 6, JAP to Merrill, 7 December 1966; Marion Porter interview 1.
45 Marion Porter comments, 7–8 July 1987.
46 Ann Porter interview.
47 Tony Porter interview 2.
48 Canada/Labour, J. Mainwaring to G. Haythorne (Deputy Minister), G. Schonning, and G. Saunders, 6 December 1966; see also Haythorne to G. Schenning, J. Mainwaring, and A. Craig, 17 March 1967.
49 LAC, JPP, vol. 16, no. 12, JAP to Pineo, 7 July 1967.
50 For a copy of the report, see LAC, JPP, vol. 7, no. 33; see also ibid., vol. 16, no. 14, JAP to G. Robitaille (Royal Commission on Bilingualism and Biculturalism), 15 December 1966 and Robataille to JAP, 22 February 1967.
51 Porter and Pineo, 'Occupational Prestige in Canada.'
52 LAC, JPP, vol. 8, no. 1, Pineo and Porter, 'Native and Foreign-Born Differences,' Report to the Department of Manpower and Immigration, 1967.
53 Porter, *Canadian Social Structure*, 1967.
54 Ibid., 1.
55 Ibid., 'Preface,' n.p., and Introduction, 1.
56 A Porterism – a term coined by his students – was a pithy aphorism Porter used in classes or conversations to drive home a point. Other Porterisms included 'Sociology is not anecdotal' and 'Voting statistics are a pile of horsefeathers' (McRoberts interview).
57 LAC, JPP, vol. 1, no. 4, Academic Registrar (LSE) to JAP, 16 September 1966.
58 Marion Porter comments, 7–8 July 1987.
59 The telephone offer was formalized in a letter from Clark (LAC, JPP, vol. 5, no. 27, Clark to JAP, 4 October 1966). For Porter's original letter of acceptance, see ibid., JAP to Clark, 28 November 1966.
60 Ibid., Clark to JAP, 6 December 1966.
61 Ibid., JAP to Clark, 13 December 1966.
62 Ibid., Clark to JAP, 6 December 1966.
63 Ibid., Clark to JAP, 13 December 1966
64 Ibid., Clark to JAP, 19 December 1966.
65 Spinks, Arlt, and Hare, 'Report of the Committee on University Affairs,' 1–6.
66 Ibid., 77.
67 Ibid., 23–5.
68 Ibid., 79, 80.
69 LAC, JPP, vol. 5, no. 27, Clark to JAP, 25 January 1967.

70 Ibid., JAP to Clark, 12 January 1967.

71 Ibid., Dunton to JAP, 1 February 1967.

72 Ibid., Merrill to JAP, 1 February 1967.

73 Ibid., JAP to Merrill, 10 February 1967 and 21 February 1967; JAP to Dunton, 23 February 1967.

74 Ibid., JAP to Merrill, 21 February 1967.

75 Ibid.

76 JAP to McFarlane, 24 February 1967 and Merrill to JAP [draft], 28 February 1967 and McFarlane to JAP, 1 March 1967, McFarlane personal papers; see also LAC, JPP, vol. 5, no. 27, Merrill to JAP, 2 March 1967.

77 As a final inducement, McFarlane reiterated that with Vallee, Whyte, and Frumhartz, he had prepared a proposal for a PhD program for the department (McFarlane to JAP, 1 March 1967 and Merrill to JAP [draft], 28 February 1967, McFarlane personal papers).

78 McFarlane interview.

79 LAC, JPP, vol. 5, no. 27, JAP to Clark, 8 March 1967. Successive letters from Merrill in mid- and late March offered additional inducements, including news that the McConnell Foundation was seriously considering a grant of up to $300,000 toward the establishment of a survey research centre at Carleton (ibid., Merrill to JAP, 16 March 1967 and 28 March 1967).

80 Ellen interview; Obituary: 'Elizabeth Edith Porter,' *Richmond Times Dispatch,* n.d. [c. late January 1991], Ellen personal papers; see also Harry Ellen to RHH, 'Thoughts about Elizabeth Porter,' 28 November 2007.

81 Ellen interview.

82 According to Marion Porter, Elizabeth contacted John not in 1967 but four years earlier, in 1963, just as he was recovering from his first heart attack (Marion Porter interview 1), but the correspondence between John and Fiona begins in September 1967 (LAC, JPP, vol. 1, no. 15). Fiona was certain that it was 1967 (Ellen interview).

83 Porter Cole interview. Cole's claim was mentioned by Marion Porter (Marion Porter interview 1).

84 Ellen interview. According to Marion Porter, John had agreed as part of the divorce settlement not to have any contact with Fiona (M. Porter interview 1).

85 LAC, JPP, vol. 1, no. 15, JAP to F. Porter, 27 September 1967.

86 Ibid., JAP to F. Porter, 27 September 1967–18 April 1968. Porter's papers contain none of Fiona's letters to him from this time. There are a few of her letters dated 1971 and 1976.

87 LAC, JPP, vol. 5, no. 27, JAP to Clark, 10 October 1967; ibid., D. Claringbold (Secretary, Board of Governors, University of Toronto) to JAP, 24 November 1967 and JAP to Claringbold, 29 November 1967. Porter confirmed

that the rumours of his impending move to Toronto were correct in an exchange of letters with Frank Jones (ibid., vol. 6, no. 18, F. Jones to JAP, 14 December 1967 and JAP to Jones, 22 December 1967).

88 R. Helmes-Hayes, 'List of Teaching Staff by Year 1963–64 to 1987–88,' in *A Quarter-Century of Sociology*, ed. Helmes-Hayes, 26–7.

89 Jeanette Wright (Graduate Assistant, Department of Sociology, University of Toronto) to RHH, 21 January 2003.

90 McFarlane interview; also LAC, JPP, vol. 1, no. 15, JAP to F. Porter, 17 November 1968.

91 Clark interview.

92 Clement interview 2. Clark did not remember this incident (Clark interview).

93 Clement interviews 2 and 3. Marion said that this decision was taken more slowly. According to her, John was 'mentally writing his letter of resignation by October' but it was not until Christmas that he had definitely decided to leave (Marion Porter interview 2). In a letter to Fiona, he wrote that 'soon after arriving' in Toronto he had decided that the University of Toronto 'would be a disappointment' and had decided to leave Toronto by January (LAC, JPP, vol. 1, no. 15, JAP to F. Porter, 9 March 1969). On this point, see R. Breton to RHH, 10 January 2003.

94 This comment about the quality of the students at Toronto is found in LAC, JPP, vol. 1, no. 15, JAP to F. Porter, 17 November 1968. Regarding his class sizes, see vol. 5, no. 28 and vol. 5, no. 29.

95 Porter was selected as a member of a fifteen-person panel to advise the Canada Council on the establishment of policies and programs (No author, 'Ottawa Men on Academic Panel,' *Ottawa Journal*, 10 December 1965, 19).

96 J. Porter, curriculum vitae, Clement personal papers.

97 Tilly to RHH, 17 January 2003.

98 Clark interview.

99 Ibid.

100 Burnet interview.

101 According to Tilly, 'several of us in the department participated with varying degrees of commitment in the Toronto anti-war movement – picketing Dow recruiters, marching to the U.S. consulate, and the like.' He recalls that 'Del certainly didn't join the ranks,' but neither did he 'express disapproval or try to stop us' (Tilly to RHH, 17 January 2003).

102 Giffen, untitled, in *Forty Years,* ed. Helmes-Hayes, 56.

103 Michelson, 'Choosing Chairs,' *Globe and Mail* (Toronto), 21 November 2003, A18; Michelson to RHH, 3 November 2003. Tilly, too, noted that

Clark's reluctance to share power was not absolute: 'Del Clark regularly consulted me when he was going to make a weighty decision, and sometimes changed his mind as a result of my intervention. What's more, at one point he broached the possibility of my succeeding him as chair, which suggests that he was not determined to hang on to the throne at all costs.' (Tilly to RHH, 17 January 2003).

104 Clark interview.

105 This phrase is in Irving Zeitlin's account: 'The old U of T tradition, in which departments were ruled by Heads appointed by the administration, was challenged, and a revolution occurred. The Head, S.D. Clark, was effectively deposed, and a new form of departmental government, based on a new code of laws called a Constitution, was established' (Zeitlin, untitled, in *Forty Years*, ed. Helmes-Hayes, 61).

106 Regarding the assembly and departmental politics during the period, see UTA, Robarts Library, accession no. A91–0001, Department of Sociology, Departmental Assembly, box 5, files 33–44; see also Zeitlin interview; Marsden interview; and Reitz interview. As well, see Giffen, untitled; Zeitlin, untitled; and L. Marsden, untitled in *Forty Years*, ed. Helmes-Hayes, 56–60; 61–73; and 74–8, respectively.

107 Zeitlin, untitled, in *Forty Years*, ed. Helmes-Hayes, 72.

108 LAC, JPP, vol. 1, no. 15, JAP to F. Porter, 17 November 1968.

109 Frank Jones interview. Tony Porter said that his father did not find the University of Toronto to be 'the type of supportive environment that Carleton had been' (Tony Porter interview 2). Raymond Breton noted, 'What your chapter says about the bureaucratic environment at the University of Toronto and the low status of sociology in the University are quite accurate' (Breton to RHH, 10 January 2003).

110 LAC, JPP, vol. 8, no. 20, 'Statement to Commission on University Government: University of Toronto, n.d., 5–7.

111 McFarlane interview; see also Blishen to RHH, 15 December 2001.

112 Vallee interview.

113 LAC, JPP, vol. 3, no. 6, JAP to C. Bigelow, 29 July 1969.

11: Measuring Educational Opportunity, 1970–1979

1 School of Journalism, Carleton University, *Hello Ottawa* (Ottawa: Carleton University, 1976), 23. On the question of economic activities, see 155, 160. On employment in the public service, see 153.

2 See LAC, JPP, vol. 17, no. 17, Application for Research Grant (#60–1410): 'An Inquiry into the Decisions of Youth about Education beyond High

School,' 15 November 1968. They requested financial assistance from the Laidlaw Foundation (ibid., Blishen to M.C. Thomas, 8 January 1969) and the Donner Canadian Foundation as well (ibid., Blishen to D. Rickerd, 8 January 1969). Re the Canada Council's request that they undertake a pilot study 'for the further development of the research design,' see ibid., F. Milligan to Blishen, 9 April 1969.

3 LAC, JPP, vol. 17, no. 17, JAP to R. Cournoyer, 18 July 1969 and Milligan to JAP, 19 August 1969.

4 Equivalent in 2008 to over $1 million.

5 The agenda and related materials are in LAC, JPP, vol. 19, no. 5.

6 LAC, JPP, vol. 19, no. 5, B. Blishen and JAP to Dear Professor, 'A Proposal to Study the Educational Plans and Aspirations of Ontario High School Students,' [enclosure with letter], 2 February 1970.

7 Ibid., JAP and Blishen to Dear Professor, 2 February 1970.

8 LAC, JPP, vol. 19, no. 6, untitled, non-verbatim typescript of seminar proceedings; see e.g., W. Sewell, 27, and A. Haller, 28; see 21–32 re the issue of comparative research.

9 Ibid., vol. 19, no. 6, M. Porter, handwritten notes, 'Seminar 20 February,' n.p. Marion's notes are a précis of the major points made during the day's discussion. A detailed but not verbatim transcript is also available in vol. 19, no. 6. One interesting sidelight in this discussion causes today's reader to stop short. Note that as recently as 1970, less than four decades ago, the Americans were alerting Porter and Blishen about some of the difficulties they would face because they would be using what was then a technological breakthrough – the computer.

10 LAC, JPP, vol. 19, no. 6, untitled transcript; see e.g., Sewell, 13 and passim.

11 Ibid., see e.g., Campbell, 18.

12 Ibid., see e.g., Campbell, 20.

13 Ibid., Blishen, 126, emphasis added.

14 See the correspondence in LAC, JPP, vol. 17, no. 19.

15 The questionnaires are in ibid., vol. 19, nos. 2, 3.

16 Ibid., vol. 17, no. 17, JAP to Milligan, 15 May 1970, including a rough copy of parts of the proposal.

17 Ibid., Milligan to JAP, 20 August 1970.

18 Ibid., JAP to E. von Conta (Canada Council), 9 October 1970.

19 LAC, JPP, vol. 3, no. 7, memorandum Mrs. H. Ryan to M. Porter, n.d. [c. November 1970].

20 The account of the PSA situation below has been pieced together from several sources, most particularly, the detailed account in Johnston, *Radical Campus*, 293–329, and the report written by Porter and his colleagues Rich-

ard Flacks and Edward Gross (LAC, JPP, vol. 5, no. 24, 'A Report on Simon Fraser University to the Committee on Freedom in Research and Teaching of the American Sociological Association' [hereafter 'A Report on Simon Fraser University'], n.d. [1970]). See also the sources cited in Johnston, *Radical Campus*, 364–7.

21 Johnston, *Radical Campus*, 293.

22 LAC, JPP, vol. 5, no. 24, Flacks, Gross, and Porter, 'A Report on Simon Fraser University,' 4–5.

23 Ibid., 6.

24 Part of this account is taken from McKenzie, *Pauline Jewett*, 94–7; see 92–108 more generally.

25 Ibid., 96.

26 LAC, JPP, vol. 5 , no. 24, Flacks, Gross, and Porter, 'A Report on Simon Fraser University,' i.

27 Ibid.

28 Ibid.

29 Flacks and Gross also contributed, and Marion Porter helped to combine the three contributions (LAC, JPP, vol. 5 , no. 24, Porter to Gross and Flacks, 1 July 1970).

30 Ibid., JAP to R. Bird, M. Briemberg, and R. Wyllie, 23 July 1970.

31 Ibid., Rossi to JAP, 10 August 1970.

32 Ibid., JAP to Rossi, 19 August 1970.

33 Ibid., Flacks to JAP, 19 August 1970; telegram Gross to JAP, 21 August 1970; telegram J. Demerath to JAP, 21 August 1970; Rossi to JAP, 26 August 1970.

34 Ibid., Rossi to JAP, 27 August 1970; and JAP to Rossi, 16 September 1970.

35 Ibid., JAP to Demerath, 16 September 1970. It appeared in abridged form in the February 1971 issue of the *American Sociologist:* 'Summary of the Report of the Sub-Committee Concerning SFU,' *AmS* 6, no. 1 (1971): 58–60.

36 LAC, JPP, vol. 5 , no. 24, JAP to Demerath, 18 December 1970. Ann Porter believed that the stress created by this incident helped trigger her father's second heart attack (Ann Porter interview).

37 M. Porter comments, 23 February 1993.

38 Phillips to RHH, 14 March 2000.

39 LAC, JPP, vol. 17 , no. 17, J. Morrison (Canada Council) to Blishen, 25 November 1970.

40 Porter, Porter, and Blishen, *Does Money Matter?* rev. ed., 186–7, 191–2.

41 The other members of the committee were Blishen, John Evans, Bertrand Hansen, Robin Harris, Francis Ireland, Pauline Jewett, John Macdonald, Robin Ross, Bernard Trotter, and Ross Willis.

42 The commission was so named for its chair, Douglas Wright, later president of the University of Waterloo.

43 This paragraph is based on Helmes-Hayes, 'John Porter: Canada's Most Famous Sociologist,' 91–2.

44 Vallee, 'John Porter: 1921–1979,' 94.

45 Porter et al., *Towards 2000*, 1–6.

46 Ibid., 25–9.

47 Ibid., 33.

48 Ibid., 36–8. Given Porter's later opposition to faculty unionization at Carleton, it is highly unlikely he concurred with this recommendation (see ch. 13).

49 Ibid., 29–38; see also 100–5, 170.

50 Ibid., 35–6.

51 Ibid., 69; see also 100, 168–9.

52 Ibid., 69–71.

53 Ibid., 66; see also 71–2, 169.

54 Ibid., 73–80, 81–94, 95–105, respectively.

55 Ibid., 134–5; see 123–37 more generally.

56 LAC, JPP, vol. 3 , no. 8, D. Sutherland (Chair, Committee of Presidents of CAATs in Ontario) to D. Wright, 18 March 1971 (attachment to J. Macdonald, Circuletter 780, CPUO, 1 April 1971).

57 It was reviewed in the *Toronto Telegram* and the *Toronto Daily Star* (see Dingman, 'Preparations for 2000 AD,' 36; Kildare Dobbs, 'Is Today's Speed-up Leading to Future Shock?' *Toronto Daily Star*, 31 July 1971, 51). There was a review of sorts in *BQ* as well, but it was written by Bertrand Hansen and Frances Ireland, two of the authors of *Towards 2000*, so it was more of a long executive summary ('Coming Changes in Higher Education,' *BQ* [Summer 1971]: 31–7).

58 Dingman, 'Preparations for 2000 AD,' 36.

59 D. Smith, 'Where Angels Fear to Tread,' *JCS* 1, no. 3 (1971): 1–2; see also D. Livingstone, 'Inventing the Future: Anti-Historicist Reflections on *Towards 2000*,' *Interchange* 3, no. 4 (1972): 111–19. For a reply by Porter and a rejoinder by Livingstone, see ibid., 120–1 and 122–3, respectively; see also C.B. Macpherson, 'A Note [on *Towards 2000*],' *STOA: CJSHE* 1, no. 1 (1971): 58–60; and G. Gauthier, 'Commentaires [sur *Towards 2000*],' *STOA: CJSHE* 1, no. 1 (1971): 55–8.

60 LAC, JPP, vol. 5 , no. 5, 'JAP, draft ms re Wright Commission report,' n.d.

61 See, e.g., Porter, Porter, and Blishen, *Stations and Callings*, 9–10. Here the authors refer to P. Bourdieu, 'Cultural Reproduction and Social Reproduction,' in *Power and Ideology in Education*, ed. A. Halsey and J. Karabel

(Oxford: Oxford University Press, 1977), 487–510; R. Collins, *The Credential Society: An Historical Sociology of Education and Stratification* (New York: Academic Press, 1979); and S. Bowles and H. Gintis, *Schooling in Capitalist America* (New York: Basic, 1972).

62 The SOSA study remained on his to-do list for several years, but it took so long to complete the final version, *Stations and Callings,* that his interest waned. It had not yet been published when he died in 1979. The SOSA study was published in book-length form three times: first in 1973 as *Does Money Matter? Prospects for Higher Education*; in a slightly amended version in 1979 as *Does Money Matter? Prospects for Higher Education in Ontario*; and in 1982 as *Stations and Callings: Making it through the School System.*

63 R. Breton, *Social and Academic Factors in the Career Decisions of Canadian Youth* (Ottawa: Information Canada/Queen's Printer, 1972). Related studies include Robert Pike, *Who Doesn't Go to University and Why* (Ottawa: Association of Universities and Colleges of Canada, 1970); R. Pavalko and D. Bishop, 'Socio-Economic Status and High School Plans: A Study of Canadian High School Students,' *SE* 39 (1966): 288–98; and O. Hall and B. McFarlane, *Transition from School to Work* (Ottawa: Department of Labour, 1962). For American and British studies see, for example, J. Coleman et al., *Equality of Educational Opportunity* (Washington: US Government Printing Office, 1966); W. Sewell, A. Haller and M. Strauss, 'Social Status and Educational and Occupational Aspirations,' *ASR* 29 (February 1964): 24–38; W. Sewell and V. Shah, 'Socio-Economic Status, Intelligence, and the Attainment of Higher Education,' *SE* 40 (Winter) 1967: 67–73; W. Sewell, 'Inequality of Opportunity for Higher Education,' *ASR* 36 (October 1971): 793–809; J. Douglas, *The Home and the School* (London: MacGibbon and Kee, 1964).

64 A copy of the questionnaire is in LAC, JPP, vol. 18 , no. 12. Porter, Porter, and Blishen, *Does Money Matter?* rev. ed., 30, 186–7. Their original preference was to do a longitudinal study following a cohort of students through the school system over time. When this proved too expensive, they opted for a cross-sectional design that would allow them to study a 'synthetic cohort' (Porter, Porter, and Blishen, *Stations and Callings,* 40, see 39–42 more generally).

65 Porter, Porter, and Blishen, *Stations and Callings,* 42–50. They asked girls a series of questions about 'attitudes to the adult feminine role' (see 48–9).

66 Ibid., 38–40.

67 Ibid., 41.

68 The test for self-concept of ability was taken from W. Brookover, A. Peterson, and S. Thomas, *Self-Concept of Ability and School Achievement* (East

Lansing: College of Education, Michigan State University, 1962), 47–8.
They used the IPAT Culture-Fair Test of Mental Ability from R. Cattell and
A. Cattell, *Handbook for the Culture Fair Intelligence Test* (Champaign, IL:
Institute for Personality and Ability Testing, 1965), 42, 46–7.

69　Ibid., 50–2.

70　Hugh McRoberts and Sid Gilbert did the preliminary data analysis
(McRoberts interview).

71　Porter, Porter, and Blishen, *Does Money Matter?* 1st ed., xvii.

72　When they re-released *Does Money Matter?* in 1979 it included updated
figures on the funding of postsecondary education and a chapter outlining
a path model of the factors affecting students' aspirations. The scholarly
version of the study, *Stations and Callings,* appeared in 1982. The discussion
immediately below draws on the 1979 and 1982 versions.

73　M. Porter to RHH, 25 November 1991.

74　Ibid.

75　Marion Porter interview 1; see also M. Porter to RHH, 25 November 1991.

76　The other two graduate students were Sid Gilbert (deceased) and Susan
Russell (retired).

77　Barrados interview; McRoberts interview; see also Blishen to RHH, 15 December 2001.

78　Blishen to RHH, 15 December 2001.

79　Porter, Porter, and Blishen, *Does Money Matter?* rev. ed., 3, 4, 5; see also x.

80　Ibid., 27–8.

81　Porter, Porter, and Blishen, *Stations and Callings,* 94.

82　Axelrod, *Scholars and Dollars,* 152–6.

83　Porter, Porter, and Blishen, *Stations and Callings,* 39–53.

84　They employed Blishen's occupational scale (based on years of education,
annual income, and a subjective prestige ranking) to place each student
into one of six ranked 'socio-economic status' (SES) or 'class' categories
(ibid., 44–5; see Blishen, 'Occupational Class Scale'). SES I is made up of
professionals, SES II of senior managers, SES III of lower-level managerial
and other white-collar occupations, SES IV of skilled occupations, SES V of
semi-skilled occupations (including farmers), and SES VI of unskilled occupations.

85　Desire to go to university seen at ibid., 56, calculated from table 5.1. Expectation of attending seen at ibid., 60.

86　Ibid., 59, calculated from table 5.2.

87　Porter, Porter, and Blishen, *Does Money Matter?* rev. ed., 34, 37, and 38, table 2.4.

88　Ibid., 39, table 2.5.

89 Ibid., 44–5, including table 2.9; see also Porter, Porter, and Blishen, *Stations and Callings*, 84–7, 182–9.
90 Ibid., Porter, Porter, and Blishen, *Stations and Callings*, 88, 116–36.
91 Ibid., 61, figure 5.2.
92 Ibid., 56, table 5.1.
93 Ibid., 57–64, including figure 5.2.
94 Ibid., 59, table 5.2.
95 Ibid., 62; and Porter, Porter, and Blishen, *Does Money Matter?* rev. ed., 94.
96 Porter and Blishen, *Does Money Matter?* rev. ed., xvii.
97 Ibid., xviii, 54–9 passim.
98 Porter, Porter, and Blishen, *Stations and Callings*, 63.
99 Porter, Porter, and Blishen, *Does Money Matter?* rev. ed., xviii.
100 Ibid., 61–2; see also Porter, Porter, and Blishen, *Stations and Callings*, 61–2, 92n6.
101 Porter, Porter, and Blishen, *Does Money Matter?* rev. ed., 152–4.
102 Ibid., 148–59.
103 In 1972 and 1976 Porter and colleagues undertook follow-up studies. In 1972, with Hugh McRoberts, one of his PhD students, Porter checked to see what had happened to the Grade 12 cohort they had surveyed a year earlier ('Follow-up of Grade 12 Students from the Blishen-Porter Study of Educational Aspirations,' mimeo, Carleton University, Ottawa, 1974). Correspondence regarding the study is in LAC, JPP, vol. 19, no. 13. A copy of the report is in ibid., vol. 19 , no. 14. In 1976, with Blishen and Maria Barrados, another of his PhD students, he checked back with the original Grade 8 cohort to see how they had fared (Porter, Blishen, and Barrados, *Survival of a Grade 8 Cohort*). Barrados claims that Porter edited and oversaw the analysis with some input from Blishen but that she wrote it (Barrados interview). The findings are reported in *Stations and Callings*, 274–91.
104 Porter, Porter, and Blishen, *Stations and Callings*, 292–310.
105 Ibid., 313.
106 In comments on a draft of this chapter, Frank Jones expressed misgivings about my decision to describe Porter as 'an American sociologist.' He believed that Porter's training at the LSE 'shaped him in quite a different direction' (Frank Jones comments, 12 June 2002). I agree that he was originally quite different in orientation. However, after being in North America for several years, he had become quite oriented to US sociology. He did not abandon his European training and roots or fail to keep up with developments in European sociology, but North American sociolo-

gists and their work came to be his primary point of reference. Nor did he give up his New Liberal views. Indeed, in the mid-1970s, discouraged with some aspects of his own mainstream scholarship, he returned to the more social democratic aspects of his New Liberal views in some important ruminative essays. See ch. 15 and afterword.

107 Ibid., 25–8.
108 Ibid., 28–38; re Blalock, see 38n8.
109 Ibid., 26.
110 Ibid., 26–7.
111 Neither Mead nor Cooley used the term 'symbolic interactionism.' It originated with Herbert Blumer. See H. Blumer, *Symbolic Interactionism: Perspective and Method* (Englewood Cliffs, NJ: Prentice-Hall, 1969).
112 Porter, Porter, and Blishen, *Stations and Callings,* 26.
113 Ibid., 26–7.
114 Ibid., 28.

12: Measuring Social Mobility, 1970–1979

1 That the initial overture came from Seymour Martin Lipset was reported to me by Daniel Bell (Bell interview). The official invitation came from the president and fellows of Harvard College (LAC, JPP, vol. 5 , no. 9, R. Sheraton to JAP, 3 April 1972).
2 Ibid., vol. 5 , no. 9, 'Statement from the Endowment Fund Book'; and H. Hanham, 'Harvard University,' *Association for Canadian Studies in the United States Newsletter* 1, no. 2 (1971): 46–8.
3 Ibid., vol. 17 , no. 11, JAP to [Blishen], n.d. [November 1973].
4 Bell interview.
5 JAP to Clement, 22 March 1974, Clement personal papers.
6 LAC, JPP, vol. 17 , no. 11, JAP to [Blishen], n.d. [November 1973].
7 Bell interview.
8 LAC, JPP, vol. 1 , no. 11, G. Sankoff to JAP, 20 November 1973, and JAP to Sankoff, 5 December 1973. The honorary degree is found at Citation, Degree Doctor of Laws (Honoris Causa), read 16 November 1973 by E. Salmon, Ann Porter personal papers.
9 LAC, JPP, vol. 17, no. 11, JAP to [Blishen], n.d. [November 1973].
10 Blishen to RHH, 15 December 2001. He was working on a follow-up to the SOSA study with McRoberts and had to rewrite a good portion of a report McRoberts had prepared for Bert Hansen at the Council of Ontario Universities (LAC, JPP, vol. 17 , no. 11, JAP to [Blishen], n.d. [November 1973]).

11 LAC, JPP, vol. 6 , no. 22, JAP to G. VanTighem, 30 November 1973; C. Wieczorek to JAP, 27 September 1973; JAP to Wieczorek, 6 December 1973.

12 The task force was mandated to assess the feasibility of establishing a minimum annual income in the province. His connection to the 'Mincome Project' was Sid Gilbert, one of his former PhD students, who was involved in the taskforce. So tenuous was Porter's health and so great his workload that in January 1974, less than two months after agreeing to take part, he withdrew, citing 'the recurrence ... of an old health problem' as the reason (LAC, JPP, vol. 3 , no. 11, M. Laub [Manitoba Minimal Annual Income Project] to JAP, 13 November 1973 and JAP to Laub, 2 January 1974).

13 Ibid., R. Stanbury to JAP, 15 February 1974, and 9 May 1974.

14 For descriptions of Porter's four courses, see HUA, Faculty of Arts and Science, *Courses of Instruction 1973–1974*, SOC 610, 611, 615, 617. The courses appear to have had only 24 students among them. These data came from 'Class Lists' kindly provided by the Office of the Registrar through the efforts of Ms. B. Donham, Department of Sociology, and Thurston Smith, Associate Registrar, Faculty of Arts and Science. Some rough lecture notes for this course may be found in LAC, JPP, vol. 5, nos. 11, 12.

15 JAP to Clement, 22 March 1974, Clement personal papers.

16 LAC, JPP, vol. 5, nos. 11, 12.

17 Ibid., vol. 6, no. 19, JAP to R. Davidson, 7 March 1972, and Davidson to JAP, 16 March 1972.

18 JAP to Clement, 22 March 1974, Clement personal papers.

19 For the official history of the Canadian mobility survey, see M. Boyd et al., 'Introduction: The Canadian Mobility Study, Approaches and Procedures,' in Porter et al., *Ascription and Achievement*, 1–27. The two studies in question are P. Blau, 'The Flow of Occupational Supply and Recruitment,' *ASR* 30, no. 4 (1965): 475–90, and O.D. Duncan, 'The Trend of Occupational Mobility in the United States,' *ASR* 30, no. 4 (1965): 491–8. The reference for the subsequent book is Blau and Duncan, *American Occupational Structure*.

20 Frank Jones interview.

21 David Glass, ed., *Social Mobility in Britain* (London: RKP, 1954). For similar studies see, for example, Leonard F. Broom, F. Lancaster Jones, and Jerge Zubrzycki, 'Social Stratification in Australia,' in *Sociological Studies*, vol. 1, ed. J.A. Jackson (Cambridge: Cambridge University Press, 1968), 212–33; J. Lopreato, 'Social Mobility in Italy,' *AJS* 71 (1966): 311–14; S.M. Lipset and R. Bendix, *Social Mobility in Industrial Society* (Berkeley: University of California Press, 1959); and K. Svalastoga, *Prestige, Class and Mobility* (Copenhagen: Gyldendal, 1959).

22 J. Porter, P. Pineo, and F. Jones, 'Occupational Mobility in Canada: A

Research Proposal,' [hereafter 'Occupational Mobility Proposal'] November 1968, 2, Goyder personal papers.

23 Goyder interview 1.

24 McRoberts interview.

25 Ibid.

26 Pineo, 'Prestige and Mobility,' 615. McRoberts claimed that Porter's decisions were 'much more incremental': 'I think it was much more a case of a general interest in the set of puzzles or problems John was pursuing … It [was] a conjunction of time, colleague, and circumstance within that overall playing field [rather] … than any sort of grand design' (McRoberts interview). The fact that Porter claimed in 1964 that he wanted to pursue a set of interrelated studies suggests he did have a 'grand plan,' though the factors McRoberts mentions likely had an impact on which studies would be carried out at particular times and who his co-investigators might be.

27 Note the following comment by McRoberts: 'Part of the motivation for these studies was to create a repository of data. There was a curiosity on his part about the outcomes, but … the data themselves were …an important heritage resource for Canadian social science' (McRoberts interview).

28 Pineo, 'Prestige and Mobility,' 615–23 passim.

29 D. Olsen, Course notes: Sociology 610–11, Fall–Winter 1971–2, Olsen personal papers, in the context of a discussion of Kari Levitt's *Silent Surrender: The Multinational Corporation in Canada* (Toronto: Macmillan Canada, 1970) and Andre Gunder Frank's *Capitalism and Underdevelopment in Latin America* (New York: Monthly Review Press, 1969).

30 Pineo, 'Prestige and Mobility,' 618.

31 Ibid.

32 Goyder interview 2. A year later, Keddie added a fifth location (Lindsay) to what the group referred to as the 'Four Cities' project (Goyder comments, 9 December 2001); see V. Keddie, 'Class Identification and Party Preference among Manual Workers: The Influence of Community, Union Membership and Kinship,' *CRSA* 17, no. 1 (1980): 24–36. See J. Porter, P. Pineo, and F. Jones, 'Description of the Project,' 'Occupational and Educational Change in a Generation: Canada,' application to Canada Council, n.d. [1972], n.p., Goyder personal papers.

33 On Ostry's perceived support, see Pineo, 'Prestige and Mobility,' 618, and Goyder comments, 9 December 2001. Ostry confirmed her support for and interest in such projects, but could not remember this case (Sylvia Ostry interview). Porter had retained an interest in the prospect of the study and, in part because he needed to find data for McRoberts' PhD dissertation, became reinvolved in the project (Pineo, 'Prestige and Mobility,' 618).

34 Goyder interview 1.

35 The project came to be known as the CARMAC project because it was carried out at *Car*leton University and *Mc*Master University.

36 For information on how Boyd, Goyder, and McRoberts came to join the CARMAC group, see Boyd interview, Goyder interviews 1 and 2, and McRoberts interview.

37 Pineo, 'Prestige and Mobility,' 618.

38 J. Porter, P. Pineo, and F. Jones, 'Description of the Project,' 'Occupational and Educational Change in a Generation: Canada,' application to Canada Council, n.d. [1972], n.p., Goyder personal papers.

39 J. Morrison (Canada Council) to F. Jones, 13 December 1972, Goyder personal papers. A copy of the fifty-page proposal to Canada Council (c. September 1972) is in Goyder's files. Between July 1972 and April 1973, Porter and Pineo solicited funds from a number of government agencies to supplement the grant from the Canada Council, though eventually the Council covered the entire $300,000 (Pineo, 'Prestige and Mobility,' 618–19).

40 The most significant suggestions concerned the following: (1) refinement of the section of the questionnaire and analysis concerning women and their labour force participation; (2) the addition of a question on income; (3) refinement of the occupational titles used in the questionnaire; (4) a more detailed analysis of the circumstances of Aboriginal peoples; and, (5) a rethinking of some of the questions and analysis concerning the unique sociocultural environment in Quebec (e.g., school systems, language, ethnic division of labour). See J. Morrison (Canada Council) to F. Jones, 13 December 1972, attachments to correspondence, Goyder personal papers.

41 J. Morrison (Canada Council) to F. Jones, 12 December 1972, Reviewer E, untitled, n.d., n.p., attachment to correspondence, Goyder personal papers.

42 Porter et al., 'Introduction,' *Ascription and Achievement*, 10–12.

43 Ibid., 10; for a description of the sample design, see 12–14. Were they to pay a private firm to do this work, said Pineo, it would have cost in excess of a million dollars (Pineo, 'Prestige and Mobility,' 618).

44 R. Corbeil (Statistics Canada) to F. Jones, 27 September 1973, attachment to F. Jones, J. Porter, M. Boyd, P. Pineo, and J. Goyder, Application for Supplementary Research Grant: 'Occupational and Educational Change in a Generation: Canada,' Humanities and Social Sciences Division, Canada Council, 12 November 1973, Goyder personal papers. For copies of drafts of the questionnaire, see LAC, JPP, vol. 16, nos. 1, 2, 3, 8.

45 See F. Jones interview. According to Jones, it might have taken even longer if Porter hadn't been able to 'pull some strings' at Statistics Canada (see also JAP to B. McFarlane, June 1975, McFarlane personal papers).

46 Application for Research Grant: 'Occupational and Educational Change

in a Generation: Canada,' n.d. [c. September 1972], n.p., Goyder personal papers.

47 Pineo noted in comments on a draft of this chapter that while the manuscript of *Ascription and Achievement* took a long time to prepare, 'it was not markedly out of line with other surveys' (21 February 2002).

48 Goyder interview 2.

49 As Porter put it in a letter to McFarlane, 'The problems now shift to our own computer centre [at Carleton] where a file of 40,000 records rather boggles all the packaged programs' (JAP to McFarlane, June 1975, McFarlane personal papers; see also Porter et al., 'Preface,' *Ascription and Achievement*, vi).

50 Goyder interview 2 and Boyd interview.

51 Frank Jones comments, 12 June 2002.

52 Goyder interview 2 and Boyd interview.

53 Pineo, 'Prestige and Mobility,' 619.

54 Ibid., and Goyder interview 2.

55 McRoberts used the data to write his dissertation, which Porter supervised (McRoberts interview).

56 Goyder interview 2; see also McRoberts interview.

57 Goyder interview 2; JAP to Goyder, 4 May 1979, Goyder personal papers.

58 Goyder interview 2.

59 Boyd interview.

60 Pineo, 'Prestige and Mobility,' 619, 622–3.

61 Frank Jones comments, 12 June 2002.

62 Goyder interview 2.

63 McRoberts interview.

64 JAP to McFarlane, June 1975, McFarlane personal papers.

65 This episode in Paris was not an attack but some pains and arrhythmia that were troubling (McRoberts interview; also Ann Porter interview).

66 McRoberts interview.

67 Goyder interview 2.

68 See Armstrong, 'Missing Women,' in *Vertical Mosaic Revisited*, ed. Helmes-Hayes and Curtis, 116–44.

69 Goyder interview 2 and Boyd interview. Jones, who was responsible for the financial side of the project, told a different story. The problem was not so much a lack of resources, though they could have used more, but that there was some resistance on the part of the Carleton group 'to obtain [his] approval if their expenditures exceeded their share of the grant.' This, he said, 'did occasion some conflict' (Frank Jones comments, 12 June 2002).

70 Goyder interview 2.

71 McRoberts interview.

72 Frank Jones comments, 12 June 2002.

73 Goyder interview 2; see also JAP to F. Jones, 3 October 1978, and Jones to JAP, 20 October 1978, Goyder personal papers.

74 F. Jones to JAP, n.d. [October] 1978, Goyder personal papers. Frank Jones confirmed this interpretation (comments, 12 June 2002).

75 Porter, 'A Note to the CARMAC group,' n.d. [c. 1973], n.p., Goyder personal papers.

76 Pineo to RHH, 21 February 2002. According to Goyder, both Pineo and Jones had these concerns (comments, 9 December 2001). Jones denied wanting the material to appear in book form first but claimed that Boyd had this concern (comments, 12 June 2002); Boyd interview; Goyder interviews 1 and 2.

77 Frank Jones comments, 12 June 2002.

78 Pineo said that he 'was one who felt that individual publications would jeopardize the completion of the book' (Pineo to RHH, 21 February 2002).

79 Pineo to RHH, 21 February 2002.

80 J. Porter, 'A Note to the CARMAC group,' n.d. [c. 1973], n.p., Goyder personal papers. McRoberts' view was the same as Porter's (McRoberts interview).

81 For findings see, for example, J. Porter, M. Boyd and H. McRoberts, 'The Canadian National Mobility Study: Some Preliminary Findings,' presented at the International Seminar on Research in Social Stratification and Mobility, Hebrew University, Jerusalem, April 1976 (also presented to the Institute of Philosophy and Sociology of the Polish Academy of Sciences, June 1976). For disputes see Goyder interviews 1 and 2; McRoberts interview.

82 Porter et al., 'Différences dans la mobilité professionelle.' The McMaster camp alleged he had contravened the group's publishing policy. See F. Jones to Dear [Professor], 11 June 1976, Goyder personal papers.

83 McRoberts interview.

84 Goyder interview 2.

85 Boyd to CARMAC group, 2 January 1979, F. Jones to Goyder, 9 January 1979, Goyder to Jones, 16 January 1979, Goyder to JAP, 23 February 1979, and JAP to Goyder, 4 May 1979, Goyder personal papers; H. McRoberts and K. Selbee, 'Trends in Occupational Mobility: Canada and the United States,' *ASR* 46, no. 4 (1981): 406–21; and M. Boyd, 'Sex Differences in the Canadian Occupational Attainment Process,' *CRSA* 19, no. 1 (1982): 1–28. Other papers followed once the floodgates had been opened, perhaps stealing thunder from the book but not affecting its time to completion.
      Goyder said he didn't think it created a delay (Goyder comments, 9 De-

cember 2001), while Pineo said the opposite (Pineo to RHH, 21 February 2002). Pineo also said that the book would not have generated any more interest, would not have made a bigger 'splash,' had it been finished earlier. He recalls chairing a session based on the study at the 1977 Learned Societies meeting. 'Attendance,' he said, 'was meagre.' 'I am dubious that an earlier appearance of the book, all else held constant, would have been a "splash" ... Quantitative sociology has had limited appeal at any time in Canada' (ibid.).

86 JAP to Goyder, 4 May 1979, Goyder personal papers.
87 Pineo to RHH, 21 February 2002; see also Porter et al., 'Status Attainment in Canada,' 1981.
88 McRoberts interview; see also Boyd interview and Goyder comments, 9 December 2001.
89 Pineo to RHH, 21 February 2002.
90 Frank Jones comments, 12 June 2002.
91 Blau and Duncan, *American Occupational Structure*, 70; see J. Porter, P. Pineo, and Frank Jones, 'Summary of the Project,' *Occupational Mobility in Canada*, application to Canada Council, n.d. [1972], Goyder personal papers.
92 For a discussion of the differences between these two approaches, see John Goyder, 'Social Mobility or Status Attainment or Social Mobility and Status Attainment?' *CRSA* 21, no. 3 (1984): 331–43.
93 Porter et al., 'Introduction,' *Ascription and Achievement*, 8.
94 J. Morrison (Canada Council) to F. Jones, 13 December 1972, Reviewer E, untitled, n.d., n.p., attachment to correspondence, Goyder personal papers.
95 Philip Cercone (Social Science Federation of Canada) to F. Jones, 9 June 1981, Reviewer A, 'Rapport de Lecture de Manuscrit,' n.d., n.p., attachment to correspondence, Goyder personal papers.
96 Pineo to RHH, 21 February 2002.
97 Philip Cercone (Social Science Federation of Canada) to F. Jones, 9 June 1981, Reviewer B, untitled, n.d., n.p., attachment to correspondence, Goyder personal papers.
98 Pineo, 'Prestige and Mobility,' 623.
99 Pineo notes that Porter attempted a third piece comparing mobility patterns in other countries but eventually abandoned it (ibid.).
100 Porter, 'The Societal Context,' in Porter et al., *Ascription and Achievement*, 61.
101 Goyder interview 2 and Boyd interview.

102 Pineo describes their respective roles in the drafting of the chapter as follows: 'This chapter was initially drafted by Pineo and thoroughly revised
in 1976 by Porter. The final portion, following the sub-heading "Effects
of Ethnic Origin: An Alternative Approach," is largely Porter's work, ex-
cepting the conclusions. I have left the material virtually as it was' (Pineo
and J. Porter, 'Ethnic Origin and Occupational Attainment,' in Porter et
al., *Ascription and Achievement*, 391).
103 Pineo, 'Prestige and Mobility,' 622–3.
104 Hiller and Langlois, 'The Most Important Books,' 513–16.
105 Pineo noted that as of 1985, 'some 17 articles had been published from the
data and another 14 uses were made for theses, working papers, etc …
And this sort of production continued. This productivity compares quite
favourably with that of the equivalent U.S. team' (Pineo to RHH, 21 February 2002). See also Goyder comments, 9 December 2001.
106 Pineo, 'Prestige and Mobility,' 623.
107 Porter, 'The Societal Context,' in Porter et al., *Ascription and Achievement*,
29–33.

13: The Shift into Academic Administration, 1977–1979

1 CU, ARC, Tina Harvey, 'Administrative Summaries,' September 1995,
117. Dunton reorganized Carleton's faculties in 1963, creating two divisions within the Arts faculty: Division I Humanities; and Division II
Social Sciences. Porter was the first director of Division II (CUA, Office of
the President fonds, Series: Annual Reports, *The President's Report 1962–
1963*, 7–8. See also K. McRae to RHH, n.d. January 2002; McRae interview
2). He had been offered many such opportunities – to be chair, to be dean
– including offers to be nominated as vice-president (LAC, JPP, vol. 3, no.
5, H. Armstrong, President, University of Alberta at Calgary to JAP, 17
February 1966) and president (ibid., vol. 3, no. 6, S. Cassidy, University of
New Brunswick to JAP, 14 May 1969).
2 After returning to Carleton in 1969, Porter served on three major university committees: Academic Planning (as chair), the Committee on Goals
and Requirements, and the Review Committee on Promotions. At the
provincial level, he served as chair of the research and planning subcommittee of CPUO that wrote *Towards 2000* and on the Committee on the
Ontario University System (LAC, JPP, vol. 3, no. 7, Ryan to M. Porter, n.d.
[c. December 1970]). At the national level, he served on the Academic
Panel of the Canada Council and, beginning in 1974, on the newly formed

Social Sciences and Humanities Research Council of Canada (see J. Porter, curriculum vitae, n.d. [1978], Clement personal papers; LAC, JPP, vol. 1, no. 11, G. Sankoff to JAP, 12 June 1974; and F. Elkin to P. Trudeau, 21 September 1974).

3 Jewett interview 2.

4 Bothwell, Drummond, and English, *Canada since 1945*, 401–3.

5 For a description of the Ontario case, see Axelrod, *Scholars and Dollars*, 158–213, especially 180–1. According to Cynthia Hardy, 'Ontario … sustained the largest decline in real operating income per student' in the country during this period (*Politics of Collegiality*, 26).

6 JAP and M. Porter to B. and C. McFarlane, 9 December 1974, McFarlane personal papers.

7 JAP to McFarlane, 1 June 1975, McFarlane personal papers. McFarlane claimed that the situation at Carleton was worse than at some other Ontario universities: 'The Ministry at Queen's Park deemed Carleton to be one of the five "old" universities in Ontario [along with] Toronto, Queen's, Western, and McMaster. Hence, [Carleton] received no "development" funds as did Wilfrid Laurier, Waterloo, Trent, etc … Carleton hobbled along under this strain for most of its past thirty-five years' (McFarlane comments, 23 April 2002).

8 Regarding the budget figure for 1958–9, see CUA, Office of the President fonds, Series: Annual Reports, *The President's Report 1958–1959*, 'Report of the Bursar,' 24–5; re the 1971–2 budget figure, see ibid., *The President's Report 1971–1972*, 'Statement of Income Expenditures and Surplus,' n.p. Re the 1958 figure for professorial appointments, see ibid., *The President's Report 1958–1959*, 6; re the figure for 1971–2, see ibid., *The President's Report 1971–1972*, under 'The Carleton Year,' n.p. Re enrolment figures, see CUA, Office of the Budget Planning, *Carleton University Data Book 1995–1996*, ed. D. Zaluska, 'Student Registration Statistics 1942–43 to 1995–96,' 24. Convocation exercises which in 1958 paid tribute to 146 students expanded in 1972 to accommodate 2,077 (ibid., 'Graduation Statistics, 1946 to 1995,' 46).

9 CUA, Office of the President fonds, Series: Annual Reports, *The President's Report 1971–1972*, n.p.

10 Downey interview 1. McEown remarked on this account, 'Maybe a tighter hand would have been better. There is no question … that after being chair of the Royal Commission on Bilingualism and Biculturalism, getting through the St. Pat's thing, getting through the building program, which at the end was terribly complicated and horrendous, … he was wiped out … But I don't know if another president would have done it better' (McEown interview).

11 For example, the largest department in the Faculty of Arts, English, would not make a new appointment until the late 1980s despite the loss of approximately half its faculty in the interim (Downey comments, 18 December 2001, and Downey interview 1).

12 Neatby and McEown, *Creating Carleton,* 163–4.

13 Ibid., 164–5; see also CUA, Minutes of the Senate, vol. 17 (September–October 1971), 24 September 1971, appendix C, 'Report of Committee on Tenure and Dismissal.' CUASA's generally favourable response to the document, written by Naomi Griffiths, may be found in CUA, Minutes of the Senate, vol. 17 (September–October 1971), 21 October 1971.

14 CUA, Minutes of the Senate, vol. 17 (September–October 1971), 13 October 1971, 1,074.

15 CUA, Minutes of the Senate, vol. 18 (November–December 1971), 22 November 1971, 1,098.

16 In March 1972, after approving a modified version of the tenure and dismissal document, the Senate established the Committee on Redundancy (Neatby and McEown, *Creating Carleton,* 165–7; see CUA, Minutes of the Senate, vol. 20 (March–April), 9 March 1972, 1,167–9 and appendix B).

17 Paquet noted that the problems Oliver inherited were nearly intractable; they remained unsolved for years to come (Paquet interview).

18 Larose interview.

19 Accounts of how Oliver and the other major figures on campus handled the situation – and the related, derivative problem of redundancy – are at odds. The paragraphs immediately below are based on the description in Neatby and McEown's *Creating Carleton,* supplemented with materials from interviews I conducted with key personnel on campus at the time. For other renderings, see Axelrod, *Scholars and Dollars,* 204–12, especially 208–9 and Hardy, *Politics of Collegiality,* 147–62 passim.

20 Most of the materials in this paragraph can be found in CU, ARC, Public Relations and Information Services fonds, Box no. PINFO–47, file: Michael K. Oliver, 1973–1978, 'Curriculum vitae – September 1972.' Dr. Oliver filled in some missing pieces (Oliver to RHH, 15 June 2002).

21 For the details in the paragraph above, see Oliver interview. Additional details may be found in CU, ARC, gathering file: Michael K. Oliver; J. Ferrabee, 'Carleton's New President Thrives on Hard Work,' *Ottawa Citizen,* 6 May 1972, 16; and Marsha Sadoway, 'Carleton's Oliver "Moderate Radical,"' *Ottawa Citizen,* 25 May 1972, 21.

22 Oliver to RHH, 15 June 2002; see also Neatby and McEown, *Creating Carleton,* 189–90.

23 Oliver to RHH, 15 June 2002; Brown interview.

24 Oliver to RHH, 15 June 2002.

25 Neatby and McEown, *Creating Carleton,* 190–3.

26 Ibid., 185–201 passim, especially 194–8.

27 *CUASA Handbook,* n.d. [2002], 8–9. Ironically, there were no layoffs. The redundancy provisions were written into the first collective agreement, signed in December 1975 (CU, ARC, *TWAC* 13, no. 9 [18 December 1975]; see also D. McEown to RHH, 15 January 2002) but, according to one senior administrator from the Beckel period, the layoff policy in the agreement was 'a joke,' so 'cumbersome' and expensive it was unlikely ever to be invoked (anonymous, cited in Hardy, *Politics of Collegiality,* 157). For other accounts of aspects of the redundancy issue and the unionization of Carleton's academic staff, see Paquet interview; Brown interview; N. Griffiths to RHH, 26 June 2003; McEown to RHH, 15 January 2002; and CU, ARC, *TWAC* 13, no. 9 (18 December 1975).

28 Kelley was a member of Carleton's Board of Governors.

29 Downey interview 1; McEown to RHH, 15 January 2002; Larose interview; see also Hardy, *Politics of Collegiality,* 150–1.

30 Brown first came to prominence as president of CUASA when it was still a faculty association. His first administrative appointment at Carleton was as assistant to the vice-president academic (Brown interview). Paquet, Larose, and McEown all said in interviews that Brown was devious and manipulative, not to be trusted. Paquet qualified this judgment by noting two things. First, he admired Brown for wanting to change Carleton and for his willingness to take the flak and make the changes. Second, he appreciated that Brown was willing to support others like himself who were willing to make changes and take risks, even if from time to time the changes did not work (Paquet interview).

31 Downey interview 1.

32 Brown interview.

33 McEown interview.

34 Ibid. According to Downey, Love's role in the negotiation of the first collective agreement prevented him from being renewed. Though Kelley did most of the face-to-face bargaining, there was a 'maelstrom of bitterness and controversy' surrounding the negotiations. Love became 'identified with Michael Oliver,' making it 'highly unlikely he would be reappointed in the wake of Carleton's difficulties and Oliver's impending departure' (Downey interview 1; see also Larose interview; McEown interview). When the committee to select a new vice-president was struck, McEown said, and Love's reappointment considered, 'the academic members of the committee said no, … a vote of non-confidence,' because Oliver had asked

Love to consider a second term. 'It wasn't so much directed at Ross Love,' McEown argued. 'He had been so long in the administrative side of the house [that] he was considered an administrator, not an academic. So that was "strike one" against him. But his loyalty to Michael was "strike two" and "strike three." "If Michael wants him, we don't"' (McEown interview).

35 Neatby interview; see also Downey interview 1; Oliver interview.

36 Oliver interview.

37 Ibid. Porter's main competition for the vice-presidency was Gilles Paquet (Paquet interview). Re the details of the appointment, see LAC, JPP, vol. 3, no. 14, Oliver to JAP, 27 May 1977, and JAP to Oliver 17 June 1977. The appointment was for six years with a three-year escape clause because a new president would be appointed in 1979.

38 Whitteker interview.

39 LAC, JPP, vol. 3, no. 14, D. Lewis to JAP, 11 August 1977.

40 Downey interview 1.

41 Ryan comments, 11 September 2002.

42 Oliver began at AUCC on 1 September 1978 (CU, ARC, Public Relations and Information Services, Series: Presidents 1958–1978, Box no. PINFO–47, file: President Oliver 1972–1978, 'Confidential Memo' [draft], D. McEown to the Board of Governors, 19 June 1978).

43 Neatby interview; Downey interview 1; Paquet interview; Larose interview.

44 Douglas Anglin helped me piece together the details of the so-called Uren affair (see Anglin to RHH, 19 March 2002, and 29 April 2002).

45 CU, ARC, 'The Uren Controversy and Academic Freedom,' TWAC 17, no. 17 (6 April 1978): n.p.

46 The motion of censure passed by the Faculty Council of the Paterson School is printed in CU, ARC, TWAC 17, no. 17 (6 April 1978): n.p.

47 On this score, Tom Ryan, dean of social science, wrote, 'One important point that has never come out in all of this (and I never saw a need to mention it) was a private meeting between Uren and myself (as Dean of Social Sciences). In writing and in person, he told me that he wanted out of the position as Director of the School, that he had had enough. So even if it can be argued that Porter was pushing Uren to resign or was too readily accepting of the resignation, it should be understood that Uren himself wanted out. I did have a few opportunities to explain this to Board members (Hamilton Southam is one I can remember)' (comments, 11 September 2002).

48 Reprinted in CU, ARC, TWAC 17, no. 18 (13 April 1978): n.p.

49 On support for Porter see Anglin to RHH, 19 March 2002. McFarlane noted

on this point that 'almost everyone associated with the School … supported John's move' (comments, 23 April 2002).
50 McEown to RHH, 15 January 2002.
51 Carleton University Corporate Archives, Office of the Vice-President Academic fonds, Administrative files (OVPAC–161), Report of the Committee on Carleton University to 1982 (1978), 3–5, and Appendix A.
52 Downey interview 1.
53 Ibid. Frank Jones saw Porter's interest in the vice-presidency as a way of realizing his view of what a university should be: 'The way to do that was through administering the university' (Frank Jones interview).
54 LAC, JPP, vol. 1, no. 9, JAP to D. McEown (Secretary to the Presidential Search Committee), 26 January 1972. *Rerum cognoscere causas* (To know the causes of things) is the Latin motto of the LSE, Porter's alma mater.
55 Ibid. One wonders whether Porter crafted these criteria with himself in mind (Lambert comments, 4 January 2004).
56 Carleton University Corporate Archives, Office of the Vice-President Academic fonds, Administrative files (OVPAC–161), Report of the Committee on Carleton University to 1982 (1978), 6–7.
57 Ibid, 7. The report urged Senate to get on with this task (9).
58 Ibid., 8, 10.
59 Ibid., 14.
60 Ibid., 7.
61 Ibid., 10.
62 See LAC, JPP, vol. 4, no. 26, J. Porter, 'Thoughts about unionization of faculty,' February 1975. Porter's colleague Don Whyte recalled that when the unionization issue came up in 1975, 'certain colleagues who were concerned that his views would be seen as anachronistic dissuaded him from fighting it' (Whyte to RHH, 1 February 2002).
63 Sylvia Ostry interview.
64 LAC, JPP, vol. 4, no. 26, J. Porter, 'Some thoughts about unionization of faculty,' February 1975.
65 Carleton University Corporate Archives, Office of the Vice-President Academic fonds, Administrative files (OVPAC–161), Report of the Committee on Carleton University to 1982 (1978), 115.
66 Ibid., 27.
67 Ibid, 113, 118, 120, 121. Faculty members were not the only ones singled out for criticism; the Board of Governors (47), the admissions office (67–8), student government (68), the registrar's office (77), and others were called to task on various issues.
68 Ibid., 11–12; see also 112–21, especially 121.

69 There is much else in the 140-plus page report. It proposes a substantial reorganization of Carleton's finances, programs, curriculum, recruitment strategies, service delivery, and the like. Porter seemed eager to oversee much of this revamping; he placed many of the tasks involved on his own to-do list (ibid., 132–40).

70 Ibid., 118.

71 Ibid., 10–11.

72 CU, ARC, Public Relations Information Services fonds, Box no. PINFO–47, file: Michael K. Oliver, 1973–1978, M. Oliver, 'These Were Good Years.'

73 LAC, JPP, vol. 3, no. 15, H. Nesbitt to JAP, 25 October 1978.

74 Ibid., G. Fierhaller to JAP, 25 October 1978.

75 Brown interview.

76 Paquet interview.

77 Downey interview 2.

78 Paquet interview.

79 Downey interview 1; see also Brown interview.

80 Downey interview 1.

81 Larose interview.

82 Oliver interview.

83 McEown related the following relevant story: 'I am told that at the dinner at the Commonwealth Conference in Vancouver the year that the search committee was on, John was very embarrassed because Michael Oliver would introduce him to other university presidents as "my successor"; not "I hope he is my successor," but "my successor," as if it was a done deal' (McEown interview; see also McEown comments, 15 January 2002; Downey interview 1; Brown interview; Whitteker interview).

84 Jewett interview 2.

85 Ryan comments, 11 September 2002.

86 Teron noted that members of the presidential search committee knew about the rumours but had 'no idea' how they got started. It was her view that there were no leaks from the committee: 'We were not hinting to any-one that he was going to be the choice. I think there just started to be a groundswell of opinion within the university that Porter was going to be chosen and it just grew … until it seemed to be an established fact' (Teron interview).

87 The classic overview of these developments is Marchak, 'Canadian Political Economy.'

88 Clement to JAP, 12 November 1971, Clement personal papers.

89 JAP to Clement, 22 November 1971; Clement to JAP, 25 November 1971; JAP to Clement, 22 December 1971; Clement to JAP, 14 April 1972; Clement

to JAP, 24 April 1972; JAP to Clement, 12 July 1972, all Clement personal papers.

90 Clement, *Canadian Corporate Elite*. His MA thesis, 'The Corporate Elite: Economic Power in Canada' (Carleton University, 1973), was less inclusive than *The Canadian Corporate Elite*. Clement did supplemental analysis to prepare the book.

91 See e.g., W. Clement, 'Power, Ethnicity and Class: Reflections Thirty Years After' in *The Vertical Mosaic Revisited*, ed. R. Helmes-Hayes and J. Curtis (Toronto: University of Toronto Press, 1998), 34–59.

92 D. Olsen, Course notes: Sociology 610–11, Carleton University, Fall–Winter 1971–2, Olsen personal papers. Clement recalls that he, Olsen, and Porter did a reading course on some related materials around that same time (Clement to RHH, 26 December 2008).

93 Olsen interview.

94 LAC, JPP, vol. 3, no. 3, typescript, untitled, n.d., review of a scholarly article.

95 Knight interview. The full reference for the Parkin book is *Class Inequality and Political Order: Social Stratification in Capitalist and Communist Societies* (London: Macgibbon and Kee, 1971).

96 Barrados interview.

97 Frank Jones interview. Recall the comments in ch. 12 by John Goyder and Peter Pineo that for the mobility study Porter saw his primary role as entrepreneurial.

98 Downey interview 1.

99 Ibid.

100 Myles interview.

101 Ibid. This was Barrados' view as well: 'I think he reached a point where ... he was feeling that his time was limited and that there were other things he wanted to do. And he was passionate about excellence in the universities' (Barrados interview).

102 Downey interview 1.

103 Ann Porter interview.

104 Ibid.

105 Tony Porter interview 2.

106 Ann Porter interview.

107 Farr interview.

108 Jewett interview 2.

109 McFarlane comments, 23 April 2002.

110 Frumhartz interview.

111 Ibid. A related observation was made by Downey: 'John was a member –

and a prominent member – of a meritocratic elite – Canada's burgeoning scholarly elite, and meritocrats of whatever kind think they would have been members of another elite if they hadn't chosen this one. John once said that he believed he could have been successful at whatever he had chosen to do, and I'm sure that included business' (comments, 18 December 2001; see also Downey interview 1).

112 Blishen interview.

113 Whyte agreed with my assessment that Porter was comfortable wielding power (comments, 1 February 2002) and recalled being 'summoned, as department chair, along with his teaching and research assistants, to [Porter's] bedside at home,' after his heart attack in 1970: 'He delivered unequivocal directives on how his seminars should be organized during his recovery, in a manner not unlike a wounded general on a battlefield issuing directives to his troops.' Really, he was, said Whyte, 'a power unto himself' (Whyte to RHH, 1 February 2002).

114 Oliver interview.

115 Whitteker interview.

116 Clark interview.

117 Barrados interview.

118 Downey interview 1.

119 Fox interview.

120 Porter, *Vertical Mosaic*, 493–5, 500, 504.

121 Marion Porter interview 1.

122 Barrados interview.

123 McRoberts interview. Whitteker said the same thing (Whitteker interview).

124 Farr interview.

125 Tony Porter interview 2.

126 McRae interview 1.

127 Boyd interview.

128 McEown interview; Paquet interview.

129 The details of Beckel's life and career have been taken from CU, ARC, gathering file: Beckel, Dr. William, 'William E. Beckel: President and Vice-Chancellor, Carleton University, Ottawa, Ontario, biographical information …,' 1981.

130 McEown interview.

131 Paquet interview.

132 Sylvia Ostry interview.

133 McFarlane interview.

134 Downey to RHH, 8 April 2002.

135 CU, ARC, Public Relations and Information Services fonds, Box no.

PINFO–40, Series: Former Employees, file: Porter, John (Part I, II, III), 1961–1979, Mike Strobel, 'Carleton Truce,' *Ottawa Journal*, n.d.

136 Teron interview.

137 CU, ARC, Public Relations and Information Services fonds, Box no. PINFO–40, Series: Former Employees, file: Porter, John (Part I, II, III), 1961–1979, Trish Irvin, 'Storm brewing over Carleton appointment,' *Ottawa Journal*, 29 September 1978, 32.

138 These letters are in LAC, JPP, vol. 4, no. 15.

139 Paquet interview; Amberg to RHH, 27 October 2004.

140 Downey interview 1; see also McEown interview.

141 Teron interview.

142 Downey interview 1.

143 Forcese to RHH, 5 January 1989.

144 Downey interview 1.

145 Two observers noted that some people on campus might have been threatened by Porter because they did not have a PhD and/or were not productive scholars (McRoberts interview; Barrados interview). Certainly, he issued such a threat in 'Carleton University to 1982' (Carleton University Corporate Archives, Office of the Vice-President Academic fonds, Administrative files [OVPAC–161], Report of the Committee on Carleton University to 1982 [1978], 118).

146 Quotations in this paragraph are from McEown (interview). Interpretations are my own.

147 McFarlane comments, 23 April 2002.

148 Downey interview 1.

149 Ibid.

150 McEown interview.

151 Downey interview 1. Tom Ryan concurred that Porter had 'aggravated many board members' (Ryan to RHH, 1 September 2004) and Carl Amberg agreed (Amberg to RHH, 27 October 2004).

152 Larose confirmed the existence of this rumour (Larose interview). Both McEown and Paquet denied that Paquet played the role of spoiler (McEown interview; Paquet interview).

153 For a description of one dispute that arose between them (i.e., over the choice of external examiners for Wallace Clement's PhD dissertation) see W. Clement, 'The "Hidden" Research Process: Developing the Habit of Research,' 1989 Davidson Dunton Research Lecture, Carleton University, Ottawa, 16 November 1989, 3–4. Olsen said that Paquet seemed 'hostile' to Porter (Olsen interview). For Paquet's side of this story, see Paquet interview.

154 Paquet interview.

155 Ibid.

156 Teron interview.

157 Ibid.; see also Paquet interview. No one mentioned Porter's history of heart attacks. However, for some of them the focus on his 'energy level' may have been a consequence of their knowledge of his long-term health problems (R. Hamilton to RHH, 8 June 2004). Amberg wrote, 'I'd forgotten (if I did know at all) that Porter had a heart attack in 1970. That in itself was surely enough not to have him get the Presidency of Carleton' (Amberg to RHH, 27 October 2004).

158 Paquet interview.

159 Ryan to RHH, 1 September 2004; Downey to RHH, 8 April 2002.

160 Ryan to RHH, 1 September 2004.

161 Paquet interview.

162 Teron interview.

163 McEown interview.

164 Ryan to RHH, 11 September 2002.

165 CU, ARC, Public Relations and Information Services fonds, Box no. PINFO–40, Series: Former Employees, file: Porter, John (Part I, II, III), 1961–1979, Mike Strobel, 'Carleton Truce,' *Ottawa Journal*, n.d.; see also LAC, JPP, vol. 4, no. 15, JAP to Oliver, 29 September 1978. Larose, then vice-president administration, also resigned when he discovered that Beckel intended to keep Brown on as director of institutional planning (Larose interview).

166 CU, ARC, Porter, 'Statement from John Porter,' *TWAC*, special edition (1 October 1978): n.p.

167 McRoberts interview.

168 Whitteker interview.

169 Neatby interview.

170 McEown to RHH, 15 January 2002.

171 Beckel to RHH, 19 May 2004. According to Whyte, the depth of Porter's disappointment helps to explain his bitter and intemperate response to the decision of the selection committee: 'I recall the various factions for and against him, and his public response at having been passed over and it seemed to me to be unlike him. John was in every way a gracious man and [his response] was a departure from that way' (Whyte to RHH, 1 February 2002).

172 CU, ARC, Porter, 'Statement from John Porter.' *TWAC*, special edition (1 October 1978): n.p.

173 Ibid.

174 LAC, JPP, vol. 4, no. 15, JAP to Oliver, 29 September 1978.

175 McFarlane comments, 23 April 2002, emphasis added.

176 Downey to RHH, 7 April 2002.

177 Paquet interview.

178 Downey interview 2; Ryan to RHH, 11 September 2002.

179 Downey interviews 1 and 2.

180 CUA, Board of Governors, the Minutes of the 297th Meeting of the Board of Governors, 25 September 1978, Confidential annex 1: Item 1, Report of the Presidential Search Committee; see also McEown interview; Downey interview 1.

181 McFarlane interview.

182 CU, ARC, Public Relations and Information Services fonds, Box no. PINFO–40, Series: Former Employees, file: Porter, John (Part I, II, III), 1961–1979, T. Irvin, 'Storm Brewing over Carleton Appointment,' *Ottawa Journal*, 29 September 1978, 32.

183 Re the letters and the petitions, see LAC, JPP, vol. 4, no. 15. One of them came from the Carleton University Support Staff Association (memorandum, G. Black, President, CUSSA to JAP, 28 September 1978). Another, from the chairs of two departments in the Faculty of Engineering, noted that faculty members in the two departments had unanimously voted to urge him to stay on as vice-president (A. Boothroyd and J. Riordon to JAP, 27 September 1978).

184 CU, ARC, Public Relations and Information Services fonds, Box no. PINFO–40, Series: Former Employees, file: Porter, John (Part I, II, III), 1961–1979, T. Irvin, 'Storm Brewing over Carleton Appointment,' *Ottawa Journal*, 28 September 1978, 32; J. Wylie, 'Porter Quits as Vice-President,' *Ottawa Journal*, 30 September 1978, 2; no author, 'Porter Decides to Continue Teaching Career at Carleton,' *Ottawa Citizen*, 2 October 1978, 51; no author, 'Carleton Truce,' *Ottawa Journal*, n.d., n.p.; D. Rogers, 'V-P Quits Carleton in Hiring Row,' *Ottawa Citizen*, 30 September 1978, 1; no author, 'Oliver nommera le successeur,' *Le Droit*, 30 October 1978, 4; no author, 'Carleton VP Says He Should Be Boss,' *Ottawa Citizen*, n.d., n.p.; and no author, 'Carleton's VP Reconsiders Future Plans,' *Ottawa Citizen*, 29 September 1978, 3.

185 Downey interview 1.

186 Bernard Ostry interview.

187 McFarlane interview.

188 McRoberts interview.

189 Downey interview 1.

190 Farr interview. Bernard Ostry, too, said that Marion was more openly

and publicly bitter about the situation than was John: 'Marion was pissed off. She thought people had let him down. That's what I recall. I may be wrong but I can remember her thrashing about a bit [over] it. In fact, I'm not so sure he didn't try to calm her down and tell her to lay off the subject' (Bernard Ostry interview).

191 McRae interview 1.
192 Whitteker interview.
193 Bernard Ostry said that though Porter was hurt, it was 'not in a very deep way.' He thought Porter's personality was such that 'he was probably thinking he wouldn't get it anyway. He had that view about not quite making things even though he might have deserved it ... So I'm sure that there was an ambivalence when he went into it' (Bernard Ostry interview).
194 Jewett interview 2.
195 Phillips interview.

14: Marion Porter, John Porter's Intellectual Partner

1 Marion Porter interview 1.
2 See Susan Hoecker-Drysdale, 'Women Sociologists in Canada: The Careers of Helen MacGill Hughes, Aileen Dansken Ross, and Jean Robertson Burnet,' in *Despite the Odds: Essays on Canadian Women and Science*, ed. M. Gosztonyi Ainley (Montreal: Véhicule Press, 1990), 152–76, and the sources cited in Margrit Eichler, 'Women Pioneers in Canadian Sociology,' 2001.
3 See the articles in Callan and Ardener, eds., *The Incorporated Wife*, and also A. Prentice, 'Boosting Husbands and Building Community: The Work of Twentieth Century Faculty Wives,' in *Historical Identities: The Professoriate in Canada*, ed. P. Stortz and E.L. Panoyotidis (Toronto: University of Toronto Press, 2006), 271–96.
4 See D. Smith, *Conceptual Practices of Power*; see also A. Innis Dagg, 'Academic Faculty Wives and Systematic Discrimination – Antinepotism and Inbreeding,' *CJHE* 23, no. 1 (1993): 1–18.
5 M. Porter to RHH, 25 November 1991.
6 Sullivan, *Shadow Maker*, 1995.
7 Marion maintained a sporadic relationship with MacEwen until MacEwen died in 1987 (see UTA, GMP, R. Sullivan interview of M. Porter, 4 February 1993).
8 See UTA, GMP, R. Sullivan interview of M. Porter, 4 February 1993, and R. Sullivan interview of Dora (Lyons) Hurford, 18 January 1993.

9   M. Porter to RHH, 25 November 1991.

10 Ibid.

11 UTA, GMP, R. Sullivan interview of M. Porter, 4 February 1993, and ibid., M. Porter, 'Aunty,' typescript, n.d., n.p.

12 'My feelings about Aunty are and were very complicated. She provided stability and gave us a feeling of security. I wanted to love her. In fact, I did love her. But she never expressed any love for me until I met John and no longer needed her. She would say when I tried to hug her: "I'm a very cold person. I can't show affection." This was not true. She showed a great deal of love and affection for Uncle. I think a major problem was that I wanted to think of her as a substitute mother and she thought of me and Dora and the other foster children … as a means of earning money' (UTA, GMP, M. Porter, 'Aunty,' typescript, n.d., n.p.).

13 M. Porter to RHH, 25 November 1991; see also UTA, GMP, M. Porter, 'Aunty,' typescript, n.d., n.p.

14 Dora lived with her father for about six years, then returned to live with the Martins (Sullivan, *Shadow Maker,* 28–9).

15 Ibid., 28.

16 UTA, GMP, M. Porter, 'Aunty,' typescript, n.d., n.p.

17 UTA, GMP, Marion Porter, interview by R. Sullivan, 4 February 1993, cited in Sullivan, *Shadow Maker,* 31.

18 M. Porter to RHH, 25 November 1991.

19 Ibid. and Sullivan, *Shadow Maker,* 29.

20 Sullivan, *Shadow Maker,* 82.

21 M. Porter to RHH, 25 November 1991. According to the account in Sullivan, Marion's schooling was paid for with a loan arranged by her social worker (Sullivan, *Shadow Maker,* 82).

22 M. Porter to RHH, 25 November 1991.

23 Marion Porter interview 1.

24 M. Porter, 'John Porter,' 5.

25 Bernard Ostry interview.

26 QUA, JMP, box 30, file 734, M. Porter to Meisel, 23 January 1963.

27 Ibid., Meisel to M. Porter, 28 January 1963.

28 Porter, *Vertical Mosaic,* xiv. When I asked Marion about the accuracy of this assessment of her role, she noted that it constituted 'an adequate expression of [her] contribution' (M. Porter to RHH, 25 November 1991).

29 M. Porter to RHH, 25 November 1991.

30 According to Tony Porter, Marion also had to 'press' John to acknowledge her contribution: 'Over time, I think it became much more of an equal relationship and I think also she began to press a little more on getting some

recognition for herself' (Tony Porter interview 2). See also anonymous comments, 13 October 2002.

31 LAC, JPP, vol. 6, no. 20; see the correspondence between Shils and his editorial staff at *Minerva*, and Porter (21 July 1969 – 27 August, 1970).

32 M. Porter to RHH, 25 November 1991; see 'Democratization of Canadian Universities,' 1970.

33 Marion Porter interview 1.

34 Ibid.

35 Ibid. and M. Porter to RHH, 25 November 1991.

36 M. Porter to RHH, 25 November 1991.

37 Ibid.; see also McRoberts interview.

38 M. Porter to RHH, 25 November 1991. Marion did not have anything to do with the writing of her husband's contribution to *Ascription and Achievement* other than preparing it for publication after his death. She helped to select the articles for *The Measure of Canadian Society*, but John wrote the introductions and she did nothing other than prepare the index after he died (ibid.).

39 M. Porter curriculum vitae, Marion Porter personal papers. The account below of Marion's involvement in CRIAW is based in part on correspondence with Ann Hall (11, 14, 17, and 21 January 2003) and Margrit Eichler (10 and 14 January 2003), comments by Naomi Griffiths (26 June 2003), interview of anonymous and the comments of the same person (13 October 2002). Hall was president of CRIAW in 1980–1 and a long-serving board member. Eichler served for many years, including a term as president in 1981–2. Griffiths helped found CRIAW and was an officer of the organization during its early years (N. Griffiths, 'Preface' in *Voix Feministes/Feminist Voices*, ed. Clippingdale, 61).

40 Bonnett, 'Building Bridges,' in *Voix Feministes/Feminist Voices*, ed. Clippingdale, 55–60; see also Griffiths, 'Preface,' in ibid., 1–5.

41 Bonnett, 'Building Bridges,' in *Voix Feministes/Feminist Voices*, ed. Clippingdale, 61.

42 Ibid., 64–5.

43 See M. Porter, 'John Porter and Education: Technical Functionalist or Conflict Theorist,' *CRSA* 18, no. 5 (1981): 627–38; M. Porter, curriculum vitae, Marion Porter personal papers.

44 Anonymous comments, 13 October 2002. By such a reckoning, Bob Phillips would be one among many who misunderstood the extent of their partnership. 'After he died, … fairly quickly she was simply dropped from the visiting lists of his friends. If she were a major contributor … that wouldn't have happened … [T]hey would have been sensitive enough to recognize

that despite the lack of formal scholastic attainment, [she had] … made a real contribution.' Phillips recalled as well that 'she felt kind of bitterly about this, … that when he died she lost so much of her social life' (Phillips interview).

45 Griffiths to RHH, 17 September, 2003.

46 The women's studies option was introduced under the umbrella of the Canadian Studies Institute at Carleton in 1982, so Marion would have been one of the first people to have this designation (personal conversation, C. Schmueck, 18 February 2003).

47 Ann Porter interview.

48 Tony Porter interview 2. Ann Porter, who was close to her mother during this period, had some reservations about this interpretation of her mother's motivation. She said that she 'would not deny it,' but that this was not her sense of it (Ann Porter interview).

49 M. Porter, 'The Church and the Status of Women in Quebec' (MA thesis, Carleton University, 1987).

50 Joan Gullen and Marion Porter, 'Sexism in Policies Related to Welfare Fraud,' in *Taking Sex into Account: The Policy Consequences of Sexist Research,* ed. J. Vickers (Ottawa: Carleton University Press, 1984), 209–18. This work resulted in changes to the law (Gullen interview; also anonymous comments, 13 October 2002).

51 M. Porter and Gilles Jasmin, 'A Profile of Post-Secondary Students in Canada: The 1983–1984 National Post-Secondary Student Survey: Summary National Data,' Barrados personal papers. Jasmin replaced Barrados at the Secretary of State after she had been there a year (M. Barrados to RHH, 30 May 2002).

52 Ann Porter interview.

53 M. Porter, curriculum vitae, Marion Porter personal papers.

54 Ann Porter interview.

55 Eichler, 'Women Pioneers in Canadian Sociology,' 2001.

56 See Smith, *Conceptual Practices of Power.*

57 Anonymous comments, 13 October 2002. According to Boyd, for a period after John's death, partly in response to being cast aside by some of John's colleagues and friends, Marion became aggressive about making people aware of her role in John's work, unintentionally creating the impression that she had done more or been more central to it than was actually the case (M. Boyd, personal communication with RHH, 12 July 2000).

58 This list includes Barrados, Boyd, Downey, Frank Jones, McRoberts, Oliver, Bernard Ostry, Sylvia Ostry, and Phillips.

59 Boyd interview.

60 McRoberts interview.

61 Barrados' opinion was based in part on first-hand experience. In the mid-1980s, when Barrados was chief of educational statistical analysis at the Secretary of State, she hired Marion to analyse some data from a Statistics Canada survey of postsecondary students in Canada. From this position she offered an assessment of Marion's working style and ability: while Marion was 'very good at sitting down with piles of data and writing reports describing the data,' she did not provide 'that *extra* amount, sort of bringing it together ... So that made me think ... it was probably John who would give that extra element' (Barrados interview).

62 Oliver interview.

63 Griffiths to RHH, 26 June 2003.

64 Hamilton's idea here is that Marion's mediated access to sociology parallels the access that women philosophers had to philosophy in the premodern era, as described by French feminist philosopher Michelle LeDoeuff: 'LeDoeuff considers women's relationship to philosophy historically. She says before the modern period, women did have access to philosophy but only through a particular philosopher ... and uses examples.' But Hamilton says this is not the same thing as having the kind of access to philosophy that men did: 'It is only through the mediation of a man that woman could gain access to a theoretical discourse ... My thought is that Marion had access to sociology through John. And that's different than having access to sociology' (Hamilton to RHH, 2 July 2004).

65 Griffiths to RHH, 26 June 2003.

66 M. Porter to RHH, 25 November 1991.

67 Ibid.

68 Ann Porter interview.

69 Boyd interview.

70 S. de Beauvoir, *The Second Sex* (New York: A.A. Knopf, 1957); B. Friedan, *The Feminine Mystique* (New York: Norton, 1963).

71 Marion Porter interview 2.

72 M. Porter to RHH, 25 November 1991.

73 See the materials in Callan and Ardener, eds., *The Incorporated Wife*.

74 Ann Porter interview.

75 Barrados interview.

76 Ann Porter interview.

77 Marion Porter interview 2.

78 M. Porter, 'John Porter,' 5.

79 M. Porter to RHH, 25 November 1991.

80 Tony Porter interview 2.

81 See for example, ibid.; and Ann Porter interview.
82 Farr interview.
83 Marion Porter interview 1.

15: Second Thoughts, Ruminations on Social Justice

1 Boyd interview.
2 McRoberts interview.
3 LAC, JPP, vol. 3, no. 15, JAP to S. Gilbert, 29 November 1978.
4 Porter delivered the McInnis Lectures February 1 and 2, 1977 at Osgoode Hall Law School in Toronto.
5 *Stations and Callings* did not appear until 1982 but was complete in draft form when he died in June 1979. Regarding the papers he presented, see LAC, JPP, vol. 7, no. 27, 'Notes: An Address to the Options for Canada Colloquium,' Montebello, Quebec, 7 May 1977; and LAC, JPP, vol. 6, no. 23, J. Porter, 'Education for Its Own Sake,' presented at a seminar on higher education, International Association of Universities, Halle, German Democratic Republic, 29 May–2 June 1978. While in office, he began preparing ibid., vol. 9, no. 22, Porter, 'Who Are Minorities? What Do They Want and Why?' and vol. 8, no. 14, Porter, 'Some Limits to Self-Determination,' [1978].
6 LAC, JPP, vol. 5, no. 2, K. Benzekvi (Canada Council) to JAP, 6 October 1978.
7 LAC, JPP, vol. 5, no. 2; see also vol. 3, no. 16.
8 Ibid., vol. 6, no. 1, André Renaud to JAP, 15 November 1978. He had served as a committee member the previous year (ibid., Renaud to JAP, 23 November 1977).
9 CU, ARC, Public Relations and Information Services fonds, Box no. PINFO–40, Series: Former Employees, file: Porter, John Memorial Service, 1979, tribute by B. McFarlane, n.p.
10 Ann Porter interview.
11 Marion Porter interview 1.
12 J. Porter, curriculum vitae, Clement personal papers; Re Ostry's invitation, see LAC, JAP, vol. 3, no. 16, S. Ostry to JAP, 7 February 1979, and JAP to Ostry, 19 February 1979.
13 Ibid., M. Gertler (Amnesty International) to JAP, 15 February 1979, and JAP to Gertler, 5 March 1979.
14 Ibid., H. Nesbitt to JAP, 26 March 1979.
15 LAC, JPP, vol. 1, no. 15, JAP to Fiona Porter, 21 March 1968; see also Ellen interview.

16 Ellen interview.

17 Ibid.

18 See CU, ARC, *TWAC* 19, no. 3 (16 January 1979).

19 LAC, JPP, vol. 5, no. 26, T. Nind to JAP, 12 March 1979; JAP to Nind, 20 March 1979; M. Doxey to JAP, 14 May 1979.

20 Marion Porter interview 1.

21 LAC, JPP, vol. 6, no. 11, '*The Canadian Condition*: John Porter: An Outline Based on Papers and Lectures'; see also ibid., vol. 6, no. 22, C. Wieczorek to JAP, 27 September 1973; JAP to G. van Tighem, 30 November 1973.

22 Marion Porter interview 1.

23 Ibid.

24 Clement thought it constituted his most important contribution to Canadian sociology save *The Vertical Mosaic* (Clement, 'Obituary: John Porter [1921–1979],' 14).

25 Porter, 'Prologue,' in Porter, *Measure of Canadian Society*, 2.

26 Clement, 'Foreword,' in ibid., xii–xiii.

27 Porter, Introduction to 'Research Biography,' in ibid., 11–12.

28 Porter, 'Prologue,' in ibid., 3. That said, Porter remarked to Dennis Olsen that he had reservations about the direct applicability of Marshall's analysis to the Canadian case: 'With "new" nations like Canada I really wonder whether you can import these European models or whether we have to create our own model; e.g., Marshall's discussion of citizenship in/for the U.K. They had a whole different legal and institutional framework within which their citizenship developed. Canada did not simply inherit the English framework; e.g., early ethnic settlers on the prairies were not even citizens. They could be deported if they caused trouble' (D. Olsen, Course notes: Sociology 610–11, Fall–Winter 1971–2, n.d., Olsen personal papers, in the context of a discussion of Barrington Moore, *Social Origins of Dictatorship and Democracy* [Boston: Beacon, 1966]).

29 Porter dealt with these same themes in detail in 'Equality and Education,' a keynote address presented at the annual conference of the Canadian Society for the Study of Education, Toronto, Ontario, June 1974. The talk was later published in two parts in *Integrateducation* 13, no. 4 and 13, no. 5 (1975).

30 Porter, 'Education and Equality,' in Porter, *Measure of Canadian Society*, 242.

31 Ibid., 244.

32 Ibid., 244–5.

33 Rawls, *Theory of Justice*, 303, cited in Porter, 'Education and Equality,' in Porter, *Measure of Canadian Society*, 247.

34 Porter, 'Education and Equality,' in Porter, *Measure of Canadian Society*, 25.

Contrary arguments are outlined in Robert Nozick, *Anarchy, State and Utopia* (New York: Basic, 1974); Robert Nisbet, 'The Fatal Ambivalence of an Idea: Equal Freemen or Equal Serfs?' *Encounter* 47, no. 6 (December 1976): 10–21; and Nisbet, 'The Pursuit of Equality,' *PI* 34 (Spring 1974): 103–20, discussed by Porter in ibid., 248–9.

35 Porter, 'Education and Equality,' in Porter, *Measure of Canadian Society*, 250.
36 McRoberts interview.
37 McFarlane interview.
38 Jewett interview 2.
39 Porter, 'Education and Equality,' in Porter, *Measure of Canadian Society*, 250.
40 Ibid., 241.
41 Porter examined, for example, Jencks et al., *Inequality*; see also Coleman et al., *Equality of Educational Opportunity*.
42 Porter, 'Education and Equality,' in Porter, *Measure of Canadian Society*, 252–4, drawing on Coleman et al., *Equality of Educational Opportunity* and Jencks et al., *Inequality*.
43 Ibid., 254–5.
44 Porter, 'Education and Equality,' in Porter, *Measure of Canadian Society*, 255–8. Here Porter draws on the Marxists Samuel Bowles and Herbert Gintis, *Schooling in Capitalist America* (New York: Basic, 1976) and radicals Paul Goodman, *Public Mis-Education and the Community of Scholars* (New York: Random House, 1962) and Ivan Illich, *Deschooling Society* (New York: Harper and Row, 1972), among others.
45 Porter, 'Education and Equality,' in Porter, *Measure of Canadian Society*, 259.
46 Ibid., 264–7, citing H. Braverman, *Labor and Monopoly Capital: The Degradation of Work in the Twentieth Century* (New York: Monthly Review Press, 1974).
47 Porter, 'Education and Equality,' in Porter, *Measure of Canadian Society*, 267–8, citing I. Berg, *The Great Training Robbery* (New York: Praeger, 1970).
48 Macpherson, *Democratic Theory*, 1973. Macpherson's ideas, like Porter's, are very similar to those of Hobhouse, Hobson, and others who worked in the British New Liberal tradition.
49 Porter, 'Education and the Just Society,' in Porter, *Measure of Canadian Society*, 273–4.
50 Ibid., 276. He was here following Amitai Etzioni, *The Active Society* (New York: The Free Press, 1968).
51 Porter, 'Education and the Just Society,' in Porter, *Measure of Canadian Society*, 276.
52 LAC, JPP, vol. 3, no. 1, '*Excalibur* interview,' by Agnes Kruchio, York University, 10 February 1977, 13.

53 Ibid., vol. 1, no. 31, 'Convocation address, University of Waterloo, October 21, 1977,' emphasis added.

54 Ibid., vol. 3, no. 16, M. Kenny to J. Porter, 26 April 1979.

55 Marion Porter interview 1; also M. Porter, 'John Porter,' 1.

56 Jewett interview 2. On this point, see also McKenzie, *Pauline Jewett*, 146.

57 LAC, JPP, vol. 1, no. 15, JAP to F. Porter, n.d. [c. early 1971].

58 McKenzie, *Pauline Jewett*, 146; Marion Porter interview 1; Barrados interview.

59 Marion Porter interview 1; see also Phillips to RHH, 14 March 2002; Boyd interview.

60 Phillips to RHH, 14 March 2002.

61 Barrados interview.

62 Marion Porter interview 1.

63 Marion Porter interview 2.

64 Marion Porter interview 1.

65 Sylvia Ostry interview.

66 No author, 'John Porter,' *Ottawa Journal*, 19 June 1979, 6.

67 CU, ARC, Public Relations and Information Services fonds, Box no. PINFO–40, Series: Former Employees, file: Porter, John Memorial Service, 1979, eulogy by Davidson Dunton.

68 *CRSA* 18, no. 5 (1981).

69 John Porter Tradition of Excellence Book Award, List of Past Recipients, www.csaa.ca/Awards/AwardsPorter.htm.

70 R. Brym, 'Comments' for a session, 'Canada Two Decades after *The Vertical Mosaic*: A Critical Evaluation of Porter's Vision,' annual meeting of the CSAA, Windsor, June 1988. Michael Ornstein has made a similar comment ('Three Decades of Elite Research,' in *Vertical Mosaic Revisited*, ed. Helmes-Hayes and Curtis, 151–2).

71 Porter, 'Research Biography,' in Coleman, Etzioni, and Porter, *Macrosociology*, 153.

72 Sylvia Ostry interview.

73 Forcese to RHH, 5 January 1989.

74 CU, ARC, Public Relations and Information Services fonds, Box no. PINFO–40, Series: Former Employees, file: Porter, John Memorial Service, 1979, tribute by B. McFarlane.

75 CU, ARC, Public Relations and Information Services fonds, Box no. PINFO–40, Series: Former Employees, file: Porter, John Memorial Service, 1979, tribute by H. McRoberts.

76 As an illustration, Jewett referred to an instance when they travelled from the cottage at Constant Lake into the local village to have her car repaired. She recalled chatting to the mechanic while he worked. Porter said noth-

ing. Later, returning home, Porter confided that he envied her capacity to chat with the mechanic so easily and that he always felt awkward in such situations (Jewett interview 2).

77　LAC, JPP, vol. 6, no. 20, JAP to R. Davidson, 8 April 1970.

78　Ibid., vol. 9, no. 5, JAP to R. Davidson, 19 May 1977. Note a similar statement in the introduction to a reprinting of the research biography of *The Vertical Mosaic*, written in 1979: 'Much more material is now available than formerly to undertake another macro-analysis of Canada in transition or to revisit the "mosaic." That would be an attractive possibility if time and energies allow' (in Porter, *Measure of Canadian Society*, 9). He said much the same thing in a letter to Clement, written in 1976: 'When I can get out from under my present grant obligations I have every intention of doing another macro-book on Canada' (JAP to Clement, 14 July 1976, Clement personal papers).

79　Excellent overviews of work in the elite studies tradition in Canada since the publication of *The Vertical Mosaic*, are R. Brym, *The Structure of the Canadian Capitalist Class* (Toronto: Garamond, 1985), and Ornstein, 'Three Decades of Elite Research,' in *Vertical Mosaic Revisited*, ed. Helmes-Hayes and Curtis, 145–77.

80　Here I am thinking of, among others, Clement and Myles, *Relations of Ruling*, 1994; William Carroll, *Corporate Power and Canadian Capitalism* (Vancouver: UBC Press, 1986); and Jeff Reitz and Raymond Breton, *The Illusion of Difference: Realities of Ethnicity in Canada and the United States* (Toronto: C.D. Howe Institute, 1994).

Afterword: Duty, Service, and Mission

1　Sections of this chapter are based in part on Helmes-Hayes, 'Hobhouse Twice Removed'; Helmes-Hayes, 'J.A. Banks'; and R. Helmes-Hayes, 'Engaged Practical Intellectualism: John Porter and "New Liberal" Public Sociology,' *CJS* 34 no. 3 (2009): 831–68.

2　Hiller, *Society and Change*, 3–39.

3　Knight interview, emphasis added.

4　Neither the British New Liberals nor John Porter used the term 'engaged, practical intellectual' to refer either to themselves or to their view of the proper role that a social scientist should play. The term is mine.

5　See Cook, *Regenerators*.

6　In *The Regenerators*, Cook describes the beliefs and activities of many intellectuals who, in resolving for themselves the science–religion debate of the late nineteenth century, developed a secular stance not unlike Porter's. Good examples are groups such as the Free Thinkers Association and the Canadian Secular Union, which linked rationalism and humanism to social progress without invoking God, religious morality, providential design, and the like (41–64).

7 The discussion below is based largely on Allett, *New Liberalism*; Clarke, *Liberals and Social Democrats*; Collini, *Liberalism and Sociology*; and Freeden, *New Liberalism*.

8 The most famous work of classical liberalism is, of course, Smith, *Wealth of Nations*. Quotation from book 1, ch. 2, para. 01.

9 Allett, *New Liberalism*, 21, emphasis added. On Hobson and Hobhouse as the leading theorists of the movement, see ibid., 15; Collini, *Liberalism and Sociology*, 4–5 and Freeden, *New Liberalism*, 253–4. Three books are regarded as exemplars of the tradition: Hobhouse, *Liberalism*; Hobhouse, *Democracy and Reaction*; and J. Hobson, *The Social Problem: Life and Work* (New York: J. Pott, 1901); see Allett, ibid., 26 and Collini, ibid., 4.

10 Dennis and Halsey, *English Ethical Socialism*, 76.

11 Hobhouse, *Democracy and Reaction*, 229, and see also 237. For a detailed discussion of the New Liberalism as an extension of the old, see Collini, *Liberalism and Sociology*, 38–9, 100–20.

12 Hobhouse, *Liberalism*, 87 and 88–127 passim; see also Grimes, 'Introduction,' in Hobhouse, *Liberalism*, 6.

13 Hobhouse, 'Leader,' *Contemporary Review*, vol. xciii, 353, cited in Clarke, *Liberals and Social Democrats*, 113; see also 139–40.

14 Allett, *New Liberalism*, 262. This socialist connection perhaps explains why Norman Dennis and A.H. Halsey place Hobhouse in the 'ethical socialist' tradition in *English Ethical Socialism*. There are many parallels between New Liberalism and ethical socialism, and they claim many intellectuals in common as part of their respective political heritages. Though Dennis and Halsey make some scattered references to the New Liberalism in their book, however, they do not outline the differences between the two approaches in any detail (see Dennis and Halsey, *English Ethical Socialism*, 75n55).

15 Allett, *New Liberalism*, 179.

16 Ibid., 54–5.

17 Collini, *Liberalism and Sociology*, 129.

18 Hobhouse, *The Labour Movement*, 2nd ed. (London: T. Fisher Unwin, 1898), 4–5, cited in Collini, ibid., 67–8.

19 Hobhouse, *Liberalism*, 66, 68.

20 Allett, *New Liberalism*, 74–5.

21 Collini, *Liberalism and Sociology*, 116.

22 J. Hobson, *Problems of Poverty: An Enquiry into the Industrial Condition of the Poor* (London: Methuen, 1891) 227, cited in Clarke, *Liberals and Social Democrats*, 49; see also Freeden, *New Liberalism*, 207.

23 Allett, *New Liberalism*, 17.
24 The issue of different forms of rent and the degree to which individuals should be allowed to keep various types of 'rental' income (earned and unearned) was a source of much debate among liberal political economists and between liberal political economists and others (e.g., socialists of various types). See, for example, Collini, *Liberalism and Sociology*, 61–6; Clarke, *Liberals and Social Democrats*, 46–54, 163. A related issue was the problem of the causes of the economic recessions. One oft-debated theory was Hobson's idea of 'underconsumption' (Allett, *New Liberalism*, 70–130). See Hobson, *The Problem of the Unemployed* (1896; reprint, London: Routledge/Thoemmes Press, 1992); and *The Industrial System: An Enquiry into Earned and Unearned Income* (1910; reprint, New York: A.M. Kelley, 1969), 284–311.
25 Collini, *Liberalism and Sociology*, 118.
26 Hobhouse, 'The Historical Evolution of Property, in Fact and in Idea,' in *Property, Its Duties and Rights, Historically, Philosophically, and Religiously Regarded*, ed. Charles Gore (London: Macmillan, 1913), 98–106 passim, cited in Collini, *Liberalism and Sociology*, 143, emphasis added; see also Clarke, *Liberals and Social Democrats*, 153.
27 On the links between Hobson's economics and Keynes', see Clarke, *Liberals and Social Democrats*, 226–34.
28 Hobhouse, *Liberalism*, 96 and 88–109 more generally; see Dennis and Halsey, *English Ethical Socialism*, 66–70.
29 Hobhouse, 'Leader,' *Manchester Guardian*, 23 February 1899, cited in Collini, *Liberalism and Sociology*, 109; see also 111, 125.
30 Hobhouse, *Democracy and Reaction*, 216, cited in Collini, *Liberalism and Sociology*, 112, 122–3. For a detailed discussion of Hobhouse's views on practical reforms, see Dennis and Halsey, *English Ethical Socialism*, 75–90. For a detailed discussion of Hobson's views on appropriate practical measures, see Allett, *New Liberalism*, 240–54.
31 Wm. Clarke, article title unknown, *Progressive Review* 1 (1896), 4, cited in Clarke, *Liberals and Social Democrats*, 58.
32 Samuel, article title unknown, *Progressive Review* 1 (1896), 258, cited in Clarke, *Liberals and Social Democrats*, 58.
33 Dennis and Halsey, *English and Ethical Socialism*, 62–3.
34 Ibid., 64–6.
35 Wallas, *Human Nature in Politics*, cited in Clarke, *Liberals and Social Democrats*, 136. For Hobhouse's views on the importance of education for raising the cultural standards of citizens, see Dennis and Halsey, *English Ethical Socialism*, 76–7.
36 See Collini, *Liberalism and Sociology*, 207. Collini argues that after the outbreak of World War I, Hobhouse became pessimistic about the prospect

of progress. For his part, Collini is highly critical of Hobhouse's views on progress (e.g., 253).

37 Hobhouse, *Mind in Evolution* (London: Macmillan, 1915), 5, 9, cited in ibid., 180–1.

38 Hobhouse, *Development and Purpose, An Essay towards a Philosophy of Evolution* (London: Macmillan, 1927), xv–xvi, cited in ibid., 150.

39 Hobhouse, 'Democracy and Empire,' *Speaker* (18 October 1902), cited in ibid., 179; see also Hobhouse, *Social Evolution and Political Theory* (New York: Cambridge University Press, 1911), 39, cited in ibid., 212. See Collini, *Liberalism and Sociology,* 150–3, 184, 186, 214.

40 Ferguson's treatment of the New Liberalism at Queen's University refers to it as political economy rather than sociology (*Remaking Liberalism*).

41 Collini, *Liberalism and Sociology,* 184–7; see also 201.

42 Hobhouse, *Morals in Evolution II,* 280–1, cited in Collini, *Liberalism and Sociology,* 218.

43 Owen, *L.T. Hobhouse,* 15, 50–4.

44 Ibid., 54–6, 76n16.

45 Hobhouse, article title unknown, *Sociological Papers* 2 (London, England: Macmillan, 1905) 188, cited in Collini, *Liberalism and Sociology,* 225–6; see also Clarke, *Liberals and Social Democrats,* 147–8.

46 Hobhouse, *Elements of Social Justice,* 14, cited in Dennis and Halsey, *English Ethical Socialism,* 84.

47 Hobhouse, *Labour Movement,* 158, cited in Dennis and Halsey, *English Ethical Socialism,* 84–5.

48 Hobhouse, *Social Development,* 78–9, 88, cited in Collini, *Liberalism and Sociology,* 233–4; see also Dennis and Halsey, *English Ethical Socialism,* 64–6.

49 Hobhouse, *Social Development,* 78, cited in Collini, *Liberalism and Sociology,* 234.

50 Collini, *Liberalism and Sociology,* 234.

51 Hobhouse, 'Sociology,' in *Hastings' Encyclopedia of Religion and Ethics,* vol. 2 (1920), 50–5, cited in ibid., 234.

52 Collini describes the New Liberal conception of sociology as a 'vocation' (ibid., 209–34). Ferguson uses the term 'mission' to describe the conception of political economy held by the New Liberals at Queen's (*Remaking Liberalism,* 41–2).

53 See Ferguson, *Remaking Liberalism*; McKillop, *Matters of Mind*; Granatstein, *Ottawa Men*; and Owram, *Government Generation*; see also S.E.D. Shortt, *The Search for an Ideal: Six Canadian Intellectuals and Their Convictions in an Age of Transition, 1890–1930* (Toronto: University of Toronto Press, 1976).

54 Though Owram does not discuss the period from the 1950s to the 1970s in

detail, he claims that immediate postwar trends continued unabated (*Government Generation*, 274). Regarding related developments in the United States, see Morton White, *Social Thought in America: The Revolt against Formalism* (London: Oxford University Press, 1976); and Christopher Lasch, *The New Radicalism in America, 1889–1963: The Intellectual as a Social Type* (New York: A.A. Knopf, 1965).

55 Owram, *Government Generation*, x.

56 Ferguson, *Remaking Liberalism*, xii–xv.

57 Owram, *Government Generation*, 8; see also McKillop, *Matters of Mind*, 101–19.

58 McKillop, *Matters of Mind*, 101–19.

59 Ibid., especially 112 and 115.

60 McKillop describes the higher criticism as 'a quest for the historical Jesus and for a critical understanding of the biblical record' (ibid., 204). For the crisis of belief see Cook, *Regenerators*, 8, and 7–25 more generally; see also Marshall, *Secularizing the Faith*. For a different view, see Christie and Gauvreau, *Full-Orbed Christianity*.

61 Cook, *Regenerators*, 229, 231; see also 3–6, 174–6, 195; and Marshall, *Secularizing the Faith*. On the roots of the social gospel and its influence on sociology in the United States, see J. Morgan, 'The Development of Sociology and the Social Gospel in America,' *SA* 30, no. 1 (1969): 42–53. For the Canadian case, see Allen, *Social Passion*, and Campbell, 'Social Reform,' in *Beginnings*, Campbell.

62 G. Smith, *Lectures on Modern History Delivered in Oxford 1859–61*, 32–3, cited in Cook, *Regenerators*, 34.

63 Cook, *Regenerators*, 105.

64 Ibid., 122; Henry George, *Progress and Poverty* (London: K. Paul, Trench, Trübner, 1890). George was influential in progressive Canadian intellectual circles in the last part of the nineteenth century (Cook, ibid., 105–22). See W. Douglas, 'The Science of Political Economy,' *Methodist Magazine and Review* 47 (June 1898): 564, cited in Cook, ibid., 122.

65 Christie and Gauvreau argue that from 1900 to 1940 the Protestant Churches constituted the fulcrum around which the social welfare agenda revolved and largely controlled the movement, using the government to achieve their reformist goals (*Full-Orbed Christianity*, see especially chapters 3, 4, and 6).

66 Owram, *Government Generation*, 14.

67 Ibid., 50, 51; see 50–79 more generally.

68 McKillop, *Matters of Mind*, 202–3.

69 Owram, *Government Generation*, 108, see chapters 4 and 5 in general.

70 There were developments at the University of Toronto as well. See immediately below. See Hiller, *Society and Change*, 8–9; Campbell, 'Social Reform,' in *Beginnings*, ed. Campbell; and Helmes-Hayes, 'Images of Inequality,' 171–7.

71 H. Ames, *The City below the Hill* (1897; reprint, Toronto: University of Toronto Press, 1972); J.S. Woodsworth, *My Neighbor* (1911; reprint, Toronto: University of Toronto Press, 1972); and *Strangers within Our Gates* (1909; reprint, Toronto: University of Toronto Press, 1972); United Church Archives, Methodist Church of Canada and Presbyterian Church in Canada, Reports of Social Surveys, 1913–14, cited in Allen, *Social Passion*, 12–13n34.

72 See e.g., Owram, *Government Generation*. For a different perspective on the role of the Protestant Churches, see Christie and Gauvreau, *Full-Orbed Christianity*, 1996.

73 Owram, *Government Generation*, 120–1, 189–90, 192–220. Owram refers to it as intellectual liberalism because until near the end of World War II it was not tied to any particular political party.

74 I. Drummond, *Political Economy at the University of Toronto: A History of the Department, 1888–1982* (Toronto: Faculty of Arts and Science, University of Toronto, 1983), 56–61. MacIver and Urwick shared a number of views (McKillop, *Matters of Mind*, 505–11).

75 McKillop, *Matters of Mind*, 672n61.

76 See MacIver, *The Modern State*, especially 311, 315–16. Owram discusses MacIver's conception of the state in *Government Generation*, 117–21. Owram refers to it as the 'service' state because in MacIver's conception it was like a business corporation that provided a series of services to its citizens (107–34).

77 McKillop, *Matters of Mind*, 498–505. The term 'architectonic' comes from MacIver (*Elements of Social Science*, 13).

78 MacIver, *Elements of Social Science*, 16.

79 McKillop, *Matters of Mind*, 500–2.

80 Owram, *Government Generation*, 121.

81 MacIver, *Elements of Social Science*, 80–95, especially 94–5; see also McKillop, *Matters of Mind*, 500.

82 McKillop, *Matters of Mind*, 502, citing MacIver, *Labor in the Changing World*.

83 Urwick knew Hobhouse and worked with him to establish the Sociological Society in England. He held Hobhousian views, like MacIver, and wrote *A Philosophy of Social Progress* (London: Methuen, 1912) and *The Social Good* (London: Methuen, 1927) (McKillop, *Matters of Mind*, 506–10). For a brief portrayal of Urwick and MacIver that plays up their differences, see Hiller, *Society and Change*, 5–6, 13.

84 See McKillop, *Matters of Mind*, 497–8; Clark, 'How the Department of Sociology Came into Being,' in *Forty Years*, ed. Helmes-Hayes, 29–30.
85 Some had studied with Keynes in Cambridge; others were influenced in some less direct way. Some people who were especially important in this regard were R.B. Bryce (Granatstein, *Ottawa Men*, 256–63), A.F.W. Plumptre (ibid., 49–50 and 135), and W. Mackintosh (ibid., 158, 165–6). See also Owram, *Government Generation*, 294–5.
86 Owram's 'reform elite' is a much bigger group than Granatstein's 'mandarinate,' comprising some forty to a hundred people in academia, the civil service, and so forth (*Government Generation*, 135–59). Granatstein's list refers to the period 1935–57 and deals with about twenty men. Almost all had university degrees. A number earned MAs, but only Skelton and Mackintosh earned the PhD. Of those for whom Granatstein provides detailed information, half attended Cambridge, Oxford, or the LSE and were thus exposed more or less directly to the ideas of the New Liberals and, if they went to England late enough, to the ideas of Keynes. At some point in their respective careers, over half taught at a university (*Ottawa Men*, 1982).
87 Owram, *Government Generation*, 160–91, 193.
88 Ibid., 200–20 passim. Citing an interview with prominent political economist Vincent Bladen and the writings of mandarin W.A. Mackintosh, Granatstein argues that the principles of reform liberalism were not popular either in Canadian academia or among the mandarinate and their political advisees more generally until about 1940 (*Ottawa Men*, 158).
89 Granatstein, *Ottawa Men*, 276.
90 Ibid., 168, 276; Ferguson, *Remaking Liberalism*, 219. According to Owram, this was not a rapid Keynesian 'revolution' but a slow working out of practical responses to economic change in Canada and the gradual and selective rethinking and reformulation of classical economic theory (*Government Generation*, 200–1). For a summary of welfare state measures included, see Ferguson, *Remaking Liberalism*, 220–31 passim.
91 Ferguson, *Remaking Liberalism*, 232–46. Owram points out that by allegedly advocating on behalf of the Canadian population at large, they differed from earlier generations of intellectuals, who tended to represent specific organizations such as the Canadian Manufacturers Association (*Government Generation*, 176–7). Whatever their professed intentions, their orientation to all matters political and economic was that of the liberal, 'managerial middle-class' (ibid., 262).
92 Ferguson, *Remaking Liberalism*, 41–2, 231.
93 Owram, *Government Generation*, 171.

94 Ferguson, *Remaking Liberalism,* 8; Granatstein, *Ottawa Men,* 10, 2.

95 Ibid., 277. Owram phrased this differently, in terms of a new notion of the efficient, managerialist 'service state' combined with the idea that civil service intellectuals were to adopt a sense of 'service' which combined two somewhat conflicting ideas. They were to be at one and the same time both professional (i.e., driven by norms of 'objectivity' and 'detachment,' yet politically 'commit[ed] to social goals and policy choices' (*Government Generation,* 163–4).

96 Granatstein, *Ottawa Men,* 276.

97 F.H. Underhill, 'The Conception of a National Interest,' *CJEPS* 1, no. 3 (1935): 404. For a less charitable assessment of the intentions of the mandarins, see Christina McCall, 'The Establishment That Governs Us,' *SN* (May 1968): 23–4, cited in Granatstein, *Ottawa Men,* 17–18.

98 Owram, *Government Generation,* 274.

99 Ibid., 166–7 and 262–73.

100 On the problems intellectuals faced when they became involved in political debates or electoral politics, see Michiel Horn, 'Running for Office: Canadian Professors, Electoral Politics, and Institutional Reactions, 1887–1968,' in *Historical Identities: The Professoriate in Canada,* ed. Paul Stortz and E. Lisa Panayotidis (Toronto: University of Toronto Press, 2006), 63–83; and M. Horn, *Academic Freedom in Canada: A History* (Toronto: University of Toronto Press, 1999).

101 Owram, *Government Generation,* 143.

102 Tomovic, 'Sociology in Canada,' appendix C.

103 On the early history of the McGill Department of Sociology, see Shore, *Science of Social Redemption;* and Thomas Palantzas, 'A Chicago Reprise in the Champagne Years of Canadian Sociology,' MA thesis, Lakehead University, 1994.

104 Clark, 'How the Department of Sociology Came into Being' in *Forty Years,* ed. Helmes-Hayes, 29–30; and Helmes-Hayes, ed. ibid., 203–4, appendix A.

105 Tomovic, 'Sociology in Canada,' appendix C provides a good basis for constructing a list of those who taught during this period.

106 See, for example, Wilcox-Magill, 'Paradigms and Social Science,' in *Introduction to Sociology,* ed. Grayson; and Wilcox-Magill and Helmes-Hayes, 'Leonard Charles Marsh.'

107 Helmes-Hayes and Wilcox-Magill, 'A Neglected Classic,' 85, 99–100n.8 and n.9.

108 Marsh, *Canadians In and Out of Work;* Research Committee of the League for Social Reconstruction, *Social Planning for Canada* (1935). Owram notes

that the authors of *Social Planning for Canada* were influenced by the Fabians and Keynes (*Government Generation*, 171–2).

109 William Beveridge, *Social Insurance and Allied Services*, Great Britain, Interdepartmental Committee on Social Insurance and Allied Services (New York: Macmillan, 1942). On Beveridge, see Lord William Beveridge, *Power and Influence: An Autobiography* (London: Hodder and Stoughton, 1953); and Jose Harris, *William Beveridge: A Biography* (Oxford: Clarendon, 1977). On differences between the British and Canadian plans and a description of options put forth by Charlotte Whitton and Harry Cassidy, see Guest, *Emergence of Social Security*, 109–15; see also 117–23.

110 For the government response, see Guest, *Emergence of Social Security*, 124. Re the Marsh report, *Social Security for Canada*, see Owram, *Government Generation*, 281–4, 290–2.

111 Marsh, *Social Security for Canada*. On the significance of Marsh's work as foundational for the establishment of the welfare state in Canada, see the essays in *Journal of Canadian Studies* 21, no. 2 (1986): 3–76. A contrary opinion is offered by Owram in *Government Generation*, 290–2.

112 Owram, *Government Generation*, 256; see 254–84 passim more generally. During the war the federal civil service expanded from 46,000 to 115,000 (ibid.) and government expenditures rose from $681 million to $5.2 billion (R. Bird, *Growth of Government Spending in Canada* [Toronto: Canadian Tax Foundation, 1970], 268–9, table 26). By contrast, during the decade of the Depression ending 1939, the number of federal civil servants increased by only 2,000, from 44,000 to 46,000 – hardly a massive response to a major problem (Owram, *Government Generation*, 256).

113 On the roots of King's cautious, reformist political economy and progressive Protestantism, see Cook, *Regenerators*, 196–213. On the ongoing efforts of those within the Liberal Party to 'modernize' King's liberalism, see Owram, *Government Generation*, 181–9, 254–84, and 285–317.

114 Owram, *Government Generation*, 302–3.

115 William Kilbourn, 'The 1950s,' in *The Canadians 1867–1967*, ed. Careless and Brown, 316.

116 Gordon to RHH, 6 August 1987.

117 Finkel, *Our Lives*, 6.

118 Ibid.

119 Owram, *Government Generation*, 261.

120 Ibid., 303, 308, respectively; see 303–8 more generally.

121 Ibid., 296.

122 Ibid., 295–7, 317.

123 Ibid., 163–4, 261–3.

124 See Ferguson, *Remaking Liberalism*, 29–30.

125 Owram, *Government Generation*, 167–8. Re Mackintosh's views on this issue, see Granatstein, *Ottawa Men*, 156.

126 Owram, *Government Generation*, 325.

127 See ibid., 261–2 and 285–334.

128 Brooks and Gagnon, *Social Scientists and Politics*, 87; see 83–91 in general. They claim that for many years other social sciences were regarded as subordinate to economics.

129 Granatstein, *Ottawa Men*, 168, emphasis added.

130 Hiller, *Society and Change*, 14–16; re McGill, see Shore, *Science of Social Redemption*, 1987.

131 I surveyed Canadian university calendars to glean this information.

132 Hiller, *Society and Change*, 23, table 3.

133 Ibid.

134 Brooks and Gagnon, *Social Scientists and Politics*, 83; see also 86, table 14.

135 Ibid., 92–3.

136 Hiller, *Society and Change*, 23, table 3.

137 Re the Royal Commission on Bilingualism and Biculturalism, see Brooks and Gagnon, *Social Scientists and Politics*, 95–8. For the situation after 1967, see 111, table 18.

138 D. Olsen, Course notes: Sociology 610–11, Carleton University, Fall–Winter 1971–2, n.d., Olsen personal papers, re Daniel Bell's 'Knowledge and Technology,' in E.B. Sheldon and W.E. Moore, *Indicators of Social Change: Concepts and Measurements* (New York: Sage, 1968).

139 Brooks and Gagnon, *Social Scientists and Politics*, 98, 104–5. They give the example of *The Real Poverty Report*, which challenged the official Senate report on poverty (Ian Adams, W. Cameron, B. Hill, and P. Penz, *The Real Poverty Report* [Edmonton: Hurtig 1971], 98).

140 Brooks and Gagnon, *Social Scientists and Politics*, 108–109, 88–9. They were generally able to ally only with oppositional and marginalized groups, which are difficult to mobilize, especially in economic good times.

141 Ibid., 104.

142 Re the role of the vanguard in Quebec politics in the 1960s and '70s, see ibid., 23–74. For a summary and assessment of later, very different, developments in Quebec, see Marc Renaud, Suzanne Doré, and Deena White, 'Sociology and Social Policy: From a Love-Hate Relationship with the State to Cynicism and Pragmatism,' *CRSA* 26, no. 3 (1989): 426–56.

143 Brooks and Gagnon, *Social Scientists and Politics*, 11–12.

144 Ibid., 112.

145 Ibid., 104, 91 respectively.

146 Ibid., 16.
147 On Ginsberg as a New Liberal, see McKillop, *Matters of Mind*, 672n61.
148 MacRae interview; John Grist interview; Jewett interview 1; CU, ARC, no author, 'Profile: John A. Porter,' *The Carleton* 5, no. 19 (21 March 1950): 16.
149 LAC, JPP, vol. 2 nos. 2–5.
150 A. Tropp to RHH, 29 August 1990.
151 Richmond, comments made at CSAA annual meeting, 6 June 1988; Richmond to RHH, 11 March 1988; see also E. Shils to RHH, 21 June 1989.
152 Halsey, 'Provincials and Professionals,' 53, 55. In the conclusion to this chapter, I discuss Halsey's argument further, drawing a series of comparisons among members of Halsey's cohort, Porter, and the generation of sociologists that institutionalized modern sociology in Canada from the 1950s to the early 1970s.
153 Tropp to RHH, 29 August 1990.
154 M. Ginsberg, *On Justice in Society* (Harmondsworth: Penguin, 1965); M. Ginsberg, *Nationalism: A Reappraisal* (Leeds: Leeds University Press, 1961); and M. Ginsberg, *The Idea of Progress: A Revaluation* (London: Methuen, 1953). See D. Olsen, Course notes: Sociology 610–11, Carleton University, Fall–Winter 1971–2, n.d., Olsen papers.
155 Porter, introduction to 'Ethnic Pluralism in Canadian Perspective,' in Porter, *Measure of Canadian Society*, 103–4.
156 Porter, 'Research Biography,' in Coleman, Elzioni, and Porter, *Macrosociology*, 151–2, emphasis added.
157 Hobhouse discusses these issues in many places (see, e.g., *Morals in Evolution I*). For more details on Hobhouse and Ginsberg's views on the place of values in scholarship, including a list of secondary sources, see Helmes-Hayes, 'Hobhouse Twice Removed,' and Helmes-Hayes, 'J.A. Banks: From Universal History to Historical Sociology.'
158 Porter sometimes claimed that facts assumed meaning only in theoretical context and argued that aimless empiricism was a waste of time. For example, in a methods lecture in the early 1950s, he noted: 'Facts by themselves are meaningless, e.g., [the] Census ... Theory gives direction to research, [and] order and meaning to facts' (LAC, JPP, vol. 2, no. 17, 'Theory and Research,' 2). But more often he stressed the primacy of data over theory. Facts, he said, 'often speak for themselves' (Porter, 'Foreword,' in Clement, *The Canadian Corporate Elite*, x). He sometimes expressed this idea as a 'Porterism.' 'Confronted with a choice between theory and data,' he said, 'choose data' (McRoberts interview). A corollary of this was that he was uninterested in purely theoretical disputation. '[Porter] thinks sociology tends to get hung up on theory as a kind of scholasticism ... He is

a positivist – i.e., insists on the primacy of social reality which is out there, ever-changing, giving us empirical problems which we have to study, explain and interpret. Theory makes sense out of the world. [It] tells us what to look for, serves as a guide to research. It should not be an end in itself. The end is the development of empirical generalizations or laws. He can't understand how anybody can say "I'm a theorist" and ... cop out of a concern with empirical reality' (D. Olsen, Course notes: Sociology 610–11, Carleton University, Fall–Winter 1971–2, n.d., Olsen personal papers).

159 According to McRoberts, Porter had great respect for Jordan's views (McRoberts interview).

160 See my discussion of the McInnis Lectures below.

161 See Porter, 'Macrosociology: Some Problems with the Nation State as the Unit of Analysis,' draft prepared for use in Sociology 622, Carleton University, Spring 1974, Clement personal papers; and Porter, 'Towards a Macrosociology: Further Notes,' draft prepared for use in Sociology 602, Carleton University, Spring 1975, Clement personal papers. I discuss this methodology below

162 Ginsberg, *Sociology,* 7–37, 38–53; Ginsberg, 'Problems and Methods of Sociology,' in Ginsberg, *Essays in Sociology,* 7–55.

163 Jewett interview 3. Jewett said one of the things Porter admired about C.B. Macpherson's 'intellectualism' was his 'synthetic capacity' (Jewett interview 2).

164 Porter, 'Macrosociology,' Clement personal papers; Porter, 'Towards a Macrosociology,' Clement personal papers; and Porter, *Measure of Canadian Society,* 3–5, respectively.

165 Porter, 'Research Biography,' in Coleman, Elzioni, and Porter, *Macrosociology,* 150; 'Macrosociology,' and 'Towards a Macrosociology,' Clement personal papers.

166 Ginsberg, 'Problems and Methods of Sociology,' in Ginsberg, *Essays in Sociology;* see also Hobhouse, *The Rational Good* (New York: Henry Holt, 1921); and *Elements of Social Justice.* For discussions of other like-minded European social thinkers see H. Stuart Hughes, *Consciousness and Society* (New York: Vintage, 1961); and F.L. Baumer, *Modern European Thought: Continuity and Change in Ideas, 1600–1900* (New York: Macmillan 1977), 367–400.

167 Abrams, 'Origins of British Sociology,' 87, emphasis added.

168 Vallee interview, emphasis added.

169 Hobhouse, 'Editorial,' *Sociological Review,* vol. 1 (January 1908): 3–4, cited in Owen, *L.T. Hobhouse, Sociologist,* 20n10.

170 Owen, ibid., 17.
171 M. Barrados, '*The Vertical Mosaic* in Everyday Life,' John Porter Memorial
    Lecture, 3 March 2004, Ottawa, Carleton University, 2; see also 4, 9.
172 Porter, 'Prologue', in Porter, *Measure of Canadian Society*, 1.
173 Marion Porter interview 1. Bob Phillips confirmed the accuracy of this
    story, which I thought might be apocryphal, noting that in the early years
    in particular Porter's colleagues at Carleton College often debated the
    issue of announcing one's personal convictions in the classroom (Phillips
    interview).
174 Porter, *Measure of Canadian Society*, 208, emphasis added. In a similar vein,
    Clement described Porter as motivated throughout his career by the pos-
    sibilities of social democracy (interview 1).
175 In this regard, Porter would seem to be like S.D. Clark (D. Nock, '"Crush-
    ing the Power of Finance": The Socialist Prairie Roots of S.D. Clark,' *BJCS*
    1, no. 1 [1986]: 86–108); and Seymour Martin Lipset (R. Collins, *Three So-
    ciological Traditions* [New York: Oxford, 1985], 104).
176 See, e.g., Hofley, 'John Porter: His Analysis of Class,' 596–9.
177 He engaged in such media activities from time to time beginning in 1954.
    See 'Two Cheers for Mental Health'; radio talks 'The Economic Elite,'
    and 'The Bureaucratic Elite,' CBC radio, *Post-News Talks*, 11 and 19 April
    1958 respectively (CUA, Office of the President's fonds, Series: Annual
    Reports, *The President's Report 1957–1958*, 66); appearance on CBC televi-
    sion, *Fighting Words*, November 1958 (LAC, JPP, vol. 3, no. 4, A.H. Robson
    to JAP, 4 November 1958); *Crossfire,* appearance with Pauline Jewett,
    February 1968 (ibid., vol. 3, no. 6, B. MacLean to JAP, 14 February 1968);
    CBC television, *Ideas,* appearance with Carl Berger, University of Toronto
    historian, 1972, n.d. (ibid., vol. 3, no. 8, D. Macpherson to JAP, 5 Octo-
    ber 1971). Note also 'Some Aspects of the Power Structure in Canada,'
    presented at the annual meetings of the Canadian Institute of Public Ad-
    ministration,' Regina, 7 September 1962, published in *CPA* 2 (June) 1963:
    140–7; 'Aims and Problems in Canadian Society and their Implications for
    Teacher Training,' presented at the meetings of the Canadian Teachers'
    Federation, Ottawa, 9 May 1966; 'Social Change in Canada,' address to
    staff training conference, United Steelworkers of Canada, Niagara Falls, 2
    December 1965 (both cited in CUA, Office of the President's fonds, Series:
    Annual Reports, *The President's Report 1965–66*, 102); 'Education, Values
    and Social Change,' presented at Althouse College of Education, Univer-
    sity of Western Ontario, 6 March 1968 (cited in CUA, Office of the Presi-
    dent's fonds, Series: Annual Reports, *The President's Report 1967–1968*,
    125); 'Post-Industrialism, Post-Nationalism and Post-Secondary Educa-

tion,' *CPA* 14, no. 1 (1971): 32–50; and 'Educational and Occupational Opportunity in the Canadian Mosaic,' *Canadian Counsellor* 8, no. 2 (1974): 90–105.

178 LAC, JPP, vol. 7, no. 27, Porter, 'Address to the Options for Canada Colloquium,' 1977, published as 'Address by John Porter,' in *Options for Canada,* 56–67; Porter, 'Education and Equality,' and 'Education and the Just Society,' in Porter, *Measure of Canadian Society,* 241–62 and 263–80, respectively; Porter, 'Ethnic Pluralism in Canadian Perspective,' in ibid., 103–37; LAC, JPP, vol. 8, no. 14, Porter, 'Some Limits to Self-Determination,' [1978]; Porter, 'Macrosociology' (1974) and 'Towards a Macrosociology' (1975) are in Clement personal papers; Porter, 'Comments on … Macrosociology,' Edmonton, University of Alberta, 1975 (LAC, JPP, vol. 6, no. 14); see also Porter, 'Prologue,' in Porter, *Measure of Canadian Society,* 1–5.

179 Two general remarks about the style of these essays: (1) Porter does not always provide explicit references to these thinkers each time he uses their ideas in these essays; and (2) there are many overlapping, indeed more or less repeated, passages in this set of essays, especially in the 'Prologue' to *Measure of Canadian Society,* the essay on minority rights, the McInnis Lectures, and the essay on the limits to self-determination.

180 LAC, JPP, vol. 7, no. 27, Porter, 'Notes … Options for Canada Colloquium,' Montebello, Quebec, May 1977, 1.

181 Ibid., 2.

182 Ibid. He took as prototypical for the purposes of his analysis the 'modern industrial society,' which was in the process of becoming a 'post-industrial society' ('Towards a Macrosociology'). The modern industrial society had a mixed capitalist economy with a solid industrial base, a large service sector, and a liberal democratic form of government. I describe Porter's model of the modern industrial society below.

183 LAC, JPP, vol. 7, no. 27, Porter, 'Notes … Options for Canada Colloquium,' 5.

184 Ibid., 11.

185 Porter, 'Education and the Just Society,' in Porter, *Measure of Canadian Society,* 278. Porter was not entirely satisfied with Rawls' work because Rawls took as basic the idea of human beings as consumers of utilities rather than as possessors of capacities. This meant that Rawls paid much more attention to the distribution of rewards when constructing his principles of social justice than to the provision of opportunities for the expression of creativity and the use or realization of capacities (see ibid., 273).

186 Interview of John Porter by J.D. Hamilton on CBC program 'Distinguished Canadians,' 26 June 1972, http://archives.cbc.ca/politics/.

187 Ibid.; see also LAC, JPP, vol. 8, no. 14, Porter, 'Some Limits to Self-Determination,' [1978].

188 Ibid.; see also Porter, 'Ethnic Pluralism in Canadian Perspective,' in *Ethnicity: Theory and Experience,* ed. Glazer and Moynihan, 288–304, especially 300–1.

189 Porter, 'Ethnic Pluralism in Canadian Perspective,' in Porter, *Measure of Canadian Society,* 104, emphasis added. Note that 'unity of mankind' is Hobhouse's precise phrase. See also 'Melting Pot or Mosaic,' in Porter, ibid., 142, 160; and LAC, JPP, vol. 8, no. 14, Porter, 'Some Limits to Self-Determination,' [1978] 6–7 and passim.

190 Porter, 'Prologue,' in Porter, *Measure of Canadian Society,* 3; see also LAC, JPP, vol. 6, no. 14, Porter, 'Comments … on Macrosociology,' 2.

191 F. Cunningham, 'C.B. Macpherson,' *University of Toronto Faculty Association Newsletter* 2 (17 March 2004): 2.

192 Porter, 'Education and the Just Society,' in Porter, *Measure of Canadian Society,* 273–4, citing Macpherson, *Democratic Theory,* 10.

193 Porter, 'Prologue,' 3, in ibid.

194 Porter, 'Ethnic Pluralism in Canadian Perspective,' in Porter, *Measure of Canadian Society,* 128.

195 LAC, JPP, vol. 6, no. 14, Porter, 'Comments … on Macrosociology,' 2.

196 Porter, 'Prologue,' in Porter, *Measure of Canadian Society,* 2.

197 Ibid.

198 Porter, 'Macrosociology,' Clement personal papers.

199 LAC, JPP, vol. 6, no. 14, Porter, 'Comments … on Macrosociology,' 1. The bulk of Porter's second macrosociology think piece described the distinguishing features of the modern industrial society ('Towards a Macrosociology,' Clement personal papers).

200 Porter, 'Macrosociology,' Clement personal papers, 15. Elsewhere in this essay he argues that to carry out such a task a macrosociology would have to examine two 'dimensions' of modern national societies: the 'temporal' (looking back into history and forward into the future); and the 'spatial' (i.e., examining the political, economic, and demographic place of each society in the international web and hierarchy of nations in order to determine its degree of autonomy) (9–11).

201 Olsen said that Porter saw James Coleman and O.D. Duncan as exemplars but confessed that he often felt 'technically inadequate.' Moreover, said Olsen, Porter stated that detailed methodological papers bored him (D. Olsen, Course notes: Sociology 610–11, Carleton University, Fall–Winter 1971–2, n.d., Olsen personal papers, re J. Coleman, 'Properties of Collectivities').

202 Porter, 'Macrosociology,' Clement personal papers, 7.

203 Ibid., 8.

204 Porter, 'Towards a Macrosociology,' Clement personal papers, 1–2.

205 Porter, 'Research Biography,' in Coleman, Etzioni, and Porter, *Macrosociology*, 152–3; see also LAC, JPP, vol. 6, no. 14, Porter 'Comments ... Macrosociology,' 4–5. The phrase 'organic harmony' is, of course, Hobhouse's.

206 Porter, 'Prologue,' in Porter, *Measure of Canadian Society*, 3.

207 Porter, 'Towards a Macrosociology,' Clement personal papers, 6–7.

208 Ibid., 20–1.

209 Porter, 'Prologue,' in Porter, *Measure of Canadian Society*, 3.

210 Interview of John Porter by J.D. Hamilton on CBC program 'Distinguished Canadians,' 26 June 1972, http://archives.cbc.ca/politics/

211 Porter, 'Ethnic Pluralism in Canadian Perspective,' in Porter, *Measure of Canadian Society*, 130, 133.

212 Clarke, *Liberals and Social Democrats*, ch. 3 passim; Allett, *New Liberalism*, ch. 5 passim, especially 143.

213 LAC, JPP, vol. 6, no. 14, Porter, 'Comments on ... Macrosociology,' 4.

214 Halsey, 'Provincials and Professionals,' 61.

215 Three of those Halsey includes in his analysis came from other countries: Percy Cohen from South Africa, Ralf Dahrendorf from Germany, and John Westergaard from Denmark (ibid., 44–5).

216 Ibid., 47–9.

217 Ibid., 57.

218 Ibid., 60.

219 Ibid., 57; see 55–8 more generally.

220 Ibid.

221 The list of those who taught sociology in Canada after attending LSE includes Porter, Bruce McFarlane, Reginald Robson, Anthony Richmond, and Aileen Ross. There may have been others.

222 An early version of this set of propositions was presented in R. Helmes-Hayes and A. Turrittin, 'Class Inequality, Social Justice and English-language Canadian Sociology, 1945–1970: John Porter as an Exemplar,' presented at the biennial meeting of the Association for Canadian Studies in the Unites States, Seattle, Washington, November 1995.

Bibliography

The text draws on archival materials, published sources (books, articles, etc.), unarchived personal/private papers, interviews, and correspondence.

A list of published works by John Porter cited in the manuscript is given in 'John Porter: Published Sources.' Citations to John Arthur Porter's correspondence in the endnotes refer to him as JAP.

Personal Papers

Abbott, Dick
Barrados, Maria
Blois, Mary
Campbell, Ian
Clement, Wallace
Curtis, James
Ellen, Fiona
Goyder, John
Jones, Eileen (Porter)
McFarlane, Bruce
MacLean, Beattie
McRae, Kenneth
Olsen, Dennis
Phillips, R.A.J.
Porter, Ann
Porter, Marion
Shaw, Ian

Interviews

Abbott, Dick	17 October 1991
Anonymous	27 June 1991
Barrados, Maria	18 February 2002
Barrie, Douglas	14 March 2001, telephone, not recorded
Bell, Daniel	20 July 1990, telephone, not recorded
Blishen, Bernard	15 April 1988
Boyd, Monica	12 July 2000
Brown, David	17 November 2004
Burnet, Jean	2 February 1995
Campbell, Ian	Interview 1, 9 April 1991
	Interview 2, 17 April 1991
Chesworth, Donald	20 July 1989
Clark, S.D.	14 February 2003
Clement, Wallace	Interview 1, 18 April 1988, not recorded
	Interview 2, 15 February 1999, not recorded
	Interview 3, 24 June 2002
Cole, Dodie	2 June 2002
Cole, Porter	2 June 2002
Downey, James	Interview 1, 19 June 2000
	Interview 2, 11 September 2002
Ellen, Fiona	10 November 2007
Farr, David	19 February 2002
Fenn, Norman	27 June 2002
Fenn, Richard	1 October 1987, telephone, not recorded
Forcese, Dennis	29 May 2001
Fox, Paul	22 August 1987
Frumhartz, Muni	20 April 1988
Gibson, James	19 April 1991
Goyder, John	Interview 1, 5 July 2000, not recorded
	Interview 2, 25 July 2000
Grist, Gill	15 July 1989
Grist, John	15 July 1989
Gullen, Joan	26 June 2002, not recorded
Helmes, Charles	12 January 2009
Jewett, Pauline	Interview 1, 20 August 1987
	Interview 2, 4 September 1987, not recorded
	Interview 3, 9 October 1987, telephone, not recorded

Jones, Eileen (Porter)   12 July 1989
Jones, Frank   25 October 1991
Knight, Graham   12 April 2006
Larose, Albert   27 June 2002
Marsden, Lorna   6 February 1998
McEown, Don   28 May 2001
McFarlane, Bruce   21 November 1986
MacRae, Donald   14 July 1989
McRae, Kenneth   Interview 1, 26 June 1991
   Interview 2, 20 February 2002
McRoberts, Hugh   18 February 2002
Meisel, John   18 January 1991
Myles, John   10 July 2000
Neatby, Blair   24 June 1991
Oliver, Michael   16 October 1991
Olsen, Dennis   10 July 2000
Ostry, Bernard   28 July 2000
Ostry, Sylvia   11 July 2001
Paquet, Gilles   26 June 2002
Phillips, R.A.J.   25 June 1991
Porter, Alan   22 February 1988
Porter, Ann   19 December 2002
Porter, Marion   Interview 1, 3 February 1987
   Interview 2, 18 February 1988, telephone, not recorded
Porter, Tony   Interview 1, 31 August 1987
   Interview 2, 29 January 2003
Reitz, Jeff   27 October 1997
Richmond, Anthony   28 March 1988, telephone, not recorded
Rowat, Donald   18 October 1991
Teron, Jean   17 February 2003
Vallee, Frank   11 August 1986
Whitteker, Doris   13 December 2005
Zeitlin, Irving   8 December 1997

Selected Secondary Sources

Abrams, P. 'The Origins of British Sociology.' In P. Abrams, *The Origins of British Sociology, 1834–1914: An Essay with Selected Papers,* 3–153. Chicago: University of Chicago Press, 1968.

Abse, J., ed. *My LSE*. London: Robson, 1977.

Adams, I., W. Cameron, B. Hill, and P. Penz. *The Real Poverty Report*. Edmonton: M.G. Hurtig, 1971.

Allen, R. *The Social Passion: Religion and Social Reform in Canada 1914–1928*. Toronto: University of Toronto Press, 1971.

Allett, J. *New Liberalism: The Political Economy of J.A. Hobson*. Toronto: University of Toronto Press, 1981.

Armstrong, P. 'Missing Women: A Feminist Perspective on *The Vertical Mosaic*.' In *The Vertical Mosaic Revisited*, ed. R. Helmes-Hayes and J. Curtis, 116–44. Toronto: University of Toronto Press, 1998.

Aron, R. 'Social Structure and Ruling Class I and II,' *BJS* 1, nos. 1 and 2 (1950): 1–16, 126–41.

Ashley, C. 'Concentration of Economic Power,' *CJEPS* 23 (1957): 105–8.

Axelrod, P. *Scholars and Dollars: Politics, Economics and the Universities of Ontario 1945–1980*. Toronto: University of Toronto Press, 1982.

Bannerman, J. 'The Truth about Our Classless Society,' *Maclean's* 78, no. 14 (24 July 1965): 47.

Berle, A., and G. Means. *The Modern Corporation and Private Property*. New York: Macmillan, 1948.

Bissell, C. *Halfway up Parnassus: A Personal Account of the University of Toronto, 1932–1971*. Toronto: University of Toronto Press, 1974.

Black, E. 'The Fractured Mosaic: John Porter Revisited,' *CPA* 17, no. 4 (1974): 640–53.

Blau, P.K., and O.D. Duncan. *The American Occupational Structure*. New York: John Wiley & Sons, 1967.

Blishen, B. 'The Construction and Use of an Occupational Class Scale,' *CJEPS* 24, no. 4 (1958): 519–25.

– 'A Revised Socio-Economic Index for Occupations in Canada,' *CRSA* 4, no. 1 (1967): 41–53.

– 'Social Structure in Canada,' *QQ* 73, no. 1 (1966): 130–5.

– 'A Socio-Economic Index for Occupations in Canada.' In *Canadian Society*, ed. B. Blishen, F. Jones, K. Naegele, and J. Porter, 477–85. Toronto: Macmillan, 1961.

Boldt, M. 'Images of Canada's Future: John Porter's *Vertical Mosaic*.' In *The Sociology of the Future*, ed. W. Bell and J. Mau, 188–207. New York: Russell Sage, 1971.

Bonnett, L. 'Building Bridges and Expanding Expectations.' In *Voix Feministes/ Feminist Voices*, ed. L. Clippingdale, 55–91. Ottawa: Canadian Research Institute for the Advancement of Women, 1996.

Bothwell, R., I. Drummond, and J. English. *Canada: 1900–1945*. Toronto: University of Toronto Press, 1987.

– *Canada since 1945*. 2nd ed. Toronto: University of Toronto Press, 1989.

Boyd, M., J. Goyder, F. Jones, H. McRoberts, P. Pineo, and J. Porter. 'Introduction: The Canadian Mobility Study, Approaches and Procedures.' In J. Porter, M. Boyd, J. Goyder, F. Jones, H. McRoberts, P. Pineo, *Ascription and Achievement: Studies in Mobility and Status Attainment in Canada*. Ottawa: Carleton University Press, 1985.

Brooks, S., and A. Gagnon. *Social Scientists and Politics in Canada*. Montreal and Kingston: McGill-Queen's University Press, 1988.

Brown, L. *When Freedom Was Lost: The Unemployed, the Agitator and the State*. Montreal: Black Rose, 1987.

Brym, R., with B. Fox. *From Culture to Power: The Sociology of English Canada*. Toronto: Oxford, 1989.

Caine, S. 'Ginsberg at the LSE.' In *The Science of Society and the Unity of Mankind: A Memorial Volume for Morris Ginsberg*, ed. R. Fletcher, 30-1. London: Heinemann, 1974.

– *The History of the Foundation of the London School of Economics and Political Science*. London: G. Bell and Sons, 1963.

Callan, H., and S. Ardener, eds. *The Incorporated Wife*. London: Croom Helm, 1984.

Campbell, D. 'Social Reform, the Social Gospel, and the Rise of Sociology in Canada.' In *Beginnings: Essays on the History of Canadian Sociology*, ed. D. Campbell, 7–52. Port Credit, ON: Scribblers' Press, 1983.

Canada, Dominion Bureau of Statistics. *Canada Year Book 1963–64*. Ottawa: Queen's Printer, 1964.

– *Canada Year Book 1964–65*. Ottawa: Queen's Printer, 1965.

– *Canada Year Book 1970–71*. Ottawa: Queen's Printer, 1971.

Caves, R., and R. Holton, 'An Outline of the Economic History of British Columbia, 1881–1951.' In *Historical Essays on British Columbia*, ed. J. Friesen and H. Ralston, 152–66. Toronto: Macmillan, 1976.

Christie, N., and M. Gauvreau. *A Full-Orbed Christianity: The Protestant Churches and Social Welfare in Canada 1900–1940*. Montreal and Kingston: McGill-Queen's University Press, 1996.

Clark, G. 'Evolution of an Administrator.' In *The Installation of Claude Thomas Bissell, Eighth President*, 36–40. Toronto: University of Toronto Press, 1958.

Clark, S.D. 'How the Department of Sociology Came into Being,' in *A Quarter-Century of Sociology at the University of Toronto, 1963–1988*, ed. R. Helmes-Hayes, 1–10. Toronto: Canadian Scholars' Press, 1988.

Clarke, P. *Liberals and Social Democrats*, Cambridge: Cambridge University Press, 1978.

Clement, W. *The Canadian Corporate Elite: An Analysis of Economic Power*. Toronto: McClelland and Stewart, 1975.

– *Continental Corporate Power: Economic Linkages between Canada and the United States*. Toronto: McClelland and Stewart, 1977.

– 'Foreword: The Measure of John Porter.' In J. Porter, *The Measure of Canadian Society*, 2nd ed., xi-xxxv. Ottawa: Carleton University Press, 1987.

– 'John Porter and the Development of Sociology in Canada,' *CRSA* 18, no. 5 (1981): 583–94.

– 'Obituary: John Porter (1921–1979),' *S/S* 3, no. 3 (1979): 14.

– 'Power, Ethnicity and Class: Reflections Thirty Years after *The Vertical Mosaic*.' In *The Vertical Mosaic Revisited*, ed. R. Helmes-Hayes and J. Curtis, 34–59. Toronto: University of Toronto Press, 1998.

Clement, W., and J. Myles, *Relations of Ruling: Class and Gender in Post-Industrial Societies*. Montreal and Kingston: McGill-Queen's University Press, 1994.

Cobb, D. 'John Porter,' *Toronto Daily Star*, 31 December 1965, n.p.

Coleman, J., E. Campbell, C. Hobson, J. McPartland, A. Mood, F. Weinfeld, and R. York. *Equality of Educational Opportunity*. Washington: US Department of Health, Education and Welfare, US Government Printing Office, 1966.

Coleman, J., A. Etzioni, and J. Porter. *Macrosociology: Research and Theory*. Boston: Allyn and Bacon, 1970.

Collini, S. *Liberalism and Sociology: L.T. Hobhouse and Political Argument in England 1880–1914*. Cambridge: Cambridge University Press, 1979.

Colombo, J., ed. *The 1994 Canadian Global Almanac*. Toronto: Macmillan Canada, 1993.

Cook, R. *Regenerators: Social Criticism in Late Victorian Canada*. Toronto: University of Toronto Press, 1985.

Cormier, J. *The Canadianization Movement: Emergence, Survival and Success*. Toronto: University of Toronto Press, 2004.

– 'Nationalism, Activism, and the Canadian Sociology and Anthropology Community, 1967–1985,' *AmS* 33, no. 1 (2002): 12–26.

Connor, D., and J. Curtis. *Sociology and Anthropology in Canada: Some Characteristics of the Disciplines and Their Current University Programs*. Montreal: CSAA, 1970.

Dahrendorf, R. *A History of the London School of Economics and Political Science 1895–1995*. Oxford: Oxford University Press, 1995.

Dennis, N. And A.H. Halsey. *English Ethical Socialism: Thomas More to R.H. Tawney*. Oxford: Clarendon, and Toronto: Oxford University Press, 1988.

Dingman, E. 'Preparations for 2000 AD.' *Toronto Telegram*, 21 July 1971, 36.

Dobbs, K. 'The Strains of Social Climbing.' *SN* 80, no. 6 (June 1965): 27.

Dofny, J. 'Book Review.' *PSQ* 82, no. 4 (1967): 654–6.

Douglas, W., and B. Greenhous. *Out of the Shadows: Canada in the Second World War*, rev. ed. Toronto: Dundurn, 1995.

Eichler, M. 'Women Pioneers in Canadian Sociology: The Effects of a Politics of Gender and a Politics of Knowledge.' *CJS* 26, no. 3 (2001): 375–403.

Elkin, F. 'Book Review [of *Canadian Society*].' *QQ* 69, no. 1 (1962): 159.

Elliot, S. *Scarlet to Green: A History of Intelligence in the Canadian Army 1903– 1963*, Toronto: Hunter Rose and Canadian Intelligence and Security Association, 1981.

Ferguson, B. *Remaking Liberalism: The Intellectual Legacy of Adam Shortt, O.D. Skelton, W.C. Clark and W.A. Mackintosh, 1890–1925*. Toronto: University of Toronto Press, 1993.

Finkel, A. *Our Lives*. Toronto: Lorimer, 1997.

Fletcher, R. 'Introduction.' In J. Owen, *L.T. Hobhouse, Sociologist*, ix-xi. London: Nelson, 1974.

– 'Introduction.' In *The Science of Society and the Unity of Mankind*, ed. R. Fletcher, 11–22. London: Heinemann, 1974.

– ed. *The Science of Society and the Unity of Mankind: A Memorial Volume for Morris Ginsberg*. London: Heinemann, 1974.

Forcese, D. 'The Macro-sociology of John Porter.' *CRSA* 18, no. 5 (1981): 651– 6.

Freeden, M. *The New Liberalism: An Ideology of Social Reform*. Oxford: Clarendon, 1978.

Gerth, H., and C.W. Mills, eds. *From Max Weber: Essays in Sociology*. New York: Oxford, 1946.

Giffen, J. Untitled. In *Forty Years, 1963–2003: Department of Sociology, University of Toronto*, ed. R. Helmes-Hayes, 56–60. Toronto: Canadian Scholars' Press, 2003.

Ginsberg, M. 'The Problems and Methods of Sociology.' In Ginsberg, *Essays in Sociology and Social Philosophy*, abridged, 7–55. 1939. Reprint, Harmondsworth: Penguin, 1968.

– *Sociology*. London: Thornton Butterworth, 1934.

Goyder, J. 'Subjective Social Class Identification and Objective Socio-Economic Status,' PhD diss., McMaster University, Hamilton, 1972.

Granatstein, J. *Ottawa Men: The Civil Service Mandarins, 1935–1957*. Toronto: Oxford, 1982.

Granatstein, J., and D. Morton. *A Nation Forged in Fire: Canadians and the Second World War, 1939–1945*. Toronto: Lester and Orpen Dennys, 1989.

Granatstein, J., I. Abella, D. Bercuson, R. Craig Brown, and H. Blair Neatby. *20th Century Canada*, 2nd ed. Toronto: McGraw-Hill Ryerson, 1986.

Grant, G. 'An Ethic of Community,' in *Social Purpose for Canada*, ed. M. Oliver, 3–26. Toronto: University of Toronto Press, 1961.

– *Lament for a Nation: The Defeat of Canadian Nationalism*. Toronto: McClelland and Stewart, 1965.

Grayson, J., and D. Magill. *One Step Forward, Two Steps Sideways: Sociology and Anthropology in Canada*. Montreal: CSAA, 1981.

Griffiths, N. 'Preface.' In *Voix Feministes/Feminist Voices*, ed. L. Clippingdale 1–5. Ottawa: Canadian Research Institute for the Advancement of Women, 1996.

Grimes, A. 'Introduction.' In L.T. Hobhouse, *Liberalism*, 1–8. 1911. Reprint, London: Oxford, 1964.

Guest, D. *The Emergence of Social Security in Canada*. Vancouver: UBC Press, 1980.

Halsey, A.H. 'Provincials and Professionals: The British Post-War Sociologists,' *LSEQ* 1, no. 1 (1987): 43–73.

Hardy, C. *The Politics of Collegiality: Retrenchment Strategies in Canadian Universities*. Montreal and Kingston: McGill-Queen's University Press, 1996.

Harris, R. *A History of Higher Education in Canada, 1663–1960*. Toronto: University of Toronto Press, 1976.

Heap, J. *Everybody's Canada: The Vertical Mosaic Reviewed and Re-Examined*. Toronto: Burns and MacEachern, 1974.

– 'The Vertical Mosaic Re-Examined: Conceptual, Theoretical and Ethical Problems in *The Vertical Mosaic*.' In *Everybody's Canada: The Vertical Mosaic Reviewed and Re-Examined*, ed. J. Heap, 89–163. Toronto: Burns and MacEachern, 1974.

Helmes-Hayes, R. 'The Concept of Social Class: Everett Hughes' Contribution.' *JHBS* 36, no. 2 (2000): 127–47.

– '"A Dualistic Vision": Robert Ezra Park and the Classical Ecological Theory of Social Inequality.' *TSQ* 28, no. 3 (1987): 387–409

– 'Everett Hughes: Theorist of the Second Chicago School.' *IJPCS* 11, no. 4 (1998): 621–73.

– '"Hobhouse Twice Removed": John Porter and the LSE Years, 1946–9,' *CRSA* 27, no. 3 (1990): 357–88.

– 'The Image of Inequality in S.D. Clark's Writings on Pioneer Canadian Society.' *CJS* 13, no. 3 (1988): 211–33.

– 'Images of Inequality in Early Canadian Sociology, 1922–1965.' PhD diss., University of Toronto, 1985.

– 'J.A. Banks, "From Universal History to Historical Sociology": A Comment.' *BJS* 43, no. 3 (1992): 333–44.

- 'John Porter: Canada's Most Famous Sociologist (and His Links to American Sociology).' *AmS* 33, no. 1 (2002): 79–104.
- 'L'analyse des classes sociales dans la sociologie canadienne de langue anglaise (1895–1965).' *CRS* 39 (2004): 15–53.
- ed. *Forty Years, 1963–2003: Department of Sociology, University of Toronto*. Toronto: Canadian Scholars' Press, 2003.
- *A Quarter-Century of Sociology at the University of Toronto, 1963–1988*. Toronto: Canadian Scholars' Press, 1988.

Helmes-Hayes, R., and J. Curtis, eds. *The Vertical Mosaic Revisited*. Toronto: University of Toronto Press, 1998.

Helmes-Hayes, R., and D. Wilcox-Magill. 'A Neglected Classic: Leonard Marsh's *Canadians In and Out of Work.*' *CRSA* 30, no. 1 (1993): 83–109.

Henderson's Greater Vancouver Directory (1915–23 incl.). Vancouver: Henderson Directory Company.

Henderson's Greater Vancouver, New Westminster and Fraser Valley Directory (1911–14, incl.). Vancouver: Henderson Directory Company.

Heron, C. *The Canadian Labour Movement: A Short History*. Toronto: James Lorimer, 1989.

Hiller, H. 'The Canadian Sociology Movement: Analysis and Assessment.' *CJS* 4, no. 2 (1979): 125–50.

- *Society and Change: S.D. Clark and the Development of Canadian Sociology*. Toronto: University of Toronto Press, 1982.

Hiller, H., and L. DiLuzio, 'Text and Context: Another "Chapter" in the Evolution of Sociology in Canada.' *CJS* 26, no. 3 (2001): 497–500.

Hiller, H., and S. Langlois, 'The Most Important Books/Articles in Canadian Sociology in the 20th Century: A Report.' *CJS* 26, no. 3 (2001): 513–16.

Hobhouse, L.T. *Democracy and Reaction*. 1904. Reprint, Brighton: Harvester Press, 1972.

- *Elements of Social Justice*. New York: Henry Holt, 1922.
- *Liberalism*. 1911. Reprint, London: Oxford, 1964.
- *Morals in Evolution I*. New York: Henry Holt, 1906.
- *Morals in Evolution II*. London: Chapman and Hall, 1915.
- *Social Development, Its Nature and Conditions*. New York: Henry Holt, 1924.

Hofley, J. 'Canadianization: A Journey Completed?' In *Fragile Truths: Twenty-Five Years of Sociology and Anthropology in Canada*, ed. W. Carroll, L. Christiansen-Ruffman, R. Currie, and D. Harrison, 103–22. Ottawa: Carleton University Press, 1992.

- 'John Porter: His Analysis of Class and His Contribution to Canadian Sociology.' *CRSA* 18, no. 5 (1981): 595–606.

Horn, M. *The Great Depression of the 1930s in Canada*. Canadian Historical

Association Booklet no. 39. Ottawa: Canadian Historical Association, 1984.

– *The League for Social Reconstruction: Intellectual Origins of the Democratic Left in Canada, 1930–1942.* Toronto: University of Toronto Press, 1980.

Horowitz, G. 'Creative Politics, Mosaics and Identity.' *CD* 3 (November–December 1965): 14–15, 28, and 4 (January–February 1966): 17–19.

Hull, R., G. Soules, and C. Soules. *Vancouver's Past.* Vancouver: Gordon Soules Economic and Marketing Research, 1974.

Hunter, A. *Class Tells: On Social Inequality in Canada.* Toronto: Butterworths, 1981.

Husby, P. 'Education.' In *The Canadian Economy: Problems and Options,* ed. R. Bellan and W. Pope, 181–96. Toronto: McGraw-Hill Ryerson, 1981.

Jencks, C., H. Acland, M-J. Bane, D. Cohen, H. Gintis, B. Heyns, S. Michelson, and M. Smith. *Inequality: A Reassessment of the Effect of Family and Schooling in America.* New York: Basic, 1972.

Johnston, H. *Radical Campus: Making Simon Fraser University.* Vancouver and Toronto: Douglas and McIntyre, 2005.

Jones, F. 'Current Sociological Research in Canada: Views of a Journal Editor.' *JHBS* 13 (1977): 160–72.

– 'Establishing the Canadian Sociology and Anthropology Association (CSAA).' *S/S* 14, no. 3 (1990): 30–7.

Keynes, J.M. *A General Theory of Employment, Interest and Money,* Vol. 7 of *Collected Works of John Maynard Keynes,* ed. Donald Moggridge. 1936. Reprint, London: Macmillan for the Royal Economics Society.

Kilbourn, W. 'In Canada's Society, No Room at the Top?' *Executive* (September 1965): 63–4.

Lapierre, L. 'The 1960s.' In *The Canadians 1867–1967,* ed. J.M.S. Careless and R. Craig Brown, 344–82. Toronto: Macmillan, 1968.

Laski, H. *A Grammar of Politics.* London: Allen and Unwin, 1925.

Leacy, F., ed. *Historical Statistics of Canada.* 2nd ed. Ottawa: Statistics Canada with the Social Sciences Federation of Canada, 1983.

Levitt, C. *Children of Privilege: Student Revolt in the Sixties,* Toronto: University of Toronto Press, 1984.

Li, P. *The Making of Post-War Canada.* Don Mills, ON: Oxford: 1996.

Longstaff, S. 'John Porter's *Vertical Mosaic*: A Critique with Some Reflections on the Canadian Scene.' *Berkeley Journal of Sociology* 12 (1967): 82–90.

Lower, A.R.M. 'Book Review.' *CHR* 47, no. 2 (1966): 158–61.

McAndrew, B. *Canadians and the Italian Campaign, 1943–1945.* Canada Department of National Defence. Montreal: Art Global, 1996.

McCann, L. 'Urban Growth in a Staple Economy: The Emergence of Vancouver as Regional Metropolis, 1886–1914.' In ed. L.J. Evenden, 17–41. *Vancouver: Western Metropolis*. Victoria: University of Victoria Press, 1978.

Macdonald, A. 'Population Growth and Change in Seattle and Vancouver, 1880–1960.' In *Historical Essays on British Columbia*, ed. J. Friesen and H. Ralston, 201–27. Toronto: Macmillan, 1976.

McDougall, R. 'War, a Narrative: The Sicilian Campaign.' In R. McDougall, *Totems: Essays on the Cultural History of Canada*, 87–99. Ottawa: Tecumseh, 1990.

MacIver, R. *The Elements of Social Science*. London: Methuen, 1921.

– *Labor in the Changing World*. New York: E.P. Dutton, 1920.

– *The Modern State*. Oxford: Clarendon, 1926.

– *Society: Its Structure and Changes*. New York: Ray Long and R.R. Smith, 1931.

Mack, J., and S. Humphries. *London at War: The Making of Modern London, 1939–1945*. London: Sidgwick and Jackson, 1985.

McKenzie, J. *Pauline Jewett: A Passion for Canada*. Montreal and Kingston: McGill-Queen's University Press, 1999.

McKenzie, R. Untitled. In *My LSE*. ed. Joan Abse, 83–103. London: Robson, 1977.

McKillop, A.B. *Matters of Mind: The University in Ontario, 1791–1951*. Toronto: University of Toronto Press, 1994.

Macpherson, C.B. *Democratic Theory: Essays in Retrieval*. Oxford: Clarendon Press, 1973.

– *The Political Theory of Possessive Individualism*. Oxford: Clarendon, 1962.

McVey Jr, W., and W. Kalbach. *Canadian Population*. Toronto: Nelson Canada, 1995.

Manley, D., ed. *LSE People, 1947–1953*. London: LSE Alumni Group, 1987.

Marchak, P. 'Canadian Political Economy.' *CRSA* 22, no. 5 (1985): 673–707.

– *Ideological Perspectives on Canada*. 2nd ed. Toronto: McGraw-Hill Ryerson, 1981.

Maroney, H.J., and M. Luxton, eds. *Feminism and Political Economy: Women's Work, Women's Struggles*. Toronto: Methuen, 1987.

Marsden, L. Untitled. In *Forty Years, 1963–2003: Department of Sociology, University of Toronto*, ed. R. Helmes-Hayes, 74–8. Toronto: Canadian Scholars' Press, 2003.

Marsh, L. *Canadians In and Out of Work: A Survey of Economic Classes and Their Relationship to the Labour Market*. Montreal: Oxford University Press, 1940.

– *Social Security for Canada*. New edition with an introduction by L. Marsh. Toronto: University of Toronto Press, 1975. First published 1943.

Marshall, D. '*Maclean's* Interviews John Porter.' *Maclean's* 81, no. 6 (June 1968): 51–4.

Marshall, David. *Secularizing the Faith: Canadian Protestant Clergy and the Crisis of Belief, 1850–1940.* Toronto: University of Toronto Press, 1992.

Marshall, T.H. *Citizenship and Social Class.* Cambridge: Cambridge University Press, 1950.

– 'Class and Power in Canada.' *CRSA* 2, no. 4 (1965): 215–21.

Mathews, R., and J. Steele, eds. *The Struggle for Canadian Universities.* Toronto: New Press, 1969.

Meisel, J. 'Foreword.' In J. Porter, *The Vertical Mosaic: An Analysis of Social Class and Power in Canada,* ix–x. Toronto: University of Toronto Press, 1965.

Mills, C.W. *The Power Elite.* New York: Oxford, 1956.

Morton, D. *1945: When Canada Won the War,* Ottawa: Canadian Historical Association, 1995.

Mowat, F. *My Father's Son.* Toronto: Key Porter, 1992

– *The Regiment.* Toronto: McClelland and Stewart, 1989.

Neatby, H.B. *The Politics of Chaos: Canada in the Thirties.* Toronto: Macmillan, 1972.

Neatby, H.B., and D. McEown. *A Brief History of Carleton University.* Ottawa: Carleton University, 1993.

– *Creating Carleton: The Shaping of a University.* Montreal and Kingston: McGill-Queen's University Press, 2002.

Nicholson, G. *The Canadians in Italy, 1943–1945.* Vol. 2 of *The Official History of the Canadian Army in the Second World War.* Ottawa: Queen's Printer, 1956.

Norrie, K., and D. Owram. *A History of the Canadian Economy.* 2nd ed. Toronto: Harcourt Brace Jovanovich, 1996.

Norrie, K., D. Owram, and J. Emery. *A History of the Canadian Economy.* 3rd ed. Scarborough: Thompson/Nelson, 2002.

Oliver, M., ed. *Social Purpose for Canada.* Toronto: University of Toronto Press, 1961.

Olsen, D. 'Power, Elites and Society.' *CRSA* 18, no. 5 (1981): 607–14.

– *The State Elite.* Toronto: McClelland and Stewart, 1980.

Ornstein, M. 'Three Decades of Elite Research in Canada: John Porter's Unfulfilled Legacy.' In *The Vertical Mosaic Revisited,* ed. R. Helmes-Hayes and J. Curtis, 145–79. Toronto: University of Toronto Press, 1998.

Owen, J. *L.T. Hobhouse, Sociologist.* London: Nelson, 1974.

Owram, D. *Born at the Right Time: A History of the Baby Boom Generation.* Toronto: University of Toronto Press, 1996.

– *Government Generation: Canadian Intellectuals and the State 1900–1945.* Toronto: University of Toronto Press, 1986.

Palmer, B. *Working Class Experience.* 2nd ed. Toronto: McClelland and Stewart, 1992.

Pineo, P. 'Prestige and Mobility: The Two National Surveys.' *CRSA* 18, no. 5 (1981): 615–26.

Porter, M. 'John Porter.' *S/S* 12, no. 2 (1988): 1–5.

– 'John Porter and Education: Technical Functionalist or Conflict Sociologist?' *CRSA* 18, no. 5 (1981): 632–60.

Rawls, J. *A Theory of Justice*. Cambridge, MA: Harvard University Press, 1971.

Research Committee of the League for Social Reconstruction. *Social Planning for Canada*. Toronto: University of Toronto Press, 1935.

– *Social Planning for Canada*, rev. ed. Toronto: University of Toronto Press, 1975.

Resnick, P. '*The Vertical Mosaic* Revisited: The Dynamics of Power in Canada.' *OG* 6, nos. 1 and 2 (1968): 134–51.

Rich, H. '*The Vertical Mosaic* Revisited: Toward a Macrosociology of Canada.' *JCS* 11, no. 1 (1976): 14–31.

Roberts, L., R. Clifton, B. Ferguson, K. Kampen, and S. Langlois, eds. *Recent Social Trends in Canada*. Montreal and Kingston: McGill-Queen's University Press, 2005.

Rosenbluth, G. 'Concentration and Monopoly in the Canadian Economy.' In *Social Purpose for Canada*, ed. M. Oliver, 198–248. Toronto: University of Toronto Press, 1961.

Roy, P. *Vancouver: An Illustrated History*. Toronto: Lorimer, 1980.

Roy, R. *The Seaforth Highlanders of Canada, 1919–1965*. Vancouver: Evergreen, 1969.

Seeley, J. 'Review.' *AJS* 72, no. 3 (1966): 321–2.

Sheffield, E. 'Enrolment in Canadian Universities and Colleges 1976/77.' Ottawa: Association of Universities and Colleges of Canada, 1966.

Shore, M. *The Science of Social Redemption: McGill, the Chicago School and the Origins of Social Science Research in Canada*. Toronto: University of Toronto Press, 1987.

Smith, A. *Inquiry into the Nature and Causes of the Wealth of Nations*. 1776. Reprint, New York: Modern Library, 1937.

Smith, D. *Conceptual Practices of Power: A Feminist Sociology of Knowledge*. Toronto: University of Toronto Press, 1990.

Spinks, J., G. Arlt, and F. Hare. 'Report of the Committee on University Affairs and the Committee of Presidents of Provincially-Assisted Universities of the Commission to Study the Development of Graduate Programs in Ontario Universities.' Toronto, November 1966.

Stacey, C.P. *The Canadian Army 1939–1945: An Official Historical Summary*. Ottawa: King's Printer, 1948.

– *Six Years of War: The Army in Canada, Britain and the Pacific*. Vol. 1 of *The Of-*

ficial History of the Canadian Army in the Second World War. Ottawa: Queen's Printer, 1955.

– 'Through the Second World War.' In *The Canadians, 1867–1967,* part 1, ed. J.M.S. Careless and R. Craig Brown, 275–308. Toronto: Macmillan, 1968.

– *The Victory Campaign: Operations in North-West Europe 1944–1945.* Vol. 3 of *The Official History of the Canadian Army in the Second World War.* Ottawa: Queen's Printer, 1960.

Stacey, C.P., and B. Wilson, *The Half-Million: The Canadians in Britain, 1939–1946.* Toronto: University of Toronto Press, 1987.

Struthers, J. *'No Fault of Their Own': Unemployment and the Canadian Welfare State, 1914–1941.* Toronto: University of Toronto Press, 1983.

Sullivan, R. *Shadow Maker: The Life of Gwendolyn MacEwen.* Toronto: Harper-Collins, 1995.

Sun Directory Limited. *The British Columbia and Yukon Directory 1935.* Vancouver: Sun Directory Limited, 1935.

– *The British Columbia and Yukon Directory 1936.* Vancouver: Sun Directory Limited, 1936.

– *The British Columbia and Yukon Directory 1937.* Vancouver: Sun Directory Limited, 1937.

– *Sun Directory British Columbia 1934.* Vancouver: Sun Directory Limited, 1934.

Tawney, R.H. *The Acquisitive Society.* New York: Harcourt Brace, 1920.

Tepperman, L. 'Sociology in English-Speaking Canada: The Last Five Years.' *CHR* 59, no. 4 (1978): 435–46.

Tomovic, V. 'Sociology in Canada: An Analysis of Its Growth in English-language Universities, 1908–72.' PhD diss., University of Waterloo, 1975.

Urquhart, M., and K. Buckley, eds. *Historical Statistics of Canada.* Toronto: Macmillan, 1965.

Vallee, F. 'John Porter: 1921–1979.' *Proceedings of the Royal Society of Canada* series 4, vol. 17 (1979): 94.

– 'Obituary: John Porter (1921–1979).' *S/S* 4, no. 1 (1980): 14.

Wallas, G. *Human Nature in Politics.* 1908. Reprint, London: Constable, 1948.

Warner, W.L. *Yankee City.* 5 vols. New Haven: Yale University Press, 1963.

Warner, W.L., and P.S. Lunt, *The Social Life of a Modern Community.* New Haven, CT: Yale University Press, 1941.

– *The Status System of a Modern Community.* New Haven, CT: Yale University Press, 1942.

Weber, M. 'Class, Status and Party.' In *From Max Weber: Essays in Sociology,* ed. H.H. Gerth and C.W. Mills, 180–95. New York: Oxford, 1946.

– 'The Concepts of Class and Class Status,' 'The Significance of Acquisition Classes,' and 'Social Strata and Their Status.' In *The Theory of Social and Eco-*

nomic Organization, ed. T. Parsons, trans. A.M. Henderson and T. Parsons, 424–9. New York: Free Press, 1947.

– *The Theory of Social and Economic Organization,* ed. and trans. A.M. Henderson and Talcott Parsons. Glencoe, IL: Free Press, 1947.

Wilcox-Magill, D. 'Paradigms and Social Science in English Canada.' In *Introduction to Sociology: An Alternate Approach,* ed. J. Paul Grayson, 1–34. Toronto: Gage, 1983.

Wilcox-Magill, D., and R. Helmes-Hayes. 'Leonard Charles Marsh: A Canadian Social Reformer.' *JCS* 21, no. 2 (1986): 49–66.

Woods, S. *Ottawa: The Capital of Canada.* Toronto: Doubleday, 1980.

Wrigley-Henderson Directories. *Wrigley-Henderson Amalgamated British Columbia Directory (1925–32 inclusive).* Vancouver: Wrigley-Henderson Directories.

– *Wrigley's Greater Vancouver and New Westminster Directory 1933.* Vancouver: Wrigley Directories.

Zeitlin, I. Untitled. In *Forty Years, 1963–2003: Department of Sociology, University of Toronto,* ed. R. Helmes-Hayes, 61–73. Toronto: Canadian Scholars' Press, 2003.

John Porter: Published Sources

COMPILED BY WALLACE CLEMENT AND
RICK HELMES-HAYES

This list of published sources cited is based on the bibliography compiled by Wallace Clement that first appeared in *The Measure of Canadian Society* (1979) and was amended and reprinted in the 1987 edition of *The Measure of Canadian Society*. Co-authors are listed where applicable.

I have altered and supplemented the 1987 version, which I prepared, by adding a few published pieces not listed there and by deleting all references to unpublished materials. Where unpublished materials are cited in the text, I provide a reference to an appropriate source (e.g., the John Porter papers in Library and Archives Canada or a set of private papers).

Co-authored works are listed with Porter's name first, for ease of reference, although he was not always the primary author in the original publications.

Books and Reports

Porter, J., *Canadian Social Structure: A Statistical Profile*. Carleton Library no. 32. Toronto: McClelland and Stewart, 1967.
– *The Measure of Canadian Society: Education, Equality and Opportunity*, 1st ed. Agincourt, ON: Gage, 1979.
– *The Measure of Canadian Society: Education, Equality and Opportunity*. 2nd ed. Ottawa: Carleton University Press, 1987.
– *The Vertical Mosaic: An Analysis of Social Class and Power in Canada*. Toronto: University of Toronto Press, 1965.
Porter, J., B. Blishen, and M. Barrados. *Survival of a Grade 8 Cohort: A Study of Early School Leaving in Ontario*. Toronto: Ministry of Education, 1977.
Porter, J., B. Blishen, J. Evans, B. Hansen, R. Harris, F. Ireland, P. Jewett, J. Macdonald, R. Ross, B. Trotter, and R. Willis. *Towards 2000: The Future of Post-Secondary Education in Ontario*. Toronto: McClelland and Stewart, 1971.

Porter, J., B. Blishen, F. Jones, and K. Naegele, eds. *Canadian Society: Sociological Perspectives.* Toronto: Macmillan, 1961. Revised editions 1964, 1968, 1971.

Porter, J., M. Boyd, J. Goyder, F. Jones, H. McRoberts, and P. Pineo. *Ascription and Achievement: Studies in Mobility and Status Attainment in Canada.* Ottawa: Carleton University Press, 1985.

Porter, J., W. Coleman, and A. Etzioni. *Macrosociology: Research and Theory.* Boston: Allyn and Bacon, 1970.

Porter, J., and E. Humphreys. *Part-Time Studies and University Accessibility.* Toronto: Ministry of Colleges and Universities, 1978.

Porter, J., M. Porter, and B. Blishen. *Does Money Matter? Prospects for Higher Education.* Toronto: York University Institute for Behavioural Research, 1973.

– *Does Money Matter? Prospects for Higher Education in Ontario,* rev. ed. Toronto: Macmillan, 1979.

– *Stations and Callings: Making It through the School System.* Toronto: Methuen, 1982.

Contributions to Periodicals

Porter, J. 'The 1971 Census and the Socio-economic Classification of Occupations: A Research Note.' *CRSA* 14, no. 1 (1977): 91–102.

– 'The Bureaucratic Elite: A Reply to Professor Rowat.' *CJEPS* 25, no. 2 (1959): 207–9.

– 'Canadian Character in the Twentieth Century.' *AAAPSS* 370 (March 1967): 49–56. Also published as 'Le caractère canadien au XXème siècle,' *Revue de psychologie des peuples* 22, no. 3 (1967): 238–47; and as 'Conservatism: The Deep Bond in an Embattled Marriage,' in *Canada: A Guide to the Peaceable Kingdom,* ed. W. Kilbourn, 263–7 (Toronto: Macmillan, 1970).

– 'Canadian National Character.' *Cultural Affairs* 6 (1969): 46–50.

– 'The Class Bias of Canadian Education.' *UBC Alumni Chronicle* 22, no. 2 (1968): 10–15.

– 'Comments by John Porter.' From a symposium on H. Braverman, *Labor and Monopoly Capital* (New York: Monthly Review Press, 1974). *Alternate Routes* 2 (1978): 23–5.

– 'Concentration of Economic Power and the Economic Elite in Canada.' *CJEPS* 22, no. 2 (1956): 199–220.

– 'Conceptual and Theoretical Problems in *The Vertical Mosaic*: A Rejoinder.' *CRSA* 9, no. 2 (1972): 188–9.

– 'Conserving the Bureaucracy.' *CF* 38 (May 1958): 27–8.
– 'The Democratization of the Canadian Universities and the Need for a National System.' *Minerva* 8, no. 3 (1970): 325–56.
– 'Dilemmas and Contradictions of a Multi-ethnic Society.' Royal Society of Canada *Transactions* 4, no. 10 (1972): 193–205.
– 'The Economic Elite and the Social Structure in Canada.' *CJEPS* 23, no. 3 (1957): 376–94.
– 'Educational and Occupational Opportunity in the Canadian Mosaic.' *Canadian Counsellor* 8, no. 2 (1974): 90–105.
– 'Elite Groups: A Scheme for the Study of Power in Canada.' *CJEPS* 21, no. 4 (1955): 498–512.
– 'Equality and Education.' Parts 1 and 2, *Integrateducation* 13, no. 4 (1975): 17–20, and 13, no. 5 (1975): 41–3.
– 'The Future of the University.' Carleton University *Arts Faculty Forum* (March 1979): 14–20.
– 'The Future of Upward Mobility.' *ASR* 33, no. 1 (1968): 5–19.
– 'Higher Public Servants and the Bureaucratic Elite in Canada.' *CJEPS* 24, no. 4 (1958): 483–501.
– 'Inequalities in Education.' *Canadian Counsellor* 2, no. 3 (1968): 136–47. Also published as 'Inequalities in Education,' *School Guidance Worker* 24, no. 6 (1969): 1–17.
– 'John C. MacDonald, 1925–1977: A Tribute.' *CRSA* 14, no. 3 (1977): 365.
– 'Karl Mannheim.' *CF* 34 (January 1955): 222–3.
– 'La mobilité sociale: Facteur de croissance économique.' *Synopsis* (March–April 1969): n.p.
– 'Political Parties and the Political Career.' *CF* 38 (May 1958): 54–5.
– 'Post-Industrialism, Post-Nationalism and Post-Secondary Education.' *CPA* 14, no. 1 (1971): 32–50.
– 'Una problema sociale: L'alta qualifizione de lavoro umano.' *Mercurio* 12, no. 1 (1969): n.p.
– 'Reply.' To D.W. Livingstone, "Inventing the Future: Anti-Historicist Reflections on *Towards 2000*." *Interchange* 3, no. 4 (1972): 120–1.
– 'Social Change and the Aims and Problems of Education in Canada.' *MJE* 1, no. 2 (1966): 125–30.
– 'Some Aspects of the Power Structure in Canada.' *CPA* 2 (June 1963): 140–7.
– 'Some Observations on Comparative Studies.' International Institute for Labour Studies *Bulletin* 3 (November 1967): 82–104.
– 'Two Cheers for Mental Health.' *CF* 34 (October 1954): 145, 152–3.

- 'Why the Shortage of Highly Qualified Manpower?' *LG* 68, no. 5 (1968): 195–239.
Porter, J., and M. Boyd, J. Goyder, F. Jones, H. McRoberts, P. Pineo. 'The Canadian National Mobility Study.' *Canadian Studies in Population* 4 (1977): 94–6.
- 'Différences dans la mobilité professionelle des francophones et des anglophones.' *Sociologie et Sociétés* 7, no. 2 (1976): 61–79.
- 'Status Attainment in Canada: Findings of the Canadian National Mobility Study.' *CRSA* 18, no. 5 (1981): 657–73.
Porter, J., and P. Pineo 'Occupational Prestige in Canada.' *CRSA* 4, no. 1 (1967): 24–40.
Porter, J., P. Pineo, and H. McRoberts. 'The 1971 Census and the Socioeconomic Classification of Occupations.' *CRSA* 14, no. 1 (1977): 91–102.

Book Chapters

Porter, J. 'Address by John Porter.' In *Options for Canada: A Report on the 1st Options for Canada Colloquium*, 56–67. Ottawa: St. Patrick's College and Carleton University, 1977.
- 'Education and Equality: The Failure of a Mission.' In J. Porter, *The Measure of Canadian Society: Education, Equality, and Opportunity*, 241–62. Toronto: Gage, 1979.
- 'Education and the Just Society.' In J. Porter, *The Measure of Canadian Society: Education, Equality, and Opportunity*, 263–80. Toronto: Gage, 1979.
- 'Ethnic Pluralism in Canadian Perspective.' In *Ethnicity: Theory and Experience*, ed. N. Glazer and P. Moynihan, 267–304. Cambridge, MA: Harvard University Press, 1975.
- 'Foreword.' In W. Clement, *The Canadian Corporate Elite: An Analysis of Economic Power*, ix–xv. Toronto: McClelland and Stewart, 1975.
- 'The Human Community.' In *The Canadians: 1867–1967*, ed. J.M.S. Careless and R.C. Brown, 385–410. Toronto: Macmillan, 1967.
- 'Melting Pot or Mosaic: Revolution or Reversion?' In *Perspectives on Revolution versus Evolution*, ed. R. Preston, 152–79. Durham, NC: Duke University Press, 1976.
- 'Power and Freedom in Canadian Democracy.' In *Social Purpose for Canada*, ed. M. Oliver, 27–56. Toronto: University of Toronto Press, 1961.
- 'Research Biography of *The Vertical Mosaic*.' In J. Coleman, A. Etzioni, and J. Porter, *Macrosociology: Research and Theory*, 149–82. Boston: Allyn and Bacon, 1970.
- 'Social Class and Education.' In *Social Purpose for Canada*, ed. M. Oliver, 103–29. Toronto: University of Toronto Press, 1961.

Book Reviews

Porter, J. 'Bilingualism and the Myths of Culture,' a review of Books I and II of the Report of the Royal Commission on Bilingualism and Biculturalism. *CRSA* 6, no. 2 (1969): 111–18.
- 'Class and Conformity: A Study of Values (by M. Kohn).' *Science* 170 (1970): 1183–5.
- 'Do Canadians Get the Best Jobs?' a review of A. E. Safarian, *The Performance of Foreign-Owned Firms in Canada. Canadian Business* (November 1969): 44–51.
- '*Elite Accommodation in Canadian Politics* (by Richard Presthus).' *CS* 4, no. 2 (1975): 120–1.
- '*Italy* (by Elizabeth Wiskeman).' *Clare Market Review* 48, no. 2 (1948): 39–40.
- 'Kvetcher in the Rye,' a review of P. Newman, *Bronfman Dynasty: The Rothschilds of the New World. Books in Canada* 7, no. 10 (1978): 9–10.
- 'The Limits of Sociology,' a review of Christopher Jencks et al., *Inequality. CS* 2, no. 5 (1973): 463–7.
- '*Minetown, Milltown, Railtown* (by R. Lucas).' *CHR* 53, no. 4 (1972): 455–7.
- '*The Origins of Psycho-Analysis: Sigmund Freud's Letters to Wilhelm Fliess, Drafts and Notes: 1887–1902* (edited by Marie Bonaparte, Anna Freud, Ernst Kris, authorized translation by Eric Mosbacher and James Strachey, introduction by Ernst Kris).' *CF* 34 (October 1954): 163–4.
- '*Philadelphia Gentlemen: The Making of a National Upper Class* (by E. Digby Baltzell).' *CJEPS* 25, no. 2 (1959): 230–2.
- '*Political Power and Social Theory: Six Studies* (by Barrington Moore).' *CJEPS* 25, no. 1 (1959): 522–3.
- '*Pouvoir dans la société Canadienne-française* (ed. Fernand Dumont and J.-P. Montminy).' *SF* 46, no. 1 (1968): 134.
- '*The Power Structure* (by A.M. Rose).' *ASR* 33, no. 2 (1968): 301–2.
- '*Problems of Power in American Democracy* (by A. Kornhauser).' *CJEPS* 24, no. 4 (1958): 589–91.
- '*The Role of Groups in World Reconstruction* (by C. Henry).' *Canadian Welfare* (May 1953): 51–2.
- '*Social Stratification: A Comparative Analysis of Structure and Process* (by Bernard Barber).' *CJEPS* 25, no. 1 (1959): 86–7.
- '*Social Stratification and Career Mobility* (edited by W. Muller and Karl Ulrich Mayer).' *CS* 4, no. 2 (1975): 166–7.
- '*Statistical Review of Canadian Education, Census, 1951* (by Dominion Bureau of Statistics, Education Division, Reference Paper 84).' *CJEPS* 25, no. 1 (1959): 73–4.

- 'Structured Inequality Down Under,' a review of S. Encel, *Equality and Authority: A Study of Class, Status and Power in Australia*. SF 50 (June 1972): 531–3.
- '*The University Question* (by W. Woodside).' CF 38 (May 1958): 46–7.
- 'The Vertical Power Trip,' a review of Peter Newman, *The Canadian Establishment*. *Books in Canada* 4, no. 12 (1975): 3–5.

Index